THE SOCIOLOGY
OF BLACK AFRICA

SOCIAL DYNAMICS IN CENTRAL AFRICA

Georges Balandier

TRANSLATED BY
DOUGLAS GARMAN

PRAEGER PUBLISHERS
New York · Washington

BOOKS THAT MATTER

Published in the United States of America in 1970 by Praeger
Publishers, Inc., 111 Fourth Avenue, New York, N.Y. 10003

Library of Congress Catalog Card Number: 72-100931

Printed in Great Britain

CONTENTS

PREFACE

Some years ago, in our Introduction to the Second Edition of this work – an edition which had been largely recast and brought up-to-date – I stressed the fact that it was a contribution to the creation of a *dynamic and critical anthropology*. My purpose in doing so was to draw attention to the originality of the questions it raised and the kind of answers it proposed, and to suggest that because of this it was in line with a number of recent developments in the field of modern comparative sociology and anthropology. Such concepts as 'colonial situation' and 'position of dependence', and phenomena accepted as revealing fundamental social relations and their specific dynamic, like the breakaway religious movements, have now forced themselves upon the attention of the specialists. But they were already centred to the research on which this book is based; though they represent only one aspect of it.

Indeed, its most obvious aspect. The theoretical inferences which are closely bound up with the presentation of the facts and their analysis, are nowhere summed up in a fully developed theory. Sometimes they are implicit in the cautious approach, sometimes expressed because of their immediate explanatory effectiveness, but they are never formulated categorically. Often they remain in the background. And indeed one of my critics expressed regret that I had not 'adequately exploited the rich theoretical content of the field-work carried out on the spot by providing a full theoretical exposition'.[*]

Undoubtedly, the possibility of doing so has influenced the direction of my subsequent work. In particular, insofar as the

[*] See the review by J. Maquet in the *Cahiers Internationaux de Sociologie*, XXXV, 1963, pp. 180–83.

political dynamic of the Fang and the Ba-Kongo constitutes in a sense the connecting thread of the present book, it was this that led me to elaborate a theory of political anthropology. In this sense, my recent *Anthropologie Politique* sets out to show that 'research conducted by politically minded anthropologists demands a differently oriented social anthropology and comparative sociology'.* These latter belong to the kind of interpretation that has been described as 'dynamist'.

This was a first assessment. It needs to be clarified and filled out with the help of this new edition of *The Sociology of Black Africa*. In this work, a study deriving directly from an anthropological project rehabilitates history, as opposed to functionalist and structuralist presuppositions. The comparison of Kongo and Fang society shows them to be part of a long process of development which led to a diversification of their formations and reactions, despite the fact that they both had to face the same situations – those arising from a slave economy, then from colonialism and more recently from decolonization. Their systems of social relations and cultural organization cannot be fully understood merely in the light of the principles that govern them or of their 'formal' existence; they only assume their full meaning when they are related to the historical movements and events that have shaped and modified them. In trying to discover not only the most obvious changes, but also those that were hidden behind a façade of formal continuity, I was forced to appreciate, at a higher level of complexity, the dynamic of the two societies and the two cultures when subjected to comparative analysis. Thus recognition of the different practices deriving from tradition, which exhibit different procedures and strategies according to whether they occur among the Fang or among the Ba-Kongo, proved to be the start of a new interpretation of *traditionalism*. It led me to distinguish, according to the kind of approach to tradition and the ends in view, four 'faces' of the phenomenon: fundamental traditionalism, formal traditionalism, the traditionalism of resistance and pseudo-traditionalism.†

* G. Balandier: *Anthropologie Politique*, 2nd ed., Presses Universitaires de France, Paris, 1969; American and English editions of which are now in preparation (Pantheon and Penguin Books).

† Cf. *Anthropologie Politique*, p. 203 ff.

Similarly, the realization that, during the colonial period, political problems were expressed in terms of religion encouraged me to attempt a clearer interpretation of the relations of *expressiveness* that arise between the various constituent elements of all social and cultural formations.

This is a feature of the method which it is important to emphasize. At the time of my investigation, both the Kongo and the Fang societies were in a state of serious crisis, the former as a result of its long resistance to the colonial authorities, the second owing to internal deterioration. Once research ceased to be merely retrospective, and concerned itself with the present day, this situation became a kind of permanent reference. It revealed the severe ordeal to which both societies had been exposed for several decades, and brought us face to face with a harsh and barely tolerable experiment. Because of this, *crisis* served as an *indicator* of definite social relations, of definite cultural configurations, and of the respective relations between them. It made it essential to understand the two societies in action and reaction, and not as hitherto in the light of timeless forms and systems. The necessity for this, which became apparent in the course of working in the field, led me to seek out the conditions of social existence that are most revealing of the relations comprising it, and to sketch a *situational analysis* which, thanks to similar efforts on the part of others, has now acquired scientific status.

Societies that constitute part of the colonial situation are under strong compulsion to ambiguity and ambivalence. This leads to a real effect of exaggeration, with the result that the discrepancy between the appearance of social reality and social reality itself is increased. At the time of my investigation, the main question was to decide whether this discrepancy (more readily discernible in this instance) was the result of the colonial situation or whether it is characteristic of every society. My later studies, especially those in the sphere of political anthropology, have convinced me that the phenomenon is a general one. Societies are never what they appear to be or what they claim to be. They have to be understood on at least two levels: a superficial one, representing what may be called the 'official' structures; and a much deeper one which enables us to penetrate the really fundamental relationships and practices that reveal the dynamic of the social system. From the moment it grasps these two levels of organization and expression, and reveals the relation between them, any social science becomes critical; and this is the only way in which it can advance as genuine science.

A considerable part of this work deals with movements that have caused the colonial situation to be challenged and subsequently repudiated. It stresses repeatedly the extent to which the rejection of an order imposed from without (by colonialism) has also been the occasion for reopening the question of some of the relations governing the internal order. The recognition of this fact has meant that I have had to define more precisely the roles of conformity and opposition respectively within the so-called traditional societies. An investigation that began with the examination of the Fang and Kongo societies and the conditions determining their existence and transformation has now widened its scope. It opens up the possibility of an anthropology of confrontation.* It differentiates between the motive force inherent in the structures themselves and that which gives rise to their profound modification and should properly be described as diachronic.

July, 1969.

---

* This research was in progress during the summer of 1968, at the time when public events in France were giving to the term confrontation its present strong political connotation, much stronger than the conceptual one.

TRANSLATOR'S NOTE

In order to relieve the reader of a mass of references in the form of footnotes, while not depriving him of convenient access to other notes, references to sources (denoted in the text by superior numerals) have been placed at the end of the book, grouped by chapters. Other notes or comments have been left in the form of footnotes in the text.

In transcribing names and terms taken from African languages, I have followed the system adopted by the author for the original French edition of this work. Each sound is indicated by one letter, accented where necessary. Thus an acute (´) or a grave (`) indicates the opening of vowels, and the circumflex (ˆ) their nasalisation (*ô on* in French). *ö* corresponds to *eu* in French; *u* to *ou*. The tilde (˜) indicates a liquid consonant, e.g. *ñ, ġ* corresponds to *ch* in German; while *š, č, ǰ* and *ž* would be represented in French by *ch, tch, dj* and *dz*.

With the author's consent and help, I have compressed some material, and have omitted a few passages, especially in Part I Chapter II.

I would like to thank **Professor** Thomas Hodgkin for his help and advice without which my task would have been far more difficult.

D.G.

Douglas Garman (born 15 February 1903, died 8 December 1969) completed this translation shortly before his death. A translator of great skill and sensibility, he was also a serious sociologist, a man of many-sided learning, of wit and critical power, an imaginative educator, writer and publisher, a farmer and lover of the country, a devoted revolutionary.

THOMAS HODGKIN

INTRODUCTION

Since 1945 there have been an increasing number of studies dealing with the social changes that are taking place in developing countries, and with the so-called phenomena of 'acculturation'. In many cases they have been influenced by the requirements of contemporary politics, but in such circumstances the specialists concerned must often be content with results that appear more like those of scrupulous technique than of scientific progress. Thanks to the 'treatment' to which the facts have been subjected, the amount of material assembled is out of all proportion to the development of theory. There can be no doubt, therefore, particularly in the minds of those engaged in this field of study, that from time to time some critical assessment is needed; and, indeed, *Les implications sociales du progrès technique*, published under my direction in 1959, was an attempt in this direction.

Unfortunately this is a field that has aroused little interest amongst French ethnologists and sociologists, despite the new material it could provide them with. This is all the more regrettable in that the tradition of French sociology would have brought to such work an original style and obviated the dangers of a naïve sort of empiricism. The critical work that is necessary as a start has here been undertaken, however incompletely, in the examination of the concept of the *colonial situation* with which the present work opens. The value of such a concept was brought home to me by first-hand experience, acquired since 1946, of African societies exposed to the processes of increasingly rapid change; it was therefore for quite practical reasons that I felt obliged to undertake a first evaluation of the existing material and conceptual equipment.

The present study is the result of field work carried out in

Central Africa between 1948 and 1951, in Gabon and the Congo, with one or two incursions into the neighbouring Congo (Leopoldville) and the Ebolowa district of Cameroun which provided additional material of a comparative nature. Apart from the fact that this investigation had been included in the programme of work for the Sociology Department that I had organized at the Institut d'Études Centrafricaines, I had also been invited to draw up a kind of balance sheet for two peoples – the Gabonese Fang and the Ba-Kongo of the Congo – who had attracted the attention of the administrative authorities by their enterprise and 'revival of initiative', and now, after accepting the colonial situation for a time, were beginning to react against it by reorganizing themselves. Before making enquiries on the spot, I felt obliged to clarify the situation that had led to this reaction. This meant undertaking some historical research, including a thorough study of the old literature and of such archives as were still available for the period 1890–1950; and part of this material was used in writing the chapter, 'The Peoples of the Gabon-Congo and the European Presence'. I should add that, for many years prior to Independence, I had been following the development of both countries 'at a distance', and in 1961 I paid a second visit to Central Africa.

The Fang and the Ba-Kongo share a certain number of common features. Both are ethnic groups scattered over relatively large areas, but *split up* as a result of the division of territory between the colonial powers; thus the Fang are to be found in various parts of Cameroun, Spanish Guinea and Gabon, and the Ba-Kongo in both Congos and Angola. This splitting up of related groups explains why movements seeking to achieve consolidation and reunification exert such influence. On the other hand, both peoples had at an earlier stage tried to make use of the colonial system: in the case of the Ba-Kongo in order to maintain and extend their economic influence; in that of the Fang to substitute economic conquest for the armed conquest they had been obliged to forego. Thus, unlike their neighbours, who continued to avoid contact, they were exposed to the process of change; and this, together with the influence resulting from their size, tended to make other peoples look up to them as leaders. It remains to add that in their relations with Europeans and the colonial groups both peoples found themselves in much the same position, characterized by the persistence of the slave trade until fairly recent times, by the influence of a primary economy established against the background of a vast underpopulated area, and by the intensive activities of the Christian missions and the French administration, who very early on sought to achieve effective control. Both ethnic groups were subjected to the same type of total domination.

Nevertheless there are also essential differences between the Fang and the Ba-Kongo, and it is precisely the differences in their reactions to the same 'contact situation', to use Malinowski's expression, that makes the comparison between them so fruitful. In their attitude to the processes of change and in their resistance to the colonial situation, the two types of society reveal significant divergences. By examining them it should be possible to distinguish how, and to what extent, they have been affected both by internal factors (their specific structure and organization) and by the external factor common to them both, the activities of the colonial power that exposed them to outside influences. Obviously, this kind of approach demands a thorough analysis of the colonial situation, and of the form that this assumed locally.

For a long time the relations with the land of the Gabonese Fang, who had been reduced by colonial expansion to the position of 'out-of-work conquerors', had been extremely loose; their mobility prevented them from developing the necessary technique of land management. Their technical level of production and the fact that they had had to learn to become farmers, the slight social influence they had exerted on the countryside and their traditional notions as to their rights to the land exploited by them, are all indicative of this. The Ba-Kongo, on the contrary, had carefully organized their relations with the land, creating 'territorial chiefdoms' whose authority extended to the clan domain. Their skill as agriculturists, at least in the case of certain tribes, had been noted by the earliest observers. With them, the land belonging to the clan, which had a special value since it contained the ancestral graves, could not be abandoned with impunity – which explains the fact that they were less mobile and that their villages were more 'resistant'.

In addition to these basic differences, it is important to

emphasize those that concern the actual organization of the two societies. Compared with the Fang, who traditionally relied upon personal and temporary authority rather than upon chiefly power, the Ba-Kongo maintained a considerable measure of centralization, expressed in the person of the 'crowned chief'. In contrast to the egalitarian tendencies of the former, the organization of the latter was based upon hierarchy and slavery, and this played a decisive part at times of social change. The Fang were less capable of adjusting themselves to the extension of social space resulting from economic expansion and modern means of communication, while the introduction of a money economy and exposure to competition affected them more deeply; in the absence of any centralized authority, their old political system depended upon a strict control by the 'elders' (the heads of extended families) of trade goods and the traffic in wives; once this primitive form of planning was upset the entire system of social relations was impaired. Moreover, the comparatively large size of the Fang villages, which had once been due to the needs of self-defence, had for some time ceased to be necessary, so that there was nothing to prevent the groups from splitting up and dispersing; and this, too, hindered the emergence of any centralized power. Among the Ba-Kongo, however, the existence of domestic slavery had helped to prevent the deterioration of social relations: because of the danger of confusing 'free men' with 'slaves', it served to check what one might call the commercialization of customary procedure that occurred among the Fang, the main result of which was to change the nature and amount of the marriage payments and to encourage the use of wives for speculative purposes. In this respect a further important fact is that, whereas Ba-Kongo society was matrilineal, Fang society was predominantly patrilineal. This is a very significant distinction, since relations with the 'affines' cannot be disregarded with impunity so long as the uncle-maternal nephew relationship remains fundamental; and, in this context, the fact that colonialism contributed to the extension of 'father right' was particularly important.

Thus the two societies were sharply differentiated, and this found expression in the very different extent to which they resisted the total and intensive intervention of the Europeans. While it is true that both peoples had experienced an unmistakable revival of initiative, it is equally important to emphasize the specific forms that this revival took. The Gabonese Fang were primarily concerned with the need to carry through a veritable reconstruction of society, as may be seen from their efforts to restore the clan and to regroup and modernize their villages. The Ba-Kongo, on the contrary, were less interested in internal problems (the most important of which was to find a modern substitute for the old 'crowned chief') than in that of their relationship with colonial society. Their early attempts to achieve unity – notably through the medium of the neo-Christian churches – were unequivocally opposed to the colonial situation; they tended to create, over and above kinship groups, petty 'particularisms' and administrative or political divisions, a unified Ba-Kongo entity, a first manifestation of emergent nationalism.

Since the Ba-Kongo were settled in the vicinity of (as well as within) the two great cities that dominate Central Africa, Brazzaville and Leopoldville, where their influence was preponderant, the proximity and mobility of an urban population gave rise to multiple forms of communication and reciprocal influence between rural and urban environments. As it would hardly be satisfactory to study either of them in isolation, we therefore undertook, in addition to this parallel treatment of the two ethnic groups, a sociological study of the black townships of Brazzaville (subsequently published as *Sociologie des Brazzavilles noires*, Paris, 1955). The process of urbanization in a country where the cities are a direct outcome of colonization, and the emergence of a growing class of wage workers to the detriment of the old subsistence economy, are phenomena of major importance. Our investigations therefore had to take into account, not only the villages, but also the urban centres and large-scale public works. These were the areas of contact where many innovations were developed, where socio-cultural models, later to spread beyond the ethnic frontiers, were constructed and where a new conception of law was taking shape which, though less effective than ancient 'custom', was on the other hand polyvalent.

By organizing our investigations in this way, we feel we may have provided an up-to-date and distinctive approach to the Central African societies now facing the shock of decolonization and economic development. We hope, too, that both by the nature of the materials and our theoretical treatment of them, we may have made some contribution to an understanding of the processes of social change. As it turns out, the theoretical and practical interest have proved to be of almost equal importance.

Part I
The 'Colonial Situation' and its Negation

I
THE 'COLONIAL SITUATION' CONCEPT

Despite the changes that have occurred, the colonial problem remains one of the main issues with which specialists in the social sciences have to deal. Indeed, the pressure of new nationalisms and the reactions resulting from decolonization give this problem an immediacy and a topicality that cannot be treated with indifference.

Anthropologists concerned with the phenomena of social change have as yet hardly taken account of the 'colonial situation' insofar as it constitutes a special combination of circumstances giving a specific orientation to the agents and processes of change. They have treated these processes in isolation – for example, the introduction of a monetary economy and a wage-earning class, the extension of modern education, or the efforts of missionary enterprise, etc. – but they have not regarded them as comprising a single entity that provides the basis for a new and autonomous society. For the most part their work has been based upon one of two points of view: either they have tended to tackle theoretical problems relating to the very nature of cultural reality, its receptivity to foreign cultural influences, its vicissitudes, etc.; or they have sought to achieve 'practical' results by undertaking enquiries of limited scope, and have all too often remained satisfied with a convenient empiricism.

Any *concrete* study of societies affected by colonization that aims at a complete conspectus of the subject can only be accomplished, however, by reference to the complex known as the 'colonial situation'. It is only by deepening our analysis of this situation, by focussing attention on its characteristics in relation to the particular place under investigation and by examining the developments that tend to negate it, that it becomes possible to interpret and classify the phenomena under observation. This recognition of the situation arising from the relations between the 'colonizing' and the 'colonized' societies, demands of the sociologist a continual critical effort, and serves as a warning against the dangers of a too one-sided approach. The examination of contemporary problems cannot but be affected by the observer's own 'reservations' or his attitude towards them; as is certainly the case with respect to the newly established states engaged in the task of decolonization. These remarks explain the importance we attach, at the start, to the theory of the 'colonial situation'. Of the early works undertaken in France, only those by O. Mannoni have devoted sufficient attention to this concept,[1] and they are confined essentially to the field of psycho-analysis. Moreover, Mannoni admits having restricted himself deliberately to an aspect that had hitherto been inadequately considered. We, on the other hand, are committed to totality, since we are of the opinion that there is a certain dishonesty in concentrating upon only one of the implications of the 'colonial situation'.

I. SOME METHODS OF APPROACH

It is possible to envisage this situation, created by the colonial expansion of the European powers during the last century, from various points of view. These include the specialist approaches of the imperial historian, of the economist, of the politician and administrator, of the sociologist preoccupied with the relations of alien civilizations, and of the psychologist concerned with the study of race relations, etc. It seems essential, therefore, if we are to attempt an all-round account, to examine what can be derived from each of these special contributions.

The historian considers colonization at its different stages and generally in terms of the metropolitan country. He enables us to grasp the changes that have taken place in the relations between the latter and the dependent territories, and shows how the isolation of the colonized peoples was brought about by the play of historical forces over which they had little or no control. He draws attention to the ideologies which, from time to time, have sought to justify colonization, and to the disparity between theory and practice. He describes the administrative and economic

systems that have ensured 'colonial peace', and that have endeavoured to make colonial enterprise profitable to the metropolis.
In short, the historian helps us to understand how the 'colonizing'
power, *in the course of time*, established itself within the 'colonized'
societies. By doing so, he provides the sociologist with a first
and indispensable set of references; he reminds him that the history
of a 'colonized' society is worked out as a function of a foreign
presence; and at the same time reveals the changing aspects
assumed by this presence.

Most historians have insisted on the fact that the pacification,
capitalization and development of the 'colonized' countries have
always been carried out 'in the interests of the Western nations,
and not with a view to local interests'.[2] They have shown the
extent to which the absorption of Asia, Africa and Oceania by
Europe has, in less than a century, 'transformed, by force and
often by bold reforms, the shape of human society'; and reminded
us that economic exploitation depends upon the achievement of
political power, for these are the two specific features of colonization.[3] Thus the historians enable us to realize the extent to which
the 'colonized' society becomes a tool in the hands of the 'colonizing' power. An example of this instrumental nature of the
relationship may be seen in the policy of compromising the indigenous aristocracy by allowing them to acquire a financial
interest,* and, still more, in the policy of transferring population
and recruiting labour solely in response to the requirements of
large-scale economy.[4] By reminding us of some of these bold
measures – movements of population and the creation of 'reserves',
modifications of the pattern of settlement, the transformation of
traditional law and of relations with authority, etc. – the historian
draws our attention to the fact that 'colonization has sometimes
actually amounted to social surgery'.[5] And this view, more or less
correct according to the regions and peoples under consideration,
is of great interest to the sociologist studying 'colonized' societies;
it explains why such societies are, to varying degrees, in *a state of
latent crisis*, and therefore in some measure in need of social
pathology.

Having defined the external pressures affecting 'colonized'

---

* Winning the ruling class over 'to our interests', Lyautey used to say; reducing
the native chiefs 'to mere tools', as R. Kennedy puts it.

societies, the historian notes the diversity of the resultant reactions; those of the peoples of the Orient, of Islam and of Black Africa have frequently been described in comparative studies. In this way, the history of Africa south of the Sahara reveals important differences in its power of resistance to European ascendancy. The historical study of colonization, having shown the importance of the 'external factor' as regards the changes affecting the 'colonized' societies, finds itself confronted by an 'internal factor' connected with the social structures and civilizations of the dependent peoples, and here it touches upon problems where the anthropologist finds himself on familiar ground. But by providing an account of the various reactions to the colonial situation, it shows how this situation can serve as a source of genuine insight. Colonization appears as an ordeal imposed upon certain societies, or, if one may risk the expression, as a crude sociological experiment. No analysis of 'colonized' societies can afford to disregard these specific conditions; they not only reveal, as some anthropologists have perceived,[6] the processes of adaptation and rejection and the new patterns of behaviour resulting from the destruction of traditional social models, but also show the 'resistance points' of the 'colonized' societies, the basic structures and behaviour patterns – in certain respects, they get down to rock bottom. Such knowledge is of definite theoretical interest (if one considers the colonial situation as a fact amenable to scientific observation and independent of the moral judgements it gives rise to); and it has real practical importance, since it suggests the fundamental data in the light of which every problem has to be approached.

The historian makes clear, moreover, how the colonial system was established and how it has been modified, and what, according to the circumstances, have been its various political, juridical and administrative features; he also enables us to bring into focus the ideologies by which men have sought to vindicate it.[7] Many studies have pointed out the considerable discrepancies that exist between the principles successively enunciated and their practical application, between the idea of a *civilizing mission* (the formulation of which, in a particularly emphatic form, goes back to Napoleon III) and the *utilitarian purpose* aimed at, which Eugène Étienne defined in 1894 as 'the sum of the benefits and profits that the metropolis can hope to derive' from any colonial enterprise.[8] In his history

of French colonization, H. Brunschwig refers to the long series of
misunderstandings that have marked its course. L. Joubert notes
'the discrepancy that has existed, ever since notions of responsibility for civilization were first adopted, between theory and
practice; the gap there has always been between them, if not the
hypocrisy of seeking to justify pure and simple exploitation on
humanitarian grounds'.[9] Thus an essential feature of the colonial
situation appears to be its *inauthenticity*. R. Kennedy, in his essay
'The Colonial Crisis and the Future', shows how every characteristic
of 'colonialism' – colour bar, political and economic subordination,
inadequate 'social' provision, lack of contact between the native
people and the 'dominant caste' – is based upon a 'series of
rationalizations', that is to say, the superiority of the white race,
the native peoples' incapacity for leadership, the despotism of the
traditional chiefs and the temptation that modern political leaders
are under to set themselves up as a 'dictatorial coterie', the inability
of the indigenous people to exploit the natural resources of their
countries, their lack of finance, the necessity of maintaining
prestige, etc.[10] With the help of such insights, the sociologist
recognizes how the European 'colonizing' society, inspired by a
dubious doctrine whose historical development he can trace,
committed to inauthentic modes of behaviour and hampered by a
stereotyped image of the native, acts in accordance with these
representations of the 'colonized' society. Elsewhere, we have
stressed the importance of this fact:[11] there can be no sociology of
the 'colonized' peoples unless due weight is given to ideologies
and to the more or less stereotyped behaviour they entail.

The historian reminds us that modern 'colonized' societies are
the product of a twofold history. Thus, in the case of Africa, there
is on the one hand African history properly so-called, ('these
communities so stable, so apparently stagnant, were all, or nearly
all, the result of various combinations of different peoples that had
been flung together, mixed up, superimposed upon one another
by history'),[12] which has given rise to homogeneous social structures;[13] and, on the other, a history largely determined by
European domination, 'which has brought into contact radically
heterogeneous social structures'.[14] A concrete study of these
societies can only be made by 'situating' them in relation to this
twofold history. It is usually accepted that colonization has

functioned through the interplay of three forces which it is almost impossible to separate – historically connected, and experienced as closely interrelated by those affected by them[15] – economic, administrative and missionary activity. Moreover, it is in relation to these three terms of reference that anthropologists have as a rule studied 'social change'. But in order to characterize European colonization and explain its appearance, certain historians have been led to over-emphasize one of these aspects – the economic factor. 'Colonial imperialism is only one of the manifestations of economic imperialism', Ch.-A. Julien suggests in an article devoted to this topic.[16] Here, history impinges upon another point of view, which is essential to any understanding of the colonial situation.

It was partly on economic grounds that the policy of expansion based its propaganda. In 1874 P. Leroy-Beaulieu insisted that it was necessary for France to become a colonial power; in 1890, Jules Ferry wrote: 'Colonial policy is the child of industrial policy . . . colonial policy is an international manifestation of the eternal laws of competition . . .'[17] Economic arguments were also employed by the colonial powers to justify their presence, development and capital investment being regarded as vested interests, and it is precisely these economic benefits that they have been most reluctant to forego, even when they have been prepared to grant political independence. Even prior to the studies undertaken by Marxist writers, certain early analysts of 'colonial imperialism' were already drawing attention to its economic basis.[18] The close connection between capitalist development and colonial expansion has also prompted various authors to compare the 'colonial question' with the 'social question' (and to insist 'that substantially there is no difference between them'), as well as suggesting a possible identification of the 'colonial peoples' with the 'proletariat'.[19] For a Marxist, this identification raises no difficulty; it provides political justification for the joint action of the proletariat and the colonial peoples.[20]

Without being prepared to reduce the colonial situation solely to its economic manifestations, the sociologist is nevertheless bound to give due importance to these points of view. They suggest to him that it is not only the contacts between technological and 'primitive', pre-industrial civilizations that explain the disruption of 'colonized' societies; they also remind him that both the 'colonizing' and 'colonized' societies stand in a certain relationship to one another (we have already stressed the instrumental nature of this relationship), and that this involves tensions and conflict.

The economic features of the colonial situation have been described by certain anthropologists, and by geographers specializing in the tropical countries. R. Kennedy, in the study already referred to,[21] notes the principal features: poor industrial equipment; large-scale exploitation, with foreign trade almost exclusively in the hands of foreign companies;[22] the 'distance' maintained between the colonizing and colonized communities, which explains the difficulties experienced by the native 'in raising himself economically'; and the poverty of the indigenous masses, which is accentuated by the decay of their traditional economies.

Of the books by French authors, those devoted to Indo-China are especially valuable. They are the work of geographers (a significant instance of that evasion of reality that is characteristic of French ethnology), Ch. Robequain and P. Gourou;[23] and they are primarily concerned with the problems of the peasantry. Apart from the attention they pay to technical methods (which have not been improved, or only slightly), they stress particularly the phenomenon of the break-up of landed property[24] and 'dispossession', resulting in proletarianization and uprooting; and also the creation of an agrarian bourgeoisie, which, like the proletariat, comes into existence 'through contact with western civilization and the weakening of traditional values'.[25] The observations they make elsewhere with regard to commerce and industry confirm, up to a recent period, the general schema advanced by R. Kennedy.

To apply this to African experience, let us consider the situation created in South Africa by the European minority.[26] It imposes both territorial segregation (the Native Land Act of 1913) and social segregation (the Colour Bar Act of 1926), which restricts the black workers to unskilled labour; a very small share of the national income in African hands, amounting in 1950 to only 20 per cent; and an economic system based on racialism, which nevertheless continues to encourage the exodus from the rural areas that leads to proletarianization and detribalization. The peculiar situation in South Africa – in a way, almost a caricature – shows how closely the economic, political and racial aspects are related,[27] and makes it clear that any contemporary study of the peoples of the Union can only be made by taking all three of them into account. We realize, therefore, the overwhelming importance of treating the 'colonial situation' as a complex, a totality.

Anglo-Saxon anthropologists have attributed great importance to the economic facts, which they regard as being amongst the main 'forces' inducing social and cultural change. Monica Hunter, in her well-known book *Reaction to Conquest*, studies the changes that have taken place in Pondo society (South Africa) as a result primarily of the economic factor, and only then of the political factor ('which, whatever non-Marxists may say, is historically economic in origin'). But these studies, of which there are already many dealing with Africa, were often organized around the 'primitive' social and economic system, and its transformation under the impact of the 'modern' economy and the resulting problems. They neglected to relate their observations to the colonial situation, and lacked any dialectical awareness of the interaction between colonized and colonizing society. Writers inspired by Malinowski display this weakness in the highest degree, merely examining the result of 'contact' between 'institutions' of the same type, and scarcely going further than the simple description of change and the enumeration of problems. This explains the importance accorded to purely rural aspects, to the changes that affect the village and the 'family', and to the problem of rural depopulation. In this field, anthropologists have established significant classifications: destruction of the economic unity of the family, increasing predominance of economic values, emancipation of the younger generation, introduction of a monetary economy that upsets personal relationships, weakening of traditional hierarchies, etc. On the other hand, such important phenomena as new types of social grouping (including political parties and trade unions), the emergence of social classes or pseudo-classes and the nature and role of the proletariat, are only described in very general terms; and the conflicts they imply are rarely analysed.[28]

Earlier studies of a political and administrative character devoted more detailed attention to these latter aspects, although of an essentially practical and 'oriented' kind. They showed the extent to which the colonized society, in both its urban and rural aspects, and the colonizing society form an entity, a system; and suggested that the study of either one of these elements must necessarily be related to the whole. They drew attention to antagonisms and conflicts that are only to be explained within the framework of the colonial situation; and, furthermore, the notion of 'crisis' was implicit in this preoccupation. By stressing, perhaps exaggerating, this, they send us back to that pathological aspect of colonized societies to which we have already drawn attention.

II. IMPORTANCE OF POLITICAL FACTORS AND ADMINISTRATIVE METHODS

The relinquishing of political and administrative ascendancy should not lead us to overlook the part it has played, and indeed still plays, in certain parts of Africa. Historians of colonization, as well as anthropologists, regard administrative activity, which for a long time was mainly concerned with economic activity, as one of the principal causes of change.[29] The pacification imposed by government, the tracks and roads it opened up with forced labour, primarily served the interests of foreign companies and traders. The taxes it levied, by forcing the native to obtain legal currency, delivered him into the hands of the buying agents. The recruitment of labour under its auspices supplied public works and other enterprises with manpower; and its control of wages and conditions of work, as well as of the movement of men and merchandise, benefited local undertakings. Thus the purpose of administrative action was, to begin with, to encourage some measure of development; or, to use a word that many people now fight shy of, to *exploit* the colonies. In this respect, it adds little to our previous analysis of the situation.

But to administer a colonial country involves other forms of activity; the country has to be controlled, 'held down', so that the administrative system becomes an integral part of all colonized societies. R. Delavignette was fully justified in saying: 'In reality, indigenous societies can no longer be separated from the colonial administration of the territory'.[30] The continually increasing number of officials and the multiplication of 'services' reveal the diversity and extent of its influence; and it is especially in terms of political control, whether exercised directly or indirectly, that it functions most powerfully and is least prepared to admit of dispute. Such action is related more or less explicitly to a theory of 'native policy', which, to use the classic term, aims either at *assimilation* or (unequal) *association*, or at a compromise.

There can be no doubt that the recognition of a theoretical context of this kind is indispensable for the understanding of colonial societies; it helps to fill out the study of ideologies, which we showed to be necessary when considering the historical point of view. But to these theories, and the policies derived from them, colonized peoples of similar type react in different ways; in West Africa alone, the different reactions of the native elites in the British and French colonies is most revealing in this respect. The structures, the cultural context, the ways of life and modes of thought resulting from the activities of the colonizers remain deeply rooted in the hearts and minds of the African peoples, even after Independence. It was in the light of this that B. Boganda, one-time leader of the Central African Republic, drew up his project for a 'United States of Latin Africa'. Similarly, when they first met as heads of state, Sékou Touré and Nkwame Nkrumah were to discover the extent to which differences in the evolution of their countries thwarted their efforts to achieve unity.

Whatever the political theory adopted, the relations of domination and subordination existing between the colonizing and colonized societies characterize the colonial situation. And the authors who have devoted most attention to this aspect have shown that political domination is accompanied by cultural domination. One of them has suggested that 'the cultural problem is closely bound up with the general problem of political and economic evolution', that 'the influence of European cultures' resulted in 'the destruction of the indigenous cultural basis'.[31] A hint of this kind deserves serious consideration, for it puts the anthropologist on his guard against any temptation to consider 'culture contacts', or 'the interpenetration of civilizations', as operating in a more or less mechanical way.

On the other hand, stress has been laid upon the arbitrary manner in which the colonial powers divided up the territory of the subject peoples, and imposed purely administrative boundaries upon them. This resulted in the fragmentation of important peoples, the breaking up of viable political units and the creation of artificial groupings. Thus many of the initiatives undertaken by the colonized peoples seem to reveal a determination to restore the old boundaries. In West Africa alone we may note the demands for reunification of the Ewe (then split up between the two Togos and Ghana), the attempts at tribal federation in South Cameroun, the more or less explicit desire for regrouping shown by the so-called 'Kimbangist' Negro churches in the Ba-Kongo country (i.e. the two Congos and Angola). This 'balkanization', and the hostility and rivalries between ethnic groups created for administrative purposes, have imposed a peculiar history upon these peoples, an understanding of which is indispensable for any sociological analysis.

Political control could only be effected through the intermediary of the 'chiefs' and, to some extent, through that of native institutions. Directly or indirectly, the chiefs had to be integrated into the administrative system as a whole. But such integration was not always easy: either because the colonized society, by means of an entirely fictitious submission, hid its real chiefs behind men of straw, or because the colonizing administration, through its failure to understand the reality of the native political system, either created the 'chiefdom as well as the chief', or else appointed to the chieftainship 'a man who neither should nor could have had any claim to it'.[32] Frequently the administration overthrew the existing authorities, and created new chiefs or chiefs invested with completely new powers; thus, in the French West African colonies, the village headman was in principle a traditional chief charged with certain administrative duties, while the district chief became a 'specialized civil servant'. Two types of authority (one arising from native history, the other from European occupation) were obliged to *coexist*, the first being subordinate to the second, and both hostile to one another; and official reports, in Gabon and the Congo for instance, monotonously refer to the lack of authority of the administrative chiefs, or to the rivalry between them and the traditional chiefs. As a result, political equilibrium within the colonized societies was seriously jeopardized. M. Fortes, in his important study of the Tallensi of Ghana, has shown how the installation of official chiefs – who established their position by the part that they played, unofficially to begin with, in legal matters – upset the stability and weakened the original character of a society, which, although it had no political head, nevertheless had a very real organization underlying its apparent anarchy. It was partly against this political distortion that the emerging nationalisms reacted, and this in some measure explains the racial character that these at first assumed. In this respect, the example of Nigeria is significant: *Nigerian* nationalism, seeking a way forward, came up against a 'tendency to adjust the old tribal loyalties within a new framework, the limits of which are difficult to determine', and also against the rivalry between 'tribal nationalisms' which find their expression in political parties competing on an ethnic basis.[33]

To all these factors the proponents of applied anthropology have devoted close attention, in the first place by endeavouring to discover that 'scientifically controlled adaptation' defined by L. Mair. The detailed studies of English anthropologists (we refer elsewhere to the important literature devoted to 'political systems' and social organization), and the place assigned to problems of a political order in their research programmes and certain specialist journals, are significant of this interest. The most recent phenomena – the rise of nationalist aspirations and political parties, the development of political opinion, etc. – are now beginning to be studied, and not merely the traditional political institutions. Such problems subject modern anthropology to a severe test; through research of this type it is brought face to face with the most immediate social reality.

III. THE CONTRIBUTIONS OF SOCIOLOGY AND SOCIAL PSYCHOLOGY

Colonizing Society and Colonized Society

In the light of the foregoing facts, it becomes easier to assess, and to appreciate, the contributions made by sociology and social psychology. In a work devoted to the colonies, E. A. Walcker draws attention to the fact that they are essentially 'plural societies'.[34] He points out that a colony (a global society) 'generally consists of a number of groups more or less aware of each other's existence, often opposed to one another on grounds of colour, and striving to lead different kinds of lives within the limits of a single political framework'. And he continues: 'These groups speak different languages, eat different foods, often pursue different occupations to which they are committed by law or custom, wear different clothes . . . inhabit dwellings of different types, cherish different traditions, worship different gods and entertain different ideas of good and evil. Societies of this kind are not communities.' In addition to these elements he makes a point that is useful for our analysis when he observes, with regard to the colour bar, that it 'translates the world problem of minorities into tropical terms'. These observations provide a starting point. What is interesting about them is not the reference to pluralism, but the specific examples of it which he notes: the racial basis of the 'groups', their radical diversity, the antagonistic relationships existing between them, and the necessity of having to coexist 'within the limits of a single political framework'. Moreover, the importance he attaches to the colonizing society being a *dominant minority* is fruitful. In a primarily political article, H. Laurentie defines a colony as: 'a country where a European minority is superimposed upon a native majority with a different civilization and different customs; this European minority acts upon the autochthonous peoples with an energy out of all proportion to its size; it is, so to speak, extremely "contagious" and, of its nature, distorting'.[35] This active minority owes its dominant position to its indisputable material superiority, to a legal system introduced to maintain its own interests, and to a system of justifications of a more or less racial character (for some writers, such as R. Maunier, the essence of colonialism is primarily the fact that it is a 'contact between races'). The more deeply rooted and opposed to fusion it is, the more it sees itself threatened by the demographic pressure of the subject people, the more reactionary it is: as, for instance, in South Africa, where the white population regards 'its position as a minority problem, whereas the Blacks see theirs as a colonial problem, a problem of tutelage';[36] or again, in Algeria, where a European minority fiercely defended its own status. This point is important precisely because it brings home to us that this numerical minority is not a *sociological minority*, and is in no danger of becoming so except through the transformation of the colonial situation.

2

This has, indeed, already been noted by certain sociologists. It is a point that L. Wirth insists upon in his definition and typology of minorities. In his view, the concept is not a statistical one. He cites as an example the Blacks in the United States, who, though they are in a numerical majority in some of the southern states, nevertheless constitute a minority in that they are socially, politically and economically subordinate; or, again, the position resulting from the colonial expansion of the European nations, which has transformed the colonizers into dominant groups, and the coloured peoples into minorities.[37] The size of a social group does not of itself make it a minority, although it 'may have a bearing upon its status, and upon its relations with the dominant group'. The nature of a minority is inherent in the position it occupies within the global society, and it essentially implies a relationship between subordinate and dominant; a relationship which we have repeatedly encountered in the course of the preceding analysis.

The sense in which the term minority, in the sociological meaning of the word, applies to the colonized society clearly shows that the latter must be envisaged in its relation to the other groups comprising the colony. But it does not indicate how the colonized society is to be distinguished from other minorities who find themselves in a different position. For this, a preliminary step is necessary: to define its place within the global society, the colony.

If one considers schematically the groups brought together by the colonial situation, by classifying them from the colonizing society (dominant group) down to the colonized society (subordinate group), one can distinguish: (a) the colonizing society, excluding foreigners belonging to the white race; (b) these other white foreigners; (c) the 'coloureds', to use the English expression, which has a very wide sense; and (d) the colonized society, those whom the English refer to as 'natives' – distinctions which rest in the first place on criteria of race and nationality. These imply as a kind of postulate: the supremacy of the white race and, more precisely, of that part of it to which the colonizing nation belongs; a supremacy that is accepted as being based upon history and nature.

But this is only an approximation, and requires filling out.

R. Delavignette devotes a chapter of his book to the question of *Colonial Society*.[38] In it he notes some of the features by which it may be defined: 'A society that is metropolitan in its origin and connections', constituting a numerical minority, capitalist by nature and inspired by a 'sense of heroic superiority' (a fact that is partly to be explained by the preponderance of men, and their youth, who are to be found in the colonies during the early stages of colonization). But what is most significant is that it is a society whose function is to dominate, politically, economically and spiritually; which, according to Delavignette, tends to give its members 'a feudal outlook'. The important fact is that this *dominant society* remains an *extreme numerical minority*: there is such a vast disproportion between the number of colonizers and the number of colonized that there is always a more or less conscious fear of seeing the traditional hierarchy restored purely as a result of superior numbers.

L. Wirth oversimplifies matters considerably, however, when he maintains that, in a colonial situation, 'the dominant group could always maintain its position of superiority merely by bringing into play the military and administrative machine', so great was the material disproportion between the two civilizations.[39] He had no understanding of the struggle for decolonization that was developing. He underestimated, too, a number of important features: the steps taken by the dominant group to make itself 'untouchable', either by reducing social contact to the minimum (segregation), or by setting itself up as a model, while withholding the necessary means of attaining this model (assimilation represented as the condition of equality – because the group knows it to be impossible, or else prevents it); ideologies justifying the dominant group's position; political procedures that serve to maintain the disequilibrium in favour of the colonists (and of the metropolis). To all of which must be added the transference of the feelings of hostility aroused by politico-economic coercion to specific groups – for instance, the Lebanese in West Africa, the Indians in the Union of South Africa, and the coloureds more or less universally. The more the gap between the two civilizations tends to be reduced, the more significant the numerical factor becomes; force ceases to be sufficient to maintain domination, and other, more indirect, means have also to be employed.

The colonizing society is not homogeneous. It has its 'factions' or 'clans', which remain more or less closed to one another, more or less in competition, and each with its own policy. The degree of remoteness of this society from the colonized society varies with each group; yet its policy of domination and prestige *requires* its absolute inaccessibility – which does nothing to promote understanding and creates 'stereotyped' reactions. The exclusiveness of the main group of colonists is expressed in the first place with regard to the other white men whom they treat as 'foreigners'. These constitute a minority in the full sense of the word, both numerically and sociologically: though their economic status may be high, they are nonetheless subject to administrative restrictions; they are suspect on account of their nationality, and often cut off from the 'real' colonizers; the more they are spurned the more they regard themselves as national minorities; and thus they are often on closer terms with the native peoples. This greater familiarity on their part, and their lower social position, explains the ambivalent reaction towards them of the native people: a certain intimacy, tinged with scorn; feelings of resentment may be directed towards them with relative impunity, and they all too easily invite this process of transference.

In the scale of discredit that attaches to the subordinate groups the least favourable position is that of the coloureds (half-castes and non-white foreigners). The more they succeed in achieving positions of economic importance the more they find themselves forced into isolation by discriminatory measures: for example, the Indian problem in South Africa is to be explained in the first place by the fact that some Indians 'are too rich and surreptitiously encroach upon the position of the Whites'.[40] Thus the overlapping of racial and economic factors is all the more complete precisely because they represent 'a racial compromise'. Only in exceptional circumstances (the example of the 'Bastards of Rehoboth', in what was previously German South West Africa, is particularly well-known) do they succeed in forming a group, in constituting a viable community and maintaining a rigid exclusiveness. As A. Siegfried notes with reference to the Cape coloureds, they are thrust back upon the black race, with which they do not wish to become confused because they are seeking assimilation with the colonizing society, which, depending upon local circumstances, either remains more or less closed to them, or else grants them a purely personal status,* thus as it were, giving some kind of legal sanction to their special position. Though representing a racial compromise, they in no sense constitute a 'social compromise'; it is difficult to imagine them as a means of liaison between the colonized and colonizing societies. Political alliances between them and the elite of the colonized society have hardly proved lasting: thus the Conference of Non-Europeans, held in South Africa in 1927 in an attempt to unite half-castes, Indians and Bantus with a view to common action, proved to be ineffective and of short duration. Owing to their better economic and political position, as well as to the racial factor, the coloureds find themselves more often in conflict with the colonized society than in agreement; it is impossible for them to make headway as leaders of the latter.†

The two most striking features of a *colonized society* are its overwhelming numerical superiority,‡ and its basic subordination. For though numerically it is a majority, sociologically it is nonetheless a minority, since, as R. Maunier puts it, 'colonization is a question of power', involving the loss of autonomy and '*de facto* if not *de jure* subjection'.[41] The function of each sector of the colonizing society is to ensure this domination in a clearly defined field, political, economic and, almost always, spiritual. For a long time the subordination of the colonized society was absolute, owing to the lack of advanced technique or of any material power other than numbers; and it was expressed in *de facto* as well as *de jure* relations. It is based, as we have several times pointed out, upon an ideology, a system of pseudo-

---

* As was attempted before 1939 in the French territories of French West Africa (1930), Madagascar (1934), French Equatorial Africa (1936) and Indo-China (1938).

† We should point out, however, that a certain degree of common danger, such as that produced by the decisions of the nationalist governments of South Africa, results in a more united opposition.

‡ For Black Africa alone, the figures given by R. Delavignette in 1939 for the so-called European population, were: Union of South Africa, 250 per 1,000; what had previously been German South West Africa, 100 per 1,000; Rhodesia, 45 per 1,000; Angola, 10 per 1,000; Kenya 5 per 1,000; Belgian Congo, 2 per 1,000; French West Africa and French Equatorial Africa, 1 per 1,000 (*Les vrais chefs de l'Empire*, Paris 1939, p. 36). As regards the last two territories, the European population increased considerably in the years 1946–51, tripling in French Equatorial Africa and Cameroun, and doubling in French West Africa and Togo.

justifications and rationalizations; and it has a more or less admitted, more or less obvious, 'racialist' bias. The colonized society is subject to pressure from all the groups comprising the 'colony', each of which exercises domination in one sector or another, and for whom it is in the first place a means of creating wealth, although, despite its numbers, it only receives a minimal part of the profits. This function determines, in part, its relations with the other groups who derive economic advantage from it; relations – such as those of exploiter and exploited, of dominant and subordinate – which are nevertheless by no means simple owing to the lack of unity on the part of the colonized society, and especially to the essentially heterogeneous nature of the culture by which it is inspired.

A colonial society is *ethnically split* – by divisions which have their origin in native history, but are utilized by the colonial power and complicated by the arbitrary allocation of territory as well as by the imposition of administrative boundaries. These determine not only the relations of the various peoples with the colonizing society (for example, those who acted as 'agents' during the period of African trade and trading-posts sought to change their function from an economic to a political plane, and now appear as 'militant' minorities), but also their attitude towards the imported culture (some ethnic groups prove to be more 'assimilationist' or more 'traditionalist' than other groups in their vicinity, partly at least as a reaction against the latter). A colonial society is also *spiritually divided*. These divisions may have existed prior to European colonization, as a result of successful Islamic invasions, for example; but, in many places, colonization introduced religious confusion, arousing antagonism between Christianity and the traditional religions, and supporting the various Christian denominations against one another. In this respect we may quote a Brazzaville African, who described this 'state of affairs as having no effect except a regrettable confusion in moral development'. He added: 'The Blacks in Africa, whoever they may be, have the rudiments of religion; to rob them of these by importing atheism or conflicting religious teaching can only confuse them.'[42] He even went so far as to suggest that the colonists ought to enforce unity – which only goes to show how painful the infliction of these new divisions on top of those already in existence might sometimes be.* Moreover, colonization gave rise to other, social, divisions, arising from administrative and economic action and the development of education: separation between city dwellers and countryfolk, between proletariat and bourgeoisie, between the elite, or as they are usually called, the 'progressive' elements, and the masses,[43] as well as between generations. We shall come back to these divisions, and suggest what their consequences may be, at various stages of our analysis; but each of them participates in the global society in a different way. The contacts between races and civilizations which are imposed by colonization do not, in every case, have the same significance or the same incidence, and they must therefore be studied as a function of this diversity.

The colonized and colonizing societies differ from one another both as regards race and civilization. In both these fields the distinction appears absolute: a distinction that is expressed by contrasting 'primitive' and civilized, pagan and Christian, techno-logical civilizations and 'backward' civilizations. It is this very obvious fact, the bringing into contact of heterogeneous civiliza-tions and the consequent antagonisms, rather than the colonial situation itself, that has attracted the attention of anthropologists during the last few decades.

Studies of 'Culture Contact'

The systematization of similar types of research was not effected until comparatively recently. Malinowski's early papers relating to this problem appeared about 1930, and his introduction to the volume *Methods of Study of Culture Contact in Africa*[44] was even later. This was the essay in which he unequivocally asserted his intention of studying societies as they actually exist ('a completely intact indigenous society would appear to be a fiction'), and of giving 'anthropology' a practical significance. It is here, too, that Malinowski defined what he called 'the contact situation', and clarified the notion of a 'new' culture which, though consisting of 'partially fused' elements, was not to be regarded as the product of some kind of mechanical assimilation of the cultural

* Sometimes these divisions were the cause of veritable 'religious wars'; as happened in Uganda on two occasions, between 1878–88 and 1890–99.

elements incorporated in it. Indeed, he criticized a similar notion, when he insisted upon the fact that the contribution of European society, which in large measure controls the situation, is 'highly selective'. He also warned against the dangers of a 'one-sided approach'; though on this point he spoke cautiously, and was careful to emphasize that it was in no way his intention either to accuse or to present a 'pro-native' case.

The phenomena of cultural change, he said, could be evaluated by starting from a 'zero point', which would define the conditions of social equilibrium prior to European intervention. But this would be a naive point of view, since it was bound to underrate the remote influences, the already existing 'discordances', and to exaggerate the possibilities of reconstructing and interpreting the earlier state of affairs. Any reference to an earlier situation, in which the tribe appeared to have been protected from any outside contact, seemed to him to be a dangerous illusion. Malinowski protested against the 'pseudo-historical passion for reconstruction'; for the research worker engaged in studying culture contact, he said, observation of the existing reality was enough.* The way in which the institutions that have been preserved function is different in the new context to what it was in the old – it is the comparative data, much more than the dubious historical data, that the specialist concerned with such problems should be looking for. Here we find that tendency of functionalists to reject history, which A. Kroeber was soon to denounce – an approach that Malinowski justified by the lack of an adequate body of established fact (*Ignoramus ignorabimus*), while at the same time recognizing that the study of culture contact and change is to some extent a micro-history, a 'short term' history. This theoretical position Malinowski was to confirm in a critical examination of the work of two of his pupils (L. Mair and M. Hunter), *The Dynamics of Culture Change*, where it appears to be very feebly sustained. In a severe critique of this theoretical work, M. Gluckman had little difficulty in showing that Malinowski's ideas with regard to history – particularly his failure to distinguish between objective and subjective history – are confused;[45] and Gluckman correctly drew attention to the existence of materials (official documents, books by explorers and missionaries, etc.) that have

* His actual words were: 'is sufficient for all he needs to know', *ibid.*, p. 32.

a definite value, and to the importance of making use of the
information contained in them in order to understand the emergence of this or that situation, the development of this or that
process. Thus, when Malinowski maintained that the peace
imposed by the colonizers 'has obliterated the old tribal
antagonisms',[46] and treated this as a phenomenon belonging to
a vanished past, he was depriving himself of an indispensable
element for understanding the present; for though European
occupation suppressed the *military* expression of tribal antagonisms
and conflicts, it nevertheless continued to make use of them for
commercial and political ends, and might well end up by provoking 'previously hostile tribes to unite against the Europeans. . . .
Without an historical study we cannot understand the drives
which lie beneath the changes in the relationships of personalities
and groups' (*idem*).

It is impossible not to accept Gluckman's criticisms, and
wherever the opportunity occurs we shall make use of them
against the historical background. The *situation* in respect of
which we study socio-cultural change already exists; the analysis
it requires is only fruitful if we seek out the essential facts of local
colonial history. We have already drawn attention to this, but it
is worth remembering also that the concept of *situation* enables
us, to a considerable extent, to integrate the various points of
view (including that of history) demanded by the present state
of the social sciences. It must also be remembered that we are
confronted by processes that have been developing over a long
period – Messianism, for example, has been active amongst the
Ba-Kongo since 1920. There can be no doubt that, in such cases,
recourse to recent history is essential – insofar as this explains how
the innovating movement is organized, how it fulfils the requirements of the new social conditions and is subject to variations
arising from the vicissitudes of the relationship between the
colonizing and colonized societies. Moreover, the persistence of
certain institutions can only be fully explained in those exceptional
cases where reference to their mode of operation in the old context is available to the investigator. This was demonstrated in
our *Sociologie des Brazzavilles noires*, where we showed how the
Témo, originally a savings association, was at different periods,
beneath its apparent formal continuity, able to fulfil a variety

of functions as a result of economic and social change.[47] It is on occasions such as this that the appeal to historical facts is essential.

In *The Dynamics of Culture Change* the theoretical views already mentioned are submitted to a more detailed examination, but the initial orientation is in no way modified. The 'contact situation' concept appears to be of very little practical significance: above all, it fails to treat the colony as a global society. Indeed, precisely what is lacking is the sense of social reality – of the field of complex relationships that it comprises and the antagonisms it gives rise to. As Gluckman has pointed out, the conceptual system elaborated by this famous anthropologist in no way lends itself to the recognition of conflict (whether more or less restricted) as an attribute of every society. 'In general', says Gluckman, 'wherever Blacks and Whites cooperate, he classifies the phenomena as "processes of contact and social change"; wherever they are in conflict he regards them as distinct and "not integrated".'[48] These latter aspects are excluded from the sphere of culture contact, even when the facts oblige Malinowski to consider them. It should be noted how easily a theoretical position of this kind can, in a situation characterized by domination and unequal relations between colonizers and colonized, become a source of error. We then see that the notion of 'maladjustment' is regarded as a strictly cultural phenomenon – resulting from the *cultural* incompatibilities created by contact and the rhythm of change – without sufficient attention being paid to the underlying conflict between groups or races. In the present work, on the contrary, we are concerned to bring out these basic motivations and to show how certain cultural phenomena – for instance, the use of specific aspects of culture for purposes of evasion or opposition – are determined by such conflicts. Having adopted a very conciliatory position (he suggested that 'in the long run the interests of both Africans and Europeans converge'), Malinowski was prompted to define the problems 'of practical anthropology' in a disconcertingly naive manner. He implies, for instance, that the forces of change, if wisely controlled, 'can ensure a normal and stable development', that a sound colonial policy involves achieving equilibrium between 'things promised and things given', and so on.[49] Thus he finds himself obliged to minimize such phenomena as emergent nationalisms and forces making for independence, racial reactions, the early social movements and the influence of Marxism; and in the concluding paragraphs of *The Dynamics of Culture Change* he reveals his fear lest his work be regarded as an indictment of British colonial policy – a reservation that only accentuates the weakness of his contribution.

At this point, it is appropriate to mention his theory of culture change, according to which three distinct realities – African culture, Western culture and that resulting from the contact between them* – confront one another, each 'obeying its own laws'. It was on the basis of this theory that Malinowski decided upon the principles and 'instruments' which he regarded as most suitable for his study. Although he recognized that these three cultural 'orders' are interdependent, he established a division between them, describing and treating each of them separately, in a way that the facts do not justify. In criticizing this approach, Gluckman correctly points out that the new cultural reality must be analysed as a function of the 'situation' – a situation similar to those that are to be found elsewhere: for example, in any society where the processes of industrialization and urbanization have already begun to operate – and not simply as a result of the 'variants' imposed by the African context. Neither of these points of view can be omitted; though it is at once apparent that this approach modifies the basic distinction put forward by Malinowski. In the same way, it is impossible to compare the 'customary' background with the 'detribalized' background, since between the two there exist a host of connections, numerous exchanges and a continual interplay of reciprocal influences. When I decided to study simultaneously the Brazzaville townships and the neighbouring peasant societies, it was precisely in order to bring out this interdependence and reciprocity.† More than this, I consider that in such circumstances a purely unilateral approach would have lost much of its significance.[50] In this sense, the recording of parallel observations in parallel columns, as advocated by Malinowski,[51] can scarcely lead to an analysis in depth: it leaves out essential links between them.

Finally, in a much broader way, this particular work calls in

* 'The *tertium quid* of contact.'
† See the chapter devoted to the Ba-Kongo groups in Part III of this work.

question his whole theory of culture. The unit of culture derived from his analysis is the *institution*, which satisfies fundamental physiological and psychological needs.[52] This was the starting point that led the famous anthropologist to regard all 'culture contacts' as occurring between institutions of the same type, each 'Western' institution having 'to direct its impact primarily upon its indigenous counterpart';[53] thus, one might say, the primary effects of the contact are treated in a purely *horizontal* way, and it is admitted, elsewhere, that any given institution can be replaced by another so long as it is capable of satisfying the fundamental needs that gave rise to it. Although Malinowski is at pains to avoid reaching this conclusion, his argument tends that way, especially when he sets out to define 'the common factor in culture change'.[54] This conception leads him to minimize the significance of relations of conflict, to treat phenomena in an essentially descriptive way, and to omit any analysis of the complex connections and interactions that occur in any social system that is subject to change. These defects are all the more apparent in that Malinowski does nothing to clarify his views when asserting that contact occurs 'between institutions'. In order to understand the full meaning and functions associated with the various forms of Bantu Messianism and the 'separatist' churches – including the 'nationalist' reactions that are bound up with them – is it enough simply to consider the impact of Christianity upon the magical cults of the Africans? Obviously not. It is because he fails to state clearly the nature of the reality represented by the 'colony' (a global society), because he does not frankly define the 'situation' in which contact occurs, as well as on purely theoretical grounds, that Malinowski's treatment of the problem remains thoroughly unsatisfactory.

On the other hand, a number of writers (as a rule, the most polemical) have insisted upon the *state of crisis* that exists in the majority of colonial societies. This is true, insofar as the dominant minority is opposed to genuine solutions; for it would certainly appear, in the case of the colonized society, that *its demand for modern norms coincides with its demand for autonomy*. This fact obliges the sociologist to adopt an almost clinical method of analysis. And, in an earlier work, we showed that the examination of colonized societies, from the angle of their specific crises, offers the investigator in certain respects 'a privileged position'.* Since such crises bring into play almost the whole of society, its institutions as well as its social groups and symbols, the mal-adjustments provide opportunities for analysis not only to per-meate and grasp the phenomena of contact between the dominant and subordinate societies but also *to understand the latter more fully in its traditional forms*, by revealing certain characteristic weaknesses or certain irreducible collective structures and representations. Such crises, since they affect the global society as a whole, throw light upon this 'totality' and upon the fundamental relations implied by it,† thus facilitating the kind of concrete and detailed study recommended by Marcel Mauss.

These crises manifest themselves, at first sight, *in the modification or disappearance of institutions and groups*. But sociological analysis cannot be restricted merely to these social aspects; it is essential to go still further if we are to grasp what G. Gurvitch has called the 'forms of sociability'.[55] It seems clear that various ties, various social relationships, subsist even when the structures within which they functioned have deteriorated or been destroyed, while new ones appear as a result of the colonial situation and the social conditions arising from it. These may coexist, and it is they that give to the new ideas conceived by the subordinate society that characteristic of being at once traditionalist and modernist; the *ambiguity* that a number of observers have remarked upon.

Race Relations and Psychology

We have frequently alluded to the importance of race relations, to the racial significance that economic and political factors assume against the background of the colonial situation. A number of writers have insisted upon the interracial character of 'human relationships in overseas countries', upon the fact that

* G. Balandier: 'Aspects de l'évolution sociale chez les Fang du Gabon', I: 'Les implications de la "situation coloniale"', *op. cit*. Similarly, the radical programmes of modernization and development undertaken after Independence were, for a time, productive of 'crises' for the traditional societies affected by them.

† Monica Hunter reaches a similar conclusion. She writes: 'The story of culture contact makes very clear the fact that society is a unity and when one aspect is modi-fied the whole is affected,' *Reaction to Conquest*, p. 552. But she merely mentions the point, without expatiating upon its methodological consequences.

underlying the 'political and economic causes of conflict that still exist between the white race and the coloured peoples, there is almost always a racial motive', and upon the fact that, even when national independence has been achieved, society often remains 'interracial'.[56]

We have already suggested that colonial anthropologists have devoted too little attention to race problems, allocating to them far too small a part of their research programmes. This is to be explained partly by the fact that their interest has been focused on cultures rather than on societies, but partly also by their more or less conscious anxiety not to call in question the very foundations and ideology of the colonizing society to which they belong.[57] On the other hand, work carried out in the United States (and in Brazil) has been largely concerned with race relations between Blacks and Whites. In these countries, the facts could not be evaded, firstly because the basic differences in civilization, language, religion and habits that operate in the case of the colonial situation are there considerably modified, and serve neither to mask them nor to complicate them; secondly, because cultural distinctions are there being obliterated and equality of rights has been proclaimed; and thirdly, because in America such phenomena only represent that part of the colonial past that still remains to be liquidated. The work that is being done is not exclusively centred upon attitudes but shows, as has been suggested by R. Bastide,[58] the connection that exists between racial and cultural reactions.

One of the most significant facts is the way the colonizing society manipulates this racial diversity in order to justify and maintain its domination: assertion of the superiority of the white race as the basis of its civilizing mission, utilization of 'local racialisms' and recourse to methods that give rise to resentment. The topography of colonial towns, and the segregation of which this is an expression, provide material evidence of the importance of the racial factor. It is during the colonial period that race relations assert themselves, becoming increasingly complex and virulent. The need for a dynamic perspective in this field is imperative; as Mannoni observes, 'racial antagonism is not a primary or spontaneous phenomenon'; it 'develops progressively, by a process of evolution'; it only 'manifests itself', and gives rise to open conflict, when the colonized people 'show signs of emancipating themselves from subjection'.[59]

Race relations, and the potential conflicts they involve, play an increasing part as the colonized society 'changes'. They are an effect of contact, though in turn they also determine its nature; according to Mannoni, 'European racialism is met by a racialism (on the part of the colonized) that is induced by the former'. It hardly ever finds expression in the relationships created by daily life, and it leads to one of two things: cultural changes, especially in the form of clandestine developments, or violent revolts that rarely affect the group aimed at, the colonizers, but more often some substitute for it – the Hindus in South Africa, for example. It is here that we find the connection, referred to above, between certain aspects of the culture contacts and certain aspects of the racial contacts; a connection that is made all the closer by the colonial situation. It is from this point of view that we must approach the facts of *counter-acculturation** (a reaction which is at the same time cultural, racial and political); such social movements as the 'Negro churches' and African Messianism; and the changes and clandestine development of traditional institutions and groups. It is equally essential to appreciate how these conditions have led sometimes to a strengthening of racial peculiarities, sometimes to the fusion of large ethnic groups, brought together on a more or less permanent basis by similar types of protest. In all these fields, writers frequently resort to concepts borrowed from social psychology and psycho-analysis – at least those who do not confine themselves merely to the external manifestations of the facts of contact but pursue their investigations in depth.[60] We must now consider, therefore, the notions derived from 'colonial psychology' or 'the psychology of colonization'.

These disciplines have been but little developed despite the comparatively early date of the first essays in this field: the earliest, by H. de Saussure[61] goes back to 1899, yet in a paper written in 1947, G. Hardy could still remind us that 'we are still at a rudimentary stage'.[62] Anthropologists working in colonial countries

---

* At the end of 1961 demonstrations in Rhodesia called upon the people to give up wearing European clothes, spectacles and watches as being 'symbols of oppression.' In this semi-industrialized region speakers maintained that, if industry proved to be an obstacle to 'Bantu nationalism', it would be destroyed.

often touched upon the psychological domain, without being interested in it specifically: the concept of 'institutions' (with all the importance this assumes in the works of Malinowski and his disciples), as well as those of primitiveness and primitive mentality (especially noticeable in French research) were scarcely orientated towards a psychology of the colonized.

A few French authors, nevertheless, did envisage problems of this kind: for example Émile Cailliet, in his *Essai sur la psychologie du Hova*, published in 1924, and Raoul Allier, whose *Psychologie de la conversation chez les non-civilisés* analyses the psychological influence of one type of colonial intervention, the effect of conversion to Christianity. He questions the value of such conversions, pointing out that they involve a transformation of the whole mentality and that, as R. Bastide put it, 'by the mere fact of acquiring Christian concepts one enters the very heart of Western logic'. M. Leenhardt, too, discusses the question of missionary influence in a chapter of his work *Gens de la Grande-Terre*, where he maintains that it tends to develop an awareness of personality and therefore leads to individualism. And again, the work of R. Maunier takes into account, though only incidentally, certain psychological factors, insisting upon the role of imitation which occurs in a variety of manifestations.

One of the few recent works to deal with the psychological factors involved in the relations between colonizer and colonized is O. Mannoni's *Psychologie de la colonisation*. Here the author compares the personality of a 'typical' Madagascan – characterized by the 'subjection complex' and an evasion of personal responsibility* – with that of a 'Europeanized' Madagascan, who has broken the bonds of subjection but finds himself in a position of insecurity. Mannoni insists upon the disturbances affecting the personality of the 'Europeanized' individual; emphasizes their more or less pathological nature (which, on the plane of psychological structures, corresponds to the state of crisis we have already noted on the plane of social structures), though without adequately relating them to the concrete social background (the new personality has difficulty in 'settling down' within the social structures created by colonization); and points out the 'apparent

* The same point is made by D. Westermann in his *Noirs et Blancs en Afrique*, p. 46: 'As far as possible personal responsibility is avoided.'

duplicity', which makes one think of 'one actor playing two parts', as well as the ambiguity revealed in the urge 'to speed up evolution' side by side with nostalgia for 'the old days'.

As for the European colonist, he is able to rid himself of his 'inferiority' thanks to the part he plays in the colonial situation (that is to say, psychological advantages are, in a sense, the complement of his material advantages). Deep in his unconscious, the colonist is bound up with the colonial system, as well as being modified by it, as may often be seen in his feeling of superiority to 'metropolitan Europeans'. Mannoni goes on to show how these two types of personality, colonial and colonized, exert a reciprocal influence upon one another. He suggests that the ways in which they are modified are closely connected with the changes affecting the colonial relationship, thus stressing the *reciprocal bond*, to which we have frequently referred. Though one has a number of reservations about this stimulating work – a tendency to generalize, its lack of concrete background and its insistence upon considering only one dimension of the colonial situation – it is nevertheless an original contribution. It recognizes and identifies a field into which any sociologist concerned with colonial societies must venture if he hopes to achieve a significant analysis.

Examples of careful investigation in the colonial and ex-colonial territories are few in number; and they are mainly the work of British and American scholars. As a rule they deal with the pathological aspects of the subject, and the facts of 'maladjustment'. Thus, when R. Firth drew up a plan of research for the West African countries under British influence, part of it was reserved for a study of neuroses and psychoses, and he justified the need for this by reference to the variety of mental disturbances that affect so many of the peasants when they start to work in industrial enterprises, and also to the cases of hysteria and other mental illness that have been observed amongst the child population in the coastal towns. Similarly, I. Schapera, when listing the priority problems that ought to determine the nature of anthropological research in Kenya, included the study of 'mental conflict' resulting from 'the too rapid development of individualism'. In the same way, A. Irving Hallowell expressed the view that European expansion is a 'source of anxiety' for the people affected by it, emphasizing the conflictual nature of the culture contact and the effort to 'readapt' that this imposes upon the individual.[63] Here the work that has been done by American authors on the 'marginal man'[64] is of some help; but the process they expound to us amounts to little more than the one that has already been elaborated in studies of 'acculturation' – periods of conflict followed by periods of adjustment, which, depending upon circumstances, may lead either to assimilation (to the so-called superior culture) or regression. They also lay great stress on certain characteristic features, such as split personality and inner conflict, with all the dangers of psychosis that these involve, as well as on some of the phenomena described by Mannoni. This facile agreement, at the level of mere generalities, is a reminder of how essential it is to return to the concrete, to consider particular 'situations'.

Social Science and Decolonization

The process of decolonization has had a direct influence upon scientific practice in the fields of social anthropology and the sociology of non-European societies, as well as upon the classic attitude to this category of societies. It has upset long established habits, made us reconsider our terminology (the use of such words as 'archaic', 'primitive', etc.) and raised doubts as to the *contemporary* bearing of anthropological endeavour. Suddenly, societies that had hitherto been regarded as static, or bogged down in mere 'repetition', have been thrown open to change and revolution; they have rediscovered their own history and ceased to be passive objects in the hands of others.

This revival of initiative also finds expression in the sphere of political and social thought; and the anthropologist, no longer having the monopoly of 'explaining' traditional societies and cultures, has, for the first time, to face contradiction at the hands of native scholars. The work of such men is often political (for example, that of L. S. Senghor, who has put forward an interpretation of African society and culture that provides a basis for a theory of socialism which would be both African and humanist), or polemical (for instance, that of A. Ly, who uses the Marxist approach to evaluate the position of the 'African masses' and assess the grounds for a 'genuine revolution').

A number of recent studies, the work of political activists or participants in nationalist struggle, show how decolonization affects social evolution, often by bringing about a veritable mutation. An example of this is Dr F. Fanon's book on the Algerian Revolution.[65] As regards both the position of women and the family in Algeria, and the beliefs and modes of thought, Fanon makes clear the nature of 'the inner mutation, the complete change in social and family structures' that has occurred. In this extreme case, the revolutionary situation resulting from the long struggle for independence accelerates the rhythm of transformation of the old society and leads to a widespread onslaught on traditional types of behaviour. In a later work, at once violent and lyrical, Fanon went further than this, and attempted to propound a methodology of decolonization, which led him to examine and assess nationalism, national culture, the role of the bourgeoisie, the function of parties and leaders, etc., with the result that the sociology of decolonization became a passionate theory of total revolution.[66]

This brief summary indicates how wide a gap there is between the sociological image constructed by the classical anthropologist and that sketched out by the political activist. Mention must also be made, however, of the reorientation of anthropological and sociological research that has led to the analysis of traditional societies becoming more dynamic, more concerned with the contingencies immediately affecting them. The study of Messianic movements, notably in Melanesia, has eventually resulted in a less rigid conception of social systems and attracted the attention of anthropologists to the phenomena of 'primitive' revolt.[67] Thanks to the research that has been carried out into developments of a prophetic or Messianic nature, into peasant revolts like that of the Mau Mau amongst the Kikuyu of Kenya and into the earliest manifestations of nationalism, there has been a similar shift of interest with regard to African society. In this respect, the little known work of E. Evans-Pritchard, *The Sanusi of Cyrenaica*, remains of outstanding importance; in it is described the birth of an effectively united form of religious nationalism among Bedouin tribes hitherto kept apart by conflicting interests. While this kind of research was in progress, a parallel attempt was being made to include the concepts of antagonism, tension, conflict and ambivalence in projects for the interpretation of traditional social systems: an enterprise of which Max Gluckman's *Rituals of Rebellion in*

South-East Africa is typical.[68] This twofold movement has helped to create the need for a social theory at once more dynamic and more critical.[69]

IV. CONCLUSIONS FOR RESEARCH

So far we have considered a number of the factors summed up by English and American writers in the notion of 'the clash of civilizations' or of 'races', but we have also shown that, in the case of the dependent peoples, these clashes or contacts have occurred under very special conditions. It is this totality of conditions that we call the *colonial situation*. This may be defined if we bear in mind the most general and obvious of these conditions: the domination imposed by a foreign minority, 'racially' and culturally distinct, upon a materially inferior autochthonous majority, in the name of a dogmatically asserted racial (or ethnic) and cultural superiority; the bringing into relation of two heterogeneous civilizations, one technologically advanced, economically powerful, swift moving and Christian by origin, the other without complex techniques, economically backward, slow moving and fundamentally 'non-Christian'; the antagonistic nature of the relations between the two societies, owing to the instrumental role to which the subject society is condemned; and the need for the dominant society, if it is to maintain its position, to rely not only upon 'force', but also upon a whole range of pseudo-justifications and stereotyped patterns of behaviour, etc. Simply to enumerate these conditions, however, is not enough.

We have chosen, therefore, with the aid of the individual views of specialists in the various fields, to treat the colonial situation in its entirety and as a system. We have considered the factors that are required for the description and understanding of any concrete situation, and, by showing how these are bound up with one another, have also shown that any partial analysis is bound to be biased. This *totality* involves the 'groups' comprising the 'global society' (the colony) as the collective representations appropriate to each of them. But the colonial situation is in process of modification, at an ever increasing pace; and this makes it essential therefore *to understand it historically*, to date it, to study it up to the moment of its extinction.

The autochthonous society with which the anthropologist is concerned has, to a greater or less degree (according to size, economic potential, cultural conservatism, etc.) some of the characteristics of the colonial situation; it is, or was, one of the groups that constitute the 'colony'. And it would be a mistake to suppose that a satisfactory study of this society can be made without taking into account this twofold reality – on the one hand, the 'colony' or global society of which it is an integral part, and, on the other, the colonial situation – especially when the avowed subject of such study is the facts resulting from 'contact', the phenomena or processes of change. If, adopting a one-sided approach, it treats these simply in relation to the traditional (or 'primitive') heritage, it can do little more than enumerate and classify them; and the same is true if, as Malinowski proposed, it confines itself to studying the contact between 'institutions' of the same kind. In fact, once the 'modernist' features have been identified, they can only be understood in terms of the colonial situation; and fortunately certain anthropologists, like Fortes and Gluckman, have come near to recognizing this by treating both black and white societies in colonial Africa as parts of a single whole, by introducing the concept of 'situation'.[70] Similarly, in his work on the interpenetration of civilizations, R. Bastide has stressed the importance of the 'situation within which the process takes place'. We have sought to go further than these early findings by showing how a colonial situation can be 'tackled' and what it implies; and also to make clear that, until recent times, no contemporary sociological problem of the colonized peoples could be envisaged except in relation to this totality. The notion of 'situation' has been forced upon a number of specialists in the social sciences, whether they speak of it in terms of 'social situation' like Wallon, or of 'special social circumstances' as does Gurvitch; the concept of 'the total social phenomenon' elaborated by Mauss had, moreover, already prepared us for such an approach.*

* The three terms are associated by Gurvitch in the foreword that he contributed for the section on 'Collective Psychology' in L'Année sociologique, 1948–9. Similarly, a psychiatrist like Karen Horney insists that all neuroses, whether individual or collective, are to be explained by a process that involves *all* personal and socio-cultural factors; see The Neurotic Personality of our Time, New York, 1937. Many other examples could be quoted.

It is significant, however, that many of the anthropologists engaged in field work in colonized societies, who have interested themselves in their current aspects and problems, have nevertheless avoided (unconsciously for the most part) describing the concrete situation peculiar to these societies. They have either relied upon such non-committal stereotypes as 'Western' and 'primitive' civilizations, or restricted themselves to problems of such a limited nature that their proposed solutions are equally restricted. Moreover, it is because they have refused to accept this attitude, which they consider to be necessary and useful only to the colonizing society, that some anthropologists have rejected the idea of their discipline becoming an 'applied science'.[71] This is something that has a bearing upon the whole question of observation in the human sciences; and it indicates the serious critical work that has to be carried out beforehand by anyone setting out to study societies affected by colonization.

What, then, from the point of view of sociological theory in general, is the significance of the kind of research whose development we have been considering? Studies concerned with the examination and explanation of the changes that are modifying traditional dependent societies throw light not only upon the future of these societies, *but also upon their previous structure and organization*. As a result of the 'ordeals' they have to face, these societies seize upon more or less tentative arrangements, more or less unreliable equilibria and overrated social models that persist despite their inadequacy in the new situation; the relative importance of the various constituent elements can thus be seen more clearly and less arbitrarily. By our analysis of the *colonial situation* concept, we have shown that the crises to which colonized societies are subject can throw light, not only upon the phenomena of contact and domination, but also upon the earlier structures of these societies. This approach has also been adopted by English anthropologists of the Manchester school. On the basis of his experience in South and Central Africa, Gluckman was able to show that modern evolution takes place in the direction of the structural weaknesses peculiar to this or that traditional society. More recently V. W. Turner, when presenting the results of his field work amongst the Ndembu of Northern Rhodesia (Zambia), has described his method as 'diachronic micro-sociology'; and has devoted himself to the detailed and fruitful study of the current 'social dramas' that disclose specific contradictions and conflicts within the traditional social system.[72]

A dynamic approach is indispensable on other grounds. It helps us to recognize more clearly the *heterogeneous* nature of any society that still contains elements of 'different ages' – as a result of its history – which coexist in a more or less contradictory, more or less effective manner. H. Lefebvre, by tracing the 'perspectives of rural sociology', was able to bring out the 'dual complexity' of peasant societies: on the one hand, a 'horizontal complexity' inherent in structures 'of the same historical date', which reveals 'essential differences amounting to hostility'; and, on the other, a 'vertical complexity' which is due to 'the coexistence of formations of different age and date'. These two complexities 'cut across and react upon one another'; they create a 'tissue of facts which can only be disentangled by a sound methodology'.[73] It was to this analysis that J. – P. Sartre was referring when he expressed his agreement with the method it involves, which, according to him, is applicable 'to all fields of anthropology'.[74] By recognizing this multiple complexity, the dynamic study of traditional societies in transition enables us to correct any oversimplified representation of social structures, which are all too often considered merely from the point of view of their 'purity' or 'primitiveness'.

Moreover, the study of social structures, in a context of frequent and rapid change, reveals, and indeed amplifies, the 'approximate' nature of their disposition within the global society. It exposes the contradictions between the various principles of structuration and organization, as well as the gaps that exist between the 'official' view of society and social practice. It is, in fact, this combination of circumstances that enables us to perceive the incompatibilities and discordances, the conflicts of interest, between groups and individuals, and the types of strategy to which they may resort. In this way, we are put on our guard against any tendency to over-rate the static aspect and to attribute (at least implicitly) a quasi-perfection to traditional societies envisaged as systems.

In an article dealing with ethnological methods, F. Boas once remarked: 'It is not enough to know what things are, but how they came to be what they are.'[75] This approach does not go far enough: it has to be seen as part of a dialectical movement, which takes into account the processes owing to which things provisionally remain 'what they are', and also reveals the forces that will impose new arrangements on them. The diachronic and relational study of societies until recently regarded as 'primitive' opens the way for this very necessary step. It will make it possible to establish that *dynamic anthropology and sociology* for which there is so urgent a need.

II
THE PEOPLES OF THE
GABON-CONGO AND
THE EUROPEAN PRESENCE

I. THE HISTORICAL BACKGROUND

In the absence of adequate historical material it is difficult to assess correctly the effect of the 'French presence' on Gabon and the Congo since the middle of the nineteenth century. Nevertheless, if we are to understand as clearly as possible the present position of these two great ethnic groups, the Fang and the Ba-Kongo, we must attempt to do so; and for this it is necessary to take into account certain historical facts. The two countries represent 'an integral part of Central Africa, the western limits of the Congo basin',[1] and ethnically as well as geographically they comprise a single entity oriented towards Central Africa, for both peoples are essentially of Bantu stock and have always resisted Muslim penetration.

First sighted by Portuguese navigators towards the end of the fifteenth century – between 1471 and 1475 Lopo Gonçalves identified a number of places on the Gabonese coast, to which he gave Portuguese names – in 1482 Diego Ção arrived with his fleet at the mouth of the Zaire (the Congo). The date is an important one: it marked the discovery of two 'states', *Loango and Kongo*, lying along either bank of the river; it was the beginning of relations with Europe; and it opened up the country to trade and the preaching of Christianity.

Of the first of these kingdoms little of historical interest is known, except that it had extensive access to the sea, consisted of 'a sovereign state and two vassal states', shared a common frontier 'with the ancestors of the Ba-Téké of today' and was in touch with the 'kingdom of the Kongo'.[2] By the end of the fifteenth century, however, it had lost control of many of the chiefdoms situated on its borders and, up to the nineteenth century, it only managed to subsist, on a much reduced scale, thanks to the part it played in the slave trade. Nevertheless, travellers' reports and naval archives show that it was sufficiently well organized both socially and politically (a king and a number of specialist functionaries*) 'to conclude agreements that had some kind of validity'.[3]

The facts relating to the kingdom of the Kongo are more numerous, as well as being more accurate.[4] In 1491, the Portuguese entered the 'capital', Mbanza-Kongo, at that time little more than a large native village, but which was to become famous as São Salvador. The kingdom, which extended to both sides of the river Congo, was 'already divided into six regions, later known as provinces' – though this was 'not so much for administrative purposes as the result of the progressive occupation by the Ba-Kongo of the territory they now occupy'.[5] Until the middle of the sixteenth century, the power exercised by the king (Na-Kongo), remained highly centralized, but since the 'great chiefs' were responsible for his 'election' it was subject to a measure of control. He appointed the most important chiefs, received tribute from them, could impose 'the blood tax' and, in the event of war, could require them to provide him with additional troops. His main prerogative, however, was that of 'supreme law-giver': he appointed judges for each of the regions, and if there was any sign of trouble he sent his representatives to the disaffected provinces – a function that the much less powerful rulers of the nineteenth century still retained.[6] It was during the reign of Alfonso I, the second of the Christian kings, that centralization reached its highest peak; as he indicated in a letter to the King of Portugal, he had taken care to establish his brother Pedro and his sons as governors of the 'provinces'. Under his successors, however, 'the ties between the central government and the provinces were progressively weakened'.[7]

Such as they are, these facts are not only interesting in themselves but also relevant to our purpose. In the first place, they demonstrate conclusively that 'states' of considerable scope, created by force, but also on a basis of genuine ethnic kinship, though they

---

* Two notables, ma-fuka and ma-ngovo, were respectively responsible for commercial and political relations with foreigners.

might flourish for a short period after their 'discovery' by Europeans, could only disintegrate, without being replaced by political organizations that were in any way comparable. By the end of the nineteenth century, the *Na-Kongo*'s kingdom had been reduced to a petty chiefdom, while the Loango had become so decadent that it was only a matter of time before they died out completely. We do not have to accept everything we read in the sixteenth-and seventeenth-century chronicles, particularly their inflated style, to be convinced that disintegration was already a fact long before the advent of colonialism in the nineteenth century. In the second place, they make it clear that these relatively complex political organizations never succeeded in creating real cities and developing an urban civilization, as was the case in Nigeria and Dahomey for example. São Salvador was a Portuguese creation, and as soon as they left it for São Paulo de Luanda, at the beginning of the eighteenth century, it declined and was allowed to fall into ruins.* Similarly, neither the 'kings' of Loango nor the slave rulers of the seaboard created genuine capitals. Towns developed in response to European requirements; without exception, they are directly attributable to colonization. And lastly, it is important to realize that the history of these kingdoms, preserved by legend in a rudimentary and distorted form, still has a definite glamour. There is hardly a single Mu-Kongo who cannot describe *Kôgo-dya-Ntòtila* (São Salvador): 'The place where we were all born, where every clan still has its own street and everyone has kinsfolk waiting to welcome him,' in the words of one of our informants. The Ba-Kongo people, split up as they are between Angola and the two Congos, still share the memory of a common past, which for some of them has become the symbol of a unity that they may yet create, a weapon in the political struggle now confronting them.

De Jonghe, in his Preface to *Études bakongo*, speaking of 'the multiple causes' of decadence lays particular stress on an internal factor, 'the use of the dispersed clan as a political organism', and he attributes this to the peculiar nature of the kingdom of Kongo,

* Luanda was founded in 1575, and the decline of São Salvador had already begun by 1668.

as having been more or less a federation of clans. But it is equally important in this respect to appreciate the effect of their relations with the Europeans. And, in the first place, those arising from the slave trade.

If we accept Father Rinchon's estimate, in his book *La traite et l'esclavage des Congolais par les Européens*, published in 1929, the number of slaves exported from the Congo to America amounted to no less than 13,250,000; and it must be remembered that it was precisely the most active and prolific elements of the Congolese people that bore the brunt of this monstrous traffic. While the overall figure may be arbitrary, and fails to distinguish between Congolese and Angolans, it is nevertheless abundantly clear that, long before the introduction of the 'concessionary companies' and the official policy of forced labour, the peoples of the Congo had suffered a demographic setback from which it would be extremely difficult to recover.

Moreover, the trade in slaves and natural produce transformed the relations between these peoples, according a privileged position to those living in the coastal areas who were therefore in a position to control trade with the Europeans. As a result, a number of relatively important chiefdoms were able to develop, beyond the Loango and along the coast of Gabon, which took advantage of the competition between 'traders' and endeavoured, by guile or violence, to preserve the market for themselves. They were on good terms with the peoples of the interior – the Echira, the Mitshogo, etc., in Gabon, and the Ba-Téké and the Ba-Fumbu in the Congo – who acted as sources of supply; and later, in the second half of the nineteenth century, during the strictly 'commercial' phase of European settlement, they did what they could to encourage this with a view to maintaining their own advantageous economic position. The 'trading' peoples, who acted as agents, supported colonial penetration; the peoples of the Haut-Ogooué and the Haut-Congo, who over a long period had borne the cost of trading with Europe and had adopted a defensive position, were opposed to it. Not only were there conflicting reactions to colonialism, but also antagonism between the people of the Haut-Congo and those of the 'coast', the Bas-Congo, who had become purveyors of European 'attitudes' as well as European merchandise. These contradictions were reflected both on the cultural plane (the *gens du Bas* tending to be assimilationist, whereas the *gens du Haut* were in the main traditionalist) and on the political plane (demands and initiatives coming primarily from the former). Thus new and deep divisions were superimposed upon the multiple ethnic divisions typical of this part of Central Africa.

When discussing the history of Kongo, Van Wing was fully justified in saying: 'The slave trade, by arousing the cupidity of the chiefs, induced them to sell their own subjects and then those of their neighbours; this was one of the main causes of the local wars that devastated Central Africa before the coming of the Europeans.'[8] As a result of the economic rivalry it led to, it certainly contributed to the breakdown of important political units like Kongo and Loango, as well as small chiefdoms. It created competition for markets and 'sources of supply'. It increased the number of rival groups, and oriented the migration of newcomers such as the Fang who, having arrived in the Haut-Gabon in the second half of the eighteenth century, made for the centres of the trade on the river Ogooué or the coast and, since they were still organized on a military basis, had little difficulty in overcoming the trading peoples already established there, especially the Galwa, Mpongwé, Oroungou and Nkomé. When the French administration, having strengthened its authority, decided to put an end to commercial privilege, it met with serious resistance. In Gabon, in 1906, the Ba-Yaka tribes, who for nearly two centuries had acted as 'agents' throughout the Bas-Congo, revolted, and were only suppressed with the help of the armed forces. But the effect of trade was not simply to split the native peoples of the Bas-Congo and the coast into rival groups; by the end of the nineteenth century it was also causing divisions amongst the Europeans: while the administration was attempting to restrict the privileges of the 'agents', the Europeans who had set up trading-posts continued to make use of them, taking advantage of ethnic antagonisms to defeat their competitors.

The slave trade did not simply exacerbate division and competition, however, it also gave the Congo a definite economic orientation. Right from the start, it had been responsible for the division into 'trading peoples', who though more exposed to European influences were also to prove more difficult to absorb into the colonial economy, and 'producers' who, while endeavouring to maintain their defensive isolation, continued to supply the market created by Europeans, though now with ivory and other natural products. It also covered the country with trade routes which, though extremely dangerous to travel by,* provided a chain of markets that were generally accepted as places of asylum, as well as places for trade and social intercourse. The coastal region had long been a place where people were accustomed to move about freely, and where most of them were more interested in their commercial activities than in farming. This mobility and passion for trade, which proved useful during the strictly 'commercial' period of colonization, were to become serious drawbacks when the administration undertook to settle the villagers and organize production. Porterage and 'caravans', as a means of distribution, had been a typical feature of African life long before they were used for colonial exploitation. The trading peoples practised slavery not merely in order to have slaves to sell, but also to provide the caravans that were the sole means of transport available. Indeed, as long as the colonial economy was primarily based on trade, it was impossible for the administration to suppress the traffic in slaves completely, and even less to establish the principle of porterage on a 'democratic' basis – i.e. by making it an obligatory service to which everybody was liable. In the same way it had considerable difficulty in transforming a barter economy into a money economy, since both the peoples who supplied the goods and the Europeans who had supplanted the old traders were opposed to it. Trade had imposed a type of economic relationship that was to subsist pretty well throughout the first phase of colonization.

Another factor that should not be overlooked is the prestige that was associated with the possession of 'trade goods'. The Ba-Kongo around Stanley Pool used to hide them away in secret encampments (*manyãga* or *šikaya*), guarded by armed men; while the Gabonese Fang kept them in chests that were looked upon as the groups' 'treasury'. The traffic in ivory, one of the most important products for the market, was so dangerous that it was carried on by clandestine methods, sometimes giving rise to

* An official report of 1922 describes a caravan 'going to sell a dozen women and children. . . . It consisted of twenty men armed with rifles, apart from the captives' (Moyen-Congo archives).

murder. According to a Fang legend, the coast was the 'country of those who distribute wealth'; wealth that was all the more highly prized because the goods of which it consisted were scarce and often paid for with men's lives. While it might lead to hoarding and become a kind of dead capital, as a rule it was transformed into the more traditional form of wealth – i.e. wives, slaves, trade goods and women were elements of a single economic system, controlled by the people of the coast as the possessors of trade goods, who competed with one another to establish their monopoly in a particular area. Rudimentary as it was, this economy did not neglect profit and the possibility of accumulating capital.

The system of distribution resulting from trade encouraged the exchange of cultural features as well as merchandise. In this respect, the part played by the *pombeiros* in the Congo was an important one: these were slaves, trained by the Portuguese of Loango and São Salvador to take charge of the caravans to *Pumbo* (Stanley Pool), who thus became the first purveyors of European goods and attitudes. But trade did more than establish this indirect contact with western civilization: since it also involved regular contact with a variety of peoples it led to a wide diffusion of *Ki-Kongo*, the commercial language adopted by the *pombeiros*. All this suggests the conclusion, which will be confirmed when we come to study the more recent period, that owing to its longstanding commercial activity, the Bas-Congo had become a centre of cultural contact and diffusion.

The first missionaries were sent by John II, King of Portugal, and arrived in Kongo in 1491, their first task being to baptize the *Na-Kongo*, his favourite wife, his heir, who was also given the name Alfonso, and some of the people. It was, says Van Wing, 'a very brilliant occasion, but little more; and, miracles apart, its effects could hardly be expected to be either profound or lasting'.[9] Up to the beginning of the eighteenth century a succession of missionaries – Jesuits, Franciscans and Capuchins – were sent to work in the Kongo, all the kings assumed semi-Christian names, and, in Europe, the kingdom was regarded as a Christian state.[10]

As regards the nature of this missionary activity, the first thing that strikes one is that it was carried out from a distance, from bishoprics established on the coast, São Tomé, São Paulo de Luanda and, for a short period, from Loango. The chapter of São Salvador, endowed by the Portuguese ruler John II, experienced many vicissitudes, depending upon the attitude of the Kongo kings and their relations with the Portuguese; but in any case, by the end of the seventeenth century, most of the missionaries had been transferred to Angola. The only effective attempt to introduce genuine Christianity to the mass of the population seems to have been that of the Capuchin friars, who stayed on for another hundred years, travelling from province to province establishing mission posts. Secondly, since the work of the missionaries was closely bound up with politics, it was a source of serious antagonisms: rivalry between the Portuguese and Spanish kings, who jealously clung to their rights of patronage, and the Holy See; competition between the powers (Portugal and Holland for a time); and disputes between the secular clergy, primarily devoted to the interests of Portuguese colonialism, and those missionaries with reforming tendencies. And thirdly, since it failed to take root in native society, the missionary endeavour remained extremely superficial, concerned with quantity rather than quality. According to Cavazzi,[11] one missionary baptized more than 100,000 people during the twenty years he spent in the Kongo; and there was a native priest who travelled about the country baptizing 'up to 300 people a month'. As Father Van Wing was to write later: 'The number of baptisms must have been enormous; once they realized that it would not involve facing difficulties or making sacrifices, the Negroes asked nothing better than to become Christians like their kings and chiefs.'[12]

The general picture that emerges, both from contemporary accounts and from Father Van Wing's study[13] of the subject at the beginning of this century, is that the majority of missionaries were quite satisfied with these statistical achievements, and made little effort to understand either the mind of the Africans or their society. All too readily the priests succumbed to the easy-going and dissolute life of the court and chiefs, with whom they mainly associated, and this, together with the poor quality of their teaching, prepared the way for every kind of syncretism. For the kings and chiefs, Christianity, which until the middle of the seventeenth century had helped to maintain a certain stability at

São Salvador, was simply a means of strengthening their own authority, continually threatened by the traditional clan organization. For the Portuguese colonists it served to reinforce their political control, since both the clergy and the 'Christian' chiefs acted as their agents. That Christianity was primarily the concern of the chiefs is shown by the fact that in the Bas-Congo the Christian cross (*nkagi*) for a long time remained one of the insignia of chieftainship and, in particular, a symbol of judicial authority (palm wine was sacrificed to it at an annual ceremony for the dead, and oaths were sworn upon it). It was thus an important instance of assimilation, against which the modern missionaries, at the end of the nineteenth century, were to react by destroying the *nkagi*, which they simply regarded as fetishes.

From the few records left by the first of these contemporary missionaries, we know that 'it was the fetishists and sorcerers who had taken over the objects of Christian worship' introduced by the old missionaries. In 1911, a 'doctor' for pregnant women still possessed a figurine of Saint Anthony, which was supposed to enable women to choose whether the child should be a boy or a girl if they laid it on their bellies and sacrificed a chicken;[14] and there can be little doubt that statues of saints must have been widely diffused throughout the kingdom of Kongo. Unfortunately, we lack the detailed information that would enable us to establish 'mystical correspondences' similar to those that the sociologist R. Bastide has discovered among the Brazilian Blacks. The only reference by Van Wing is to the appearance, in 1911 near Stanley Pool, of a fetish called *Dombasi* (Dom Sebastian) that was used against evil spells.* And in that part of the Congo (Brazzaville) where we were working such survivals no longer existed; it was the person of Christ who occupied the outstanding position in the syncretistic movements while among the Loango Christ and the Virgin were associated with Bunsi, the earth goddess. But it was the cross, the Christian symbol *par excellence*, that was most widespread and seems to have acquired the greatest religious potential. One finds it in the Loango country as one of the symbols

---

* *Etudes bakongo, Histoire et sociologie*, Brussels, 1921, p. 113. In 1705, however, a young Congolese woman (Dona Béatrice) identified herself with Saint Anthony; the first known example of Congolese syncretism (see the *Relations* of Father Laurent de Lucques 1700–10).

3

representing the elements (earth and air) and, in the huts, in the form of 'fetish nails' in the shape of a crucifix. In the Bas-Congo and Gabon it was associated by many peoples with the cult of the dead; and Van Wing came across it among the Ba-Mpangu, where it was used as one of the protective *mikisi* against enemies and sorcerers, fixed to the walls of the huts to drive away ghosts. Slight as it is, this evidence nevertheless reveals an attitude towards Christianity that was to appear again later on, despite energetic action on the part of the new missionaries. The rapid spread of such movements as Kioka (Angola), Kimbangism (specifically Ba-Kongo) and Kitawale or Watch Tower (Central Africa), though they were doubtless due in the first place to individual initiative, were also the result of a still living tradition of the free use and interpretation of Christian teaching.

II. THE COLONIAL PERIOD

By treaties concluded with 'King Denis' in 1839 and 'King Louis' in 1843, the French were eventually established on the estuary of the river Gabon, an area where the European presence had long made itself felt. Du Chaillu, who explored the coastal region ten years later, refers particularly to the skilful way in which the Mpongwé 'make themselves at home with the whites and understand how to flatter the peculiarities of the different nationalities, American, English, French and Spanish', who had the greatest commercial experience. It was not until 1880 however, that de Brazza made his way into the interior and reached the Congo, and only in the course of his third mission, in 1883–5, that he succeeded in creating a preliminary form of administration throughout the territory which was ultimately conceded to the French by the Berlin Convention (February 26, 1885). Even then some time was to elapse before the administration established its authority. Until 1914, the policy pursued was one of 'pacification and domestication', and the regions of Gabon-Cameroun, Gabon-Congo and Congo-Oubangui were still regarded simply as 'zones of influence'; a fact that explains why the part of the country known as *Vieux-Gabon* for so long continued to play a dominant role as the centre of cultural contact and modernist tendencies – a place that, until about 1910, was occupied by Libreville.

From the start, the colonists found themselves faced by a highly unstable population, whose fragmentation was one of the factors that helped them to establish themselves. There can be no doubt that the trade that had been carried on in the coastal region had deeply affected the people of the Gabon-Congo, creating a network of commercial routes and markets, and determining their relations with other ethnic groups.

Transformation of Economic Conditions

The mere fact of opening up the interior had immediate effects on the economy: it modified the established relation of force between peoples and, consequently, the orientation of trade; and it also established the ascendancy of the trading peoples of the coast. From the start, the policy of conquest took on an economic aspect, creating an upheaval of which certain ethnic groups sought to take advantage and opening a new era of competition. Later, the setting up of the 'concessionary companies' greatly enhanced the economic power of colonialism,[15] for though they scarcely affected the actual mechanics of trade they considerably extended it, and firmly established it in European hands. It dispossessed the native traders without resulting in any significant economic development, as was shown by the Pobeguin mission in 1920.

Prevented from pursuing their longstanding commercial activities, the Congolese found themselves caught up in an economic system which they neither controlled nor understood. Obliged to participate in it, either directly or indirectly, the need to obtain cash obliged the peasants either to produce for the 'colonial sector' or else to become temporary wage-workers. In the consequent upheaval, the demographic structures were seriously damaged by the massive movements of labour, while owing to the growing demand for cash crops the old subsistence economy deteriorated.

Suddenly the villagers found themselves occupying a very minor position in an economic system for which nothing had prepared them. The mechanism implied by the very notion of 'trade', which continued to operate until comparatively recently, was largely destructive: it entailed speculation in colonial produce without leading to any economic growth. The disorganization it gave rise to was in no sense a preparation for the development of those areas that had been surveyed.* The villager's ability to sell his produce depended essentially upon the vicissitudes of the export market and the prices that the trading-posts were prepared to pay, knowing full well that his need for cash was to their advantage; he became permanently indebted; and the indifferent commercial network that was created meant that the cost of transport was often a heavy burden for him.

The system of porterage had for a long time encouraged mobility, contributed to the spread of endemic diseases and led people to escape to the least accessible areas. But it was the actual conditions of work that did much more to cause the demographic deterioration referred to in the official reports. In 1931, an administrator in the Moyen-Congo, discussing the reasons for depopulation, wrote: 'A considerable number of natives work for commercial companies, which establish labour camps for them, or else send them to gather rubber in the forest. The majority of them leave their wives behind in the village and do not see them again for several months or even years, during which time they enter into adulterous relationships and have no hesitation about getting rid of the children that result from them. As for the wives who accompany their husbands, for them, too, maternity would be an intolerable burden. . . . The means by which abortion is procured are so brutal that it leaves the women incapable of further child-bearing. As a result there is a continual exodus of the young men to the commercial centres'.[16]

From this may be seen what a price the village groups had to pay for integration in the new economy, even prior to the introduction of the most up-to-date means of exploitation. The Compagnie Minière of Mindouli (Moyen-Congo) began extracting copper in 1910, but only on a very small scale, and it was not until after 1930 that the mineral wealth of the Congo and Gabon was seriously exploited. Similarly, it was only in the thirties that prospecting for oil started in the Bas-Ogooué, whereas large-scale development of the timber trade in Gabon had begun in

* Cf. E. Trezenem: 'A.E.F.', in *La France équatoriale*, Paris, 1947, pp. 86–7. 'The big companies are usually content to exploit to the full local resources and natural products such as ivory without contributing anything to the country or assisting in its development. In the Alima region there was practically only one company that attempted to establish the production of palm oil on a viable basis.'

1920. The human problems created by this period of economic development were further accentuated by the fact that the building of roads, railways and the port of Pointe Noire were all taking place at approximately the same time. The cost in human lives and the demands for outside labour that this gave rise to are well-known; the local contribution of labour for the construction of the Congo-Océan Railway was high – the 1931 Annual Report put the number of workers recruited from the Bas-Congo alone at 25 per cent of the adult male population (i.e. fifteen years and upwards). A figure of this order indicates clearly enough the effort that was called for, as well as the serious disruption it caused in the villages.

The building up of roads and railways gave rise to a process of proletarianization. The effect of the insatiable demand for labour, typical of colonial economies, upon an already depleted population whose traditional social organization had been seriously affected, was exceptionally grave. Though most of the villages suffered from it, it still did not solve the problem of providing labour for the European sector, despite the methods of compulsion that were employed. Later we shall see how the policy of forced labour for forestry work affected a particular ethnic group, the Fang of Gabon, but what we wish to emphasize here is the failure to integrate the workers adequately in the new economy, and the fact that, by the time they returned to their villages, they had ceased to be typical agriculturists. Owing to the rudimentary nature of the economy, most of the men uprooted from their villages became wage-earners, but, as may be seen from the figures for Gabon even as late as 1947, compared with 83·1 per cent labourers, the number of so-called skilled workers amounted to only 13 per cent.

While the appearance of European trading firms had led to the break-up of the groups, the early stages of large-scale exploitation resulted in extensive proletarianization, owing to the numerical decline of the population and the methods of exploitation. At the same time the Congolese and Gabonese communities became extremely sensitive to economic crises – an experience that was completely new to them – which made it increasingly difficult for them to meet the growing demand for cash. Thus both their subjection and their sense of economic insecurity continued to increase.

As we shall see later, particularly when we come to consider the Messianic movements,* such periods of crisis often coincide with the most violent outbreaks of protest on the part of the colonized society. In 1921–2, when exports were falling off, the Kimbangist movement was organized in the Brazzaville area, and there was a rising of the Haut-Gabonese Fang against the N'Goko Sangha Company. During the 1929 crisis, several violent incidents occurred among the Ba-Kongo and in various parts of the Haut-Congo. In 1931, a number of official reports insisted upon 'the activities of the sorcerers, who are exploiting the economic crisis by spreading a rumour that the Whites have been seriously weakened and no longer have any money'. And, in the same period, the fact that the administration adopted measures to ensure a minimum price for native produce reveals both the precariousness and the inadequacy of their financial resources, though as the Lieutenant-Governor of the Moyen-Congo pointed out, the essential purpose of these measures was 'to enable the natives to pay their taxes'.[17] Thus the old forms of insecurity, which traditional organizations and techniques had been more or less competent to deal with, were replaced by a new and more insidious kind, all the more acute because of the deterioration of society, for which the Congolese were quite unprepared.

Mobility and Instability of Social Groups

Almost every administrative document of these years stressed the mobility of the village groups and the difficulty of 'regrouping' and 'settling' them. A report drawn up in 1927 is a case in point: 'We continually find that the largest and most coherent groups are the least accessible. Domestic warfare, incessant invasions and, above all, the slave trade have driven the natives away from areas that are easy to get at. . . . Even the large villages that were developed for purposes of defence have split up into small groups always on the move.'

In addition to the causes of mobility that operated before the colonial period, to which we have already referred, a new factor was now affecting the distribution of population: whether the

* See Part III, ch. 3.

various ethnic groups were more concerned to establish contact with the Europeans or to escape from them. For instance, the Ba-Téké preferred to retreat into the high, sandy uplands which today bear their name,* while the Ba-Sundi groups were only too anxious to occupy the territory thus vacated. The modern antagonism between the two peoples was in part determined by this different attitude to colonization. In a country where communications were rudimentary and the administrative forces widely extended, flight was the easiest and least dangerous form of opposition. It made it more difficult to recruit men for porterage† and to enforce administrative measures involving stricter control and fuller acceptance of the system of forced labour.

Colonization increased mobility by imposing peace between the various ethnic groups, and by making it possible for them to enter into relations with one another by facilitating communication, all of which encouraged the break-up of villages and the free movement of individuals. Administrative action, however, often seems to have been contradictory: it did its best to maintain the groups in easily accessible places, or to settle them near the roads, railways and economic centres, but at the same time it sought to direct the displaced populations towards development areas – such as the lumber camps of the Bas-Gabon, for instance. From the start, the government was opposed to the 'craze for migration', yet its actions encouraged it, since demands for porterage and forced labour and the transference of people to the vicinity of roads planned for the future sometimes led to the flight of entire lineages. Around 1930, a systematic policy of 'regrouping the villages', and resettling them near the network of newly built roads and the C.F.C.O. railway, involved a complete reorganization of the population, which in some districts, like the Haut-Gabon, met with violent resistance. Moreover, it is clear that the lack of centralized organization and the likelihood

* Referring to the Ba-Téké, the Annual Report for the Moyen-Congo (1914) says: 'Proud and independent, many of them were unwilling to accept our authority. Relying upon their reputation as redoubtable warriors, they displayed the utmost contempt for those who accepted our orders and influence.'

† Cf. H. Cuvillier-Fleury: *La mise en valeur du Congo français*. Paris, 1904. 'By requisitioning Negroes for porterage on the main trails and rough commercial routes, and forcing them to perform the heaviest and worst-paid kind of work, the Europeans simply achieved the magnificent result of making them run away, like unarmed people confronted by wild animals.'

of social units splitting up, once the need to defend themselves and the ties that bound them together were relaxed, were also factors that led to fission.

Above all it was the economic structures that encouraged mobility. Owing to the method of collection and the shortage of European commercial centres, to obtain a steady flow of produce over large areas involved considerable displacement, while dependence upon a cash economy stimulated commercial activity and the development of suitable markets. Thus the creation of a 'market for local produce' at Brazzaville in 1915 attracted the native producers, since it seemed to them to be more effectively organized and better adapted to their interests.* The shortage of trading-posts in the Bas-Congo led to increased trade not only with the capital of the territory, but also with the Belgian Congo and Cabinda, while in Gabon some of the ethnic groups (especially the Fang) were drawn to Spanish Guinea and the Cameroun as centres of economic attraction. And this in turn resulted in a revival of traditional or recently organized native markets. Relations were established, not only between individuals, but also between ethnic groups that hitherto had had no contact with one another, and these increased as communications improved, leading to the diffusion of new forms of socio-cultural contact.

In a second phase of economic development, the policy of labour recruitment produced profound changes in the distribution of the population, since certain areas where a modernist outlook prevailed, as well as the towns, attracted the countryfolk as centres of economic and administrative power. To such an extent was the exodus from the countryside accelerated that it created a dangerous state of disequilibrium – in a period of ten years the population of the 'native townships' increased so rapidly that they accounted for a fifth of the whole population of the Moyen-Congo[18] – and if this phenomenon was not so marked in the Gabon, it was simply because a larger part of the active population was employed in forestry and mining. The inadequacy of the economic structures accounts for the difficulty of absorbing

---

* Report for the Ba-Kongo Region, March 1915: 'The decision to set up a market for local produce at Brazzaville is bound to encourage the producers. . . . All the natives have been told that they will be paid in cash, and that in future they cannot be stopped on the road and sent to some particular trading post.'

these groups of uprooted people and settling them usefully, while the impoverishment and demographic deterioration of the villages, by reducing their standard of living to an intolerable level, was a further cause of fission and increased mobility. And on top of this, as experience showed, those men who left the villages were prepared to face long periods of instability before returning to their birthplace.

It is clear that the changes affecting the traditional social structures, the effects of a type of social intercourse that had scarcely existed before colonization and the consequent changes in mental outlook, were all conducive to the same result. In a social setting in which relationships play so large a part, the multiple effect of the phenomena of contact, diffusion and cultural contamination produce a more or less lasting effect – as may be seen from the way in which various religious innovations spread from town to country, and from one area to another. Instability is not only an obstacle to any lasting reorganization, it also involves exposure to many influences that are usually ephemeral because contradictory. The conditions that exist today in many Central African societies are due to their weak resistance, but especially to economic developments that gave rise to a far-reaching disturbance of the population and almost limitless mobility. Wherever a modern economy has been created on a viable basis that makes it possible for the groups to settle, attempts to reconstruct society have quickly ensued, and this was particularly so in the case of the Fang peasants of North Gabon.

Nature of Reactions to the Colonial Situation

Apart from changes affecting the very basis of the traditional organizations, the political, cultural and religious ascendancy of the colonists gave them great scope for substantially transforming these organizations – modernizing and 'Christianizing' them. Under pressure from this combination of forces, the colonized societies reacted in a more or less direct way, thus proving that they did not accept their position passively.

Once the period of conquest was over, violent opposition on the part of any major group was unusual. In 1906, there was a revolt of the Ba-Yaka in Bas-Gabon because they were convinced that their privileged trading position was threatened, And in 1928–9, in the Moyen-Congo, there was an uprising among the peoples of the Haute-Sanga which, since it spread to the neighbouring territories, would appear to have been on a larger scale. It was caused by the influence of a religious leader, Karinou, who, having invented a crude form of Messianism, proclaimed 'the forthcoming expulsion of the Whites, whose hearts he had eaten', to be followed by an endless period of abundance and prosperity. Those who opposed the movement were massacred, while its members, driven back by the police, destroyed bridges and burnt their dwellings and possessions. The brutal nature of the rising shows the strength of the feelings which had hitherto been kept in check, the xenophobia being encouraged, moreover, by a religious association (the *Labi*), whose members lived in isolation and refused to see white men. Yet once the prophet was killed – in a clash with the army – the movement rapidly declined: it proved to have been simply an explosion, without any capacity for lasting resistance. More significant, and representing the permanent demands of a whole number of ethnic groups, were the disturbances led by different branches of the Ba-Kongo in the villages around Brazzaville, for although still in a crude form they were nevertheless an expression of nationalism, of an attitude of almost permanent resistance.

Given the much greater power at the disposal of the colonizing society, most forms of opposition almost inevitably tended to be clandestine, achieving results indirectly. The intermittent manner in which the country was occupied, and the fact that the indigenous cultures were completely alien to the colonists, favoured such under-cover tactics,* but no observer who attempted to penetrate beneath surface appearances could fail to be aware of this. It was unmistakably manifest in the tacit understanding which, very effectively, concealed from European eyes many social features and local events. Those practices and institutions which struck

* M. P. Mus gives a good example of this, with regard to Vietnam, when he describes the French people in 1930, 'deeply involved though unconscious of the fact', watching the Vietnamese women of all classes performing their regular evening ritual beside the sacred lake, Lê Loi, and wondering what they were up to. 'We were soon to realize', he goes on, 'that they were silently praying to the spirits of earth, air and water for the success of the revolt that their men-folk were preparing, and which on that occasion failed' (see *Viêt-Nam: Sociologie d'une guerre*, Paris, 1952).

officialdom as being most deplorable – ordeal by poison, the persistence of certain forms of slavery, etc. – were protected by a conspiracy of silence, as we ourselves were to discover when investigating the survival of slavery in the Moyen-Congo. And when the administration attempted to obtain information about the hidden life of the societies for which it was responsible, it met with considerable difficulty: for example, all its efforts to discover the underlying causes of Ba-Kongo Messianism after 1930 (also in the Moyen-Congo) proved to be fruitless.

In certain circumstances, the method of evasion was a *dual* process: administrative orders were carried out, but only in an entirely superficial way. This might take a very practical form: for example, a 'regrouped' village, that had been rebuilt with model dwellings of the prescribed type, would be abandoned for bush camps and traditional huts; or, again, the official quota for the growing of new crops might be treated simply as a concession to the authorities. But this method was much more difficult to distinguish at the institutional level. It occurred particularly in the sphere of political organization: the crisis of authority referred to in the earliest official reports is to be explained, not merely by the type of structure peculiar to the societies of Central Africa (where centralization was exceptional and organization relatively classless), but also by the fact that the exercise of real power often succeeded in escaping administrative supervision. We came across a very clear instance of this among the Ba-Pounou, in Gabon: up to a quite recent period, the position of village headman was frequently filled by men selected from 'slave' lineages, while, unknown to the authorities, the real chiefs maintained their accustomed authority.[19]

The rivalries and disputes arising from this kind of dualism were all the more serious in that they involved very considerable material interests. At first it was a source of difficulties for the colonial government, but later on it caused disequilibrium within the indigenous societies themselves. Typical of this was the position of the 'judges' or 'arbitrators', who managed to survive, to begin with on account on their traditional prestige, and later because they represented a form of justice that was complementary to that provided by the administration. In 1920, an official document notes with reference to the $\chi\hat{o}\chi i$, the judges peculiar to the ethnic groups of the Bas-Congo: 'The *zózi* are the only natives who are feared and respected by their compatriots. They live in remote villages, with no external indication of their status to attract the attention of Europeans. Yet it is through them that the traditions and customs of the country are transmitted.' This concealment of authentic social reality behind official appearances had two effects: in the long run it led to semi-secrecy losing its dynamism and, because of its ambiguity, it brought into the open antagonisms within customary society that had previously been held in check. In these circumstances, customary society is much more likely to deteriorate than to adapt; or rather, by exaggerating the significance of 'secret' institutions and groups, it tends to develop abnormally. It is this, as well as the rejection or distrust of the type of organization and religion introduced by colonialism, that explains why new religious cults so readily obtain a hold and have such lasting effect. These cults have at least three common characteristics: they claim to provide an overall cure for the state of crisis affecting the society in which they occur; they make use of traditional forms, but invest them with a radically new content; and, though they would strongly deny it, they imply a protest against the colonial situation. In the respective chapters devoted to the Fang and the Ba-Kongo, we shall be studying in detail their response to the current problems that arise from the social conditions in Central Africa.

From another angle, if one considers the black townships, one finds that here, too, despite the very different economic and social relations and cultural influences, the Congolese for a long time preferred *forms* of organization and protest that were familiar to them. This was one reason why trade unionism, and political activity in its modern sense, were slow to develop when they were first introduced; it was not simply a question of the colonizing society's opposition to them. In the native townships of Brazzaville, politico-religious associations attracted more members than the modernist organizations based upon foreign models, whether political parties or trade unions.[20]

Latent Contradictions within the Colonizing Society

In the preceding chapter we pointed out that, despite its being a very small minority, a colonizing society is not on that account a homogeneous entity. It consists of different elements pursuing different objectives, all with their own policies which almost inevitably conflict with one another – a fact that most writers dealing with the problems of culture contact disregard. Yet it is impossible to appreciate correctly the effects of Christianity on the Congolese communities unless we take into account both the rivalry that existed between the various Christian denominations, and the relations between them and the administration. In a sense, European society introduced its own divisions and conflicts, and transmitted them through the followings that each of its component elements succeeded in attracting. Thus it is not surprising to find a lively reaction with regard to what some of the young literates called 'imported divisions'.

Among the groups concerned with economic matters, these contradictions were largely determined by competition for goods, markets and labour. During the trading period, the rivalry between European business men had the effect of reviving the rivalry between ethnic groups; and the same thing occurred, among comparatively large units, when it came to marketing cash crops – such as cocoa in northern Gabon – which involved the circulation of large sums of money. During the years of economic expansion, the ever-increasing demand for labourers and skilled workers intensified the antagonisms. But in this case they were not due merely to the conflicting aims of different economic groups, but also to the effects of government intervention: the administration's attempts to restrain the catastrophic recruitment of forced labour and to supervise the markets led to longstanding disputes.

On top of this, the fact that the Christian missions pursued an independent policy was frequently a cause of antagonism. In many instances, the organizations they created appeared to be in competition with the secular administration. A whole number of official reports point out that Christian villages were often looked upon as places of refuge for 'those natives who wish to evade the jurisdiction of the official chiefs', with the result that they 'tend to become states within the state'. Others protest about 'the activities of certain catechists, who create hostility between Christians and pagans', and about the protection given to individuals whose behaviour 'disrupts native society', at the same time drawing attention to the disputes between Christians belonging to different churches.[21] Apart from the fact that this represented a crude form of 'transference' of the long-standing quarrel between secularism and the Church, it was almost inevitable that missionaries and administrators should have conflicting policies. In order to create the most favourable conditions for the extension of Christianity, the former attacked those features of traditional society that were most hostile to their efforts – polygamy and the cults associated with the exercise of authority; in other words, forms of organization that were important factors of internal equilibrium. They also sought to exert their influence through the medium of the most vulnerable social categories: children, 'slaves', women and the younger men. The administration, on the other hand, anxious to prevent any encroachment upon its own authority, was opposed to any sudden interference with the existing structures; whereas the Church thought in terms of conversion, the administration was primarily concerned with development.[22]

Moreover, the administration itself also had its disagreements, particularly those between members of the executive branch (whose powers had been curtailed by the recent reforms) and technical advisors to the various services. As a result, the influence it exerted on native society was far from being uniform, the differences being most marked in the urban centres, where individual officials had greater freedom of manœuvre. Reference should also be made to the contradictions that arose in the course of carrying out the early programmes of modernization and development: the emergence of the European workers as a privileged proletariat, for instance, and the rivalry between the political parties that sprang up in the post-war period. The more the territories were developed, the more the contradictions inherent in the colonizing society increased and were intensified. The time had come when the contradictions within Congolese society were beginning to assume the form of a struggle between classes and political parties – thanks to the confrontation of European groups, seeking to strengthen themselves by African support.

Recent Tendencies

The changes that occurred as a result of the final orientation of colonialism to economic and political problems were multiple and, because of their ephemeral and sometimes contradictory character, difficult to assess as a whole. In a very schematic way, they may be summarized as follows.

New attempts to develop and expand the economy coincided with a period of reforms that recognized the freedom to work and set up organizations for the protection of the wage-earning class. Though legislation did nothing to check the growing numbers of workers, the increase remained far short of the demand, partly because the advantages of being a wage-earner remained quite inadequate. Competition between employers and failure to control the movement of employees created yet greater instability, resulting in a state of near anarchy, all the more marked because the number of wage-earners continued to increase rapidly (from 21·5 per cent to 30 per cent of the adult male population of the Moyen-Congo, between 1947 and 1949), and also because the labour market remained very vulnerable.[23] The effects of this proletarianization were serious, not simply because of its extent, but also because of the ruthless and precarious conditions of existence that it involved as people were suddenly brought into contact with modern forms of organization. The first appearance of social conflict was an important date for this part of Central Africa. Similarly, the development of the labour force was bound to have important results: it increased the number of rootless, more or less regularly employed men and women in the towns, while at the same time it filled the countryside with a surplus of unemployed wage-earners who became active agents of social change.

Expansion and the post-war situation benefited a minority of native 'planters', traders and transport operators, while at the same time the growth of the wage-earning population, which was therefore almost completely subject to a money economy, enabled African business men to make higher profits from money-lending as well as from increased sales. It is permissible, therefore, to speak of an emergent bourgeoisie, still small in numbers, whose appearance in the towns aroused the hostility of their impoverished fellow citizens. Whether or not it would succeed in consolidating itself as a class seemed dubious, however, since this was dependent upon continued economic progress and the success with which its members established their position in the European business community. The fact that some of them became members of local or metropolitan assemblies, and the contact this involved with business circles, was a move in this direction.

In the political sphere, the effects of the reforms initiated from 1946 onwards were very uneven. By establishing a system of representation that favoured certain social categories, they accelerated the transition of power from the 'elders' to the younger men, from the traditionalists to the modernists, from the typical notabilities of the past to the wealthy educated European-ized elements. But these new elites were not satisfied with a role that was restricted to electing representatives to the assemblies: they wanted to take part in the management of public affairs. The pressure exerted in various urban and rural centres, and the demands put forward by the Gabonese Fang when the move-ment for village 'regroupment' was taking place, were significant in this respect – they were an assertion of their determination to exercise real authority in the towns and villages. There was, however, a considerable difference between participating in political life at the most remote level (i.e. by electing representa-tives to the assemblies) and the almost complete impossibility of doing so at a more immediate level (i.e. in the villages, cantons and native townships),* and this distinction gave rise to consider-able tension between the administration and the most dynamic elements among the Africans. As early as 1949 quite small ethnic groups, like the Ba-Vungu and the Ba-Pindji in Gabon, began to appoint 'committees' with a view to replacing the official chiefs. Reactions of this kind, however, were ambiguous, for although they were modernist in form they still bore the marks of the traditional environment. Partly as a result of opposition to the new legislative and administrative organizations that sought to promote equality and unity, partly because of the almost complete inability to extend the basis of 'clan civilization', they

* The proposals with regard to municipal reorganization adopted by the National Assembly in August 1954 were a first step to the solution of this problem in the main urban centres.

tended to exacerbate particularism. Nevertheless the new legislation did create opportunities (however restricted) for political
life in the modern meaning of the word. The great variety of the
movements and associations that sprang up under the leadership
of the most advanced elements did not, at first, achieve the desired
impact, whereas, on the other hand, those politico-religious
organizations that adopted familiar forms attracted considerable
membership. Yet because the latter were still associated with
ethnic particularism, and often dominated by the forces seeking
to return to an idealized past, they were unsuitable for resolving
contemporary problems.

The societies of the Congo and Gabon, whose demographic
and material bases have been disrupted and whose traditional
equilibria have been largely destroyed, are slowly advancing
towards social reorganization. Yet it is difficult to conceive of
such a transformation taking place without a veritable social
mutation, requiring economic and cultural conditions that as yet
do not exist, or rather, which exist only as tendencies. Nevertheless
there has been a genuine revival of initiative, of which the post-
war period was merely a beginning and whose chances of success
were enormously enhanced by the Independence achieved in
1960. It is in this context that we have to assess the distinctive
changes that are taking place among the Fang and the Ba-Kongo,
two great ethnic groups of exceptional dynamic energy.

Part II
Social Change among the
Fang of Gabon

I
FANG SOCIETY

I. THE COUNTRY OF THE FANG

Fang migration towards the Gabon coast continued until the
beginning of the twentieth century. This endless thrust and the
terror it caused among the peoples that were driven back soon
attracted the attention of the earliest explorers and settlers. As
early as 1856 P. du Chaillu was drawn to the country of the
Fang: he described them as 'a stirring and enterprising race',
who were set upon seizing possession of the whole seashore
as they realized that this provided the key to trade with the
interior. In 1884 A. Fourneau, at that time undertaking his first
expedition, was surprised by the all-conquering vitality of the
Fang. He said of them: 'Intelligent, with highly developed commercial instincts and as yet free from the vices of the coastal
tribes, there can be no doubt that before long they will overwhelm
all the autochthonous peoples by absorbing them'.[1] Throughout
the period of European penetration a kind of Fang mirage was
developing, which led particularly to an over-estimation of the
size of the group: 'an extreme density ... extending over a distance
of more than a hundred leagues', according to the Marquis of
Compiègne (about 1875); according to Lesieur-Trilles (1900), 'a
population that must amount to several millions'; while Captain
Cottes, more exact and positive, put the figure at '2–3 million' at
the time of his mission in 1905–8. In fact, the Europeans who
were discovering the interior during the second half of the nineteenth century were surprised by the considerable amount of
migration that was still going on towards the coast and along
the river Ogooué, and therefore in the opposite direction to
themselves.

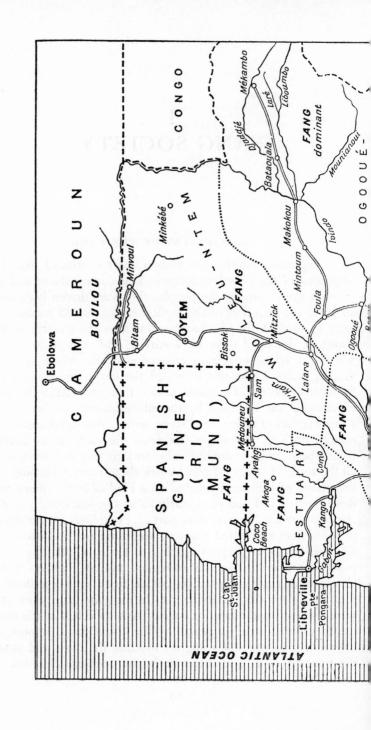

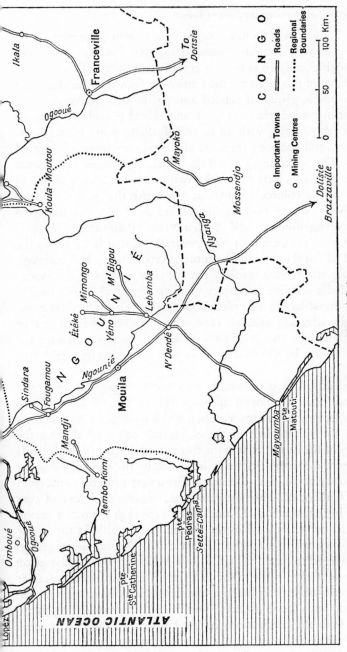

Figure 1. Map of Gabon

The Fang – or Pahouin – occupy the north western part of Gabon, an area roughly bounded on the south by the river Ogooué (Figure I). In 1950, they comprised 127,000 of the 415,000 inhabitants of this country; the Cameroun frontier separates them from a whole group of related and particularly active peoples, comprising more than 550,000 individuals;[2] and in Spanish Guinea (Rio Muni), with an essentially Fang population (somewhere around 100,000), there are also a number of closely related groups. This splitting up into three 'blocks', governed by different policies and for a long time unknown to one another, was due to the hazards of colonial expansion. As regards the Fang settlement in Gabon, one or two landmarks are available. According to our investigations in the Woleu-Ntem, their arrival in this district goes back eight or nine generations, that is to say to the second half of the eighteenth century. According to E. Trezenem, the Fang must have reached the Moyen-Ogooué at the beginning of the nineteenth century,[3] and their arrival in the Gabon estuary must have taken place about 1850;[4] at the furthest point of their advance, around 1890, they reached the district of Setté-Cama (the shores of Lake Sounga),[5] having been attracted to this region by the trading-posts that were already established there.

Originally, this considerable movement of population would seem to have developed in response to the advance of the victorious Peul people (pl. Foulbé), which took place in Cameroun during the second half of the eighteenth century,[6] driving the peoples of the bush towards the forest zone.[7] Most of the legends speak of the country originally inhabited by the Fang as being far away to the north-east – a country with a very different fauna from that of Gabon, inhabited by white men, who rode horses and were skilled in the working of iron.[8] Their arrival in the forest region seems to be symbolized in the legend of the 'hole in the *adzap*' (*aẕa mbura*), which refers to the fact that all the migratory groups were obliged to pass through a hole hollowed out in the *adzap* tree. Even today, some of the Fang still pride themselves on their traditional origin, emphasizing the linguistic connection between the Fang and Zandé dialects,[9] and in this way associating themselves with the civilizations of the Upper Nile (and so perhaps with Egypt), and recalling the time when their ancestors dressed 'exactly like the Haoussa people'.* This more or less explicit determination to provide themselves with 'noble' origins corresponds to a more or less conscious desire to impress the forest people of Gabon.

It is necessary to examine the disposition of the Fang throughout Gabon carefully, and to describe their relations with the neighbouring territories, Cameroun and Spanish Guinea. A first distinction, division by 'territories', was attempted by early writers:[10] *Betsi* territory, the region north-north-west of the Gabon estuary, and extending into Spanish Guinea; *Maké* territory, the region to the south-west of the estuary and including Ogooué-Ivindo; and *Ntoum* territory north of the Woleu-Ntem and extending as far as the river Cameroun. This rough and ready division does not take account of all the groups in Gabon, nor does it reveal the overlapping between tribes resulting from a migratory movement that even today has scarcely ceased. Moreover, these designations are now hardly used;† they have given way to the general term 'Fang', and to precise names (of the tribe or clan, and above all of the lineage) expressing the local situation. According to G. Tessmann and I. Dugast,[11] it would seem that these appellations referred in the main to migratory groups which had overthrown and assimilated different foreign groups, and thus acquired distinctive cultural characteristics.

Father Trilles however maintained, in a paper published in 1912, that such distinctions may be explained 'from the point of view of the dialects, and not from that of the customs and practices, which are exactly the same'.[12] But the dialect variants themselves, which occur particularly in the clan names (those beginning with *Esa, Esé, Esi* . . . amongst the Betsi, and those with *Eba, Ebi* . . . amongst the Maké), have become blurred: at the time of the migrations several groups changed their clan name and became so disintegrated that the linguistic map is no longer applicable to the original divisions.

From these facts two conclusions emerge. In Gabon, Fang settlement does not take the form of large homogeneous zones as is the case in Cameroun (where Evondo country, Boulou country,

---

* In the modern version of a legend relating to the Ndong tribe found in the Woleu-Ntem.

† Fifty years ago Maignan already considered such a division to be fictitious.

etc. are clearly distinguished). Various Fang groups have become interspersed and, in the course of their almost incessant migrations since the second half of the eighteenth century, have 'digested' foreign characteristics peculiar to the peoples they have encountered. And it is in southern Gabon, at the end of their journey, that the Fang groups present a state of maximum confusion.

Thus, from the outset, one is amazed by the complexity of the Fang country: apart from the Upper Woleu-Ntem, the clan groups are not restricted within the limits of even small areas; they live in villages that are often very remote from one another, which are scattered and overlap. Indeed, only the village group and the land it tills can be precisely located; and even so it must be realized that the village itself has only been stabilized, or stabilized itself, in recent times. Fragmentation is maximal at the furthest point of the Fang thrust, in the coastal districts and the 'contact zone' that has been created in the vicinity of the Moyen- and Bas-Ogooué. If one calculates the average size of a clan in each region, the figures vary from a minimum of 64 in the old sub-division of Chinchoua to a maximum of 1,000 in the Kyé-Nyé district (previously Oyem) and the villages around Bitam-Minvoul. In other words, there is a considerable difference between the reality and effectiveness of clan and lineage groups in the various parts of the Fang country: it may be seen, therefore, that attempts to revive the clan could only occur in regions where this form of social organization still retained its vitality. It should also be noted that the average size of the clan is greatest in those districts where the Fang population is most numerous, and the demographic situation most favourable: such centres of vitality are to be found in the Woleu-Ntem (excluding a large part of the district of Mitzik) and in a smaller zone in the immediate neighbourhood of Libreville. These two regions have competed in the attempt to extend their influence throughout the entire Fang country, their rivalry extending later to the electoral plane; and it will be readily understood that, in the different parts of the Fang country as a whole, one does not find either the same modification of traditional social structures or the same capacity for adaptation to present-day conditions.

If one were to draw a map of the groups that can be identified in each of the regions, other facts would become clear, as for instance the direction taken by various migrating groups. Thus from the Cameroun frontier the Effak skirted the boundaries of Spanish Guinea and continued as far as the coast between Coco-Beach and Libreville; the Angonâmvé from the Woleu-Ntem reached the Ogooué (they were seen in the Ndjolé sector at the beginning of this century), and then the southern part of Gabon beyond Lambaréné, and so on. Moreover, certain groups did not spread out and are only found in clearly demarcated zones: the Oyèk in Spanish Guinea and the Gabonese districts to the south (Médouneu, Coco-Beach and Libreville); the Kòjé in the neighbourhood of Bitam and Oyem; the Ožip only in Oyem, and so on. Lastly, it seems that certain minor groups are only found in the outlying areas of Fang country, where they lead an independent existence. The Yéngwi of Oyem still preserve the memory of one fragment of their clan which emigrated in the direction of Kango (without knowing either its present-day name or situation), although none of the groups included in the census in this district claims a common origin with the Yéngwi of the Woleu-Ntem. Thus the last bond has disappeared, the only one observed at the beginning of the century by an administrative official who described the extreme disintegration of lineages that live 'hundreds of kilometres apart from one another'.[13]

This fragmentation and entanglement are to be explained, on the one hand by the comparatively recent nature of the migrations into Gabon and the search for economically suitable bases; on the other, by the pacification of the country which made it no longer necessary to create numerically powerful units. The latter had already been noted by early observers: Maignan mentions 'families settled near the Ivindo' who 'found it necessary to unite in order to defend themselves against the attacks of their neighbours, and who have remained together forming an unbroken succession of villages'.[14] Lastly, it is important to emphasize the effects of administrative action: firstly, the policy of attracting labour to the urban centres and the fact that certain groups reacted to this by flight ('no sooner is a trading-post set up in a populous region than the whole neighbourhood is deserted in the twinkling of an eye', as Périquet reported;[15] secondly, the policy of setting people to work constructing roads; and thirdly, the policy of regrouping and consolidating the villages (1930). The nomadic habits of the

Fang have always been the despair of administrators. But it must be assumed that apart from these causes of fragmentation – the most obvious ones – there were others; for instance, the fact that there is an *upper limit to the concentration of villages*, an idea that we shall have to clarify when we come to study social structures.

Successive splits and repeated migrations make it difficult to define at all strictly the nature of the groups at present scattered throughout Fang territory. As regards certain recognized major units, we have suggested that here it is a question of migratory groups who, having been displaced at different periods and having been affected by different cultural influences, were the first to occupy the Fang country in Gabon (this would explain the attempts of old observers to outline a division into 'territories'); and we have shown how their significance has become blurred. It can be proved that these territorial names are *later* than those of the tribes and clans (at least in the case of the oldest clans); the Ožip include groups who call themselves Ntumu, *Fang* and Maké;[16] Tessmann attributes the Ndôg and the Bökwé to two different groups, Ntumu and *Fang*,[17] whereas according to our investigations (confirmed by various observers) there is in fact only one tribe, the Ndôg, of which the Bökwé (a corruption of Ebikwé) constitute a clan; and Curault gave a further example of this at the beginning of the century when he described a tribe then living at Ndjolé, the Okana, as having 'produced' clans known as Bétsi, Maké and Nzaman.[18]

If we confine ourselves to the names, we notice that they are differently constructed: some beginning with *Yé* or a consonant, others beginning with *Ésa* (*ésé, isi*) or *Éba* (*ébi*), refer to groups which are today identical in appearance, apart from the fact that those beginning with *Ésa* or *Éba* occur much more frequently. The word *yé* (meaning 'valley') is accompanied by an epithet that usually indicates a plant, an animal or some other natural phenomenon (*yé-ngwi*, 'a boar', *yé-moâg*, 'rain', etc.) whereas the prefix *Ésa* or *Éba* (meaning 'genitor') is used to indicate descent from a more or less remote ancestor. We can therefore assume that, in the latter case, it is a question of denominations indicating groups of more recent date, of secondary formation, such as clans and lineages; whereas the other names refer to earlier groups, of

legendary origin and at one time localized, which were split up and
scattered in the course of multiple migrations, that is to say, to
tribes. The first people to study the Fang, Trilles and Martrou,
were quite definite on these matters, as indeed are tribal traditions:
those of the Yénžòk preserve the memory of the first division into
four clans, which took place after crossing the river Sanaga[19] (a
decisive stage in the migrations which divided the Fang between
Cameroun and Gabon). Each major phase of migration accentuated the fragmentation and created new leaderships. This happened
with the Yénžòk: crossing the Sanaga led to their splitting up into
fragments, which are still known as Yénžòk; crossing the Ntem
(which gives access to Gabon) resulted in the creation of the important Effak group, which, in order to reach the coast, broke up
into sub-groups that called themselves simply Effak.[20]

The relations between groups thrown up by such a succession
of splits became loosened, although units with names beginning in
Yé (known as females) intermarried by preference with those
whose names began in *Ésa* (known as males), especially in
Cameroun. But in many cases close relationships eventually broke
down, owing to the conflicts which had often caused fragmentation, to the distance between fragments, to the situation created by
colonial occupation, i.e., pacification, which no longer required
'powerful solidarity on the part of the tribe',[21] and to the organized
collective displacement of people and their settlement within
administrative boundaries, which eventually reduced association
between them to a very localized scale. Proof of this loosening of
ties is to be found where we compare the composition of the tribes
as established by L. Martrou (on the Ogooué in the first decade of
this century), by the leaders of the clan consolidation movement
(in Upper Gabon from 1945 onwards), and by the members of the
Commission of Historical Enquiry (at Libreville in 1949) – these
documents all reveal considerable disparities, which are primarily
to be explained as the result of local conditions. And it is thanks to
this ambiguity that the leaders of the clan movement were prepared
to accept fusions which, simply from the point of view of clan
logic, would have been very debatable. Moreover, the fact that in
the course of their migrations the groups modified their names
(as vouched for by Martrou, Maignan and Mba[22]) only adds to the
confusion. This explains why, over the last few years, the only

effective groups have been small in numbers and strictly localized
– while at the same time enjoying semi-autonomy.

II. THE DEMOGRAPHIC SITUATION OF THE FANG

It was not simply the officials, but also the villagers themselves,
who were aware that the demographic situation in the Fang
country was unsatisfactory. For more than thirty years administrative and medical reports had been insisting upon 'the gravity of
the demographic problem'; and the Fang, alarmed by the
numerical decline of their communities, expressed their concern
by demanding that their wives should receive medical treatment
so that they should 'be able to have plenty of children as in the
past'. This sense of demographic deficiency, combined with
fragmentation and the powerlessness of village units, has been
one of the chronic features of the various Fang 'crises'. Unfortunately the necessary documentation for a detailed study does
not exist: until recent years the census figures were inaccurate
and the administrative districts to which they apply were frequently being changed.

The only overall study available to us is that prepared by
General Le Dentu of the Army Medical Service. It is based on
information provided by local health reports and involves more
than 84,000 people.[23] It draws attention to 'the great local
variation'; the Fang people, who are declining in the Ogooué-
Maritime and Estuary districts – where the replacement indices
vary from 0·5 to 0·7 – reveal much 'greater vitality' among the
Woleu Fangs and the Bakwélé of the Sangha, who have indices
of 1·05 and 1·08. The author tends to explain these considerable
variations by the different stages of development of the groups,
but this view requires some modification: we have to take into
account not only the different types of development (for instance, the present-day peasants of the Woleu-Ntem remain some
of the healthiest, although widely exposed to modernist influences), but also the natural conditions affecting each group.
These, as well as economic factors (intensive timber exploitation)
and factors of social disorganization, have played their part in
creating in the Bas-Gabon the least favourable demographic
situation (the highest rate of sterility and the weakest reproductive

capacity). As to the Fang people as a whole, its numbers remained more or less stationary throughout the decade 1930–40 (2·3 per cent births as against 2 per cent deaths).

How then are we to explain this feeling of demographic crisis which was so strongly felt? One can only assume a state of dis-equilibrium, which, as a result of, or at any rate accentuated by, colonial settlement and exploitation, could not have been checked until recently. It is difficult to be certain, for the information available is fragmentary and not always reliable. The earliest estimates of population density, made about 1910 by G. Bruel[24] and Périquet,[25] give much higher figures than those obtained recently. G. Sautter, a geographer who was able to make careful comparisons as far as the Woleu-Ntem was concerned, came to the conclusion that 'from the beginning of French penetration until around 1930, the population . . . decreased considerably'. He notes that 'in places where Périquet estimated the density at 4·5 people to the square kilometre . . . twenty years later we find less than 2'; and he pointed out that this big difference could not be accounted for by optimism on Périquet's part, since 'he seems to have been a reasonable man'.[26] Sautter maintained that a population of this order, 'already inadequate' (partly owing to natural causes, it would appear, 'which affected the whole stretch of equatorial forest from one end to the other'), must have been grievously afflicted by endemic disease and famine, as well as by emigration and labour recruitment. The stabilization that was achieved in the course of the first three decades of this century, together with the development and enrichment of the whole region, is still precarious; so much so, that Sautter was not pre-pared to make any forecast as to population trends in the Woleu-Ntem, although he admitted that the Fang, in this part of their territory, represented 'a flourishing population when compared with their kinsmen from the Ivindo, the Ogooué and the coast, whose position was a great deal worse'.

The precariousness of this equilibrium was revealed during the period of the 'war effort'. A political report on the Woleu-Ntem, made in 1944, drew up a balance sheet that was concerned essen-tially with the 'problem of depopulation': it notes the large proportion of deaths compared with births (22·1 per thousand, as against 15·9 per thousand) and draws attention to the serious recrudescence of emigration – an official estimate speaks of 4,500 adult men (that is to say, more than 20 per cent of the adult male population) having at that time crossed over into Spanish Guinea. This means that the success of the population policy from 1930 onwards remained extremely dubious. The Fang, while remaining one of the most vigorous ethnic groups in Gabon, suffer from a handicap that makes them very sensitive to any critical situation. Unlike the early observers, not a single medical report boasts of the robustness and fecundity of the Pahouins.

As a result of investigations carried out in the Woleu-Ntem, it is possible for us to study the structure of Fang population in this relatively favoured region. The most obvious fact is the disproportion between the number of adult men and women in the official censuses up to 1950, ('adult' refers to anyone over fifteen years of age). This may be seen from the censuses carried out between 1936 and 1951,* which nonetheless reveal a reduction in the disparity over the fifteen-year period:

TABLE I

Ratio of Male and Female Inhabitants†

Number of females per 1,000 males (in population as a whole)	Year	Region as whole	Bitam-Minvoul	Oyem	Mitzik	Médouneu
	1936	1,283	1,170	1,239	1,241	
	1951	1,147	1,184	1,142	1,161	1,125
Number of adult women per 1,000 adult men	1936	1,521	1,443	1,598	1,523	
	1951	1,373	1,443	1,337	1,323	1,300

To see the position more clearly we carried out a demographic inventory of eleven villages in the old Oyem district which we were investigating, with a total population of 1,570. As regards

* Though in 1936 Médouneu was not included administratively in the Woleu-Ntem.

† Recent figures do not show any marked change. For example, according to the 1959 census the overall sex ratio of Woleu-Ntem was 1,175 female per 1,000 male.

age and sex (see Figure 2) this confirmed the figures in Table I: in the eleven groups there were 838 women compared with 732 men – equivalent to 1,144 per 1,000 as against 1,142 per 1,000 for the district as a whole; but the disproportion between the sexes varied greatly according to the age group.

TABLE II

Age group	0–10	10–20	20–30	30–40	40–50	50–60
Number of women per thousand men	955	868	996	1,083	1,728	2,127

Excluding the drop revealed in the 10–20 year age group (which can partly be explained by errors in estimating the age of the

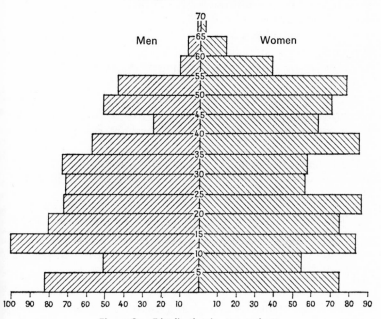

Woleu-Ntem

(Previously Oyem district)
11 villages, 1,570 inhabitants

Figure 2.—Distribution by age and sex.

4

women, which census takers usually tend to exaggerate),* it will be seen that the number of women increases from one age group to the next, an increase that attains drastic proportions from forty onwards. One can only assume a much higher male death-rate, which appears to be the case if one compares the figures provided by the censuses: in 1936, for instance, the number of male deaths represented more than 60 per cent of the total mortality, reaching a maximum of 66·6 per cent in the vicinity of Oyem. But this fact alone is not enough to explain the disproportion. If we take the year 1930, which marked a slowing down of emigration and the end of compulsory labour,[27] it will be seen that the men who at that time were over twenty years old were those who, in 1950, would be more than forty; the decline in the number of men in the higher age groups is accounted for in the main by those who had emigrated for good or died while engaged on public works. The smaller disproportion, between 1936 and 1951, tends to confirm this. In addition we have to bear in mind a factor that is inherent in the social organization: the young women in the 10–20 year age group are handed over in marriage to alien groups before they can be replaced, as a result of the bride payments received, by the alien women who become the wives of the men belonging to the lineage – a misleading time lag, which finds partial expression in the marked falling off in numbers in the 10–20 year age group.

According to Dr Le Dentu's report, the child population for the entire Fang people in 1936 was quite inadequate: the numbers in the age groups up to fifteen years old amounted to only 28·4 per cent of the total, whereas amongst other peoples in Gabon, such as the Eschira, it was nearly 36 per cent. The figures in the 1951 census show no signs of improvement, at least as far as the Bitam-Minvoul and Mitzik districts were concerned:

TABLE III

District	Bitam-Minvoul	Oyem	Mitzik	Médouneu
Child population as percentage of whole	29·3	35·3	25·4	32·3

* When the date of birth is either disputed or forgotten the census officials simply make an estimate.

The fact that the least satisfactory position was in Mitzik partly explains the fall in population in that district between 1936 and 1951 amounting to 2,092 people – that is to say, more than 20 per cent of the population, or about half the decline suffered by the whole Woleu-Ntem region in the same period.

The most satisfactory demographic position appears to have been in the old Oyem district: nevertheless, from 1936 to 1948 its population, to within a hundred or so, remained stationary. Our investigation, covering eleven villages, shows how quickly the situation reacted to changes in economic and political conditions. The years of the 'war effort' (1940–45) showed a drop in the 5–10 year age group, whereas the return to normal conditions and the relative prosperity due to increased cocoa production led to a broadening of the demographic basis at the 0–5 year level (see Figure 2). Furthermore, careful censuses carried out in nine villages in the neighbourhood of Oyem in 1945, 1946 and 1948 showed an increase in the number of people from 1,090 to 1,133 with a replacement index of 1·32; what is more, although the increase in births only amounted to thirteen, the total population increased by forty-three, mainly due to the return of emigrants.

These figures reveal an extreme demographic sensitivity, and suggest a swift reaction to modifications of local policy. But this sensitivity was only so marked because the general position remained bad: despite normal fecundity (the average number of pregnancies of women of child-bearing age for the whole district was 4·2), the number of children was insufficient as a result of the high infant mortality (see Table IV), and also, it would appear,

TABLE IV

(Based on the Medical Report for the 4th Quarter of 1944)

District	Live birth-rate per cent	Mortality-rate during first year as percentage of deaths	Overall infant mortality-rate as percentage of deaths	Child population as percentage of whole
Bitam	1·3	7·1	27	29
Minvoul	1·3	7·3	13	25
Oyem	1·7	10	26	34
Mitzik	0·8	6·7	18	25

because of the ageing of the female population. Serious malarial complaints, as well as intestinal parasites, were responsible for this mortality.

To complete these figures, it should be pointed out that infant mortality, which is very high up to one year of age, decreases from one to five years, and only shows a net decline from five years onwards. In 1936, taking the Fang as a whole, the number of deaths per cent given by Dr Le Dentu for these three categories, were: 16·5, 12 and 8·9 respectively – figures that suggest the catastrophic situation that existed in certain parts of the Pahouin country.

Such, then, were the facts revealed in this privileged part of the Woleu-Ntem. They would have been still worse had the administrative division as a whole been taken into account, especially at the end of a period of crisis, (as may be seen from the 1944 health report), or if the survey had been restricted to the smallest village groups, which seem to have been the worst affected. This is illustrated diagrammatically for three typical Oyem villages in Figure 3.

Nevertheless this demographic position seems excellent when compared with that of the Fang in other areas, as may be seen from the position in the Ogooué-Ivindo (based on information obtained in 1947):*

Replacement index	0·43%
Birth-rate	0·77%
Child population rate	24·7%
Overall mortality-rate	1·79%
Infant mortality-rate	25% of deaths

An earlier report (1946) gives additional, and even more significant, figures with regard to the single district of Booué, which is almost entirely populated by Fang: a child-bearing capacity of 2·7, and, amongst the 'young women', a fecundity rate (number of pregnancies declared) of 1·2 – figures which are far lower than those for the Fang of the Woleu-Ntem; moreover, '35–40 per cent of the young women remain sterile, whereas the

* Economic Report for the Ogooué-Ivindo, 1947, section on demography. In the decade 1949–59, the *global* population of the Ogooué-Ivindo increased by less than 1,000 units. The reversal of this tendency had scarcely begun.

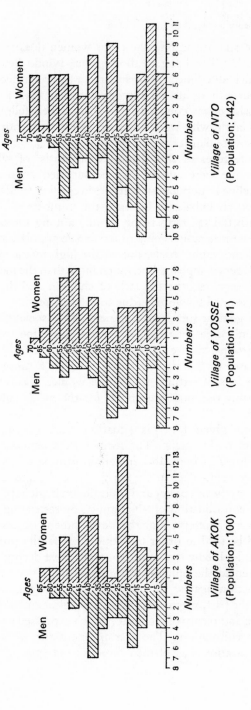

Figure 3.—Age Structure in three small Oyem villages.

Village of AKOK
(Population: 100)

Village of YOSSE
(Population: 111)

Village of NTO
(Population: 442)

percentage of sterility among the older women does not exceed 8–12 per cent'.[28] The Fang in the Ogooué-Ivindo belong to a region in which all ethnic groups suffered a demographic decline, losing one-seventh of its population between 1934 and 1947. Here, the position was comparable to that of their fellow tribes-men in Bas-Gabon who were suffering, as Dr Le Dentu pointed out, from a severe deficiency.

The main features of this demographic crisis, of which the Fang as a whole were aware, may be summed up roughly as follows: a decline in population, varying according to district and circumstances; an imbalance between the numbers of men and women – with the sex ratio rising rapidly among the older age groups – and a more rapid ageing of the female population; and an inadequate demographic basis, due to the high infant mortality. What the villagers complained of, much more than the inadequacy of the health services, was the lack of children and the sudden importance assumed by women (due to their increasing numbers, as well as to general social development). In a society in which *numbers* not only differentiate between and determine the impor-tance of the groups, but are also the basis of personal pre-eminence, the acute phases of this demographic crisis are a cause of deep concern. The loss of fertility among the women was one of the reasons, possibly the most important, for the men's antagonism towards them.

The reasons given for this situation were of two kinds: modernist and traditionalist. The former were expressed at the Pahouin Congress in 1947, and, in certain groups, at the time of the clan movement. They took the form of definite demands: insistence upon a health policy and education in hygiene; control of prostitution; consolidation of 'the family', by restricting divorce and suppressing adultery; and the development of cash crops, 'which could be sold in order to support the family properly'.[29] But it was undoubtedly the latter that were most deeply felt, and which represented the opinion of the majority. They revealed a powerful reaction against the modern state of Fang society, a yearning for the past, when everything was better and 'there were plenty of men and plenty of children', which expressed a tendency to 'counter-acculturation'. The disruption of the whole socio-cultural organization was blamed directly: the splitting up and dispersal of groups, which had led to the breakdown of basic prohibitions (especially those applying to exogamy, since, in the existing state of confusion, a man was in danger of marrying his 'sister' and thus being 'condemned to a childless marriage'); the giving up of traditional religious practices, above all of the *Biéri* cult, which resulted in the ancestors taking 'vengeance' by making the women sterile; and the borrowings from European civilization and from neighbouring tribes, which had led to the deterioration of 'Fang customs' and the adoption of rules of behaviour that threatened the very basis of social existence. These were the main reasons that were advanced. We mention them here because they illustrate the subjective aspect of the demographic crisis, and the extent to which the search for fertility and potency still affected the reactions of this people, expressing itself ambiguously in the recourse both to contemporary foreign methods and to traditional Fang methods. For the people of the Fang villages the crisis was the most serious result of the situation arising from colonization – or, as some of them oddly put it, from 'civilization'. This only goes to show that these phenomena must be viewed as part of the entity that we have undertaken to interpret.

III. THE TYPE OF SOCIAL STRUCTURE[30]
Tribes, Clans, Lineages

The movement of clan revival referred to above, is evidence of the still fundamental role of the social groups based upon 'kinship'. This had been immediately noted by the earliest observers and administrators of the Fang, all of whom insisted upon the 'family' character of the Pahouin groups, and therefore concluded that any solid social framework was lacking – as one report drawn up at the beginning of the century put it, 'scarcely a trace of organization' apart from the more or less 'extended families'.

In the past, the system of education had provided the young Fang with detailed knowledge of his genealogy (*abara*). The first thing he was taught, according to Father Trilles, was 'the individual names of his forebears, which consist entirely of his male ancestors, for the women are ignored' – and, moreover, never receive any education of this kind.[31] By learning the names of

his paternal ancestors, each man knew what basic group he belonged to, which women he was forbidden to marry and the
relations he was expected to maintain with the former, both living
and dead. By means of these increasingly tenuous bonds he was
attached to wider and wider groups of more and more ancient
origin.

The first of these groups, of which he immediately became a
member, was the *nd'è bòt*: a patrilocal group, based upon the village,
often with its own quarters and communal household, which
brought together under the authority of the 'elder' (*ntòl-mòt*) the
latter's descendants, his younger brothers and their descendants,
and sometimes the descendants of his paternal uncles; and, in
addition, such individuals as were attached to them by bonds of
kinship, adoption or friendship. The largest of these groups was
the 'tribe' (*ayôg*, originally *ayòm*) – which was first studied by Martrou and Trilles, but has since been scattered throughout almost
the whole Fang country – the origin of which, being neither
localized nor dated, was purely legendary. The intermediate social
units spread out concentrically, the relations between the individuals belonging to them being expressed by a form of 'fraternity',
which became less and less real, less and less binding.

Like the earliest students of the Fang, we use the word 'tribe' to
designate the group which was the first to be formed, and which
is actually the most comprehensive, the most widely dispersed and
the least influential, originating with a legendary ancestor (or
mvam) who is nowadays sometimes given a 'Christianized' name
(for example, Adam-Nzamö, amongst the *Ndôg*). The unity of the
tribe was expressed by a name, a motto, and its own tattoo and
symbols;[32] before the last great migrations, it was strictly localized
and divided into a limited number of clans (six, for example, in
the case of the Yévò). The migrations to and across the Cameroun
and Gabon rivers gave rise to a long series of splits, as may be
seen from various tribal legends which connect serious cases of
fragmentation with crossing the upper Sanaga (*Lom*) and passing
through the 'hole in the *adzap*' (symbolizing entry into the jungle).
Thus the Yévò[33] relate how, after this 'crossing', they broke up
into ten groups, six of whom set off for the region of the Ntem,
three for Gabon and one, after following the course of the Nyong,
towards the coast. All of these themselves underwent a further

process of splits and hivings-off, which we shall analyse with the help of recent examples. Father Trilles was able to demonstrate that, after this dispersal, the tribal name was only used by 'the clan of the founder of the tribe or by one that was created by one of his sons or direct descendants';[34] in the latter case, the fact that it was a secondary grouping was indicated by a prefix – thus the tribal name Yémvi still persists in the two forms, *Yémvi* and *Esamvi*. Such clans, however, owe their authority to a basic principle of social organization, the pre-eminence accorded to the 'elder son' and his direct descendants, the legitimacy of this authority, moreover, being guaranteed by their possession of the ancestral skulls (*évora biéri*), which are handed down 'from eldest son to eldest son'.[35] Nowadays, owing to the extreme dispersal of these tribal fragments, to the more or less complete disappearance of the *Biéri* cult, to the small number of such groups and to the loosening of the bonds between lineages, by no means all such clans enjoy a privileged position, nor did they always play a leading part in the clan movement – indeed, by that time, some of them had even been assimilated by more vigorous tribes.* They were unable to maintain either the feeling of tribal reality or the solemn gatherings (*bisama, bisulan*) that were periodically summoned to keep that feeling alive, whereas the groups in Cameroun, being less split up and fragmented, succeeded in doing so, which explains the impressive role they have played during the last few decades.

The term 'clan', then, is reserved for those groups that can trace their descent from a *real* ancestor (*ésa*: the *ésa* being distinguished from the *mvam* in the same way that 'physical kinship' is from 'spiritual kinship') and which, more than the tribe, express themselves locally (by clan marks or strung-out villages), have maintained strict exogamy, share in the systems of affinity created by marriage and, unlike the smaller groups, have specific denominations. These clan names are the ones by which the Fang groups were known to the colonial adminstration; names that often have a characteristic morphology on account of the prefixes *ésa* or *éba*. The clans, too, have undergone the process of splitting

* 'Those groups that used to consider themselves tribes (*Ayong*) find themselves demoted to the status of clans,' observes the author of a *Rapport sur le regroupement des Fan*, March 1948.

up; groups descended from the same founding ancestor may thus live considerable distances from one another, or even in foreign territory (Spanish Guinea or Gabon, for example). Nevertheless, whatever their average size may be, and this varies according to the region, they remain entities that exert a clearly defined influence upon individuals, both by the fact of membership (a man is an Esibil, an Esakòra, etc.) and by 'fraternity' (expressed in the term *mwanayôg*). Today, the word *ayôg* is also used to mean clan, which seems to have been its original sense: it only took on its present vague meaning when, in the course of migration, the tribal reality became blurred and, as a consequence, the word describing it, *ayòm*, almost disappeared. This interpretation is specially significant taken in conjunction with the observations made by Tessmann, who, at the beginning of the century, drew attention to the existence of groups known as *ayôg*, which were more or less federated at a higher level and formed the largest group which he calls 'tribe' (*ayòm*). This terminological confusion is indicative of the profound upheavals that had occurred, and explains the doubts expressed by Father Trilles on this subject.

Elsewhere, this writer insisted upon the existence of totemism amongst the Fang, from the tribe to the individual and extending to various social groups, though he was careful to point out that this was already beginning to disappear at the beginning of this century, both on the Ogooué and in the coastal areas. Van Gennep was fully justified in his criticism of this theoretical fantasy when he wrote: 'All our efforts to restrict the terms totem and totemism to a category clearly defined by the facts are disregarded by Father Trilles, who goes so far as to equate totemism with the Latin *genius*, or any other spirit that protects individuals and groups.'[36] This is not the place, however, to become involved in an out-of-date dispute, particularly as the rapid changes that have taken place in the course of the last fifty years have modified or destroyed the necessary basis for reaching a conclusion; but, from the facts provided by Father Trilles, we can accept the suggestion that some protective being, some religious substance (*akamayôn*), an agglomeration of symbols and a body of beliefs and legends did supply the Fang clans with some other kind of unity than the purely genealogical one.

Agnatic lineages, consisting of a more or less limited number
of generations, played and still play an important role: it is
around them that the villages or groups of villages are organized,
and that the nomadic groups described by the earliest observers
were created. In this respect, the history of their progressive
distribution throughout Gabon is significant. As an example of
this we will consider the Yéngwi, a fragment of whom, represented by twenty-five villages, are settled in the Oyem district in
the Woleu-Ntem. They all claim descent from an ancestor called
Esònò Angò, who is said to have come from the legendary Adža
Mbura and to have led the first migrations through South
Cameroun, and who is still regarded as the founder (abial)* of
the groups that exist today. These comprise some 3,300 individuals and are mainly concentrated in the southern part of Kyé-Nyé
canton, north of the river Woleu. From this region, where the
first Yéngwi villages were established and where a compact
nucleus of more than 1,500 individuals still remains, there was a
further hiving-off in the direction of present-day Spanish Guinea
(ten villages), and toward the mouths of the rivers Ntem, Ogooué
and Gabon. This large group, consisting of descendants of
Esònò Angò, settled in a clearly demarcated area and having the
same abialö bòt, forms a major lineage (nlam). Although these
descendants are spread over ten generations, real bonds subsist
between the members of the nlam, even though their 'kinship'
goes back to Esònò Angò; bonds which are strong enough
to ensure the admission of dissident elements to one village or
another.

The word abial has the implication of locality; it can mean
'birth place', 'place of origin'.[37] Groups belonging to the same
abialö bòt are, in fact, distinguished in two ways: both genealo-
gically, that is to say, having a common ancestor, and geographi-
cally, having a clearly defined locality. All the groups we studied
in the Woleu-Ntem trace their descent from an ancestor who had
led the last migrations through present-day Cameroun, crossed
the river Ntem and set up the first settlements on the other side
of this river, from which various clan fragments hived off as they
increased in size. In the case of the Yéngwi referred to above,
Esònò Angò established the first village on the south side of the

* Abial (ö) comes from bialö, to give birth.

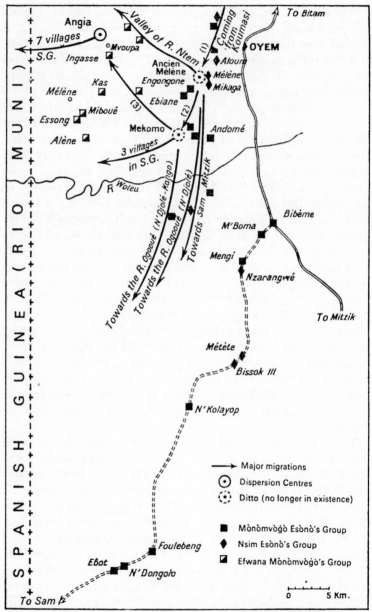

Figure 4. Dispersion of Yéngwi in the neighbourhood of Oyem

Ntem; his two sons, Mònòmvògò Esònò (the elder) and Nsim Esònò, after living there for some time, broke away and founded the first two Yéngwi villages in the Oyem district. It was from these two centres that, from the third generation onwards, line-ages began to organize themselves independently and split up further as shown in Figures 4 and 5.

Before the administration changed the structure of the villages – moving them and reconstituting them primarily for admini-strative purposes – each of them consisted of men who could trace their descent through a variable number of generations, together with their 'followers'. The Yéngwi village of Ebiane, for example, still comprises the major part of the lineage descended from Egwâga Mònòmvògò, the second son of Mònòmvògò Esònò, which takes us back eight generations, the only elements to break away having created the comparatively unimportant villages of Nkoum and Bibasse (22 and 65 inhabitants respectively), which have remained on the outskirts of the original group. But the village itself, once it had reached an average size, included a certain number of minor lineages, consisting of the descendants of the group of real brothers and half-brothers (*bòbéñâg*) who constituted the *initial cell*, Ebiane has three of these minor lineages, corresponding to the three lines of descent from the three sons of Egwâga Mònòmvògò, after whom they are called. These are the *nd'è bòt* (a term including the idea of descent, although the idea of locality is also strong) which we have already described – the minor lineages which form the basis of the hierarchy of groups. (Figure 6, on pages 112 and 113, shows how they are divided up among the Kòjé villages in the neighbourhood of Oyem.)

This *structure of interconnected patrilineages* appears to be the dominant feature of Fang society. It explains the importance that was attributed in the past to each individual having a detailed knowledge of the members of his paternal descent. Thanks to the system of nomenclature devised by the Fang – each individual is known by two names, his own followed by that of his father – the list of ancestors forms a series from which it is impossible for a single member to be omitted. Thus Ntutum Ngéma of the village of Sam in the district of Mitzik (a member of the Esabökâ clan) could trace back the names of his male ancestors to the fourteenth generation:

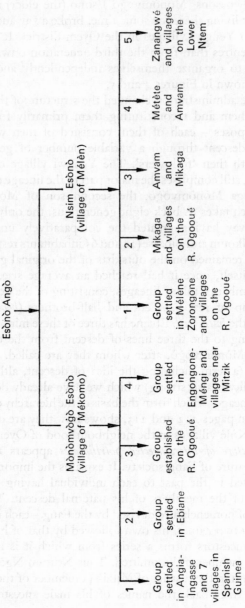

Figure 5. Yéngwi in the neighbourhood of Oyem

Esònò Angò

Mònòmvògò Esònò (village of Mékomo)

1 — Group settled in Angia-Ingasse and 7 villages in Spanish Guinea

2 — Group settled in Ebiane

3 — Group established on the R. Ogooué

4 — Group settled in Engongone-Méngi and villages near Mitzik

Nsim Esònò (village of Mélèn)

1 — Group settled in Mélène Zorongone and villages on the R. Ogooué

2 — Mikaga and villages on the R. Ogooué

3 — Amvam and Mikaga

4 — Météte and Amvam

5 — Zanangwé and villages on the Lower Ntem

Generations	Known ancestors
X	Y
↑	↑
14	Éba Zi
13	Möbyèn Éba
12	Zògò Möbyèn
11	Ékwikwi Zògò
10	Mâfò Ekwikwi
9	Sé Mâfò
8	Étògò Sé————————————Nki Sé
7	Tsa Étògò ↓
6	Ökwò Tsa
5	Bitògò Ökwò————————————
4	Édu Bitògò ↓ ↓ ↓
3	Bògò Édu 2 3 4
2	Ngéma Bògò
1	Ntutum Ngéma

By learning this list Ntutum Ngéma was able to define his position as a member of the clan descended from Éba Zi, who initiated the migrations across the Cameroun, and of the major lineage descended from Sé Mâfò who led one part of the Esabökâ clan as far as Gabon; it also explains his relationship to the intermediate lineages (those of Étògò Sé and Nki Sé), as well as to the minor lineages (the four sons of Bitògò Ökwò) which are still represented in the district and in the village itself.

Moreover, the type of personal nomenclature peculiar to the Fang stresses the importance of a basic social segment – the group consisting of his siblings and half-siblings; for example, the sons of Bitògò Ökwò who became the 'heads' of four minor lineages, still in existence:

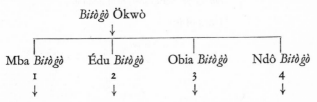

Thus the names emphasize this twofold orientation – a vertical one denoting the real line of descent, and a horizontal one denoting the real fraternity – which is characteristic of the Fang social

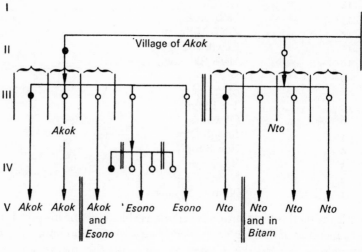

I

II   `Village of *Akok*

III

    Akok   *Nto*

IV

V *Akok* *Akok* *Akok* `*Esono* *Esono* *Nto* *Nto* *Nto* *Nto*
              and   and in
              Esono   *Bitam*

VI   *Akok* (202 inhabitants)   *Nto* (150 inhabitants)

Legend: ● Eldest brother

             ○ Younger brothers

             ⌐ ⌐*Nd'è bòt* recognized in the village

             ‖ Lines of fission

Kòjé living near Oyem

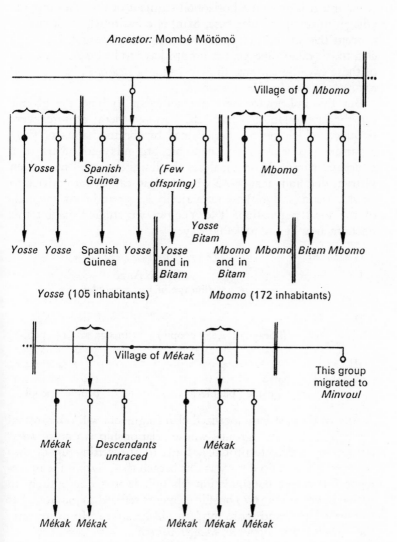

Ancestor: Mombé Mötömö

Village of Mbomo

Yosse

Spanish
Guinea

*(Few
offspring)*

Yosse
Bitam

Mbomo

Yosse Yosse Spanish Yosse Yosse Mbomo Mbomo Bitam Mbomo
Guinea and in and in
Bitam Bitam

Yosse (105 inhabitants)   Mbomo (172 inhabitants)

Village of Mékak

This group
migrated to
Minvoul

Mékak   Descendants   Mékak
untraced

Mékak Mékak   Mékak Mékak Mékak

Mékak (152 inhabitants)

Figure 6. Example of fragmentation

structure. It is around a horizontal segment of this kind that the village (in this particular case, Sam) is constituted, while within it occur the fissions that give rise to separate lineages. From the clan to the minor lineage, the groups have to be defined in terms of these two dimensions, thus revealing a *structure that one might call both segmented and interconnected.*

But this imbrication was not sufficient to bind the groups together and establish a hierarchy between them; ruptures were frequent, which are to be explained by the mechanics of Fang expansion, as well as on economic grounds and others of a structural nature. If one analyses the lineages settled in a given district, one finds that those whose origin can be traced back to an eldest son (*ntòl-mòt*) are numerically larger and form the basis of the local population. The Yéngwi we studied exhibit this phenomenon in a remarkable way:

Generations		Yéngwi in the vicinage of Oyem	
I		Esònò Angò	
		(lineage of 3,325 people)	
		↓	
II	S_1		S_2
	(lineage of 2,175 people)		(lineage of 1,150 people)
	↓		↓
III	s_1 s_2 s_3 s_4		s_1 s_2 s_3 s_4 s_5
X	950 people	1,225 people	510 people	640 people

Any of these strictly localized clan fragments will often reveal the existence of two groups whose relationship is one of *latent antagonism*, which, territorially, leads to the setting up of two separate villages. So deep was this breach that, during the movement for village consolidation (though it was due entirely to native initiative) the two hostile elements refused to join together to create larger and more modern village units.* In every case, the rupture was between *lineages descended from 'elder sons' and lineages descended* from 'younger sons', as was clearly shown by the five clan groups we studied in the Oyem district; and in each case it dated from the time of their settlement (see Table V).

---

* In a Kòjé group that we were questioning, for example, most of our informants kept repeating: 'If all the Kòjé were mixed up the village would go smash.'

TABLE V

Clans	Group descended from elder son	Group descended from younger son or sons	Villages corresponding to first group	Villages corresponding to second group
Yéngwi	Lineage of Mònòmvògò Esònò	Lineage of Nsim Esònò	Ebiane, etc.	Zorongone, etc.
Effak	Lineage of Ngu Mâmvé	Lineage of Môndu Mâmvé	Nto, etc.	Mékomo, etc.
Ožip	Lineage of Enduma Eswa	Lineage of Emvélé Eswa	Nkang	Mbenga, etc.
Yébimvé	Lineage of Ekòrò Mési	Lineage of Obiré Mési	Aféname, etc.	Angone, etc.
Kòjé	Lineage of Mòzògò Mômbé	Lineages of five younger sons	Nto, etc.	Mbomo, etc.

This state of tension, amounting more or less to actual fission, has to be seen in relation to a form of social organization that accords economic and political pre-eminence to 'elder sons', that favours the lineages descended from them and, above all, that has no hierarchical system for maintaining social cohesion, apart from the requirements of defence and expansion and the prestige of temporary 'chiefs'. There is no effective means of offsetting the desire for independence expressed by the 'heads' of lineages, once their group attains a certain size. Investigations carried out at the beginning of this century, chiefly by Martrou and Trilles, all insist upon this process of fragmentation, which was intensified when the Fang gave up their warlike activities. Similarly, there have been frequent examples of extensive agglomerations being disrupted upon the death of the 'chief' who had created and maintained them. Thus, to a considerable extent, the size and cohesion of the groups seems to have been *dependent upon the personality of the leaders* who had attained power (for all rights of succession could be contested on the pretext of incapacity), *and upon circumstances*. This accounts, in part at least, for the frequency with which, as a number of writers have noted, fissions occur in the third and fourth generations.[38] Thus the size of the localized groups, especially since the country has been pacified, is subject to extreme variation, extending from the major lineage, which is distinguished by the use of 'clan marks', to the minor lineage (*nd'è bòt*) forming an isolated hamlet. But all this is very far from exhausting the possible explanations. We also have to take into account the organizational effect of the antagonisms and antagonistic dualism of which the dynamic of the relations between young and old is but one manifestation.

Kinship

So far our examination of Fang society has only considered the groups from two fundamental points of view: *patrilineal affiliation* and *real fraternity*. We must now examine the ties of kinship, such as the alliances that may be established with 'alien' groups as a result of marriage.

Through the mediation of his father (*ésa*, whom he calls *taga*) and his mother (*nya*, whom he calls *nanö*), a man becomes a member of two kinship groups, patrilineal (*ésinyâg*) and matrilineal (*dzânanö*). To the young Fang, these two groups are far from being of equal importance or significance. The major events of his life take place within the former, whereas his relations with those 'kindred' who belong to the latter are largely adventitious; it is from the former that he derives his clan membership. The basic relations of patrilineal kinship are, as we have already pointed out, governed by descent (the term *émò*, accompanied by an epithet indicating the nature of this descent, *émò wam*, for example, meaning my son) and by 'fraternity' (the term *mwanö* designating the descendants of the same generation belonging to the same segment). By means of these two coordinates, certain relationships may be represented, as shown in Table VI.

It seems, in the first place, that the word *mvam*, which strictly speaking designates the grandfather and great-grandfather, has a very general meaning: it can also be applied to the great-uncle, and to all the ancestors both in the direct and collateral lines of descent. According to Trilles, the word *mvam* 'comes from the root *va*, which implies not the idea of begetting (which is *sa* or

TABLE VI

Generations	Terms of filiation (vertical)	Terms of fraternity (horizontal)
X	Mvam (sg)	
I	Mvam (sg)—Ngibâg (col)	
II	Esa (sg)	
III	Mwanö (sg)	Bobéñâg (pl)
IV	Bèndè (pl)	Bobéñâg (pl)
V	Nwabâg (col).................	Bobéžâg (pl)
Y	Nwabâg (col).................	Mwan'ayôg (sg)

Abbreviations: sg., singular; pl., plural; col., collective

ba, meaning "to plant"), but of production, augmentation, growth . . . '.[39] The *mvam* whether living or dead (the latter being regarded both as ancestors and tutelary beings) constitute in a vague way the *ngibâg*, or ancestors. This intentional confusion of terminology, which is a sort of throwback to the past, to the dead members of the clan, must be seen in conjunction with the way in which the Fang keep the men who have become too old for public life in the background, reducing them to an almost marginal existence.* Similarly, the men of the fourth generation are regarded as belonging to the ambiguous group known as *nwabâg*, which (while at the same time strictly designating the great-grandchildren as a whole) also signifies progeny, descendants, related in an unspecified way; and these latter are, among themselves, *mwanéžâg* (pl. *bobéžâg*), a term that might be translated 'lineage brother', or simply 'kindred'. This transition, which occurs in the first and fourth generations, reveals the privileged position accorded to the two intermediate generations: those of *ésa* (father) and *mwanö* (son). In the case of this warlike people, which used to rate its villages solely in terms of the number of warriors available, this fact has to be related to the importance that society attributed to 'a man in the pride of his strength'

---

* H. Trilles, *Le Totémisme chez les Fân*, p. 106 'Among the Fang an old man with white hair is not often looked up to. Once he is no longer strong enough to carry a gun no one pays much attention to him, and he himself accepts this position and jokes about it.'

(*nyamòrò*),* and 'a man in the prime of life' (*ékwar*). These were the two age groups upon which the cohesion of traditional Fang society was based.

Moreover, the strong sense of fraternity expressed in the concept of *mwanéñâg†* only subsists as far as the third generation, with respect to a common grandfather (*mwam*).‡ This is confirmed by the order of succession, which, among the collateral descendants, only includes the 'cousins-germane' and paternal nephews of the dead man,[40] that is to say, all the *émò mwanéñâg*, sons of his *mwanéñâg*. It is in connection with this relationship that the most closely knit and smallest group in Fang society, the *nd'è bòt*, is organized, apart, that is to say, from the individual family, which has no independent existence. This factor, which ensures the cohesion of a social group of this kind, also contributes, in a quite opposite way, to the loosening of the bonds of kinship, to the fissions that frequently occur in the fourth generation.

On the same horizontal segment, there are certain important distinctions that must be noted. Firstly, as regards sex, between brother (*ndum*) and sister (*kal*), both of which terms are used in a very wide sense, since according to L. Martrou they can also mean by extension 'brother and daughter of the same village'.[41] Secondly, as regards birth, the children of the same mother ('of the same womb', *abum avòri*) constitute with her a distinct group known as *abumò bòt*, that is to say, the matricentric family, although no privilege is conferred upon the siblings – a relationship which as a rule can only be specified with the help of the periphrasis *mwanéñâg abum avòri*, 'brother of the same womb'. Thirdly, and above all, as regards seniority: a distinction which is expressed by the use of different terms for the elder brother (*ntòl* or *nyamòrò*) and the younger (*ndzimö*), and which confers a marked precedence upon the former, of the same order as that which unconditionally subordinates the generation of the *mwanö* to that of the *ésa*. The eldest son inherits not only most of the property (at least 70 per cent according to Bertaut), but also certain religious

* *Ibid.*, p. 106. '*Mur* means "individual" and the particle *nya* suggests the idea of plenitude or superiority.'

† According to Trilles this word means 'real kinship or affiliation, and not one by adoption or blood . . .', *ibid.*, p. 251.

‡ An expression we often used to hear was: 'They had the same *mwam*, so they belonged to the same *nd'è bòt*.'

privileges (he is the sole legitimate guardian of the ancestral skulls) and, if he shows sufficient ability, political privileges.

On the mother's side, the most important relationship is that between the nephew (*mwanö kal*) and his maternal uncles (*nya nduma*). Proof of this is to be found in an early monograph devoted to the Fang of the Ndjolé district, and also in a document that was prepared more recently for a clan gathering. In the former, Captain Curault[42] examines the avuncular relationship in detail: 'The relations between uncle and nephew are very close: throughout his life the nephew continually gives his uncle presents to increase still further the bride-wealth paid for his mother to his uncle. Similarly, whenever his nephew comes to see him the uncle kills chickens, etc. for him in the same way as a father-in-law does for his son-in-law. . . . If a poor nephew needs trade goods to pay for a palaver or to get married, he can appeal to his uncle knowing in advance that, even if his poverty has prevented him from giving his uncle many presents, the latter will help him. It is the supreme disgrace for a man to send his sister's son away empty-handed.' Uncle and maternal nephew share the inheritance. An account of a clan meeting of the Yémisèm-Éba still laid down, as late as 1948, the 'indemnity' to be paid on the death of a *nya-nduma* (a sum *equivalent to the value of a wife* and a sheep), and on the death of a *mwanö-kal* (a slightly smaller sum, 'depending upon the amount of the inheritance', and a sheep).[43] The position of the latter with regard to the former is, in certain respects, the same as that of the son-in-law to the father-in-law, or that of the receiver of wives to the giver of wives.*

The significance of these facts is understandable in the light of the Fang principle governing the payment of bride-wealth; 'A brother obtains a wife with the marriage payment made for his sister', *nduma a luĝ nö biki kal*. In this process, the marriage of a man and woman involves not only the two principals, but also the husband's sister who has indirectly 'contributed' the payment enabling the marriage to take place, as well as the wife's brother who has indirectly 'recovered' the same payment in order to get

---

* The strong kinship existing between nephew and maternal uncle strengthens the marriage. When either of them dies, the handing over of the equivalent of a marriage payment to the survivor is an inducement to renew the marriage and thus restore the strong maternal relationship which has just been broken.

married. This helps to explain the close tie between nephews and maternal uncles, and also the rights which, according to Curault, a paternal aunt (*sôna*) has 'over her brother's children, since it is thanks to the sum paid for her that her brother is able to marry, and consequently to have children'. This relationship is sufficiently strong to permit, in exceptional circumstances, of the nephew being admitted to the family group of his maternal uncle, or of the husband of his paternal aunt. We were able to observe an example of the former, which had led to a change with regard to clan membership: a man belonging to the Yéngwi by birth left his own lineage as a result of a death which he was suspected of being responsible for, and, having gone to his maternal uncle and settled down with him, was accepted as a member of the *Esabâg* (he was said to be *ña ayôg*, 'received into the clan').

In the Fang system, the kinship terms apply not only to a precise class of individuals, but are often used in an extended sense. *Ngwé* may be used to designate any maternal kindred. *Nya nduma* (literally 'mother's brother') is applied to a number of male kindred on the mother's side: her grandfather and his brothers, her uncles and their descendants;[44] in fact, to all the men belonging to the *nd'è bòt* of the maternal grandfather. *Mwanö kal* implies kinship with the descendants in the female line, through the paternal aunts (the term *sôna* having a classificatory equivalent, *kal ésuô*, father's sister), the maternal aunts (to whom the term *sôna* is applied on a symmetrical basis) and, obviously, the sisters (*kal*); but its meaning is extended to include, as Martrou points out, 'any child whose mother was originally a member of the village or the tribe'. When the term is intended to designate the closest kinship in each of these classes, it is qualified by the epithet *fogo*, meaning 'true', which emphasizes it; for instance, *mwanéñâg fogo* would be translated as 'brother by the same father'. Whereas the relationship of *mwanéñâg* essentially refers to the paternal filiation, the relationship of *mwanö kal* is concerned with descent through the 'sisters' and the system of distributing the marriage payments. These relationships are in a sense complementary; they refer to the procedure which makes it possible for a couple to get married and beget descendants; and any one of them can make up for another's failure to do so. This is suggested by Curault, in the case already referred to, when he says: 'An orphan who does not get on with his father's brothers can also find a "brother" in the household of his maternal uncle, or of his paternal aunt's husband, or of his sister's son, provided she is considerably older than he and already the mother of adult men.' In this way, if a man wishes to escape the unjust exercise of authority by the 'head' of his own *nd'è bòt*, an alternative is open to him.

This account of the main features of kinship is enough to show that Fang society, while according primary importance to the 'paternal' kindred, also recognizes those on the mother's side by attributing important functions to them.* This double recognition is confirmed by the obligation of double exogamy: a man is forbidden to marry a wife belonging to his father's or mother's clan (or to a clan related to the latter if their common origin is still known). We have mentioned certain circumstances in which maternal kinship becomes effective. It should also be noted that it operates from childhood onwards, making it obligatory for the *mwanö kal* to visit his *nya nduma* (mother's brother) so that he may be granted the right of guardianship, receive the marriage payment, share in any inheritance by taking the place of the paternal kinship that has ceased to exist and also play a part in the various phases of funerals and mourning alongside the 'relations by marriage' (*abè*). It would seem, therefore, that, as this last fact suggests, the power of maternal kinship – though remaining subordinate – may be recognized in this way in order to strengthen relationships established by marriage: the father's relations 'by marriage' are the *nyanduma* of his immediate descendants; and in this way the bonds that are essential to the very existence of traditional Fang society are consolidated.

Marriage and Marriage Relationships

The earliest explorers, du Chaillu and Mary Kingsley, were quick to note the importance of the relationships created between 'alien' groups as a result of multiple marriages. Father Trilles, also, in a study carried out at the beginning of this century, refers to the

* This had already been noted by Mary Kingsley in her *Travels in West Africa*, London, 1897, when she writes: 'Among the Fang, kinship is recognized on both the father's side and the mother's, and not, as with the Galwa, restricted to consanguinity.'

personal advantages that are inherent in an extended network of
'relationships' resulting from marriage. 'A Fang', he says, 'will
therefore marry a girl in order to procure for himself relations in
other tribes, thus acquiring greater influence through having more
men connected with him by the ties of blood.'[45] All three authors
stress two *social* consequences of marriage: an increase in personal
prestige and in the power of the family group.

These observations need to be amplified by explaining why
every Fang attaches such importance to the 'possession' of several
wives, and why the competition for wives is so intense. As for its
importance, this was put very vividly by Dr Cureau, who said:
'The women's quarters are a kind of savings bank. . . .'[46] And L.
Mba, a Fang from the Libreville district, explains it in a similar
way in his book on Pahouin customs: a wife 'becomes part of the
property (*bioum*) of the group of which her marriage makes her a
member'; and he goes on to point out that the reason why
adultery by a married woman is 'so severely punished is because
it is regarded as theft'.* A wife has no legal status, and little
personal property apart from objects of everyday use; she cannot
inherit, but is passed on by inheritance in exactly the same way as
trade goods and other forms of wealth (which may virtually be
regarded as wives). Nevertheless she is a special kind of property,
the most important kind: a form of productive capital. Thanks to
the part women play in agriculture, all the more valuable nowadays when they help with the growing of cash crops, a wife is a
source of profit; and also, owing to her various domestic duties,
of service. She is, too, a source of power, 'cooperating in the
defence of the group or in procuring alliances through the pro-
creation of children',[47] and of personal prestige. And, lastly, she
is a source of 'affinities' and of kinship: it is through her that the
number of people participating in the exchange of services and
gifts, and who are able to provide help and support, is enlarged.
Thus marriage has a predominantly social significance; it creates
the bonds (*abe*) which consolidate the family and clan groups. As
Curault correctly pointed out, 'despite the diversity of languages
and the palavers, it brings about a close unity between the different

* In the same way Martrou, in a study written in 1918, quotes a remark made by a
young Fang from Libreville to his wife: 'What are you grumbling about, you are one
of my animals. . . . I have paid enough for you!'

sections of the Pahouin people'. But at the same time marriage
also has a personal significance: in traditional Fang society, the
possession of numerous wives is the main indication of wealth
and the necessary condition for any increase in wealth; and it is
this wealth that partly determines a man's social status and enables
him to acquire a kind of personal authority in a society in which
the sense of hierarchy plays but little part.*

It is due to this personal element that the rivalry for wives
sometimes becomes extremely acute. In the early days, official
reports were already drawing attention to the number of 'palavers
that are devoted to the question of wives'; and they continue to
complain about this, regarding it as a distinctive feature of 'Fang
society and psychology'. It may be said at the outset that this
rivalry does not primarily arise from the sexual demands that are
made upon women. For an unmarried man a variety of alternative
possibilities are available, though only on the plane of 'pure sexual
indulgence', as R. Bastide points out.[48] Before marriage, the young
folk enjoy complete sexual freedom with one another – the custom
known as *azòya-angòn* (*azòya*, fornication; *ngòn*, girl). In a monograph on the Fang of the Ogooué, Trezenem maintains that 'a
wife's virginity is not considered of any importance', and that
'the girls are free to give themselves to anyone they choose'; but he
goes on to make the important reservation 'that there are not
really any "girls", as they are married by their parents at a very
early age, sometimes even before they are born'.[49] This reservation is only relative, however, for according to Mba 'custom
permits a girl who is engaged to have as many lovers as she likes
during the period of her engagement'; and, similarly, Bertaut
points out that 'a young girl has complete sexual freedom as long
as she has not got *a husband*', which may well mean a long period of
licence in view of the considerable time that it takes to find the
money for the marriage payment, which is always high. Furthermore, a kind of prostitution used to be tolerated, if not actually
organized, because the husband was able 'to force one of his wives
to earn money for him by prostituting herself with strangers'.[50]
A number of practices, such as putting a wife at the disposal of a
guest, lending or exchanging a wife as a mark of friendship (the

* It is worth noting that two words from the same root, *éval* and *évala* mean respectively 'polygamy', and 'support' or 'stay'.

wife becoming *munöga ângôm*, 'wife of friendship')*, show, in precisely the same way as the freedom we have just described, that the harsh repression of adultery is primarily to be explained on social grounds.

Above all, the possibility of carrying off women from neighbouring tribes during the period of conquest, and of buying 'alien' women cheap so long as the slave trade continued, enabled the 'heads' of the lineages to deal with the problems arising from the young men's unsatisfied appetites. The Fang do not appear, as is the case with some peoples,[51] to show any sign of being sexually deprived because women are the property of the men of mature age. One might almost say that what is sought after is the *legal possession* of a wife, on account of the many benefits she confers, rather than mere *sexual possession*. And in this sense, one can understand the point of view expressed by Mba, when he says: 'It was not the physical satisfaction of the senses that drove the Pahouin to polygamy, but needs of a very different kind. . . .'

Once the marriage is consummated, the wife passes from a state of almost complete freedom to one of complete sexual control. The physical penalties for committing adultery, which applied only to the woman, were harsh: to be exposed naked before the village assembly; to be tied to an ant-tree; the removal of the clitoris, or 'pepper torture', as well as other forms of mutilation. Moreover, the public nature of the punishment shows that the group as a whole regarded itself as being wronged. When a woman, either by running away or being abducted, leaves the lineage into which she has married, all its members react violently: it results in fighting, rape and looting, at the expense of the village that takes her in.† This control, and the collective sanctions by which it is enforced, are in complete contrast with the tolerant morality that allows a girl to 'make the most of her youth', as expressed in the proverb: 'A woman is a dried corn cob, anyone with teeth can take a bite.' Marriage

---

* Cf. V. Largeau: *Encyclopédie pahouine*, the article on 'Adultery': 'The rules of hospitality require the host to put one of his wives at the disposal of his visitor; similarly, for two neighbours who respect each other, to exchange wives for a time is common practice and an unmistakable sign of mutual trust.'

† 'As a result, there are quarrels that last for years, leading to wives being carried off and ending in shooting,' Libreville archives, 1909. See also the proverb: 'If a wife is a vessel at which everyone slakes his thirst, it is best not to carry her off.'

reinforces the *social* status of a wife; it imposes upon her unconditional submission. To quote Bastide, it marks the point at which
'libidinous sexuality' gives place to 'social sexuality'.

The social character of marriage is stressed symbolically; the
acceptance of the wife into her husband's lineage is marked by a
whole series of ceremonies. The husband's mother recites his
genealogy for her, and she has to spend a week in isolation, after
which she is bathed and anointed with oil by the eldest of the
kinswomen and is given a new name, expressing a wish that is
formulated by the other women to the accompaniment of singing
and dancing.[52] The 'affinity' that has been created between the two
family groups is manifested by the eating of meals in common and
rejoicing (*éyalö*). It is then consecrated by the gift of an animal to
the bride's relatives, which will be sacrificed on the *biéri* (the
ancestral altar) – emphasizing that the bonds that are created are
not only with the living, but also with the community of
ancestors.* Great stress is laid on her becoming a part of the
lineage (in this respect, the recitation of the genealogy appears to
be very significant), and on the creation of an affinity (the same
word, *abè*, designating both the bond and the affines) which will
ensure peace and mutual assistance. Thus two of the wife's
essential functions are revealed: she represents the principles both
of fertility, and of peace and help. Such were the relationships upon which traditional Fang society was based; and this
explains the control exerted by the lineage, on the one hand by
limiting the man's freedom of choice – through the mediation of
the head of the family it sought to ensure an alliance which would
prove advantageous[53] – and on the other by intervening if the wife
ran away or was abducted, which upset the equilibrium achieved
by the marriage.

The process of marriage leads to the development of reciprocity,
to the exchange of gifts and even of challenges between the two
family groups concerned. From the first stage of the betrothal
(*dzâ ga*), the man establishes ascendancy over the girl he has chosen,
through his right to live with her for several days; but his family
has to provide the first gifts for her relations and to assist with
various kinds of work such as clearing scrub, building huts,

* Probably the collective violence that 'quarrels over wives' give rise to is also
connected with the *sacred* character of marriage.

hunting and fishing. It is during this stage that the girl's father decides the amount of the marriage payment, *nswa*. It is followed by a second, during which the payment is actually made, which may be done over a period of time (provided the first instalment has been a substantial one), and which usually leads to arguments and palavers. On the other hand, the *nkia* ('the recipient of the marriage payment') is bound to reciprocate with gifts, usually of animals, known as *mévalö*. Both the marriage payment and the 'counter-gifts' have to be handed over in a formal ceremony that involves both challenges and banter. When the women of the husband's village present their gifts, they boast of the wealth of their village and make fun of the poverty of the bride's presents, and are in turn mocked by the latter when they bring the counter-gifts. Finally, there is a third stage, the 'handing over of the betrothed', when the wife comes to live permanently in the husband's family group. This requires a further ceremony, since, according to Largeau, 'the woman only becomes a true wife (*mônöga*), and not merely a concubine, when she is allowed to cook for her husband, her mother helping her to prepare the first meal'.[54] This final ceremony, as Leenhardt has pointed out elsewhere, 'takes the form of a communal feast';[55] it marks the end of a phase during which the bonds resulting from reciprocity are reinforced by intimate communion between the members of the two lineages related by marriage.

Later on, exchanges between the two groups continue in the form of reciprocal visits, help and presents, especially when children are born and the husband has to make presents to his wife's family. In the past, this reciprocity must have been more direct, for we met Fang who could remember marriages that took the form of exchanging wives. A Pahouin writer, François Meyé, says that 'examples of such marriages (called *bikour mêngong*) are known', but very rare.[56] Despite the payment of bride-wealth, this sustained reciprocity is unmistakable; moreover, the endless interchange it involves – which led Dr Cureau to compare the family-in-law to 'a swarm of leeches'* – guarantees the persistence of the marriage.[57]

The circulation of the marriage payment creates a network of

---

* And to write: 'There are endless demands on the most curious pretexts: a fiancée's first menstruation, the first conjugal cohabitation, the first signs of pregnancy, the confinement.' See *Les populations primitives*, p. 117.

ties between groups, which, were it not for the insistence upon
exogamy, would have continued to live as so many independent
political, economic and biological units turned in upon themselves.
It ensures cooperation. It creates areas of security in a country
where, during the period of conquest, there was bitter economic
competition for the best farmland and hunting grounds, for trade
routes and centres. Moreover, the double exogamy increases the
number of *abè* (bonds), and the clear recognition of the maternal
kin further strengthens their efficacy. The circulation of wives,
and, parallel with this, of the marriage payments, therefore has to
be scrupulously controlled. This responsibility falls upon the
head of the *nd'è bòt*, the *ntòl* – a term which implies not only
'elder', but also 'arbitrator, envoy, ambassador' – who is the possessor of wealth and giver of wives. At the level of the fraternal
segment (*bobéñâg*), the principle that the bride-wealth received
upon the marriage of the daughters enables the sons to get married
in order of birth is strengthened by the eldest son's obligation to
help provide the bride-wealth required for the marriage of a
younger son who is not in a position to do so himself. It is clear
that this principle, which was intended to regulate the distribution
of wives and to limit competition, has not always worked out
successfully. Antagonism between 'eldest' and younger sons, involving the splitting of lineages, are often to be explained by failure
to carry out this obligation:* the older men may take advantage of
their seniority to acquire a larger number of wives; or, again, the
younger men may be tempted to leave the group in order to
earn their own marriage payments, or to become involved in
raiding and abducting wives – it is they who represent the most
dynamic and mobile part of the group.† Nevertheless, it is clear
from the earliest observations that a limited polygamy was established. Fourneau says: 'In fact, more often than not, the Pahouin
is monogamous, but only because the price of wives is too
high,'[58] and Dr Cureau goes further: 'Amongst the Fang', he
says, 'where wives are expensive, the maximum scarcely ever
exceeds five; it would seem that even thirty years ago only the very

* Cf. *supra*, pp. 114–5.
† It is probable that their lineages comprise the major part of the Fang population
in southern Gabon; this would help to explain the more or less restrained rivalry and
hostility between the 'Fang du haut' and the 'Fang du bas'.

rich could hope to avoid the humiliation of monogamy by taking one or two additional wives.'[59] These two authors confirm the existence of a *restricted* monogamy, and therefore of a tendency to equality in the distribution of wives, and attribute it to the high value of marriage payments.

We must now consider the material aspects of the marriage payment. In the nineteenth century it consisted mainly of iron objects (small reproductions of assegais, knives and axes), the best known of which were the *bikki*,* used solely for this purpose, as well as animals, ivory and salt. With the development of trade, imported trade goods began to take the place of these symbolic objects; and in the 1860s the explorer du Chaillu commented on the continually increasing demand for such goods.† Up to 1918–20, the marriage payment still usually took the form of this symbolic money and valuable trade goods; it was only after this date that cash began to be used, and gradually came to represent a larger and larger part of the whole. This development must be regarded as an attempt to maintain *the equivalence in terms of wives* (the outstanding form of wealth) *with the most valuable goods* available to the Fang; and to ensure that the marriage payment comprised the rarest objects: *bikki* and trade goods in the trading period, cash when this gradually became acceptable in the villages. To begin with, it was not so much a matter of having to pay a high price – the notion of purchase only very gradually supplanted that of exchange – as of ensuring a restricted circulation, only open to the heads of lineages and subject to maximum control.‡ In these conditions, the unusual instances of polygamy were a mark of exceptional success; which explains the prestige of the *nkukuma*, the man with a large number of 'wives' and considerable property (*bioum*). The concept of price, which the marriage payment has acquired today, is the result of recent changes. Originally, its payment in full sealed a marriage

* Cf. M. H. Kingsley: *op. cit.* Moreover, the old word for marriage payment was *bikki* or *nswa bikki.*

† And he goes on to say: 'Copper rings, white beads, and the copper pans called neptunes on the coast, are the chief articles of trade which are a legal tender for a wife among The Fang'; cf. *Exploration and Adventures in Equatorial Africa*, London, 1861, p. 86.

‡ The efficacy of this control is noted in a study, *Le mariage fang*, in the Oyem archives: 'In the old days, indeed, the authority of the head of the family was very considerable, and he often used to appeal to family solidarity to enable the poorest members to get married and to ensure a fair division of wives.'

which could only be broken by a lengthy procedure of 'divorce'; which even survived the man who allowed it, since the wife was passed on to the eldest son or the eldest brother; and which, above all, established a legal right to the children. If the bride-wealth was not fully paid, the new-born child belonged to the wife's kin; and, similarly, in the event of a 'divorce', until it was completely re-paid, the child belonged to the father. The fact that the bride-wealth was not refunded on the death of the wife, provided she left children, is no reason to assume that it was a question of 'paying for the wife', but rather of a reciprocal exchange, emphasizing that by means of the offspring *affinity* had been transformed into *kinship*.

We have endeavoured to bring out the social aspects of marriage by indicating the importance of the bonds it creates between groups and, particularly, of the control it makes possible over the circulation of wives and marriage payments. But it is obvious that this system did not always operate smoothly: its significance for the lineage does not necessarily coincide with its significance for the individuals directly concerned. Certain procedures, sanctioned by custom, help to modify the conflicts that may arise. It is possible for a marriage to take place by agreement between a man and a girl, against the wishes of the heads of families, by the abduction (*abòm*) of the girl;* there are various expedients open to a woman if her marriage proves to be seriously detrimental to her (on the basis of charges brought by her she may be married to another of her father-in-law's sons, or she may be allowed to go off with the man of her choice, provided he pays compensation, or she may 'publicly curse her husband');[60] and lastly, if the dispute threatens to become dangerous, she may be granted 'a divorce', although, traditionally, this is only possible in clearly defined circumstances and 'with the consent of the heads of the two families concerned'.[61] Thus, although in the old days they were only resorted to in the most exceptional cases, there were a number of ways in which personal considerations could be taken into account – and these were what Meyé had in mind when he said that, given the expedients available to her, 'a Fang woman can in no sense be

* Cf. E. Trezenem: 'Notes ethnographiques sur les tribus Fan du Moyen-Ogooué', in *Journ. Soc. des Africanistes*, VI, 1, 1936, p. 88: the young man 'offers what he has in the way of money and trade goods, and the kinsmen are obliged to consent to the marriage by accepting this as a payment on account.'

regarded as a slave'. Moreover, the personal element that most frequently proves to be the disturbing factor is the fact that the number of wives is a sign of wealth and social importance;* when the circulation of goods ceases to be rigorously controlled, it results in keen competition and frequent disputes.

We now have to consider the people affected by marriage and, at the outset, to recall that certain persons are excluded from this relationship. Apart from the rule of double exogamy, which involves 'fraternity' in the widest sense, marriage is forbidden between a number of clearly defined degrees of kinship: firstly, between members of the *taġa* category (father, mother, uncle, aunt) and of the *mwanö* category (sons and daughters, nephews and nieces), as well as between members of the same segment, including cousins as far as the third generation; secondly, with regard to 'relations by marriage', between a man and 'any woman whatsoever, even divorced, who is related to him by marriage', and between 'the members of the son-in-law's household' and any divorced woman related by marriage;[62] and lastly, as regards 'adopted' members (*ntobö*) of the clan. It seems worth while mentioning that these various prohibitions exclude from the affinity created by marriage individuals who already have clearly defined relationships with one another: those due to effective kinship (including 'cousins' as far as the level at which the *nd'è bòt* is most likely to break up into different segments); those that exist between groups already related by marriage; and those arising from the status known as 'adoption'. Thus everything points to the fact that one of the purposes of marriage was to effect an alliance with *the most alien* elements, alien and hostile being more or less synonymous throughout the period of conquest.† The obligation to respect both double exogamy and the prohibitions just referred to helped considerably to widen the lineage's circle of relationships involving cooperation. Incest, that is to say any

---

* This element is to be seen particularly in the custom reported by L. Mba: 'In well-to-do families the kinsmen arrange for the betrothal of the boys *before* puberty and the girls *after* puberty.' 'Essai de droit coutumier pahouin', in *Bull. Soc. Rech. congolaises*, 25, June 1938, p. 14.

† Cf. E. Trezenem: *op. cit.*, pp. 91–2: 'Relations with alien tribes are unusual . . . a stranger is only received with reserve, and then only if he can produce trade goods to prove that the purpose of his visit is simply to find a wife. Most of the tribes are hostile to one another.'

infractions of these principles, came within the category of *nsêm*, defined by Martrou as 'ritual impurities or moral blemishes'; it resulted in infertility or sickness and, in traditional society, called for collective action. Largeau describes the expiatory procedure that was then customary,[63] requiring intervention by the 'men's association' and the rites connected with the *makuma*, a dance peculiar to the latter.

Marriage creates the 'restricted' or 'individual' family, for which the Fang have no special term. Husband and wife are known to each other as *nomö* and *nga*, both terms which emphasize the biological character of their relationship, since they can also mean 'male' and 'female'. The parents-in-law are described as *mînki* or *nkia*, 'those who receive the marriage payment', referring to the final act which makes the marriage legally valid, in the same way that the word *mbòm*, meaning 'a newly married woman whose bride-wealth has just been paid', is used to designate the daughter-in-law. The principle of precedence inherent in seniority, subsists in the relations between the 'affines' or *abè*: for the husband, his wife's eldest sister is *mînki* (mother-in-law), while the youngest is *ngòm ʒam* (my daughter). The authority of the first wife with regard to the co-wives is based on the same kind of precedence: whereas she is known as *nanö* (mother), the others are looked upon as her *mbòm* (daughters-in-law), which explains both her supervisory position as regards the various kinds of work to be performed and the moral responsibilities with which she is entrusted. Finally, it is important to note that the personal factor operating within these relationships is typified by the position accorded to the favourite wife (*nluga* or *ntômba*). This so surprised one of the early government officials that he said: 'While as a rule they profess to feel more or less indifferent toward their wives, and do not scruple to hire them out or lend them, they are nevertheless deeply attached to the one they select as "favourite".'[64] Here it is the least social of the two aspects of marriage that encourages the development of spontaneous relations.

Residential Units

The colonial administration regarded the Fang country as consisting of a series of villages, the name they gave to any group, whatever its size, provided it occupied a clearly demarcated area. According to the earliest observers, however, the Fang distinguished at least two types of village: the *žal*, which 'is inhabited by the family of the *ésa* (head or patriarch), his kindred, and his followers'; and the *mfaĝ*, 'where several families live together . . . though without any intermingling . . .', the different sections being 'separated from one another by guard-houses built in the middle of the single street . . .'[65] From this description it may readily be seen that the *nd'è bòt* (minor lineage) constituted the basic element and occupied clearly defined quarters. For the most part, the larger concentrations were due to reasons of security (they were mainly observed in the most remote part of the Fang country during the period of conquest), or to the influence of some powerful personality.* They represented more or less extended lineages, and Martrou notes that all the members of these villages 'can trace their descent through four or five generations from a common paternal ancestor'.[66]

Old books and documents make it clear that the village group was an eminently *mobile* unit. Father Trilles quotes the example of a village which, under the leadership of the same man, had migrated a distance of five hundred kilometres (1910); and Dr Aujoulat refers to a group which, in the course of twenty years, had travelled 'more than two hundred kilometres' (1935). Such facts are characteristic of a semi-nomad people, not of a peasant people tied to the land; and for a long time the administration found itself at odds with what it called the Fangs' 'craze for migrating'. In Gabon, this instability was reflected in the laws: Martrou points out that there was no definite ownership of land for purposes of cultivation, hunting and fishing, but simply roughly defined 'zones of influence'.[67]

Basing himself on these suggestions, J. Bruhnes, the geographer, described the Fang as the very type of *Naturvoelker*, and maintains that 'the most general cause of migrations . . . is their destructive occupation of the soil'.[68] It is, however, important to correct this view, since it was derived from inadequate knowledge of facts that have a direct bearing on our analysis. On various

† Maignan in his 'Etudes sur le pays pahouin' in *Bull. Soc. Rech. congolaises*, 14, 1931, refers to the authority exerted by a man who 'by reason of his age, experience, eloquence and wealth, is most capable of defending everybody's interests'.

occasions we have pointed out that there are a number of Fang settlements in a clearly defined region (the Woleu-Ntem) that have been there for a very long time;* we have shown how they spread out from definite 'hiving-off centres', and explained the way in which the organization of society encourages lineages to break away. These facts suggest that the instability is *relative* and due to internal causes.

Modern geographical studies maintain that the 'methods of cultivation adopted by the Fang could not, by destroying the forest, have led to the displacement of an entire population', and point to 'an early and genuine settlement' in southern Cameroun, the heart of the Fang country;[69] citing as legal evidence of this the existence of landed property amongst the Cameroun Pahouin.[70] It must be assumed, therefore, that the migrations into Gabon took place more recently (probably the starting-point of a new phase on a larger scale), and that if the Ogooué represents the boundary of the Fang country it is only because of the French occupation. The Fang did not readily relinquish the policy of conquest, in which they excelled thanks to their courage and their capacity for assimilation. Right up to the eve of 1914, the authorities were often involved in conflict with the warrior associations, the *Bizima*, that operated in the neighbourhood of the river Okamo; and, as late as 1922, a report notes: 'The natives are not yet under control.' There can be no doubt that the Fang had for a long time been striving to monopolize and control the trade routes and trading centres established in the old days as is clear from their legends, which often associate the discovery of great wealth with the advance to the west.[71] As early as the middle of the nineteenth century, the explorer, du Chaillu, noted that their military pressure was supported by peaceful conquest, thanks to the 'alliances' created by inter-marriage with 'strangers'.† And fifty years later Dr Cureau observed that 'the control of trade on the Ogooué has fallen into the hands of the Fang people'.[72] After

* This is confirmed by Maignan, *op. cit.*, who speaks of villages 'that have occupied the same territory for more than a century'. This was written in 1912.

† P. du Chaillu: *Exploration and Adventures in Equatorial Africa*, p. 87: 'The poor Fang, who are farthest of all from the coveted white trade, are but too glad to get a son-in-law nearer the seashore; and I have little doubt they will even succeed in intermarrying with other tribes to a considerable extent.'

they settled in Gabon the economy of the Fang groups underwen
a twofold transformation: it established contact with that of the
forest tribes, who were primarily hunters and collectors of trading
produce; and their expansion was slowed down by their attempt
to annexe the trade of southern Gabon, where it might almost be
said that only French colonization prevented a kind of Fang
colonization. While the responsibility for fighting and trading fel
upon the men, the subsistence economy was almost entirely lef
to the women, thus resulting in a division of labour that left the
acquisition of wealth and capital entirely in the hands of the
former.

Factors of this kind help us to understand the relative mobility
of the social groups: attachment to equally productive plots o:
land somewhere in the forest zone was not likely to exert much
influence on a people who were not primarily interested in agriculture.* Besides, their role as a conquering people imposed a definite
lay-out on the old Fang villages, which has often been described –
two continuous rows (*nkara*) of dwellings, enclosing a kind o:
courtyard, with a 'guard house' (*abèñö*) at either end; sometimes a
palisade of stakes, surrounding a banana plantation, to ensure
protection in the rear; and, inside the huts, a few easily transport-
able goods and chattels (any valuable merchandise being stowed
away in chests, while the ancestral skulls, *biéri*, were kept in large
cylindrical boxes).† It is clear that, for much of the time, the group
lived in a state of insecurity. This was the chief reason for
maintaining it at a minimum size, since otherwise any real protection would have been impossible; the causes that led to fission –
the basic organization of Fang society, the quest for wives and
trade-goods and, in the last place, agricultural methods – were
largely offset by this necessity. It appears that when the French
first began to take over the country there were still villages of
considerable size. Largeau mentions *mfaġ* with as many as eigh
to ten guard-houses; Grébert speaks of ten to twenty;[73] and Meyé
asserts that 'the usual population of a village consists of between

* Consider what was still being said in 1934 by Le Testu, one of the most competen
observers both of the people and of the country: 'Lacking any taste for work on the
land, which the Pahouin will never take to because he finds it humiliating, he may
however develop a liking for the profit to be derived from such work.'

† Very similar to the 'ancestor baskets' which the Ba-Kongo always took with
them on their long migrations.

80 and 170 warriors, not counting the women and adolescents'.[74] According to estimates arrived at fifty years ago, this would mean a total population of from 350 to 700 or 800 people, whereas today the size of the villages rarely exceeds 100. As the pacification of the country proceeded, the need for groupings of this size diminished and they broke up into their constituent elements, which were often strung out in neighbouring hamlets; these were called *ngòra*, and they were regarded as still belonging to the same lineage unit.

Undoubtedly there was a connection between the virile nature of Fang society and the marked separation between the sexes that was expressed in their everyday life: for women, the place they lived in was the hut; for men, it was essentially the guard-house. Mary Kingsley says: 'The men spend the greater part of their time in the palaver huts that are built at each end of the street, where the women bring them bowls of food throughout the day'[75] – though without being allowed to enter the *abèñö*, from which they were strictly excluded.

Father Trilles describes the latter as the place 'where the men gather to discuss the affairs of the community, war, marriage, disputes, etc.', and where strangers were entertained. It may be added that it was there also that the boys acquired much of their education and, according to Mba, learnt the most important prohibitions (*biki*). The *abèñö* brought together the men belonging to the same *nd'è bòt*, thus constituting a male kinship group. It was there that the authority of the 'elder' was established, the symbol of unity and organizer of the group's life as well as their intermediary with the ancestors; there all important decisions were taken, and the whole rhythm of work was organized; and there, too, each man's life was subject to almost continual control and criticism by all the others, creating a sense of solidarity that made this group *the most enduring element* in Fang society. Traditionally, it was in this way that a Fang acquired individual status and identity in the eyes of strangers; instead of being known as X, he was regarded primarily as a member of Y's *abèñö*. A social group of this kind enjoys a deep sense of community, since its members are bound together by the closest effective kinship (i.e. based upon direct lineal descent as well as on 'fraternity'), a common ancestral cult and the sharing of the same duties. On the other hand, the women it controls form no such coherent entity: they represent different clans, different types of kinship; they are a potential source of conflict (between 'kindred' and 'affinity', as well as between co-wives); and, apart from the co-wives of one man who live together, they rarely take part in any communal family life.

The *nd'è bòt* – or more precisely this masculine community of kinsfolk belonging to the same *abèñö* – is not, however, completely immune from latent antagonisms, arising from the privileges connected with seniority. Such tensions often come into the open as a result of disputes about economic issues, such as the distribution of wealth and wives, or the allocation of agricultural land. This *helps* to explain the great disparity in the size of the groups regarded as villages, and the processes of growth and disintegration that affect the latter according to circumstances. But both these developments occur as a function of this minor lineage, which is what the *nd'è bòt* amounts to.

It is possible for this group, amounting to a few dozen people or a village with some hundred inhabitants to break away on its own. But this is exceptional. When a village is well established and has a considerable population (200–300 people, or more), it cannot remain organized around a *single* communal household. Its inhabitants attach themselves to various centres, corresponding to the sons of the founder or their successors: for example, the village of Ebiane (Yéngwi, in the vicinity of Oyem) has a population of 235, divided into three groups, each of which is descended from one of three brothers. We have already insisted upon the fact that it is at the level of the same segment that the 'heads' of minor lineages are to be found. The village of Afénane (Yébimvé, in the Oyem district), with 300 inhabitants, also consists of the descendants of three brothers; and each of the three *nd'è bòt* occupies a definite part of the village street, as shown schematically below:

The groups are arranged in order of rank, the eldest son's being in the background, in immediate contact with the chief's hut. It should be added that Group 1 does not include the whole of the lineage descended from the eldest brother (Ekòrò Ngòm); the latter, starting with the sons of Ekòrò Ngòm, split up into three factions, one of which still lives at Afénane, while the other two have formed villages *nearby*: Messia, with 139 inhabitants, and M'Fagne, with 97.

This agglomeration of Yébimvé, consisting of nearly a thousand people settled in a fairly small area, is interesting in that it shows how the 'major' lineages (which we have previously referred to as being descended from the same remote ancestor – *abialö bòt*) and the 'minor' lineages determine residence in a particular area and village. Two brothers led a migrant group of Yébimvé from Cameroun to the territory now occupied by their descendants. A dispute, about the unfair division of wives acquired from

TABLE VII

Yébimvé in the district of Oyem

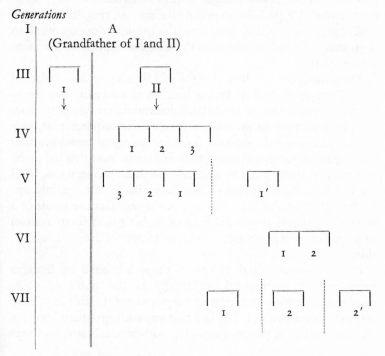

NOTE: Double line indicates separation of the two major lineages; dotted lines, fragmentation in alternate generations.

villages belonging to other tribes, brought about the first breach, each of the two brothers breaking away, and taking with him the group under his control. The memory of these past antagonisms has remained sufficiently strong to prevent any attempt at reunification.

The initial split, which became an irreversible structual phenomenon, may be represented as shown on previous page.

This split, which occurred within a major lineage having a common ancestor (A), is shown here by double lines. The two *nd'è bòt* broke away from one another, but nevertheless settled down in *neighbouring* districts. Since that time, however, these two groups have themselves suffered further fragmentation, which we show here as it affected the second of them, where it occurred in alternate generations (III, V and VII), thus giving rise to the creation of a number of villages quite close to one another, able to cooperate and, especially, to reunite if circumstances demanded it. Although it occurred so long ago, the original cleavage went so deep that it helped to minimize the dangers implicit in the more recent splits.*

These observations show that the *nd'è bòt* is a genuine residential unit. They make it clear that a breakaway becomes possible as soon as it reaches a certain size (size determining its viability, from the point of view of security and economic requirements, as a separate unit), but the distance (in the sociological sense) between the fragments varies according to the circumstances that led to the rupture and to the need to maintain potential cooperation. Until recent times, the instability of the Fang village was certainly due to the nature of the old economy, but it was also the result of a type of organization that did little or nothing to facilitate control of large numbers of groups – only the impact of danger could do this.

In the case of mixed villages – those inhabited by lineages belonging to different clans (usually as the result of some administrative reorganization of the population) – this instability was even more marked. The fact that any such grouping involves the coexistence of people belonging to 'stranger' clans increases

* The initial breach, which more or less split the Yébimvé into two camps, was a major source of antagonism and overshadowed the antagonisms within the two groups.

the divisive forces referred to above, even in the case of comparatively small villages. A case in point is Atout, a village in the Mitzik district, originally established by the Esibil, who were later joined by Yémödâg and Esakòra. The founder group and a large part of the Yémödâg had already seceded and the Esakòra group was divided into two *nd'è bòt* (the eldest son's and his brother's), representing a first stage in the loosening of ties, since in this case the split was not attributable to the small size of the lineage.

TABLE VIII

Village of Atout

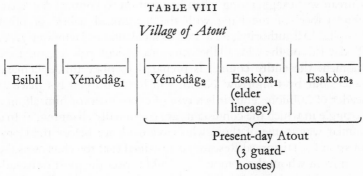

Present-day Atout
(3 guard-
houses)

(Here the double lines indicate final separation; the single, division into the *nd'è bòt* comprising present-day Atout).

These mixed villages – known as *mfulana möyóg*: 'mixture of clans' – made it necessary to set up embryonic chieftainships, in recognition of an authority *not* dependent upon kinship. When this involved a number of groups, the chief took care to remain *aloof* and to have his own guard-house, separate from the one where the members of his own *nd'è bòt* met. But apart from the administration's efforts to 'build up' the chieftainship, there was nothing to justify such an organization, nor to ensure the cohesion of the village group under its control. In fact, for Fang society, which has been classified among the 'anarchies' or 'stateless societies', any future progress will depend upon whether it succeeds in solving the political problem of maintaining stable village units of adequate size.

Political and Judicial Authority

Speaking of Fang society, Dr Cureau refers to the way in which

the social group is, as it were, 'drawn out . . . into a hierarchy
based either upon lineal descent, or upon intellectual, and particularly moral, superiority, principles which, according to the times,
both have a practical value'.[76] This emphasizes a feature to which
we have already drawn attention: the lack of any organized
hierarchy. This is borne out by the language, which has no special
word for 'chief': if the pre-eminence is of a genealogical nature
the word *ésa* is used; if it is based on wealth, *nkuma*; and if it is due
to eloquence and skill in leadership, *ŋoé* (from *ŋu*, to speak). But
Cureau was exaggerating when he went on to contrast the 'anar-
chist tribes' of the Fang with the 'organized tribes' of other
peoples. 'All authority', he writes, 'is incidental and temporary. . . .
Today Edvoughe wins all the votes in a difficult palaver, and for a
moment the entire council is prepared to obey this ephemeral
chief; but by tomorrow Nzokh will have usurped his place as
leader of opinion. Thus it is a case of every man for himself, in a
struggle in which the contestants are continually changing.'[77] In a
similar way, some of those who gave evidence before the Commission for Historical Research maintained that the chief 'was the
man from whom the community could expect the most outstanding services';[78] and the same point of view is continually echoed
in the complaints of officials who failed to win over powerful
traditional chiefs and persuade them to act as government
agents.

It should be noted, however, that as long as the ancestral cult
continued to be observed throughout all the sub-divisions of the
clan, precedence 'based upon lineal descent', to use Cureau's
expression, was maintained without much difficulty, since compared with the temporary authority depending upon events it was
lasting. This precedence was determined by *seniority*, it was justified
and made effective by possession of the receptacles containing the
ancestral skulls. This authority of the 'elder', who was at the same
time *primus inter pares* and in charge of the *Biéri* cult organized
within the framework of 'kinship', did not however enable
effective chieftainships to be created that were in any way comparable with those established on similar principles among the Ba-
Kongo.* An official report insists on the fact that a man *became*
chief, explaining that the *nyamòrò* (elder) 'became a chief when his

* See Part III below.

impartiality and his executive efficiency were *recognized* within his sphere of influence'.[79] Thus neither the villages nor the localized clan fragments, and still less the extended clan and the tribe, reveal the existence of a differentiated political hierarchy; what they do show is the pre-eminence of the *ésa* (which may simply take the form of a certain deference), or, temporarily, of some man who had succeeded in extending his 'sphere of influence'.

How are we to account for such a position? If we compare it with that of the Ba-Kongo, which we deal with later, we find that, with them, the fundamental social bond is that between the ancestors (owners and guardians of the soil), the land and the lineage; it involves the necessary relationships between related lineages and it limits the mobility of the groups. With the Fang, there is nothing of the kind: their connection with the land has no such importance, and, until recently, their whole economy remained oriented towards military and economic conquest. Even in districts where the Fang appear to have been established for a comparatively long time, instability is usual for a large number of the groups. As a result, a kind of vicious circle has been created: the mobility imposed by long-range conquest prevented the setting up of any hierarchic organization, and the lack of this has continued to encourage an ill-contained instability.

The social system includes no elements conducive to a better organized hierarchy. Though the precedence of 'the elder' is accepted, that of the 'elder lineage' (and it is to this that the Ba-Kongo turn when choosing their 'crowned chief') has hardly been sustained; indeed, quite the contrary, for as we have pointed out there is an almost continual state of tension between the senior and junior lineages. On the other hand, the absence of domestic slavery indicates a determination to prevent any development of inequality. Throughout the period of their major conquests the Fang had had two ways of disposing of their defeated enemies: they either killed them, or else they adopted them. And although the 'elder' continues to make some show of organizing economic and political life, and as the ultimate guardian of the ancestral rites of the lineage, the authority he enjoys appears to be subject to effective control. It operates within groups of *limited extension*, is subject to criticism by the other members of the *nd'è bòt* (who regard themselves as the equals of the 'elder', who can only act as their representative) or, if the village includes several minor lineages, of the *council*, and is always liable to be challenged by temporary leaders.

Though it is true that seniority confers authority almost automatically, the latter is nevertheless limited, and often threatened, by the principle that the most able man should be the most influential. In villages of some size, the position of chief (it would be better to speak of 'organizer and representative', which is what the word *ntòl* properly means) is generally handed down from eldest son to eldest son (or failing this, to a younger son belonging to the same segment) of the lineage directly descended from the founder, but only on condition that the successor is accepted by everyone 'on account of his courage, wealth and eloquence'.[80] Where this is not the case, someone else, who is considered to be 'stronger', is chosen from among the elders of the other *nd'è bòt* comprising the village. Furthermore, the chief's authority is controlled by a council, which is seen not merely as representing the different minor lineages but may include rival authorities – the best warrior (*éyènö*), a particularly wealthy man (*nkuma*), or one specially skilled in resolving disputes (*nté bété*), not to mention the officials of various 'associations'. Traditionally, possession of the *biéri* altar provided the legal authority; it was evidence of the antiquity of his lineage and a sign that the authority he exercised was legitimate. With the disappearance of this cult, as a result of colonization, the elder has either to make use of the new 'associations', or else to impose himself by fear by resorting to magic practices, otherwise he finds that his position as chief is threatened by the competition which is implicit in the social logic of the Fang.

The part played by personal prestige may be seen from the number of words or expressions that are used to denote an 'important' or 'honoured' man: *éguma* (from *gum*, to honour); *muramo* and *fâm ndên* (from *mura* and *ndên*, great or worthy); *nkurödi* (a very important man); *mfum* (a man with many relatives); *nkuma* (already mentioned, a man of wealth), etc. The authority derived from prestige of this kind tends to limit the authority dependent upon seniority, though tradition also imposes definite restraints upon it. Any kind of pre-eminence acquired on purely personal grounds involves certain risks for its possessor, for it means that his power or wealth or knowledge must be used in the service of all the members of the group.*

Several early writers refer to the danger of displaying outstanding opulence or prosperity. Le Testu stresses the part played by 'the fear of arousing jealousy': 'Bigger and more successful plantations, a better hut, more fruitful wives, more prosperous trade . . . any of these may be a cause of jealousy; and the result of this feeling may well be, as many people have good reason to know, death for the man who arouses it.'[81] In the same way, Briault, a very careful observer, notes that the death of a chief or any other notability is always open to suspicion, and has to be much more thoroughly investigated than that of an ordinary individual. 'Anyone who is in any way privileged', he says, 'is envied, just as the exercise of authority always gives rise to discontent; many chiefs have died unexpectedly, and few people who are envied live to make old bones. This must be generally accepted since there are so many proverbs that confirm it . . .'[82] Until the colonial authorities were in a position to protect the wealthy and successful, it could be said that anyone whose behaviour endangered the fundamental unity and egalitarian tendencies of the group simply in his own interests ran the risk of being murdered.

Through this interplay of more or less conflicting forces, varying in intensity according to circumstances, Fang society was preserved from any excessive concentration of power; this is why, despite its essentially military character, it has never exhibited the slightest trace of feudalism. Authority, and then under rigorous control, was only to be found at the level of small units – a village, or a group of related and adjacent villages. Only exceptionally (and precariously) did it extend beyond such groups; and since the 'associations' did little to improve this position, Fang society continued to display a complete lack of centralization which contributed to its rapid decline during the colonial period.

In a social system which affords considerable scope for conflicting relationships, courts of justice and conciliation play an

* 'A rich man had, so to speak, to "buy his safety" by generosity to his own people.' 'Society accepted the presence of a "rich" man on condition that his wealth, *akum*, benefited everyone.' See H. M. Bot ba Njock: 'Prééminences sociales . . . dans la société traditionnelle bulu et fang'.

important part. The Fang not only established a classification of offences – *nté*, a simple difference of opinion; *étôm*, a serious dispute that might involve war; and *nsêm*, ritual offences – and a scale of punishments that included the taking of hostages (*étéa*), but also evolved a judicial system that made use of 'arbitrators' and a 'jury' and had various ways of establishing proof (including several forms of trial by ordeal). In an unpublished paper,[83] L. Mba refers to the existence of (1) a 'family tribunal' – in fact, of the minor lineage – dealing purely with internal matters, in which the *ntòl*, acting as conciliator, was assisted by one or two members of the group acting as arbitrators; (2) a tribunal functioning at the level of the major lineage, which intervened in disputes between two or more *nd'è bòt* and, in principle, constituted a court of appeal, consisting of a judge (who was not necessarily the chief, but might well be an arbitrator of proven ability) and representatives of the groups involved; and (3) of a clan tribunal, constituted in a similar manner, which exercised the same functions in respect of larger groups, and which could also hear appeals. Furthermore, the members of the jury (*bétolö*) were only appointed on the day when the hearing was due to take place. This brief account is sufficient to show that it was a question, not so much of permanent judicial officials, but of principles that made it possible to deal with offences and disputes without recourse to violence. The status of 'judge' was not nearly so clearly defined as we shall find to be the case when we come to study the Ba-Kongo; in this respect, his position was an unsatisfactory as that of 'chief'. The latter might be the judge for the lineage or clan, but he often found himself supplanted by a really fluent speaker. In this sphere, practical knowledge and personal prestige were all-important, so much so, indeed, that, particularly in criminal cases, the judge might well be selected from some other clan.

As regards the functioning of the judiciary, it appears that, like that of the chieftainship, the framework of groups based on lineal descent and kinship hardly lends itself to any centralization of power. On the other hand, some of the 'associations' are organized in such a way (often effective outside the clan) that they fulfil (or attempt to fulfil) a compensatory function. This is certainly the case with the *Ngil*, which has played a part as regards both pacification and justice beyond clan boundaries – and, in fact, despite them.

Associations

We have frequently referred to the fairly loose nature of the bonds existing between different sections of a clan. In Gabon, owing to the extreme dispersal and confusion of the various fragments, the periodical gatherings of the clans were long ago abandoned: apart from a vague reference by Father Trilles, none of the early writers even mention them. Nevertheless such gatherings (*bisulan*) continued to be held in Cameroun, for the purpose of reviving the sense of solidarity between all the members and giving expression to it in the form of 'mutual help in kind, in cash, or in workdays'. [84]

These bonds, however, were drawn closer during the initiation of the young men into the *Biéri* cult, which was also an occasion for strengthening the association of fully adult males. The *Biéri*, which according to Father Trilles seems to have borrowed its form from neighbouring tribes, though 'its content remained Fang', was a cult paid to the shade of the ancestors through the medium of their skulls. For its observance, it required an altar, to be set up by the principal *nd'è bòt* in the 'elder's hut' or its immediate vicinity, at which regular sacrifices had to be offered, and the *Biéri* had to be consulted before any activity of general interest.

This cult confirmed the continuity of descent and periodically expressed the profound unity created by the succession of generations; when food was sacrificed, 'it was first offered to the *Biéri* and then eaten', but only by the initiates (*mvôma biéri*) during a solemn meeting in the guard-house. It involved a number of prohibitions (with regard to non-initiates and women) and duties. It 'set apart' the men who had been initiated, thus ensuring a privileged position – justified by their right to communicate with the ancestors and 'to see the *Biéri*' – for the most active elements of Fang society.

The initiation consisted of a series of ceremonies, and culminated in a state of intoxication, produced by eating a plant known as *alan*,* which sometimes caused a prolonged period of unconsciousness. [85] As a result of this, the new member was convinced that he had experienced a revelation and that from then on he was

* *Strychnos icaja.*

in direct communication with the ancestors. He felt himself at one with society as a whole, and at the same time discovered the significance of this: he had become capable of making prophecies which would always be fulfilled.* He had, so to speak, asserted himself as a Fang in the full possession of his powers. Thus the *Biéri* cult was, in the highest sense, an act of solidarity. It must be emphasized that the initiation was carried out in the same place for all the lineages belonging to the same clan; thus it strengthened the bonds of kinship between the most closely related fragments of the clan, and tended to revive, to give reality to, a still wider sense of unity. From another point of view, this initiation, like circumcision (which was performed on a different occasion, and appears to have been recently adopted by the Fang), created groups of young men (*bijula*) who clearly belonged to the same age group; and it was also a reminder of that close relationship between the generations (the initiation ceremony was performed by the 'fathers' or 'elders') which was fundamental to traditional Fang society.

The social group created by the *Biéri* remained closely connected with the kinship system. At the same time, as we have just shown, it had a distinctive role: it established real relations, all the more binding because of their religious nature, between members of the same clan who did not belong originally to the higher type of unity that chieftainship would have provided. But other 'associations' developed outside the kinship system, exempt from the diversities, particularisms and antagonisms that this gives rise to. Of these, the best known was the *Ngil*, a multi-purpose organization that sought to restore order in times of exceptional crisis. [86]

Members of the *Ngil*, when acting as such, were 'guaranteed against attack wherever they might be', and could move about with impunity among tribes who were 'involved in open vendetta'. [87] The *Ngil* (the word means the power responsible for order, as well as the 'association' itself and the masked man who acted in its name) 'has the right to beat, wound and even kill'. The solemn nature of its activities was marked by the complete

* Cf. E. Trezenem, *op cit.*, p. 75: 'All the Pahouin that we questioned maintained that predictions made by the *biéri* to people under the influence of *alan* always turned out to be correct.'

toppage of life as soon as it entered a village: the doors of the
huts were closed, the fires put out, the women shut up and none
of the men dared show himself in the inner courtyard. The final
ceremony involved the setting up of a hollow clay figure[88] (also
known as *Ngil*), before which 'all the members of the village and
of the villages belonging to the same lineage' had to appear, its
purpose being to expose the guilty, that is to say, those responsible
for unexplained deaths or for some calamity involving the whole
group, etc. Intervention by the *Ngil* was only called for at
moments of serious crisis. It gave rise to widespread activity,
involving whole lineages, for whom it had a therapeutic value:
by attributing guilt (indisputably, since it represented a superior
and anonymous form of justice), by restoring unity (on an
emotional basis) through the punishment imposed, and by impart-
ing a new energy as a result of this 'cleansing'.

  Its absolute and compelling power was justified by the religious
nature of the 'association'. Unfortunately little is known about
this, except that an appeal was made to the dead by means of
skulls, bones and sacrifices, and that it included fertility rites,
since the *Ngil* had a companion called *Omore*.* Here we have the
usual dialectic: recourse to the collective past, that veritable
storehouse of powers accumulated over the ages, to inform and
fecundate the society of the future; the past and the future, the
ancestors and the living, standing in the same relationship to
one another, of progenitor and offspring, as the generation of the
ésa to that of the *mwano* – a relationship that expressed a fundamental interdependence, a certain basic social order. The intervention of the *Ngil* tended to restore this elementary order; it
was a summons to normality, a pledge of fertility and power.
It would appear that the *Ngil* resembled a number of other
associations' that used to exist in Gabon, especially the *Mwiri*
of the peoples of the Ngounié.[89] In the first place, it was a way
of fighting against the power of the 'sorcerers' (*böyêm*), insofar
as they attempt to interfere with the normal order of things;
but it was much more than this – it proclaimed the existence
of a higher power than that based upon kinship, of a group

* H. Trilles: *op. cit.*, p. 62, says: 'The participants have to perform various actions
connected with sexual intercourse before the statue of *Omore*'; and Poupard speaks of
shameful ceremonies'.

with a great capacity for authority and almost certainly more powerful.

The Fang also had various specialized 'associations' like the *akûm*, which was responsible for organizing the ceremonies connected with the male dance known as *makuma*. The *akûm*, who also appears to have been a kind of bardic chronicler, took part in funerals and all matters appertaining to fertility, such as seeking out the 'sorcerer' responsible for an abortion that might lead to complete sterility,[90] or the rite for removing a charge of incest which resulted in childless marriages. In everyday life the *akûm* was distinguished from the uninitiated by his acceptance of a code of special prohibitions. He was 'treated with much respect, or rather fear', for he was considered to have 'great power'. 'To attain this position, he had to study under another *akûm*, to learn those interminable chants that go on all night, and then to kill one of his close kindred with his own hands . . .'[91] In this all too brief account, the last point is significant: it shows that he was subjected to a test; and, above all, it indicates unmistakably that the only way to acquire authority outside the clan, outside kinship, was by making, at least symbolically, the gesture of 'killing kinship'. It was under the influence of social groups of this kind that the logic of the system of kinship and affinity was transcended.

The *meaning* and relative importance of these 'associations' varied according to the particular circumstances. At times when insecurity called for at least a minimum of unity between related villages, they helped to create a closer cohesion between the clan fragments, as may be seen from the activities of initiates of the *Biéri* in Gabon, or of the *Ssò*, a rite practised in Cameroun and known to the frontier villages. In different circumstances, when it was only possible to deal with disputes peacefully and when conciliation was all-important, they sought to strengthen the authority inherent in organizations whose importance was increasing, for example, the groups that controlled the ancient 'dance of justice' (*sòmana*). They might also, as was the case with the women's 'associations', help to reduce the oppression of those belonging to an inferior social stratum; this is borne out by the fact that these specialized groups declined when the relations between the sexes began to improve.

When speaking of the *Ngil*, we said that the 'associations'
sometimes functioned as peace-making organizations; it is equally
important to point out that some of them adopted an attitude of
almost permanent opposition to the existing social order. This
was the case with the 'association' of so-called sorcerers (pl.
böyèm), who set out to acquire, on purely *personal* grounds, 'wealth,
strength and power'. All of them were admitted because of an
absolute *differentiation* – possession by a 'spirit' (*évur*)[92] that was
physically identifiable* – and a special initiation, the latter
involving an obligation to break, at least symbolically, the bonds
of kinship and affinity, by sacrificing the first child in the case of
a woman, or the maternal uncle in the case of a man.

The *évur* took possession of the future sorcerer either before
birth or during the following week, and drastically modified the
latter's organism, since it could be seen if an autopsy was performed.† Biologically the *nnèm* (singular of *böyèm*) and the *évur*
were inseparable: 'it grows with the child and only attains full
vitality when the child becomes adult'; its energy was dependent
upon that of the *nnèm*, and sacrifices had to be offered to maintain
it. The close bond between them was expressed in a number of
special prohibitions and obligations, from which the *nnèm* 'cannot
free himself'. Everything conspired to make the *nnèm* feel that
he belonged to a different order of nature, including the ritual at
the two fundamental ceremonies, those representing the 'birth'
and the coming to 'maturity' of the new *nnèm*. Lavignotte says:
'The *évur* lives in its owner's body, enabling him to lead a double
existence by leaving his body and acting on his behalf, to discover the secrets of other *böyèm*, to multiply his strength tenfold,
to do extraordinary things that would make him wealthy and to
kill without trace.' And Trezenem completes this description by
adding: 'Except when acting *in the interests of its owner* . . . the *évur*
is always malignant.'

Here, then, we have confirmation of an unusual power being
used for strictly personal ends: the power called *sân ngwèl*, that
of the *évur* in action. The characteristics of domination and

* This belief, it should be pointed out, is widespread in Southern Gabon, amongst
the Loango and also the Ba-Téké.
† M. Briault, *Sur les pistes de l' A. E. F.*, 1948, describes it as: 'A creature with
paws, eyes, a mouth and tongue . . . which can travel through the body',

radical differentiation are accentuated (so much so that possessio
of an *évur* 'is indispensable for anyone who wishes to be'
magician)[93] as against the system of kinship (implying 'fraternity
and a tendency to equality) and affinity (implying reciprocity an
cooperation). Whereas 'associations' like the *Ngil* or the *akún*
functioned lawfully, and so remained within the global society
the *böyèm* as a whole were regarded as an alien body, essentiall
heterogeneous and therefore in the highest degree dangerou
The relations between the *böyèm* themselves, which were expresse
in the two ceremonies of possession and initiation, did not exclud
rivalry: the *évur* might fight against one another. The fact of bein
a *nnèm* to a large extent freed the individual, enabling him t
assert himself against the established order (and to threaten thos
who supported it), but it also imposed upon him a considerabl
degree of solitude and a continual state of aggression; an extremel
dangerous existence, as may be seen from the violent collectiv
reactions when the sorcerers were punished.* Both the symbol
used and the formula pronounced when the *évur* 'is given
indicate the benefits that could be expected (fame, wealth and
numerous posterity), but they also stress the qualities that ar
required (virility and courage). The very term *böyèm* originall
referred to 'those with knowledge', a knowledge from which the
derived an invulnerable pre-eminence.

These facts reveal the existence of a *radical form of opposition t*
the old clan order; they represent the most highly individualized
the most revolutionary, side of Fang culture. They may be see
as a kind of 'fixation' of the feelings of aggression and individual
ism that counteract the feelings imposed by tradition[94] (the *nnèn*
is tolerated so long as there is no actual proof of his harmfu
activities). They must also be recognized as a means of differentia
tion, a factor of profound inner transformation.[95] The *böyèm* ar
individuals who carry on the most violent and persistent struggl
against the global society, yet the reaction towards them
ambiguous, as may be seen from the fact that a distinction is mad
between 'good' and 'bad' *évur*. Although both are dangerous fc
the ordinary man, they supply a necessary threat.

---

* Cf. V. Largeau: *op. cit.*: 'When he is discovered he is burnt alive, or else kille
and eaten.'

IV. RELATIONS BETWEEN SEXES AND GENERATIONS, AND THE SYSTEM OF TABOOS

The contemporary study of Fang society, as we shall see in the next chapter, raises two main types of problem: those concerning the changing relationships between men and women (typified by the frequently heard expression: 'our wives don't obey us any longer'), and those relating to modification of the typical relations between the generations. Where there is no doubt that it is the morphological changes affecting the community (atomization, personal mobility, abnormal sex ratio) and the process of economic development that give rise to these phenomena, it is equally true that the acuteness of the problems thus raised is to be explained by internal, and specifically Fang, conditions.

Oral tradition provides significant information as to the old relations between the sexes. From this it appears that women were originally regarded in terms of their *fecundity* ('Go and find yourself wives and people the earth,' Nzamö told the first man[96]) and of their *usefulness* ('Old woman, worn out gourd,' as the proverb has it). They were looked upon as being subordinate to men ('I am nothing beside a man, I am as silly as a chicken,' says another proverb) and protected by them, since in the old days they were essentially 'warriors'. All the early ethnographical studies insist upon this inferior status. Writing at the beginning of the century, Father Trilles said: 'Girls are not regarded as members of the tribe';[97] and this was confirmed by Trezenem in a more recent work: 'Women are scarcely considered to be more than domestic animals . . .'[98] At the same time, and apparently in complete contradiction to this, most of the early writers were surprised by the tremendous importance that seemed to be accorded to women, who were the subject of innumerable palavers. In addition, most of them described Fang women as being the principal means of production in a society where slavery was unknown, and therefore a means of procuring wealth. Such were the opinions generally held; the question is, what do they amount to?

In our view, the main emphasis was laid upon the *childbearing capacity of a legally acquired wife*. A wife enabled a man to assert himself as the genitor (*ésa*), and guaranteed him that posterity which, to every Fang, was the most important asset. In this way, not only did he prove his masculinity, but he also obtained real social promotion, acquiring an influence that increased with the prosperity of his family group and taking his place in the generation of 'fathers' which comprised the highest social stratum. In a warlike society, such as the Fang were until recently, a man's influence was determined more by the number of warriors attached to him* than by his personal fighting capacity; one might say that his importance depended upon his aggressive and defensive potential.

A Fang without offspring was of inferior status because he was powerless; and it is significant that the word *ki* means not only strength and virility but also power. This explains the importance of fertility magic and the various techniques that made it possible to identify the causes of sterility, as well as the fact that sterility was looked upon as a punishment for the most serious offences, particularly incest. In the light of these facts it is clear, therefore, that the production of human beings was considered to be more important than the production of the means of existence.

The chance discovery of a notebook, in which a young man from the Oyem district had jotted down some of his dreams and the rules of conduct he imposed upon himself, reveals how obsessional the desire for descendants could become. As an example, we quote the most 'obvious' of these dreams: 'I dreamt that a woman told me when I was asleep how my wife could have a child. I was to roast a banana, go down to the river, cut up the banana and give half of it to my wife; and after we had eaten it both of us were to drink the water of the river. Then I was to make love to my wife. After that, you will dip her in the water, saying: "Who is this woman you come from?"' Another passage, purporting to be a 'dream', though scarcely deserving the name, is nevertheless extremely revealing. It consists of a recipe for fertility: 'I dream that the Devil tells me of three herbs for a sterile woman, that will make her conceive . . .' The meaning is unmistakable, especially as various precepts, collected under the title 'personal resolutions' provide an obvious commentary: '. . . I shall find a way of ceasing to live, unless I leave behind a child; what studies enable a man not to die without leaving

---

* As a proverb puts it quite unequivocally: 'Another kinsman means another gun.'

a child? To choose for himself what is necessary, to marry a woman who bears children . . .'[99] One might almost describe this as 'the childless man's complex' – the quest for a numerous progeny still being the most highly esteemed undertaking. If the reasons for potency just described no longer exist, others have taken their place: the fear of breaking the line of descent, of becoming simply 'a dead man' and not an ancestor (*mvam*) revered by his descendants, the fear of a lonely old age and, nowadays, the desire to enrich the family group – which is an economic unit – by leaving behind the greatest possible number of active members. Moreover, as we have said before, to be the head of a large group is the surest guarantee of freedom because it enhances one's influence.

A wife is a means not only of reproduction – and therefore subjected as soon as she is married to the most strict control – but also of production. While the men build, clear land for plantations and, in the past, had the primary responsibility of 'defending the women and children',* the women are first and foremost peasants. They undertake most of the subsistence farming, and even take part in hunting. With the development of colonization this side of their work acquired a new importance and a new meaning: as a result of the opening of more and more markets and the established use of money, the produce they grew became a source of income, and they themselves, as workers, a source of profit. Thus a wife acquired an economic value, becoming so to speak doubly fruitful. At the same time her dependent and implicitly instrumental position was accentuated: she tended to become literally a 'thing', an object that was all the more desirable in that polygamy (despite the freedom granted to young people before marriage) gave her scarcity value.[100] While remaining the most put-upon members of Fang society, women were at the root of all competition because they were most in demand. It seems that although the women were kept apart from male society, that is to say from the most highly organized and active section of society, the impurity of their nature was periodically proclaimed in order to confirm their subordination. This is all the more readily explained in that the egalitarian tendency (within male society)

* In 1890 Fourneau commented on the 'long files of women laden like mules . . . escorted by men armed with flint-locks'.

and the rejection of slavery did not permit any institutionalization of relations between dominant and subject groups.

This position implies a certain ambiguity. A 'mother' has a relative authority over her sons and, by publicly cursing them (yoğö, to curse), can disclaim her position as mother;[101] similarly, the principal wife is allowed to curse her husband; a 'son-in-law' and 'step-mother-in-law' are bound by a system of taboos; the mwanö are expected to show respect to the 'generation of mothers'; and the deference due to seniority is also observed in the relations between the sexes. Thus it is possible for a woman both to be respected and to inspire fear. Moreover, 'associations' of women, with their own hierarchy and teaching, their own initiation rites and a whole system of symbolism expressed in a specific form of dance, are referred to in various documents – especially the Mévungö,[102] a Fang version of the Nyèmbé, a feminine sect that was well-known throughout Gabon and was observed by du Chaillu in 1860 among the Ba-Kélé, most of whom were subjugated by the Fang. This admirable observer wrote at the time that the Nyémbé 'protects women against their male enemies, avenges their wrongs, and serves them in various ways'.[103] Here the compensatory role played by groups of this kind is well brought out. By joining such an 'association' a woman could overcome the submissive and marginal position which was her lot in everyday life. It involved her cooperation in important community events and in spheres of activity from which she was normally excluded; for instance, in the old days, the dance of the Mévungö had to be performed 'when a Pahouin tribe was preparing to wage war or raid another tribe for women', and it was also part of the preparations for the great elephant hunts.[104] In a more general way the Mévungö took part in the principal events of village life, especially when marriages were solemnized and new 'alliances' were publicly announced. Today such 'associations' only persist sporadically, and then in a very degenerate form, as for example, the N'nup, based on a theory of 'queens', which appeared recently on the borders of Spanish Guinea.

This ambiguity with regard to the position of women results in a certain measure of equilibrium. On the other hand, this is not the case with regard to their emotional relationships: the man, who admits that marriages are arranged primarily for social reasons, lives in the hope of one day acquiring a 'favourite' wife, and has less to fear from the sanctions against adultery, whereas the woman, who is married at a very tender age, remains a prisoner of the system and is always threatened by severe sanctions. This seems to have led to frequent quarrels, as noted both by the early administrators – 'A wife very often leaves her husband to return to her parent's village or to *go off with the man of her choice* . . .'[105] – and by the first educated Fang – 'A Pahouin wife has no hesitation about running off with a lover; often married against her will, she *takes revenge for this state of affairs* by a considerable degree of infidelity'.[106] In both cases the language is significant: what might be described as an emotional pretext produces a more general reaction corresponding to frustrations of another kind. This may be seen as a sign of tensions finding expression at the only level at which this is possible; though we should add that the conditions resulting from colonization have to a large extent freed women from them, by destroying the comparative stability created by the traditional system.

These are not the only tensions one finds. Between generations, those of the *ésa* and the *mwanö*, and within the same segment between elder and younger brothers, relations of dependency develop that may become antagonistic. Soon after he is born, a boy is 'marked' by his kinsman, receiving a double name, which consists of the name of one of his paternal ancestors (of a *mvam*), and the first of his father's two names.* Apart from particular taboos imposed upon him by his father, the child is subject to various general prohibitions which are gradually relaxed as he achieves the status of manhood: for instance, until he reaches the age of puberty, he is forbidden to eat pork† or anything caught by him when hunting or fishing. According to Martrou, the significance of this is that 'useless mouths' are not wanted within the family group, 'but only arms and hearts capable of defending

---

* This double name implies that a man is created and moulded by his lineage as well as by his father.

† Pigs are highly prized throughout the whole of this part of Central Africa, since owing to sleeping sickness cattle are scarce.

and enriching it'.[107] He is also prohibited from living with a woman before he has been circumcised.[108] Moreover, various rituals mark the stages of his development: at ten years old the rite of *Ssò*;* then circumcision, which requires no initiation but appears to have been a public recognition of the fact that a youth had reached the age of virility; and, most important of all, the 'revelation' of the *Biéri*. Thus, by the time he is admitted to the male assembly, a young man has experienced, at varying levels of intensity, a sense of his biological, social and spiritual dependence upon his ancestors (*mvam*) and his 'elders' (*nyamòrò*), to whom he owes both life and safety, his social existence. Yet before he is allowed to participate fully in the assembly, he has to accept a number of further prohibitions, attesting his new position in society and reminding him of his obligation to submit to those who have made him a man and a full member of Fang society.[109]

For a long time he accepts the superior status of the 'elders', who intercede for him with the ancestors and enable him to fulfil himself through marriage and the possession of descendants, since it is they who control the distribution of marriage payments and wives. Thus the curve of a man's authority reaches its peak when he begins to influence society as one of the elders; then, as old age sets in, it declines (we have spoken of the tendency to push the 'grandfathers', *mvam*, into the background); and finally, after his death, which confers upon him the rank of 'ancestor' and enables him to intervene at will in the world of the living, it once more increases indefinitely.

In traditional Fang society, dependency ensured material and spiritual security, and was based upon the relationship between genitor (*ésa*) and offspring (*èmò wâm*), rather than upon that between ruler and subject. We have frequently insisted upon the egalitarian tendency within the *nd'è bòt*, and upon the dangers attendant upon any pre-eminence achieved on purely personal grounds. What is expected from the 'elder' is not domination, but a fair division of wives, wealth and communal tasks. Moreover, during the period of conquest, the considerable influence of the 'warrior', and the continual danger of the line of descent being broken in a group

* Bertaut, in his thesis on the Boulou of Cameroun, a related tribe, describes a less decadent form of the *Ssò*, which was central to any genuine 'men's association', that has now almost disappeared.

which had to remain sufficiently numerous and coherent, served to check any attempt to establish a harmful personal ascendancy. A state of equilibrium was achieved between the authority of the 'elders', based on their religious and political pre-eminence, and that of the young men, based on their fighting qualities. This involved strict control of the circulation of wives, and confidence on the part of the young men that, having passed beyond the stage of simple dependency, they in turn would have an opportunity of 'capitalizing' human lives, in the form of wives and descendants. The changeover from military to economic conquest, then to subsistence farming in which women played a fundamental part, and the enforced pacification which prevented them from remedying any shortage of wives by raiding other tribes, upset this equilibrium. The capitalization of wives became closely bound up with that of property, the one being more or less a condition for the other. The social function of the wealthy man (*nkumakuma*) became more and more important;* the relationship between generations, between older and younger men, tended to become a relationship between owners (of wives, property and political status) and dispossessed; and dependency began to assume the character of subordination leading to tensions and conflict.

So far we have considered a number of points of equilibrium within traditional Fang society; now it is important to clarify the considerable part that the system of taboos plays as regards social control. According to Briault, the word *éki* (pl. *biki*) comes from the root *ki* meaning 'strength, constraint, virility, power'; it expresses a ritual interdict, and designates 'any person or thing regarded as sacred with whom contact is forbidden'. Briault considers the *biki* essentially from the point of view of the constraint they exercise and the social order that they help to maintain: 'They almost convey the idea', he says, 'of an effective means of maintaining a spirit of submission to those in authority among those members of society, young people and women, from whom obedience is demanded. . . . Their political significance is reinforced by a supernatural aspect which ensures their

* So much so that Bertaut notes that among the Boulou, whose economy has long been on modern lines, *nkuma* is the only word for designating the head man of a village group.

acceptance'.[110] Mba describes them as 'rules of conduct which the Pahouins have imposed upon themselves with regard to personal behaviour and manners, and in matters concerned with marriage, religion, medicine, witchcraft and morality';[111] he emphasizes their application to every aspect of social life, their significance as categorical imperatives, and the effectiveness of their hold upon people. His description and that given by Martrou[112] suggest a distinction between collective *biki* (those of a general, moral kind, affecting sex, age categories and 'associations') and personal *biki*. When describing the 'guardians' responsible for maintaining the *biki* – male relatives in respect of children, husbands of wives and 'elders' of young men – Mba reveals the importance of the taboo as a means of maintaining and strengthening social precedence. In the same way, Martrou notes the number of prohibitions upon women, with a view to keeping them 'in a position of inferiority'. An *éki* would appear to be a rudimentary kind of regulation, issued without any definite justification, asserting the authority of the agent responsible for enforcing and 'proclaiming' it, and, in the event of violation, calling for a more or less vigorous reaction according to the nature of the authority involved (from simple blame to expiatory sacrifice). In particular, it reveals *the form assumed by law* in a society which does not possess specialized institutions, and which, in the absence of written signs enabling it to give permanent expression to every law, has to resort to material symbols. It should be noted that the same word *biki* is used to designate both the special kind of 'money' that was used in the old days for marriage payments, and 'taboos'. The system of *biki* may, perhaps, have originated in the method of controlling the distribution of wives, the first and most important of regulations. This may be regarded, by those authors who consider the 'incest taboo' to be the essential element of so-called primitive societies, as yet another proof of their contention.

If the *biki* help to preserve the social order and the precedence this implies, they also confer rights upon those who are governed by them; for while they certainly have to respect the prohibitions that affect them, they can also insist that the obligations be respected by everyone else.* It is in this double sense that the role of

---

* Thus the husband is strictly obliged to respect the *biki* appropriate to each of his wives.

'giver of *éki*' is important: on the one hand a sign of authority, on the other, primary evidence of the rights of the individual. In the study referred to above, Martrou pays special attention to the *biki* relating to 'status' and 'social conditions'. These are concerned with the important events in the life of the individual (there are, for instance, a whole number of taboos relating to pregnancy) and of the community (for example, periods of preparation for war or hunting), as well as to special situations (every 'association' has taboos peculiar to itself). Here we have an important function of differentiation, which leaves its mark on men's minds and increases the number of distinctive behaviour patterns. The *n'nèm*, upon whom *biki* are imposed at the same time as the *évur* which makes him a 'sorcerer', thereby feels himself to be so radically changed that his whole physical existence is devoted to their strict fulfilment. Trezenem describes definite cases in which the involuntary transgression of some *éki* or other resulted in almost immediate death, which could be attributed to no other cause.[113] Often the content of the *éki* is of less importance than the mere fact of giving or receiving it. This clearly indicates some authority: that of the ancestors who have handed down the 'tradition',* or of some ancestor who has revealed himself in a dream, or of a practising magician or a father, or of the 'association' of adult men, etc. It aims at efficacy by effecting a modification of the individual or of the social conditions; and in the case of taboos automatically connected with certain illnesses the aims of differentiation and therapy are perfectly clear.

The *biki* do not constitute a closed, immutable system. They are relevant to the life of the global society, increasing in number or falling into disuse according to circumstances. Mba states that as a result of Fang contact with other peoples in Gabon their taboos developed 'in the direction of amalgamation and multiplicity'. The point is an important one; it shows the extent to which the *biki* were used within the framework of the policy of assimilation and power of the Fang contact groups, to which they tended to adapt themselves to new conditions. It should be added that this 'multiplicity' also reveals factors of differentiation operating outside the clan structure. Mba represents the taboos

* The Fang have a word *eyêm* (pl. *biyêm*) to designate individual or collective 'ways of behaviour'.

as being not only a 'certain code of morality', but also 'the
secret and atavistic springs of the Pahouin soul'. Thus he insists
upon the part they play in the creation of a kind of 'national
character' and upon the essential values that they promote and
defend.

V. FIRST REACTIONS TO MATERIAL INFERIORITY

The arrival of the Fang in areas where trade had already been
established was of capital importance; imperceptibly, an enterprise that had begun as one of conquest and 'colonization'
was transformed into a quest for manufactured 'wealth' (*bioum*)
and competition for roads and trading posts. The quest for
'trade-goods' became the primary objective of masculine endeavour, involving the whole apparatus of military and magical
skills.

Many of their legends insist upon the attraction of the West as
the country of the white man, the owners of material wealth. One
of these, quoted by Largeau, suggests the almost mythical
significance they attached to access to these trading districts: 'At
last we reached the Ntem and the Ogooué, where we met those
who dispose of wealth. . . . They gave us everything, we became
rich.'[114]

The legendary stories collected by Father Trilles under the title
Noirs et Blancs are especially significant. The theme of some kind of
wealth that had passed the Blacks by – owing to their lack of
technical skill and passive rather than dominant attitude[115] – or
had been stolen from them,* occupies a major part of the book. It
appears that the Whites symbolized wealth; they were the *mitâgö*,
'the men of account', whose coming had been foretold in mythology, who would have the physical appearance of ghosts and
possess all the wealth that had accumulated in the land of the
ancestors. From this one can form some idea of the ideological
background to the arrival of the white man, the bearer of 'merchandise', and of the value attributed to the latter. A form of

---

* See 'The Legend of Bingo': 'And in order to steal Bingo's treasure from him and
to get hold of his secret, they killed him and took the green stone that they should
have left for us. Since that time the men from beyond the mountains own the riches of
the earth, whereas we have kept the laws of Bingo.'

questions and answers, widely used at the time of the clan consolidation movement for instructional purposes, still associated
these two ideas: the power of white example and the pursuit of
wealth:

Q. 'What way of life should be followed?'
A. 'The European way of life.'
Q. 'What example should we set ourselves in order to follow
the European way of life?'
A. 'We should work to make money . . .'[116]

At the beginning of this chapter we insisted upon the attraction
exerted by the centres of economic power – the coast, the Bas-
Ogooué and Spanish Guinea. A map of the migrations would show
these as *points of convergence*. From the outset, the Fang either
established themselves in the neighbourhood of these centres of
activity, or else encouraged the setting up of trading-posts for
which they had a real feeling of ownership. Both du Chaillu and
Cureau carefully noted this phenomenon: the first, by showing
how, when he became a certain chief's 'white man', his 'well-
being and security' were assured, though at the same time he
found himself continually subjected to requests for 'presents';[117]
the second, by studying the trade on the Ogooué that had fallen
into the hands of the Fang: 'Business firms found themselves
obliged to set up their establishments in definite localities and were
prevented, under threat of war, from moving them further up-
stream. The European agent was respected; his warehouses, far
from being interfered with, were closely guarded by the warriors
of the village. The trader was the prisoner of the people, and
found himself obliged to operate an enforced monopoly'.[118] The
first government reports also commented, as du Chaillu had done,
upon the anxiety of every important group to have 'its own
trading-post', which, 'when satisfied, led to an easing of the
situation and eventual submission'.[119]

Here we have a reaction which is not to be explained merely by
the economic advantage of maintaining a monopoly and having
immediate opportunities for barter. To establish a trading-post in
direct contact with the village meant that migration to the West
in search of wealth had achieved its object. Henceforward, a
permanent share in this wealth and a better life were assured. To
be on terms with the white man, who was regarded both as an

6

'elder' and, with all his wealth and knowledge, as more than human, meant participating in an endless round of power and fecundity, transcending an existence that was under some kind of curse in order to attain 'real life'.

From another angle, the Fang legends show that very early on, confronted with the technical superiority of the Europeans, they experienced a feeling of inferiority, both in knowledge and wealth, which they attributed to a divine decree, a veritable *curse*. One of these, also noted down by Largeau, refers to two of Nzamö's* children – Ekouagha (the subordinate one) and Ndan'-gho (the dominant one) – and the wishes expressed on their behalf. For Ndan'gho, the father proclaims: 'Wealth! Authority! Knowledge!' adding that 'All these things are contained within you!', and concludes, 'You shall beget white children.' But to Ekouagha he explains: 'Alas, my other son has taken everything. . . . For you there are no riches . . . you will beget black men and always remain poor . . .'[120]

A similar theme occurs in the 'Legend of the Nsas', quoted by Father Trilles, in which Nzamö ends up by saying: 'You, Black Man, get up, go and find wives and people the earth. . . . You will remain for ever as naked as you are now. . . . But you, White Man, will be rich, richer even than you have ever dreamt of. . . . The White Man will always be white, and the Black Man black; the White Man always rich, the Black Man always poor . . .'[121]

The theme of malediction suggests the high potential that was associated with imported wealth and the winning of it. Here, too, one can see a dawning awareness of the colonial situation and, especially, of the technical inadequacy of a social organism pre-occupied with 'the production of human beings'. In the legend, 'Go and find yourselves wives and people the earth' is part of the curse. The illusion of sharing in this new wealth was quickly disappointed, and the hold of the agents of colonization became more clearly defined and more complete: the theme of a curse connected with race expresses the depths of this disappointment. To go back to violent methods was now out of the question. As a result, recourse to magic procedures, to the knowledge revealed under the influence of certain forms of strychnine, increased; and, with the help of borrowings from Christianity, the belief in a better

* *Nzamö*, the individualized form of the divinity.

ife after death took a firmer hold.* The strain of adaptation
primarily affected religious and magical techniques. In both these
ields there were considerable borrowings from neighbouring
peoples (for instance, the *Bwiti* cult with which we shall be dealing
ater); customs changed, no longer in an attempt to assimilate the
aims of victory but simply with a view to defence. Reduced to the
status of out-of-work warriors, the Fang people lost the most
essential feature of their moral energy. As we shall show in the next
chapter, they were one of those that were hardest hit by the crises
arising from the colonial situation; but they were also one of those
who responded to this 'challenge' most wholeheartedly.

---

* Colonial intrusion, in various forms and at different stages, has had remarkable
effects upon African legends and myths. It has led to rearrangements and modifications which, in the language of *myth*, manifest the various vicissitudes and problems
that have confronted man and society as a result of colonization.

II
FANG CRISES

Already at the beginning of this century, Father Trilles wa
expressing concern about 'the weakening of authority' amongs
the Fang and 'the disappearance of ancestral customs'. He con
sidered that the two main causes for this were 'the intermixture o
tribes belonging to different races', and the influence of the whit
man 'through his presence, his religion and the fear he inspired'.

The Fang drive towards the coast and the European penetratior
of the interior were actuated by opposite motives. The forme
sought to capture the direct trade routes in order to control them
and to subjugate peoples who were few in number or divided
amongst themselves;* the latter to extend its advance toward
the Haut-Ogooué by making use of the internal trade route
and endeavouring to establish regular communications betweer
a chain of outposts extending from Gabon to Brazzaville. Te
some extent the Fang tried to relate their conquests to thi
endeavour. By 1880 the labour force required for the operation o
the Ogooué 'convoys' had so far increased that, according te
Fourneau, it almost had the effect of an 'enforced exodus'.†
This temporary agreement between certain Fang groups and th
European settlers gave the latter a more favourable opinion of th
whole ethnic group.

Before 1900, however, the first incidents began to occur

* The explorer du Chaillu points out that trade with the interior was in the hand
of a whole number of *intermediaries*, who attempted to safeguard their position b
frightening the European traders with tales about the tribes living in the interior a
being cannibals, while at the same time assuring the latter that the white men who ra
the trading-posts on the coast carried on the slave trade because they ate huma
flesh.

† In his *Au Vieux Congo*, he says that, in 1889, 'A cargo vessel put in at Ndjol
almost every day of the week.'

esulting from various forms of colonial activity and generally
ttributed to the failure to achieve pacification. There were
»bjections to the spread of missionary work, which was multi-
»lying the number of mission posts along the banks of the
)gooué;[1] and, particularly, an increasing number of economic
eactions. The granting of large-scale concessions was the first
erious threat to the old economic order: speaking of the Ndjolé
listrict, Curault says that, 'by killing the trade carried on by native
ntermediaries, [this system] caused a serious decline in the
»opulation'. Competition between individual traders, and between
hem and the companies, took advantage of the disputes between
ocal groups or provoked them to rebel. The opening and closing
lown of trading-posts, without any control, led to the revolt of
hose villages that had recently been established purely for this
»urpose. Disputes of a more or less economic character became
nore frequent, owing to 'the dishonest methods employed for
ttracting native labour', as well as to the brutality[2] and 'theft'
»ractised upon individuals (for example, the dollar was valued at
·5 when a native trader 'handed in produce', but at 2 to 2·5
vhen he was 'paid in trade-goods').[3] These were some of the ways
n which the Fang made contact with capitalist economy in its
nost primitive and brutal form; and they account for the first
igns of lack of confidence in the white man, and the resort to
tealing, dishonesty and flight.

Moreover, before 1910, two of the distinctive features of a
:olonial economy had already been experienced: the serious
epercussions of crises affecting colonial produce (the rubber
:risis of 1907 led to a particularly 'delicate' situation); and the
iecessity of supplying the labour required by European enterprises
n the terms laid down by the latter. A report of 1907 puts this
·learly: 'The problem of labour has become so serious that, *if it is
ot already too late*, steps must be taken to ensure the strictest
upervision; labour is becoming scarcer and scarcer, and more
lifficult to recruit.' This admission is significant. The new
:conomy – distinguished by arbitrariness, lack of organization
ind the reckless exploitation of men and materials – was not
:ontrolled by the administration, which so far had not succeeded
n occupying the whole territory. Often its activities were directly
»pposed to official intentions.

In 1910, Gabon was still divided into three 'military districts' (Ivindo, Okana and Ofoué-Ngounié), where the Fang groups wer' numerous and particularly insubordinate. The Annual Repor' notes that every period of 'complete business stagnation revives hostility that is almost always latent'; and this was based on th' feeling of the natives that the Europeans were opposed to thei' trade. All the attempts to administer the country effectively, fror 1910 onwards, merely added to this acute awareness of economi' domination a growing realization of increasing political oppres sion, typified by the obligation to pay taxes. This last requirement which made it necessary to obtain cash, still further strengthene' the sense of economic dependence, and the already confuse' situation was aggravated by the migrations that were undertake' with a view to 'escaping tax'. Between 1913 and 1915, the admin' stration endeavoured to attract new groups of natives to Bas Gabon, where the main European businesses were established; th archives of Médègue, situated to the north-east of Libreville o' the trails leading to the Woleu-Ntem and Spanish Guinea, revea the considerable part that this trading-post played in organizin, these modern migrations.* These were the beginning of a move ment that the 'discovery' of *okoumé* wood was to accelerate while at the same time superimposing upon the declining tradin, economy an economy of exploitation that was *totally* immun' from native control.

The year 1925 was a significant one: it was then that the recruit ment of labour for forestry work was intensified, enabling timbe exports to exceed 200,000 tons in 1927 (in 1900 they had onl amounted to 4,000 tons);[4] that the 'submission' of the disaffecte Fangs of the Woleu-Ntem and Okano was obtained; and tha the first political party created at Libreville, the 'Jeune Gabonais' ceased all 'public activity'. The period 1920–25 witnessed th setting up of an economic and administrative system that was t' remain essentially unchanged until the last few years. And a though to symbolize the profound changes affecting Fang societ'

---

* 'The head of the sub-division is actively engaged in encouraging the Pahouir to migrate to the coast,' Report for 1913. 'During the last two months of the yea the exodus of the people to the coast was encouraged and important movements hav begun to take place . . . and vigorous steps have been taken to organize contingent of immigrants from Spanish Guinea,' Report for 1915.

during this period, it was in 1919 that 'Abbé Jean Aubame became the first priest belonging to the savage Pahouin race'.[5]

I. THE TRANSFORMATION OF DEMOGRAPHIC AND ECONOMIC STRUCTURES

We have already pointed out that the Fang economy was based on conquest rather than production. This weakness of their material basis, coupled with the fact that they were the most numerous people in Gabon, having at first enabled them to resist colonialism, was later to be the cause of their complete subjection to it. Certain groups were only able to retain a measure of freedom insofar as they became 'Europeanized' – as was the case with the active minority in Libreville and, thanks to their transformation into a peasantry engaged in a 'prosperous' agriculture, with the villagers of the Woleu-Ntem, who from 1930 onwards developed the production of cocoa. These were to remain, moreover, the two centres where the Fang people displayed the greatest activity and initiative.

At a time when the interior of Gabon was still only partly explored and as yet unoccupied, some of the 1915 Reports, as well as the documents collected by the Commission of Enquiry into Marriage and the Family appointed in 1918, reveal that Fang society in the coastal districts was already seriously impaired; and they attribute this demoralization to the population crisis, which was beginning to worry the administration because of the economic development envisaged. The following is a quotation from one of these documents:

'Today, the Pahouins of the Gabon estuary and neighbouring districts are living in complete anarchy. The primitive laws that they used to obey rapidly became a dead letter when they came into contact with Europeans and the peoples of the coast. ... The Pahouin, once he was freed from his 'women palavers', could become – what at present he is only intermittently – a robust and intelligent worker, indispensable for the economic development of Gabon.'[6] Here we have an account of a situation that was rapidly to grow worse. Moreover, it was in this 'affected' region that the exploitation of timber was to increase rapidly after 1920; the encouragement of emigration 'to the coast' proved to be inadequate and the practice of forced labour recruitment was adopted.

Demographic Effects of the Policy of Recruitment

Until recent years, when there has been some attempt at mechanization, forestry required a labour force that varied from 20,000–30,000 men. Since the majority of the men employed in the industry are in the 20–40 year age group, it will be seen that a labour force of this size roughly corresponds to a total population of from 150,000–180,000 individuals – that is to say, almost half the population for the whole of Gabon. This gives some idea of the effort demanded from those districts outside the zone of exploitation!

The annual reports provide detailed information as to the number of workers asked for, and the number actually taken on; and from them some significant figures may be extracted:

TABLE I

Year	Number of authorizations requested	Number of authorizations granted	Number of workers engaged
1925	16,300	12,500	6,500
1926	18,940	9,350	4,120
1927	18,736	7,996	4,500
1928	17,300	6,750	6,000
1933	5,299	5,095	Figures not available
1947	14,030	3,120	Figures not available

This simplified table shows that until comparatively recently the demand for manpower remained fairly steady, if one omits the sharp fall between 1929 and 1932 which was due to the local effect of the world economic crisis. In contrast to the sustained demand, one notes a continual diminution of administrative effort and a rapid decline in the number of workers available, so that by 1927 the local authorities were beginning to consider the recruitment of foreign labour.*

The significance of these figures becomes even clearer when we remember that the period of engagement was only two years (although this was often extended under pressure from the employers, either because men were seriously in debt, or on the pretext of some administrative irregularity) and when we consider 'the proportion of engaged men who returned'. The official who raised this latter question answered it as follows: 'On the basis of admittedly out-of-date figures, I feel practically certain that, of the 10,000 men who, in the past, used to be engaged annually, almost half were lost to the colony, either because they died in the course of their engagement, or because they did not return to their homes, and therefore could not be relied upon to produce any children.'[7] As regards the mortality amongst those engaged on public works, G. Sautter was able to show that Fang workers were especially hard hit. He quotes a report referring to 'large numbers of deaths among the imported gangs of exclusively Pahouin workers', and to one particular case of a gang of 175 men, taken on at Oyem in January 1922, 30 of whom died during the first month's work.[8]

It will be readily appreciated how seriously this steady drain of manpower affected the already unsatisfactory demographic position in the recruiting areas: a large part of the young male population was lost, either by death or because they failed to return to their native villages. A document of 1946 refers to 'a subdivision particularly hard hit by recruitment, Makokou (with a mainly Fang population), where there are only 4,603 men to 7,018 women'.[9] This represents the very abnormal sex ratio of 1,526 women per 1,000 men – at a time (1936–51) when certain parts of the Woleu-Ntem were beginning to improve upon this figure thanks to the large-scale peasant economy.[10] In this same report, M. A. Maclatchy suggests that the policy of recruitment transformed the organization of those societies in contact with large-scale undertakings: 'Thousands of unmarried workers have been transferred to the coast, 75 per cent of whom will never return to their native country. In this way, in the areas of exploitation, a rootless proletariat has been created which has broken every

* Eventually tried out in 1950 with workers from southern Nigeria.

link with its ancestral way of life. . . .' And well before this date, in 1933, the Governor of Gabon had expressed concern about the problems created by 'villages of aliens' and 'tramps who wander from one undertaking to another'.

Very early on, the local administration realized the social and demographic consequences of this policy, which was seriously damaging the peoples of the Gabon without satisfying the demands of the contractors. The Fang were doubly affected, since they lived in the zones of exploitation as well as in the recruiting areas. The officials in the interior (especially in the Woleu-Ntem and the Ogooué-Ivindo, two 'reservoirs' for labour recruitment) recognized the dangers threatening their district and tried to oppose the old official policy of drawing workers away and settling them near the forestry centres.

As early as 1921, the Woleu-Ntem provided 939 of the 2,167 labourers recruited from the whole of Gabon. In 1923, 'more than 2,000 young men were forced or induced to work in various enterprises in the colony and Spanish Guinea', a figure that represents about 10 per cent of the adult male population. In 1925 it was estimated that in the single sub-division of Oyem 'almost a third of the adult men were already employed on public works'. In 1928, from one of the cantons attached to Mitzik, 450 workers were taken, that is to say, more than a third of the young male population.[11]

The weakening of the physical structure of the groups resulting from this labour policy was still further accentuated by the fact that men were leaving the country 'voluntarily' (especially for Spanish Guinea) because of the need to obtain cash. These emigrants did not return for a considerable time; in the Woleu-Ntem, for example, not until after 1935, precisely the period when this district was experiencing the earliest development of a 'modern' peasantry. The men, or groups, who did return to their native villages proved to be an important evolutionary factor, for their long absence from their usual surroundings meant that never again would they be typical Fangs. They brought with them new ideas and behaviour patterns. From the number of men affected by recruitment and migration one can form some idea, not only of the consequent demographic upheaval, but also of the wide-spread influence of 'modern' innovations.

The Position in the Areas of Exploitation

The Economic Report for 1947, which presented a detailed list of the problems affecting Gabon, insisted at the outset that the most important of these was the high proportion of 'workers' in relation to 'peasants'. This was to recognize the existence of an *extensive proletarianization*, and to admit the disequilibrium created by an elementary economy that had developed only one industry (first forestry, then mining) and destroyed, or seriously undermined, the agricultural subsistence economy. The same report also expressed the view that 'Bas-Gabon was worked out'. In the preceding chapter, we saw how severely this region, the ancient centre of trade and later of large-scale industry, had been hit by depopulation. It was here, too, that multiple contact with alien elements, as well as with foreign socio-cultural influences, was most widespread. Working in gangs led to new types of human relationships, as well as to cultural adaptations or borrowings. And, lastly, the people of Bas-Gabon were subject to the attraction of the two towns with which they were in contract – Libreville, the administrative centre, and Port-Gentil, the timber town – and were in touch with a larger number of European firms. The effect of this was to strengthen the 'factors of demoralization', as many officials had pointed out well before 1920. One of these, in a paper written in 1915, speaking of the Fang, expressed surprise 'at the weakening and decline of a people previously so prolific, who had apparently hoped to overrun the greater part of Gabon and absorb the indigenous peoples'.[12]

From the demographic point of view, what was just as important as the overall numerical decline in these Bas-Gabon subdivisions was the predominance of men – in sharp contrast to the sex ratio for the territory as a whole, which was 1,264 adult women per 1,000 adult men. There was an almost continual intake of unmarried men and workers under contract, separated from their families. The figures for the villages within the zone of exploitation are significant, especially when compared with those for the villages in the interior which served as the main labour reservoirs. As may be seen from the following table they are in a sense complementary.

TABLE 11

Old districts	Number of adult women per 1,000 adult men (1951)*	
	Zone of exploitation	Zone of labour recruitment
Libreville	835	
Port-Gentil	965	
Lambaréné	845	
Oyem		1,337
Bitam		1,443
Booué		1,413
Makokou		1,411

The Maclatchy Report, upon which we have already drawn, may have exaggerated these facts by speaking of 'the segregation of the sexes due to the young male members of the villages being transferred to the zones of exploitation'. Yet the situation does explain the keen competition for wives, and the importance assumed by prostitution and the trade in wives. Long before the main period of public works, the Bishop of Gabon had protested indignantly against this state of affairs, attributing it to polygamy: 'The polygamists hire out their wives to the men working under contract or serving in the army, as well as to the traders passing through.'† It seems likely that the principle of making commercial use of wives, which originated in a well approved 'custom', was confirmed by the setting up of workers' camps. These were established in the vicinity of major enterprises, and consisted of young men, whose only access to the local women took the form of semi-organized prostitution – a number of women 'hired themselves out', in fact, after freeing themselves from their matrimonial ties by repaying their bride-wealth.‡ It is probable

* Unless otherwise stated 'adult' in all statistical tables means 'over 15 years of age'.

† L. Marttou: *Notes sur le projet de réglementation du mariage indigène*, an unpublished manuscript in the Libreville archives. The passage continues: 'Which of us has not seen, on the last day of every month, one of these old men going to pick up his monthly payment from his clients and, if his demands are not met, coming home with his wives or, if it suits him, setting them to work elsewhere . . .'

‡ J. Keller: 'La dot dans l'évolution de l'Afrique noire', in *Journ. des missions évangeliques*, July-September, 1951. The writer, who had previously been a missionary in Gabon, says in fact that the women 'hired themselves out when, as was the case in the Bas-Ogooué, they had managed to buy themselves back by selling the produce of their plantations'.

that the anti-feminism that has been so energetically expressed for the last two decades, arose directly from the experience of conditions in these workers' camps. In addition to this, it is in southern Gabon that the *relations between the sexes have been most radically modified* and that the capacity of women to bear children has been most deeply affected: the highest percentage of sterility (29·37 per cent) is to be found in the Ogooué-Maritime district.[13]

The Maclatchy Report goes on to point out that 'at the present time, certain recruitment areas are inhabited only by young women and old men'; and this draws attention to another aspect of the question. In addition to a certain segregation of the sexes, there was also a *physical rupture between the generations*, which weakened the traditional relations between them (typified by the precedence of the 'elders' and 'fathers') and gave contemporary expression to the implicit tensions. This led to an equally important *differentiation*, due, as far as the young were concerned, to modern economic conditions and the new social relations and cultural models encountered during their stay in the zones of exploitation. It is demonstrable that Bas-Gabon, first as a trading area, then as the oldest established economic sector, indirectly influenced the evolution of the indigenous groups in the interior.

Instability of Population

We now have to consider various forms of reaction provoked by the increasingly heavy demands of the government – attempts to escape taxation, labour recruitment and innumerable levies, either by evasion or by escape to some part of the country that was less strictly controlled. A report of 1922 illustrates the difficulties of the government's task, pointing out that the Pahouin's 'most ardent desire is to avoid any kind of authority, whether native or foreign'. Spanish Guinea is mentioned by the officials, not only as a place where higher wages were available, but also as a refuge; though they were certainly exaggerating when they spoke of it as a country 'where censuses, native taxation, levies and native justice are unknown',[14] and it was possible to live 'in complete freedom'. In 1933, the head of the Woleu-Ntem district notes 'as an important fact . . . the discovery of villages hidden in the bush in the Minvoul-Minkébé district . . .'[15] Nevertheless, in the following

year, the process of evasion began once more: 'The people of
Minkébé cling to their district because they know that it is difficult
for government officials to visit it frequently; many natives, who
were originally settled along the motor road from Minvoul to
Oyem, have now abandoned it and gone elsewhere . . .'[16] In 1940,
an attempt to recruit labour for a mining enterprise on the Ogooué
caused a real 'panic' in one of the cantons of the Mitzik sub-division. During the period of the war effort, up to 1944, the gathering
of natural rubber, which involved very heavy work for poor pay,
was started up again; and a report comments that 'the tremendous
effort required of the natives in order to obtain worthwhile
quantities of rubber has led to many of them fleeing to other sub-
divisions where less effort, or even none at all, is demanded of
them . . .' Every official made strenuous attempts to prevent such
'flights' from the territory under his control.

These few facts are enough to show that the *reaction of evasion*
persisted, despite increasingly strict administrative control. It
contributed to the mobility of the groups, and it was the most
elementary form of escape from economic and administrative
demands that were sometimes extremely oppressive. In this
respect, in the Woleu-Ntem the border provinces of Cameroun
and Spanish Guinea acted as a magnet, inducing a considerable
part of its population to settle there, not merely for economic
reasons but also because of the advantages of living in a frontier
village. In 1942, an administrative report noted that 'at the
slightest provocation, the natives leave their village to become
vagrants, or even seek refuge in Spanish Guinea'.[17]

Traditional causes of an internal nature, pacification and other
causes due to the particular colonial situation, all encouraged
the break-up of the social groups and kept them mobile. Around
1930, in an attempt to check this state of affairs and to obtain
a firmer grip on the country, the administration carried out
a systematic policy of 'regrouping' or consolidating the 'villages',
which would enable them at the same time to carry out a programme of road-building and provide them with a stable labour
force responsible for upkeep. Between 1930 and 1935, the official
reports are concerned with the progress achieved, as well as with
the difficulties experienced in certain districts, where the villagers
simply disappeared and returned to their 'bush encampments'. In

fact, the regrouping was only successful in those districts where it was not merely of advantage to the administration. Thus, in the Woleu-Ntem, it came just at the time when cocoa growing was beginning to be profitable, and when European colonists were establishing a successful trade with Cameroun. In this case, a movement that had begun on orders from above, was eventually found to be fulfilling a need, with the result that over the last few decades the villagers have themselves been taking the initiative in settling near the road and opening up access to it. Whereas the old maps of the Woleu-Ntem, dating from 1910 to 1915 show a fairly dense network of tracks with a scattered population, those of recent years show that the people have been settling along all the main roads.

It is important to examine the consequences of this transformation. After a long period of confusion, between 1915 and 1930, the village groups at last began to show signs of taking root – the cocoa and coffee plantations, and then the road, contributing to this stabilization – and of once more attaining a satisfactory size. This was particularly obvious in the cantons of the old Oyem district:

TABLE III

Cantons in the old Oyem District

Canton	Population of canton in 1948	Number of villages in 1948	Average population of villages
Kyé-Nyé	11,400	87	131
Woleu	7,610	57	133
Bissok	5,025	52	96
Ellelem	3,095	35	88
Oyem	2,615	15	174

This consolidation led to closer neighbourly relations and organized intercourse between the lineages, which could no longer remain unaware of each other's existence. In certain cases, fragments of different clans and tribes were forced to settle within the same village unit, particularly between Mitzik and Minvoul;[18] thus new ties were established, based upon place of residence instead of simply on 'kinship'. Moreover, the existence of the road made travel easier; the ideas and initiatives of neighbouring peoples soon became known in the Woleu-Ntem, and the influence of Cameroun increased.

In southern Gabon, with the development of forestry, the population was affected in two ways: there was increased fusion, due to the introduction of labour recruited outside the territory; and there were larger agglomerations of workers – around Lambaréné, a fifth of the population was employed on public works in 1936. Moreover, this region had access to two towns which between them accounted for more than 20 per cent of the population of the two administrative areas they controlled: the population of Libreville, the long established capital, rose from 2,653 in 1918 to 5,444 in 1935, and to around 18,000 (including the floating population) in 1957 – moreover it was more and more dominated by the Fang element, who comprised the majority; while Port-Gentil, the chief business centre, which was particularly sensitive to the needs of the colonial economy, had a population of nearly 10,000.

Economic Changes

Analysis of the relevant documents shows that, until around 1915–20, the economy was in the main based upon trade. It was distinguished by the high value set upon imported goods, and by the process of repeated barter, which reduced the price of local products (ivory and rubber) and raised that of trade goods and salt. Depending upon the position it occupied in this system, a group was either restricted to collecting natural produce, or enjoyed the more profitable role of intermediary in contact with the European traders. In the mid-nineteenth century, du Chaillu noted that the Fang – then a people of the interior – were simply collectors of ivory, and explained how, through the alliances formed by marriage, they had been able to establish a commercial circuit with the minimum of risk.[19] This was the starting point of a process of economic conquest that soon proved successful.

In 1908, when he published his monograph on the Ndjolé sector, Curault observed that agriculture, cattle raising and industry were 'non-existent', and that the Pahouin were simply concerned with trade. He went on to say that 'the Pahouin in the Ndjolé sector merely served as agents between their kinsmen in the interior and the European traders established on the banks of the river'.[20] The Fang were all the better placed in this respect in that they had no reason to oppose the advance of the Europeans who sought to put down the traffic in slaves; at the time when they established contact with the European firms, the traditional trading peoples were doing their best to keep clear of them so that they might continue to deal in slaves;* and, as the archives at Libreville show, the Fang of Bas-Gabon (in the Como, Sindara and Setté-Cama districts) continued to play a decisive part in commercial affairs up to about 1905.

Old travel books, like those of Mary Kingsley at the end of the last century, state specifically that the collection of rubber and ivory[21] involved numerous groups, and sometimes entire villages. The same was true as regards control of the trading-centres and trade routes: a particular village regarded the trading-post in its vicinity as 'its own', and lineages would split up and spread out in order to protect the trails used by the collectors. These activities, therefore, represented *an economy still associated with the basic groups*, while at the same time arousing keen competition between them. They also led to the capitalization of 'trade goods', only a very small part of which were consumed; and it was this that produced a state of disequilibrium. It was this accumulation, directly resulting from the extension of the Fang commercial empire and the multiplication of trading-posts in the interior, that upset the circulation of marriage payments, increased their value and led to an abnormal capitalization of wives – in short, to the serious weakening of the very foundations of social organization. It was to remedy this state of affairs that, from 1918 onwards, the administration sought to accustom people to making marriage payments in cash; they considered 'that this solution would make it easier for young men to get married', since it would prevent the women 'from being monopolized by the old men who owned all the trade-goods'.[22] But this proved to be an illusion: the number of wives a man had still remained a sign of his wealth and social status.

* Fourneau points out that in 1885 the slave trade was still being carried on by underhand means, but that 'since our occupation it has been checked'. A report from the N'Gounié in 1903, however, states that: 'The Pahouins are the only people who do not have slaves. . . . The villages in the vicinity of Sindara used to deal in slaves whom they obtained from the Issogho region on the right bank of the N'Gounié, whence they would be sent overland either to Lambaréné or to Setté-Cama.'

The period 1905 to 1915 was one of transition: from an economy based upon trade and barter to one based upon the use of wage labour. On the other hand, it was not until about 1930 that a peasantry began to take shape in the Woleu-Ntem, its develop- ment being encouraged by the economic crisis. This was due to the initiative of local officials,* who in 1925 set out to revive the growing of cocoa, which had been started by the Germans when part of the Cameroun was still a German colony; at the same time the building of the road from Cameroun and the settlement of European colonists helped to improve commercial relations with that country. However, the traditional division of labour, as a result of which the Fangs had never looked upon themselves as peasants, as well as past experience, made it difficult to get the scheme under way. There were, too, the further difficulties inherent in the geographical position of the Woleu-Ntem, for whereas the natural outlet for this region is Cameroun and New Guinea, frontiers and tariff problems made trading difficult. A report written after an official inspection in 1935 points out: 'The Woleu-Ntem region needs to be settled and developed. If this is to be achieved, the payment of customs dues must not be allowed to paralyse trade and interfere with the agricultural development of the country. The natives have little inducement to extend their cocoa and coffee plantations, because there is nowhere locally where they can use the money obtained from their labour.'[2]

Despite this, the growing of cocoa did develop in the Bitam- Minvoul and Oyem districts, and cocoa now forms 'the basis of production': in 1947, it amounted to 1,670 tons, rising to 2,000 in 1949 and about 2,600 in 1960. Thus, thanks to high post-war prices, we have here an example of an expanding economy which nonetheless remains at a rudimentary stage. This remunerative crop, together with a small trade in coffee and palm kernels, was looked upon as a substitute for old-fashioned trading, though despite the introduction of such techniques as the drying of the beans on large, movable hurdles, it was carried on under unsatisfactory conditions (in some villages the loss resulting from failure to treat the trees properly was estimated at 90 per cent).[†]

* Auréas and Saint-Yves.

† In 1949, a technical worker in the Agricultural Service remarked that the cocoa trees were as a rule badly looked after.

urthermore, the fact that disposal of the cocoa was for a long
ne left in the hands of local business men dominated by the
olicy of the all-powerful Haut-Ogooué Company, and that the
easant had no means of resisting the pressures to which he was
bjected, accounted for the material losses incurred by the latter:*
: was often cheated over the quantity and quality of the cocoa he
pplied, and he remained a victim of extortion. In addition to
is, there was little inducement to increase production; the local
arket was not organized in terms of local consumption, either
cause the shopkeepers did not stock their shops properly, or
cause they were anxious to recoup the money they had invested
  the cocoa campaign as quickly as possible by creating an
tificial shortage of goods.†

By 1960, cocoa growing had ceased to be of real importance
cept in the Bitam-Minvoul and Oyem districts, the former
pplying almost three-quarters of the total amount exported.
:lling at an average price of 100 francs a kilo, the peasants were
ole to make 255 million francs (C.F.A.) in the course of the
mpaign, representing about 5,600 francs per head in the Bitam-
invoul villages and 2,400 per head in Oyem. To this must be
lded the profits (almost impossible to calculate, and realized
ainly in the form of goods) from selling coffee, palm kernels
id potatoes to dealers in the adjacent countries. The total incomes
mained very small, but in comparison with those in other parts
' Haut-Gabon they seemed quite comfortable.

It is clear that a large part of these incomes was used for marriage
iyments rather than for improving the standard of living. With
e help of figures registered by the Catholic Mission at Minvoul
1 the occasion of Christian marriages, we have studied the
:oportion of the marriage payments that was made in cash in
e years 1938–48 (see Figure 7) – a figure that was certainly lower
ian in the case of non-Christian marriages. It is interesting to
ote how closely‡ the curve representing this proportion cor-
:sponds to that showing the increasing turnover in the cocoa

* The setting up of a cooperative for the African planters was delayed for a long
ne.
† A position that was scarcely modified until very recently.
‡ This close correlation was confirmed in a recent paper by G. Sautter (1961).
creased returns from cocoa after 1959 *immediately* resulted in higher marriage
yments.

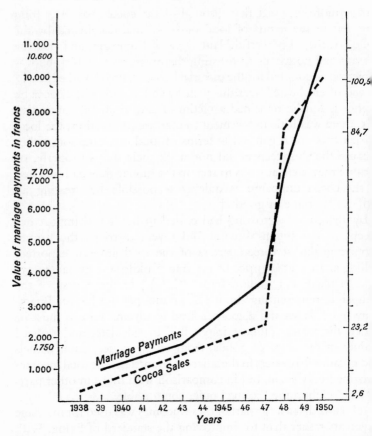

Figure 7, Cash Value of Marriage Payments in relation to Expanding Coco
Sales

trade,[24] for this indicates both the use to which earnings we
put and the increasingly economic function of the marria
payments. It must be remembered, however, that capitalizati
also took the form of 'trade goods' (*bioum*), obtained at gre
expense and locked away in chests, which represented t
traditional part of the marriage payments, presents from t
bride's family and prestige gifts.

As soon as the traveller arrives in the cocoa district of tl
Woleu-Ntem he is struck by the improvement in living condition

revealed by the houses and the people's clothing. This transformation of the village scene was mainly due to official action
the policy of 'consolidation' that was begun around 1930. The
administration did what it could to replace the old rows of huts
made of bark by individual houses built of dried clay. Despite
the resistance to this innovation – noted in the official reports for
the years 1934 and 1935, and mainly due to the separation of the
kitchens from the sleeping quarters, which meant that the men
had to sleep in rooms without a fire – the new type of dwelling
was finally adopted. The greater permanence of the villages,
which was due to the cocoa plantations and the building of the
road where markets were held, as well as to the acquisition of
household goods (wooden beds, tables, chairs, chests and trunks,
etc.) facilitated this transformation. But, in addition to this,
psychological factors were involved: the need to assert their
superior economic status, and the growing influence of the
forces of modernization, have meant that during the last fifteen
years the native people (particularly functionaries, business men,
planters, ex-soldiers and chiefs) have been anxious to own houses
copied from those of the colonists. Sautter, who gives a detailed
account of these material changes, notes as evidence of 'the
connection between economics and habitat . . . the coincidence
between the regions where cocoa production is highest and those
where new huts are most plentiful'.[25] We may add that it was in
the same areas that the need for radical modification of the
village was to be expressed most forcefully after 1945.

As regards dress, the improvement was most noticeable
amongst the women: most of them now wear dresses instead of
in cloths, and dressmakers have sprung up in the large villages
and in the vicinity of the markets. As for the men, they have
adopted European dress, though sometimes when travelling they
will carry an imitation spear, which serves as a walking-stick and
the only survival of the ancient costume of the Fang warriors.
These changes, slight though they may be, show that the Fang
of the Woleu-Ntem, despite having been the hardest hit by labour
recruitment and famine, are gradually regaining their equilibrium
and vitality by becoming modern peasants.

We must next consider the social evolution resulting more
or less directly from the new economy. In the first place it was not

only the villages that had become stabilized:* the cocoa plant:
tions, which require continual care and supervision, had so 1
speak 'anchored' the villages – but the men themselves, now th:
they were peasants, were also attached to their own plots. If th
villagers had to move, they were still determined to maintain the
ownership of profitable plantations – evidence of new ties wit
the land, which under the old economy 'did not belong to an
body'.[26] In the districts where the growing of cocoa was lea
developed, around Mitzik for example, the work could still b
carried out without upsetting the old unity of the nd'è bòt. In th
majority of cases, however, each married man had 'his own' coco
and coffee trees, while some of those with larger plantation
would even display some sign of ownership, usually a boai
with their name on it. The elementary family tended to becom
the unit operating this form of modern agriculture, whereas th
growing of vegetables for consumption had been carried on withi
the nd'è bòt or by groups of friends. The most 'advanced' indiv
duals (administrative chiefs, men who had served in the army c
lived in towns, etc.) were also those who cultivated the large
areas (anything from 3 to 5, or even 6 hectares) and who mo
conspicuously asserted their right of ownership. Many of ther
claimed to be regarded as 'planters', though none of ther
succeeded in achieving a position that enabled them to escape th
exigencies of the local traders.

It was thanks to cash crops that the Fang became peasant:
The division of labour between the sexes was modified: th
growing of such crops was essentially the men's business, th
women only lending a hand occasionally, though it was they wh
had to carry the cocoa beans to market. While subsistence crop
remained the wife's property, in the sense that any money mad
by selling them belonged to her, her share in the proceeds from th
sale of cocoa was decided by the husband – and she took care t
adapt her efforts to his generosity. This led to a considerable modi
fication of the relations between men and women, for the latte
now began to assert themselves as productive workers in a more o
less contemporary sense. Moreover, some of the 'planters' (thoug
their number remained small) began to employ hired workers

---

* A village in the vicinity of Oyem was called Ažébé (meaning 'to bury') becaus
the notables were anxious to show their determination not to move it.

Clearly, therefore, the traditional social relationships were upset; all the more so since the new economy, and the new demands it gave rise to, brought about still further differentiation by increasing the number of business men, traders and artisans (cabinet makers, tailors and even a painter, who decorated the huts along the Minvoul road with motifs taken from Christian and pagan legends).

By creating local resources, the economy based on cocoa limited the amount of voluntary emigration, and therefore tended to stabilize both the family and the village group. Moreover, as the population became more settled, social intercourse increased: the cocoa markets encouraged relations between the villagers; and the growing trade with Cameroun, centred upon Ebolowa and Kribi, multiplied the contacts with the related peoples that were established there.* Whereas forced migration to Bas-Gabon and the attraction exercised by that region had previously strengthened its socio-cultural influence (for instance, the introduction of the *Bwiti* cult into parts of Cameroun by way of the Woleu-Ntem), after 1945 these new relations increased the influence of Cameroun, especially during the clan consolidation movement.

This was particularly so as regards Bitam and Oyem, due to the economic functions they fulfilled, rudimentary as these were. Whereas previously people had avoided them as being centres of administrative control, now they were drawn towards them. If

TABLE IV

	Average population of 5 main villages	Average population of 10 main villages	Average population of 15 main villages	Average population of 20 main villages	Average population of 25 main villages
Road to Bitam	677	211	179	—	—
Road to Mitzik	166	133	154	145	134
Trail to Mbenga	236	166	146	130	—
Trail to Woleu	151	137	115	105	—

* The Political Report for the Woleu-Ntem for 1942 states that: 'The setting up of a regular postal service between Gabon and the Cameroun resulted in a movement of "strangers" into the urban centres.'

one looks at a contemporary map of the Oyem district, one finds that the further one gets from the township, along the two major trails (to Mbenga and Woleu) and the motor roads, the more the population of the villages declines.

As regards the Mitzik road, the numbers decrease less rapidly owing to the large number of villages on the outskirts of Oyem that are very close to one another.

The political importance of the Africans in this area grew rapidly: they set up organizations like the Committee of Ntumu Youth in 1948, and a movement founded by the deputy, Aubame, was supported by local representatives; then in 1950 a number of personalities led a campaign to obtain an accurate plan of Oyem, and to create a 'mixed commune'. These manifestations of political consciousness were due to the economic upsurge, rather than to any new liberal orientation on the part of the European authorities.

A further point that should be noted is that a monetary economy had now been established throughout the whole Fang country, the idea of price and profit having replaced that of exchange and reciprocal gifts. From what du Chaillu says, it is clear that in the early days certain products, widely diffused in the course of trade – for instance, sheet copper – were highly esteemed as a form of money. In southern Gabon, too, the Fang soon became familiar with 'dollar-merchandise', through contact with business firms. An official document of 1905 criticizes this type of transaction:

'The natives agree with the business firms in not wishing to see the introduction of money. . . . What they need when they go into the interior to purchase rubber and ivory is trade goods. . . . And the same is true as regards the dowries they pay for their wives. . . . The business men will do their utmost to retain the system of 'dollar-merchandise', since it is a convenient way of fleecing the Pahouin'.[27] This system, arbitrary as it was, did however establish an *exchange value*, though also making it possible to obtain a monstrous *profit*; and it did not take the Fang long to grasp the meaning of these two concepts – as may be seen from the violent measures, described in old reports, that they took to reduce the price of trade goods.

In 1891, a government decree fixed the daily wage for labourers and gang leaders, as well as the food ration. The fixing of wages, in a country where the number of wage workers increased rapidly between 1910 and 1920, and of the poll tax (the collection of which was the main task of the chiefs), hastened the introduction of a monetary economy, particularly as the administration insisted upon taxes being paid in cash. On top of this, the development of forestry and mining, the growing of cocoa and coffee and the multiplication of markets increased both the amount of money in circulation and the number of people using it.

The changeover, from a concrete and personal system of exchange to an abstract and anonymous economy based on money, opened up all sorts of opportunities for speculation. Property began to assume a personal character, as shown by the owners' names that now began to appear on village shops and modern houses, and at the entrance to plantations. Incomes tended to become individual: women, who were now helping to grow marketable produce and not simply food, and unmarried men who could find employment as wage workers, also contributed to this development. But personal wealth as the basis of authority was not tolerated, unless the individual was backed by a lineage of some importance that was prepared to guarantee it. In a village where we spent some time, a shopkeeper had acquired a unique position on account of his wealth; but he was also obliged to contribute to all public feasts, and in some cases to provide material assistance, as well as entertaining temporary visitors.

Amongst the Fang belonging to the Ntumu group (straddling the frontier between Cameroun and Gabon), an institution known as *bilaba*,* which was mainly found in the Cameroun villages that had made money out of cocoa much earlier, manifests the *collective* and *public* aspects of wealth and, in certain respects, resembles *potlatch*.[28] The word designates the defiance that two individuals hurl at one another with regard to their wealth or power. Both of them, accompanied by their wives, kinsfolk and friends, pay one another visits, in the course of which gifts and counter-gifts accumulate, to the accompaniment of public singing

* According to Martrou's *Lexique*, the verb *lab* from which this word is derived, can mean either 'to throw, to bespatter' or 'to obtain a large quantity of, to monopolize'.

and dancing and, when it comes to discussing the value of the gifts, an exchange of banter and insults.[29] Among its other functions, the *bilaba* was an attempt to make an adjustment between the traditional economy and an economy based on money; it also sought to cope with the fundamental dangers involved in any personal and lasting accumulation of wealth.

Lastly it should be noted that the extension of a monetary economy very quickly affected the substance and significance of marriage payments. Mba points out in his *Coutumier pahouin* that cash only began to be 'offered as marriage payment' in 1922, a time when large numbers of men were employed in forestry work, and which is referred to in a number of official documents as 'a period of affluence'. The part of the payment made in cash continually increased, until it came to represent about 25 per cent of the total, the remainder being paid in 'trade goods', mainly of a symbolical nature (animals, salt, loin cloths, pots and pans), or in the form of 'gifts' over and above the marriage payment. As a rule, the money used for this purpose was no longer kept for purposes of matrimonial exchange but *could be used* in exactly the same way as money earned by growing cocoa or by trade; it was regarded as money available for investment, rather than as a sum to be kept in reserve for further marriage payments. Thus the latter increasingly assumed the nature of a price, varying in accordance with other local prices, and since wives had considerable scarcity value they became a means of speculation.* The effect of divorce and remarriage was to encourage speculation, in the hope of a rise in the 'price of the marriage payment'; and similarly adultery, whether by agreement or purposefully provoked, became a source of profit, owing to the compensation that had to be paid. This emphasized the tendency to regard a wife simply as 'property'. It was against this that a Fang author, F. Meyé, was protesting when he wrote: 'The ideal would be if fathers behaved in a more disinterested fashion, and realized that their daughters are not simply for sale.'[30] But, as we have pointed out elsewhere, the concern to provide a marriage payment remained

* In 1961 the average cash value of marriage payments was 100,000 francs in Bitam, 80,000 francs in Oyem and from 30,000–40,000 francs in Mitzik. In addition they included a considerable amount of 'trade goods': clothing, materials, loin cloths, blankets, ironmongery, etc. (Information provided personally by G. Sautter.)

the chief stimulus to any kind of enterprise, and polygamy, as well as asserting a man's economic status, continued to confer pre-eminence in a society in which all attempts to achieve a different basis of organization for a long time proved unsuccessful.

It was principally to these modifications of the demographic and economic bases that an official report of 1938 attributed the collapse of Fang society. 'Traditions have been weakened; personal wealth has developed; visits to the coast and spells of working for forestry contractors have given rise to a spirit of independence. Ordinary members of the family, one time "dependents", have become chiefs, and have in turn surrounded themselves with "dependents". Families have become intermixed, as well as villages, and long and grievous famines have contributed to this confused dispersal and regrouping.'[31]

Here we find, simply enumerated, some of the facts that we have been describing. They will provide the necessary background for the study of the 'crises' referred to by this European official and experienced by the Fang who were trying to cope with them independently. By analyzing these crises, we shall be in a position to interpret the real relations between the colonizing society and Fang society, and to bring out more clearly certain fundamental characteristics of the traditional structure, as well as certain features peculiar to the state of subordination.

II. THE FANG 'CRISES' AS VIEWED BY THE COLONIAL ADMINISTRATION

A methodical examination of official documents, periodical reports and findings of Commissions relating to the period 1915–50 reveals on the one hand a series of stereotyped judge ments and criticisms with regard to 'the Pahouin' and the society of which he is the moving spirit, and, on the other, an attempt to get to grips with the subject by means of detailed investigations undertaken in the two post-war periods. In 1920, as in 1946–7, the situation called for a serious stocktaking; in both cases, this revealed a genuine desire to restore order after the upheavals caused by the war effort, and a concern to revive the local economy – in 1920 by developing the timber industry, and in 1945 by pursuing a policy of investment and more intensive production – thereby creating the conditions conducive to recovery. The effect of this stocktaking, however, was rather to focus attention upon a number of problems than to offer any solution to them.

As regards the periodical reports it is remarkable how little their contents were to change during the last forty years of colonization. Their primary concern, a kind of *leitmotiv*, is how to establish complete authority over an essentially elusive community which was not itself organized in such a way as to permit of even indirect control. Complaints about the restlessness of lineages and their 'mania for migrating', about vagrancy and the 'floating population', and proposals for the reclamation of 'lost villages' in parts of the country that were difficult of access, manifest a desire to create the human basis, so to speak, for political domination; to have *all* the groups 'well in hand', to use an expression that occurs frequently. But this endeavour was always disappointed, as were the attempts to establish an administrative hierarchy and, by this means, effective control over the smallest hamlet. The critical passages blame Fang psychology (their 'spirit of anarchism', their refusal to accept 'any kind of authority, whether native or foreign',[32] their 'individualism' and 'tendency to hold aloof', etc.) and their social organization (lack of 'tribal chiefs' on whom the officials 'could count', 'inability to control any sizable group of people',[33] rivalry between tribes, instability of families and excessive preoccupation with 'wife palavers'). Thus government intervention, aimed at maintaining order and ensuring payment of taxes and the satisfaction of local economic requirements, never went very deep. It took the form of hesitant action that was often contradictory and always on its guard. When, after 1945, the Fang tried to revive their community by consolidating the clans, the government at first held back, then became hostile, because the initiative for the movement, being strictly Fang, could be interpreted as the first indication of a developing national consciousness.

As is usual with the French colonial authorities, it was their preoccupation with politics that primarily and most frequently found expression, though they also showed concern for economic matters. For a long time they had been worried about the 'recruitment' of labour, and it was through this that they came to realize the serious demographic situation of the Gabonese peoples and their state of exhaustion; the Fang, who up till then had been regarded as an exceptionally vigorous race, were proving to be such a disappointment that some of the authors of these reports foresaw their eventual 'disappearance'.[34] Moreover, one finds references to the difficulties experienced in persuading the Fang to accept a peasant economy; there is talk of the 'lack of will to work' and 'their dislike of agricultural labour', though there is also occasional mention of the poor return for such labour and the heavy burden of taxes and levies that increased the difficulties of the administration. The introduction of an economy of large-scale development, which was a considerable strain on peoples who were few in numbers and ill-adapted to it, led to a number of setbacks which are duly admitted in the official reports from 1920 onwards.

Such are the two groups of problems that emerge from the perusal of these documents; to which must be added an obvious uncertainty as to the attitude to adopt towards the movement of 'evolution' arising from the colonial situation. This finds expression in a sense of distrust, with regard both to the older men, who based their opposition on the 'fetishes' of which they were the guardians, and to those who were younger and more Europeanized, because of the demands that they were beginning to put forward. By examining the documents relating to special investigations, we hope to clarify these very general observations.

Balance Sheet for 1918–20: *Problems of Family Organization*

The first Commission responsible for studying the serious problems affecting Fang society was appointed on January 1, 1918. Its avowed purpose was to consider 'the question of marriage amongst the M'Fans', and to suggest the best means of encouraging 'the establishment and development of the family'. In its report, it spoke of the 'civilizing mission' of the colonial government, and expressed its intention of promoting 'the moral and social development of the native peoples'. But in various passages other issues appear: the desire to minimize 'wife palavers', a constant source of dispute between 'the different tribes', creating 'a state of affairs . . . which is one of the principal obstacles to our civilizing mission'; the search for means of preventing polygamy amongst the older men and, in consequence, 'of reducing the authority derived from their comparative wealth, of which, in most cases, they make bad use'; and the need to free the Fang from a state of social 'anarchy', in order to turn them into 'the robust and intelligent workers that are indispensable for the economic development of Gabon'.[35] This preoccupation with political and economic matters – corresponding to the strengthening of the government's twofold hold upon the country during the period 1915–20 – is in fact the dominant feature of these documents.

The best informed report, by a civil servant called Guibet, describes the most immediately apparent features of social development; in the first place, the *relaxation of social control*. He maintains that, 'as a result of contact with Europeans and the peoples of the coast, the old laws of the Pahouin tribe . . . are rapidly falling into disuse', and that the first to benefit from this were the women. Both the Christian missions and the government were opposed to the traditional sanctions, which they regarded as 'inhuman' (although they prevented adultery and sexual intercourse with girls before the age of puberty, etc.). Recourse to these two alien authorities (the missions often serving as places of refuge) enabled women to escape from complete subjection, and to expose themselves to the risks of emotional licence referred to in the last chapter: 'Thus adultery has become an everyday matter and the misconduct of the Pahouin women from an early age has become truly excessive.' The document goes on to attribute this to the influence of 'the peoples of the coast', who have been profoundly affected by long-standing contact with European colonization. The example of the Mpongwé minority in particular, seems to have extended throughout the estuary region, inducing considerable freedom with regard to sexual behaviour, the rejection of marriage and the use by women (the notorious 'Gabonese women' of travellers' tales) of more or less open prostitution as a means of attaining freedom and improving their living standards.* The development of communications and the pacification of the country encouraged the spread of such behaviour.

In the second place, the report stresses the *effects of the colonial economy* which led to the accumulation of 'trade goods', in exchange for natural products, and intensified the 'conflict of interests'. To begin with, this accumulation had resulted in the more rapid circulation of marriage payments. Later, in the pacified areas of Bas-Gabon, the mere fact of the official relationship resulting from marriage appears to have been of less importance than the individual and economic advantages that it provided (the son-in-law was plagued with demands for gifts and services, to which he had to submit on pain of divorce, which had now become easy).

The distribution of wives was beginning to be completely tied up with the circulation of 'trade goods', that is to say, with *strictly economic* transactions; and this at a time when the wife was becoming a producer of wealth and no longer merely of consumer goods ('To be rich is to possess several wives, and the more a man has the more his fortune increases'). Some 'Notes' drawn up during the same period by Martrou, after attributing the 'low birth-rate' to 'the breakdown of the family', deal with the same two features. 'Custom', he says, 'being no longer protected by sanctions (which the Church had fought against, as being "bound up with immoral notions contrary to our principles and based upon inadmissible fetishistic beliefs") has lost all authority and is completely obsolete.' Moreover, the same author notes the aggravation of the economic approach implied by the position of women (regarded simply as 'things' or 'property') as well as by polygamy (which leads to a 'scarcity' of wives and 'monopolization'), a custom which, if encouraged, would result in women being treated as merchandise. In conclusion, he recalls the efforts made by the Catholic missions to eliminate polygamy (the sacrament of Christian marriage being accorded only to the 'first wife') and especially the encouragement and support given to such young

* In 1918, out of '935 married or marriageable women' in Libreville 'more than 400 were in one way or another pledged to celibacy'; and of these '65 were cohabiting with Europeans' and 'about 100 were effectively prostitutes', (Administrative Report).

women as expressed a desire for Christian marriage to an unmarried man.*

Thus it may be seen that the disorganization of the old Fang society, though sharply criticized and posing serious problems to which solutions were sought, was at the same time to some extent desired and encouraged by officials and missionaries; the former seeking to weaken the traditional political authorities in order to replace them by new ones under their own control, the latter attacking the upholders of 'fetishism' and the polygamous family. Both encouraged those elements who were traditionally in a subordinate position: women, to whom the pretext of a Christian marriage was a means of gaining their freedom,† and young men, whom they wanted to see trained as 'good workers'. By giving rise to an ambiguous policy, this more or less conscious approach accelerated the changes arising from the relaxation of social control and from the economic activities of the Europeans.

The measures envisaged by this 1918 Commission – prohibition of marriage before the age of puberty, restriction and control of divorce, limitation of the amount of the marriage payment and payment of it in cash, and sanctions to prevent adultery – remained a dead letter. In 1936, a new project to control native marriages reasserted the same principles,[36] while in 1946 and 1947 respectively the Commission on Population and the Pahouin Congress once again gave priority to the same problems. At the time of the movement for clan consolidation, the Fang themselves showed that they were clearly aware of the crisis affecting the family group and the relations between the sexes. They supported some of the official proposals (raising of the marriage age, control of divorce and adultery), though they also wanted to revive some of the traditional sanctions. Here we have a group of problems

---

* Martrou: *Notes sur le projet de réglementation du mariage indigène* (unpublished): 'Recently His Excellency the Governor of French Equatorial Africa informed Mgr Augouard that if the young wives of a polygamist ran away from their husbands and took refuge in a government post or mission, they should not be disturbed or forced to return home. It would be enough if the young man who wished to marry one of them repaid the equivalent of the bride-wealth to the previous husband when the new marriage took place.'

† Mgr Martrou's study speaks of divorces being encouraged to enable people to make Christian marriages ('Hundreds of cases every year', he says, 'in the parish of Gabon') and of the financial support obtained in France to ensure 'freedom for the young wives of polygamous marriages'.

which appeared at a very early stage and have not yet been resolved; these we must now examine in detail.*

In 1945 we carried out a detailed investigation of polygamy, village by village, in the cantons surrounding Oyem. By way of comparison, we have included, in addition to the data obtained in this way, information provided by a monograph on a canton near Sangmélima, a neighbouring district in Cameroun inhabited by related groups,[37] which had been transformed at an earlier date by the growing of cash crops and was deeply influenced by missionary activity.

The first fact that strikes one is the large number of unmarried men: for the Oyem district, out of a total population of 25,000 we found that 39·8 per cent were bachelors as against 60·2 per cent married men; and to this already high proportion must be added those men who were 'obliged' to remain monogamous: that is to say, 51·3 per cent of all those who were married. The number of wives to each man may be seen from the following figures:

TABLE V

Number of wives	1	2	3	4	More than 4
Percentages	52·3	25	11·1	5·1	6·5

These figures may be compared with those in what was regarded as a 'Europeanized' district – the canton of Ndou-Libi – as well as with those for all the Fang living in Gabon in 1938, the year when the head of the Army Medical Service, Le Dentu, carried out his enquiry. The figures overleaf reveal a limited polygamy (it is only exceptionally that a man had more than three wives) and a predominant monogamy, the latter being most marked in the areas influenced by the missionaries.

* After Gabon achieved Independence a number of regulations were adopted; notably the fixing of the marriage payment at 10,000 francs. In fact, the actual price is much higher and this sum is barely enough to secure an 'option' on the girl. Eventually this led to the revival of a kind of marriage by seizure – the carrying off of the girl taking place after a certain sum had already been paid and enabling pressure to be brought upon the 'givers of wives' to restrict the amount of cash they could demand.

7

Number of wives	1	2	3	4	More than 4
Ndou-Libi, per cent	66·8	17·1	8·1	2·9	5·1
Fang Gabon, per cent	63·1	22·2	9·6	2·4	2·7

This was the case in Ndou-Libi, with an average of one 'catechist' per 162 inhabitants, and was even more marked in the Protestant villages:

TABLE VI

Professed religion	Percentage of monogamists	Percentage of polygamists	Percentage of total population
Catholic	63	37	56
Protestant	73	27	39·4
Animistic	43·5	56·5	4

Monogamy was also accentuated in the poorer districts, which had lost many of their women to the richer ones. Along the banks of the Mid-Ogooué, a particularly impoverished area, the 'marriage rate' (i.e. the number of married women compared with the number of married men) was 1,330 to 1,000 in the subdivision of Ndjolé, whereas for the Fang population as a whole it was 1,630.[38] But it should be pointed out that this tendency to monogamy was to some extent only apparent. The increase in the number of divorces made it possible for a state of polygamy to be extended 'in time'; in the canton of Ndou-Libi, with a population of less than 6,500, there were 206 known divorces compared with 521 marriages in a period of about a year. This extension of divorce, and the remarriage of the divorced wife* – already regarded as showing a serious decline in customary behaviour at the beginning of the century – had, even before this took the form of speculating on the rising cost of marriage payments, become one of the expedients by which polygamy was maintained when the seizure or purchase of wives from alien tribes had ceased to be possible. Another method was to increase the gap between

---

* As regards the 'instability of families', a report from the Lambaréné sub-division in 1939 suggests that 'it is not unusual to see a wife pass through the hands of four or five husbands in quite a short time'.

the age at which girls were given in marriage (from early days, the growing number of girls who were married before puberty had been looked upon as yet another abuse of custom) and the age at which young men were in a material position to earn the money for marriage payments. These attempts at adjustment, however, were offset by the growing competition for wives, as well as by the fact that some of the women were no longer prepared to submit passively to the schemes of the 'givers of wives'.

On the basis of the percentages shown in Table V, in the Oyem district 100 men succeeded in procuring 115 wives between them, that is to say, a higher proportion than the ratio of women to men for the entire Fang population (105 to 100, according to Le Dentu). This figure is more or less the same as the sex ratio for the Oyem district (1,142 women per 1,000 men) and for the whole of the Woleu-Ntem region in 1951 (1,147 per 1,000).* One would therefore assume that only a small number of wives came from other regions; and, in fact, a detailed study of two groups, the Kòjé and Yébimvé, revealed that marriages occurred as a *result of proximity*. Three groups living in the vicinity of the Kòjé – the Effak, Esèngi and Esatuk – accounted for 28 per cent, 26 per cent and 14 per cent respectively of all Kòjé marriages; and in the case of the Yébimvé, the Esèngi, Yéngwi and Kòjé groups accounted for 52 per cent, 32 per cent and 15 per cent respectively. The circulation of wives thus took place within zones of restricted size and formed relatively closed systems; and this served to accentuate the competition within them.

However, a study of the 'marriage rate' in each of the five cantons that used to constitute the Oyem district, revealed a rate of about 1,600 per 1,000 for three of them (corresponding to the average figure for the whole Fang population), and higher rates, 1,823 per 1,000 and 2,175 per 1,000, in the cantons of Kyé-Nyé and Oyem. In both the latter, the one in touch with Spanish Guinea and the other with the town of Oyem, economic conditions were better, providing additional sources of income. Moreover, the 1938 enquiry had shown that the highest rate, 1,780 per 1,000, was in the sub-divisions situated along the Gabon estuary, which were precisely those where the large-scale exploitation of timber had brought about an economic development of

* Cf. Table I in Part II, ch. 1.

real importance. Thus it appears that within any clearly demarcated area there is a *direct connection between the extent of polygamy and the economic potential*; and this is what the Fang writer already quoted was saying indirectly when he wrote: 'The system of marriage payments . . . eventually became the basis . . . of the whole Fang economy.'[39] When describing the economic changes peculiar to the Woleu-Ntem area, we pointed out that a considerable part of the money in circulation took the form of marriage payments, and that the value of these varied in accordance with local prices; similarly we stressed the worsening of the economic implications of the marriage system.

The economic boom that began in 1920 with the intensive exploitation of *okoumé* wood resulted in a sudden injection of money into the economy and accelerated these changes, while at the same time the control of marriage payments, now made increasingly in the form of money, like the obligation to pay taxes, involved a greater number of people in the colonial economy. A careful observer, assessing the position of the 'Pahouin family' in 1931, wrote: 'The value of the marriage payment having increased excessively during the years of prosperity with the export of Okoumé wood, many young men were only able to get married by leaving their villages and becoming employees of the white man in the timber trade.'[40] Thus a system as basic as that regulating the circulation of women (i.e. marriage and kinship) became bound up with economic and administrative conditions that were alien to Fang society; more and more it ceased to be within the control of the Fang themselves. The study we have just quoted shows that, contrary to its intention, official intervention encouraged the break-up of the system without replacing it by any effective new organization. By establishing 'a tacit price list used in the conduct of palavers' and 'by preventing sons-in-law from supplementing the original marriage payment with the customary series of further payments', it gave official sanction to the idea of wives having a price. The men, 'feeling that they were supported by the government, claimed complete possession and disposal of their wives; they "bought" their wives'. Since this increased the number of disputes, it was necessary to increase the number of official arbitrators, who were not slow to take advantage of their position. Grébert maintains that 'the village where the tribunal was held became a court of abuses, of prostitution and haggling, as well as of exploitation of the labour of those involved (i.e. the wives who were the subject of litigation) in return for feeding them'.[41] Here we may see the two main features of the break-up of the system of matrimonial exchange;* we have described them, and discussed their economic effects, in order to stress the importance of those conditions that were due solely to the colonial situation.

Moreover, there can be no doubt that this situation brought into the open antagonisms that were already implicit in the traditional organization. By not allowing either genuine economic development or any effective adaptation of the political structure, the administration made sure that the old capitalization of wives remained the only way of winning supporters† and thus achieving a position of importance and a margin of independence. But the level at which competition occurred was altered, from extended groups to restricted groups and individuals; and at the same time the nature of the competition changed, since it could only be effected by economic and peaceful methods. How intense it became may be seen from the modification of the two fundamental rules, the insistence upon exogamy and the prohibition of incest: methods of negating kinship and removing the prohibition ceased to be exceptional,[42] while competition became general and *tended to be free*. Marriage, which had been a means of creating affinity and relationships based upon reciprocity (symbolized by the exchange of marriage payments and counter-gifts) became a pretext for seeking personal advantage. Having a wife encouraged the practice of blackmail and continual pressure for divorce; and since wives were extremely scarce they became objects of speculation.

In the preceding chapter we showed that precedence based upon seniority was only accepted provided the 'elder' (*ŋyamòrò* or

---

* An administrative report of January 4, 1937 also refers to 'illegal practices of canton chiefs with regard to wives and their husbands in cases of divorce or separation', and to 'the asylum that married women can find in the villages of canton chiefs'. From the archives of the sub-division of Kango.

† F. Grébert, speaking of 'important polygamists', refers to 'young men seeking to be adopted by them . . . to each of whom they give a wife whom they can take away again if not satisfied with the young man's behaviour': 'La famille pahouine en 1931', in *Africa*, V, 2, 1932.

ntòl) used his position equitably and was seen to be a genuine 'giver of wives'[43] and creator of alliances. When this requirement became blurred, the relation between 'elders' and 'juniors', between the generations of the *taɓa* and of the *mwanö*, tended to become a relation between owners and non-owners and took on an antagonistic character. There is no doubt that changes of this kind were an incitement both to the dependent element (younger men) and the subjected element (women) to react against the traditional social order.* The activities of the former were encouraged after 1920 by the physical rupture between the generations resulting from the shifting about of labour and the relative economic independence that the payment of wages conferred upon young men who could find employment; the fact that they could now provide marriage payments *for themselves* freed them from the most oppressive cause of their dependence. But by insisting upon participating directly in the competition for wives they raised the struggle between generations to a plane at which it was bound to assume a particularly violent nature and undermine the very foundations of the old order. Colonial society (missionaries and officials) drove them to a kind of radicalism which, until the last few years, continued to deepen the rift between the 'young Fang' and the 'old Fang'.

With the Fang women the reaction was even more rapid. Grébert reminds us of this by noting how, as early as 1931, the men were beginning to complain of the 'refractoriness' of their wives.† We have insisted at length upon the fact that wives were the most exploited element, but we have also shown how they made use of the means available to them to restrict this exploitation. They had a margin of freedom: firstly, with regard to the family of which they became a part; secondly, with regard to their husbands, by restricting their 'services' in proportion to the benefits they derived from them;‡ and thirdly, with regard to men in general,

* The writer Mongo Béti, in an unpublished study of a Cameroun group related to the Fang, writes: 'The wife, shockingly exploited though she was, was always the one potential factor, the spring-board of an eventual mutation.'

† Insubordination (*nlo abé*), like bad temper (*nlem abé*), might involve an appeal to sorcery; hence its gravity.

‡ A dissatisfied wife may break off her marriage and go back to her family; a widow is free either to choose one of the heirs for a husband or to return to her family, provided she returns the marriage payment; a wife may also, if she is ill, go back to her kinsfolk to be looked after.

by becoming objects of competition and by joining women's organizations. With the relaxation of taboos (due principally to missionary activity) and of the traditional methods of coercion (which were condemned as 'barbaric') this margin of freedom was considerably extended.

The men's attitude to these changes was ambiguous. They reacted violently when they encroached upon their marital rights; but they endeavoured to maximize their privileges when, as fathers, uncles or elder brothers, they were in a position to exercise control over their wives. It seems that the men as a whole were scarcely prepared to admit women's new position in society. At the time of the Pahouin Congress at Mitzik, none of the delegates expressed any opinion with regard to the position of women and polygamy; even the African representatives of the Christian missions remained silent. The suggestions put forward for a 'revision of custom' were essentially concerned to protect the husband's rights with regard to his 'in-laws'. Later on, during the time of the consolidation movement, the 'statutes' prepared by the various tribes were to do little more than grant certain concessions to the women: by forbidding marriages before puberty, by insisting upon respect being paid to the wife, and by creating various more or less fictitious official positions for women, etc. Nevertheless the determination to reassert masculine control was plain enough: by strict enforcement of the rules of exogamy, prohibition of divorce for a wife 'who had already had children', limitations on divorce in general, sanctions against adultery and the seduction of married women, and, above all, restoration of the punishments for disobedient or unfaithful wives.* For almost thirty-five years the same group of problems had been confronting the colonial government. It had attempted to deal with them, but only by means of partial, legal solutions, which, since they were imposed by an outside authority, proved to be ineffective or simply added to the confusion.[44]

---

* *Regulations for the Yémisèm tribe*, Article 13: 'Wives who refuse to accept their husband's authority may be punished in the following ways: smacking, flogging, forced labour or a few days' imprisonment by the adminstration (sic) . . .' At certain gatherings women whose misbehaviour was notorious were publicly chastised.

Observations of the Commission on Population in 1946

After 1945, the obligation to renounce colonial rule, to restore the economy and to prepare the reforms required by the new constitution led to the drawing-up of an overall balance sheet.

The Commission on Population, appointed in June 1946, was therefore made responsible 'for studying not only the demographic problem but also the problem of the existing population structure; for the present situation is extremely serious'. Once again it raised all the questions related to demographic decline, the disorganization of the family, workers' camps, labour recruitment and malnutrition. The members of the Commission relied especially on observations carried out in Fang country; they asserted, somewhat naively, that 'the present breakdown . . . with all its effects upon the birth-rate is fundamentally due to the deterioration of customary law and the disappearance of old established institutions'. Displaying a surprising ignorance of the social situation, the Commission envisaged 'a revival of customary law' and a 'return to ancestral morality'. It also proposed a radical solution: the creation of a *reserve*, to 'save' the Minvoul and Oyem groups in the Woleu-Ntem – though it was careful to say nothing about those village groups upon which the various European interests were dependent.[45] The sole interest of the Commission's labours, which had no practical consequences, is that they drew attention to the problems and showed how closely interdependent they were.

The Pahouin Congress and the Crisis in Political Organization

'Summoned as a result of the good offices of the Governor of Gabon', the first Pahouin Congress was held at Mitzik from February 26–8, 1947. After the event, the organizers claimed that it had inaugurated 'a policy of broad contact with all elements of the population' and had provided an opportunity for 'bringing into focus the present-day tendencies of traditional society'.

The fifty delegates or so were mainly officially appointed chiefs, accompanied by Fang representatives from the local assembly, and a group of 'Libreville progressives' and their leader. In the working sessions, the latter were the only ones to adopt a critical attitude and provide any real opposition; thanks to them the Congress, a purely official undertaking, managed to avoid complete domination by the authorities. They were the only ones who were not satisfied with passing 'resolutions' and, in the hope of getting something done, endeavoured to have their leader officially elected as *N'Zoé Fang*, Leader of the Fang people.* Such was 'their tactical skill' that the authorities stressed the undesirability of their being present, which led the 'chiefs' at what was a 'traditional Congress', 'to vote against their own interests, against traditional custom, and against good administration'.[46] This situation revealed that the chiefs (incorrectly described as 'traditional chiefs') were closely tied up with the administration and therefore obliged to behave ambiguously, and that the administration was, in official terms, 'opposed to the "progressives", who might succeed in dominating the rural masses; the danger of which is unfortunately all too clear from the present colonial situation'.

This reaction was merely the revival of a hostility that had been first expressed in 1920, at the time of the first demonstrations by the 'Libreville progressives'. This time, however, they retained the initiative; their leader at the Pahouin Conference did his best, when he returned to the capital, to take political action through the movement known as the Mixed Gabonese Committee, by creating and controlling 'customary tribunals' and setting up a 'Mutual Aid Society for the Fang People'.† The increasing awareness of the modernists, their determination to recover a certain measure of autonomy, led the authorities to put forward a policy of 'evolution within the framework of traditional institutions', whereas, twenty-five years earlier, they had done their best to weaken all traditional authority. This was due to the colonial situation, which forces the dominant society to adapt its policy to those social strata that offer the most powerful resistance.

Apart from these disclosures, the Pahouin Congress brought to light a number of major problems and suggested solutions to them.[47] Judging from the minutes, it seems that those relating to 'custom' and 'the organization of chieftainships' gave rise to the

* See the letter sent to the territorial chief in Gabon, May 19, 1947, enclosing an account of the 'elections'. The leader referred to was Léon Mba, who was later to become the first President of the Republic of Gabon.

† All these steps were closely supervised by the administrative authorities, and were the subject of a whole number of police reports.

most lively debates. As regards the proposals with regard to customary law, we have already given the essence of them when dealing with the crisis in the relations between the sexes and family organization. It may be added, however, that *à propos* of religious matters, a resolution was moved opposing the *Bwiti* cult;[48] this was mainly the doing of the chiefs, 'who see the *Bwiti* as a threat to their authority', and of certain delegates 'connected with the missions'.[49] As we shall show, this was indicative of the political and religious importance of the cult in modern Fang society. Before considering the special questions of 'the chieftainships' and 'the crisis of authority', which were the main concern of the delegates, we will briefly mention other matters that were raised.

Economic questions were dealt with 'dispassionately'. The demands put forward were indicative of the rudimentary stage of development, since they called for the introduction of new industries, mechanization, the drawing up of a plan for industrialization, the creation of a stock-raising industry, the organization of internal trade* and the improvement of the means of communication. As regards 'labour policy', the delegates, who were lacking in personal experience (there were practically no wage workers amongst them) ended up by passing a number of vague resolutions concerning the safety of workers and the raising of wages. As against this, the demand for increased 'land grants in the rural areas'† was a sign of the developments in agriculture; and parallel with this was their concern that ownership should be clearly vested in village communities and individuals. This approach, which involved a profound modification of traditional law, was due not merely to the new features of Fang economy, but also to a determination, still recent and confused, genuinely to possess their own country and to protect themselves against the extension of European enterprise. Lastly, the modernist outlook of the delegates was revealed in their demands for public

* For example, the demand (III. 3), 'That supplies for native trade should be guaranteed; and particularly that a definite proportion of goods imported from abroad should be allocated to it' indicates the small part of trade that was in native hands, and the need for 'trade goods'.

† Cf. the Report. It was proposed that 'a request should be included in the minutes of the session to the effect that liberal concessions of land should be made to individual natives and even to whole villages'.

health measures and education. Thus it will be seen that the attention of the Congress was centred upon problems arising from the breakdown of basic institutions (the system of allocating wives, marriage and the stability of the restricted family) and the distortion of the politico-judicial system by official interference. These were the only questions that gave rise to detailed discussions.

Despite official reticence,* the majority of the delegates supported 'the election of a supreme chief'. The fact that the only opposition came from the representatives of the Woleu-Ntem was due partly to the greater pressure brought to bear upon them (the preparations for the Congress had been supervised by local officials); partly to the fact that, in their case, the social structure had been less fundamentally affected, so that they did not feel the same urgency about having a symbol of unity and a common centre of authority; and partly to the political rivalry that had existed, since 1945, between the Fang leaders of southern Gabon and those from the Woleu-Ntem. The meaning of this demand was clearly understood by the government. A circular, commenting upon the resolutions put forward, stated: 'It seems, therefore, that the desire [of the Fang] to have a supreme chief, who will represent the tribe and consolidate their energies, represents in their opinion a vital necessity if they are to maintain the strength and coherence of the ethnic group in the face of the dangers of disintegration that threaten it'; and, at the same time, it reveals 'a very interesting reaction on the part of certain natives to recent legislative measures'.[50]

The war effort, with the increasingly coercive measures it had involved (higher production, the collection and porterage of produce, etc.) had made all these problems dangerously acute; and the period of relaxation and reform that followed it, while adding to the confusion, had encouraged a certain revival of native initiative. It is in the light of this twofold impulse that we have to consider the reactions that took shape after 1945: a growing awareness, to which the Pahouin Congress contributed,† of the

* Cf. the Report: 'The question of a supreme chief of the Fang was raised. . . . I think that most of the canton chiefs must have been instructed beforehand since almost all of them supported this proposal, which was opposed to their own interests.'

† For which the organizers of the Congress were blamed by the more conservative elements in the administration.

real position of the Fang groups, and a desire for consolidation and reconstruction around a symbol of unity; and a certain 'racial' particularism, running counter to the new legislation, which took no account of ethnic differences and was based upon the glorification of typically Fang characteristics.* These were the two aspects of the situation that the clan movement was to accentuate soon after the Pahouin Congress.

(a) *The Problem of Chieftainships*

Despite the majority of official chiefs, the Libreville delegates managed to raise the problem of chieftainships. One of them forcefully insisted that 'the crisis of authority' was bound up with the question of dispersal (the splitting up of lineages that had only recently ceased), which had destroyed the normal political unit, the *clan*, and also with the fact that the chiefs were 'purely administrative creations' (the 'real chief is the chief of the clan'). Thus attention was drawn to the artificial nature of the regional entities created by the government and of the 'authorities' imposed upon them. For a considerable time past, all the reports had insisted that 'the distinction between the official and the real chiefs is considerable', and that generally speaking the former, 'on account of their origin, have very little control over their people'.[51] They were compromised by being upholders of an authority created from outside by the colonial government, and the fact that they did not correspond to any element within the old social organization still further accentuated the fact that they were 'imposed'. At the same time, the real village leaders had the advantage that they represented, more or less openly, the opposition to the exigencies of the administration. The movement for clan consolidation was deeply influenced by the idea of dismissing the 'chiefs'; all the more so in that the 'progressives, who aspired to playing a political role', were at one with the traditionalists in attacking them.

In the previous chapter we showed that in traditional Fang

* For instance, the letter from the Libreville Fang demanding a supreme chief confirms their hostility to their rivals, the Mpongwé: 'The Fang . . . will never agree to be ruled by the Mpongwé.' In another region of Gabon the Political Report for 1949 speaks of 'a revival of local racialism' among the N'gounié; which shows that it was not only the Fang who reacted in this way.

society there had never been a genuine hierarchy, but rather a variety of authorities subject to public control; thus it was impossible for the administration to base its authority upon established chieftainships. Furthermore, we pointed out that the principal authority, that of the *ésa* (genitor or father, in the broadest sense of the word) was based upon a more or less extended lineage and derived its power from ancestor worship (the *ésa* being the possessor of the *évòra biéri*, the basket containing the skulls of the ancestors), and that the *ésa* only became the 'chief' insofar as he was able to impose himself as an outstanding personality, 'by extending his sphere of influence'. The very nature of the old Fang economy, orientated as it was towards conquest, together with the instability of the groups, which prevented any attachment to the land or lasting settlement, meant that 'biological patriotism' was more effective than 'geographical patriotism'.* Moreover, during the recent period, the centripetal forces tending towards the consolidation of affiliated lineages and clans† had been less effective than the centrifugal forces leading to fragmentation and dispersal; while intensive missionary activity, by attacking the *Biéri* cult, had seriously weakened the religious basis of the fragmented clans. Since the administration was therefore unable to exercise its authority, either through a stable hierarchy or through a clearly localized political unit, it had created arbitrary divisions (cantons and territories) and chosen as its agents those who seemed best fitted to serve its interests. The latter, unless they happened to be men of straw 'sacrificed' to the colonial government,[52] were usually unpopular, and content to exploit this inevitably compromising position.‡ The political organization of the Fang (based upon a system of precedence and the balancing of antagonistic forces) had thus been irreparably damaged; and there was nothing to replace it but dubious expedients.

* This distinction between 'biological' and 'geographical' patriotism was first suggested by the geographer E.-F. Gautier.

† Tessmann speaks of this comparatively loose federation of the *ayôg* as constituting a higher group, which he calls the 'tribe'. Cf. *Die Pangwe*.

‡ An inspector's report (January 1937) on the 'complaints' of the Fang in Kango refers to 'the abuses practised by the canton chiefs' with regard to taxes, divorce procedure and the abduction of wives, and speaks of 'the exactions imposed'. Cf. also F. Grébert, *op. cit.*

At the Pahouin Congress, the chiefs, knowing that they were there primarily as representatives of the government, nevertheless accepted the principle of election (IV.5), despite the fact that it was obviously 'against their own interest', as the official report noted – but they refused to accept the *ayôg* as a basis for the new chieftainships.* The progressive minority endeavoured to re-interpret the traditional clan structure in a modern sense, by combining the principle of a genuinely Fang political unit (the *ayôg*) with that of election by all adult males. The experiment made in Cameroun, among peoples related to those of the Ntem district, of a reform that recognized 'group chiefs' elected by 'all the men of the clan'† was later to impose this type of solution upon the most active Gabonese Fang. Though the Pahouin Congress achieved nothing practical, it nevertheless gave a lead; and the 'village resettlement movement' and the 'clan consolidation movement' (*Alar Ayôg*) were soon to give expression to the political concern it had displayed.

(b) *Example of the Fang groups of the Woleu-Ntem*

Before considering these initiatives, we propose to illustrate the above observations by one or two examples taken from the Woleu-Ntem region. The division of the country into 'cantons' and 'territories' could only be done by taking the geographical factor into account and, even more, the government's convenience. The system of control envisaged was completely artificial as far as its territorial and human basis was concerned and the form of authority it was supposed to provide. It incorporated in a single 'unit' large numbers of individuals belonging to alien clans who, though related by ties of affinity, often lived on the memories of ancient feuds. The example of the cantons of the Woleu-Ntem, where the original clan basis remained least impaired, was none the less typical of this kind of mix-up.

Official documents, referring to the setbacks, maintained that 'there is often bitter rivalry between the clans',[53] hindering any

---

* One of the chiefs, referring to the wars between *ayôg* in the past, declared: 'This would mean war!' The proposal for the restoration and official recognition of the leaders of the *ayôg* was rejected.

† Known as the Bourdier-Granier reform, 1944–5.

TABLE VII

District	Canton	Dominant group	Percentage of population of canton	Number of clans
Bitam	North	Effak	34	27 for
	South	Eba	31	district as
	Ekorité	Kòyé	23	a whole*
Oyem	Kyé-Nyé	Esèngi	40	12
	Woleu	Ožip	32	17
	Bissok	Esèngi	23	10
	Ellelem	Bökwé	24	18

attempt at consolidation; that only 'small groups'† were at all
stable; and that, in general, authority was only effective within
the limits of the 'guard-house', that is to say, of the *nd'è bòt* or
minor lineage. The 1943 Report for the Ogooué-Ivindo district
says quite clearly: 'There is no lack of chiefs; there are as many
as there are guard-houses, which is saying a good deal. . . .
Official appointment will never succeed in making a canton or
territorial chief out of someone who is, and always will be, simply
the head of a family.' Indeed, on the contrary, such appointments
had a quite negative effect; at best, the 'chief' would only be the
representative of a clan. Antagonisms (particularly between senior
and junior lineages) still persisted, concealed when it was a
question of confronting alien elements, open as regards internal
affairs. The Ožip of the Ellelem canton (Oyem district) explained
to us that the rivalry between the heads of the two groups of
villages, one of whom was chief of the canton, was due to the
kind of hostility between lineages referred to above. Lastly, the
'chiefs' often found themselves competing, within their own clan,
with new personalities aspiring to play a political role.

* A figure taken from the 1936 census, which is the only reliable source, though it
does not show the number of clans for each canton.

† Le Testu, in his report on the Woleu-Ntem for 1934, after expressing his
preference for small groups, goes on to declare that 'without exception, the natives
have neither the perseverance, the *method*, nor the mental application that are necessary
for governing any considerable group of people'.

It should also be pointed out that the position of 'chief' was equally distorted on account of the judicial power – derived from the administration and based on an 'adopted' system of rules – that was granted him. He was nothing more than a court of appeal, an arbitrator, from whom one of the parties hoped to gain advantage on the basis of a decision that was not in accordance with custom.* He often tended to abuse his authority, which could only be over-ruled by the colonial government, thus driving the villagers, as Grébert points out, 'into the arms of unofficial arbitrators, the real village chiefs'. In the important sphere of the palaver, arbitrary decisions affecting the settlement of differences and the question of punishment had destroyed the very principle of authority (hitherto based upon 'knowing how to speak' in the name of custom, as well as upon the status of genitor (ésa) or military valour) especially when at the same time the impossibility of resorting to violence and the increasing number of disputes arising from economic change and the decay of 'traditional morality' had strengthened the position of the 'conciliator' (nté mözö).

It was the clan movement, rather than the Pahouin Congress, that was determined to create genuine chiefdoms extending beyond the village. It reasserted the relationship between clans belonging to the same tribal unit, in order to discover within a limited area groups of some size associated by 'the brotherhood of the ayôg'. It based its authority upon elections in which all the adult males who were present at a meeting took part – a modern approach, which nevertheless corresponded to the egalitarian tendency that existed at every level. In 1948, when the administration withdrew its opposition to the movement, the chiefs elected in this way asserted their authority in the Oyem district, and a number of reports suggested that it was better to recognize the fait accompli than to provoke 'the open hostility of the real chiefs'.[54] This tolerant attitude was not to last for long. Few of the official chiefs could accept this innovation and expect to derive from it a confirmation of their own powers; most of them turned to the

* A report from the Lambaréné sub-division (1939, first quarter), where the Fang were in contact with an unrelated ethnic group, the Galwa, is a typical example of this approach. 'It is not unusual to find the Pahouin getting the Galwa to adjudicate in family matters in the hope that, with judges who are not acquainted with their customs, it will be easier to win their case.'

colonial apparatus for support, thus revealing how little their authority was based upon Fang society.

Similar problems arose in the village groups, particularly when they lived in close proximity with alien clans (*mfulana möyôg*). This was the case in the Mitzik district, where 45 per cent of the villages situated on the main roads were 'mixed',* and some of them, according to the Annual Report for 1935, were 'completely artificial'. Here, the real unit remained the *nd'è bòt*, with its separate guard-house and 'communal hearth'. At the time of the clan consolidation some of these villages broke up into their constituent elements, though material interests (for instance, the desire to remain near an urban centre) and particularly recourse to the system of 'affinity' (which made it possible for two lineages to live in peace by reciprocally assisting one another) did provide a genuine basis for living together, however easily upset. In fact, this kind of amalgamation was more stable in small communities, the mark of it being a single guard-house, which was unusual. In 'mixed' villages, authority scarcely extended beyond each of the juxtaposed clan fragments. 'Sometimes', one report notes, 'five or six *ayôg* are represented in the same village, with as many chiefs', and the chieftainship appeared to be even more artificial, being restricted to carrying out with great difficulty only those duties imposed by the administration.

When it was a question of a homogeneous village consisting of several related *nd'è bòt* (corresponding to the minor lineages created by the brothers or sons of the founder), there was real unity. Cohesion was encouraged by the *principle of alternation*, which distributed authority between the main lineages, though giving preference to that of the founder. Table VIII shows some examples of this, taken from Mitzik and Oyem.

It was very rare for authority to be continually transmitted in direct line of descent from father to son; this only happened when the elder lineage, being also that of a father, had succeeded in maintaining undisputed authority. This arrangement, based more or less upon the principle of alternation, did not conflict with the Fang system, for as one delegate to the Pahouin Congress recalled,

* Whereas in a remote part of the interior, only 13 per cent of the villages on the trail leading to Médègue were mixed, and the inhabitants of those that were adjacent to one another were intermarried.

TABLE VIII

Village	Fouk Solé (M)	Nkar I (M)	Nkang (O)	Mékak (O)	Mbomo (O)	Akoko (O)	Nto (O)
Alterna-	1	1	1	1	1	1	1
tion of	1	1	1	2	2	2	1
real	2	2	3	1	2	2	1
authority	2	3		1	2	1	2
among	1			1	1	2	1
the nd'è	2				2	2	
bòt					3	2	
						1	
						1	
Number of nd'è bòt	2	3	3	2	3	3	4

(M) = Mitzik; (O) = Oyem

'There is no custom that insists upon power being hereditary.' It tended to encourage cooperation between lineages that were obliged to live together, if only because for more than twenty years the administration had opposed any further fragmentation.*

Within the limits of the village group, the authority created by the government was little more effective than it was in the larger units. In a village created by orders from above, not far from Mitzik, the founder-in-chief was given the nickname *Amvöné kâ*, 'the man who will put up with anything'† – which expresses the ordinary man's opinion of the role of intermediary. In 1934, the Political Report recognized that 'the majority of natives are not the least concerned about becoming chiefs'.[55] The process of evasion could clearly be seen in certain villages where the official power was independent of the real power; for example, at Engongone (near Oyem) which consisted of a very active Yéngwi group:

* Innumerable reports of duty tours refer to splinter groups being officially sent back to the main village.

† From the word *âmvön*, meaning 'patience, endurance'.

Village of Engongone

Devolution of real power	Devolution of official power
(1) Mözögo Mötulu (founder)	(a) Paternal nephew of (1)
(2) Son of (1)	(b) Relation by collateral descent
(3) Paternal nephew of (1)	(c) Chief of a small affinal group settled at Engongone
(4) Son of (3)	(d) Son of (3)

It was not until 1925, with the accession of the last 'chief', that the two types of powers coincided for the first time, but the same evasion was liable to occur again as soon as circumstances required it. Usually the real chief would hand over official authority to a paternal nephew or son, thus enabling him to act through an intermediary over whom he exercised strict control; on the surface, this also satisfied the government, which, in a society where

Village of Akok

Succession to official 'chieftainship'	Succession within the three nd'è bòt		
(1) Asumu Mômbé (founder)	(1) Asumu Mômbé		
(2) Son of (1)			
(3) Son of (1) (1915)			
(4) Son of (2)	(2) Mômbé Asumu	(3) Evònò Asumu	Òlò Asumu (3rd son)
(5) Son of (2)	↓	↓	↓
(6) Son of (3)	(4) [S]	[S]	[S]
(7) Grandson of (3)	↓	↓	↓
(8) Great-great grandson of (1)	[S]	[S]	[S]
(9) Great-great-grandson of (1) present official chief (a)	(9) ↓	present ntòl (a)	present ntòl (a)
	[S] present ntòl and village chief (a)		
	(a) in 1951		

seniority still played a decisive part, was nevertheless obsessed by the search for 'young and energetic chiefs'. If one compares the devolution of official power with the succession of 'elders' in the *nd'è bòt*, one sees not only the incompatibility between these two forms of authority, but also *the instability of the authority* created by the government. A typical example from the village of Akok (near Oyem), which was the centre of a small Kòjé population, is shown on the previous page.

This dualism, which reveals the existence of an official power alongside a real power, did not merely serve as a means of evasion, weakening the administration's control. It was also a frequent cause of serious disequilibrium: firstly, because it helped destroy authority in a society with but little sense of hier-archy and profoundly disturbed by the colonial situation; secondly, because it divided the groups into supporters and opponents of collaboration with the government;* and thirdly, because, if the official chief was a man of personality and ambition, he could rely upon considerable government support and assert his authority in opposition to the *real* authorities. We have already noted the extent to which the clan movement brought disputes of this kind into the open.

(c) *New Types of Differentiation*

So far we have only considered the first group of problems in terms of the traditional context. We now have to examine those that arose from the internal transformation of the Fang groups; and, in the first place, those that affected the process of differentia-tion taking place within Pahouin society. At the very moment when the powerful unifying factors of clan, lineage and kinship were being seriously weakened by fission and dispersal, as well as by the loss of their religious basis, the colonial situation was in-creasing the number of these processes and changing their direc-tion. The social structures had been transformed in varying degrees according to local circumstances, and new political forces were seeking expression. This was clearly seen by one official, who

* An official report makes the same point: 'In the villages, especially among the Fang, one finds that there are always two factions, those who support the head man and those who are opposed to him. . . . The young, educated folk are always against the headmen, except of course when their immediate interests dictate otherwise.'

wrote: 'The reform of the chieftainship is desired by all natives, at whatever level, whether advanced or backward.'[56] New social categories, arising from colonization, were beginning to compete with the old, more or less direct opponents of governmental authority, determined to play their part and to achieve representation. What were these categories?

Though Europeans had been in Gabon for centuries, there were comparatively few of them (in 1950 they represented only 9·2 per 1,000 of the African population); but since almost all of them lived in an area which brought them into contact with the Fang, this brought the figure there up to 18·2 per 1,000. This contact, which had been one of the purposes of the later Pahouin migrations, and the position of the Fang in the local economy had strengthened the colonizing society's hold upon them and accelerated the process of differentiation. As the part played by Europeans in effecting the socio-cultural change has been well-explored in English and American studies of 'culture contact', we shall here content ourselves with a brief account in which we shall be mainly concerned with the changes in social structure and political relations.

Missionary and educational activity had created two new social types, 'Christians' and 'literates', who, though few in number, had imposed themselves on the village communities by the different attitudes they adopted, sometimes in addition to, sometimes as an alternative to, traditional attitudes. They regarded themselves as belonging to more or less distinct categories, maintaining relations of hierarchy or rivalry: among the first type were native priests and 'catechists', Catholics and Protestants; among the second, school teachers and pupil teachers, those who had obtained 'certificates',* and clerks. From a merely religious point of view, differences existed between 'Christians', traditionalists and members of the *Bwiti* cult, and between Catholics and Protestants, though all these antagonistic relationships also had a political significance, since in Africa it is impossible to conceive of any religious influence that is not also political. Periodical reports frequently allude to disputes between the administration

* Anyone with a certificate of primary education enjoyed considerable prestige; his diploma guaranteed his social importance.

and the missionaries,* and to signs of 'a kind of religious war between Catholics and Protestants'.† The divisions existing within the colonizing society were also to be found within the colonized society, and involved the latter in struggles for ascendancy that were on the whole alien to it; struggles which became particularly lively at election time, when 'government candidates' often stood against 'mission candidates'.‡ As for the members of the *Bwiti* cult, they were opposed both to the 'Christians', because of their desire to create a genuinely Fang religion, and to the 'chiefs', because of their attempt to revive the political role that used to belong to the old 'men's associations'. They represented a social force which, in certain areas (Libreville, Kango and Médouneu), achieved a position of leadership by the fear it inspired. As a typical example of these essentially religious divisions, we will take the little village of Nkoumadzap (Médouneu), where there was both a Catholic mission station and a *Bwiti* church, and where the population, though small, was split up into a so-called Catholic majority, a traditionalist minority and four members of the *Bwiti*. The fact that these different elements could coexist proves that the tensions involved, which in certain circumstances came into the open, were dominated by unifying factors (kinship, and membership of the Òyèk clan which still functioned in this area) and were restrained by the complementary use of various religious observances.

As for the 'literates', as they used to be called in colonial days, they were the only ones who had a directly political influence; though for a long time restricted to the main centres, later it spread owing to the part they played in the villages. The introduction of a new method of marriage payments – preparing lists (*kalaġ*) of the gifts made to the wife's family – increased

* See, for example, a report from the Booué sub-division for the 3rd quarter of 1935: 'Our difficulties have been increased by the fact that there are two missions in the area, whose catechists secretly undermine any kind of authority by representing the missions as places of asylum for women who are dissatisfied with their husbands and the work they force them to do, and for idlers who like spending a few days there in order to escape their village duties.'

† References to this war, 'which in normal times might have rather serious consequences', occur in the report on Booué and Makokou for the 2nd quarter of 1943.

‡ Particularly at Oyem in the Woleu-Ntem, where the Catholic Mission tried to rig the local elections in order to pursue its own policy, which was sometimes opposed to that of the administration (1949–50).

their influence, as did the part they played as assistants to chiefs and business men, as interpreters and, in some cases, as correspondents to local newspapers such as *Méfoé*, published by the American Protestant Mission at Elat (Cameroun). There were abundant signs that a civilization based upon oral tradition was turning into one based upon writing. In this sense, the clan consolidation movement was revealing. Legitimatized by two basic documents – the 'legend of origin' and the 'statutes' of each *ayôg* – it gave rise to a whole number of bureaucratic manifestations, such as the minuting of meetings and 'decisions', and a system of book-keeping for all monies paid into the tribe's bank (*mbâk*). The more general the reliance upon documentation became, the more closely the 'literates' were integrated with Fang society, since their role was no longer restricted to that of intermediary between the colonizing society and the villagers. This explains their political aspirations, which were often hostile both to the government and the 'old Fang'.

Among the processes of differentiation that were specially effective, mention must be made of *those that resulted from closer contact with the colonizing society*, whether as agents of the latter or as individuals returning to their villages after spending several years away from their customary environment. The first category included official 'chiefs' and their assistants, and the employees of European firms; the second consisted of Africans who had lived in the towns or were ex-soldiers. What distinguished the former was the fact that they were more or less 'hangers-on' of one class or another of colonial society. They were able, however, to offset this inferiority by using the power of their 'masters' to assert their authority over the other villagers; thus there was always something ambiguous about their behaviour, which suggested an elementary form of 'double bluff'.[57] This was exemplified by one of our informants, Florentin, an ambitious young man, educated by Catholic missionaries, who compensated for his position as assessor to the Conciliation Tribunal in one of the districts of the Woleu-Ntem by playing an important part in one of the principal *Bwiti* 'parishes', as well as by being very active in the clan movement, for which he was rewarded with a post in the new hierarchy. Despite his official position, he utilized each of these means of asserting his authority over various local groups.

As to those who returned to their original environment after living in the city or away from Gabon, they found reintegration difficult. They were convinced that they were in some way superior to the villagers – like a certain young man who, returning to his village after a long stay in Libreville, very soon broke with his family 'because their huts were not sufficiently clean and up-to-date' – and they were no longer prepared to accept the harsh official constraint they encountered 'in the bush'; after 1944, there were many examples of this amongst ex-soldiers, whose lack of discipline is referred to in a number of reports.[58] These marginal individuals became the bearers of new cultural models and behaviour patterns. The *Bwiti* cult was adapted and spread throughout the Fang country by men who had worked in southern Gabon. In the Woleu-Ntem, the village modernization and re-settlement movement was kept going by a few ex-soldiers who tried to set up large-scale groups in imitation of those they had come across during their service in France and the North African countryside. As a result of their increasing numbers, these men exerted a growing influence and aspired to become leaders in a Fang society modernized through their efforts.

Finally, in addition to these, there were the types of differentiation resulting from the development of the local economy, though it is impossible to distinguish them clearly since they partly overlap. The small Fang 'business man', the modern avatar of the old 'trader', enjoyed a privileged status as the owner of coveted wealth in a country where the market for consumer goods was far from being saturated, and where, in addition to the old capitalization of 'trade-goods', there was an ever-increasing demand for consumer goods. He was the *'nkumakuma'* (the rich man), *par excellence*, and we have already pointed out under what conditions his wealth was recognized as entitling him to authority. Moreover, owing to his mobility, he was a means of liaison between the village communities, a pedlar of ideas as well as of goods; and as a rule he seems to have had a progressive outlook.*
All the interviews we conducted in the Woleu-Ntem in the course

---

* A report on the Ogooué-Ivindo for the year 1948, drawn up by a government ethnographer and primarily dealing with political problems, speaks of 'agitators among the small shopkeepers who frequently visit the coast' – an indication of the exaggerated suspicion with which these modernist elements were regarded.

of investigating the village resettlement movement showed that he supported it; he felt the need for larger communities, so equipped as to raise the standard of living, in which, taking account of the new conditions, power would not only be based on geneological authority or the requirements of the administration.[59] One of these business men was not afraid to assert forcefully: 'We shall act under the leadership of our Deputy, even if the white people are opposed to us.'

With the extension of cash crops, some villagers hoped to be accepted as 'planters', believing that in this way their position in the 'social scale' would be enhanced.[60] In the cocoa country, these were usually young men who owned more than five hectares of cocoa trees and were at pains to mark their ownership in some obvious way – although the only planters on any considerable scale were a few in the neighbourhood of Oyem and, particularly, of Bitam. This recent development (1930–35) was, however, of considerable importance. It conferred a new standing and significance upon the village, and modified social relations. Not only was the position of the village determined by the cocoa plantations, but the area under cultivation was carefully laid out, in plots with well-defined boundaries (*'ni*). Property rights, to which all the men who worked them were entitled, were established and tended to become permanent, so that leaving the village no longer involved giving up one's rights in the trees one had planted.* Groups which until recently had appeared to be nomadic, were transformed into agricultural communities. The men became farmers, and were responsible for the 'money-making' crops. They discovered that their economic power was directly related to the amount of labour they contributed, so that one of the 'commandments' they were taught at the time of the clan movement was: 'We must work to earn money.'[61] The most active of the young men realized the need to help one another, on the basis of groups of 'comrades' (*miö*), if they were to clear more ground; and the need for some kind of cooperative organization that would enable them to obtain better marketing conditions was understood

* We once attended a palaver in the village of Metsui between a group which had broken away and established itself about a kilometre further on, and was asserting its rights to the cocoa and coffee trees that it had previously planted, and the villagers who had stayed where they were and claimed that the trees belonged to them.

by the more thoughtful elements. As a result of the different amounts of money they earned, inequality became more marked, and began to create relations of the employer-employee type. More and more a villager's wealth depended upon his agricultural activities, tending to find expression in the size of his plantations rather than in the number of his wives. The most enterprising individuals wanted a form of village organization that would recognize their influence, guarantee their rights, and be based essentially upon this developing economy.

To these two types, arising from the new village economy, must be added that of the semi-artisans who established themselves in areas where they could make a living; these consisted mainly of tailors,* and one or two carpenters or carpenter-blacksmiths. This category of skilled workers in no way represented a revival of the old class of craftsmen who, as Grébert had pointed out almost twenty years previously,[62] had completely disappeared. They came into existence in response to new needs, and their numbers were far too small for them to be responsible for any major demands.

Such, then, were the *social types that tended to become differentiated*, that tended to express themselves outside the fundamental relations of 'kinship'. The result was confusion rather than the

TABLE IX

Tribe and locality (a)	Social status	Position at time of clan movement (b)
Yémisèm (E)	One-time Protestant pastor	Inspired the Yémisèm tribe, and attempted to federate the Fang tribes in Cameroun
Yémisèm (B)	Dismissed canton chief	President
Yémisèm (O)	Planter	President
	Business man, ex-pupil of Catholic Mission	Vice-President
	One-time cook	Vice-President
	Ex-agent of the agricultural service	Tribal inspector

* For instance, in an impoverished district like Mitzik, according to the official census there were no less than eleven tailors in the capital alone.

Tribe and locality (a)	Social status	Position at time of clan movement (b)
Yémisèm (M)	Business man	President
Yémisèm (Me)	Assessor to Conciliation Tribunal	Vice-President
	Business man	Director of Commerce
Yémisèm (Bo)	Ex-Service man	President
Yémvâg (O)	Cocoa planter	President
Yémvâg (M)	Ex-Service man	President
	Village chief	Vice-President
	Assessor to Conciliation Tribunal	Vice-President
	Cabinet-maker	Governor
	Planter	Governor
	Planter	Governor
Yémvâg (Bo)	Ex-Warrant Officer	President
	Business man	Vice-President
	Territorial chief	President
Yémödâg (O)	Tailor	President
Yémödâg (M)	Territorial chief	President
Yémödâg (Bo)	Ex-Service man	President
	Territorial chief	President
	Business man	Governor
	Government interpreter	Vice-President
	Ex-Service man	Vice-President
	Business man	Governor
Yénzòk (B)	Large-scale cocoa planter	President
Yéngwi (O)	Planter, ex-pupil of Catholic Mission	President
	Shopkeeper's assistant in Libreville	Vice-President
Ožip (O)	Ex-Warrant Officer	President
	Assessor to Conciliation Tribunal	Vice-President

(a) the abbreviations indicate: (B) Bitam, (Bo) Booué, (E) Ebolowa, (M) Mitzik, (Me) Médouneu, (O) Oyem

(b) The exact meaning of these 'positions' is explained below in our analysis of the clan movement

outline of a new structure, since, until the fifties, the government opposed any attempt at reorganization that was due to native initiative. The clan movement, however, which was one of these attempts, showed which elements derived advantage from the new hierarchy, and from a choice based upon election. In the preceding table some examples of this are given from an investigation carried out in 1949 among the most active tribes.

This list reveals, not only the increasing number of social categories, but also the almost complete rejection of the official candidates. The election in Bitam of a previous canton chief, dismissed in 1937, typifies the opposition to an administrative order that had proved to be less and less adequate. It is difficult to explain these 'elections'. The people's choice seems to have been determined on one of two grounds: either because the candidate was 'wealthy', and they hoped to secure his wealth by giving him authority over the tribal group; or because he claimed to know the Europeans, and was therefore expected to teach people how to adopt 'the European way of life'. On the other hand, the rivalry for important positions, as well as the complexity of the hierarchy created by the clan movement, revealed an intense desire to obtain power. The struggle was expressed in terms of the old antagonisms between lineages, but it also left room for the genuinely political influences that came from Libreville and the towns in Cameroun.* Moreover, the exploitation of personal prestige in the old society had prepared people for competition of this kind. The recent movements, which were due entirely to Fang initiative, indicated the power shifts that had occurred in Pahouin society: from 'genealogical' values to economic values; from the older generations to the younger, who were more active in the economic field and were determining the course of social evolution; from the traditionalists to the modernists, who relied upon the experience and knowledge obtained from contact with Europeans. It must be remembered that, during the period of clan consolidation, the promotion of Fang women had been to some extent recognized – positions such as 'woman chief' (*évèt mininga*), 'woman president', 'governor', etc. were created for them – although, as

* For example, the *Comité mixte gabonais* (Libreville), the *Union tribale Ntem-Kribi* (not officially recognized) and the *Union des populations camerounaises* (in South Cameroun).

against this, the men were striving to reassert their authority and to subject the women to stricter control. The administration, while actively engaged in 'undermining the traditional cadres',[63] at first encouraged the exercise of these new powers; but later, by opposing them in order to preserve its own authority, it simply frustrated a social reconstruction that was deteriorating into a series of abortive ventures. After the breakdown of the colonial system, the processes that had hitherto been contained were suddenly set free. Access to political and administrative positions, partial control of an economy that was no longer entirely in the hands of 'foreigners', created overnight a governing elite and enlarged the class of those performing modern economic functions. Here, then, was the starting point of a structural transformation that appeared to favour the creation of genuine social classes.

III. FANG 'INITIATIVES' UP TO THE 1950S

We have frequently pointed out that the colonizing society asserted its political and economic domination in the years 1910 to 1920. For the Fang, this period marked the end of their conquests and of the large-scale trading which had forced them to compete with peoples who had previously held a monopoly. It was also characterized by their first positive reactions to the European presence and to the problems created by the breakdown of their social structure. Bas-Gabon, where 'contact' had existed longest and been most active as a result of the number of urban centres and public works there, and where the process of disorganization was most rapid, was for a long time to remain the focal point of Fang initiative. The first, almost simultaneous attempts were of two different kinds: the first, which had a religious basis and showed itself to be capable of winning a certain measure of traditional support, was the *Bwiti* cult; the second, which had a political basis in the modern sense of the word, expressed the reactions of the Europeanized social category, and was the beginning of an organized political opposition.

The Bwiti Cult: a Reaction Based on Religion

According to the aged African Abbé, A. R. Walker, who had a scholarly knowledge of the ethnography of the Gabonese people,

the *Bwiti* cult was first introduced among the Fang people half a
century ago; but 'such was their enthusiasm, at least on the coast
and along the banks of the Ogooué, that it exceeded that of all
other peoples'.[64] In his paper, 'Totemism amongst the Fang',
written in 1912, Father Trilles was content to note the connection,
based especially upon certain common symbolic features, between
the 'Fang *Biéri*' and the 'Fiot *Bwiti*' – the Fiot forming a large
ethnic group that extends as far as the river Congo. Earlier
writers do not even mention the term, so that presumably
'contamination' was spread, between 1900 and 1910, by the Fang
groups that had penetrated furthest and were by then settled on
the Fernan Vaz, and as far south as Setté-Cama, these being the
two 'contact zones' at the end of the trade routes.

According to the most reliable information,[65] the *Bwiti* cult had
originally been spread among the peoples of the coast by slaves,
and Blacks engaged in the slave trade. It should be added that,
later on, the ethnic groups driven back by the Fang invasion
became, in their turn, admirable propagandists; among these were
the Ba-Kélé, whose 'clan idol', as the explorer du Chaillu noted
about the middle of the last century, was known as the *Mbuiti*.
From what he says, it appears to have been a basically clan cult,
only open to men (the women belonged to the *Njambai*), which
was responsible for the protection of the members and property of
the group.[66] If the majority of the peoples of southern Gabon
(Eshira, Ba-Varama, Ba-Vungu, Ba-Lumbu and Galwa, Nkòmi,
Oroungou, Mpongwé, etc.) knew about the *Mbuiti* most of
them only regarded it as being 'supplementary' to their main
religious activities. In a monograph devoted to the Mpongwé, A.
R. Walker notes that 'it is extremely unusual for genuine
Mpongwé to be initiated into this society'.[67] The country where
the *Bwiti* cult seems to have originated is the Haute-Ngounié; but
the peoples living in this region, the Mitshogo and the Masango,
who must have been its actual creators, also had other 'associations', like the *Mwiri*, which appears to have been a masculine
organization of a religious nature, fulfilling a variety of functions,
judicial, disciplinary and economic.[68] It was only among the
Fang, in those areas where it succeeded in establishing a firm
hold, that the *Bwiti* cult was developed exclusively, seeking to
monopolize the greater part of all religious and political activities.

This is the first point that has to be made clear if we are to understand the reason for their 'enthusiasm'.

None of the studies devoted to the Fang in the period around 1910 – whether those from the Gabon estuary, the Ogooué or the Woleu-Ntem[69] – makes any reference to the existence of the *Bwiti* cult among these groups. At that time, its influence was very restricted, and most of our informants assured us that it was the work-sites in Bas-Gabon that were the real training ground for the *Bwiti*, since there the 'labour recruits' from Ngounié were in continual contact with those from the Fang country, the two main reservoirs of labour. It was during the period of large-scale development between 1920 and 1930 that the cult increased the number of its 'churches' (*mbáža mbwiti*) in the Lambaréné and Kango districts, established itself at Libreville and spread to the Ogooué and the Woleu-Ntem along the trail connecting this region with the coast, penetrating as far as the Ntoumou villages in Cameroun. The ex-labour recruits became the bearers of the new cult. Its diffusion was, until recently, a sign of the preponderant influence of the Bas-Gabon Fang, and particularly of those from Libreville who wanted to make this city the '*Bwiti* capital'. By that time the organization was sufficiently established to issue slogans of resistance to the authorities; and around 1930 M., whose position as leader of the opposition was by that time assured, was prosecuted for his activities as 'head of the *Bwiti*'. Official hostility was supported by the missionaries; in 1931, incidents occurred in the outskirts of Médouneu, following the destruction of *Bwiti* 'churches' on orders from a Fang abbé, and adherents of the cult in Spanish Guinea received harsh prison sentences. Many villagers fled to less accessible areas, and the clandestine development of the cult increased; it was not until after 1945 that it was possible for 'churches' to be built near the motor roads. This clandestine development explains the concentration of *Bwiti* villages in the marginal areas, between Coco-Beach and Médouneu, for example.

Such are the facts we have been able to gather about the history of this institution. They enable us to understand certain characteristics of the Fang *Bwiti*. The fact that it was a widespread socio-cultural system which, as a result, underwent various adaptations, explains the liberties that the Fang took with the original cult.

They overlaid it with a variety of meanings, which have changed considerably during the last thirty years, strengthening its material content to such an extent that Abbé Walker could say: 'So many additions have been made that the Fang *Bouiti* is quite different from the primitive *Bouiti* of the Apindji and the Mitsogo'.[70] On the other hand, the very conditions in which they took it over, in the *contact zones* where the *Bwiti* had already acquired an inter-tribal character and in the workers' camps where it served as a link between ethnically disparate elements, and its diffusion by men returning to their villages after a long absence, explain why the new sect was largely independent of the kinship groups. It was relatively easy for 'strangers', and even women, to join it (though the latter was exceptional), provided they were initiated and prepared to accept its rules. Moreover, the antagonisms that developed in opposition to the missionaries' efforts to suppress it (they attacked it as a revival of 'fetishism'), and against officials who were afraid of it becoming established as a politico-religious organization, meant that its manifestations took on an anti-European character. Thanks to these disputes, as we found on a number of occasions, some of its adherents felt convinced that they were being subjected to persecution.

The word itself, *Bwiti*, designates not only the superior divinity who reveals himself to the initiated, but also the carved post which is the central feature of the church, as well as the organisation itself; however, it is impossible to determine its etymology since the word is found in various forms, *Bwiti*, *Bwété* and *Butu*, throughout a large part of Gabon. It should also be pointed out that, owing to the extension of the cult, the vocabulary of the *Bwiti* raises a number of linguistic problems that could not be broached within the terms of our enquiry. Each of the various peoples who have adopted it has contributed some original and distinct development; in addition to the basic terms, which are found everywhere, one comes across others that belong to the linguistic groups of the south, such as the Omyène and the Fiot, whilst it owes its essential linguistic structure to groups from the Haute-Ngounié, the Mitshogo and the Masango. Thus, apart from their own direct contributions, the Fang members of the cult took over a whole body of words, only to be understood by 'equivalents' or 'translations', which now constitute part of the special knowledge that enables initiates (*ba'âzi*, pl. *böba'âzi*) to distinguish one another from outsiders.

(a) *Material Features and Symbolism*

Among the groups that were entirely favourable to the cult, the 'church', *mbâza mbwiti*, usually occupied a privileged position at the end of the central alley and was regarded as the apex of the village. Otherwise it was hidden away in the part of the village where the members lived. The church was built over the 'relics' (skull and bones) of a man noted for his ability (a chief, rich man or trader), though in the Mitshogo country the bodies of Europeans were also used for the purpose.* When a new church was built a sacrifice had to be offered by the founder, who then became the priest (*nkòbé-bwiti*). For the cult to be effective, it was supposed to require a human sacrifice, either a relative or an adopted member of his group. Obviously, it is not possible to say how far this demand was complied with, but it is similar to the obligation to 'kill kinship' which we have already come across in the case of the 'associations' that used to be formed outside, and above, the kinship groups.†

It was over these 'relics', with which pieces of the '*Biéri* baskets' of some of the members were included,[71] that the carved post (also known as *Bwiti*) supporting the central structure of the church was erected – an object whose significance may be compared with that of the 'centre-post' of the voodoo sanctuaries in the New World.‡ When the *Bwiti* were being hunted down by the missionaries and certain officials, the post was often taken down and the relics disinterred so that they could be transferred, together

---

* Cf. *Rapport Etat-Major, 2e bureau*, Libreville, August 21, 1947: 'Best of all would be to have the skull of a white man. Those of M. Ourson and Sgt. Sampique were particularly famous *Bwiti* among the Mitshogo.'

† Sillans, *Rites et croyances*, Paris, 1962, denies that such sacrifices occur; which was true at the time he was writing. But it is nevertheless a fact that the sacrifice, either real or fictitious, of a kinsman or of an adopted member of the group was one of the ways of breaking the bonds of kinship and setting oneself outside normal society. Thus the founder of the *Bwiti* church could act on behalf of all the members and not only of his own lineage.

‡ Considering the large number of slaves exported from the Congo and the part that slaves undoubtedly played in spreading the *Bwiti* cult, this is certainly more than a coincidence. A more detailed study of the *Bwiti* would certainly have to take into account the practice of voodooism.

8

with a number of other sacred objects, to a secret sanctuary (*nǰimba*) in the forest. This led to some discrepancies between the public and private aspects of the cult, the former tending to assume the form of a secular counterpart of the latter, and laying particular emphasis on the 'holiday atmosphere' of its gatherings in an attempt to justify itself and win official acceptance.*

It is the design of this centre-post, decorated more or less richly with conventional symbols, that expresses the personality of different *Bwiti*. We managed to distinguish three types, all fairly strictly localized: a rudimentary type, with only one diamond-shaped groove near the base, representing the female sex organ; an intermediate type, where the symbol is essentially the carved figure of a woman, with the sex and breasts clearly shown, representing Nyingòn Möbòga, the female principle of divinity, the 'first woman', sister of Nzamö (the supreme being), pillar of the world and the link between heaven and earth;† and, thirdly, a much more elaborate type, where the rich and complex symbolism incorporates borrowings from Christianity, which may also be seen in the structure of the church itself. The first type was found in the marginal zone already referred to, between Kango and Médouneu and in the vicinity of Médouneu, whose remoteness led to a certain conservatism and 'freezing' of institutions; the second, in the villages of the Moyen-Ogooué, towards Mitzik and Cameroun; while the third was peculiar to the earliest and most profoundly 'acculturated' region between Libreville and Kango and slightly further on towards Lambaréné. Everywhere the *Bwiti*-post was an object of fundamental importance, which was never left behind when a village moved, particularly, as we saw for ourselves, when the members had had to go as far as Libreville to obtain it. These brief comments show the extent to which the institution has been modified by local circumstances and how its symbolic potential varied according to the particular 'parish'.

* In the course of our investigation, a *nkòbé bwiti* of a *Bwiti* in the Bas-Ogooué asked us to approach the local government official to obtain a document, recognizing his group as being 'the best dancers' and authorizing them to perform outside the village.

† Cf. Trezenem: *op. cit.*, pp. 67–8: 'When Nzame reached the end of the earth, which is flat, he found his way barred by the sky, an iron roof covering the earth as a roof covers a hut, supported in the middle by an invisible post which is kept in position by Ningone Maboere, the sister of Nzame.' From this it is clear that the new cult had adopted the Fang cosmogony.

In the Fang country the church has no special shape, whereas among the Mitshogo its flattened construction and the carving on the master beam remind one of a dug-out canoe turned upside down. A large, rectangular building entirely open at one end, not unlike the traditional 'guard-house', it has benches running along each side for the 'congregation' and spectators. Where the *Bwiti* reveals Christian borrowings, there are in addition one or two side-rooms (not unlike vestries), where the priest gets ready to officiate; and the altar, which is at the far end of the temple, is larger, has steps leading up to it decorated with astral symbols* either painted or modelled in clay, and is supposed to resemble the altars in Christian churches.† This altar, on which the sacrifices are performed (of kids, chickens, eggs and money), seems to have been added, as an appendage so to speak of the *Bwiti*-post; it is not found in the Mitshogo country, nor even in all Fang churches.‡ Its shape varies considerably, from a simple base made of logs to a small erection of baked clay containing little recesses. On the other hand, the objects that are *always* to be found as an integral feature of the church are set along its central axis: at the front the *Bwiti*-post; in the centre, a fire that is always kept burning; and, at the back, the *obaka*, the branch of a palm tree, supported horizontally by two stakes, on which an assistant beats out a rhythm with two sticks. Along this all-important area, and attached to the master beam, are ratten rings, marking the spot where you have to stand to 'address the *Bwiti*'.

We must now consider each of these essential features, in order to explain their significance.

(i) As an example of a particularly heavily decorated *Bwiti*-post, we will take the one in the church at Abogotome, in the Médouneu region. It is covered with a considerable number of emblems, some of which are painted:

On the front (facing outwards): 'The bird of death', which only

---

* For instance, in the *Bwiti* church at Abogotome, the sun, moon and stars were represented on the front of the altar.

† An example of this is the *Bwiti* at Akournam, referred to in the document submitted by the Libreville sub-division for the Enquiry into Native Housing, in the Brazzaville archives.

‡ It is not mentioned by Trezenem in his account of his investigations in the Moyen-Ogooué, and we ourselves found no trace of it in the churches we visited in the Médouneu region.

sings at night and brings death to anyone who hears it; a lizard, which represents thunder (light and fire playing a considerable part in the Mitshogo rite);* the 'first woman'; 'a monkey'; a saw, which is emblematic of destruction; a symbolic representation of a kind of lemur (which never lets go of its prey, even after it is dead), suggesting the solidarity of the group (it is said to 'hold on to the *Bwiti*') and the determination of its initiates not to renounce their beliefs, however harshly they may be treated.

On the back (facing into the church): Emblems of the spider (the earth), of the stars, and of night and day (on some posts a line is drawn between these two latter symbols, indicating the division between night and day, heaven and earth, the land of the dead and the land of the living); the 'door' and the 'four windows' of the world; a series of crosses ('the crosses of the dead'); and a tortoise.

On the sides: A python representing the rainbow, which in Bas-Gabon plays such an important part in the *Bwiti* that Father Trilles could maintain that 'the entire *Bwiti* cult is dedicated to it' † (in fact, though it occurs everywhere, it does not have the same priority in all parts of the Fang country); ‡ a row of notches representing the female sex organ; and a knife, which is a reminder both of the punishment that awaits anyone who attempts to harm

* This may be compared with one of the *Chants du Bwiti* collected by Abbé Walker (though not published), which pays tribute to the power of *Bwiti*, under his various names, by evoking the lightning:

> *There where the lightning struck, mushrooms have sprung up.*
> *O Mother! My Mother! Truly Digôjé performs wonders!*
> *Truly Dibôji performs wonders!*
> *There where the lightning passed, two shapes in*
>   *the form of diamonds appeared.*
> *O my people!*
> *O! o! o! it is Botuda himself who achieved this*
>   *extraordinary thing.*

† H. Trilles: *Le totémisme chez les Fân*, p. 52; *ibid.*, quotations from Father Le Scão's paper on 'The *Bwiti* of Setté-Cama,' which contains information about the large number of designs derived from the serpent. Among the songs collected by Abbé Walker there is one in honour of the python; the dancer-singers follow one another through the village 'bearing on their shoulders a long rope to which are attached torches made of okoumé resin. The rope represents a python uncoiling itself.' The song says: *The great python swims down the river like a rope unfurling*.

‡ In the Ngounié region, the rainbow occupies a special place in a 'cult of wealth'. Cf. J. W. Fernandez: 'Christian Acculturation and Fang Witchcraft', *Cah. Ét. africaines*, 6, 1961.

the initiates and of the function of defending people against maleficent sorcery that has devolved upon the *Bwiti*.

Here, then, we have a composite entity, where it would only be possible to determine the significance of the various additions by a detailed investigation of the *Bwiti*, but where, directly one begins to make comparisons, the original contribution of the founders appears considerable. One finds reflections (more accurately, survivals) of a cosmogony, the suggestion of a religious idea centred upon notions of fertility and death, and indications of a defensive reaction to the danger of sorcery that has developed as a result of social disintegration. It is precisely this last characteristic that Trezenem insists upon when speaking of the *Bwiti* in the Ogooué, thus providing an important indication of the growing number of personal disputes and rivalries.

(ii) The fire permanently fed by three logs, which is in the centre of the church and is kept burning by one or other of the members, is one of the features that is to be found in every *Bwiti*,* It seems to be like the 'communal hearth', where a fire, that still has religious significance, is always kept burning in 'every guardhouse' – a significance even further accentuated by its similarity to the sanctuary lamps in Catholic churches. The fact that it is always alight is connected with a whole number of ritual gestures and invocations that accord an important place to fire and to the stars. In this respect, it is worth quoting from an old study, part of which deals with the Fang: 'Before every service, the fetishist takes a lighted torch, walks round the hut with it, and then goes outside and invokes the stars; and similarly everything that is to be used in the service is passed through the flame.'[72] Here we find elements of a cult in which purifying fire and natural forces played a considerable part; one which did not originate with the Fang but among the indigenous peoples of Haut-Gabon, and which, if we consider the part played by fire in certain voodoo rituals, may well have been taken with them by slaves.

(iii) The *obaka* is a musical instrument found among the peoples of Bas-Gabon, as well as the Mpongwé, where it has the same name. It seems to be regarded not merely as a musical instrument

---

* Among the Mitshogo, as described by Abbé Walker; among the Fiot of the Bas-Gabon, as described by Father Le Scão, who says that the fire 'is like the sanctuary lamp'.

but also as of symbolic value. Among the Mpongwé, the various synonyms used to designate this instrument and any other where raffia is used, also mean: 'origin, immemorial time' (*ikókó*).[73] This sense of 'origin' – of 'genesis' would be more exact – seems to be borne out by the fact that the player of the eight-stringed harp (*ngòma*) takes his place in the immediate vicinity of, and slightly behind, the *obaka*, *ngòma* symbolizing 'the first woman', woman as creator. The combination of these two instruments represents the female antithesis of the *Bwiti*'s personality, which is always male. The importance of the *ngòma* may be judged not only from its presence in every church, but even more from the fact that it receives the blood from the sacrifices and is so sacred that, as a protection against theft, many copies are made which have no value except as musical instruments. The *ngòma* has a head, indicated very schematically, on the forehead of which a metal cross ('the cross of the dead') is inscribed; a neck with an iron band in which the strings are inserted, emphasizing that part of the nape of the human victim's neck where the sacrificial blow is struck; a back, over which the blood from the sacrifices is poured, forming the sounding board; and a belly, the skin with which the latter is covered being scored with three circles representing the breasts and sex.* It creates a link between the couple *Bwiti-Nyingòn Mòbòga* and the human victim (who in the past used to be a woman) sacrificed at least symbolically when the church was founded. This is one of the features of this complex cult (grossly elaborated by the Fang, who have continually loaded it with a whole variety of borrowings) in which *dualism*, in the form of antagonistic pairs, plays a considerable part: male-female, day-night, sky-earth, birth-death and good-evil.

(iv) The assistants to the *nkòbé-bwiti* take their places on either side of the fire and the *Bwiti*-post, on wooden stools of a peculiar shape that are only found inside their churches, the most remarkable of these being made of two flat, circular pieces of wood, held together by two pairs of crossed, spiral legs. There can be no doubt that these, too, have a ritual significance, though the explanation is not easy to discover.

---

* The harp described here is used by the Nkoumadzap *Bwiti*, on the Médouneu road.

To conclude this brief account of the external features of the cult, it may be noted that the dances sung by the 'priest' and certain members of the congregation are accompanied by rattles or sistrums; and that for these dances the initiates have to wear a garment made from the skins of tiger-cats and monkeys over a raffia loin-cloth (a reminder of the costume worn by the old Fang warriors), and a feathered headdress, with painted designs on the face and body. Here again it is a question of residual cultural features that tend to disappear or be transformed under local influences. In the Libreville-Médouneu region, the initiates have even taken to wearing, as a sign of membership, such an exotic form of headdress as a red tarboosh.[74]

We have described these physical features of the cult, not only because there is no serious work that deals with them,[75] but also because they show the extent to which the *Bwiti* remains a repository of cultural forms gravely impaired in the course of social evolution. It preserves a whole body of knowledge and myth, including part of the ancient *Biéri* cult, which was 'abandoned mainly because of the way it was attacked by the Christian missionaries'[76] (so much so, indeed, that one writer confuses *Biéri* and *Bwiti*), and fulfils, or seeks to fulfil, the functions once performed by the old 'associations'. But, as we shall show further on, the *Bwiti* is none the less exposed to modern influences and needs. Its syncretistic aspects are in this respect significant.

(b) *Sociological aspects and functions of the sect*
Villagers who do not belong to the sect frequently refer to its members as 'those who have drunk *iboga*', a powerful drink made from the grated bark of a plant (*Tabernanthe Iboga*), which produces aphrodisiac effects and hallucinations, and is drunk for the first time at the initiation ceremony. This shrub, which is often grown near the huts, is a distinctive mark of membership and, by the considerable part that it plays in the cult, reveals the dual preoccupation with personal 'revelation' and acquired 'potency' (manifested in the exacerbation of sexual desire) that actuates all the initiated. The teaching that is given is of less importance than the personal experience resulting from intoxication with the *iboga*; whether or not a candidate is admitted to the sect depends entirely upon the quality of his revelation. In the preceding

chapter we noted a very similar orientation with regard to
initiation into the *Biéri*; and long before this Father Trilles had
reported that a candidate for the position of *akûm* was tied for
several days to the corpse of his human victim, and by the time he
managed to get away had become a victim of hallucinatory
visions.[77]

Thus one can see how important revealed knowledge, as
distinct from ordinary knowledge, is in Fang eyes; it alone
ensures individual commitment and can provide a certain type of
qualification. Revelation, though judged by the form it takes in
each individual case, is nevertheless *profoundly socialized*; the aspects
of *Bwiti* (the divinity), like those of 'the country of the dead', which
manifest themselves during a hallucinatory crisis, are to a large
extent stereotyped. One might almost describe it as a state of
partially controlled mental derangement, which nevertheless
involves a personal experience and 'grades' the initiate according
to the intensity with which he experiences it; and an experience
involving a return to the group past and a state of close communion with the dead,* which was one of the reasons for the
success of the *Bwiti* at a time when insecurity was at its height and
the old means of protection had almost disappeared. Moreover,
this cult shows that religious experience had not changed its
character despite the extension of Christianity: in this sense the
Bwiti is recognized as a living, intensely experienced religion,
whereas Christianity is looked upon as a religion that is not only
imposed from outside, but also 'taught' in a rational way, and not
discovered as a result of a spiritual revelation. This was one of the
reasons for the setback sustained by the missionaries. The *Bwiti*
not only saved part of the Fang cultural heritage, but also preserved certain specifically Fang behaviour patterns. In this sense
it was a reaction against the distortion implicit in the colonial
situation.

The cohesion of the sect is reinforced by its members' feeling
that they have some higher form of knowledge: candidates for
initiation are reminded that they have 'the honour' of learning

---

* It should be noted that, for peoples without writing, this is an example, of 'the
appeal to history'. The lineage, which goes back to the origins of time, represents
both the past (the succession of ancestors) and the present (the living descendants
of these ancestors) of the group to which the individual belongs.

'how the things of the earth function'.* It is sustained by the rule
of secrecy (on pain of death) and the occult character of some of
its manifestations – though this secrecy is beginning to be relaxed
insofar as the *Bwiti* aspires to become a major religion available to
the greatest number of people. It is confirmed by periodical
sacrifices in which all the members take part, as well as by public
ceremonies and the festivities connected with initiation (*abâji*),
when for a time the sect becomes the centre of village activity.
Above all, the active opposition of the missions and the administration intensified its sense of solidarity and imbued the whole
venture with a fundamentally racial as well as socio-cultural
significance.

This solidarity is all the more effective in that membership is a
matter of personal choice (anyone who is opposed to the sect can
always avoid the pressures of its members) and that the organization of the cult is not hampered by clan or tribal boundaries. A
'stranger' may be admitted, once he has been initiated; and even a
few Europeans have become members on the understanding that
they would obey the rules strictly (obviously this is an extreme
case, and has only happened with one or two extremely 'Africani-
zed' individuals). Moreover, having incorporated various Christian
elements into its myths and rituals, the *Bwiti* is able to recruit
certain lapsed Christians. It offers them an indigenous religion that
does not make exaggerated or incompatible demands. The most
enlightened members insist upon this characteristic, contrasting
the 'public' nature of the *Bwiti* with the 'private' nature of the
ancient *Biéri* – the one appealing to the totality of ancestors,
whereas the other is concerned only with the ancestors of the
lineage – and representing it as a great religion capable of competing with Christianity (since syncretistic additions have encouraged
the extension of the original cult), while at the same time changing
its nature.

The diffusion of this new cult may be regarded as a first attempt
at 'solidarity' on the part of the Fang, and as their first organized
reaction against the Christian missions. Its aim is to recreate
cohesion and to provide a practical religion which the old,

* The formula employed is that of the *Bwiti* of the Mitshogo; it is applied to the
profane, or people of small account (*zésé bòt*), to exalt the knowledge they have
received.

degenerate groups could no longer maintain. Its very organization implies a longing for unity; a hierarchy is created between
the different *Bwiti* centres, based on the length of time they have
been in existence, the distinction they have achieved and the
prestige of the *nkòbé-bwiti* in charge of the churches. Zones of
influence, not unlike 'parishes', have been established in the
neighbourhood of Libreville, Kango and Médouneu. These show
that the status of a particular centre depends not only upon the
authority of its 'priest' (who is mainly responsible for initiations)
but also upon material factors (the way in which the church is
built), symbolic factors (the design and ornamentation of the
Bwiti-posts), and mythical and ritual factors (for example, the
particular type of dance). During our investigation the priest of
the *Bwiti* at Ngonéki (in the Médouneu district), who was one of
our informants, was an example of how important it was locally to
have lived in Libreville; for it was while he was there that he had
learnt a new version of the myth of creation* and a type of dance
more disciplined than the old one. There are four villages whose
Bwiti are directly dependent upon Ngonéki, one of which, Efulana,
is so situated that its influence extends to a further series of villages
lying along the Mitzik road as far as Nkamenvi. Thus, as a result
of some personal innovation or success, the sphere of influence of
some of the leaders is widespread. In several districts a form of
organization copied from the Christian missions (periodical
meetings of those in charge of the churches, tours of inspection,
etc.) strengthens the hold of the *Bwiti* cult; indeed, one influential
priest, when visiting the centres in the Kango district, was not
afraid of introducing himself to a Catholic priest, who was
inspecting mission stations, as the '*Bwiti* bishop'. The tendency
to regroupment and reorganization is clearly marked, which is why
the administration remained hostile to the movement, whereas the
missionaries pretended to regard it simply as a revival of 'fetishism'.
It takes the form of a *total* reaction, in which the religious element
predominates – this being the only level at which the most energetic elements amongst the Fang were able to act – and in which the
socio-cultural, as well as the political, aspects are of importance

---

* A highly Christianized version, telling how the world was created in a night
lasting five days, and how, on the sixth day, the sky and stars were created and dark
ness was succeeded by light.

It also has some of the characteristics of the Negro churches of the Bantu that indicate an awakening of nationalist feeling. Nevertheless this unifying tendency is offset by other factors: the *Bwiti* has not succeeded in effacing the memory of tribal, and even clan, antagonisms; the fear of more or less direct repression restricts its capacity for expansion; and the rivalry between its own leaders, between initiates and 'Christians', between officials of the cult and government authorities, combine to hinder its development.

How then are we to explain the hold that this new cult has obtained over a large part of the Fang country in less than thirty years? Apart from the sociological and cultural reasons just referred to, there are others of a strictly psychological nature. In a society that has seriously deteriorated, where the machinery of social control has either been destroyed or depends upon a foreign power, it offers a measure of security by offering protection against 'sorcery' and dangerous competition, by providing methods of therapy consistent with tradition and by giving assurances about the after-life – a sphere in which it has been deeply influenced by Christianity. It creates centres of intense life; it permits those flights from normality to which the secret names adopted by the initiates bear witness; it represents a complete reaction of the individual, a liberation from a social environment that has been rationalized by the colonial administration and a capitalist economy.* Moreover, it has the attraction of offering the elements of organization to a society that had been almost destroyed.[78] Some of the Fang leaders realized how greatly a movement of this kind might appeal to the village masses, and endeavoured to orient it in this direction; but they were very few, the so-called 'progressive' minority being primarily concerned to achieve leadership on a strictly political level and condemning themselves to a form of activity that for a long time remained extremely vulnerable.

Reactions of a directly political nature

The first political reactions of the Fang groups were determined

* Certain recent versions of the *Bwiti* – for instance, the *Ndeya Kâga* in the Libreville region – minimize the physical attributes of the church, emphasizing its organization and the ritual aspects that glorify mystical communion. For a brief account, see G. Lasserre: *Libreville et sa région*, Paris, 1958, p. 315 ff.

more by their concern to supplant the dominant tribes of southern Gabon than by the colonial situation. Government reports up to about 1940 reveal the anxiety of the Fang to prevent the Mpongwé (in the Libreville district), the Galwa (in the Lambaréné district) or the Oroungou and Nkomi (in the Port-Gentil district) from achieving any ascendancy. One of these reports, dated 1938 and referring to 'the well-known hostility between the Fang and the Mpongwé', suggests that it was a question of 'rivalry between two neighbouring groups, both claiming to exercise the major influence, one by virtue of its intellectual superiority, the other because of its greater vitality and superior numbers'.[79] The active Fang minority in Libreville, the main political centre, was for a long time kept out of the leadership by the influence of the Mpongwé and half-caste elements who were better prepared for political action.

It was not until after the First World War that a Gabonese branch of the *Ligue des Droits de l'Homme et du Citoyen* was set up. Neither the founder nor its principal leader were Fangs, though the latter did join the 'sub-sections' that were formed in the villages, whose 'activity extend throughout the whole Libreville district'. The administration saw in this an organization directed essentially against itself ('to thwart government action by every possible means and on any pretext'), though recognizing that 'the majority, inspired if not by the highest intelligence at least by good intentions, only seeks to improve the well-being of the native population'.[80] The purpose of the *Ligue* was to counteract the domination of the colonizing society; it was an expression of the progressive minority's desire to participate in the management of public affairs and to overcome its political alienation. This intention was proclaimed more openly with the creation of the first political party, the Young Gabonese Movement, and the first political paper, the *Echo Gabonais*, (later to become the *Voie Coloniale*). The very titles show that here was a direct reaction against the colonial situation, led by the younger generation and those individuals who had become most westernized. This group acted as an unofficial opposition until 1924, when the local authorities in Libreville and Port-Gentil realized that it was thwarting their activities and attacking their decisions more and more frequently. From then on, the movement declined – as a result of official hostility, of the

acute rivalry between the leaders due to their exclusion from any
share in the exercise of power, of inter-tribal disputes, and, above
all, of the economic position, which had become more favourable
with the intensive exploitation of *okoumé* wood. After 1926 the
official reports claimed that the opposition, which had previously
been so active in the political sphere, had given up its demands and
'no longer dreams of putting any obstacles in the government's
way'.

The economic crisis of 1930 was to put an end to this comparative calm. In 1933, M. was dismissed from his position as canton
chief, and from then on emerged as leader of the Fang opposition.
During the same period, the Association of Half-Castes was
organized in Libreville to put forward the demands of this
important section of the population, which had the advantage of
outside support. In 1937, a Pongwé Committee was formed and
attracted 'the most enlightened elements of the population' by
expressing their intention 'to play a more effective part in the
administration of their country'.[81] This provoked a hostile reaction on the part of the Fang, who set up a Committee for the
Defence of Pahouin Interests. Official policy benefited most from
this split; nevertheless it proved that a progressive minority had
appeared amongst the Fang, capable of adopting an independent
attitude towards political problems.

The Second World War, followed by a policy of reforms that
led to the introduction of an electoral system, enabled the Fang
not only to seize the initiative but also to assume the lead as the
largest racial group in Gabon. They took their seats in the local
assemblies, and the deputy elected to the Upper Chamber of the
National Assembly was a Fang, born in the Woleu-Ntem. In
Libreville, M. founded a progressive movement, the United
Gabonese Committee, which was more or less directly inspired by
the *Rassemblement Démocratique Africain* (R.D.A.), while at the
same time he endeavoured to assume responsibilities that had
hitherto been the preserve of the colonizing society: intervention
in labour disputes, attempts to organize a mutual aid society and
customary tribunals, etc. The movement only achieved limited
success, however: the government remained hostile to its attempts
to take things into its own hands, and tribal antagonisms affected
the Committee, which was intended to be 'mixed' while ensuring

Fang leadership. The hostility of the Libreville leaders to those from the Woleu-Ntem indicates the position that the latter region counted on achieving as a result of its economic development. This rivalry which was still further complicated by the struggle between the 'Europeanized' elements (those who were aware of the achievements of the national movement abroad) and the 'reformists' (who were content with improvements within the existing political framework).

As a result of past experience, the leaders realized that they would only be able to act effectively if they could win the support of the rural population. Thus the movement functioned at two very different levels: in a borrowed form, which was inspired by party activity (each of the two rival leaders having his own political party, the United Gabonese Committee, later the Gabonese Democratic Bloc, and the Gabonese Democratic and Social Union); in a more traditional form, which made use of influential individuals and organizations in the villages (for instance, some well-known sorcerer or the *Bwiti* society) and which endeavoured to give direction to the confused aspirations expressed by the most active clans. In this way the tendency to unity displayed by the latter took on the form of clan consolidation and village reunification. The political leaders had to adopt complicated tactics varying according to circumstances: for example, any of them might be called upon at one moment to assume the functions of the leader of a political movement, and, at the next, those of the priest of one of the important *Bwiti* in Bas-Gabon. Their influence also transformed from within the content of institutions like the clan or tribe, which seemed to be most typical of traditional organization. It was thus essentially ambiguous; and more recent developments have done little to modify this ambiguity. The two Fang leaders continued to oppose one another after 1952, one subscribing to the ideas of M. Senghor, the other to the political views of the R.D.A.; and their entente after 1957, under which the first coalition government was formed, was always precarious. However, not even membership of the same political party has been enough to overcome tribal and personal rivalries.

The 'Consolidation' Movement

We have often referred to the clan movement as the most important attempt at social reconstruction undertaken by the Gabonese
Fang; a movement that was particularly active in the Woleu-
Ntem. The political reforms achieved after 1946, by overthrowing
the previous administrative structure for a time, encouraged the
revival of Fang initiative.

The plan for reorganization was borrowed from the related
tribes in Cameroun who, thanks to their more prosperous
economy, had successfully maintained their clan structure while
at the same time modernizing it. There, the groups had been able
to keep up the periodical gatherings (*bisulan*) that proclaim the
unity and solidarity of the clan; they had managed to force through
a reform of the chieftainship (1944–5), which recognized the clan
chief as part of the administrative machinery; and they had expressed their desire to bring about unity amongst the Cameroun
Fang by means of tribal federation. The latter involved the setting
up, in July 1948, of the Ntem-Kribi Tribal Union, the leading
body of which was to be the Tribal Assembly, based upon a
variety of clan councils and committees representing the traditional political units, and of local councils and committees
representing the official units created by the tutelary power.[82] But
the Union never obtained permission to function legally: the
administration was radically opposed to a powerful organization
that would be in a position to put forward political demands and
to develop still further.

This example, however, made a deep impression on the
neighbouring clans in Gabon. Moreover, the Pahouin Congress
made it possible to raise the serious problems affecting Fang
society and appeared as an incitement to resolve them; it thus
precipitated clan revival. Its earliest meetings, prior to 1947, had
only involved a limited number of villagers; nevertheless this
date marked the starting point of a movement – the *Alar Ayôg*
(from *lar*, 'to unite', and *ayôg*) – that was to spread rapidly throughout the Woleu-Ntem, extending as far as the Ogooué and Ogooué-
Ivindo regions. The tremendous enthusiasm shown during the
festivities that accompanied the *bisulan* made it clear that this initiative had aroused hopes of a genuine social transformation.

(a) *Tribal Meetings and Methods of Propaganda*

The *ésulan* (sing. of *bisulan*) brought together in each administrative division the members of the various clans belonging to the same tribal unit. Its primary aim was to counteract fragmentation and dispersal by recreating local aggregates that would feel themselves to be bound together at the *level of the tribe*, not merely of the clan. A 'Book of the Tribe' provided a list of the lineages that *ought* to be united – which only goes to show the part now played by a written tradition and by the 'literates' who decided what this should be. It was with this in view that the statutes of the Ntem-Kribi Tribal Union devoted two clauses to 'tribal genealogy', the tribal delegates being 'obliged to bring to the assembly the genealogy of their own clan, which will be read at the opening of the Congress', and which will 'represent the delegate's mandate' (Article 18), and those genealogies 'constituting the basis of the Tribal Union's archives' (Article 19). In Gabon, such was the confusion and so seriously impaired were their traditions, that little was known about the relations between clan fragments. Distinctions between clan and tribe were often vague (the same group being looked upon as a 'tribe' in Haut-Gabon and as a 'clan' in the coastal districts), so that they had become a matter of merely local importance. The clan relationships were therefore decided upon in a fairly arbitrary manner – several of our informants assured us that 'before the *Alar Ayôg* we did not know we were related to this or that group' – but the prestige of the written word legalized this state of affairs. It was among the leaders that the most lively disputes occurred: those from Bas-Gabon did their best to restrict the influence of those from the Woleu-Ntem by accusing them of having 'invented' the *Yémisèm* tribe, which had been one of the most active from the start.* The purpose, however, was clear: to bring together, under a single tribal appellation, the largest possible number of clans and fragments of clans. In the Woleu-Ntem, the *Yémisèm*, *Yémvâg*, *Yémödâg*, *Yéngwi* and *Ožip* succeeded in reuniting respectively twenty-eight, forty, eighteen, eleven and eight such groups; some of them even, as may be seen from the names of the incorporated groups, assimilated tribal remnants.

Such incorporations were supported by a very modernized

* This is a large group belonging to the Boulou of the Ntem (Cameroun).

version of the 'tribal legend' (often influenced by knowledge of the Bible) which was transcribed in the 'Book of the Tribe'. An example of this is the legend of the Ndôg, published under the title of *Endan Ayôg Ndôg*, which, after a short introduction, begins with the usual formula: 'We are going to make known to you how the Ndôg tribe was created, and the other tribes that are attached to it.' The long first part consists of an adaptation of a passage from the Bible entitled 'David, adulterer and murderer',[83] and then goes on to use the symbol of the tower of Babel to describe the unity of the human race before the dispersion that differentiated races and tribes. The second part describes the migrations (to Cameroun, and later to Gabon) and names the groups descended from the common stock, as well as their subsequent divisions. This is typical of the new legends entrusted to the care of the dignitaries chosen during the *bisulan* and passed on by them from village to village. Apart from these specific accounts, a very general kind of document was circulated, recalling the migrations of the various branches of the Fang tribe and proclaiming its unity. This contained a version adapted from the myth of the Fang migrations (the legend known as the 'Hole in the *adzap*'), which sought to justify unity by a tradition refashioned in terms of contemporary requirements and concluding with the words: 'We represent *only one part of our Negro race*.'* The more or less confused idea of tribal federation began to spread, and the old spirit of conquest and assimilation reappeared, some of the particularly active tribes endeavouring to absorb fragments of neighbouring peoples on the most varied pretexts.

In addition to these basic documents, the list of clans and the local legends, there were the 'statutes' or 'laws' of the tribe. Often preceded by a solemn declaration,† they consisted of a series of 'commandments', aimed at overcoming the breakdown of Fang society and inducing it to modernize itself, and reasserting the values necessary to strengthen social solidarity. These 'statutes' clearly reveal the ambivalent nature of the movement: on the

---

* 'Thus all of us, Fang, Yaoundé, Okak, Mévoumendem, Boulou and Ntoumou, are descended from the same father Afri Kara and from Kara Kouba Ta, Ta Ma and Ma Mgôo, and we form *one part of the Negro race*.'

† Thus the statues of the Yémisèm of Makokou are preceded by the following formula: 'God being He to whom all wisdom, power and intelligence belong, nothing must be begun or undertaken without first having asked him for his help.'

one hand a return to the values (race, blood and tribal brotherhood) which had been the strength of the old clan organization;
on the other, an affirmation of modern requirements in the field
of politics and economics. They provide for a period of education
during the dry season – for which the tribal dignitaries were made
responsible – that would instruct the young folk in the history
and genealogies of the tribe.* This teaching was of a very for-
malized kind, often based upon the method of questions and
answers used by the missionaries.† It should be noted that they
were often printed in French, not in dialect – which shows the
important part in the movement played by the 'literates', as well
as revealing the desire to represent the movement as an elaborate
reaction by people who were now civilized. The style in which
they are written, moreover, shows how much they were influenced
by the two main sources of 'literature' known to the Fang: school
books used by the missionaries, and official documents. In the
light of such literary influences, it is easier to understand the
bizarre character of this clan literature. [84]

Observers have emphasized the holiday atmosphere in the
villages when tribal meetings were taking place. The part of the
village where the *ésulan* was held was decorated with arches made
of interwoven branches, with a temporary shelter (*dubana*) put
up for the dignitaries of the tribe. The *ényêngé* dance, apparently
a recent invention, was performed at these gatherings, and seems
to have been their especial symbol. Unlike the old dances, where
the sexes were separated, it is a mixed dance, indicating the
tendency to new relations between men and women. The fact
that a number of texts describe it as 'a dance in which the women
do not strip' shows that it deliberately omits the obscene or erotic
gestures that used to accompany the traditional dances, whether
sacred or profane; and, in this respect, it reveals the puritanical
effect of missionary teaching. Nevertheless, despite these changes

---

* Cf. the statutes of the Yémisèm of Makokou: 'Courses are organized every dry
season to study the genealogy and history of the tribe. This is an extremely important
decision, for the history of the tribe includes the moral, intellectual, civic and
scientific facts that are suitable for young people to learn.'

† The following example is taken from the teaching notes of a dignitary of the
Yémisèm of Oyem: 'What race do you belong to? – We belong to the Yémisèm
tribe, because we all have the same blood. – Who brought you into the world? – It is
because of Missam Mivoġo that we should respect birth, etc.'

the dance retains its essentially social function. It is only performed at these tribal gatherings to proclaim the settlement of
matters concerning the clan groups and as a way of welcoming
the dignitaries of the tribe or honouring influential guests. It has
rightly been compared with the ancient *somana* dance which was
performed when a 'chief' or 'traditional judge' paid a visit and
which was regarded, since it was a preliminary to serious palavers,
as a 'dance of justice'.* Finally there were certain manifestations
directly symbolizing the unity of all the members of the tribe, in
which everyone joined in. The culminating point was the eating
of a communal meal, for it was said that 'by eating the same food
during the *ésulan* festivities our blood is mixed' (the Yémöžit of
Mitzik); while certain tribes insisted, at the start of the meeting,
that members of different clans 'should embrace like brothers'
(the Yémisèm of Oyem).

In accordance with the dynamism peculiar to Negro-African
societies, the movement had a religious as well as a political
aspect. The statutes of various tribes insisted upon obedience to
God, Nzamö, the vague deity who might just as well be the God
of the Christians as the God of the traditional cults; and, in many
districts, meetings could not begin until 'his name had been
invoked'.[85] At certain *bisulan* religious hymns were sung by the
Christian members, split up however into Catholics and Protestants, immediately after dancing the *ényêngé*. This was due to
Cameroun influences, particularly that of the American Mission
at Elat (near Ebolowa) which, through its teaching and the
circulation of its paper, *Méfoé*, printed in Boulou, had unintentionally created a kind of 'national' Christianity. Moreover, for
Westernized individuals, the acceptance of Christianity was the
indisputable mark of their transformation; in this respect, one of
our informants assured us that 'religion is a form of progress
introduced by civilization; it doesn't matter whether you are a
Protestant or a Catholic, so long as you are a Christian'.[86] This
insistence upon Christianity reveals the influence of the 'literates',
most of whom had been taught by the missionaries, and their

* In his unpublished *Rapport sur le regroupement des Fang*, Trezenem gives the
following description: 'A dance which required a hierarchy consisting of:
otsamedzang, someone responsible for keeping order; *everman*, a bodyguard; *monekule*,
a boy appointed to accompany him. During the dancing of the *somana* certain disputes
were settled.'

desire to represent the movement as being progressive – not just a return to traditional socio-cultural organizations. It should be added, however, as we shall show in Part III, that the development of African forms of Christianity was often bound up with the adoption of a nationalist outlook. In the case of the Fang, this was only true as regards the Cameroun groups. In Gabon, relations were much less favourable to the Christian elements; besides, there the Christian features of the *Alar Ayôg* movement had been modified or transformed to make it acceptable to members of the *Bwiti* cult. This brief account shows the extent to which the *ésulan* was able to sustain the atmosphere of exaltation and community characteristic of traditional festivities; in this way, it sought to give meaning and life to a tribal institution that had already deteriorated.*

The solidarity movement spread from Cameroun by stages, more or less following the lines of the old migrations. The tribal dignitaries appointed in one official district were responsible for introducing the *Alar Ayôg* into the neighbouring district. In the course of preparatory meetings they taught the historical and genealogical facts about the tribe, as well as the 'statutes' peculiar to it, and showed them how to dance the *ényêngé*. Once this teaching had been assimilated, the date of the *ésulan* could be fixed. The gathering was controlled by the dignitaries until a local leadership could be set up; and at the end of the festivities they were paid for the 'knowledge' they had imparted. Little by little the movement spread to almost all the villages of the Woleu-Ntem and the Ogooué-Ivindo, though scarcely touching the southern regions, where there was a state of extreme confusion and the Fang were much intermixed with 'strangers'. These regions, moreover, coincided more or less with those where wage labour was employed, and where the problems were very different from those confronting the cocoa country. It is understandable

* The following account is taken from an administrative report for the Ntem region. 'The *ésulan* in certain cases still retain the festive character referred to by M. Bertaut; they are held in daylight in various village squares that have been brightened up for the occasion; usually the local authorities are invited to the final session, and when I recently attended one of these, I was greeted on my arrival with the *ényêngé* dance. . . . Welcomed as an opportunity for dancing and rejoicing, they are looked upon primarily as popular gatherings for the serious discussion of matters concerning the community, particularly questions of marriage and the rate of marriage payments . . .' Ebolowa archives, 1948.

therefore that the movement did not arouse the same enthusiasm there, especially as it reached this last stage just when the administration was beginning to show its hostility.

Up to 1949–50, the results of consolidation were very conspicuous: villages had moved in order to regroup themselves according to their clan affinities (around Mitzik); huts were rebuilt and decorated according to the instructions of the tribal dignitaries; a number of villages put up notice-boards announcing the name of the *ayôg* to which they belonged,* and in some places (among the Cameroun Fang) even the houses had signs indicating the name of their tribe;† meetings were held to launch undertakings of common interest. These were the material manifestations of a whole number of activities intended to exalt the honour of the tribe and tribal brotherhood. The authorities were taken by surprise: for the first time they found themselves confronted by an organized popular movement that gave rise to a genuine mystique of Fang renaissance – so much so that certain officials professed to see 'foreign' influences at work.

(b) *The Creation of a Hierarchy*

The tribal hierarchy was created within the framework of the administrative divisions, all the most important positions being at district, canton and village level. The purpose was obviously to replace the appointed chiefs by authorities elected by the tribal assemblies. We have already pointed out that the aim of the whole movement was to resolve the problem of authority and to revive *a minimum of political initiative* in the smallest groups. The official chiefs were in no way deceived by what was happening and for the most part, in Cameroun as well as Gabon, were hostile to the movement. Many of the reports drawn up during the years 1947 and 1948, on the other hand, realized that the chiefs elected by the tribe (*jé ayôg*) exercised 'a powerful authority over the members of their groups, and represented a much more genuine power than those appointed by the colonial administration'. Most of the

---

* These were 'decorated with arches made of plaited palm leaves, surmounted by the Christian cross,' Political Report for Booué, March 1948.

† 'Among the Yékòmbò, all the women's huts have special inscriptions painted on the front. The purpose of the inscription is to inform any member of the tribe who happens to be passing through the village that they will be able to find food and lodging.' Report for the sub-division of Sangmélima, 1942.

dignitaries, moreover, did their best to prove that their power was effective: they controlled palavers, concerned themselves with restoring order in the villages and improving the plantations, and undertook to interpret the wishes of the villagers to the European officials; by their skilful tactics they managed to enlist the latter's support.

During the tribal gatherings, when the 'statutes' were being handed over, there was almost always some expression of obedience to the government. The slogan adopted by the Yémisèm of Makokou was the most striking example of this: 'High above all, the thrice blessed God; at the level of our hearts, the French administration and government; below this, at knee level, the tribe.' Every precaution was taken to prevent the movement being regarded as an attempt to secede or as an expression of xenophobia.

The hierarchy continually caused surprise by the terminology it employed and the multiplicity of duties it appeared to undertake. The titles given to the dignitaries were borrowed from the administrative and military organizations by which the colonizing society maintained its authority locally. This procedure, which some people derided as a childish parody and which others were disturbed by, seeing in it the germ of a subversive organization, has an interesting psychological aspect. It shows a weakness for those French words that emphasize the idea of power,* and also, by a kind of magical turn of thought, the need felt for having the former in order to achieve the latter; in addition, it reveals a concern to represent the clan movement as a progressive attempt to modernize the tribe and create 'civilized' institutions. Apart from the president and vice-president, who held the two most important offices with authority over all the members of the *ayôg* living in the district, there was also a whole hierarchy of governors, commandants, etc. at canton and village level, as well as 'technicians' – assessors (a kind of assistant in the law courts), plantation organizers, trade inspectors, commissioners responsible for public order, etc., not to mention a whole swarm of petty

* The statutes of the Yémisèm, of Makokou state clearly: 'At the head of each tribe there shall be a leader, an intelligent and powerful man to be known as President. The word President is borrowed from the French for there is no word in our language which expresses his function so clearly.'

officials. On top of this a number of positions were created for women – such as tribal president, or governor, and women's chief (*évèt mininga*) – and it was their function to organize and control female labour, to constitute a court of conciliation to deal with 'differences arising in the household', and to ensure that the men's meals were provided on a communal basis (certain tribes even envisaged penalties for those who held aloof), in order to show the unity of the group. All this was significant of the part that women were beginning to assume – no longer as a form of wealth, but as people.

This kind of hierarchy was not unlike that of the 'work teams' in Haiti, in the days when these were prosperous and powerful. In a study of the villagers of the Maribal valley, the ethnologist, Alfred Métraux, noted that all these organizations were 'miniature armies or republics', and that 'the peasant weakness for complicated hierarchies and high-sounding titles was given free rein'.[87] In Africa itself this phenomenon is widespread, and now well-known. In the Haut-Katanga region of the Congo, an eye-witness in 1936 referred to the 'swarms of organizations . . . which were causing the government some concern and which, with their statutes grossly parodying our own institutions, express their desire for discipline'. In 1944, in the Dagana sub-division in Senegal, the official in charge noted a modification of the organization by age groups: the various groups were forming federations, known as 'committees', at the village level. A hierarchy, comparable to that created by the Fang, was set up; there was a 'savings bank', supported by a system of subscriptions and fines; and the 'committee' was aiming to play a leading part in all undertakings of general interest, in the village courts and in the organization of great periodical festivities. An official report on this attempt to revive a traditional institution provides a pretty fair appraisal of it: 'Here we have what is essentially a symptom of the profound development among the rural population, a manifestation of the progressive outlook of the younger generation of black peasants.'[88]

These African examples show that a transformation of such traditional institutions as the 'fraternal age-group' and the clan was taking place *from within*. They reveal the emergence of new social strata, and express the outlook of those elements that were most aware of the state of dependence created by the colonial situation. The multiplicity of offices appears to signify *a desire for prestige and political responsibility* on the part of an increasing section of the village population; a desire asserted by the Fang through the movements for clan consolidation and the regrouping of villages. Moreover, according to some of our informants, many of the positions were created simply 'to give pleasure': they were essentially honorary titles, and only of any practical use during the *bisulan*. They may be seen as a precaution against a head-on clash with egalitarian tendencies, and an attempt to avoid any cause for jealousy. Nevertheless we must insist upon the fact that this revival of old organizations was only apparent; it was in no sense a question of 'counter-acculturation' as usually understood by anthropologists. These organizations were only used some-times in a quite arbitrary fashion, with a quite new meaning, determined by economic developments and the existing situation. Moreover, they were used at a higher level, which tended to create a sense of tribal unity at a time when tribal and clan anta-gonisms were in the ascendant, to encourage consolidation and the development of new forms of political organization in place of the existing fragmentation and arbitrarily imposed administra-tive organizations, to bring into being economic groupings (work teams, *ékip*, and cooperatives amongst the Cameroun Fang*) adapted to modern requirements, and to establish a type of authority that would restore initiative to the villagers and develop new social forces. What we have, then, is a veritable mutation, which, because the colonial authorities radically opposed it, only prolonged the state of crisis it sought to remedy.

(c) *Work Teams*

The introduction of work teams (*ékip biséñö* from *ésa*, 'work', 'labour') was due to the initiative of the clans in the Cameroun whose economy was more highly developed and who had the temporary advantage of being on good terms with the local authorities. Whereas in western Africa, amongst the great agricultural peoples, this type of organization had long been in

* In 1945, during one of their *ésulan*, the Yé-Mbong declared that they wanted an 'association of planters' to be formed within the group, which would be responsible for putting cocoa growing on a business footing.

existence, here it represented an innovation arising from very definite conditions. The work team encouraged adaptation to the new labour legislation, which had made forced labour illegal, by offering its services for carrying out public works; thus, in the Ebolowa region, each team undertook two ten-day periods of work a year. The purpose was to demonstrate in the most practical way the constructive nature of clan consolidation – and in this way to win the government's agreement. Furthermore, it was an attempt to organize the youngest and most dynamic elements who, owing to the disappearance of the traditional cults and associations, no longer received any collective education.[89] The setting up of the teams was carried through 'with great enthusiasm'; they used to set out for work preceded by a brass band and special banners, and the tasks they undertook were of considerable value; at Ebolowa, for instance, they put in a sewage system. The fact that, by 1947, there were no less than seventy-nine teams in the single sub-division of Ebolowa is evidence of the interest the movement aroused. In the following year, in the canton of Ndou-Libi (in the Sangmélima region), every tribal fragment had one or two teams, involving altogether 830 men, that is to say, more than a third of the 'adult' male population. The government, disturbed by the rapid growth of these new groups, did their utmost to prevent them from becoming a state within a state; and this in itself bears witness to the dynamic quality of these young men's organizations.

In Gabon, the only place where work teams functioned was the Oyem district, among the Yémisèm and the Yéngwi. They undertook to make a road from Zorongone to Oyem, to build a school at Ebiane, to be responsible for the upkeep of the district capital and to help the younger folk improve their cocoa plantations. The decline of the groups was bound up with the vicissitudes of the *Alar Ayôg* movement, and the lack of material support. The creation of the Yéngwi team was the work of a dignitary who had come from Cameroun to promote clan solidarity; the president elected during the first *ésulan* was in charge of the team and organized their work, while a new official, *évèt mbarlè biséñö* (supervisor-in-chief) saw that it was carried out. The Yémisèm team in Oyem, which was organized on the same elementary lines, never became very active.

In Gabon the work teams did not play much part. This was because the main effort had gone into rebuilding the clan and tribal organization, which had been much harder hit than in Cameroun. Above all it was due to the still very rudimentary state of the economy: there was no 'bourgeoisie' of planters and business men strong enough to influence the economy and give it direction; nor was there the same need for economic development and the strict allocation of work.

(d) *Solidarity within the* Ayôg

Solidarity between 'brothers of the tribe' was one of the most frequently proclaimed principles of the movement. The statutes proclaimed it in stereotyped phrases: 'Each for all and none for himself. . . . If your brother suffers an accident, help him cheerfully . . .' (the Yémisèm of Makokou). 'The Yémvâg family swears to help any of its members who fall upon evil days' (the Yémvâg of Booué). All such 'commandments' bear the imprint of Christian teaching, which had changed the way in which clan morality was expressed; one finds this not only in the above precepts but also in those condemning adultery, theft and murder. In practice, solidarity took the form of mutual assistance when a hut had to be built or plantations to be cultivated or extended, etc. But, thanks to the modest funds (*mbâk*, from the French *banque*) available to the *Ayôg*, there was a tendency for it to take the form of financial help.

The *mbâk* consisted of sums levied during the *bisulan*, when every member of the tribe had to make a financial contribution, and of the fines that had to be paid whenever the tribal laws were broken. The management of this money was entrusted to the *mbâk mözö*, or banker, under the guidance of the president, who periodically checked the accounts. In theory, the *mbâk* was supposed to help any member of the clan in need of financial assistance (in fact it was a low interest loan, usually at 5 per cent) to enable him to complete his marriage payment, settle his poll tax, pay fines imposed by the European authorities, or provide treatment for a sick person. It also had to contribute to the needs of orphans and help any young boy who had an opportunity of attending one of the 'big schools'. It tried, too, to prevent the practice of usury within the *Ayôg*, though in the long run this tended to limit its effectiveness: the most influential elements, often those who had been appointed to important positions because they had made the highest contribution to the *mbâk* at the time of the *bisulan*, were not prepared to see this source of income permanently cut off. At Makokou, the Yémisèm organized a Tribal Security Fund, as part of the native Social Assurance Society, on the lines of the social security system introduced by the government. Its title indicates a desire on the part of the villagers to participate directly in the management of their own affairs, even at the level of such restricted groups as the village or tribal fragment. It was a phenomenon similar to that observed in Senegal when the associations were first set up, to which we have already referred. Not long after, a local official commented on the profound change that had occurred as a result of this 'embryo budget'; its initiators, he said, 'had invented a new form of municipal organization, much closer to our own conception of the commune'.

(e) *The* Alar Ayôg *movement and subsequent reactions*

A study of the movement as a whole reveals not only the motives that inspired it, but also the genuine support that it received from the majority of the villagers. It is worth asking what reasons were given, and what pressures exerted, to obtain this backing. The arguments put forward were inevitably ambiguous, since it was necessary to obtain agreement from all social categories. Thus a movement that was created by the 'Young Fang' appears to have emanated from the 'Old Fang'. At every opportunity, it asserted its wish to collaborate with the colonial government, while at the same time doing all it could to weaken its grip – which shows how the dynamic of social reorganization is *directly related* to the dynamic of the struggle for autonomy.

Judging by the public opinion polls we carried out, it appears that this line of argument was put forward because of a *general* feeling that the Fang community was in a serious state of 'crisis'. This feeling was confused but strong. In the first place, there was a conviction that the population was declining because 'the race had become mixed', because the law of exogamy had been transgressed and sexual morality relaxed – great importance was attached to the fact that the prohibition of sexual intercourse during the daytime was no longer observed, probably because this break with the past corresponded with an increase in adultery. Secondly, there was a desire to put an end to the uncontrolled competition for wives, which was the starting point of most disputes ('all the divisions between us are due to trouble about women'). Thirdly, as a result of contact with the outside world, there had been the discovery that the standard of living was very poor, and a determination to improve it through better economic organization. And, lastly, there was the realization that the fragmentation and dispersion of the clans, and the consequent weakening of authority, facilitated colonial domination.

The movement was represented as being a *total solution* that would enable the Fang groups to recover their lost power – the concept of the *Ayôg* was at the very heart of this bid for revival. And in order to arouse enthusiasm, the leaders turned to a past which, though more or less falsified, nevertheless recalled the prestige they had enjoyed during the period of conquest – alluding to the communal migrations, to the power of the lineages, then numerous and united, to the kinship existing between the members of the tribe and to the identity of 'blood' and 'race'. Mutual aid between 'brothers of the *Ayôg*' was represented as a sign that unity had been restored; and the threat that was held over the heads of recalcitrants was precisely that of being 'turned out of the tribe', since they would no longer be entitled to be housed or helped by the members of their own group. This illustrates the emotional use that was made of this concept, despite the fact that both tribe and kinship had been seriously weakened; and it also explains the support of the most traditionalist elements, who interpreted the movement as a return to the past when no one challenged the established authorities. But alongside these somewhat reactionary arguments others were advanced that corresponded to the desire for advance and the hopes of the 'progressives'. The aim of the latter was, primarily, to be recognized as 'civilized beings'. One of the dignitaries told us: 'To prevent us from making *Alar Ayôg* is the same as wanting us to remain savages.' This demand constituted the very basis of the political responsibilities that they were anxious to assume. All the statutes express a concern for modernization: compulsory education for all the children, proposals for schools and public health measures, propaganda for building hospitals and for more rapid economic development.

Thus the movement had two aspects, one 'reactionary' and the other 'revolutionary'. Though the initiative was everywhere in the hands of the modernists, the relationship between the two tendencies varied from region to region; the second growing weaker the further south one went from Cameroun to the Ogooué, from the districts that were in process of economic development to those that were still undeveloped. It was in the latter that the conflict was most actively concerned with Christianization, with the regulating of marriage and of women's position in society. At the same time, the movement everywhere revealed the same hankering for consolidation – as opposed to a process of atomization – and for the setting up of a system of social control that would counteract family and political disorganization and the weakening of the basic laws. This attempt at reconstruction also gave rise to the first large-scale move to throw off the state of dependence to which they had been subjected.

By 1950, however, everyone was convinced that the movement was dying without having brought about the changes anticipated. To understand what had happened we must consider the interplay of internal and external influences affecting modern Fang society. One of our informants went straight to the point: 'I didn't accept office, because I knew the Fang were not sufficiently tenacious.' And a number of villages did, in fact, adopt an attitude of reserve or indifference once the government revealed its opposition. Moreover, the bitter competition for office revived ancient antagonisms between tribes, clans and lineages; it destroyed the unity of the movement, and it was difficult to exalt the tribe without immediately reviving ancient rivalries. The behaviour of the political parties in their efforts to save the movement also encouraged splits: the leaders of the Gabonese Fang did their best to prevent the Cameroun leaders from winning power (by playing on the old colonial hostility between the peoples of Gabon and Cameroun) and in this way cut off the Gabonese lineages from the most dynamic centres of activity; the Gabonese leaders quarrelled amongst themselves, thus giving rise to two different factions, that of the Gabonese Joint Committee in Libreville, and that of the Gabonese Democratic and Social Union in Uyem. Lastly, it appears that in Gabon the tribe did not provide a suitable framework for modernization and adaptation; despite all attempts to consolidate it, it remained an artificial unit; owing to the fragmentation of the groups – which had gone so far that only a radical popular upheaval could improve matters.

The reactions of the colonizing society to tribal revival sustained and aggravated the confusion, directly or indirectly. In the first stages (in Cameroun, at the time of the chiefdom reforms, and in Gabon, immediately after the Pahouin Congress) the government behaved tolerantly, seeing an opportunity of restoring order among the Fang, and possibly of resolving the crisis of authority that had been thwarting its activities for so long. During this phase, every *ésulan* was the occasion for solemn manifestations of loyalty, with the tricolor flag much in evidence; then, as the organization of the movement became stronger and its intention of establishing tribal federation was proclaimed, the government either withdrew or became hostile. This second phase started with its refusal to recognize the statutes of the Ntem-Kribi Tribal Union in Cameroun, and not long afterwards 'official' Gabon adopted a similar policy. During this period, some local officials warned the higher authorities that the movement appeared to have become simply a 'nationalist political organization', closely associated with 'groups' said to be under Communist influence. It is scarcely possible for social reorganization, *especially when it assumes a modern form*, to be achieved within the framework of a typical colonial situation: it soon reaches a point where it appears to constitute a threat to the dominant society, arousing its opposition on pretexts that are often purely stereotyped. On the other hand, an innovation like the *Bwiti*, which accepts traditional principles of organization, which conceals itself behind a cultural facade that is not easily penetrated, and which develops in semi-secrecy, is far less open to attack – although it arouses the same kind of reaction amongst the colonizing society.

The Christian missions were all in favour of a movement that encouraged its members to be Christians and taught them that man's primary obligation was 'obedience to God's will'. Moreover, in Cameroun, its principal organizer was an ex-Protestant minister, a Boulou by birth, who had been educated at a mission station near Ebolowa; with a team mainly consisting of Protestants, but also including Catholic representatives, he created the Tribal Union. In general, it is clear that the most dynamic elements belonged to the reformed church: an official report of that period expressed the opinion that the native Protestants 'are serious cadres, more dependable, and harder to manipulate' than the Catholics. Once it appeared that there was a danger of Protestants dominating the movement, the Catholics began to show signs of withdrawing; so much so, in fact, that a civil servant responsible for the Fang in Spanish Guinea had no scruples about attributing the movement to the machinations of a foreign Protestant mission which, 'anxious to counteract the influence of the Catholic clergy, has dreamt of appointing, with the help of a highly organized tribal movement, clan chiefs who will give it their support'.[90] Thus the religious question became yet another divisive factor: the Catholic missions, after a moment's hesitation, decided that it was necessary to adopt the same attitude as that of the government authorities. Both outside and inside the groups, forces hostile to tribal consolidation carried the day; especially in Gabon where competent leaders were far too few.

The movement had partially failed, but the issues that had provoked it remained, as did the determination of the modernist elements to find a remedy for the Fang 'crisis'. A project put forward at the time by the Deputy Aubame, a Fang from the Woleu-Ntem, seeking to ensure modernization within the framework of 'regrouped villages' so as to create units of an adequate size, aroused fresh hopes of a solution. A mystique of 'village regroupment' developed in the Woleu-Ntem which was often barely distinguishable from the *Alar Ayôg* movement. Word went out that it was now necessary to build villages comparable to those in the French countryside; this involved not only consolidation – now desired by the villagers, whereas the earlier attempts at regrouping had only been achieved by constraint and had not caught on – but also a programme of practical demands (for schools, dispensaries and markets) and reforms (politically, the setting up of an elected municipal authority; economically, the organization of producers). This project, which respected the territorial divisions created by the colonial administration, was no longer concerned with tribal organization, but sought to recapture the two basic units that were dependent upon native control: the village and the canton. The purpose of the proposed reforms was to ensure, within the limits of the existing organization, an improvement in the standard of living and acceptance by the villagers of a certain number of political and economic responsibilities.[91]

Thanks to the Pahouin Congress and the attempts to reorganize the clans, not only did the project meet with a favourable reception in the Woleu-Ntem, it also benefited from the skilful propaganda carried out by the associations and their local representatives. The support of the 'literates', the so-called 'Europeanized elements' and the younger generation proved to be decisive; they felt themselves to be working in a field that no longer looked to tradition but to an understanding of 'European behaviour', and this strengthened their position; they expressed their determination to participate in the 'village councils' that were to be created, and insisted upon being allowed to work side by side with the traditional authorities (the heads of the *nd'è bòt*).

To carry out the programme would have required considerable financial resources (for which they appealed to the government) and a profound upheaval of the people and the socio-economic structure. The reservations of the authorities were due to lack of funds, to the fear of disorder having a bad effect on the production of cocoa, to an unwillingness to create villages too densely populated to produce sufficient food by subsistence farming, and, in the last resort, to a definite scepticism as to the possibility of 'settling' large village groups. The Woleu-Ntem peasants interpreted this lack of confidence as yet another indication of the opposition of the authorities to any attempt to rebuild and modernize society. They therefore found new ways of demonstrating their support for this new hope of resolving their most urgent problems: bringing pressure to bear upon the local authorities, moving villages in order to create larger units, constructing a motor road to link up with the main road from Gabon to Cameroun and, at a higher level, actively defending the project in the 'representative assemblies'. From the propaganda campaigns it was clear that all the 'modernists' were involved in organized activity, the leaders of the regional associations as well as those of the Gabonese Democratic and Social Union. They voiced the opinions of a minority which, freed from traditional constraint, aspired to a role in society that was no more available to it under the colonial administration than in the traditional social organization.

This minority, which asserted its leadership in the course of this new initiative and aimed at radical social reform, nevertheless had to win the support of the traditionalist majority. It took up once more the arguments that had been used during the movement for tribal consolidation: the need to revive the large villages of the past which had once been the source of Fang power, and to settle their old disputes in order to restore 'the brotherhood of the *Ayôg*'. Sometimes it resorted to such exaggerated slogans as 'It is better to go and join your brothers than to stay on your plantation', and it exalted the virtue of obeying the Deputy, who was able to speak for all the Fang.

In order to assess this initiative and examine the practical possibilities of realizing the project, we were invited to organize two enquiries, which were carried out mainly in the Mitzik and Oyem districts.[92] It at once became clear that the outlook of the villagers varied considerably. This was due to the uneven socio-economic development: in the Oyem district, we found general support for regrouping, because the majority of villagers expected either to obtain economic advantages from it (possibilities of extending their cocoa plantations and improving marketing conditions) or to have their new political demands satisfied; in the Mitzik district, social disorganization and the low level of investment meant that the project was tolerated rather than accepted, whereas the *Alar Ayôg* movement, which relied upon more traditional solutions, had a large following. The opinion polls we conducted among the groups in the Oyem district also revealed that, although the region was more exposed to modernist influences, the 'revolutionary' aspects of the undertaking were checked by the persistence of the traditional type of social relations. The creation of 'regrouped villages' was only accepted on the basis of tribal unity; but within this unity the antagonisms between clans and lineages continued to operate, often kept alive by economic competition, rivalry for wives and disputes

9

about leadership. Here we have a tragic example of a community that can neither revert to a degenerate traditional organization nor, because of the control to which it is subjected, carry through the necessary reforms: all it can do is accumulate antagonisms. The ending of colonization in 1960 is still too recent to have produced a final solution; all the more so because it simply substituted for a dominant 'colonizing' minority a 'new native class' which is also a minority. It should be noted however that, in the Woleu-Ntem, the resettlement movement did not stop: between 1956 and 1960 'large villages', comparable to towns and admirably planned, continued to be built in the vicinity of Bitam, Oyem and Mitzik.

III
THE DIRECTION OF
SOCIO-CULTURAL CHANGE
IN THE FANG COMMUNITY

While it is true that Fang society changed profoundly during the colonial period, it should not be assumed that the agencies responsible for this only operated for the worse. Deterioration cannot go beyond a certain point – varying according to individual circumstances – without compensatory processes coming into play or attempts at reorganization achieving more or less lasting success. There was therefore a twofold movement of acceptance or of submission to the agents of social change and renewal, though for reasons that are inherent in the very nature of Fang society and the colonial situation the former outweighed the latter.

Some of these reasons fall within a single category, which has been studied by English and American sociologists concerned with the problems of the so-called under-developed countries and with the conditions of 'progress' and 'modernization'. Others represent a field that academic sociologists have as yet scarcely begun to tackle; as far as France is concerned, only the economist F. Perroux has advanced the idea of a *dominant economy*, and indicated the *effects of domination*. It is with both these approaches in mind that we have attempted to analyze the 'Fang situation', which we have already described in some detail because it is important to combine an overall view with a body of carefully attested fact.

A society of this kind, as it exists today and in the light of its history over the past fifty years, raises a preliminary series of problems that must at least be mentioned: those concerned with the breaking down of group exclusiveness, those created by the decline of 'clan democracy' and those resulting from new technological requirements.

I. THE DESTRUCTION OF 'FRONTIERS' BETWEEN
SEMI-AUTONOMOUS GROUPS

We have seen that the traditional groups constituted semi-autonomous units, able to form alliances through marriage, but more often finding themselves in competition rather than in cooperation. In many cases equilibrium could only be established within these units, which had been organized for the purpose of conquest and were semi-independent and small in size. Direct relations between the members of these groups and 'strangers' were limited by their sense of insecurity, while relations with the outside world remained the *exclusive* responsibility of outstanding individuals and specialized associations. Colonization encouraged or imposed the breaking down of this almost total exclusiveness.

Apart from the part played by pacification and the improvement of communications, this phenomenon of 'opening up' was largely dependent upon economic development. Whereas the rudimentary trade of the early colonial period only brought a comparatively small volume of goods into circulation and was of a purely collective nature, the introduction of a monetary economy led to a continually increasing circulation of currency and 'merchandise', individualizing competition and the search for sources of income. We have emphasized the fact that the Fang villagers, who to begin with only became wage workers by compulsion, later became so of necessity owing to the growing importance of production for the market. Thus the basic mechanisms of society were affected, whilst the traditional authorities were incapable of mastering the complex processes resulting from developments over which they had little or no control.

The consequences of this situation were particularly serious in the case of inter-relations between economic phenomena and the principles governing the circulation of wives. In contemporary Fang society, the capitalization of wives still remains the means of acquiring (or maintaining) prestige and rank – at once a survival from the period when power was primarily determined by the number of men and a consequence of the part played by women as producers. The provision of marriage payments remains the basic, and today almost unique, condition for this capitalization. Marriage payments may be seen as one of the last, if not *the* last, obstacles to free competition. They are looked upon by women as a factor of stability (in the absence of traditional social and religious forms of protection), and as a sign that the wife's personal worth is recognized. The men are in favour of them because they see in them either an indisputable proof of the legality of marriage or, if they happen to be 'givers of wives', an opportunity for doing business. They will continue to be accepted as long as polygamy is practised, and as long as marriage takes place within the legal and social context of custom. However, and it is at this point that disequilibrium occurs, the circulation of marriage payments – in cash and merchandise of considerable value – has acquired all the characteristics of an economic transaction.

The system has been maintained despite the fact that its effective functioning requires more or less closed lineages and a scarcity of *external* wealth.* The development of a monetary economy is radically destroying these conditions, particularly as it is not yet well enough established to permit of capital accumulation in the form of landed property, real estate or commercial enterprise. *It has gone at once too far and not far enough.* Under these conditions, as we have seen, a wife becomes in some ways a commodity, and the marriage payment a price; an increase in the amount of money in circulation, such as occurred with the extension of cocoa production in the Woleu-Ntem, leads to the inflation of marriage payments. Here the market economy was introduced into a social environment still based upon kinship, affinity and the physical energy of the family group; to begin with it was bound to have a destructive effect, to become a blind alley. The competition for wives became all the keener owing to the greater possibilities of acquiring *individual* sources of income, and to the considerable gap between the size of incomes and the volume of goods actually consumed. It is important to remember that the total amount of marriage payments, though continually increasing, represented a capital that was used unproductively, since its sole purpose was to regulate the allocation of wives. It

* The regular functioning of the traditional 'marriage exchange' depended upon strict control of the marriageable women as well as of the trade goods and symbols circulating in the opposite direction. It therefore presupposed the existence of 'spheres' of marriage exchange, controlled by a small number of outstanding individuals.

is undoubtedly in this respect that the maladjustment created by the opening up of Fang society to a money economy first made itself felt. This can only be overcome insofar as the 'biological' and mythical determination of human relationships disappears and is replaced by the *real* relationships imposed by modern economic and cultural conditions; in short, when these conditions have acquired sufficient dynamism to produce a fundamental social mutation.

Schematically speaking it might be said that there are two predominant types of problem: those arising from the difficulties experienced by a society in which the various elements are adjusted on a basis of collective action and reciprocity of integrating all forms of individual action and competition; and those that result from the deterioration of semi-autonomous groups and the widening of the field of social relations. The latter process gives rise to initiatives aimed at *defining new social areas* and tending towards unity; and all the projects that originated with the Fang reveal this tendency. The *Bwiti* was an attempt at 'consolidation' under the aegis of a syncretistic religion – a sort of monotheism, influenced by Christianity, that broadened the basis of the ancient cults and reorganized the mythical content implicit in them. The clan revival, with its objective of tribal federation, had similar unitary ambitions, though expressed in terms of modern political concepts and a tacit recognition of Christianity. An orientation of this nature was almost bound to result from the unifying role that, in their own interests, the administration and the missionaries sought to play.

There were many obstacles, however, to all such attempts to achieve unity. Starting from a common socio-cultural basis, the various regions of the Fang country were subject to significant differentiations as a result of local conditions, and this meant that they were not all equally successful in adopting the same innovations. The apparent agreement was often based upon a misunderstanding. On the other hand, 'micro-particularisms' were always able to find expression on one pretext or another, whereas the Fang villager had scarcely any opportunity of making the necessary adjustments. He was caught up in an administrative system and subjected to a form of direct control that operated against any initiative on his part; all the more effectively in that traditional Fang society had no organizations that could offset this influence. At the same time, the difficulties must not be exaggerated: processes had been set in motion that were to involve the transformation of this society in the direction of a greater unity and effectiveness.

II. THE DECLINE OF 'CLAN DEMOCRACY'

We have already mentioned the features of Fang society that were responsible for its 'virile democracy', for the egalitarian tendency to be found within the groups. In this respect, the significant points of equilibrium were: the way in which the young men (representing military power) acted as a counterweight to the generation of the 'elders' (possessing political and religious authority); the fact that rank was determined by seniority, which gave any mature man (*nyamòrò*) a social importance primarily based upon age;* the quasi-equality existing between members of the 'village council' and the fact that the authority of a notability was primarily dependent upon circumstances, and closely related to personal ability.

The colonial situation and the consequent economic changes definitely weakened this system. When the government created chiefdoms and established a hierarchy between them by basing them upon a specific territory (village, district or canton), it introduced a dual principle of organization that was fundamentally alien. Among the Fang, these administrative chiefdoms were from the start completely at odds with custom. This explains why the position was mainly filled by men who were 'put forward' by the real leaders of the groups, or by individuals who were anxious to make use of it for personal ends. In some cases, their right to collect taxes and their extensive judicial authority, backed up by the colonial apparatus, favoured the emergence of a *quasi-feudal* form of power. An official report of January 1937 mentions signs of this: abuses in the collection of the capitation tax, use of government loans to obtain free labour, exacting of fees 'for

* Among the Bantu of South Africa, promotion to adult manhood was marked by a custom involving a material symbol, 'the putting on of the wax crown'. The notion of rank being connected with age seems to be widespread. Cf. H. A. Junod: *Mœurs et coutumes des Bantous*, vol. I, Paris, 1936.

conducting palavers';[1] and to this should be added the fact that the chiefs could obtain government assistance in establishing a powerful economic position for themselves, notably by increasing their agricultural holdings. The latter did not occur frequently, however, thanks to the powerful resistance of the lineages to any such extension of 'feudalism'.

The clan movement exposed the seriousness of the crisis of authority. It formulated, with considerable clarity, precise demands: the need for an effective native authority at a higher level than the village, acceptance of a straightforward differentiation of function (political, judicial and economic), and the setting up of a native administration. Thanks to the activities of the 'literate' elements, the exercise of power was now seen from a modern point of view, and both in this and other ways the movement represented an experiment in establishing a bureaucracy within the framework of the clan. This is only one example of the multiple implications of this enterprise; it showed, as the movement for modernization of the villages was to do later, how persistently the progressive minority sought to establish itself as a governing elite. And, indeed, it is upon the number and energy of this minority, and therefore upon the country's economic and cultural development, that the whole future of the Fang depends.

The question that arose was whether these progressive elements would succeed in maintaining their position as leaders. The political void, resulting from the official chiefs' lack of authority, favoured them in this respect; as did their position as an opposition. On the other hand, distrust of any kind of power established on a permanent footing and not under more or less continual popular control, coupled with the ill repute in which the very notion of 'chieftainship' was held when seen in an administrative context, had a beneficial effect. The clan movement revealed not only an intense competition for office, but also the precariousness of the authority achieved by most office-holders. This may be seen from one of the 'Questions and Answers' used in their propaganda by the Yémisèm of the Oyem district.

'Q.–What threatens to destroy our tribal religion?'

'A.–What threatens to destroy our tribal religion is disobedience and the election of several presidents.'

This was followed by a number of 'commandments', indicating the same approach: 'We must respect our superiors in the same way that our children respect us; we must never be jealous of a brother who has become president and maintains order within the tribe'.[2] It is clear that the old attitudes to power persisted and, *outside the traditional framework*, served as a brake upon the re-organization required by the new social relations. The men who acquired some kind of position were: those who stood out as *conciliators* – one might almost say as 'creators of law', since they imbued customary law with the requisite inflexibility; those who contributed to the material development of more or less extended groups; and those who could hand on to the group the social and political experience they had gained elsewhere. At the time of the clan movement, certain tribes, such as the Yémisèm and the Yéngwi, were urged to choose their officers solely on grounds of 'authority', that is to say because of their ability to settle the disputes that inevitably increase in any society 'in transition'. Considerable importance was also attached to anyone capable of suggesting new methods of village administration (those who could read and write became clerks in the clans' business affairs), and this was a sign of the profound changes that were taking place amongst certain sections of the Fang. Moreover, our investigations convinced us that an economically powerful individual could enjoy genuine prestige, provided he was able to create equally favourable economic conditions for the group – by establishing a 'market', attracting trade or initiating improved methods of production, etc. This was the modern form of the prestige once enjoyed by the *nkumakuma* or the giver of *bilaba*;* a rich man set the pace of village economy, and eventually came to be looked upon as a kind of 'friendly society' for those who were worse off.

As an example of what we mean, here is a brief description of two such leaders whom we knew some ten years ago: one with a growing influence that eventually became nation-wide, the other

---

* Cf. J. Guilbot, 'Le bilaba', in *Journ. Soc. des Africanistes*, XXI, 2, 1951, pp. 172–3: 'A notable really deserves the name when he has distinguished himself at the *bilaba*. . . . The authority of many of the Bulu chiefs and the respect in which they are held are in large part due to their exploits at the *bilaba*. . . . Wealthy men who are in a position to assist those who are in distress . . . are involved in a public and private undertaking.'

known to a smaller number of groups. M. was a Fang from southern Gabon, belonging to the Éssòké clan. He had had a comparatively advanced education and was able to use it to study customary law and analyse the urgent problems confronting the Fang community. His attainments attracted the attention of the colonial authorities, who made him a canton chief. Having been born in one of the regions most seriously affected by social decline and the fragmentation of groups, he soon realized that the first job to be tackled was to re-establish the links between individuals and between the smaller social groups. He recognized in the *Bwiti* cult an effective instrument for the purpose; and there can be no doubt that he did everything he could to achieve a leading position in it,[3] and quickly grasped the fact that the various 'parishes' could become organized cells, free from official control. His activities became suspect and in 1933 he was dismissed from his position as chief, which was the beginning of a period of quarrelling with the colonial authorities that soon won him the support of the less amenable Fang. By 1947, the time of the Pahouin Congress, his influence over a considerable part of the Fang people could no longer be ignored; he took part in the debates and tried to get himself recognized as leader. His unique prestige among the Fang people – extending to the most remote regions – was due to the great skill with which he won the support of the most 'backward', as well as of the 'modernist', elements. M. understood how to turn an electoral struggle into a competition between magical and religious methods, and how to base his esentially political activity upon the power wielded by the *Bwiti* in Bas-Gabon. In order to give meaning to such a radically new type of organization as a political party, he did not hesitate to transform it into an instrument that could function within the framework of everyday life, adapting his actions both to customary rule and to modern attempts at cooperation. In the last resort, M. owed his influence not merely to his oppositional stand and initiative, but also to the way he succeeded in exalting the concept of 'the Fang people'.

If one attempts to define the reasons for this exceptional personal influence, one must take into account his position as a symbol of opposition to colonial authority, his ability to make up his mind quickly as to the possibilities offered by every socio-cultural innovation (the *Bwiti* cult and the clan movement), and the skill with which he succeeded in giving political action an ambivalence that enabled him to appeal both to the old and the young Fang. He knew how to project his modernist ideas in a form that would be familiar to those still bound by custom. Thus he was able to compete for influence with the first elected representatives, who relied upon a system controlled by the colonial government and were not seen as an explicit symbol of the entire Fang people. His success led to his becoming the first architect of Gabonese independence and a national leader on authoritarian lines – though he was to discover his limitations when confronted by the representatives of racial minorities, and by the rise of young intellectuals and technicians.

Z.O., born in the Médouneu district, though still a young man of thirty in 1950, had nevertheless acquired real influence over a section of the people. Brought up by a Christian mission, he soon obtained an official post, which encouraged the village people to accept him as intermediary since he was on good terms with the colonial authorities, and they enabled him to study local questions and acquire a working knowledge of administrative methods. In addition to his leadership of the Christianized and 'modernist' elements, Z.O. succeeded in combining it with a more traditional appeal. On the one hand he impressed people by his skill in settling differences; on the other, he achieved an outstanding position in one of the most important *Bwiti* 'parishes'. At the time of the clan movement, he managed to become 'President' of all the clans and lineages of the Yémisèm tribe; a leaflet supporting his election stressed his 'good behaviour', his 'determination to serve the whole Yémisèm tribe', and the 'knowledge' that fitted him to act 'as intermediary between the government and the tribe'.[4] This many-sidedness, his capacity for influencing the various tendencies that were then actuating the Fang community, was one of the factors that helped to extend his authority beyond the limits of 'kinship'.

However, although these two examples might suggest that the leaders succeeded in establishing their authority over fairly extensive groups, it should be added that the number and efficacy of such new representatives for a long time remained limited. Very early on, the centrifugal forces were predominant, preventing every attempt to concentrate power. Deterioration of the physical basis of Fang society, the weakening of the mythical context and the still active role of kinship – all these had the effect of retarding the appearance of new social categories and the rise of new leaders. There was an imbalance between society's requirements and the actual possibilities of more rapid adaptation. The hold of kinship remained such that it hindered the accumulation of wealth by some and of power by others; it continued to slow down the organization of groups outside its boundaries, and to impose a notion of obligation towards one's 'kin' at the very moment when the notion of 'public service' should have been paramount. So great was the imbalance, that it was a question not only of conservatism becoming more and more formal, but also of a conservatism that was even more highly prized because it preserved the last traces of the traditional edifice.

III. PROBLEMS ARISING FROM NEW TECHNICAL REQUIREMENTS

The development of cash crops – the cocoa plantations in the Woleu-Ntem – was a technical innovation, the relative success of which was facilitated by the villagers' desire to avoid as far as possible the necessity of working for wages, that was to have great consequences because of the stimulus it gave to the market during the post-war years, and the increasing need to have access to money. It was in this way that the Fang eventually became genuine farmers. The technique of growing cocoa* was easily acquired, but owing to the small inducement to increase the size of plantations and the lack of interest in improving them by better treatment of the trees and improved methods of fermentation, drying and seasoning, it remained at a low level for a long time. This was a strictly technical problem arising from the inadequate education of the peasants and the unsatisfactory methods put at their disposal. But, as we shall see, it was not merely a technical question, inasmuch as it required a higher level of organization on

---

* Cf. G. Perrault: 'Les Fang du pays Yaoundé', in *op. cit.*: 'This is a crop that suits the native marvellously. All he has to do is to clear a suitable area of scrub, plant the cocoa trees, and then, when the beans have ripened, harvest them once a year.' The drying and preparation of the beans is carried out with the help of women.

the part of the producers – the thought of which scared the business men engaged in buying and exporting the cocoa.

The mere fact of introducing an export crop involved a new relationship between men and the land. The latter assumed a new value once it became a source of revenue and not simply of subsistence farming, as may be seen from the fact that in Cameroun, where various related peoples had already settled down to producing cocoa, it was possible during the cocoa crisis of 1928 to surrender plantations in payment of debts. This practice shows how highly land planted with cocoa trees was valued.* Moreover, this right to a plantation on the grounds of having cultivated the land was a permanent right, established outside customary law (the plantations had been developed under pressure from the local administration) and as a result of individual initiative. It had only gradually assumed importance, and it did not apply to more than a small area of the land under cultivation, but the circumstances under which it occurred meant that it had made *the notion of private ownership* a part of customary law. We referred to this evolution previously when describing some of the practical manifestations of the new right; and we also drew attention to the fact that one of the demands put forward at the Pahouin Congress related to official recognition of these 'rural concessions'. The effect of cash crops was to stabilize the population, while at the same time the rights they created led to the carrying out of a survey showing more clearly the distinction between land belonging to the village and individual plantations. In principle the right to choose where one would plant cocoa trees was not affected: it was enough if the headman of the village gave his consent, provided this did not lead to competition or prevent the extension of the village, etc – indeed, the right involved an obligation to develop the land properly.

Even when the idea of property in land was accepted and became a source of income, it was always dependent upon the ability to develop the land. An 'important man' who was in a position to employ wage labour could thus base his authority upon his ownership of land – and among the Cameroun Fang some of

---

* Although, traditionally, 'the land belongs to whoever takes it; it has no value in itself and is not accepted as security for debt'. Cf. League of Nations Report, 1922 (unsigned).

these new 'landowners' later invested in real property or transport undertakings that brought them in a higher return.[5] In the Woleu-Ntem, however, where cocoa growing was more recent, the number of large-scale 'planters' remained small* and the accumulation of capital took the old form of wives and 'trade-goods'. The poorer villagers, particularly the young men, nevertheless felt that this was a definite cause of social inequality; and in some cases they tried to avail themselves of mutual help within the 'comradeship groups' and to show a spirit of enterprise so as not to be left too far behind. Either because of this effort, which tended to offset the power of the leading elements, or as a result of threats aroused by jealousy, the mechanisms restricting the development of a landed aristocracy remained effective.

It is important to clarify the difficult problems that this more or less improvised peasantry encountered when it came to organizing themselves as a productive group. In a community that had never experienced any form of slavery or servitude, and where, in addition, there was still a strong egalitarian tendency, the formation of a labour force and the creation of a class of wage workers within the clan or lineage inevitably met with hostility.† The clan movement gave expression to this ambiguity, on the one hand by exalting the 'brotherhood within the *Ayôg*' and on the other by demanding the right 'to work in order to earn money', but without offering a solution that could reconcile the two principles. Apart from the rare cases where a planter succeeded in winning over his employees, it was mainly a case of resorting to expedients that seemed to fit in with the traditional context – and in the first place, the use of wives (based on polygamy) as workers in the plantations. This involved a complete upheaval in the customary division of labour, since it required agreement on the part of the wives and the payment of wages, thus giving them a hold over their husbands that they would never have dreamt of previously. They became closely concerned with the husband's wealth, and therefore freer in their relations with him. Such a situation inevitably led to change and disequilibrium: on the one hand, contributing to

* Plantations of more than 3 or 4 hectares were unusual.

† The same problem was found in the cocoa districts of the Ivory Coast. In fact, the wage-earners working for African planters were 'mainly strangers'. But this did not prevent disputes between the 'strangers' and the local inhabitants.

the emancipation of women; on the other, encouraging pressure from the 'in-laws', who tried to obtain advantages on the pretext of their right to control the standard of living imposed upon the wife, as well as accentuating rivalry between the co-wives. A man of standing, who was therefore polygamous, had an additional chance of obtaining a few workers by the hold he had over the young men who were allowed access to some of his wives* – the 'lending of wives' being permissible by custom, as noted by Largeau at the end of the last century. Furthermore, a *nkumakuma* was able to make up a labour force by 'obliging' some of his kindred, particularly by helping them to get together a marriage payment and so hasten their marriage. Thus the possession of several wives or virtual wives (the elements comprising marriage payments) was at the very heart of this system of expedients – a wealthy man having scarcely any other opportunity of directly exploiting the other men of his clan.

The rapid increase in the production of cocoa and in incomes accelerated the pace of social change. As the movement developed, the relations between individuals were bound to assume the form either of 'landowner – agricultural wage worker', or of partnership based on solidarity within specialized groups of producers. The influence of capitalist commercial firms operated mainly in the first direction, local influences mainly in the second, while the Cameroun tribes hesitated between the two alternatives: increasing numbers of planter-employers and even of capitalist types of partnership (taking over European coffee and cocoa plantations), or 'planter companies' within the clans and the co-operative organizations.[6] This goes to show the extent to which the introduction of new agricultural techniques not only transformed the one-time Fang warrior into a farmer, but also changed his relations with the land, the principles of the division of labour and, ultimately, the relations between individuals.

A second group of problems arose from the need for new

* Cf. F. Grébert: 'La famille pahouine en 1931', in *op. cit.* With reference to the position in the Camerouns, Sister Marie-André of the Sacred Heart notes: 'There are also some far-seeing planters who use the profits from their plantations as marriage payments so as to increase the number of their wives (in other words, of their labour force), turning a blind eye to their relations with other men, since they are afraid of losing them if they are too strict,' *La condition humaine en Afrique noire*, Paris, 1953, p. 104.

administrative techniques governing men and property. The most obvious example was the gap between the extension of the field of social relations and, in Gourou's phrase, the 'techniques of organizing space' acquired by the Fang. Poor means of communication, both material and otherwise, and administrative incompetency at all levels of social organization larger than the village, exposed the vulnerability of this type of society. To begin with, the achievements of the colonizing society made up for this, but only imperfectly, owing partly to the inadequacy of their efforts, partly to the resistance of the colonized society. The attempts made during the clan movement to redefine 'custom', to set up 'judges' or 'arbitrators' within the framework of the tribal groups or a federation of these groups, were an indication of the steps that were necessary. In the religious field there was a similar weakness: the 'associations' operating outside the family cults soon disappeared, while the *Bwiti* cult, with its emphasis upon unity, was only a recent innovation. What the Fang lacked was an extensive network of religious relationships – like that of the Komo society in western Sudan, for instance – which might serve as an effective means of linking up widely dispersed groups.

A number of problems that have not yet been properly elucidated arose from the spread of the written word within a cultural system built up on an oral tradition and the use of material signs and symbols, and from the necessity of making use of this technique. It was necessary not only for official purposes (census-taking and tax-collecting, for instance) but also in the interests of the Fang themselves. We have insisted upon the urgency of a complete overhaul of custom, which in many instances had become ill-adapted and ineffective. This was made clear at the clan gatherings, though at the same time suggestions were put forward for modernizing and rationalizing it. Those that were held in July 1948, by twenty-five Yémisèm villages in the vicinity of Oyem, set themselves the aim 'of dealing with certain questions relating to the adaptation of custom to modern life', and in a document that was produced with great solemnity an attempt was made to regularize the system of marriage payments, divorce trials, conditions of inheritance, etc.[7] The problem that arose as a result of these attempts was how best to win respect for the rules that were adopted and make them *effective*. By making use of the authority associated with any apparently official document, and by presenting this as expressing the agreement of all the adult men who had taken part in the gatherings, the leaders of the movement sought to impose the necessary adaptations of custom definitively. In a colonized society that lacks any centralizing body – whether 'chieftainships' or 'assemblies' – this problem appears to be almost insoluble however. Every initiative inevitably arouses distrust, either on the part of the administration (which regards it as the work of authorities not mandated by themselves), or on the part of the villagers (if it is put forward through the intermediary of 'official' chiefs). As long as there were no administrative cadres or effective agents outside the village group, the results of this attempt to reorganize custom, undertaken for the first time by a rudimentary 'bureaucracy', had no chance of being permanent. The authorities that have been set up since Independence have realized this, and are doing their best to strengthen their own power and their hold over the people through the instrumentality of a political party, and to provide the country with a coherent body of legislation adapted to present-day social conditions.

Recourse to the written word is necessary not only as a means of introducing 'customary' innovations, but also as an alternative to the old methods of legal proof. In a community where disputes over financial transactions and insurance claims are becoming increasingly frequent, the use of written proof is bound to assert itself. Marriage payments, one of the main causes of litigation, now consist of money and goods, instead of the symbolic objects used in the old days; their value is subject to the 'market' and they are part of a process that encourages the abuse of 'gifts' (*avö nzòm*, 'greasing the palms' of the wife's kindred); because of the growing risk of divorce, they make some form of book-keeping essential, since their value can no longer be clearly proved, as it could be in the past when the circulation of marriage payments corresponded exactly, though in the opposite direction, to the circulation of wives. This explains the importance of the list of gifts (*kalaǵ*) that is now drawn up, and the concern of some of the younger men to have their marriages registered. Here, too, the need for a simple bureaucratic apparatus and, consequently, a new function for the village 'literates', are obvious. Lastly, we should note the use of written documents as confirmation of the validity of legal judgements, which made their first appearance in cases relating to financial settlements. As a footnote to the above, one might even mention the use of notice-boards as a proof of ownership, in connection with the new laws affecting landed property.

This increasing reliance upon the written word, which is also to be seen in the case of individuals – with the 'books' kept by business men and planters, or the 'complaints' addressed to the administration, for instance – shows the extent of the changes that have occurred. In particular, they have introduced a principle of *rationalization*, the force of which we noted with reference to the tribal legends drawn up at the time of the clan movement. It not only required the knowledge of 'literates' and clerks, it also modified the actual processes of thought.

IV. CONSERVATISM AND SOCIAL AND CULTURAL CHANGE

In considering the cultural and social changes affecting typical Fang society, we have repeatedly stressed the part played by conservatism and traditional attitudes, and the maladjustments that often resulted from these. Certain changes, though accepted as necessary, were therefore not carried out. The causes of this kind of resistance were complex and are not easy to identify: they could have been the result of a certain inertia with regard to innovation, and a fear of fundamental change, or the result of group and individual interests being involved, or because hiding behind 'tradition' was one of the best ways of evading the authority of the administration.*

The *Bwiti* cult, that complex of borrowings, innovations and Fang additions, is a useful starting point for studying the connection between conservatism and the processes of change. We have already shown the *Bwiti* to be a veritable storehouse of dying cultural forms, including 'a whole body of knowledge and myth' as well as certain features of the ancient *Biéri* cult. In a culture where the monuments created by its artisans and artists have disappeared, and where writing only plays a minor part, an organization of this kind is tantamount to a national archive. Nor

* In the first part of this work, we showed how a subject society can use its cultural specificity to conceal its rejection of authority.

is it a unique phenomenon, when one remembers that for the Africans transported to the Antilles and Brazil *Voodoo* and the *Candomblé*[8] still serve as a repository of tradition for those utterly deprived peoples. In such cases, conservatism is far from being sterile.

Due in large measures to the reactions to Christianity, the cult was also an attempt to establish a unifying religion. It therefore accentuated and enriched those aspects or ideas that appeared to have parallels in the Christian religion. This phenomenon, at least in its most recent versions, is apparent at the level of myth. In the 'parishes' where attempts to elaborate it have gone furthest, the *Bwiti* sometimes assumes the characteristics of God the Creator, as may be seen from the fact that one form of its teachings, associated with the (foreign) name *Ivâgi Vâga*, describes the creation of the world in six days. The *Bwiti* is also represented as God the Father, inasmuch as Jesus Christ – whose blood is said to be found in the red-barked *dèmbò* tree* – is associated with him. Furthermore, in at least one of the churches that we examined, we found that *Nyingòn Möbòga* (the first woman) was identified with the Virgin Mary, whose statue had been stolen from a Catholic mission. Similarly, the old initiation names, which were those of the individual's tutelary animal, were beginning to be replaced by names derived from those of saints or angels,† especially Gabriel. Such cases were still rare and the correspondences only approximate; nevertheless they did represent an attempt to establish a connection between indigenous and Christian notions: for instance, a young man who had been given the name *Mayâža* (which means 'the angel guarding the gates of Heaven when Christ passed through them') was initiated on a Friday because of the significance of that day for Christians.

As to borrowings from Christianity, the most revealing seems to be its mythical topography. In the old days, during the stereotyped revelation that initiation involved, considerable

* The colour red (*èvelé*), symbolizing menstrual blood, has also been identified with Eve, the Virgin Mary and the female principle of the divinity, *Nyingòn Möbòga*.

† The transition from the idea of an individual protector to that of a guardian angel is unmistakable. It was encouraged by the 'translations' used in religious teaching.

emphasis was placed on *Bwiti*'s role as chief of the 'village of the dead'* – and this physical contact with death, whether experienced in reality or as a result of controlled hallucination, was also a feature of initiation into traditional society. As taught nowadays, however, the myth provides a much more detailed and significant topography of the 'country of the dead'. It consists of six villages: the first, called *Tsômbo*,† is where the dead are sorted out according to their deserts; the second, *Misòbanpay*, is the dwelling of 'the Lord Jesus Christ'; the third, *Lubanasêgé*, is the resting place of the 'good dead', while the fourth, *Mavindi*, is recognized as 'hell'. Next comes *Mbulakômbo*, the home of the 'Creator' (that is to say, of *Bwiti*), in his capacity as master of all things; and, finally, *Dumakâga*, where the 'angels' live (i.e. the dead who have earned the right to wait upon *Bwiti*).‡ This brief account of the new structure of the myth is enough to illustrate the significant changes that have occurred in religious attitudes. Christianity§ introduced the idea of salvation, of reward or punishment after death; it modified the traditional conception of the way the dead are able to intervene on behalf of the living – only those who have behaved well (the 'angels') are capable of interceding effectively with *Bwiti* – and it has transformed the ritual for the treatment of the dead – the funeral rites are an attempt to ensure that they will remain in the 'village of the good dead'. As Reinach points out, at the present stage of synthesis, the cult exhibits features of the 'religions of antiquity' as well as features of 'modern religions', the faithful 'pray both *to* the dead and *for* the dead'.[9] But we may be sure that it is the first of these aspects – concern for the efficacy of the works of the living – that is the more important.

* An anonymous account of the *Bwiti* contains the following: 'The initiate sees a long procession of bald, grimacing corpses pass before his eyes, giving off an unbearable smell and practically all crippled. The chief of this city of the dead, even more repulsive than the others, asks the candidate in a terrible voice: "What have you come here for? – I've come to see *Bwiti*. – Well, I am *Bwiti*!" '

† Possibly derived from the root *tsâm* (passive, *tsâmba*), 'to disperse', 'to wander at will'.

‡ This version was found in the churches of the Médouneu region.

§ The Catholic missionaries translated the concept of sin by the word *nsem*, a word that primarily suggests incestuous behaviour, offences against purity, etc., although there is a more general word, *ebiran*, meaning *any* act that is harmful to society. Traditional ethics were concerned with the social, rather than the individual, consequences of irregular human behaviour.

In the preceding chapter we showed that the material organization of the cult – the building of the church, the assimilation of the
vestments of the *nkòbé-bwiti* to those of Catholic priests, the setting
up of 'parishes' and a hierarchy – was borrowed from the Christian
missions. Here we see an obvious concern to establish the *Bwiti*
cult unmistakably as a religion. Its members proclaim their
determination 'to be as strong as the Catholics' and protest against
the 'persecutions' to which they are subjected, convinced that
they are simply 'practising a religion like anyone else', worship-
ping God in a way that is more effective and better suited to their
needs. Above all, by resorting to 'models' suggested by the
Christian churches, they are creating an institution that can reach
out beyond the boundaries of the village or small kinship group
and impose some sort of order upon a society in which the old
methods of social control have largely broken down.

There can be no doubt about the originality of the attempt:
the propagandists of the cult, ex-employees of the big contractors,
as well as the composition of the *Bwiti* congregations, which were
dominated by the younger members, are evidence of it. To understand how closely new and traditional elements were bound up
with one another, one must study their relations, not only at
the cultural level, but also in terms of their social relations,
direct and indirect, with the colonizing society. To approach the
matter solely from the angle of cultural anthropology is not
enough.

By comparing this religious experiment with various other
Fang attempts to overcome the 'crisis' in their society, we have
shown that it was the beginning of a *positive* period of reconstruction, following upon a long period of deteriorating social relations.
It was a reply to exigencies determined by forces outside Fang
society – to what may be regarded as tactical exigencies – as well
as to those of an internal nature. Among the latter may be noted:
the need to 'reintegrate' individuals who had been separated for a
considerable time from their kinship group; the role that the
young men aspired to play now that they had become an 'economic
force' instead of merely representing the military strength of the
lineages; the urgency of giving the many 'atomized' groups some
effective authority (of a sacral nature) that would promote consolidation; the importance of allowing a certain freedom of expression

to the new desire for personal affirmation (the *Bwiti* provided for this, thanks to the fervour of its revelations);* and the need to restore a system of prohibitions that would be binding – to which end, the Christian idea of salvation has been incorporated with the ancient religious preoccupations. From the point of view of what we have called 'tactical' considerations, we would lay special emphasis on the determination to resist the religious and political influence which, up to 1960, was exercised by the colonizing society. The *Bwiti* did what it could to counteract this twofold control: the incorporation of genuinely Fang contributions encouraged people to join, while the concept of salvation, here as in the Negro churches, seems to have encouraged resistance.† Neither the most conscious leaders of the movement, nor the European officials, were unaware of the striking potentialities of the cult. At this stage of our analysis, it therefore seems that the objectives aimed at might lead to the reorganization of Fang society, even if certain of its old features (those borrowed from the religious 'associations' that had been active in the past) still predominated.

The facts of syncretism only have meaning when they are seen as the result of a choice that is made in response to certain social and individual needs. The modifications of the *Bwiti* cult in the course of the last few decades were significant of the former. As far as its supporters were concerned, by insisting upon a new form of religion, what they were primarily seeking for was two of the cardinal traditional values: strength or power, fertility in the widest sense of the word; and secondly, protection for the individual in a society where the dangers were increasing.‡ But the *Bwiti* offered them more than this: some of our informants clearly showed that they were anxious to obtain knowledge of 'the things of the other world' – that 'other world' which, according to the ancient myths, belonged to the white man, and which still remained the place where the secrets of European wealth and

---

* A feature that is also to be found in the Negro churches of South Africa and the Congo; see Part III of the present work, chs. II and III.

† *Ibid.*

‡ In this sense, Léon Mba explained to us that the function of the *Bwiti* was not only to protect, but also 'to bring to justice those whose behaviour was harmful to the community'; punishment could be immediate, and might come either from the ancestors or from God. On the other hand, J. W. Fernandez rightly emphasizes that here the tendencies to power, fecundity and prestige are 'sublimated', *op. cit.*

power were to be found.* Their interest in the notion of salvation, derived from Christianity, was encouraged by the traditional mythical context, which enabled them to equate 'rewards after death' with participation in the riches of 'the other world'. A member of the *Bwiti* glimpsed the possibility of compensating for his present inferiority (forced upon him by the presence of the European) either by access to the sources of genuine knowledge, or, after his death, as a reward for his faith. As one of our Fang informants, a young assistant pastor, put it, the cult combined the principle of traditional magical and religious therapies ('the short way', i.e. the one that takes effect quickly) with the Christian principle of the 'long way' (which decides man's fate after death). One can see, therefore, that the *Bwiti*, while taking into account the traditional religious needs (duties to be paid to the ancestors of the lineages, access to the cardinal values) was much more deeply influenced by the need to respond to new needs. Its development was bound up with the rise of individualism and the first reactions against the alienation resulting from the colonial situation.

These new developments, however, also had recourse to traditional models. For the Fang, there can be no important social phenomenon without the creation of a specific kind of dance. Dancing remains the most effective means of communication; one could almost say that every major institution is *danced* – in the past there used to be a special dance for the *akûm* association and another, the *somana*, for the meetings at which justice was dispensed. All the recent innovations like the *Bwiti* or the clan movement had their own dance, which emphasized their importance and their particular characteristics; and in the case of the *Bwiti*, the development of the movement itself involved new forms of choreography. Thus, in a living way, a form of association and communication that had always played a great part in Fang society was still maintained. From another point of view, the *Bwiti* reveals the significance attributed to revealed knowledge and the various techniques by which it is induced; the whole machinery of initiation, and the use of fasting to the point of hallucination, were derived from very ancient knowledge. At the same time, it is

* The white man was described as the favourite son of God, the possessor of the knowledge that is the source of power. He was said to be able to perform miracles (*akungé*).

important to grasp their contemporary meaning as a reaction to all the forces that are giving rise to and developing rationalization, and as an adaptation to a state of social and cultural instability that limits the efficacy of conformism and, in consequence, appeals to personal initiative and originality. The emergence of the individual depends upon the quality of the knowledge that he manages to attain. In this sense, the background to his 'hallucination' provides more opportunity for him to orientate himself, more points of reference common to all the adepts than obstacles to individual discovery.

If one attempts to isolate systematically some of the connections between conservatism and the process of change, what conclusion does one come to? The experimental innovation, inspired by those who have freed themselves most completely from their traditional background, strives after *totality*. It elaborates a religious system, sketches out a system of authority (the transition from a seriously impaired 'patriarchal authority' to a 'charismatic' authority, and the extension of its field of force) and initiates a whole new pattern of behaviour. This advance, which is operative at *every* level, is to be explained by the fact that it takes place in a society whose constituent elements have a smaller margin of autonomy than exists in modern communities. The various elements are as united during a period of decline as they are in a period of reconstruction; and the partial solutions previously attempted by the colonial government are inoperative, because they run counter to this. In the second place, an experiment of this kind *primarily* attracts those individuals within the socio-cultural unit most affected by the processes of change: which explains why, in certain respects, it serves as a kind of 'cultural repository', despite the fact that it is built up around those who most strongly support thorough reorganization. Furthermore, the use of traditional models and the choice of models borrowed from the colonizing society are carried out in a *functional* manner – that is to say, as a result of the new needs expressed by the most sensitive social groups and individuals. This equilibrium between genuine Fang elements and acquired elements, which gives the institution its syncretistic appearance, was conditioned by the relations (of relative power and interest, in the main) that had been established between and within the groups, as well as between them and the European community. The nature of the equilibrium varied as a result of the modifications affecting these relations. We suggested this by showing how the *Bwiti* cult endeavoured to 'respond' to the exigencies of a nascent individualism, to the need for political reconstruction on the basis of enlarged groups and to the concern to limit the domination of the colonizing society. There was a continual process of modification which led, in fact, to the emergence of a new type of society. Any study which only took into account relations of a cultural order, and not the relations of 'forces', or which was carried out from a static point of view, would inevitably miss the fundamental significance of this type of situation.

In pointing out the difficulties that prevented effective adaptation, we stressed the ambiguity of the behaviour patterns, an ambiguity resulting from the tactical opportunities created by the current 'political void' between a regime based on custom that is no longer adequate and a modern ethic in process of elaboration.[10] To this must be added the obstacles to the creation of new social relations that arise from particularism and a continual harping on old quarrels between alien groups or related lineages; and the consequent difficulties did not fail to make themselves felt, in a quite brutal manner, during our first investigations into the policy of village resettlement.[11] The past weighs most heavily on those societies that rely exclusively upon oral tradition, where the collective memory still seems to be saturated with events (rape or abduction of wives, cases of incest and adultery, quarrels over trade routes, etc.) that once led to the breakdown of alliances, war and the splitting up of lineages. Moreover, in the case of the old Fang groups that were not closely enough associated to form really large units – and in Gabon this was typical – one might almost say that the events that most affected them amounted to little more than a *micro-history*. This lack of historical preparation remains one of their major weaknesses; it is all the more serious in that, during the recent period, there has been a continual need for large-scale cooperation, in the first place to weaken the hold of the colonial government, and then to ensure national reconstruction.

V. ORIENTATION DUE TO A POSITION OF SUBORDINATION

1. The colonial situation subjected Fang society, in a completely *physical* way, to processes over which it had no control – to which, as a rule, it reacted by rough-and-ready methods of self-defence. Whether it was a question of forced labour (the extent of which we have described), or of attempts to redistribute the population, or, in a different way, of health measures, the effect upon the groups, both *quantitatively* and *qualitatively*, must not be underestimated. The destruction of equilibrium between the sexes and the generations was primarily determined, directly or indirectly, by the essentially physical activities of the colonial authorities. In certain areas, and we have in mind particularly the villages built along the Moyen-Ogooué, the impact was so violent that the groups were reduced below the point of equilibrium (demographic or economic) necessary for their preservation. Confronted by a threat of destruction that continually grew more acute, they remained inert: only the techniques of protective magic that distracted their sense of insecurity made any progress, whereas proposals for the reconstruction of society met with very slight response.

Two facts, therefore, have to be considered: on the one hand, the change in the *size* of the groups, together with the *opening up of their relations* with the outside world, called for genuine reorganization;* on the other, these purely physical modifications, once they failed to reach the threshold of toleration, eventually created a situation that demanded a positive reaction. There is undoubtedly a moment when the deterioration of the colonized society also becomes a threat to the colonizing society; this was shown by the vicissitudes of labour recruitment. At this point, there was a chance of 'recovery' – of which the villagers of the Woleu-Ntem managed to take advantage.

The risks of material intervention arising from economic exigencies are aggravated by the *insecurity* that is characteristic of any primitive economy. Whether it is the income derived from trade in the old days, or nowadays from cash crops like cocoa and coffee, or the wages paid in the mining and forestry industries, is

---

* There is a close correlation between these changes in the size of the groups and their relations on the one hand, and some of their new structural features on the other.

immaterial: the state of the external market has a direct and brutal effect. Thus the Fang found themselves at the mercy of a 'crisis' they could do nothing to control.* They were thrown into a world far more dangerous than the one they had succeeded in taming by tradititional techniques. This situation not only led to protests against the Europeans whom they held responsible, but also aroused in them a sense of their own weakness and destitution. We have shown that the new legends they created were an expression of a 'technical inferiority complex' and related this inferiority to the decision of the supreme power, to a veritable curse.[12] The corpus of modern myth collected by Father Trilles at the beginning of the century is of the greatest interest, precisely because it enables us to follow the effort of rationalization that was made in an attempt to explain this sense of inferiority. This step was indubitably the starting point of an understanding of the relations imposed by the colonial situation. But one cannot help wondering whether this psychological orientation did not encourage the evolution that occurred within the *Bwiti* cult: the recourse to the idea of rewards in the after-life, and the need to establish the same close relationship with God as had been established by the Europeans, which was looked upon as the real reason for their material success. The teachings of the missionaries may well have proposed a solution to needs – to compensate for their inferiority and overcome it – which come very soon to find expression in the creation of new myths and legends. As may be seen from the development of the Black Churches among the Bantu, this often gives rise to innovations of a purely Utopian nature, which nevertheless create a basis for the first manifestations of 'nationalism'.

Once the economic and cultural processes arising from the colonial situation have seriously affected the colonized society, the consequent reactions are more directly appropriate. They become the expression of definite interests and are the concern of the newly differentiated social categories. The contribution made by the colonizing society, in the form of the techniques that are necessary for the exploitation and administration of the country's

---

* This sensitiveness to 'crises' was intensified by rumours about the international situation and the relations between the Great Powers; so much so indeed, that some of the members of the *Bwiti* lived in expectation of a world-wide cataclysm.

wealth, is still looked upon as being useful, but the native peoples now have sufficient experience to realize that *they themselves can acquire these techniques*. The discovery was to have important consequences. Inferiority ceased to be looked upon as inevitable, once it was understood to be the result of a temporary situation. The Pahouin Congress put forward demands directed towards obtaining a larger share in economic progress. The clan movement showed that the most widely accepted precepts were those that urged people 'to live like Europeans' and to work to make money by increasing the cultivation of cash crops. But at this point, the *real* conflicts, like those between the native planters and the European entrepreneur who bought up their products for the market, were beginning to come into the open. In 1950, Fang society had only reached the stage at which basic antagonisms become a reality and give rise to specific demands. Thereupon, the Fang began to react as wage workers, 'planters' or 'literates' who held no part in the administrative system. And it was at this point that their belief in illusory compensations began to decline.

2. The entirely empirical way in which the colonizing nation carried out its native policy was contradictory, both in the short and the long run. This can be explained by the heterogeneous nature of a colonizing society, which often has divergent aims, each with its own 'supporters' among the local population. We have brought out the disagreements and disputes that were, so to speak, transferred to the colonized society; the Woleu-Ntem, as well as southern Gabon, was subjected to contradictory influences from the three main strongholds of the European community: the administration, the Christian missions, and the commercial or industrial enterprises. In addition to this, the same policy – that of the administrative authorities – may well appear incoherent when considered at different periods. We have seen for instance, how, having first sought to restrict the power of the traditional authorities by supporting the emancipation of the younger men, the same policy was later thought to be capable of reviving tradition and containing the influence acquired by the most progressive elements.[13] The dialectic of the relations between a colonized society and a colonizing society means that the former is continually threatened at the level of those who constitute its centres of

strength and, inevitably, of resistance. And this restricts its capacity for reorganization, at a time when it is exposed to contradictions that it has not engendered.

3. The position of subordination explains the frequent recourse to processes of evasion, and the number of cases of indirect or ambiguous reaction. The straightforward breaking-off of contact, the appearance of institutions that duplicate one another (as in the case of the chieftainships), or the ostentatious pretence of collaboration (during the first phase of the clan movement, for instance) are all significant examples of this. Readiness to accept any kind of innovation is not merely a sign of the inability to master any one of them effectively; it also shows an interest in experiments not yet domesticated or thwarted by the colonizing society. To maintain institutions at a certain level of instability, makes it *more difficult to control them*. Recourse to traditional socio-cultural means in order to achieve essentially new ends is necessary partly for the same reason – to preserve a facade, confronted with which the colonizer always feels himself to be a foreigner and, in a sense, defenceless; quite apart from the need to maintain a sociological environment familiar to the least 'modernist' individuals. Thus it is possible to speak of a *tactical formalism*. The *Bwiti* cult, with the orientation that some of the Bas-Gabon leaders endeavoured to give it, is an illustration of this. Similarly, the clan movement was an attempt to achieve contempory aims beneath a mask of traditionalism.

This formalism, determined by internal as well as external exigencies, may however become an obstacle to a viable reconstruction of society. Our analysis of the specific 'crises' of Fang society has shown how maladjustments and disequilibria piled up upon one another because of the failure to find a solution in time. The new lines of force that were taking shape were not yet accepted because they called in question the basic relations that characterized typical Fang society, and above all because they required a new approach to the relations established with the colonizing society. Since 1960, decolonization has modified these problems, and the Fang have had to face the basic structural facts, the defects in internal cooperation, that have retarded the inclusion of *their* society in a stable, modern state.

Part III
Social Change Among the Ba-Kongo
of the Congo

I
CHARACTERISTICS OF
BA-KONGO SOCIETY

I. THE BA-KONGO OF THE CONGO

The ethnic groups in the Congo (Brazzaville) who regard themselves as having originally come from *Kôgo dya Ntòtila* (São Salvador), represent the most advanced of the peoples who, since the sixteenth century, have inhabited the provinces that once comprised this ancient Christian kingdom. The capital of *Kôgo* is looked upon both as a real place – it is known to have been in Angola – and a mythical one, a magnificent town in which each of the scattered branches is said to have its *own* street and everyone is sure of finding his own kindred ready to welcome him.

The clans established in the Congo,* in the Stanley Pool region, are descended from migratory groups who succeeded in crossing the river and driving out the Ba-Téké, the withdrawal of the latter at the time of the French penetration enabling them, in a final surge, to advance as far as the high plateau dominating the river Congo. Historical tradition, as well as surviving place names, bears witness to this major changeover throughout a large part of the region – a process that took place gradually once a settlement had been established on the right bank of the river.[1] In Dr Cureau's Annual Report for 1909, the only sign of the Ba-Téké on the ethnic maps of the region is an enclave on the right bank of the Foulakari; by that time almost all the Téké having been driven back to the Haut-Niari and the Léfini.

According to somewhat confused traditions, the migratory

---

* For purposes of simplification we use the terms Congo, or Republic of the Congo, when referring to the Republic of the Congo (Brazzaville).

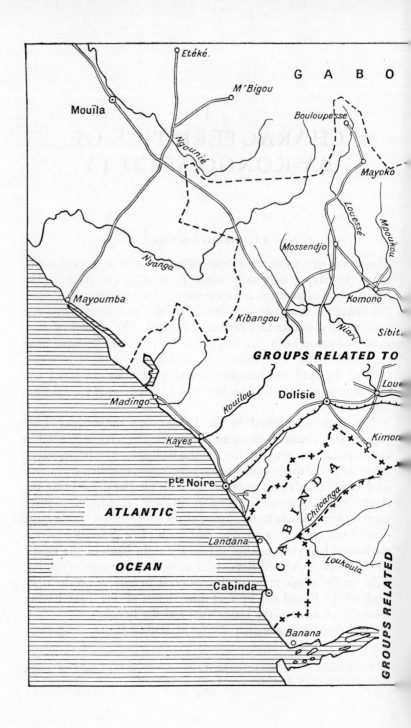

Map of the Ba-Kongo country

groups seem to have crossed the Congo near Manyanga, and then, having partly conquered the zone between this river and the Foulakari, to have split into two groups: one occupying the Brazzaville-Mayama-Pangala region; the other, the Mindouli-Mouyondzi region. Today, this whole geographical area is occupied by two ethnic groups known as the *Ba-Kongo* properly so-called* and the Ba-Lali. Meanwhile, a third stream of migration, the Ba-Sundi, who came from groups established further up the Congo and crossed the river at the end of the sixteenth century, settled partly within the two zones inhabited by the earlier invaders. The rise of the Ba-Sundi continued throughout the colonial period, whereas the other two groups had already become stabilized, as may be seen from observations made at the end of the last century. These three names correspond to the three principal ethnic entities recognized by the administration.

All these migrations, even the earliest, were relatively recent. One of our informants, the crowned chief Bwâgo, an old man renowned for his knowledge of 'custom', put the crossing of the river Congo by his own clan (Ki-Kwimba) at only three generations before the coming of the Europeans. According to the remarkable work of Father Van Wing,[2] it would seem that here we have the final results of a period of instability which had begun in the sixteenth and seventeenth centuries with the invasion of the Ba-Yaka and then been aggravated by the rivalries and conflicts caused by the slave trade and the slow disintegration, continuing into the nineteenth century, of the kingdom of Kongo. Chief Bwâgo could remember the names of six important migratory groups that had given rise to the *Ba-Kongo* and Ba-Lali (also known as Lari or Laadi):

1. *Ba-Kongo*: Ba-Kongo Banséké   2. Ba-Lali: Bisimingèngé
              Ba-Kongo Bayantatu   Bisimizuka
              Ba-Kongo Manyâga   Bafumbu†

---

* Here, and in future, the use of italics indicates this specific meaning of the term; in its generic sense it is printed Ba-Kongo.

† Van Wing counts this group separately, attaching it to the Ba-Téké or Téké. Essentially it was a group that had acted as agent in the trade between the Haut- and Bas-Congo, and gave its name to the region around Stanley Pool.

He could only approximately identify the Ba-Sundi,* the Ba-Ângala, and the Ba-Yumbé (who occupy the massif of the Mayombe).

In fact, these migratory groups only include, under names whose 'equivalents' (it is a question of detached branches having attained a certain independence) are known, a small number of clans (twelve, according to the most generally accepted tradition); the migration, according to Van Wing, having been carried out by groups of related clans. Their names are distinguished by the prefix *Ki*, and we give them here in the form obtained from the most reliable sources in the Boko country.

TABLE I

List of the Twelve Original Clans

1. Ki-mbèmbé – Ki-nkumba – Ki-sunga
2. Ki-ngoi – Makôdo – Kimbâda
3. Ki-nsundi – Ki-mbwéya
4. Ki-mpâzu – Ki-bwèndé
5. Ki-kwimba – Ki-lòza – Fumvu
6. Ki-vimba – Ki-nkala – Ki-nsaku
7. Ki-ndâmba – Ki-fuma
8. Ki-mpâga – Kaunga – Ki-ngoma
9. Ki-mbuzi – Manéné – Ki-mbènza
10. Ki-ndunga – Ki-sèmbo
11. Ki-ngila – Ki-mazinga
12. Ki-sèngélé – Sèngélé

To give some idea of how the groups are distributed over the various regions, we take as an example the administrative divisions where our investigations were actually carried out.

The Boko country

The 'Boko country', as it used to be called, lies between the river Congo and the frontier. It enjoys particular prestige, being one of the crossing-places of the river at the time of the migrations and the first place to be settled by groups from the left bank. It is (and long has been) a lively economic centre, controlling the trade

* Themselves divided into three groups, according to J. Tchikaya: 'Étude sur las race bassoundi', *Bull. d'information et de documentation de l'A.E.F.*, 59, 1950.

routes and closely linked with Brazzaville. It is also one of the most highly populated regions in the whole Gabon-Congo area, having, in 1950, some 30,000 inhabitants, representing more than twelve people to the square kilometre.* The population comprises four homogeneous groups, corresponding to the four entities referred to above, which had been established as administrative chiefdoms as early as 1915:

1. *Ba-Kongo* canton, 8,560 inhabitants
2. *Ba-Kongo* Nséké canton, 7,732 inhabitants
3. Lari canton, 4,536 inhabitants
4. Sundi canton, 8,462 inhabitants

The *Ba-Kongo* occupy the banks of the Congo and control most of the frontier – a key position for an ethnic group which, from the time of the earliest official reports, was described as having 'a real vocation for trade'. From an official study carried out in 1937–8, we know exactly how the different clans were distributed in each of these cantons regarded as tribal units. Here we can only indicate this in a very simple manner by noting the dominant outlines; the following list shows the number of groups belonging to each of the clans enumerated in Table I, to which the numbers in brackets refer.

1. *Ba-Kongo*: 116 clan fragments, of which: 24 belong to (1), 17 to (8), 15 to (4), 9 to (6), 8 to (10), 7 to (5), 6 to (9), 5 to (3).
2. *Ba-Sundi*: 172 clan fragments, of which: 26 belong to (1), 25 to (8), 21 to (7), 19 to (4), 12 to (11), 11 to (3), 8 to (Kiimbi), 7 to (6), 6 to (5), 5 to (12).
3. *Ba-Lali* (or *Lari*): 106 clan fragments, of which: 15 belong to (8), 15 to (4), 14 to (1), 10 to (3), 10 to (2), 6 to (7), 5 to (6).

From this it may be seen that the clan disparity, especially when related to the size of the population belonging to each group, is much less marked in the case of the *Ba-Kongo*, though three clans stand out particularly – the Ki-Mbèmbé, the Kaunga and the Ki-Kwimba. This explains the relative cohesion (and vitality) of the groups settled in this administrative region.

* At the census published in January 1959, the number was 37,760.

The old Kinkala District

Owing to its situation, near Brazzaville and connected with the railway that takes its farm produce to the port of Pointe-Noire, this administrative unit is an island of relative prosperity. It has a population of around 33,000 (in 1950), the *highest density* in the whole of the Gabon-Congo area,* 15 per square kilometre. The population is split up homogeneously into what used to be, until 1917, administrative chiefdoms, and later became cantons. The Ba-Téké had been driven out early on: according to the 1950 census only 930 of them remained, compared with 1,800 in the Annual Report for 1916. The Ba-Fumbu, of whom there are a considerable number, form a group on their own.

1. Ba-Sundi canton, 12,500 Ba-Sundi
2. Ba-Fumbu canton, 9,990 Ba-Fumbu
3. Ba-Lali canton, 8,890 Ba-Lali

The old Mindouli District

This is a transitional zone, occupied solely by Ba-Sundi who, in 1950, numbered 6,450, divided into six 'territories' comprising one homogeneous canton. Their closest neighbours are two related ethnic groups, the Ba-Ângala and the Ba-Dondo, but they do not maintain such close relations with them as those between the three constituents of the Ba-Kongo group (in the generic sense). However, their common historical background and genuine cultural kinship means that the ethnic groups extending from Brazzaville to the coast are all susceptible to the same innovations and unconsciously exposed to influences that tend to draw them together. On the other hand, the Stanley Pool region, despite the fact that it is the heart of the Ba-Kongo country and that tribalism plays a predominant role in Brazzaville, provides easy access to the large northern zone where the Ba-Téké are paramount.

The old Brazzaville District

In the immediate vicinity of the capital the population is predominantly Ba-Lali, comprising 16,500 out of a total of 24,000 in 1950.

* At the 1959 census, 37,132.

The Ba-Sundi and the *Ba-Kongo* remain small minorities, 1,000 and 125 respectively; while the Ba-Téké, who have done their best to maintain a footing here, account for some 4,000.*

As regards the relative importance of the *Ba-Kongo* group in the 'centres' adjoining the European town, we may perhaps refer the reader to our *Sociologie des Brazzaville noires*. At Bacongo, it represents 91·5 per cent of the population, or approximately 17,500 people. At Poto-Poto, in the six main 'wards' that we studied methodically, it accounts for 21 per cent of the population, and the number of people belonging to the group could be put at about 11,500.

The old Mayama-Pala District

This administrative unit is essentially a contact zone between the *Ba-Kongo* and the Ba-Téké; the replacement of the latter has been continuous but slow, the former often having to adopt the 'Téké' suffix in order to be tolerated. Out of a population of more than 18,000, in 1950 there were still 5,165 Ba-Téké (tied up, literally, with one or two Babinga groups). The Ba-Sundi predominated, with 11,185 of them compared with 1,250 Ba-Lali.† From an analysis of the official map, showing the clan territories for the whole area lying between the rivers Djoué, Ndouo and Léfini, it would appear that the dominant clans are identical with those to be found in the Ba-Sundi country in the Boko region; that is to say, Kaunga, Ki-Ndâmba, Ki-Kwimba and Ki-Nimbi (a clan that we did not succeed in identifying), whose appearance seems to be mainly typical of the Ba-Sundi branch.

Thus, in 1950, within a radius of about 150 kilometres of Brazzaville, this relatively homogeneous and expanding ethnic entity comprised almost 97,500 people: 39,600 Ba-Sundi, 31,350 Ba-Lali, 9,990 Ba-Fumbu and 16,450 *Ba-Kongo*. But to these 'country folk' must be added the 'town dwellers': nearly 30,000 in the townships surrounding the capital (predominantly Ba-Lali); 1,600, or about 22 per cent of the population, at Dolisie, an important

* The total population in this administrative area is also increasing: 30,549 in 1959.

† And their expansion continued during the decade 1950–60, the population as a whole exceeding 22,000.

junction on the C.F.C.O. railway; as well as the groups of Ba-Kongo origin settled at Pointe-Noire. The overall size of the Ba-Kongo, their relative mobility (both to and from the towns), the fact that they extend throughout the Bas-Congo and are in contact with closely related tribes, and the part they play in Brazzaville, all help to explain their political dynamism and the capacity for leadership they have shown with regard to Congolese nationalism.

Under the impact of their most active group, the Ba-Lali, their guiding influence soon came to be accepted by all the groups between the Ba-Téké highlands and the ocean. Even the peoples living in the Haut-Congo could not fail to recognize the special role of the Ba-Kongo, nicknaming them *Kôgo Mindèlé*, 'those who look upon themselves as the Whites of the Congo'.

Inevitably each of the branches comprising the Ba-Kongo ethnic group has its own characteristics, resulting from its history, its contacts and its particular specialization; and, according to the circumstances in which it finds itself, displays a more or less aggressive particularism. In a study written at the beginning of the century, Rouget described the *Ba-Kongo* as 'travellers, go-betweens, business men, involving themselves in important matters with considerable energy and not without a certain breadth of vision', whereas he referred to the Ba-Lali as being 'careful, small-scale farmers, looking for a reasonable return for their labour'.[3] On the other hand, the Annual Report for 1916 says: 'The Bakongo are hard-working fishermen, craftsmen and traders. As employees they are reliable. . . . The Balali specialize in agriculture. As young men they readily emigrate to Brazzaville and Kinshasa, where they find themselves casual jobs. The Basoundi, more backward and less energetic . . . are in the process of changing for the better . . .' This brief summary, while stressing the most obvious differences, also reveals incidentally two important features of the Ba-Kongo: their *commercial ability* (connected with the institution of 'markets' and the relatively open character of their society, even at a time when security was far from being assured), and an *aptitude for farming* which an unsettled people like the Fang do not possess. It should also be noted that from very early times they have been anxious to increase their contacts with the colonizing society.

A paper published in 1937 in connection with a project for

reorganizing the chieftainships notes both the favourable and hostile attitudes affecting relations between the various factions of the Ba-Kongo tribe. After recalling that the Ba-Lali and the Ba-Sundi had refused to give up their own names for the generic one of Ba-Kongo, the author continues: 'They have the same origin, belong to the same families, speak the same language. They are strictly endogamous in respect of other races, whereas amongst themselves such exclusiveness is unknown. But this does not mean that they do not oppose one another as friendly enemies.' And he adds: 'They have one common enemy: the white man.'[4] This portrait reveals quite unintentionally the extent to which factors of cohesion may in practice outweigh manifest particularisms.

This comparatively united ethnic group owes its strength to the support of related groups living in the Congo (Leopoldville) and even in territories under Portuguese influence (Cabinda and Angola), to its leading role in the two capital cities, Brazzaville and Leopoldville, and to its economic influence throughout the Bas-Congo. It owes its strength, also, to a whole common mythology, based upon historical events glorifying the might of the ancient kingdom of Kongo. It consists of the descendants of groups which, at an early date, were on close terms with the Europeans, and which, mainly as a result of the slave trade, were in contact with unrelated tribes; it was therefore better prepared than other peoples to withstand the shock of colonial occupation at the end of the nineteenth century. We shall see – indeed, it is the essential purpose of this comparison – how very differently from the Fang the Ba-Kongo responded to the same kind of colonial situation. The fact that they were able to resist, and to adapt themselves more effectively, raises important questions about the dynamics of social change. In the present chapter, where we shall be considering some of the characteristics of their society, we shall confine ourselves in the main to questions of social structure and traditional economy, referring the reader for further information to the admirable works of three Belgian authors, J. Van Wing, I. Struyf and J. Mertens.[5]

II. TYPE OF SOCIAL STRUCTURE[6]

At first sight Ba-Kongo society strikes the observer as one of those that have been readiest to accept modern influences (in contrast to their predecessors the Ba-Téké, who did their best to avoid European contact by withdrawing and maintaining a kind of defensive conservatism), and also as one of the least adversely affected by them in this part of Central Africa. Among the factors contributing to this immunity of the Ba-Kongo we would instance the following: their genuine attachment to the soil (*tsi*), the persistence of chiefdoms, the effectiveness of their clan organization and the fact that they belonged to an original culture of real scope (we refer to the ancient kingdom of São Salvador) and were prepared to accept radically alien influences. The division of the country between the imperialist powers split up the existing clan entities into three parts, weakening the relations between them though without completely destroying their sense of kinship, as may be seen from the unitary tendency expressed in a number of modern movements. This brief characterization is enough to indicate the marked difference between Ba-Kongo society, influenced by still operative factors of cohesion and centralization, and Fang society; it suggests that it reacted differently to a colonial situation of the same kind. The interest of the comparison and the lessons to be derived from it depend in part on the interplay of these differences.

Clans and Lineages

The essential feature of the social system is still the *kâda* (or *nkâda*); that is to say, the clan in its various local forms. In his monograph on the Ba-Kongo of the neighbouring territory, Father Van Wing gives the following definition of the clan: 'It is a community consisting of all the uterine descendants of a single common ancestress, and all bearing the name of this community. It includes all the individuals of both sexes "whether living on the earth or beneath it" . . . the living and the dead.'[7] As far as the groups established in the Congo are concerned, we have already pointed out that this was a matter of twelve clans. However, the facts about their origin appear to be scanty and confused: the 'head' of the clan is always traced back to the time of its sojourn at *Kôgo-dya-Ntòtila* – a place that has assumed a mythical significance – and the only definite information we have relates to the period of the earliest settlements in what is today known as Ba-Kongo country.

Nowadays the clans are identified by a specific name (beginning with the prefix *Ki*), by a motto (recalled on special occasions and sometimes used to soothe a crying child), by their connection, which no one today can explain,[8] with a symbolic animal (particularly the leopard, *ngò*) and by the prohibition of certain foods (*nlôgo*). The clans remain effective, not only because they determine where the groups shall live and enforce the rules of exogamy, but also because they create a field of forces which includes both the living and the 'ancestors', and within which the individual is expected to attain a state of healthy equilibrium. The fact of being a member of the clan (*musi kâda*) is of particular importance since it distinguishes a free man (*muntu a kâda* or *mfumu*) from the so-called slaves (*muntu a mbôgo** or *mwana gata*, 'child of the village', as distinct from 'child of the clan'). In traditional society to be born 'in the clan' conferred immediate superiority.

In addition to the clan, the elders of the lineages have some vague idea of still larger organizations, which at one time used to incorporate a number of related clans. These were the *luvila* (or *mvila*) described by Father Van Wing as 'tribes', but all our informants could tell us about them was that 'no one knows exactly the relationship' between the groups and individuals they comprise. Today, the *luvila* is as a rule simply described as an aggregation of clans traditionally related by marriage. To distinguish the lineages which, unlike the clan (a dispersed unit), are strictly localized, the same word *kâda* is now used; though among the Ba-Kongo of the left bank, the term *ngudi* (group of uterine descent) is still used to designate the clan fragments. A distinction is drawn between the most extended lineages (*kâda dyadinnéné*),† which enjoy both genealogical and numerical precedence and are temporarily able to play a unifying role, and the secondary lineages (*kâda fioté*). A

---

* *mbôgo*, the raffia loin-cloths that were used with other trade goods for buying slaves.

† In Van Wing the term is used in the form *dianéné* (without the duplication of the prefix): 'He ... received the title of *Neakon dianéné Kongo* – which, according to Cavazzi, means ancestor of the Kongo king', *Etudes Bakongo: Histoire et sociologie*, Brussels, 1921, p. 18. Thus the word connotes the idea of rank, of authority over the other fragments of the clan, as well as that of seniority.

study carried out in the Boko region in 1937 states: 'The "great families" are always the creation of one man, rich in wives and land. . . . Less powerful families place themselves under his protection, though they preserve their autonomy. . . . The largest *kâda* of this kind never includes more than four to ten small *kâda*.'[9] In the more populous villages, and those in which several unrelated fragments cohabit, the minor lineages take the form of *mbôgi*, 'households', where the men of an 'extended family' come together to eat their meals, rest and argue.

The more extended lineages are those descended from an elder son (the hierarchy between lineages being a function of seniority), or those that have grown up around some outstanding individual. In the genealogies, the founders are only referred to by an honorific name consisting of the prefix *mi-** and the clan name (for example, *mi-ngâdu*, *mi-ndâmba*, *myaunga*, etc.). As a rule it is from their descendants that the 'crowned chiefs' (*mfumu mpu*) are chosen, men whose authority extends to all fragments of the same clan living in a given area. In principle, it is on these two grounds – order of seniority and mode of dispersal of the groups – that relationships and precedence between lineages are established.

The way in which the groups split up and separate explains how they have been weakened and the rearrangements that govern the relations between the clan fragments – a phenomenon that is particularly marked throughout this part of the Congo, which, as we have pointed out, was originally colonized by the Ba-Kongo. The continual acquisition of new plots of land enforces fission, since *all* of them have to be occupied without any of them being surrendered – indeed, it would be unthinkable to abandon the land and the ancestral tombs. Little by little, as expansion takes place, the ties inevitably become weaker; and this, quite apart from serious disputes leading to secession, and the considerable opportunities of acquiring rights over new territory that encourage attempts at emancipation. Once a lineage, even a minor one, is settled on land that has been 'bought', it acquires a relative autonomy and its landowner-chief insists upon being treated as *mfumu kâda* (head of the lineage).

This progressive occupation has led to the overlapping of clan territories, in spite of the boundaries (*ndilu*) between them being

* Similarly, Van Wing notes the use of *ma-* as indicating respectful affection.

clearly defined. The old official policy of village resettlement accentuated this phenomenon still further, at the same time provoking energetic protests on the part of villagers who, driven from their own land, had to seek refuge among strange clans and pay them compensation for doing so. If one looks at a map showing the present distribution of villages, it is unusual to find a group of clans with exclusive rights of settlement over a region of any considerable size. Most of our informants insisted that this was the result of recent interspersion, and blamed the colonial authorities for causing the confusion. The phenomenon of fission is one of several causes that led to the decline of the position of 'territorial chief' (*mfumu tsi*), thus inevitably producing a state of imbalance within a cultural system in which the sacral nature of the ties with the land (and consequently the very notion of land ownership) was clearly defined. This was forcefully put by Father Van Wing: 'It was the Bakulu (the good ancestors) who conquered the clan domain, its forests, rivers, ponds and springs; they were buried on their property, and continue to be its rulers. The members of the clan . . . are entitled to enjoy the ancestral domain, but it is the dead who remain its owners.'[10] Since then, the whole of modern evolution has stimulated a continual process of desacralization; a fact that involves serious consequences for a society in which the *ancestor–land–lineage* bond is fundamental. From what we were told by the few 'crowned chiefs' who are still recognized, they possess, among the other material attributes of their office, a number of highly sacred objects symbolizing both the ancestors and 'lands' left behind at the time of the major migrations.

The Kinship System

In a paper that sets out to establish a typology of family structure for the Bantu peoples of Central Africa, A. I. Richards mentions that the region occupied by these peoples is sometimes referred to as 'the matrilineal belt'.[11] He goes on to say that he has chosen type A, the Mayombe-Kongo group, as being 'typical of a group of peoples which practise matrilineal descent, succession and inheritance and give marriage payments with the right of immediate removal of the bride, but with the return of her children to her brother's village at puberty.' Whereas a child acquires the status of *musi* by virtue of its relation to its mother (*ki-mamma*), which admits it to a group of lineages and to the clan, through its father it is only linked with a small group to which it belongs by virtue of *mwana*.

As *musi kâda*, Ego is involved in significant relations with four categories of kin, which are defined in terms of two fundamental coordinates: 'blood' and seniority. Blood is the seat of the soul: transmitted solely by women, it constitutes an uninterrupted flow, a system of energy that is essentially bound up with the power of the clan (its whole capital of ancestors and living members), though it also reveals the internal agencies that govern the relations between individuals. Moreover, what makes the whole machinery of witchcraft within the clan (*ki-ndoki*) so dangerous is the fact that it operates through this flow of energy.

The decisive relationship is that between genetrix and offspring, between *ngudi* (mother, known as *mamma*) and *mwana* (child). It is the basis of the 'category of *mothers*', comprising the real mother, the maternal aunts and, by extension only, the maternal aunts 'by affinity' (the affinal maternal aunt is known as 'the wife of the mother's brother', *nkènto ngudi a nkazi*), and the father's wife or wives. At the same time, between the generation of the genitors and that of the offspring, the basic male relationship is that of *nkazi* (literally meaning 'brother in respect of a wife') between maternal uncle (*ngudi a nkazi*) and nephew (*mwana nkazi*); no two men are more closely related by blood. These relationships create two of the four categories of kinship: that of the *ngudi nkazi* (maternal uncles and the mother's maternal uncles, and that of the *mwana nkazi* (maternal nephews and children of the mother's niece); categories that are extended in as far as preferential marriage between cross cousins is still practised in accordance with custom. Finally, there is the category of *ba-mpâgi*, consisting of those who, being of the same blood and belonging to the same clan segment, look upon one another as brothers and sisters, the sister being known as *kibwisi* with regard to her brothers, whether junior or senior. At this level the fundamental distinction is that between seniors (*yaya*) and juniors (*mpâgi*), which operates between brothers and uterine sisters as well as between maternal first cousins, and is extended to children of the same father (and different mothers) and to paternal first cousins – a reminder of the time when, as a result of cross cousin marriage,* the blood relationship also included the *kitata*. This precedence according to seniority was carefully noted by Van Wing, who insists on the fact that it finds expression within the lineages: 'In every lineage there is the *ndonga i bayaya* (category of seniors). . . . This distinction is always observed at every level throughout the clan: a *yaya* mother has a *yaya* son and a *yaya* daughter . . .'[12] The lineages descended from seniors enjoy superior status.

Vertically, the chief relationships are those between the grandparents (*nkaka*) and grandsons (*ntékòlò*), and between great-grandfathers (*nkaka*) and great-grandsons (*ntékòlòlò*). The category of *nkaka* and *nkaka na kèntò* ('female grandfather'=grandmother) extends to the brothers and sisters, and is duplicated on the side of the patrikin. A *nkaka* can marry his granddaughter provided both of them belong to different clans: in certain groups a marriage of this kind used to be considered a 'good' one, since it avoided 'handing over women to outsiders'. This arrangement, which Father Van Wing condemned as 'a shocking anomaly' was one of the methods employed to reduce the loss of women, who were obliged to leave their own clan when they married, and to limit the imbalance resulting from the fact that the father does not control his own descendants. It is important to note the care with which all the classificatory relationships within the four generations likely to be living at the same time are specified by name.

As regards the patrikin (*kitata*), the basic relationship is that between *Ego* and his father (*sé*, whom he calls *tata*), from whom he is considered to receive a part of the 'blood'.† He is *mwana* with regard to the category of fathers, which comprises his real father and the father's brothers and sisters (*tata na kèntò*, 'female father'), and the husbands of maternal aunts (whereas the spouses of the paternal uncles and aunts may belong to *kimamma*, where preferential marriage, i.e. between cross cousins, is practised). The purpose

---

* Van Wing comments: 'He (the *mu-kôgo*) has no real kinship with the children of his paternal uncles and paternal aunts; although between themselves they often refer to one another as *mpangi*,' *op. cit.*, p. 132. But he did not take into account preferential marriage, which was regarded as compulsory 'in the old days'.

† Cf. *ibid.*, p. 187: 'As a man's blood was supposed to be transmitted only to his descendants of the first degree, marriage between a paternal grandfather and his granddaughter was allowed.'

of this last relationship was to establish symmetry between the
two kinship groups. We have already pointed out that the grandparents and the great-grandparents on the father's side are similarly *nkaka* (or *nkaka na kèntò*) to their grandsons (*ntékòlò*) and
great-grandsons (*ntékòlòlò*).

The following table does not give a complete list of everybody
belonging to each of the categories of kinship; but, by leaving
out the basic relationship, that of maternal uncle and nephew, the
categories can be represented schematically by two coordinates:
vertically, the relations of ascent; and horizontally, the relations of
'fraternity'.

TABLE II

Categories of Kinship

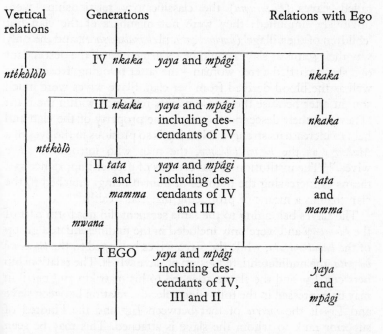

Vertical relations	Generations		Relations with Ego
ntékòlòlò	IV *nkaka*	*yaya* and *mpâgi*	*nkaka*
	III *nkaka*	*yaya* and *mpâgi* including des- cendants of IV	*nkaka*
ntékòlò	II *tata* and *mamma*	*yaya* and *mpâgi* including des- cendants of IV and III	*tata* and *mamma*
mwana			
	I EGO	*yaya* and *mpâgi* including des- cendants of IV, III and II	*yaya* and *mpâgi*

Here it should be noted particularly that the category of *ba-
mpâgi* includes, in addition to the 'brothers' (*ba-mpâgi*) who may be
regarded as closely related, the distant cousins with whom *Ego*

is also in relationship. In the fifth generation, whose living members will be few, we find the 'elders' of the lineages: which explains why the category of *ngudi a nkazi* (maternal uncles) reappears at this level. Acceptance of this basic relationship, the origin of the groups, remains part of the logic of the Ba-Kongo system. It is important to insist upon the fact that *ki-mpâgi* (true fraternity) is the essential element of this system and is determined by 'blood' – so much so, in fact, that in the past two important chiefs could become *mpâgi* by performing a ritual in which their blood was mixed.* Furthermore, a title that legitimately belongs to an individual may equally well be assumed by his legitimate successor: 'Thus the great-grand-nephew of a *Mukongo* (his *mwana nkazi*) may be called grandfather by the grandsons of the same *Mukongo*.'[13]

In the past, Ba-Kongo society practised (and still shows traces of) what is usually known as 'slavery'. With regard to these so-called slaves (*ki-mfumu*) the classificatory relationships were obviously simplified; they were not members of the clan but 'children of the village' (*mwana gata*. pl. *banaba-ngata*), and the only way their status as slaves could be redeemed was if the descendant of a slave married a free woman – the latter bringing 'freedom' as well as the blood derived from her clan. Slave wives were much sought after because their descendants remained within the clan: 'They and their descendants remain the property of the clan and help to increase its strength. Nothing is so precious in the eyes of a *Mukongo* as the *nkuni bakento*, the man who introduces slave wives.'[14] The institution of slavery was of greater importance as a means of increasing the number of human beings attached to the clan than as a means of producing material wealth.

The slaves belonging to the same segment did not form part of the *ki-mpâgi* and were only included in the undifferentiated group of the *banaba-ngata*, while the slave wives belonged to the *ba-kèntò ba-gata*, the undifferentiated group of slave wives. The relationship between *Ego* and the slaves attached to his matrikin and patrikin may be expressed in the following rule: the relation between slave and *Ego* is the *inverse* of that between *Ego* and the kindred of superior rank to whom the slave is attached. This may be seen from the following examples:

* According to Van Wing this rite was known as *vukana menga*.

TABLE III

Relations of an individual with the slaves of the kindred

EGO

tata	Slave wife of the—— father	is to	——Slave wife of the *ngudi a nkazi*	*ngudi a nkazi*
tata	Slave wife of—— paternal uncle		——Slave co-wife of maternal aunt	*mamma*
tata na kèntò	Slave co-wife of—— maternal aunt		——Slave co-wife of the maternal grandmother's brother	*nkaka*
nkaka	Slave co-wife of—— paternal grand-mother			

In every case the free person is regarded as being superior, whatever the slave's position may be.

Marriage and the Effects of Affinity

Marriage not only establishes affinity between two clans, but also gives rise to a new kinship group: the group of 'affines' *ba-nkwézi*. The relations between a man and his wife are those of 'male' (*yakala*) and 'female' (*nkèntò*), of husband (*munkazi, nkazi**) and wife (*lumyani, mulumi, nlanni*).† The wives of a polygamist regard one another as *yaya* and *mpâgi* according to the date of the marriage;‡ to the husband they are simply *bakèntò-bani* (my wives). The children look upon all the co-wives as mother, *mamma* – and regard each other as *mpâgi* amongst themselves.

* An expression which we came across among the Ba-Lali and Ba-Sundi of Mayama and Boko, and which was also observed by J. Chaumeton in the Kinkala region (in his unpublished study: *La parenté et la propriété foncière chez les Balali-Bassundi*). Possibly this may be a contraction of *mwana nkazi*, in which case it would be connected with traditional preferential marriage: the young people marrying a *mwana* of the maternal uncle (*ngudi nkazi* or *nkazi*).

† Expressions which no one could explain, but which represent local variants and are an indication of foreign influences affecting affinal relationships.

‡ A usage which seems to confirm the place previously occupied by marriage between cross cousins (who are each other's *mpâgi*).

In addition to these relationships, two others define the 'categories of affines': that of *buko* and that of *nzari*. The reciprocal relationship *buko* exists between the husband and his relations-in-law and corresponds to the concept of *nzitu* observed by Van Wing among the Ba-Kongo in the adjoining territories. It extends horizontally to all those who are 'brothers' (*ba-mpâgi*) of the *buko*. The spouses also stand with regard to each other's brothers and sisters in the reciprocal relationship *nzari* (among the Ba-Kongo, *nzadi*); this being similarly extended to all the *ba-mpâgi* of the brothers- and sisters-in-law. We should add that between *nzari* the same kind of familiarity is permissible as that which exists between cross-cousins, that is to say, between potential spouses. While the relations of *buko* and *nzari* are expressed horizontally throughout each of the segments comprising the *ki-mpâgi*, they are expressed vertically in alternating generations, as shown in the following diagram:

Generations		Relationships	
	III		*nzari*
	II		*buko*
	I EGO		*nzari*

This alternation, which is found in other tribes related to the Ba-Kongo,[15] is connected with the fact that the 'grandfather' can marry his 'granddaughter', so that the members of generations I and III appear in their turn as potential spouses.

The aggregate of these relationships, starting from husband and wife, determines the extent of the *ki-nkwézi* – the totality of individuals between whom there is affinity or *nkwézi*. This term was noted by Van Wing (in the form *nkwese*), but it seems to have been used sparingly by the Ba-Kongo on the left bank of the Congo. The literal meaning of the term (*the man to whom the niece has been given in marriage*)[16] according to this author, and, according to Mertens,[17] the fact that it is applied to the 'category of grandparents', taken in conjunction with its wide use among the lineages that we studied, are a reminder of the importance of marriage between cross-cousins as well as between *nkaka* and *ntékòlò*. That this type of marriage (we collected a considerable body of evidence) played an important role cannot be doubted; Father Bonnefond and J. Lombard attribute a special place to 'marriage between

kindred', which is considered to serve the purpose of 'continuing
the affinity' and is distinguished by a simplified ritual, which
includes the right to carry off 'the bride' as soon as the betrothal
has taken place.[18] We have to ask ourselves what were the reasons
for a custom that is so clearly specified in the language used to
describe kinship. Unfortunately, we can only venture a supposi-
tion. In a society in which *all authority* (whether of the maternal
uncle, of the elder of a lineage or of the headman of a senior
lineage) is based upon blood, which can only be transmitted by
women, this type of marriage tends to *restore an imbalance* that
would be detrimental to the patrikin. Such are its results that
so keen an observer as E. Torday could maintain that among the
Ba-Kongo descent is bilateral.

Moreover, here we have what Lévi-Strauss refers to as a society
with a 'dysharmonic' structure,[19] where the role of wives in
respect of affiliation is confirmed, despite the fact that it is not
they who determine where the matricentric family shall live:
the mother (in her capacity as wife), and the children who have
attained the age of puberty, live in two different groups. A. I.
Richards insists upon this: 'The problem in all such matrilineal
societies is similar. It is the difficulty of combining recognition of
descent through the woman with the rule of exogamous marriage.'[20] The man is either obliged to hand over his children (to
their maternal uncle), or else he finds himself in a position of
inferiority in his wife's village (supposing the marriage to be of
the uxorilocal type). The system we have just described provides
certain correctives. The man, being *nkaka* as a result of cross-
cousin marriage, is able to make up for the members of his own
descent whom he loses when his own children leave him – a form
of compensation which operates as between the two clans.
Furthermore, the fact that the maternal grandfather is able to
marry his granddaughters means that at no time is the affinity lost.
Above all, slavery enables the husband to keep with him the
children born to him by his slave wives, i.e. to pursue a matrimonial policy that contributes directly to the growth of his
lineage. Torday points out that for this reason the Ba-Kongo were
specially concerned to find themselves slave wives.[21] In Kimpala,
the village of the Ba-Sundi chiefs of Boko, which was organized
in three joint households (*mbôgi*), we found among the thirteen

adult men who had social standing: one affine who should be considered separately, two of the chief's younger brothers (*mpâgi*), the chief's sole maternal nephew (his future heir), five of his sons (children of slave wives, though no one dared say so), and two sons (also children of slave wives), one of the *mpâgi* and the other of his maternal nephew. This example shows the importance attributed to marriages that produce 'children who will remain in the family'. Furthermore, in the past, the desire to maintain affinity between two clans was connected with the occupation of two neighbouring territories, which, at a time when the slave trade was causing a general state of insecurity, constituted a single peaceful unit, and this necessary cooperation between two clan groups explains why the breach between father and son was never final. Our informants explained this aspect of the matter to us by saying 'In the old days all the children stayed with the father. Now the maternal uncle tries to take the nephews away in order to keep the money they earn for himself.'

Although this is mainly a question of mechanisms of compensation, it is important to note the concern that is shown to maintain the affinity between two clans. Van Wing observes that, when they first left the neighbourhood of São Salvador, 'the related clans set out together in the same direction under the leadership of a superior chief or *Ntinu*'.[22] And in this respect it is worth recalling that the first settlement of the Ba-Kongo and Ba-Lali in the Congo began with six migratory groups comprising exactly twelve clans. The need to conquer or obtain new land, and the state of mobility and insecurity that existed throughout the whole region between Stanley Pool and the sea from the seventeenth century onwards, must have determined this joint movement of the groups belonging to *two closely united* clans who were in a position to interchange wives. And, similarly, the coexistence of affines in the same area may still be seen in the practice, not always easy to observe, of only ceding land to those with whom *nkwézi* already exists. A 1934 map showing the division of land between the rivers Djoué, Niari and Léfini, that is to say in a zone recently taken from the Ba-Téké, clearly shows its settlement by nuclei of villages belonging to related clans.[23] Not only was there the usual kind of mutual assistance with work that is expected between *nkwézi*, but also agreement as to the location of garden plots, so that they might take turn and turn about in cultivating those nearest the villages. Despite the upheavals resulting from the effects of colonial policy upon the population, as well as from recent developments, affinity is still predominant in the villages: in a dozen lineages that we studied in the Mayama region, we found that the dominant affinal clan was responsible for 50 to 64 per cent of all marriages.

Linguistically, there is no distinction between the concepts of marriage and affinity. To begin with, marriage implies certain taboos, some of which have already been mentioned. A man and woman of the same blood may not marry – a principle which obviously applies to any clan 'sister', as well as to the relations between the category of 'fathers' and the category of *mwana*. Moreover, to the extent that cross-cousin marriage is insisted upon, marriage between parallel cousins becomes impossible – a sanction that continues to be strictly observed.[24] In the past any infraction of the rule of exogamy, which might cause death and general sterility, used to be punished by death; and, unlike Fang society, there was no ritual method of 'killing kinship' and thus making an incestuous union acceptable. A second category of taboos applies to affinal relationships. Since relatives-in-law are in the relation of *buko* (of the general type, son-in-law/mother-in-law) to one another, they are bound by strict rules– taking the form of 'avoidance taboos'[25] – and may under no circumstances marry one another, even when the individual establishing the affinity has been removed by death or divorce. This is why it is said that 'the bond (*nkwézi*) cannot be broken',[26] even if the customary rules reciprocally involving affines are relaxed. On the other hand, relatives-in-law who are bound by the relationship of *nzari* (of the general type brother-in-law/sister-in-law) treat one another with a certain familiarity and may even regard themselves as potential spouses. On his brother's death, the Mu-Kongo inherits all the wives left by the dead man, and may marry them. By a custom known as *lutsomo*, when a wife died the husband had to be given another wife, 'usually a sister', in compensation; and the same thing applied when a wife was sent back to her family group because she was considered to be too old. Nowadays this compensation often takes the form of reimbursing the marriage payment. Nevertheless, here again, it should be noted that custom is concerned to maintain affinity: by reducing the importance of the marriage payment it has prevented the mercenary approach that has so distorted the allocation of wives among the Fang. This concern to maintain affinity is associated with the desire to restore to the clan the largest possible number of individuals belonging to the third generation; this is what is meant by the Ba-Kongo proverb: 'The twisting tendrils of the bean turn back upon themselves.'

Marriage is essentially a process, demanding a whole series of meetings and exchanges of gifts in addition to the settling of the marriage payment (*mbôgò za lôgò*); the book-keeping involved used to be carried out traditionally by means of a conventional system using the leaves of a palm frond. Just as the ceremonial drinking of palm wine (the young man's maternal uncle,* the girl and the young man himself taking it in turns to toast the recipient of the payment) marked the moment of their betrothal, so each important stage of the process required a similar ceremonial between those who would become affines as a result of the marriage. Four or five days after the payment of the bride-wealth (*kwéla lôgò*) the bride was taken to her husband's hut by her mother or an elder sister. The marriage was not fully completed however until a feast provided by the bride's maternal uncle had been eaten communally in the husband's village and the ritual *n'kungu* dance had been performed in the village of the bride's parents.

This brief account[27] needs amplifying in two ways. It must be emphasized that the father's rights were recognized at various stages of the ceremony, and that a part (*mikinka*) of the marriage payment was given to the bride's father. Mertens insists upon this unequivocal recognition of paternal right: 'The role of the father', he says, 'is nowadays of considerable importance in every marriage.' In the next chapter we shall have to consider the various ways in which this right is confirmed in the modern context. Secondly, the marriage payment is still unanimously accepted as an indispensable tradition; it bears witness to the 'respect due to the wife', and it legitimizes the union; it is the equivalent, so to speak, of registration. It distinguishes the wife both from the concubine and from the slave wife (since the latter

---

* That is to say, the *eldest* maternal uncle, who receives the marriage payment, entrusts part of it to the other maternal uncles (his *mpâgi*) and hands over what is left to the young woman's father.

is *bought*). For this reason, despite the growing importance of a monetary economy, the marriage payment tends to preserve its *symbolic* nature, instead of appearing to be simply the 'price' paid for a wife. The fact that, until quite recently, there was greater competition for slave wives (whose children remain in the clan) than for 'free' ones, helped to prevent the debasement of the marriage payment. There is nothing in the ancient traditions to suggest that the payments were ever of great value, and the rate in money terms remains low compared with the figures resulting from the kind of matrimonial speculation commonly found in the Fang country and South Cameroun – in 1950, in the Mayama region, it was about 2,000 francs. These indications of stability are very different from the facts observed amongst the groups settled on the left bank of the Congo. We believe they are to be explained by the greater part played by slavery in a country where the expansion of the Ba-Kongo took place only recently, and also by the continued recognition of affinity which has checked such abuses as speculation in divorce. Despite the transforming energy that is due to the proximity of Brazzaville, the major fact remains the tendency to maintain the structures of kinship and the matrimonial systems associated with them as the basis of Ba-Kongo society.

Residential Units

Generally speaking, the relations of the people comprising a village, provided it has managed to remain homogeneous, are determined by their descent from a common ancestress – only exceptionally going back further than the fifth generation. Thus the central feature is the lineage (sometimes called *ngudi*, with reference to this common mother), to which must be added the individuals maintained within the clan: descendants of slave wives, kinsfolk who have returned to the clan as a result of preferential marriage, and wives living with their husbands. To illustrate this, we will take the village of Mambio, the home of an administrative chief in the Mayama region. Its nucleus consists of the descendants of a woman called Nkusu, of whom all that is known is that she lived in the Boko country, the starting point of the last migrations.

TABLE IV

Village of Mambio

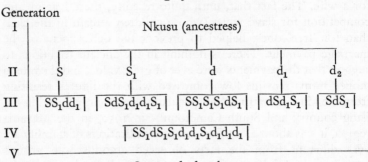

Generation					
I			Nkusu (ancestress)		
II	S	S_1	d	d_1	d_2
III	SS_1dd_1	$SdS_1d_1d_1S_1$	$SS_1S_1S_1dS_1$	dSd_1S_1	SdS_1
IV			$SS_1dS_1S_1d_1d_1S_1d_1d_1d_1$		
V					

S: son; d: daughter

The constituent element of the village is all the sons descended from Nkusu's daughters d, d_1 and d_2. S, the eldest daughter's eldest son, enjoys precedence and real authority: the numerous descendants who remain attached to him (fourth generation) are evidence of the part played by the slave wives inherited by him. The descendants of the daughters d_1 and d_2 are similarly attached to the village of Mambio, since their maternal uncles live there. Nkusu's sons, S and S_1 provide, through the medium of their male children who married paternal cross-cousins, a group of descendants who return to the clan in the fourth generation. While recognizing the dominant authority of S, there are sufficient people in the village to be divided into three households (or *mbôgi*) at the head of which are the eldest sons of Nkusu's three daughters.

Each of the seniors of a segment of uterine brothers is therefore in a position to create a group that will enjoy partial autonomy. His authority extends to his younger brothers, his maternal nephews and their restricted families, his sisters and maternal nieces who have not yet married, and those of his children who are too young to have been sent to their maternal uncle's village. On the other hand, the division of the *mbôgi* into restricted families is not customarily recognized: it only occurs exceptionally, either in the case of men who have been living in the town and have now settled down at some distance from their kinsfolk who have remained in the village, or in the case of individuals who, hoping to escape from 'witchcraft within the clan' (the most dangerous kind), have built themselves 'an isolated camp'. And here again, in most of such separated groups, the 'maternal nephews' will have taken the place of the free children of the family menage. Topographically, the huts (or 'kitchens') of the wives, of the adult children who have remained in the village and of the 'maternal nephews' are arranged around the husband's hut which is the largest and best furnished. An agglomeration of this kind constitutes a group of dwellings that is scarcely distinguishable from others in the village, except for those of the leading members of the lineage, where there are more and bigger dwellings, often built of mud bricks.*

In the case of a composite village, separate 'wards' (*mbélo*) are allotted to the different clans, each of which has its communual household where the men of the clan foregather. This type of arrangement helps to reinforce the importance of the *mbôgi* and of the headman (sometimes known as *mfumu a mbôgi*) who has authority over this minor lineage. But such heterogeneous groupings usually have a precarious existence in regions where material development, which helps to stabilize villages, is least advanced; as antagonisms, and the dangers of witchcraft that these involve, develop, there is a growing tendency to fission. We will confine ourselves to one example of this: Mindzo, lying along the Mayama-Pangala road, whose inhabitants belong to four clans: Ki-Ngâdu (the predominant one), Ki-Ndâba, Ki-Mpâga and Ki-Sèngélé. Here the weakening of cohesion may be seen from the fact that there are seven households and one camp (the greater part of the Ki-mpâga) for a small number of men: the most important *mbôgi*, that of the chief, only includes six men out of a total of twenty-four. Despite the fact that relations of affinity existed between the clan fragments, conflicts arose amongst them and even spread to some of the fragments; dissident elements were to be found among the Ki-Mpâga and Ki-Ngâdu. There can be no doubt that villages artificially constructed on orders from the administration encourage every kind of centrifugal tendency.

At village level, the centres of power are the ancestral tombs – symbols of the defunct part of the clan and of its continuity – and

* Particularly in the 'wealthy', modern Boko district.

the communal household in which men of the same blood foregather.* We have clearly emphasized the care lavished on the tombs, which has given rise to an original type of funerary art, in which the use of cement and brightly coloured composite forms creates a rather baroque impression.† In the villages of outstanding heads of lineages, the tombs dominate the countryside and are the undoubted spiritual centre of the community. By contrast, the *mbôgi* are extremely modest: often little more than a simple hearth surrounded by benches, which, in some villages, is to be found under a rough shelter, quite unlike the carefully built guardhouses in the Fang villages. As a minor lineage the *mbôgi* tend to form an entity with a certain measure of autonomy and organized around the *nkazi* (or *mfumu a mbôgi*), who is not necessarily the senior but may sometimes be the man considered the most capable. In another sense, it is a unit of mutal aid and enterprise. Nevertheless it remains dependent, subject to the orders of the *mfumu nkâda* – that is to say, the eldest member of the senior descent group with authority over a region of varying size. The latter, who generally manages to maintain his dominant position, is at the centre of the customary chiefdom.

Political and Judicial Authorities

The Ba-Kongo have preserved the memory, however confused, of the *Ntòtila* of the ancient kingdom of São Salvador; the same word, *king*, is currently used by religious and political propagandists concerned with national unity;‡ and at an earlier period the chieftainship still retained sufficient vitality to serve

---

* Previously, boys and girls, as soon as their early childhood was over, slept in communal huts: the *nzo kiyakala* for the former, the *nzo kinkèntô* for the latter. These two centres of collective life, reserved for the children, were to be found in each neighbourhood.

† For instance, the tomb of Chief Biza in the Boko region, which consisted of an old-fashioned protective structure beneath which was the grave itself, was surrounded by a complete set of miniature furniture cast in concrete and painted.

‡ The words 'king' and 'kingdom' are misleading, since they suggest a far more highly centralized organization than was ever the case. Nevertheless, though borrowed from Portugal in the sixteenth century, the word 'king' is still highly prized. President Kasavubu of Congo (Leopoldville), who was the foremost leader of the Ba-Kongo on the left bank of the river, was always referred to by them as 'King Kasavubu'.

the interests of the colonial administration. The notion of chief (the word *mfumu* means at the same time a man who possesses freedom as well as power) originally applied to what was the most remarkable feature of traditional society, the *mfumu mpu* or 'crowned chief'. This was an ancient institution whose symbols of authority – especially the headgear (*mpu*) and the bracelets (*nlunga*) – are to be found in descriptions by seventeenth-century chroniclers; but in addition to these authentic Ba-Kongo features there are today others that bear the mark of recent vicissitudes and reveal borrowings from the autochthonous groups who have had to cede territory or with whom neighbourly relations have been established.

According to Van Wing, the number of 'crowned chiefs' used to be very small; it only increased with the decline of the central authority of São Salvador and, in a second phase, as a result of the dispersal brought about by the long period of migration.[28] Following the upheavals that occurred among the population, the chieftainship lost the homogeneity that was once its justification, and where a *mfumu mpu* now exists it is mainly because of the specialized judicial or cultural functions that he performs in a region whose extent varies according to his reputation. In the old Mayama-Pangala district we counted seven 'crowned chiefs' for a population of some 12,000 Ba-Sundi. They were the rulers of the dominant clans: the Kaunga, Ki-Mbèmbé, Ki-Kwimba, Ki-Nimbi, two other clans, the Ki-Nsundi and Ki-Hinda, and their associates.

The considerations that determine the choice of a crowned chief are intimately bound up with clan logic: he must belong to the most vital part of the clan, that is to say, the senior lineages which enjoy precedence and have the most members; and he can only be chosen if he has some distinguishing mark indicating the approval of the ancestors – a swelling on his body, for instance, which goes down after special treatment carried out by young boys, usually grandsons not belonging to the clan.* In the complex field of forces that constitutes the clan, he represents the meeting-point between those derived from the dead and those derived from the living, as may be seen from his behaviour

* The danger of infection reveals unmistakably the sacred nature of the *mfumu mpu*.

towards the ancestors, his unquestioned right to the land (he is *mfumu tsi* for the whole area over which his power extends) and the acceptance of his authority by his people. His whole personality is unusual. In addition to his physical and spiritual person (body, breath, soul and protective spirit) he shares in, and partially possesses within himself, the collective strength of the clan symbolized by the aggregate of the ancestral spirits and its animal emblem, both of which are known as *čiba*. It is by this means that he has access to the revealed teachings indispensable for the salvation of the whole clan. According to Mertens, in the remote past a 'ritual putting to death' of the crowned chief used to take place when he was on his death-bed, as a preventive measure 'against the danger of sterility'; which shows that an important part of the *mfumu mpu*'s functions were concerned with ensuring fertility. At the time of his enthronement he was given two names as a mark of his changed status: the one, highly honorific, recalling the clan of which he was the representative (for example, *Mi-Nsundi, Mi-Ngâdu*, which may be translated 'Our father in the *Ki-Nsundi* or *Ki-Ngâdu* clan'); the other, drawing attention to some individual quality or achievement, which took the form of a kind of motto (for example, 'He who summoned us', 'He who has the strength of the anvil', etc.). In addition to these names, a number of songs accompanied by instruments signifying power – the double bell and the antelope horn – glorified the office of crowned chief or were improvised in honour of the *mpu*.

The choice of an eventual successor could be made as soon as the chief was threatened with death from old age or sickness – an ancient procedure that made it possible for the candidate to the succession to be carefully prepared. Nowadays, with the decline of the institution, the crowned chief finds himself competing with religious and political authorities whom he knows little about, and there is some confusion; though the *mpu* songs[29] stress the importance of not allowing the chieftainship to fall vacant, certain groups have remained without a crowned chief for as long as a year or two. But as soon as there is any serious need for a higher court of customary justice the investiture of a new *mfumu mpu* becomes essential. The ceremony (*yadika*) takes place in public, as soon as the festivities marking the end of the period of mourning in honour of the dead chief are concluded, and requires

the attendance of the notables and secondary chiefs who acknow-
ledge the *mfumu mpu*'s authority. It involves the putting on of the
raffia cap and bracelets, which is performed by young boys who do
not belong to the clan. These are the true and traditional insignia
of power, to which are added the buffalo tail (*mu-ŝyéŝyé*), the
ceremonial knife (*nẓinẓiku*), and certain objects adopted from the
Ba-Téké chiefs: the iron collar (*mu-lônga mpu*), with linear incisions
on the smooth surface, the meaning of which is unknown, and a
distinctive border of wide notches,* a piece of forged iron
(*kibiya*) in the shape of an anchor, obtained from the smiths of
Gamboma in the Téké country,† etc. When the chief has received
the material attributes of power he is lifted up on a shield (*miyalu*)
borne by four men, where he executes a prescribed dance as the
procession passes through the village streets. The *miyalu*‡ is a
kind of litter made from antelope and leopard skin, only a chief
being entitled to stand on the skins of these animals, which denote
the idea of personal power as well as that of the clan's animal
emblem. It is more a question of an emblem of the descent group
to which authority may be transmitted,§ than a specific mark of
the clans, who possess other animal and vegetable affinities. So
debased has this particular institution become – as Van Wing was
pointing out more than thirty years ago – that it is impossible to
discover its precise origin. Nevertheless the *miyalu* continues to
inspire religious respect: it has to be kept in the 'house of the
ancestors' and can only be exposed to public view on occasions
when its use is obligatory. It is through contact with it, among the
attributes of power and the relics from 'the time of the ancestors',
that the crowned chief is able to experience the revelations
necessary for the conduct of any serious business.

* This was observed in the Mayama region; the necklace was said to have come
from the Ba-Kukuyu craftsmen (a branch of the Téké) and to be a mark of
authority.

† As in the case of Chief Bwâgo, our main informant, whose chiefdom was in the
Pangala region.

‡ Van Wing, *Et. Bk.*, p. 138, writes: 'In the sense of "being stretched out on the
leopard skin", the word *yala* came to mean "to rule".' The term *mi-yalu* is derived
from the same root and is closely connected with the idea of royal power.

§ It suggests a sign of nobility, a degenerate survival of the ancient royal order of
São Salvador, rather than some remote form of totemism. To quote Van Wing
again: 'As for the leopard, it is *mbisi i kimfumu*, the animal of the great lords,' *ibid.*,
p. 147.

All our informants insisted that the *mfumu mpu* has never acted as a military leader, his authority is essentially religious and judicial. The sacral nature of his person may be seen from the number of sanctions to which he is subjected: in principle he must not be associated with the kind of work undertaken by ordinary men; he is surrounded by objects symbolizing his power or bequeathed to him by the ancestors – if he is parted from them for any length of time he falls ill; and he must never finish eating the food and drink set before him – which is connected with the obligation to present the crowned chief with part of every animal that is killed (a quarter and a heart), and with the offering of the first fruits that is demanded by the ancestors. It could be said that the *mpu* stands at the meeting-point between the 'ancestral' and the 'human' aspects of the clan; he belongs to both.

Van Wing describes the crowned chief as the high priest 'of the only cult that is socially obligatory', that of the ancestors. The power of the *mfumu mpu* derives entirely from his constant attendance at the 'ancestors' hut', *nzo a bakulu* (*Ba-Kongo*) or *nzo ya kiba* (Ba-Lali and Ba-Sundi). This shrine resembles a very small dwelling, built with special care and entered by one narrow door. The two most sacred features of it are a short central post, covered with red material on which there are motifs suggesting a leopard, and a hole in the ground to receive the offerings of palm wine and chewed kola nuts. No images are allowed in the 'ancestors' hut', and all it contains are the chief's stool, the various insignia of his authority and objects that have been left there for or been requested by the ancestors. The cult has been considerably simplified, and may originally have been based on the ritual of conversion practised at the time of the supremacy of São Salvador, but its formal expression has also been influenced by certain religious practices originating among the Ba-Téké. Though directed particularly to the spirit of the dead chiefs it also calls upon all the ancestors of the clan fragment: their power is entreated to act on behalf of everyone and to protect them against witchcraft. It performs the most vital function in a society in which every enterprise undertaken by its living members is influenced by the intervention of the dead members of the clan. Moreover, the activities of the high priest are concerned less with personal problems – treating an illness, for example – than with public matters, such as ensuring the success of the hunt, obtaining good harvests, and struggling against natural calamities, etc. The revelations he receives through visiting the 'ancestors' hut', or in dreams induced by contact with the objects connected with his office, are applicable to all those under his authority. When he stands up in the middle of the village and addresses the shades of the ancestors, he speaks collectively, in the name of the whole group; and similarly when he conducts sacrifices at the tombs.

In the old days, the authority of the *mfumu mpu* extended throughout the territory occupied by the lineages he controlled. He alone was capable of negotiating with the ancestors as owners of the land, and of making the land fruitful; de Cleene's investigations of the *pfumu tsi* (territorial chief) among the Ba-Yumbi reveal many parallels between his position and that of the crowned chiefs in the Ba-Kongo country.[30] Even today, the *mfumu mpu* possesses vague rights to the land as a whole and can intervene in disputes relating to rights of ownership. This role is one of his duties as supreme arbitrator, which he still exercises in legal disputes about property and inheritance, in matters affecting the solidarity of the clan, in arguments about the rights of individuals (particularly in respect of slavery), and in disputes arising from accusations of witchcraft. All the *mpu* songs we heard extolled the crowned chief as judge (*nzôzi*) and 'mainstay'.[31] And he, rather than the priests of the lineages accepting his authority, has become the highest authority in all questions of custom. Thanks to this conservative function, and especially to the fact that his activities have nothing to do with matters involving European intervention, he therefore became a symbol of opposition to colonialism.*

The *mfumu mpu* appears to have been the *central* element of traditional Ba-Kongo organization: he stood at the cross-roads of those forces favourable to the group and the potential antagonisms threatening its solidarity; he was the symbol of the clan's permanence; it was on him that fertility depended; and he was responsible for maintaining the strength of the lineages by preventing fission. He symbolized the unity of the clan, and controlled the system of intercourse between the ancestors, the living,

---

* Cf. *Et. Bk.*, p. 144. During his investiture a chief, when presenting his successor, used to declare: 'See that he is never mixed up in any business with the White Man.'

and the land belonging to the clan. At one time he used to have a female counterpart, known to the Ba-Kongo on the left bank by the Christianized name of *Ndona-kèntò* (woman-wife), and to the groups that we were particularly concerned with by the title *mfumu a bakèntò* (women's chief). Van Wing speaks of this woman chief as performing both a religious function – she contributed in a minor way to the ancestor cult – and a pacificatory function – it was she who drew 'the white line of peace'. According to the same author, the institution appears to have been considerably influenced by Christianity:* the *Ndona-kèntò* may have served as intermediary between the female population and the missionaries established at São Salvador. This feminine aspect of the chieftainship, which still accords precedence to one of the *mfumu mpu*'s sisters, has become singularly debased. The old chief Bwâgo assured us that the position no longer exists in all 'families' (only among the great chieftainships) and quoted the example of his maternal grandmother who, as *mfumu a bakèntò*, 'never touched cassava' (i.e. did not work in the garden plots,) and ordered all matters in which women were engaged. Today the number of woman chiefs has increased, and their essential role consists in organizing agricultural work, a responsibility for which they receive a certain part of the harvest (for example, the ground-nuts). Van Wing suggests that this institution may go back to the time 'when matriarchy attributed a more important social role to women';[32] without accepting this view, it is nevertheless a fact that the institution was created in a society and a culture in which women enjoyed a high status, and in which a whole series of 'female' bonds and activities played an important part.

In groups that do not have a crowned chief, many of the duties attributed to this dignitary are performed by the 'elder of the clan' (*mbuta kâda*), or the 'elder of the lineage' (*mbuta muna ngudi*). These elders are first and foremost arbitrators; they are also responsible for maintaining custom and educating the young men, and they are in charge of the sacral objects handed down from the ancestors and from the 'land' from which they originally broke

* As indications of this he points to the name itself, the insistence upon monogamy and the observance of a strict moral code. But documents of the sixteenth, seventeenth and eighteenth centuries make it clear that women shared in political power – at the time of enthronement and in connection with certain fertility rites, at the head of certain chiefdoms, etc. See, for example, Laurent de Lucques: *Relations.*

away. Their prestige depends primarily upon their ability to
settle disputes – people look up to them for their knowledge and
procedural skill, even if they happen to be strangers engaged in
some 'business' (*mambu*) that has nothing to do with the clan they
represent. In addition to these higher authorities, it is the headmen
of the villages (*mfumu gata*), of the restricted lineages comprising
these villages (whence the more usual name of *mfumu nkâda*), who
exercise day to day authority. Their functions are essentially
economic (controlling the garden plots and especially the markets)
and judicial, and they are also responsible for relations with alien
groups; but they do not intervene in private matters unless a
dispute is specifically referred to them. In any important decision –
which is taken irrevocably and in principle cannot be further discussed or criticized – they accept advice from the council (*milôgi
mu nkâda*), in which, until recently, the opinion of the older men
(*ba-mbuta*) always prevailed, although all the free married members
of the clan have the right to attend. This organization, which
ensured the chief's authority though not his absolute power, does
not, however, prevent him from having 'secret counsellors'.*
The life of the village is closely bound up with the person of its
chief; when he died, the village used to move on, settle somewhere
else and begin a new cycle of its existence; nowadays the village
remains, gathered around the grave of the dead *mfumu*, which
becomes a symbol of unity. The headman is forbidden to appoint
a successor before he feels himself to be on the point of death: to
do so would be 'to ask for trouble', to invite his own death and
therefore that of the village. The *mfumu* may only choose his
successor in secret, without being obliged to comply with the
ordinary rules of succession (by which power and property pass
to the younger brothers and maternal nephews in order of seniority), but rather by indicating a preference for the most able of
them. Thus personal influence can modify even such a basic
principle as that governing the transmission of power. This is not
simply a matter of preventing the dangerous situation that might
arise from the formal application of the rules, but also an opportunity of strengthening the chief's authority – a tolerant attitude
that serves a double purpose. Shortly before his death, the *mfumu*

* *Et. Bk.*, p. 157. 'The chiefs often had various secret advisors: old men, a favourite
wife, sometimes even an old slave.'

designates his successor before the women's assembly, which acts
as witness: he hands him a branch of the *musâga* tree, having first
raised it to his lips and moistened it with his saliva; he takes his
successor's hand and spits and breathes upon it; then he utters his
last words of advice as to the precepts to be respected, the education of children, the administration of wealth, etc. By the transmission of his breath he hands over power; but the latter can only
be effectively assumed and used after the ceremony that marks the
end of the period of mourning; whereupon a leading judge from
the clan proceeds to enthrone him, at the same time adjudicating
the inheritance of property and people. From what has been said it
will readily be appreciated how profoundly the appointment
of chiefs by the administration desacralized and devitalized
the function that the latter were called upon to fulfil in the
villages.

As a commercial society needing to establish markets and
reasonably secure trade routes, as well as to increase contact with
alien groups in order to trade with them, the Ba-Kongo have always regarded the peaceful settlement of disputes as a high priority. There is no right, not even the right of the conqueror to the
land he has seized, that is not open to negotiation. The institution
of markets moreover shows how closely legal practice is bound up
with trade: they are regarded as places of refuge and pacification
(at the beginning of the century a gun used to be buried when
they were first opened), as creators of law (the 'market laws'
accepted by the chiefs responsible for their foundation), and as
the appropriate spot for the carrying out of the most serious
sanction of all, execution. Through this institution, whose diffusion was mainly effected by the *Ba-Kongo* (in the limited sense),
the social importance of trade and negotiation is clearly revealed.

The *nzôzi* (judge, arbitrator) and the *ba-nzôzi* (court of justice)
were regarded, next to the crowned chief and the village headman
and his council, as the third mainstay of society. In the old days,
each lineage had its arbitrator – assisted by a deputy (*kilândi*), who
served his apprenticeship by taking the less important cases – who
combined the functions of judge and chief, but who, as a local
judge, could be replaced by an arbitrator of greater repute. In the
most frequent cases, those concerning villages belonging to other
clans, the *nzôzi* who were involved would meet at some spot

outside both villages and endeavour to come to an agreement; if they failed, the matter would be referred to an arbitrator chosen by common agreement and usually resulted in an oratorical contest in which the public played an active part.[33] In serious cases (theft or some other crime), both parties were allowed to have two principal judges with their assistants, who were solely concerned to point out mistakes in procedure.

Every trial depended upon reference to proverbs and maxims, and on the skill with which these were used and interpreted. Its purpose was not so much to punish and pass sentence ('the arbitrators are not concerned with carrying out their sentences') as to assert a right; Mertens observed that the 'aim of all procedure is the recognition of a right'.[34] Any infraction creates a dangerous situation for the whole group to which the culprit belongs; it causes real contamination. Mertens puts the point clearly: 'In cases concerning more than one clan, any breach of the law exposes the man who commits the crime, and in his person the whole of his group, to damaging intervention by the ancestors of the group that has been injured, intervention which, if it is not prevented, will eventually lead to the death of the contaminated individual. . . . He is "saved" by the carrying out of the sentence.'[35] Some such metaphysic is certainly implied, but this conception of guilt primarily corresponds to a more readily comprehensible reality. It must be seen in terms of a social and economic system where the actions of individuals cannot be isolated, and where the consequences of such actions affect the whole network of social relations, involving entire groups, and may well compromise the real relations maintained by the latter. But once the terms of the arbitration have been fulfilled, the normalization of relations, the ending of antagonism, is marked by a variety of ceremonies, such as receiving the white chalk-mark and drinking palm wine together. Thus the kind of positive contact that is essential for cooperation and trade once more becomes possible.

In addition to the machinery imposed by the clan system, the judicial organization involves the practical application of two principles that we referred to when discussing the chieftainship: the right to control, or rather to take part in, public affairs, which is the privilege of every free man, of every *mfumu*; and the power to manipulate the rules for the devolution of office so that a choice may be made that will take individual ability into account – the *nzózi* may be appointed, under pressure from the free men of the village, because of his knowledge of custom and his skill in palaver. There is a certain equilibrium between the authority acquired on personal grounds and the power possessed by the groups as units of kinship; any extension of the former is limited by the tendency to separate the three kinds of power – religious, political and jural – and by the fact that these can only be exercised within the limits of the kinship groups. It is this last point that de Jonghe insists upon in his preface to Van Wing's book. According to him, 'It is not surprising that it has been impossible to create a strong central authority, because political functions have been exclusively confined to social groups.' It is therefore appropriate to consider the *control* that the lineages can exert and, as we now propose to do, that other system of counterbalancing forces, the 'associations'.

The Function and Importance of the 'Associations'

A report drawn up in 1937, in the Boko region, draws attention, naively but very revealingly, to the important role of the 'fetishist' as 'the ferocious guardian of custom' and an authority with 'a hold over the chief' because of the prestige he enjoys. Unfortunately, any investigation of the facts is extremely difficult. The old 'associations' have not only been debased – contacts with alien tribes have led to multiple borrowings and the contamination of institutions which were once specifically Ba-Kongo but which from early times the Christian missions did their best to destroy – but have also been split up into numerous specialist groups in response to the demands of insecurity and instability. The more profoundly traditional powers and balances are impaired, the greater the number of new magical and religious organizations that spring up, endeavouring to compete with the former and to remedy the collapse of the latter. This is particularly clear as regards magical 'inventions' which, it is claimed, will maintain or restore the physical health of the group – remedies for sleeping sickness (*Matômpa*), for infertility in women and protecting the health of young children (*Nzumba, Wumba, Ndundu, Mbumba*) – and as regards methods of opposing the effects of witchcraft, which often lead to a craze for foreign 'fetishes', and become a means of political pressure.

In this way, from 1951 onwards, a movement known as *Munkunguna*, which originated in the then Belgian Congo, became extremely popular. Its rapid, though ephemeral, success was due both to its claim to protect people against witchcraft and sterility, and to its ambition to purify social relations. It insisted upon a ritual initiation and purification, accompanied by collective festivities in which both men and women took part. It organized the intercession of the ancestors who had lived *before* the country was colonized, the only ones who could be openly revered and had sufficient strength to counteract the machinations of witch doctors. It made its adherents swear to renounce evil, after having first made a public confession. Thus the *Munkunguna* appears to have occupied an intermediate position between the specialized associations and the 'churches' influenced by Christianity.

We found practically no trace of traditional associations comparable with the 'secret societies' described by de Jonghe among the Bas-Congo tribes,[36] or with the *Kimpasi* society observed by Van Wing.[37] In the latter case, the hostile nature of the organization, its opposition to the whole socio-cultural system based upon kinship, is unmistakable: 'The literature of the secret society of the *Kimpasi* shows that its members shamelessly violated every law, whether human or divine, the fetishist chief taking upon himself the prerogatives of Nzambi (God) himself.'[38] Of the associations on the right bank of the Congo, the closest to this seems to have been the *Lèmba*, the model for which is known to have been imported from the coastal region, and which disappeared about 1930 under the influence of Catholic missionaries. It was an exclusively male group, membership of which involved initiation and the concealment of its rules from strangers, as well as taking part in periodical meetings and communal meals, at which a pig was sacrificed and eaten,* and the performance of certain duties (particularly looking after the sacred fire in the 'churches'). Joining the *Lèmba* seems to have been a fairly simple

* This use of the pig in magic and religious rites is an indication that the institution was borrowed; it was a feature peculiar to the peoples living near the mouth of the Congo. Cf. A. Even: 'Coutumes des Badondos et Bassoundis', in *Bull. Soc. Rech. congolaises*, 21, 1935.

matter compared with the traditional 'men's societies' which insisted upon initiation at the time of puberty; and membership was mainly due to a desire to avoid dying of some physical ailment such as fever or swollen limbs. The association claimed to give protection against witchcraft (de Jonghe particularly stresses the 'warding off of evil spirits'), yet at the same time it tended to make use of the powers of the latter – hence the fear in which the *Lèmba* was held. Illness involving a breakdown of the personality could not be treated by any member of the family, only by a priest of the association (*ngâga lèmba*); the treatment including the patient's admission to the association under the direction of a clan kinsman who prepared his initiation. What we have here is a marginal institution, for though on the one hand it constituted a threat to the clan system, on the other, it had not yet succeeded in detaching itself completely from this system. In his preface to *Études bakongo*, de Jonghe long ago pointed out this inability of the associations to create a form of organization that could function effectively outside the clan.[39] But it must also be realized that, with the development of politico-religious and neo-Christian movements, the struggle between clans and associations has continued and grown deeper.*

In their *Notes sur les coutumes lari*, Bonnefond and Lombard distinguished between (a) 'family fetishes' and (b) 'minor fetishes' which are independent of the family. In fact, the former (the 'major fetishes') are those that are supposed to be effective collectively – for instance, in the case of an epidemic, as happened with the *Matômpa*, which required the participation of all the villagers, kinsfolk and friends and imposed a lengthy initiation upon the young folk who 'entered into the fetish', as well as ceremonies in which everyone took part.[40] The second kind are those that concern individuals, who 'pay for' the services of specialists in magic: *ngâga ngômbò* (soothsayer), *ngâga mpiatu* (magician and medicine man with various functions), *ngâga mpori* (medicine man in the true meaning of the word), *ngâga kiba* (one who implants a protective spirit), etc. The first category of fetishes is more like a public service; the second, a commercialized magical technique. Here it is a question of official positions, especially in the case of the former, to which men are admitted

* See chs. II and III below.

partly on the grounds of uterine descent, partly as the result of individual qualities displayed during the phase of testing and initiation. These specialized associations, and these 'specialists', multiplied during the period of contact with alien tribes, as well as during the period of upheaval resulting from the colonial situation. Their luxuriant growth is to be explained by the need to resolve new, or newly realized, problems and integrate new types of personality, and by the fact that the magico-religious field is the one that offers the best opportunities for asserting personal ascendancy.

Even a rough inventory shows the considerable number and diversity of fetishes that were used; in addition to those already mentioned are those that were concerned with techniques of production and acquisition, those that sought to prevent disputes and to give protection against physical attack, as well as many others which ensured protection against witchcraft, etc. It also shows how many of them were borrowed from the Ba-Téké and from the peoples of the Haut- and Bas-Congo. Moreover, even a brief glance at what happened to them reveals the extent to which they became involved in the struggle for power. For instance, seven or eight years ago the propagandists of the *Nzòbi*, which was taken over from the peoples in the Franceville region, did their best to destroy all other fetishes – and their use for political purposes. Or again, it is well-known that the most powerful chief in the vicinity of Mayama was only able to transform his *official* authority into *genuine* power by representing himself as the 'greatest fetishist of the region'. Lastly, the existence of such groups reveals the process of differentiation taking place within the clan, and increases the number of organizations functioning on the fringes of the kinship structures. An association as specialized as that of barren women, the *Muziri*, constitutes a stable, female group whose members recognize one another by a particular name and are bound by precise rules, while at the same time receiving a special form of treatment restricted exclusively to the association.* Before pursuing our study of them, however, we must first complete the description and analysis of the type

---

* In this case the association takes the place of the kinship group, which is where the Mu-Kongo is usually looked after.

of Kongo social structure by a description of the most characteristic social relationships.

III. MAIN SOCIAL RELATIONSHIPS

At the beginning of this chapter, referring to the kinship that
exists between the peoples settled in an area stretching from
Stanley Pool to the Atlantic coast, we suggested how important
this ethnic and cultural entity, within which the Ba-Kongo are the
most dynamic element, might become for the whole of the modern
Congo. However, these affinities, and the relative identity of their
reactions to strangers and Europeans, do not exclude internal
antagonisms. It is this question of the *relationships between ethnic
groups* that we now have to examine in greater detail insofar as it
concerns the Ba-Kongo groups that are the subject of this study.

In the 'townships' of Brazzaville, as our investigations of urban
sociology made clear, 'Bas-Congo people' are looked upon as a
homogeneous bloc which is striving to assert its supremacy; so
much so, that a sort of superficial dualism has developed, giving
rise to occasional disputes. This is a question of negative rejection
relations much more than of positive aggressive relations. A
socio-metrical test we carried out among school-children showed
that the pupils of Ba-Kongo origin constituted a group which,
while itself lacking cohesion, nevertheless remained more or less
closed to strangers. Though capable of reacting relatively effectively towards alien groups, the Ba-Kongo themselves were at
the same time weakened by internal particularisms.[41] An opinion
poll of the schools in the Boko country indicated that the part
played by clan membership and identification with a particular
village group was even more significant than tribal particularisms.
The affinities existing between the four tribes we are discussing,
the multiplicity of relationships among lineages belonging to
different tribes, and the redistribution of the population which
imposes neighbourhood relations, have all contributed to this
change. One might almost say that the particularisms tend to
break down, and to some extent become dulled.

This easing of the position does not however mean that any
of the tribal entities have given up their own characteristics –
which are to be explained by their different historical background

and take the form of specific linguistic, socio-cultural and traditional economic variants. Colonization, moreover, helped to
confirm this tribal diversity. In what used to be the Boko district,
one finds administrative endorsement of its division into tribal
territories, exposure to a variety of missionary influences (*Ba-
Kongo* and Protestant missions, Ba-Lali and Ba-Sundi and Catholic
missions) and, at certain periods, political use of this diversity.
The messianic and politico-religious movements that developed
after 1920 corresponded to the tribal divisions and drew attention
to the differential effect of the influences to which they were
subjected; it was only later that reactions to the colonial situation
assumed a more unified orientation. As opposed to the splitting
up of the groups, which encouraged micro-particularisms, at the
tribal level one notes a tendency to adjustment. At first this only
manifested itself in hostility to the colonists; in 1937 an official
document could maintain, not without exaggeration, that 'they
have only one common enemy, the white man'. When Africans
were admitted to political responsibilities, from 1957 onwards,
electoral rivalries and personal ambitions sometimes coincided in
a dangerous way with tribal rivalries. But owing to the political
pre-eminence of the Ba-Kongo, typified by the election of the
Abbé Fulbert Youlou to the Presidency, Kongo solidarity
eventually triumphed.

The relations with the previous owners of the land, the Ba-Téké,
have been particularly ambiguous. Often the takeover was only
effected in an insidious way, with the victorious groups apparently
prepared to submit to Téké influences: the adoption of Téké
scarification, intermarriage and the borrowing of such cultural
features as type of dwelling, insignia of chieftainship, hunting
magic, etc.; so much so indeed, that the authors of *Notes sur les
coutumes lari* maintain that 'the two tribes have many points in
common, particularly with regard to their folklore'. In the interior
of the Kongo country, the takeover spared the sacred places of
the Téké, their ancestral tombs, where ceremonies are still regularly performed.* The withdrawal of the Ba-Téké is partly to be

* The fact that a woman belonging to a Ba-Kongo village had inadvertently
planted cassava on the ancient graves of the Ba-Téké meant that the cassava fields of
the entire village became barren. This could only be put right by a collective
ceremony of reparation involving the participation of the Ba-Téké chiefs and priests.

explained by the attitude of rejection they adopted towards colonization and their very slight involvement in the monetary economy; their resentment was directed against the colonists rather than against the Ba-Kongo, whom they tended to despise because of their 'modernist' outlook. Nevertheless, competition between the two peoples exists, and finds expression in the relations between chiefs, within the administrative chiefdoms, and especially over questions of prestige and material privilege; the most notable instance of the latter being the efforts made by the Ba-Sundi in the Mayama region to attract groups of bushmen (Ba-Binga), who had previously been controlled and exploited by the Ba-Téké chiefs.* In the areas where the two peoples are in contact, good neighbourly relations are often precarious; but there can be no question of breaking off contact because they are both bound by sacral relations with the land – the Ba-Kongo still need religious assistance from the Ba-Téké, to whom they make ritual offerings. This is certainly the most obvious of the relationships requiring collaboration between the two ethnic groups. Apart from the special relations established with the Ba-Téké as the real 'owners of the soil', the Ba-Kongo adopt an attitude of superiority towards strangers which, under certain conditions, transcends their own particularisms. The importance they attach to the notion of 'racial purity', their concern to play the part of leaders with regard to tribes whom they look upon as being more backward, are the clearest evidence of this. Having preserved a very keen sense of their own individuality, while at the same time being prepared to accept modern influences, the Ba-Kongo have undergone an evolution that fits them for assuming a privileged position in the Congo – and also, to the extent that their ethnic group extends beyond existing national frontiers, in Central Africa as a whole.

In a society like this, in which women, the founders of descent, the creators of the most effective bonds of kinship and associated with the chieftainship, possess a relatively high social status, some

* The aim being to profit from the game killed by the Ba-Binga without having to buy it from the Ba-Téké, and at the same time to lower the prestige of the latter. But the attitude of the Ba-Sundi towards the Ba-Binga was nevertheless 'racialist' – they accused them of being savages, of having a filthy smell and not deserving to be treated as human beings, etc.

333 Characteristics of Ba-Kongo Society

definition of the *relations between the sexes* is essential, even in a study as wide-ranging as the present. The separation between the sexes is one aspect of a dualistic conception: the female side is linked with air and water, the male with earth and fire; mourning the death of a women involves the prohibition of fish, of a man, the prohibition of meat. The associations concerned with the fight against barrenness forbid the use of precisely those foods exclusively associated with the female principle (fish and other fresh water creatures, flying ants, pumpkins, etc.); the techniques they use tend essentially to avoid any exaggerated strengthening of femininity. This division of the sexes applies to the cultivation of plantations and of garden plots, as well as to the various methods of catching wild animals – fishing is women's work,* hunting is men's. And this essential division is also characteristic of their dances, with men and women drawn up in rows facing one another, then moving together with gestures suggestive of copulation. Writers like Torday have sought to identify this sexual dualism not merely within the kinship system but as permeating the entire religious background of the Ba-Kongo;[42] and our own observation of daily life revealed many examples of the division between the sexes.

From childhood, at least in groups that have retained traditional habits, boys and girls live in separate dwellings, and as they grow older treat one another with reserve and modesty (*nsoni*). As opposed to the sexual freedom characteristic of Fang society, there is a certain strictness about their behaviour, which Father Van Wing was quick to recognize, comparing it favourably with contemporary bad manners; despite the fact that customary attitudes have today been largely abandoned, spontaneity is still far from being an outstanding feature of relations between the sexes. Once a woman is married, she has her own sphere of activities, on which it would be difficult for anyone to encroach. She is the real owner of her hut, and complete mistress in it; she is only expected to undertake the kinds of work prescribed by custom, and her husband cannot order her to do more than is laid down – the existence of slavery serves as a genuine safeguard, since the husband can only exert his authority over a slave-wife. The wife can claim a share of the income from her own labour;

* Apart from small groups of specialized fishermen at Stanley Pool.

she is part of a marriage system in which the complete separation of goods is accepted;[43] she undertakes *all* responsibilities affecting her own clan. It is sometimes said that 'the ordinary woman is little more than an irresponsible minor, kept in tutelage by her clan'. But the essential point is that those who exercise authority over her live elsewhere – and the fact that they are at a distance allows her a margin of freedom of which she can avail herself, while at the same time being able to look to her clan for adequate protection.

Women represent a social force not merely because of the feminine associations and quasi-groups to which they alone belong, but also because of the place they have maintained within the basic systems. This has led certain observers to speak (in a somewhat confused way) of the existence of matriarchy.[44] Apart from any reserves that such an exaggerated assumption must arouse, it should be noted that the relatively high status of Ba-Kongo women is nevertheless *limited* by their function as producers of children and of consumer goods. The allocation of wives is strictly controlled, because it is the basis of the groups and determines the mutual relations between them. The reasons for acquiring a wife are that she is the source of life (if she is too old she can be sent back to her family and exchanged for another), the medium of affinity and, in the last resort, the surety of peace between two opposed groups. Until recent times, the accumulation of wives remained one of the few methods of accumulating wealth. 'The number of wives is the criterion of wealth . . . in fact they represent productive capital, almost the only possible form of investment.'[45] Here once again we are up against the phenomenon which we noted earlier, in a particularly acute form, in our study of Fang society. There the instrumental function of a wife, the outstanding form of wealth, is clearly apparent; but, as we have just shown, in the case of the Ba-Kongo this submission does not take such a complete form because the terms of cooperation between the sexes at various levels is definitely prescribed. It is interesting to find that the upheavals arising from the colonial situation did not, as they did in the Fang villages, lead to a kind of anti-feminism; and to note that, in this case, commercialization of the marriage relationship is less marked. These observations confirm unequivocally what we have said about the position of women in traditional Ba-Kongo society.

A third group of relationships, the basis of the majority of instances of rank, is connected with the notion of *seniority*. In its typical form it is to be found in the relationships between *yaya* (seniors) and *mpâgi* or *nléké* (juniors). It takes the form of the right of the former to dominate the latter – the very word *nléké* implies the idea of subordination. Van Wing illustrates the nature of this type of relationship when he says: 'The *banléké* have to carry the bundles of their *mbuta*, or senior, to accompany him to market, to help in clearing scrub and in building huts. As a rule they are kept busy from morning till night and are often exploited, particularly if the *mbuta* happens to be a trader.' And again: 'The *nléké* must yield precedence to the *mbuta* or *yaya* in all matters and everywhere'.[46] Seniority creates prerogatives to which everyone is entitled when he himself becomes a respected senior, that is to say, a *mbuta* – or man of ripe age who has acquired his full rights. It also constitutes, definitively, the groups occupying leading positions: senior lineages, for instance, are always regarded as being superior to junior lineages. It determines the superior status of individuals: the senior member of a lineage, the 'elder', occupies the highest clan position and his classificatory brothers are superior to the members of junior lineages. It is in this sense that Van Wing distinguishes between 'two kinds of *ki-yaya*'; the first applies to any younger classificatory brother within a narrow range of kinship, the second concerns the hierarchy between the lineages. Thus seniority creates a kind of immediate hierarchy to which all the members of Ba-Kongo society belong – apart from the slaves, whose subordinate position is unconditional. It affects both women and men; it determines the relationship between co-wives; and, until recently, it was an automatic means of classification because it provided an undisputed criterion. The close connection between seniority and authority is to be seen in the privileged position enjoyed by the 'elders' of the clan or of the lineage, quite independently of any formal consecration as leaders; one might almost say that their rank does not require any official sanction precisely because it is accepted as being 'natural'. In this sense, and because it is a type of hierarchy that is everywhere present and active, the positions conferred by seniority have a greater resistance to the debasement resulting from social evolution than the chieftainships; the atomization of the groups, which is fatal to the latter, does not prevent the former from remaining effective even in comparatively small units.

This automatic organization of authority, the importance of which we have already demonstrated in the case of Fang society, finds its justification in a system of ideas not unlike that described by Father Tempels as 'Bantu philosophy'. According to him: 'The senior member of a group or clan is, for the Bantu . . . the living link that strengthens the relations between the ancestors and their descendants. It is he who intensifies the life of his people and of all the inferior forces, animal, vegetable or inorganic, which exist, increase and live for the benefit of his people.'[47] Here, the idea of seniority is associated with that of greater vitality, of a greater capacity for acting in a way that will increase the group's fecundity. The very word *mbuta*, which among the Ba-Kongo is used to designate 'age', may equally well be applied to a young man who has only just attained the age of fatherhood. We have already pointed out that a conception of this kind is connected both with a genuine classification by age (which in the old days, as far as the men were concerned, took concrete form in the rites of initiation performed at puberty)[48] and also with the inequality which is to be found within the smallest groups. We should add, however, that at this level the existence of slavery has the effect of modifying the unequal relationships thus created. The lesser degree of tension, by comparison with that to be found in Fang society, which at present exists between the generations is doubtless to be explained by this greater harmony in the relations between the different age categories.

The fact of *domestic slavery*, to which we have already referred on a number of occasions, has resulted in a system of inter-personal relationships, some of which remain operative despite official attempts at suppression; but their illegality makes any detailed investigation difficult. The information obtained from our informants, however, as well as that acquired from various authors, enables us to form some idea of the importance of the phenomenon: field-workers have assured us that the descendants of slaves (*mwana gata*) are actually more numerous today than free men, and examples given by Van Wing from the adjacent territory bear this out.* But the difficulty one has nowadays in inducing a slave to behave typically, coupled with the fear of witchcraft, means that one rarely comes across any allusion to the condition – even the language has various conventional euphemisms for the word 'slave'. It is chiefly in the course of disputes about property or problems of inheritance that this distinction still has its full significance.

In the old days, slaves were obtained by purchase from other tribes (hence the name *ba-ntu a mbógo*, the latter word meaning any kind of wealth), by compensation representing the price of dead people, by pledges guaranteeing a loan (in such cases a child was regarded as a human pledge, *muntu a mfuka*), by the surrender of people in settlement of a debt and by sanctions involving 'civil death' – the ejection of 'reprobates, thieves, troublemakers, murderers and incorrigible adulterers'. It is clear that the threat of being sold as a slave, on top of having to submit to ordeal by poison, was a powerful means of social control. But the system involved considerable risk of abuse, and could then all too easily become a shameful traffic in human property. This is stressed by Mertens: 'To the extent that in any given case a man allowed his paternal rights to degenerate into despotism, he would begin to dispose of the members of his family as though they were his property, even going so far as to alienate them completely.'[49] Famines, which living men can still recall, or the mere desire for trade goods, multiplied the pretexts for selling and increased the danger of the institution becoming commercialized.

A slave loses his tribal or clan membership, and none of his descendants can recover his position in the clan or his rights as a free man unless either his mother is a free woman or he is bought back (*kula*) individually or collectively, in which case his freedom and individual attributes are restored to him. The inferior position of slaves is justified on the grounds that their birth (*buta*) did not take place within the clan. Cut off from their own lineages, their only ties are with the free men who have authority over them; in

* More up-to-date examples will be found in J. Mertens, *Les chefs couronnés chez les Bakongo orientaux: Etude de régime successoral*, Mém. Inst. Roy. Col. Belge, XI, 1, 1942, ch. I, section D, pp. 205–6,: 'At Nsongo Lwafu, a village in the valley of the Nsélé, of the 250–300 people living there no more than a dozen enjoyed the status of free men. . . At Mbéko Nséké, in the valley of the Luméné . . . in 1942 precisely two of the 50–60 people living in the village were members of the clan'.

principle no one may criticize or interfere with the way they are treated. Nevertheless, fear of public opinion, anxiety not to provoke a slave to run away and the desire to have a large number of slave descendants attached to the group* mean that the slave enjoys a measure of protection. He has no political status, however, unless he becomes, in a more or less confidential capacity, an advisor to some leading man, or else attains temporary powers because of the incapacity of the legal heir or while waiting for the appointed successor to come of age. From the economic point of view, the slave only 'enjoys the usufruct of property resulting from his labour'; but this is of less interest to his master than the number of human beings he produces for him, the prestige of having a large lineage and the variety of services he can call upon him to perform.† The justifications offered by our informants were social rather than economic, and they all insisted, as indeed does Van Wing, that the slave is usually treated as an ordinary member of the family group; they count upon him for other things than merely increasing the group's property.

Apart from the direct advantages derived from slavery, *indirectly* it had important consequences. It permitted an investment in human beings that did not imply the total domination of certain members of the clan; to a considerable extent it gave protection to the most vulnerable social categories, those most at the mercy of despotism – women, and the young men born into the clan; it enhanced the status of clan membership (*musi kâda*), as may be seen from the language, which uses the same word to designate both 'free man' and 'leader'.‡ Furthermore, slavery made possible veritable *transferences* that protected the clan group from internal tensions or the threat of external pressures. A good example of this may be found in Van Wing's account of the ritual for discovering who has committed murder by casting a spell; usually in such cases the lineages belonging to the clan are found

---

* One of our informants made the significant comment: 'A slave produces plenty of children, as a tree bears fruit.' This is why the names of trees occur among the various conventional substitutes for the word 'slave'.

† The most gifted slaves were often employed as confidential agents.

‡ We were told by a Catholic missionary that once when he was marrying a slave girl and asked her 'What is your family?' the whole congregation immediately replied: 'She has no family, she's a slave.' Membership of the clan is still a source of a keen sense of superiority.

to be innocent, while the members of affinal groups are rarely accused because of the risks involved. 'It was simpler and less dangerous to accuse a slave, which is precisely what the sooth-sayer used to do in most cases, unless he happened to have a grudge against a particular family. . . .'[50] During the European occupation the same mechanism continued to be used: in many cases the people who were picked upon and subjected to the exigencies of the colonial administration were slaves. Some of them, however, learnt to take advantage of this situation, and even managed to reverse the position in their own favour. Nowa-days, this institution, that was once so closely bound up with every aspect of traditional social organization, has declined. It has none-theless left behind attitudes (which the reserve with which the question is treated does not always conceal) and sources of conflict that have been exacerbated by the new economic conditions.

IV. TRADITIONAL ECONOMY AND TRADITIONAL RELATIONS

When the geographer Georges Sautter tried to define the Kongo economy, he stressed the fact that it is 'an almost exclusively African economy, stimulated by a relatively high level of popula-tion', and insisted that its vitality is 'closely bound up with tradition'.[51] It has succeeded in adapting itself dynamically to modern requirements without completely destroying its earlier framework. The reason for this is not merely the comparatively slight intervention of European business but also the nature of the economic structures that persisted up to the colonial period.

Always drawn to the relationships and activities of trade and exchange, the Ba-Kongo attributed such exceptional importance to the institution of markets that the neighbouring tribes were inspired to follow their example.* The names by which the markets were known were the same as those of the four days of the Ba-Kongo week,† and the fact that they were held at intervals of four or eight days gives some idea of the volume of trade that

* An indication of the regard in which commercial transactions are held is the longstanding existence of money (particularly in the form of *mbôgo*, small pieces of material made from raffia), and their understanding of price as representing an agreed exchange value.

† That is to say: *nkol, bukôžo, ntsila* and *mpika*.

went on, as well as of the close relations between groups. The creation of a market was a manifestation of power and of the need for a centre of pacification where business could be transacted without danger. An official report of 1916 says: 'Creating a market was, and still is, the prerogative of men who are distinguished by their position and wealth.' It required an agreement with the neighbouring dignitaries, which was celebrated by the drinking of palm wine and an exchange of gifts. The setting for the market, which had to be outside the villages, was the summit of a mountain, a high plateau or an open plain, in order to obviate the risk of surprise attack. A spot dedicated to peace, beneath which an old rifle was symbolically buried, it was also a place of refuge, for 'a market was regarded as being inviolate'.[52] The inauguration used to take place in the presence of friendly chiefs and their subjects; and was followed by festivities, accompanied by singing and dancing and communal meals at which pigs and kids were eaten and palm wine drunk, which continued for some two months. The laws of the market were solemnly promulgated in the course of the collective meal: 'The man who provides the meal is the law-giver, and the man who eats it thereby signifies his acceptance of the laws laid down.'[53] These prescribed freedom of access (at the same time prohibiting any magical interference with people coming and going) and liberty to buy and sell; they refused admittance to the market to anyone bearing arms and decreed severe sanctions (including the death penalty) against anybody creating trouble, stealing or causing bloodshed. A strict police force, under the orders of the market chiefs, carried out continual supervision.

The markets were, and still are, holy places. Trees (the *nsâda*, or wild fig) were planted at the inauguration, not only to bear witness later on to the age of the market, but also because of the sacral nature of the institution. In this respect one is reminded of Huvelin's pleasing comment: 'The boundaries and the markets themselves are sacred; the peace of the market merges with the peace of God.'[54] In the Ba-Kongo country, the final ceremonies of certain initiation rites were held in the market-places, as well as the courts of justice dealing with important cases; the execution of criminals and those accused of witchcraft was also carried out there, after the guilty individual had been stoned by the crowd.

The observation of a certain solemnity was the guarantee of subsequent economic relations.

A young Kongo writer says that 'the market' used to have considerable social importance and refers to the more natural relationships that this institution encouraged. The market was a place where young folk could show themselves off and meet one another, a suitable background for trying out new fashions and new dances, or performing recently improvised songs. It increased contact, served as a centre of information and the spreading of news, and encouraged intercourse and bargaining between chiefs and notables. The markets created a network that was not only economically important but also had sociological significance; it created a social field in which different types of relationship could be strengthened and cultural influences diffused. The colonial officials, both French and Belgian, were well aware of the extent to which these economic networks encouraged the development of initiatives that challenged their authority. This network of relations, which long before the period of colonization covered a large part of the southern Congo, was an unusual phenomenon; it revealed a type of activity much superior to the Fang's economy of conquest, or the Ba-Téké's economy of itinerant traders.* It was a sign of considerable progress; it facilitated the adaptation of the Ba-Kongo to the commercial economy introduced by the colonists† – which is why, being wealthier, they were able to purchase the right to land belonging to the Ba-Téké; and it explains why the notion of a 'Ba-Kongo country' gathered strength and became the basis of the first 'nationalist' aspirations. In this institution, which was the specific creation of the *Ba-Kongo* branch, is to be found one of the reasons for the modern superiority of the ethnic group as a whole.

A second institution, the *Témo*, seems to have been equally important economically; its purpose today is to accumulate 'wealth' that will subsequently be shared out equally among its members. This is the contemporary form of a type of relationship that has nevertheless retained its sociological role and still

* 'Like the Hausa, the Ba-Téké is a pedlar . . . he doesn't think much of the noisy Ba-Kongo markets.' Report quoted above.

† Referring to the Boko district, a 1933 report comments: 'Enormous difficulties for European trade: two-fifths of the sub-division are in business.'

involves a certain ceremonial. Its modern economic function, to provide for saving on a scale beyond the scope of merely individual resources, is accompanied by strict discipline and the formal drinking of palm wine. It is a temporary association, whose duration depends upon the number of members and the routine of payments, which nowadays has been simplified.* Nevertheless, the terminology employed – the two organizers are known as *ngudi a témo* (mothers of the *témo*) and the members as *banab' a témo* (children of the *témo*) – the typical cycle of payments based on the Ba-Kongo week, the frequent habit of meeting at the market as being a neutral place, all suggest the remote origin of the institution and its one-time social importance. It is connected with the idea of 'femininity', that is to say, of fertility and peace.† But the term *ngudi* means 'filiation' as well as 'mother', and in certain villages the association is still divided into two segments, each with its own *ngudi*. Our enquiries convinced us that this was a survival from the time when it was groups and not individuals who were brought together by the *témo*. Originally the purpose of the institution seems to have been to promote peaceful commercial relations between hitherto antagonistic elements.‡ It was a way of coming together and being of mutual assistance, and was thus one method, perhaps the oldest of all, of breaking down the isolation of the lineages and establishing relations with the outside world that were neither merely aggressive nor temporary.

Finally, reference should be made to an institution which, unlike the previous ones, appears to have originated with the Lali-Sundi: this is the *malaki* festival, briefly described by the authors of *Notes sur les coutumes lari* as a 'festival of the villages and of affinity', which took place each year during the dry season. Here again, in an indirect way, it was a question of establishing relations between individuals and groups by getting them to take part in a system of exchange. The purpose of strengthening kinship and affinity was

* As early as 1916 the Annual Report for the Ba-Kongo Region notes: 'There is scarcely a single native who does not belong to a *kitémo*, whether large or small, and as soon as one *kitémo* closes down, another starts up.'

† It must be remembered that the essential function of the woman-chief associated with the *mfumu mpu* is 'to bring peace'.

‡ This was understood by E. de Jonghe – in *Les sociétés secrètes au Bas-Congo*, Brussels, 1907 – where he spoke of the *Témo* as a 'relic' of the secret associations and ritual manifestations by which traders and pedlars were linked together.

confirmed, in the first place, by the fact that the festivities that marked the end of a period of mourning, which were held in honour of all the ancestors, often served as the pretext for holding the *malaki* – so much so, in fact, that the two occasions have frequently been confused. The organization of the feast, for which a *malaki* chief (*mfumu malaki*) was responsible, required a long period of preparation, depending upon the amount of food and manufactured goods to be consumed, for it was the occasion for a display of ostentatious prodigality. A number of temporary shelters had to be built and supplies of prepared cassava, fish-dried meat, palm wine and firewood had to be accumulated, the essential principle being the host's obligation to provide more than he himself had received on some similar occasion, more food and drink, more comforts and more entertainment.

The invitations (*kitumisa*) to a *malaki* were usually sent out two or three months in advance, in the form of a letter couched in naively pompous terms, or of a traditional calendar showing the dates. The list of guests (*ba-bitsiki*), some of whom were obligatory, others a matter of choice, is significant. In the first place there were the relatives-in-law (*ba-nkwézi*), whose refusal would be an extremely serious matter involving the breaking-off of relations between husbands and wives, which would require a long process of conciliation. Next came those with whom the host was on friendly terms, the *ba-nduku*; followed by those with whom he was in touch because they took part in the system of exchange implied by the *malaki* – these were the *bissi-mafundu*, distinguished by the fact that they were expected to bring gifts (*fundu*). The invitation to kinsfolk belonging to the clan, and to unrelated people living in his village, was of a quite different character, especially as it did not imply any obligation to take part in the competitive exchange of gifts; their presence and cooperation was looked upon as obligatory, since the *malaki* was connected with the feast in honour of the ancestors.

It is clear therefore that, in the first place, the purpose of the *malaki* was the periodical strengthening of existing alliances (hence the importance of the relations with the *ba-nkwézi*), and especially extending the scope of such alliances. The friends and other individuals who favoured, or wished to establish, closer relations with the giver of the *malaki*, came to widen the limited field of matrimonial alliances which the latter could create. In this case it was wealth, and not merely wives, that formed the basis for these new relations; in other words, the circulation of wealth tended to take the place of the circulation of wives. This feature of the *malaki* was connected with the point that we have made previously: that among the Ba-Kongo marriage had been less commercialized than among the Fang. Only it must be realized that the possibility of extending the field of alliances through the *malaki* was not unlimited: it depended upon the wealth available. The bonds that were created by no means excluded the idea of *peaceful competition*, of *manifest superiority*, with regard to the individuals and groups participating in the system of exchange.*

At this point the question of the consumption or circulation of wealth and its eventual capitalization requires further considera-tion. Apart from the everyday use of consumer goods, which was necessary for subsistence, reference must be made to the *wholesale consumption* of a ritual or sumptuary nature, that was called for in connection with initiation festivities, the inauguration of markets and the annual ceremonies in honour of the ancestors. As regards the circulation of goods – apart from the markets and the economic challenges implicit in the *malaki* – it was mainly gover-ned by matrimonial exchanges (marriage payments, and the succes-sion of gifts and counter-gifts up to the moment of solemnization), and by the obligations arising from kinship (to the benefit of the maternal uncle and the 'elder') or from affinity (reciprocal gifts between relatives-in-law and incidental presents to the wife). This brief list is sufficient to show that a considerable part of the goods produced was not merely for subsistence, but was a means of expressing certain social relations or of acquiring social and ritual benefits. As far as the capitalization or accumulation of wealth was concerned, traditionally it took three forms that cannot easily be separated. In the first place it depended upon the wives and dependents, and secondly upon the domestic slaves, who repre-sented 'wealth in human beings' (*mbôgo bantu*). But it also involved goods imported from abroad, which were highly prized – weapons, blankets, lengths of material, etc. – all of which used to be stored away in secret hiding-places when times were unsettled.

* These latter aspects are considered at greater length in section IV of the Conclusion, see below.

These trade goods, which entered into any major transaction, represented potential slaves and wives, as well as the land that might possibly be won from the Ba-Téké. All the above facts go to show the complexity of Congolese economy and its dependence upon social relations.

If the various modes of exchange and commerce played a major role, it must nevertheless be remembered that the Ba-Kongo villagers – especially those belonging to the Ba-Lali – were from early times looked upon as excellent farmers; and their agricultural activities had been greatly stimulated by the steady flow of produce to Brazzaville – exports from the Ba-Kongo area of prepared cassava alone amounted to more than 10 million 'loaves' annually, weighing 2 lbs apiece (at least in theory). Here, then, due to the proximity of the capital, agriculture formed the basis of quite an active trade – cassava, palm wine, garden produce and fruit for the luxury market, and cash crops such as palm oil and palmetto, tobacco, etc. being the most important products. As may be seen, this involved a considerable range of goods which were far from saturating an expanding market.

Some of these crops were grown in the forest zone (*Musitu*), others in the savannah country (*Nséké*) or in the districts best adapted to those that had been recently introduced – the swamps and humid lowlands, for instance, being used for growing rice, tobacco and vegetables. In the *Musitu*, where the main crops are cassava, bananas, yams and certain species of taro, the trees first have to be cut down and burnt – work traditionally reserved for the men; whereas the *Nséké*, where such preparation is unnecessary, is the exclusive domain of the women. A specific feature of Kongo farming is the use of burn-beating, stripping off the surface turf, piling it up in great mounds and then burning it; this gives a very orderly appearance to the countryside, for 'the fields are laid out in great rectangles with the mounds arranged in straight lines'.[55] The new crops, introduced in response to the possibility of trade or under pressure from the colonists, were thus regarded as men's work, in which the women were only allowed to take part as voluntary helpers. It was only in special circumstances, such as a sudden demand for garden produce, that the women contributed to an economy that was no longer based simply on subsistence farming but had become a source of revenue. This helped to strengthen still further the high status they enjoyed in Kongo society.

This agricultural economy has given rise to specific types of social relations. It is still unusual for farm work to be carried out individually. When a man has to fell trees in the *Musitu*, he calls in his friends to help him, and pays them either by working for them or – a more modern but still rare solution – employs labourers to take his place. In practice, the men usually form a mutual aid society, known by the borrowed term *Sošyéti*, which they regard as a *kitémo* in which labour is pooled instead of contributions. The provision of food (cassava, meat and palm wine) is the responsibility of the member of the association on whose behalf the gang works, and in order to equalize their contributions there is a system of payment for days lost which operates to the advantage of those members with the smallest plantations. This type of organization recalls the 'labour associations' that exist in many parts of the black world, but it differs from them in that it is entirely voluntary and has none of the formalism and adventitious developments connected with the latter. As for the women, the *mfumu a bakèntò* (women's chiefs) play a decisive role: they encourage the setting up of small mutual aid groups; they lead the women out to work and urge them to increase production; they act as their advisors and, when the area under cultivation is extensive, delegate part of their authority to 'plot leaders'. Their authority is much more effective than that of the *mfumu nkâda* over the men. For their part in the various traditional tasks they receive various gifts in kind; in particular, a share of the groundnuts harvested on the *Nséké*.

Particular mention should be made of the exploitation of the palm tree. This is still such an essential source of income that one might almost speak of a *palm civilization*: it not only provides the material for building and other crafts, but also, in the form of palm wine, contributes to every solemn or sacred occasion in the life of society, as well as to casual encounters between friends and fellow workers. The palm is considered to be 'masculine', and in a certain sense 'noble' – the tree having belonged to the chief who ordered the natural palm groves to be planted and cared for in the time of the ancestors. The responsibility for drawing off the palm wine (*musôgi*) requires not only a kind of apprenticeship but also the confidence of the chief who controls it; he also keeps the 'bank' (*môgussa mâba*) where the money provided by selling the wine is kept, and decides each year how this money (half of which belongs to him by right) shall be divided between the married men of his lineage.*

In the field of agricultural production techniques, despite the changes resulting from the insatiable demands of Brazzaville and the requirements of a modern economy, the traditional institutions that they gave rise to have persisted. In the words of Sautter, whom we have already quoted, farm economy remains 'closely encapsulated in tradition'. That this has a restrictive effect, as he maintains, is certainly true; but insofar as it has been possible to make certain adjustments without impairing the effectiveness of the system it is also one reason for the relative stability. Here again, as with their type of social structure, one is astonished to find how much more resistant the Ba-Kongo as a whole have proved than the Fang, while at the same time displaying a higher capacity for adaptation. Since both societies have been tested by the same colonial situation, it is therefore possible, by comparing them, to discover how far the changes that have occurred are specific and how far they have been determined by the kind of relations maintained with the colonizing society.

* This office was looked upon as a kind of bank into which people could pay the money received from sales, but it could also lend money for expensive purchases.

II
THE NATURE AND DIRECTION
OF SOCIAL CHANGE:
SPECIFIC PROBLEMS

Of all the peoples in this part of Central Africa the Kongo were
one of the best fitted to face the multiple changes involved in
modernization. Relations with Europeans, though sometimes
indirect, had existed since the time when São Salvador was built;
the groups had long been in contact with the principal trade
routes leading to the markets on the coast and at Stanley Pool –
from very early days 'Mpumbu', as it was called, has been the
meeting-place of the trails from the Haut- and Bas-Congo; and
their constant association with other peoples had encouraged the
diffusion of the Ki-Kongo language, thus giving them a capacity
for assimilation that in some cases had enabled them to 'digest' the
Ba-Téké groups overrun in the course of their advance. This
aptitude for the role of intermediary that the majority of the Ba-
Kongo seem to possess had at first been of help to the colonists,
but it soon proved to be an important influence in the transformation of their own society. Moreover, the geographical position of
the Ba-Kongo country exposed it to the stimulating influence of
social change: it has two capital cities, Brazzaville and Leopoldville; it is connected by rail with the ports of the Belgian, as well
as the French, Congo; and it has a relatively highly developed
road system. If our study of the changes that have occurred is to
be fruitful, therefore, we must start by examining in greater
detail the conditions that were conducive to them.

I. EUROPEAN INTERVENTION

Apart from a mining company in the Mindouli region that has
never been very active, the most noteworthy fact is the small
extent to which Europeans have interfered with the technique of

production. Until the years immediately preceding Congolese Independence, they were content to operate within the existing trading system, practically monopolizing the production of palm oil and palmetto by means of a network of agents. There were no large-scale public works that might have led to a policy of forced labour; even in the days when the building of the Congo–Ocean Railway required an extensive labour force the contribution required from the Ba-Kongo villages was not onerous, and did not involve uprooting the workers from their homes. Nevertheless, though they were spared the large-scale displacements that weighed so heavily upon the peoples of Gabon, there was a spontaneous orientation of the Ba-Kongo towards Brazzaville as the administrative and economic centre of their country. Thus, directly or indirectly, they have been subject to the influence of one of the focal points of social transformation – an influence that has been all the more effective because, owing to the close ties that have been maintained between town and village, leaving the countryside has not prevented them from returning to their native communities. The fact of *urban concentration*, a direct result of the European colonial presence, is one of the dominant features: not counting that other pole of Kongo society, Leopoldville, it seems that in Congo (Brazzaville) alone more than 30 per cent of the Ba-Kongo live in urban conditions.* But it should be noted that, for them, this urbanization has not involved, as it has for other ethnic groups, a complete break with their traditional background. In a sense, the city has become a Kongo phenomenon.

Though it is impossible to reproduce here the material contained in our *Sociologie des Brazzavilles noires*, it will be helpful to recall briefly certain fundamental facts. The two main townships adjoining the 'westernized' city of Brazzaville, Poto-Poto/ Wènzé and Bacongo, afford two different types of urban experience. In the former, where the Ba-Kongo are in a minority and have to compete with other dynamic ethnic groups (particularly from the Haut-Congo), the environment is such that they might all too easily lose their bearings owing to the disparity between urban conditions and their traditional background. In the latter, where almost the entire population is Ba-Kongo (predominantly

* This figure takes into account Brazzaville and the townships along the railway, particularly Dolisie. Cf. M. Soret: *Les Kongo nord-occidentaux*, Paris, 1959, p. 17.

Ba-Lali), the influences conducive to detribalization are much less marked; the kind of life they lead facilitates the adaptation of customary behaviour patterns to the novel conditions imposed by town life. It is this numerical preponderance in the capital city that explains why the Ba-Kongo came to play an earlier and more effective political role: since 1930 it has always been they who have reacted most violently against the dominant European minority.

Moreover, the dynamism generated by the city has affected the Ba-Kongo country as a whole. It created a movement of population on a scale that may readily be seen if one compares the number of people leaving the countryside with the number of those returning to their native villages. In this respect Sautter writes: 'Samples I took in several villages in the Brazzaville and Boko districts convinced me that a high proportion of the men had spent some time in town. At Bissindza, for example (in the Brazzaville district), out of 29 men belonging to three family groups selected at random 13 were living in town and 16 in the village; while twelve of the latter had lived for a longer or shorter period in one of the Stanley Pool settlements.'[1] Above all, the city affects the economy, providing a market for labour, creating a steady demand for agricultural produce and stimulating trade. Indeed, as regards employment, it attracts far more people looking for work than there are permanent jobs available – a situation that not only leads to instability but also, since so far no effective solution has been forthcoming, creates resentment.[2]

The Ba-Kongo country is exposed to the influence not only of the capital, but also of the centres established by the C.F.C.O. and of the port of Pointe-Noire. In addition, it has a comparatively elaborate network of roads, which the peasants willingly help to extend so long as there is a chance of opening new markets. The principal reason for this rather exceptional position is the fact that the Ba-Kongo villagers have become purveyors of food to the urban centres – mainly processed cassava, in the form of loaves. In a single year (1949), at a time when the 'African townships' were developing most rapidly, thirty-eight markets supplied them with more than 10,000 tons of cassava bread, not counting the very considerable amount that was purchased direct from the producer. Nor has this been the only form of economic development. Because of easy access to the towns, there is a considerable trade in palm oil and palmetto, a commercial enterprise in which European traders soon became active; as long ago as 1917 the Ba-Kongo district was supplying more than 1,300 tons of palm kernels for the market.[3] Since this is a crop that is very sensitive to the vicissitudes of the world market, it was to reach its highest level during the period of rising prices immediately after World War II; in 1946 the Boko district alone exported 1,776 tons of palmetto and 1,270 tons of oil.

These, then, were the two principal forms of modern development, but while they had the advantage of being feasible within the framework of traditional society, they also raised problems of a technical and economic nature. The rapid expansion of food growing and the resultant acceleration of the rhythm of production threatened the future of the country by causing soil erosion. In some areas this gave rise to a feeling of insecurity, which the inadequate financial returns did little to offset. Owing to the poverty of the consumers, the urban working class, the production of prepared cassava was not very profitable; in the Kinkala district, in 1949, the average income amounted to less than 2,000 francs (C.F.A.) per villager.[4] The cultivation of palm trees and its associated industries seem to have been more remunerative; although as a result of the collapse of the market in 1949 production decreased, incomes that year in the same district were 'equivalent to those obtained from cassava though involving considerably less effort'.[5] The serious problem was the irregularity of earnings brought about by the fluctuations of the market; how serious this was may be realized from the fact that maximum tension between Ba-Kongo society and the central authorities has always coincided with periods of economic crisis. At the same time, however, in addition to these major industries, one must also take into account such complementary activities as the retail fruit and vegetable trade, the sale of tobacco and the harvesting of textile fibres, as well as a number of others of a marginal or semi-clandestine nature – resulting from the survival of traditional systems of barter, smuggling across the Congo frontier and the illicit sale of palm wine – whose value it is impossible to estimate.

The region occupied by the Ba-Kongo was one that had been economically active for several centuries, a situation that had led to a relatively high population density. Colonization encouraged the further opening up of the country, created new centres of activity and took advantage of a population potential conducive to business enterprise. This twofold experience, traditionally and more recently, explains why the Ba-Kongo economy, despite its precariousness, has remained dynamic. The groups, especially in the southern districts, have achieved a relatively high standard of living compared with that of neighbouring tribes,* while higher incomes and closer contact with the European centres have resulted in appreciable changes in their way of life.[6] This can be seen in their housing (of the dead as well as the living); there are more permanent buildings constructed of durable materials, and these reveal a concern for ornamentation that has given rise to a kind of African baroque art. It can be seen, too, in the demand for furniture; as long ago as 1917 a report spoke of 'the manufacture of Ba-Kongo (more accurately Ba-Lali) wicker furniture', and contemporary cabinet-makers are still producing modern examples of this craft. And lastly, clothing has become completely Europeanized (forty years ago hand-weaving had practically died out†); while the abundance and diversity of manufactured goods displayed in even the smallest markets testifies to the important part they play in local consumption. There is thus a facade of modernism that is much more marked among the Ba-Kongo than in most other regions of the Congo-Gabon.

It was not only the economy, however, that was stimulated by contact with the European minority; its effects were soon felt at other levels. It was in the vicinity of Stanley Pool that missionary activity was strongest and assumed the most varied forms. It was conducted within a socio-cultural framework that still bore traces of the work accomplished by the earliest missionaries, who had continued to operate within the kingdom of the Kongo up to

---

* In a fairly isolated Ba-Kongo region – Luozi, in the Congo (Leopoldville) – H. Nicolai commented, in 1958, on the comparatively small farm incomes (about 2,000 Congolese francs a year per family). But he also noted, paradoxically, that the peasants seemed to be reasonably comfortably off, owing to the money obtained by casual labour and the wages earned in the cities. See *Luozi*, Brussels, 1961, pp. 58–67.

† According to the Annual Report for the Ba-Kongo Region, 1917: 'The weavers making small rectangular loin cloths of raffia have practically disappeared.' This was about the time when the use of raffia cloth for money (*mbôgo*) was given up.

the beginning of the nineteenth century. As Van Wing observes, survivals of Christianity had become freely incorporated in traditional beliefs,[7] though the effect of this had been to strengthen syncretistic tendencies rather than to facilitate the task of modern missionaries. The first of these were the Fathers of the Congregation of the Holy Ghost and the Sisters of St Joseph of Cluny; and, as one would expect, the two most important Catholic mission stations were those at Brazzaville and Linzolo, the latter having been established as early as 1884 in the centre of the Ba-Lali country. From these a whole network of missions gradually spread throughout the Ba-Kongo country: Kibouendé and the seminary at Mbamou, as well as Linzolo, in the old Kinkala district; Voka in the old Boko district; Kindaba and Vindza in the old Mayama district; and, in addition to these main centres, there were the mission posts in the villages with native catechists in charge. Catholic activity, reinforced as it still is by private teaching, remains the most widespread and effective.[8]

It was not until later that the Swedish Evangelical missionaries arrived. Their two most active centres, at Musana near Brazzaville and Madzia in the Boko district, were established around 1910, the latter directing its attention to the *Ba-Kongo* (in the limited sense) who were rapidly, if not conclusively, won over to Protestantism. During the last few decades, the quarrels between Ba-Lali Catholics and *Ba-Kongo* Protestants have affected the political life of the whole region; the fact that the Swedish pastors were less deeply involved in politics, as well as the more liberal content of their teaching, accounts for the profound, though involuntary, impulse that they gave to the earliest Ba-Kongo aspirations to independence. Later on they extended their activities to the old Kinkala district, where in 1950 the Hamon mission had more than 250 pupils and some 400 converts, thus giving them an influence which, though less widespread than that of the Catholic missionaries, was at least as profound. As a result of this dualism, the religion of the Congolese converts acquired a dynamic energy which, in the event, led them to oppose any form of 'imported' Christianity. At a much more recent period, local religious life, already affected by disputes between traditionalists and Christians on the one hand, and between Catholics and Protestants and the members of the Negro churches on the other, was still further complicated by the establishment of mission-stations under the auspices of the Salvation Army.* The latter's field of operations varied according to conditions, but some of their missions remained open long after their control had ceased to be effective. Thus a situation arose that was favourable to syncretistic interpretations: in some of their outlying stations the exorcism of evil spirits (*nkundu*) was said to be practised, and on occasion, owing to the greater freedom of movement it afforded, the Salvation Army served as a means of evasion.† The effect of all these conflicting tendencies was a state of utter religious confusion, especially as by this time traditional standards had practically disappeared, the missionaries having resolutely pursued a policy of destroying any fetishes (*mi-kisi*) that might serve to inspire new cults.

In addition to these major factors of change, reference must also be made to the part played by Europeans in teaching and education. By about 1930 there was already a wide gap between the demand for education and the provision of opportunities for satisfying it. Because of their contact with the capital and the position they had achieved there, it was the Ba-Lali who supplied most of the 'literates', who not only had little difficulty in finding employment in the main centres of activity but were also the first to be attracted to modern forms of political organization. It was primarily against them that a project for 'rationing education' was drawn up in 1934.[9] Its purpose was to increase the percentage of pupils drawn from other tribes, with a view to their 'finding employment in the administration in those positions which the Ba-Lali have hitherto regarded as being theirs by right'. But despite these attempts to weaken the influence of the Ba-Lali by depriving them of their dominant position in 'the administrative aristocracy', the development of education was still insufficient to satisfy the growing demand. Moreover, this attitude towards the Ba-Lali only served to strengthen the anti-colonial opposition inspired by the first modernist elite to have appeared in the

* According to a religious census of 1959, the Christians in the whole of the Congo (but highly concentrated among the Ba-Kongo) consisted of: Catholics, 187,000; Protestants, 48,194; and Salvation Army, about 22,000.

† For instance, at a time when his movement was threatened by suppression, André Matswa recommended his followers to join the Salvation Army temporarily.

Congo – an opposition whose influence and organization were to increase precisely because it tended to fill the 'political void' resulting from the diminished authority of the chiefs, whether traditionally elected or officially appointed. At first, the institution of tribal chiefdoms by the government had led to greater cohesion within each of the main Kongo groups; but later on it proved incapable of adapting itself and lacked the margin of autonomy that might have made it effective.

It is in the light of these facts that we have to consider the nature of the social changes that were occurring and the problems they gave rise to. The most distinctive features of the Ba-Kongo situation appear to be the persistence of a typically African economy which, if not sufficiently profitable, was capable of development; their changing relations with Brazzaville, where the Kongo element was still preponderant; and the long-standing and direct contact with Europeans, which accounted for greater fluidity in the sphere of social relations, but which, in the event, was to increase their capacity for resistance to the colonizing society. On the whole, therefore, the Ba-Kongo must be seen as a dynamic group, aspiring to the leadership of the peoples of the southern Congo. A report by a senior colonial official speaks of their 'tendency to regard themselves as being called upon to play an outstanding role in the development of the native spirit, and having a mission to fulfil with regard to the other ethnic groups'.[10] And this 'conviction' was far from being utopian, for they did in fact achieve political leadership, and it was a Ba-Kongo, the Abbé Fulbert Youlou, who was to become the first President of the Independent Republic of the Congo in 1960.

II. MORPHOLOGICAL AND ECONOMIC CHANGES

Both the form and size of the groups comprising Ba-Kongo society were affected by the direct or indirect intervention of Europeans. During the early decades of the colonial period the process of fission was accentuated: new conditions of security made it possible for certain groups which previously would have been unable to do so, to break away – as the slaves did for example. Thus internal conflicts were resolved, at least temporarily, in a quite mechanical fashion: by division, generally on a limited scale. A careful study of official reports reveals that splits of this kind were taking place continually and were dealt with in the same way, at least in certain regions like Mayama-Pangala. In a study of the Boko chiefdoms written in 1937, the author writes: 'I have already mentioned this tendency to dispersal. A man, with his wife or wives, leaves the village and sets up camp somewhere else. The next year someone else does the same, and so on.' Twelve years later, another report, referring to a much less settled area, the old Mayama district, presents a similar picture: 'It is unusual for a whole village to move at one time; more often part of it breaks away, then another, though as they seldom settle in the same place the village is gradually broken up. . . . As a rule they do not go much further than from two to twenty kilometres.'[11] This type of fission, determined by internal factors, gave the villages a scattered appearance, though it was very unusual for a family to move any considerable distance.

The colonizing society also intervened more directly, inasmuch as the authority it imposed and the demands it made led people to seek refuge in concealment or flight – a reaction that had already been observed by Van Wing. The tendency to seek refuge in the least accessible areas – which usually meant that they were neither so healthy nor so rich in material resources – was only checked comparatively recently, often by the increasing necessity of obtaining cash. In this respect, the Annual Report for 1917 is relevant: 'Once again, as in 1916, though perhaps on a smaller scale, we have assisted one-time deserters from Kinkala, Boko, Kimpanzou and elsewhere to return to their native territory. All things considered, since it is no longer possible for them to evade the demands of the administration, they still prefer to go back to the fertile regions which they have only recently left. In view of the present economic situation here, it looks as though we can expect further demands of this kind in 1918. . . . It would therefore be as well to allow the natives to return to their own "concentration centres".'[12] One can only assume that what we might call this *tactic* of dispersal was closely connected with the political situation in the area. Certainly this was so in 1930, the year when the Ba-Lali leader, André Matswa, was tried and imprisoned; and again after 1940. And it was with this political aspect that the administrative authorities were primarily concerned when they embarked upon a policy of 'hunting down the encampments'.[13]

In reaction to this tendency for residential units to split up, which was *also* attributable to internal causes, a contrary movement developed: the regrouping of villages, either on orders from above or as a result of the new economic situation. The policy of village resettlement was an old one – it is mentioned in a report for the year 1914; but it was not until 1930, when the present system of communications was more or less complete, that it was implemented on any considerable scale. A 1932 report on the successful conclusion of the operation enables us to judge of its extent: 'A number of large villages have been established, especially along the motor-roads and major trails. On the road between Brazzaville and Mindouli, where previously there were only four or five small villages, there are now about thirty. . . . Several villages have also been built along the Congo–Ocean Railway, particularly near the stations . . .'[14] Since this compulsory redistribution of the population was, from the villagers' point of view, unaccompanied by any immediate benefits and merely simplified official supervision, it was sooner or later bound to increase mobility; the lineages that were brought together were anxious to recover their autonomy. Nevertheless, under modern economic conditions this policy, although it drastically modified the traditional links between the groups and the land, sometimes had a positive aspect. This was so as regards the villages established in the vicinity of trade routes and markets; and, similarly, when rising living standards encouraged people to invest in housing, as was the case in the Boko region, where the increasing number of brick-built dwellings was an inducement to composite units (*mumfuka*) to settle down. The only way, apart from compulsion, by which people not traditionally adjusted to one another can be integrated is if they are able to acquire common material interests. The alternative is simply an endless succession of dispersals and more or less artificial regrouping.

From these observations certain general conclusions emerge: that there is a reciprocal relation between the degree of stability of the groups and the stage of economic evolution they have attained; and that, in the less stabilized areas, the point at which the tendency to fission is maximal is when relations with the

central authorities reach a definite state of crisis.* However, apart
from the very few family units living on the fringe of customary
society, there is also a minimum point below which small groups
prefer to return to their own lineages rather than to remain
isolated. For this reason, dispersion tends to occur within the
limits of the clan territory, in the neighbourhood of some centre
where there is a resident chief recognized by the administration,
and where the men can therefore be included in the census and pay
their taxes.

The problems arising from the redistribution of population are
complex. In the first place, they were connected with the factors
that determined the original settlement of the various fragments
comprising the Ba-Kongo ethnic group, since the greatest confusion and overlapping of territory was in those areas furthest from
the initial dispersal centre. Thus a 1935 report, dealing with the
furthermost expansion zone (towards Pangala), speaks of 'the
confused situation' created by 'the jumbling up of villages' and
'overlapping' of territory.[15] In the second place, as we have just
seen, they were the result of intervention by the colonial authorities. The policy of resettlement created artificial units, sometimes known as 'official villages', the precarious nature of which
may be seen from the fact that the villagers often refused to give
them a name. These haphazard agglomerations not only brought
together lineages that were 'strangers' to one another or had been
brought up on memories of bitter hostility, but in many cases it
also meant they had to settle far from their own territory, and thus
found themselves permanently in debt to the owners of the land
they occupied. It is readily understandable, therefore, that unless
the benefits proved to be substantial such groups tended to return
to their own territory as soon as opportunity occurred. Lastly, the
problems were particularly acute owing to the very considerable
gulf between their new economic conditions and their traditional
relations with the land. The need to obtain cash meant that they
had to settle in areas where the system of communications made it

* In the old Mayama district, the village of Vindza, despite the fact that it was the
home of a very powerful administrative chief, was broken up, and this led to the
creation of sixteen encampments at a time when the villagers were at odds with the
administration because they refused to join the Native Social Insurance Association
and pay their dues.

possible to sell their produce; but the obligation to hold on to the clan land because of their ancestral tombs, the difficulty of obtaining land from strangers and the relatively high concentration of population tended to counteract all attempts to redistribute the population.

The Ba-Kongo were faced by a basic problem. Land had acquired a value that it had never previously had. It could be used as security for debt. Fewer and fewer people were prepared to dispose of it (all our informants insisted that 'nowadays there is too little land and too many people wanting it', and that it was scarcely ever given up except to 'relations by marriage', and then only on condition that there were not too many of them); and it was now possible to demand rent for it (50 per cent of the crop)[16] from 'strangers'. At the same time this process was to some extent offset by various 'correctives': it was possible for lineages to exchange land, and sometimes it might be sold to 'strangers' who had occupied it for a considerable time, simply as a way of regularizing an accomplished fact and avoiding argument when the *mfumu nkâda* died; and occasionally, in the case of a bequest, it could be bought, provided the heir already owned property that he himself had purchased. These attempts to sort matters out could not possibly be adequate. Often there had been so many upheavals that disputes were almost inevitable: sometimes the existence of ancestral graves on a particular plot made it possible to blackmail the new owners;* and again, the role played by slaves as temporary successors to the chiefs, and their attempts to establish independent groups, frequently led to litigation. Whereas among the Fang most disputes were concerned with the rights affecting people (wives and descendants), among the Ba-Kongo they were usually over the ownership of land.

Parallel with the instability of the population, there was a similar confusion as to the groups' legal rights to the land; and the consequent litigation was all the more acrimonious as a result

---

* An example of this from the Mayama region was a law suit between M'Foumou (to whom the graves belonged) and Marc (who had recently acquired the property). M'Foumou had 'touched' each of the graves, while at the same time uttering the following curse: 'May there be panthers to eat Marc's cattle! May no game be killed on this land! May no cassava or maize grow until this land belongs to me again! May the hunters find no game here and may all the grass be grazed by other people's animals'.

of the increased value of land and the fact that the price varied according to its situation in relation to a trading centre. Thus the owners of the best situated land were to some extent transformed into landed proprietors, who looked down on those who were dependent upon them and drew rent from the 'stranger' groups whom they 'harboured'. A typical example of this was the Senior Chief of the Ba-Sundi (Boko, 1951) who was said to have methodically extended his 'wealth and authority' by buying up plots of land conveniently close to roads and markets, on which he had settled five lineages directly under his control. There were also cases of enterprising chiefs who set out to obtain new plots in order to consolidate their holdings and so prevent fission. The significance of this is unmistakable: there were many ways of exerting pressure to induce people to sell, and clearly the most effective was recourse to magic. At the same time, however, custom provided a means of checking the danger of abuse: land belonging to a lineage could never be 'sold' all together; transfer could only be effected with the consent of the younger men (*ba-mpâgi*). While it could be purchased by an individual with funds to which he was personally entitled, selling it (*tékisa*) remained a collective matter[17]; in no case was it possible to transmit land by deed of gift. In this respect, clan law was still so deeply ingrained that land purchased on an individual basis, and regarded by Europeans as being private property, could not be transmitted from father to son, despite the extention of 'father right'. In this instance, custom was an effective safeguard.

From the sociological point of view, this analysis leads to certain fundamental conclusions. Despite all the upheavals, whether enforced or spontaneous, land belonging to the clan tended to remain a means of support for the groups; even the fact that property rights could be inherited individually had not yet resulted in breaking the multiple bonds between the lineages and the soil. Here we have a *continuity*, and consequently a factor of stability, that we did not find among the much less settled Fang: we came across many examples of men returning to their native villages because they had inherited land left to them by a 'maternal uncle' (*ngudi nkazi*). Furthermore, individual rivalry now found expression in terms of land rather than of people; it was the extension of the former, and its value, that determined the social importance of the *mfumu* as much as, and often more than, the size of the group under his immediate control. A change of this kind was bound to reduce the tensions implicit in the older form of competition for 'wealth in human beings' (*mbôgo bantu*). Moreover, the increased value of landed property reinforced the authority of the heads of the lineages, who held the land on behalf of the group, received any rent it brought in and sometimes pursued a genuinely expansionist policy. It was these dynamic individuals who were responsible for the emergence of what might be called a landed aristocracy; a description that is all the more appropriate in that some of them managed to maintain a retinue of one-time slaves and faithful dependents, and their authority and land were bequeathed intact to their nearest heir.

The semi-rural, semi-urban character of the Kongo people was undoubtedly the most remarkable phenomenon that resulted from colonization. In the preceding chapter, we showed that this urbanization did not involve the serious imbalances that it gave rise to in other parts of Central Africa. The exodus from the countryside was not irreversible and the distribution of the population as regards both age and sex reveal an overall progressive tendency. The reasons for this comparatively privileged position are fairly clear. In the first place, Brazzaville was not only a centre of attraction: while it certainly did attract people, both as a market for labour and as a novel kind of social environment, at the same time, by stimulating economic activity in the neighbouring regions, it also created conditions that encouraged them to return to their native villages. Moreover, living in the city, at least in the native township of Bacongo, did not involve putting up with the kind of haphazard, improvised conditions that were to be found in the second of the two capital cities. Bacongo remained, unequivocally and exclusively, an extension of the Ba-Kongo countryside, with a homogeneous population which, as any observer could see for himself, still retained the impress of tradition. This in itself was proof of the vitality of Ba-Kongo institutions, and of their capacity for adaptation.

The ties between the lineages and their urbanized members in most cases remained close. A young man might be despatched to the city by his *ngudi nkazi*, with the obligation to contribute to the finances of the family unit out of his wages; but if his 'uncle' called upon him to return to the village because his presence there would be more useful he would obey his instructions. Again, members of a lineage living in the city might be expected to contribute to the upbringing of the children, as well as to assist in forwarding their education or apprenticeship to a trade. Thus, despite the cleavage between town-dwellers and countryfolk, the family group maintained its organic unity, with all its members playing an appropriate part in an economic system that depended upon the exchange of farm produce from the village against manufactured goods from the town. In this way, some of these economic units were able to purchase their own oil presses, shops and means of transport. How close the ties with the family group remained is also apparent from the amount of money saved out of wages that found its way back to the villages; even thoroughly 'westernized' elements like government employees would set aside part of their monthly salary. The desire to remain a part of the kinship system, to be able to count on the solidarity of the family and eventually return to the village, was still keenly felt. This readiness to accept the traditional framework helped to minimize the deterioration of Ba-Kongo society; and this was due not merely to the fact of proximity, but also to a genuine concern for the preservation of the customary environment and its maintenance as a source of energy – and, above all, to the spontaneous character of the population movement which created a functional bond between the cities and the countryside.

It would be a mistake, however, to conclude from such observations that the result was a sterile conservatism – like that of the Ba-Téké, who, in similar circumstances, had lost the leading position they occupied in Brazzaville in the early days of colonization as a result of their deliberate insularity. The mobility in the villages and urban centres, which was all the more lively because of their close proximity, increased the basis for differentiation as well as the tendency to innovation. The first of these processes may be seen most clearly, perhaps, in the case of newly acquired professional skills. As an example of this, consider the village of Kihinda (on the outskirts of Boko), the seat of the Sundi chieftainship, which in 1951 comprised 45 male adults. Of these, 20 represented the following occupations: 5 business men, 1 Protestant pastor

and 2 mission teachers, 2 employees at the Swedish Evangelical
Mission, 2 administrative chiefs, 2 tailors, 2 shoemakers, a
building-worker, a carpenter, a gardener and a general labourer.
This brief list clearly illustrates the important changes that had
taken place within a group that was in no sense exceptional.
Moreover, urban influences provided a constant stimulus, the
effects of which were much more widespread and varied than
might appear at first sight, especially when one realizes how few
people there were to transmit them to the hinterland. Typical of
this was the village of Makana, in the Mayama region, where the
only dynamic element was the chief's nephew, Gabriel B., who in
1951 would have been about thirty years old. After attending a
school run by the Evangelical Mission, he was sent to Brazzaville,
where he became a chauffeur but later, under pressure from
his mother and 'uncle', he returned to his native village. At that
time he was the only genuinely urbanized individual in Makana.
Nevertheless his influence made itself felt in almost every sphere:
with regard to furnishings and fashion (he was responsible for
introducing a hair-style copied from that of the Europeans); to
domestic economy (he encouraged the production of cash crops,
and undertook to sell them on the Bacongo market with the help
of his connections there); and to religious matters, where he
advocated exclusive membership of one of the 'great religions' –
though in the event this turned out to be the local Negro church.[18]
Thus even one isolated individual could exert an influence upon
many aspects of social life.

Inevitably, the close links between town and country gave a
specific character to socio-cultural innovations. These had to
have meaning for the Ba-Kongo villager as well as for people
living in the city; they thus acquired a kind of ambivalence,
assuming forms that would facilitate their acceptance in a sociologically traditional environment. Careful study of the *Témo*
reveals the rural aspects of the institution (the tentative capitalization of certain farm incomes and labour), as well as its urban
aspects (the saving of money to meet exceptional expenses without having to resort to moneylenders, and its use as a model for
setting up commercial or cooperative companies). By employing
essentially the same type of organization in both cases, the *Témo*
did not strike the typical villager as being a radically new, and

consequently 'alien', innovation. Similarly, when we come to consider the political and politico-religious movements to which a considerable part of this study is devoted, we shall find that institutions imported from abroad – like the Friendly Societies (*Amicales*) introduced from France by André Matswa – were profoundly modified by traditional society. Apart from one or two groups that settled in Poto-Poto in order to escape from customary restrictions, the cleavage between city-dwellers and country-folk was never decisive.

The Interpretation of Change

Before leaving this question of the social changes determined by modifications of a morphological order it may be as well, perhaps, to summarize their main features. The upheavals due to direct intervention by the colonial government at first stimulated fission, but the smaller groups that this led to nevertheless eventually settled on territory belonging to the clans. The connection with the land was intensified as its value increased thanks to new opportunities of disposing of farm produce; and inheritance of land was sufficient inducement to men who had settled in the cities to return to their villages. Since the economic development of cultivated land was due to the existence of a growing *local market* it was possible for it to become part of the traditional system, though at the same time it gave rise to greater commercial activity and widened the field of social relations. It was thanks to the latter that, despite the persistence of particularism, the conception of a Ba-Kongo nation began to take shape. Lastly, the dominant position achieved by the Ba-Kongo in the Brazzaville townships, while it involved an increasing interchange of ideas and growing mobility, did not inevitably result in the break-up of Kongo society; instead of a complete cleavage, town and country folk continued to exert a reciprocal influence on one another. There can be no mistaking the vitality of a society and culture that displayed such genuine powers of assimilation and adaptation.

These general observations were borne out when we came to examine the economic changes that were taking place. On two occasions we have drawn attention to the significance of the

Témo, where successive modifications produced a number of variants adapted to very different requirements. In a similar way, the traditional markets and trading network constituted a system of exchange of which the colonial economy availed itself from the start; thus 'trading' could be carried on without direct intervention by the European business firms in the capital, since the markets had become 'genuine fairs, so attractive to the natives that they were prepared to travel two or three days in order to get there'.[19] Later, the markets served as centres for supplying food for the Brazzaville townships, and as convenient meeting places for the conduct of important business.

Economic innovations were often carried out *without disturbing the traditional framework*. In this respect we have drawn attention to the way in which essentially family units were responsible for cooperation between townsfolk and villagers; and this was also the case with modern economic developments, most of which were only viable with the help of the descent group. In the Boko region the production of palm oil, at least on any scale, was organized around depots established by well-to-do individuals (business men, chiefs or catechists) who could rely upon their kinsmen for harvesting, purchasing and treating the palm kernels. As regards agricultural concessions of any considerable size and run on up-to-date lines, here too we find that the main role was played by kinsmen with the help of a paid labour force employed as labourers or even simply forced to work.[20] One of the most convincing tests of the hold that tradition still has upon those most actively engaged in the Kongo economy is the fact that the property they acquire 'remains within the clan', and is shared out in accordance with customary rules. Land, like accumulated wealth, is still closely tied up with the clan group, whatever personal advantages an individual may temporarily derive from greater activity. Despite the tendency to atomization of the residential units, it is this triple bond that constitutes the real core of resistance of the Ba-Kongo system. We shall be returning to this question, but for the moment will simply state our view that what led to the disintegration of this complex of forces was the recognition of 'father right', particularly of his right to bequeath his prophecy to his offspring.

In his study of the Ba-Kongo economy, the geographer

G. Sautter observes that 'tradition is a hindrance to its further development'. He writes: 'The maintenance of the pre-existent system of agriculture and land-tenure, and of the family in its widest sense as the basic economic unit, shackles individual effort and prevents technical progress.' While this is valid as regards technique – as may be seen from the failure to carry out any rational reorganization of the land under cultivation, the inadequate development of agricultural methods and the poor return on investment – from the sociological point of view it requires modification. From this angle, it depends upon one's personal ideas as to the kind of stimulus likely to encourage individual effort. The Mu-Kongo continues to react as a member of a family unit, of a more or less extended lineage; as a rule he accepts the fact that his activities (and the profits resulting from them) are part of a system that extends beyond himself and the restricted family to which he is immediately attached; he is therefore primarily concerned, often as a result of his improved economic position, with increasing the aggregate of kinsmen, dependents and affines so that his own group may become large enough to enhance his personal prestige and authority. It was only by taking advantage of economic opportunities of this kind that some of the descendants of slaves succeeded in escaping from a position that was fundamentally detrimental to them.

It should be pointed out, however, that there are other and more personal factors serving to stimulate effort. A wife has her own 'savings' (and some of the peasant women risk relatively large sums of money when they join the *Témo* that they organize for the sale of cassava), of which part is set aside for the head of her own lineage, but which she can also use to give 'presents' to her husband. In this way she is able to modify her dependence upon both of them. The relatively high status she used to enjoy in traditional society, as a free woman, is more easily maintained when the economic situation is favourable to her – as may be seen in the Boko and Kinkala regions. Equally, a man who had not yet acquired the privileges dependent upon age (including the rank of *mbuta*), or who occupied an inferior position as the descendant of slaves, was able to obtain financial resources by increasing the cultivation of cash crops (which were outside the traditional system of organization),* by selling the products of local craftsmanship (basket work), or by engaging in retail trade, selling from door to door or even smuggling. Here too, the multiplicity of new sources of income, however un-remunerative, helped to weaken the authority of the chiefs and notables. For the Mu-Kongo, the most effective stimulus was not only the opportunity of increasing his personal wealth (as earned by his own industry), but also the possibility this provided of extending his freedom of action.

The real reason for this lack of 'individual effort' is rather to be found in the nature of the economy. At a time when the pos-sibility of obtaining cash incomes was becoming increasingly important, the economy itself remained extremely precarious, not only because it was insufficiently differentiated and too closely dependent upon the fluctuating Brazzaville market, but also because it was not very profitable, since the main outlet for its products were the impoverished inhabitants of the urban town-ships. Moreover, the general pattern of behaviour was still ill-adjusted to a cash economy, although a growing proportion of earnings was absorbed by consumer goods. Insofar as increased savings became possible, it was *the purpose of such saving* that was in question.

The opportunities for accumulating wives had decreased with the decline of slavery and a less effective control of the marriage system, and also as a result of the influence of Christianity and modern education. In addition to this, the social position enjoyed by a Kongo wife, unless she was a slave, had always enabled her to resist any attempt at the kind of commercialization we have seen in the case of Fang wives. The form of accumulation most in demand was land, but this could only be acquired in the name of a lineage. This remained exceptional, partly on practical grounds (a number of groups complained of the scarcity of good land), but more particularly for social reasons – the fact that clan

* When the missionaries wished to influence the traditional context that en-couraged polygamy, they were careful to base their activity on economic as well as moral grounds. This was why they tried to introduce new crops which could be sold on the market and were accepted as being the responsibility of the men. In this way, the missionaries hoped to create 'producers of *mbongo*, material wealth', who would make a sufficient margin of profit to enable them to remain monogamous. For further details, see Van Wing, *Et. Bk.*, pp. 234–5.

territory, owing to the ties involved, was central to the entire Kongo social system. On the other hand, investment in cattle scarcely existed and, in general, was looked down upon (for ritual purposes, offerings of palm wine and the sacrifices of a chicken sufficed); there were practically no pigs and even fewer goats, while the rearing of calves for the butchers in the towns was mainly restricted to women. The accumulation of wealth continued to take the form of property that had prestige value (brick-built houses not fully occupied, ostentatious furnishings, decoration, etc.), or of the trade-goods that traditionally represented the 'treasure' (*mbôgo*) of a man of standing. Such savings as the villagers managed to put by were only very occasionally used in a productive way. Indeed, when we consider an institution like the *malaki*, it would seem that there was still a lively concern on the part of the lineages to compete with one another in destroying part of their accumulated wealth in collective feasting. The persistence of an institution, which in the past had involved both the living and the dead, is to be explained not only by the fact that it had taken on the modern characteristics of a speculative gamble, but also by the difficulties involved in creating personal property. By presenting a financial challenge that affected the prestige of the groups, and providing ample opportunity for the consumption of the goods required by the ceremony, the *collective* character of wealth was periodically reasserted.

The existence of behaviour patterns corresponding to two essentially different types of economy is to be seen most clearly in the choice confronting anyone who had managed to accumulate capital. Either he could use it for 'a genuine economic investment' with a view to making profit and benefiting himself, in which case his 'capitalist outlook' cut him off from his native social environment (and in any case instances of this were unusual and almost entirely restricted to the towns). Or, on the other hand, he might choose to invest it 'sociologically', taking advantage of the new economic conditions to achieve or strengthen a social position of the traditional kind, in which case the number of his dependents and the extent of his generosity would be the measure of his success, and his profit would take the form of prestige and authority. This was the choice that was usually made: economic activity was still regarded simply as a means of achieving objectives

f a kind determined by the traditional social and cultural
ystem.[21]

III. FACTORS OF EQUILIBRIUM AND DISEQUILIBRIUM
IN MODERN BA-KONGO SOCIETY

Suicide and Sorcery

n the course of our enquiry, our attention was drawn to a fact that
; rarely met with in Negro-African society: the existence of
uicide. In 1949, in the Kinkala region alone, five cases of suicide
vere known to the police and officially reported.* That this was a
henomenon of some significance is shown by the fact that the
uthors of *Notes sur les coutumes lari* considered it worth mention-
1g. 'There have always been suicides' they write, 'but they seem
o be restricted to ordinary people faced by exceptional difficul-
.es. The most frequent cases are to be found among women who
ose their babies. The methods employed are hanging, or shooting.
uicide is not looked upon as a disgrace, though there is no funeral
eremony or mourning period.'[22] Here three points stand out:
uicide appears to be connected with the 'lower' social categories;
is not illegal, and *seems* to be regarded as commonplace; and
hose who commit suicide are usually people living on the fringe
f society. Suicides resulting from an overwrought emotional
ondition are rare; and the manifestations of grief at the death of
chief or venerated elder that simulate suicide, are as a rule con-
rolled. Van Wing refers to the latter, but points out that 'in such
ircumstances authentic cases of suicide are exceptional'.†
 In fact, the investigation we carried out convinced us that most
ases of suicide were associated with possession by the *nkundu*,
hat is to say, with individuals accused of having the power to
:at the souls of their fellow men' (*ba-ndòki*). Whether the suicide
vas accused of practising sorcery or was himself the victim of
orcery, the individual concerned was no longer fully integrated

---

* I.e. 1·56 per 10,000 of the population; the same figure as that given by R.
astide for the Brazilian Negroes of São Paulo in the year 1885.

† *Et. Bk.*, p. 276. 'Men become excited and howl. Others snatch up a gun as though
 kill themselves. As a rule, however, all this is simply a way of displaying their
rief, for they know very well that they will be prevented from doing so. Cases of
uicide do occur under these circumstances, but usually these noisy outbursts of grief
ontain a considerable element of play-acting.'

with society nor subject to the laws affecting the relations between people and ensuring their protection. The effects of being accused of sorcery or subjected to the nefarious influence of the *ndòki* were much the same; for the individual concerned the lineage ceased to be 'inhabitable'. This is a very widespread phenomenon observed by Bastide among the Brazilian Negroes. 'The most significant fact', he writes, 'is that the individual no longer feels himself to be a part of a complex of institutions and customs that he can rely upon, and that gives him a sense of security: he does not know where to turn.'[23] Similarly, when we were studying the native townships, we came across people who, because they felt themselves to be 'threatened', had left their villages to seek refuge in the town, where they refused to join any association that might bring them into contact with their own group; they were trying to lose themselves in the impersonal society of a great city.[24]

Here we have a series of facts which cannot be explained solely on metaphysical grounds (a body of beliefs about sickness, death and the whole system of forces to which human beings are subject), but which are determined also by sociological factors. To be accused of possession by a *nkundu* necessarily involved submitting oneself to ordeal by poison (*nkasa*),* the outcome of which was either death (accompanied by outbreaks of public violence that sometimes included cutting up and burning the victim's body) or a declaration of innocence with the right to indemnification by the accusers. The part that sorcery played in traditional society explains the importance of detecting and suppressing it. If a group was threatened by some serious crisis and the ordinary forms of therapy proved ineffective, seeking out the *ndòki* and putting him to death established his guilt, thus exculpating the other members and restoring the confidence of the group as a whole. Bonnefond and Lombard quote examples of 'heads of families' who were prepared to submit themselves to *nkasa* in the hope of putting an end to a series of calamities affecting the people for whose safety they were responsible.† This shows how

---

* A poison made from the bark of the *nkasa* tree (*Erythrophleum guineense* Don. Leg., to which a more active poison known as *nbundu* is sometimes added.

† *Notes sur les coutumes lari*, p. 156. 'It sometimes happens that the head of a family who suffers a succession of deaths amongst his close kindred is so upset that he asks to be put to the poison test. His kinsfolk prepare the poison and, if he dies of it, his family does not grieve and his nephews do not wear mourning for him.'

closely the idea of collective salvation is bound up with the sacrificial putting to death of the sorcerer. The group survives by
expelling and destroying that part of itself that symbolizes all that
is anti-social or a-social. Negro societies are no more perfect than
our own. When confronted by a crisis they feel the need for self-
renewal: putting to death the sorcerer temporarily restores a kind
of ideal society.* One of our most helpful informants, the old
chief Bwago, was of the opinion that abandoning ordeal by poison
and the execution of the *ndòki* was, together with the decline of
the ancestor cult, one of the changes most seriously imperilling
the future of Kongo society. He was afraid that by foregoing
this means of self-protection society would find itself defenceless.

In addition to this general function, a custom of this kind had
other, more limited, effects: by making it possible to get rid of
refractory individuals, it was politically helpful to the chiefs;
and, particularly in recent times, it has been a means of expressing
the rivalry between social groups and individuals. Earlier writers
emphasize the effectiveness of the *nkasa* ordeal when the accused
man was looked upon as an 'undesirable', living on the fringe of
society.

Van Wing, for instance, speaks of the publicity given to
the execution, and its exemplary significance; it was a way of
getting rid of individuals who threatened to disturb the social
order, and of reaffirming its integrity. An official document,
produced in 1935 in the Boko region, maintains that the accusation of sorcery 'virtually amounts to excommunication'; the only
alternative to suicide,† for a man presumed to be guilty, was to
undergo ordeal by poison, his one chance of proving his innocence. The document makes it clear that anyone suspected of
being *ndòki* was regarded as an alien element within society. In the
hands of a chief who had won the complete confidence of the
fetishists responsible for administering it, the ordeal might well
become an adjunct of despotic power. It was in this way that

---

* Slaves were the most frequent victims of this sacrificial therapy: cf. *Et. Bk.*,
pp. 286–7.
† Since suicide sometimes appears to be the solution suggested by the party who
feels himself to be in danger. An example of this is given by J. Mertens in *op. cit.*,
XVI, 4, pp. 203–4.

Biza, a powerful chief of the Ba-Lali of Boko, maintained his authority over a whole number of lineages, who, on his death, reverted to a state of relative autonomy. The fact that this superior chief should have been especially feared is not, perhaps, surprising, when we find that in 1935 forty-eight people were subjected to the *nkasa* in less than six months.[25] Biza used to maintain that *nkasa* was an essential means of keeping order, and he 'defied the white men to put an end to this custom'. Furthermore, it must be remembered that an accusation of sorcery was all the more frightening in that it concerned not only a particular individual but, through him, his whole lineage.

In contemporary Kongo society, sorcery still plays an important part, sometimes even leading to individual or collective migration. It even constitutes a more serious danger than it did in the old days, because it gives rise to a state of *anxiety* of which a number of religious movements engaged in the struggle against possession by the *nkundu* are ready to take advantage.* The reason for this is clear. Social change has gravely affected traditional organization, upsetting a hierarchy that used to impose unequal status on the individuals comprising Kongo society. Colonization challenged the very basis of this inequality: by a kind of boomerang effect, sorcery, as a means of exacting vengeance, came to be feared most when employed by the descendants of slaves, since it was precisely they who, in the past, had been most frequently accused of being *ki-ndòki*. Moreover, modern economic conditions have intensified competition, thus creating new forms of inequality. Personal envy has become a factor of increasing social importance, bringing with it all the dangers, especially that of sorcery, that it has always engendered.† Lastly, the Ba-Kongo are convinced that European opposition to their methods of defence against sorcery has brought them to a state of permanent insecurity. They are bewildered by changes which they are no longer permitted to deal with in their own way, and as a result of this

---

* As was the case with certain Salvation Army missions that were only subject to very remote European control.

† Cf. *Et. Bk.* pp. 176–7. 'The most execrated of vices is *kimpala*, ill-natured and hateful envy. Its existence is due to the workings of the whole mysterious basis of the human being, heart, liver, viscera, soul and the soul's double, everything that is called *ntema, mbundu, moyo, mfumu, kutu*. Sorcery springs from envy. The Mu-Kongo is very susceptible to this vice, and knows it. . . .'

feeling, by a kind of vicious circle, there are now more people suffering from possession than ever. A similar phenomenon has frequently been observed by English anthropologists in 'transitional' Bantu societies.

In the light of these facts, we came to the conclusion that there is a significant connection between the accusation of sorcery (signifying '*social* death'), suicide (the ensuing *physical* death), and certain 'areas', or moments, of disequilibrium in Kongo society. One might almost say that explanation in terms of *ki-ndòki* is typical of any situation where established techniques, typical behaviour patterns and customary law have proved ineffectual; it is, so to speak, an 'emergency measure'. This would explain why the colonial situation has led to an extension of sorcery – though obviously unconsciously, and often as a result of trying to suppress it. Moreover, in contrast to most current ideas on the subject, it is important to emphasize the positive aspects of *ki-ndòki* (this was already implicit in what we said above about the connection between the sacrificial putting to death of the sorcerer and the temporary restoration of order). The fear of sorcery being practised within the lineage (the most dangerous kind of all) has to some extent helped to prevent the breakdown of restricted groups that would have resulted from uncontrolled competition between members of the same kinship group. Lastly, by a kind of paradox, sorcery could not develop beyond a certain point without producing a progressive form of counteraction; thus the development of religious movements opposed to fetishism, and seeking to achieve the unity and genuine reconstruction of society, were assisted by the fear inspired by the *ndòki*.[26] Apart from the moral judgements that a 'custom' of this kind involves (and how often do we stop to ask ourselves what will be the human cost of our own 'emergency measures'?), one cannot feel satisfied that it should be allowed to disappear until other institutions have been developed that are capable of taking over its positive functions.

Then again, the way in which it operates draws attention to an aspect of Ba-Kongo psychology that we shall later be considering in greater detail. It reveals the sense of guilt that is experienced at any violation of the law that constitutes a serious threat to society, and explains why, once the crime has been publicly exposed, it is accepted in all its consequences with apparent indifference.* In a case that was tried before the District Officer of Boko in 1932, he was amazed at the way the prisoners, who were accused of sorcery, stuck to the confessions they had made under duress. 'One felt completely nonplussed', he wrote, 'by their repeated admissions of complicity in a monstrous crime, and by the obstinate way in which they insisted that they had actually eaten human flesh.'[27] Another case, that occurred in the same district two years later, shows what strenuous efforts one of the villagers had made to put a stop to a series of disasters for which a dead man, one of his closest relatives, was accused of being responsible – he even went as far as to dig up the body and burn it. When interrogated, he made it quite clear that if he had failed to take effective action he would have considered himself to be guilty.† These documents are interesting for another reason; they show how the treatment of the ba-ndòki has been adapted to the new socio-cultural context: the essential fact is still the *admission of guilt*, publicly confessed; while the payment of a fine (in these two cases blankets and cash) is accepted as proof of the confession, tantamount to making material compensation.

If one accepts a category invented by certain American anthropologists, Kongo society may be described as a *guilt culture*.[28] The importance of this sense of guilt is seen not only in such examples as those we have just cited, but also in the part played by public confession in general. For instance, in cases of polygamous marriage or adultery, whether proved or assumed, involving hardship for the children, the ritual of *maguga* has to be observed. This ceremony, conducted by an elder, entails public confession of the illicit sexual relations between the man and woman, or women, followed by the 'blessing' (*kuguga*: hence the name of the

* This may be compared with a passage from a study by M. Sinda, who is himself a Kongo: 'A sorcerer cannot face up to being pointed out publicly. . . . He becomes an outcast, who simultaneously loses both his natural powers and his skill. In short, he becomes the victim of society,' *Le messianisme congolais et ses incidences politiques*, Ms., 1961.

† See the N'kouka case, June 27, 1934, Boko archives. The following is an extract from the preliminary cross-examination of the prisoner N'kouka: 'My brother, Bemba Fonda, died on May 8, 1934. Since then he has caused the death of five goats, a dog and ten pigs. I was afraid that he would end up by killing people, and that I should be accused of sorcery. I sent for the fetishist. He came, and put a spell on him.'

rite) of the guilty parties with a whisk made of small twigs; a cock
is then sacrificed, and subsequently eaten communally. Father Van
Wing, who describes the ceremony in detail, goes on to say: 'It is
the only way of curing the diseases by which the pagans and the
children of the harem are afflicted as a result of the misbehaviour
(*késa*) of a husband or his wives.'[29] The efficacy of the *maguga*
appears to be dependent upon the public admission of guilt, which
alone makes possible a return to normal relations. Obviously the
profound influence of Christianity upon the Kongo people has
helped to reinforce the significance of confession: the messianic
movements that led to the setting up of Negro churches attributed
considerable importance to the practice, sometimes insisting upon
it as a preliminary condition of membership. Moreover, this
publicizing of everyone's sins has another salutary effect: it helps
to restore their confidence when faced with the activities of the
ki-ndòki or the spreading of malevolent illnesses by clandestine
means.

Without accepting any of the theories that seek to equate a
culture's sense of guilt with a progressive outlook, one nevertheless has to recognize that the Mu-Kongo are extremely sensitive
to any transgression of the social order, quick to draw attention
to it and ready to adopt the necessary means of restoring order.
They seem to have acquired an acute sense of social reality and
of the fundamental relations that must be maintained, as well as a
deep attachment to a social order that helps them to avoid any
'deviation' that might endanger them personally. This is a factor
making for both cohesion and stability.

At this point, however, it is time to consider those factors that
tend to produce disequilibrium, the most remarkable of which
is the tendency for 'father right' to replace the authority of the
maternal uncle (*nkazi*). Though instances of this are still rare, the
tendency is unmistakable.

The development of 'father right'

Adopting the terminology used by J. Mertens in his studies of
Kongo jurisdiction, one might say that the physical father tends
to become the 'legal father'. In the light of field work carried out
in the Congo (Leopoldville) on modifications of the marriage

system, V. Mertens makes the same point, though in a rather different way. 'The importance of the natural father's social role', he says, 'is increasing at the expense of the excessive authority of the clan.' This phenomenon of *partial* substitution does not occur, however, without setbacks, as we ourselves had occasion to discover. It is often said that, nowadays, the *nkazi*'s sole purpose in seeking to obtain control of his nephews is to get hold of their earnings. Clearly that is a tendentious interpretation, that betrays the economic effects of intensified competition. If control of the children's property is transferred to the father, instead of being in the hands of the maternal uncle as hitherto, land must eventually cease to belong to the clan and become private property; and it is this fundamental question of private property that underlies the deepening antagonism between the father and the *nkazi*.

Direct attempts to assert the priority of father right are still rare: only those who have recently attained social pre-eminence, and are therefore in favour of social reorganization, have any strong inducement to set themselves up against custom. It is more a matter of tendencies. With the consent of their *nkazi*, children on reaching the age of puberty may continue to live with their father, but this is only agreed to on the understanding that the gifts the *mwana-nkazi* make to their *nkazi* are not regarded as a form of compensation, but rather as a periodical reaffirmation of the *nkazi*'s prior rights, even if he does not insist upon exercising them. This is a transitional solution, which is only viable provided both lineages agree to this adaptation of customary procedure. In other cases, on the death of a *nkazi*, or when a man returns to the village after a protracted stay in the city, the sons are encouraged to settle down near the paternal compound. We observed a number of similar instances and found that in many cases the sense of mutual solidarity and assistance existing between father and son was stronger than the relations between *nkazi* and *mwana-nkazi*. This development was directly connected with the new economic conditions – the increasing importance of individually earned incomes, the growing accumulation of cash as well as of personal chattels (private ownership of which had always been recognized by custom), and the emergence of new forms of property (tools, means of transport, small businesses, etc.) which, although of considerable value, were outside the traditional context.

It was also connected with the cultural influence exerted by Europeans, especially with the continual struggle of the Christian missionaries to establish monogamy, which meant not only that the married couple was accepted as the basic social unit, but also that their children were expected to go on living with them.* In addition to this, the effects of modern legislation must also be taken into account: in particular, the admittedly rudimentary projects for family insurance for wage-earners, and a whole body of more recent regulations that are either based upon 'father right' or tend to encourage it. At the same time, the transition from mother right to father right is not as subversive as might at first sight appear. In an earlier chapter we insisted on the partial recognition accorded to the patri-clan, on the bonds of affection and obligation existing between sons and their father's descent group and on their recognition of a direct blood relationship with him (though not with the other members of his lineage). Moreover, the father has real power over his descendants: not only can he resort to the dreaded weapon of malediction, which destroys its victim's peace of mind and condemns him to a miserable death,[30] but when the time comes for his daughters to get married his rights are recognized and he is also expected to contribute to the bride-wealth which his sons need to obtain a wife.

However, these are opportunities of which he can only occasionally avail himself: there are still formidable obstacles to the full acceptance of father right. To begin with, there is the whole complex of notions relating to the system of forces which, for good or ill, affect the lives of every individual: most Ba-Kongo, for instance, still believe that illness can only be cured 'within the family', that is to say, in contact with the *nkazi*. Again, the concept of servile descent – only the offspring of slave wives live permanently with the father, because they have no clan to go to when they reach the age of puberty – has a negative effect: as yet, men 'born in the clan' are not prepared to be confused with those 'born in the village'. The main obstacle, however, to the transfer

* See *Et. Bk.*, pp. 233–8. From what Father Van Wing says, it is quite clear that the efforts of the missionaries to encourage monogamous marriage is inseparable from the struggle to establish paternal authority. He himself expresses the view that the law should entitle a monogamous father to a large measure of paternal authority.

of rights is the attitude of all those who are not prepared to support a change calling in question the very nature and basis of Kongo society; and among these are to be found many of the younger men whose outlook, in other respects, is progressive.

It has always to be remembered that the fundamental bonds at the heart of this society and its culture are those between the land belonging to the clan, the matrilineal lineages, and the ancestors. These constitute a complex of intense and deeply felt relationships, integrated with one another through the medium of the marriage system. All the main social and economic relations are organized and interconnected in terms of this complex, which is represented schematically in the following diagram.

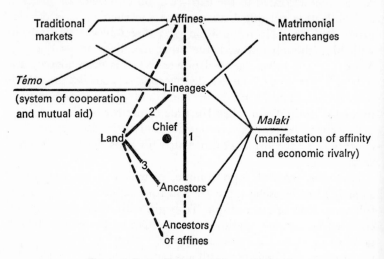

Figure 9. Basic Social and Economic Bonds

The seriousness of what is at stake in this struggle between mother right and father right, which results from colonization and the evolution of society, is readily apparent: if the latter were eventually to gain the upper hand, the essential relationships (1, 2 and 3 above) would be broken, and this would involve a radical breakdown of the traditional system.

There are plenty of signs, however, that traditional attitudes are not accepted merely from some kind of lazy conservatism, but are respected and capable of arousing positive attitudes. In Mayama, a government chauffeur, having managed to save enough money to buy a plot of land, established his *nkazi* (less well off than himself) on his newly acquired property; he was satisfied that by complying with custom his rights would be effectively guaranteed. In general, people still look to their *nkazi* for the most reliable advice and instruction. The common expression *kâda dyani* ('my family'), which means the whole group of a man's nephews and nieces, though not his sons and daughters, is still the one that arouses the strongest affective reactions. These are no more than straws in the wind, yet they imply that the fundamental social relations still persist. But though they may retard the contrary phenomenon, the extension of father right, the latter nevertheless continues to develop; and since in a sense its development provides us with a means of assessing the changes which, at any given moment, are taking place within Kongo society, it deserves the closest study.

Decline of the traditional hierarchy

If one considers the history of Ba-Kongo society, from the days of São Salvador (when its unity was most marked and its hierarchic organization most effective) up to the present, one cannot help noticing that the authority of the most comprehensive groups tended to break down unless they were directly connected with the kinship system. In his preface to *Études Bakongo*, de Jonghe stresses this process of decline, and attributes it mainly to 'the use of the dispersed clan as a political organism'.[31] In the absence of historical documentation, it is impossible to trace the stages of this decline prior to the main epoch of colonial expansion. Nevertheless it is clear that the colonial government seriously weakened the traditional hierarchies, not only by abolishing the basic distinction between free men and slaves, but also by creating an official, and often alien, hierarchy (by investing men who belonged to minor lineages, or who had bought their freedom, with administrative authority).[32]

In Fang society, as we have seen, there was a strong egalitarian tendency, and those individuals whose authority was due to their own initiative were more highly regarded than those who owed it to government patronage. But this was not so with the Ba-Kongo. As long as the kingdom of Kongo managed to survive there had been a central government, a 'nobility', a hierarchy of chiefs (as may be seen from the fact that their vassals paid tribute, *nkòtò*), a hierarchy of tribes (dominated by the Ba-Mpangu) and a hierarchy of clans, which in those days had specific functions.[33] During the modern period traces of this hierarchical organization persisted in the superiority of the senior lineages, who alone enjoyed the right of *tukisa* (i.e. of submitting candidates for the position of 'crowned chief'*), the superior status of the *ki-mfumu* (free men) and the respect accorded to the elders, compared with the relatively subordinate status of the younger men (*niéké*).

We have already mentioned some of the factors tending to off-set the inherent inferiority of men born 'outside the clan', the most important of which was direct intervention by the colonial government and missionaries. This did not prevent the practice of slavery from being carried on surreptitiously, but at least it provided an opportunity for the less submissive of the slaves to react against it – though few cases seem to have been reported to the authorities, for the archives contain no evidence of any significant resistance on their part. It is also true that, in the early stages of colonialism, the free men who were unwilling to become involved tended to push the slaves into the limelight: not only were they sent to the mission schools and public works, but they also acted as men of straw for the real leaders, especially for the *mfumu mpu* who refused to have anything to do with the Europeans. In this way they were in a position to further their own emancipation, and were the first to acquire the modernist training that was to make them indispensable when the traditional environment began to change. They were often to be found – though accurate figures are difficult to come by – among the more powerful chiefs and leaders of politico-religious movements. Lastly, it appears that with the development of the Ba-Kongo economy a number of 'slaves' succeeded in buying their freedom, thus becoming *kulu ba-ntu*, that is to say, entitled to break away and found their own lineages, the *size* of which depended upon the

---

* Even today, when the *mpu* chieftainships have lost their efficacy, the head of the eldest lineage still enjoys considerable status; he remains an instrument of conciliation and a higher judicial authority.

conomic resources available, while their prestige was determined
by the number of free wives they were able to accumulate who
ould provide them with children 'born within the clan'. Moreover, the fact that the administration treated them equally, especi-
lly as regards political promotion, in addition to the equality of
opportunity afforded by modern society, meant that in the areas
most exposed to European influence the distinction between 'free
men' and 'slaves' gradually ceased to have any meaning. Now that
both free men and slaves were subject to the same central
authority, and that religious life was dominated by Christianity
and the new cults, the political and religious criteria which had
been the essential basis of the distinction between them disappeared. At the same time, a new process of differentiation was
beginning to take effect, all the more significant in that it was due
to the new economic and political conditions.

Today, the gradual elimination of slavery does not present very
acute internal problems. They only arise incidentally – with
regard to litigation over an inheritance, or a sudden crisis due to
an outbreak of sorcery, or in personal disputes when a reminder
of a man's slave antecedents may serve to humiliate one's
antagonist.* Where discrimination chiefly persists is in the case of
slave wives; they are still treated as 'family property', and what
becomes of them is solely a matter for the head of the lineage to
which they belong. There are a number of reasons for this: it is
much more difficult for a slave woman to purchase her freedom;
he husbands, even when themselves descended from slaves, are
anxious to maintain a distinction that entitles them to keep these
producers of men'; and thirdly, in polygamous families, the subordinate position of free wives is minimized by the yet inferior
status of slave wives. As far as the male slaves are concerned, on
the contrary, the potential antagonisms are 'suspended', since on
the one hand any economic activity entails a large measure of
cooperation, and on the other the political situation has created
a relatively uniform standard of behaviour in the new institutions,
and particularly in political parties.

The integration of one-time slaves within the existing structures has often been achieved (unlike the case of the Ba-Pounou, a

* But this is exceptional, for there is always the danger that it would provoke a
further act of sorcery by way of vengeance.

related people settled in the Gabon-Congo*) without there being any special lineages whose very designation denotes their servile origin.[34] In general, however, at least among groups who have been prepared to accept modernist influences, there is a certain reserve – one might almost say a conspiracy of silence – with regard to past slavery; just as with other peoples, like the Fang, there is a similar reserve with respect to ancient rites involving cannibalism. Then, too, the concern of the most dynamic sector of Kongo society to assert its leadership of the less advanced ethnic groups, and to demonstrate its acceptance of civilized standards, also helped to accelerate the processes conducive to emancipation. At the same time, the achievement of emancipation entailed important modifications: it contributed to the weakening of the traditional authority that was based upon the numerical size and accumulated wealth of the lineage; and it affected those social relations that *indirectly* guaranteed favourable conditions for other socially subordinate categories – for instance, a free wife could not be treated in the same way as a slave wife, nor could a younger son be subjected like a man born outside the clan. Lastly, this major emancipation set off a chain reaction. In particular, it led to the emancipation of the younger men, thus creating a genuine crisis in the troubled period at the end of the Second World War, when the young dissidents were known as 'Gaullists' because they had grown up in the days when General de Gaulle was establishing his position.† While it cannot be said that the gradual disappearance of slavery was in itself conducive to disorder – the Ba-Kongo succeeded in eliminating it much more successfully than other African peoples – it was nevertheless one of a number of factors that contributed to the breakdown of the traditional hierarchy.

At this point, we must consider in some detail the position of the *chief* in modern Kongo society. A report published in 1937 stressed the ambiguity of a situation in which the chiefs found themselves 'being pulled in two directions at once': 'Our efforts to strengthen their authority all too often result in an appreciable decline in their traditional prestige.'[35] Since his authority was

* Among the Ba-Pounou only the name of the lineage is used, not that of the clan (for example, *Dibura Simba*, lineage of the slave Simba).

† In 1950 they were accused of knowing nothing about custom and of rejecting the basic behaviour patterns and the essential forms of authority.

derived from a foreign government, the more the latter sought to extend his official duties the more the chief found his real power diminishing. Judging from the Political Reports from 1915 to 1920, it seems that the period when the chiefs provided an effective form of administration did not last long. From 1926 to 1928 onwards, one or two of them even attempted to revive their prestige by joining the opposition movement, which by then was beginning to make headway among the Ba-Lali. But a reaction against colonial domination, of which they were the instruments (it was they who collected taxes, transmitted official orders, served as intermediaries between Europeans and villagers, etc.), was not *of itself* enough to explain their loss of authority and moral influence.

In the first place, the office of chief had to a considerable extent become secularised. This is a well-known phenomenon: writing about Vietnam in its colonial days,[36] Mus points out that as soon as people realized that the authority of the traditional rulers was derived from the French Government, instead of being 'a mandate from heaven', it lost its religious significance and gradually declined. In the old Ba-Kongo society, the essential functions of the chief were those of a priest – he was the focal point of all the forces that linked together land, ancestors and lineages – and judge. Nowadays, when the religious role of the lineages has been taken over by the Christian missionaries, and more recently by the neo-Christian churches, the 'priesthood' has ceased to be a province of the chieftainship. Many of the *mfumu mpu*, like our old informant Mbwâgo, would like to see a revival of the ancestor cult, which they regard as their only chance of restoring their diminished authority. In the same way, though not to the same extent, the chiefs have lost their authority as judges and arbitrators. Many disputes are now settled by the authorities, who have introduced new legal principles that cannot always be reconciled with customary law. The compromises made in the cities, where two rival legal systems conflict, have also contributed to the impoverishment and secularization of custom (inasmuch as it represents a complex of intangible precepts imposed and 'guaranteed' by the ancestors); nor has the precaution of associating with the chief, in the execution of his judicial functions, representatives of the lineages subject to his jurisdiction prevented the decline of his authority. Traditionally, the purpose of the chief-tainship was to protect the interests both of the individual and of the group, not simply to administer people and property. But the government has tended to transform the chief into a mere agent, with little or no concern for personal relations – an administrative functionary, responsible for counting heads, keeping accounts and issuing orders. These two conceptions are almost impossible to reconcile, and in fact the result has simply been a *duplication of authority*: on the one hand, the 'clerk', a more competent admini-strator who often supplants the chief;[37] and, on the other, the kind of man best described as a 'prophet', who is capable of restoring the essential links between syncretistic structures. Faced by this split, which involves choosing the best means of control-ling considerable bodies of people, the traditional chiefs have often proved incapable of maintaining their influence.

In addition to these changes, which we have dealt with first because they affect the whole conception of traditional political authority, we now have to consider the general, overall con-ditions that have led to the virtual disappearance of the tradi-tional chief – though the position is not as serious as that of the Ba-Kongo on the left bank, of which Van Wing wrote in the 1920s: 'All authority is at an end. Things have reached such a pitch that in many villages there is no longer either chief or judge.'[38] In the first place, we have to bear in mind the serious upheavals to which the lineages had been subjected both by arbitrary uprooting and resettlement at the hands of the admini-stration, and by the spontaneous process of fission, the mechanics of which we have already discussed. The consequent intermixing of incompatible clan fragments had sapped the very basis of any widespread authority – without which the chieftainship can have little meaning. At the same time, new economic conditions and the growing importance of a market economy were leading to more and more active competition. Political power relations tend to adapt themselves to economic power (in the modern sense), as we saw with the mock battles, in the form of cash gifts and counter-gifts, that are fought out at the *malaki* festivals.* The struggle between traditional authority and economic power was

* See also section IV of the Conclusion below, where the *malaki* is discussed at greater length.

intensified by the fact that the primitive control of the economy exercised by the chief had been progressively replaced by competition between restricted groups or individuals, which tended to concentrate power in the hands of outstanding individuals, who nevertheless often belonged to secondary lineages.

On top of this, there were factors of a more directly social character. In a rapidly changing society, where the declining authority of the chiefs was causing a growing sense of insecurity, the rival power of the associations – which were springing up on all sides, sometimes surprisingly enough calling themselves *sindikats* (trade unions) – and of men with new ideas, especially inventors of new magical techniques, was inevitably enhanced. And finally, there was the colonial administration, which was able to intervene in various ways according to circumstances: sometimes by helping to establish a kind of local dynasty, as in the case of Bôgo, the *Ba-Kongo* chief in the old Boko district, whose customary authority 'extended well beyond the limits of his own tribe';* sometimes by supporting a notable who had managed to gain control over a number of heterogeneous groups, despite the fact that his authority had no traditional sanction. (This was how the superior Kongo chief in the Mayama region came to be responsible for a mixture of ethnic units, including not only Ba-Sundi and Ba-Lali, but also Ba-Téké and Mikéngé). Then, too, the attitude of the chiefs was not always the same: some of them were content with an essentially passive role, simply transmitting the administration's orders 'correctly'; while others, in response to public opinion, took a more active line, for it was often the extent to which they were prepared to resist government policy that determined the villagers' confidence in them.

The fact is, the position of the chieftainship varied from one part of the country to another and a chief's personal ability counted for more than it had previously. But the chieftainship as such was not directly attacked; the fact that it had become an instrument of 'officialdom', was even in some cases debased, did not mean

---

* See the 'Projet de chefferies', Boko, 1937, which emphasizes the status of 'great chief in the fullest sense of the term'. It also insists upon the *customary* nature of Bôgo's authority, and reveals the dynastic character of an authority that went back to the negotiations between Chief N'Zabi and de Brazza, the order of succession being (1) N'Zabi, (2) his uterine brother, (3) his uterine nephew, (4) Bôgo, the uterine nephew of (3).

13

that it had ceased to have any meaning. At moments of crisis, involving relations with the colonizing society, the chiefs, despite their official position, tended on the whole to identify themselves with the rural opposition. In 1930, for instance, when André Matswa was arrested, they systematically refused any form of generosity offered them by the authorities, particularly the payments they were entitled to after the annual tax collection. If the role of the chieftainship was scarcely affected, the chiefs, for their part, usually allowed themselves to be swayed by the positive tendencies among the groups under their authority. With the coming of Independence, they adapted themselves to the new conditions; and so long as the Ba-Kongo political leaders maintain their national status, continue to need the chiefs' support locally and do not adopt a programme of radical transformation of existing structures, their position is not likely to be endangered.

Kongo society is still deeply influenced by the *idea of kingship*. We find this expressed in the Annual Report for 1932: 'In this country, it would be disastrous to apply the egalitarian tendencies typical of our own people. Here, if anarchy is to be avoided, the maintenance of the existing social hierarchy is essential.'[39] The very image of 'king' represents a definite reality; it is derived from that of the *Ntòtila* (sovereign) of São Salvador, whose memory is kept alive by popular myths, crystallizing the people's aspirations to national unity. In modern times the concept has been extended to include biblical representations of the 'king', victorious war leaders like de Gaulle and the Ba-Kongo 'saviours' – prophets like Simon Kimbangou, and political pioneers like André Matswa. These interpretations are interrelated, and recent myths show how concretely the relations between them are understood. Between the idealized representation of the chief, projected in the persons of Presidents Youlou and Kasavubu, and the *mfumu nkâda* of the lineages, is a whole range of administrative chiefs whose function tends to be reduced to the purely technical duties resulting from the modernization of the customary environment. Broadly speaking, it is in terms of this triple orientation that we can best understand the way in which the notion of chieftainship has been diversified and enriched.

The role of the 'évolués'

The part that the évolués (especially the educated ones) have played in the opposition movement shows how completely the government underrated their influence. It tended to regard these atypical individuals as people without roots, 'renegades';[40] and it was not until the first organized anti-colonial movements that the authorities began to appreciate the prestige of the 'literates in the townships' and the influence that 'their demagogy had . . . upon primitive intelligence and embryonic consciences' (sic).[41] Only in 1930 was the problem of 'native elites' clearly recognized – at a time, that is to say, when their pressure was already increasing and no policy towards them had as yet been formulated.

The numerical growth of this social category was, as we have shown, initially determined by the nature of the Kongo economy, long oriented towards the outside world, by the proximity of urban centres as zones of attraction and by the spontaneous character of the migration movements. This rapid growth had certain specifically Ba-Kongo features. It was facilitated by the peculiar qualities of a people who have been described by a careful observer as 'inquiring, willing to accept innovations, anxious to educate themselves and appreciative of a higher standard of living'.[42] Their readiness to acquire and make use of modern techniques is unquestionable; it is confirmed by the Inspector-General's Report for the year 1937, which speaks of the many ways in which they were showing their determination to improve their lot. We will confine ourselves to one or two facts with regard to education: in 1935 there were no schools in the Kinkala region, but so strong was the demand that by 1948 'at least 2,500 children' – i.e. 15 per cent of boys and girls under 15 years of age – were receiving some kind of education. Moreover, the document from which these figures are taken goes on to point out that the Ba-Lali region was soon providing a number of government functionaries, the majority of native priests and the first doctor born in French Equatorial Africa.[43] This attitude towards change not only stimulated the formation of modernist cadres – for example, family solidarity made it possible for pupils and apprentices to live in the towns – but often created favourable conditions for the integration of these atypical elements. Moreover, it entitled the

Ba-Kongo to assume the leadership of less dynamic and adaptable ethnic groups; so successfully, indeed, that they were said to be 'aspiring to play the same role in French Equatorial Africa as the Senegalese in French Oriental Africa'. As a result, there was a more intense and precocious awareness of the inferiority created by the colonial situation, referred to in an official report of 1937 as 'a mystique of racial revival . . . through assimilation with the white man, who is still accepted as the representative of civilization'.

It is this collective tension and drive for progress that explains the profound influence exerted by the évolués; and particularly the fact that the kinship groups and lineages, having retained their vitality, provided a social environment in which even those who had been cut off from it for a considerable time could feel at home. We have already given a number of examples of the way in which the organic unity between town and country was maintained, and others may be found in our *Sociologie des Brazzavilles noires*.[44] In addition to this, Africans living in the cities took every opportunity of 'visiting the village':* women went back to have their babies, children spent the holidays with their family; and in many cases villagers continued to send food to their relatives in the town. It was the strength of these relationships that enabled the évolués, atypical as they undoubtedly were, to become so effectively integrated in the Kongo communities; it determined the influence they were able to exert and, at the same time, made them more sensitive to any reaction in the customary environment. In this way, the modernist movements they created were adapted to the needs of the villagers who were to join them. But while it is important to stress this real reciprocity of influences, it would be a mistake to assume that there were no grounds for antagonism. There were, but it was mainly at the two poles of Kongo society that they were openly expressed: in the urban centres, where there was a growing division between the educated and the illiterate, and in the areas most remote from the centres of modernization, where an évolué often found it difficult to fit in unless he accepted traditional values.

---

* So much so, in fact, that it led to a considerable development of communal transport between Brazzaville and the nearby villages; while carrying passengers on long-distance lorries meant a welcome addition to freight charges.

Compared with the other socio-cultural entities of Equatorial Africa, Ba-Kongo society seems to be both one of the most advanced and, at the same time, one of those that have most successfully avoided social deterioration; though, as we have just seen, this does not mean that it contains no areas of disequilibrium. Among the reasons that account for the relative smoothness with which changes have been achieved, we have stressed certain historical factors: on the one hand, its richer past, which encouraged cultural contributions from abroad and at the same time stimulated the development of Kongo culture; and, on the other, the actual way in which relations with the colonizing society were established – politically, by making use of the customary authorities and, economically, by allowing the traditional economy to develop without any violent disruption either of the labour force (by large-scale compulsion) or of farming methods (by the sudden introduction of export crops). In addition to this, certain internal factors must be taken into account: the maintenance of the land–property–lineage linkage; the continuity of the minor lineage as the basic social unit – a continuity that depends upon the 'maternal uncle–nephew' relationship, whereas the 'father–son' relationship encourages fragmentation into restricted families, with a tendency to autonomy; and lastly, the fact that the positions of elder (*mbuta*) and chief (at once king and priest) still retain their significance. It is this two-sided aspect of modern Kongo society that explains why its most serious crises are usually due to its relations with the outside world, the dominant colonizing society, rather than to its internal relations. With these considerations in view, we must now turn to the first organized political movement.

IV. THE 'AMICALIST' MOVEMENT AND ITS SOCIAL IMPLICATIONS

It was in 1926 that a Mu-Kongo, André Matswa, born near Brazzaville but then living in Paris, founded, with the moral and material backing of certain government officials, and in collaboration with four other Congolese, an association known as the *Société amicale des originaires de l'Afrique équatoriale française.** The

* The society was founded on July 17, 1926, in a café in the First Arrondissement, which at that time was frequented by Congolese living in Paris.

declared purpose of the organization was to carry on the work of a friendly society (*Amicale*), though its founder later admitted that it was also an attempt to rid 'his fellow Africans of their inferiority vis-à-vis the white man'. Once it had been formed, the organization was transferred to the Congo, where it became known popularly as *Mikalé*, and later to Libreville and Bangui. There seems little doubt that, at the outset, it had been Matswa's ambition to create the cadres for an organization covering the whole of Central Africa, but it was mainly among the Ba-Kongo that the association succeeded in establishing itself in the rural areas. Towards the end of 1928, two delegates from Paris began visiting the villages and collecting subscriptions. It cannot be denied that membership was represented as ensuring a measure of freedom from the colonial authorities: already by 1928 the Annual Report was beginning to speak of 'demonstrations at public works sites, where on several occasions the employees quit work', and of 'Europeans being threatened'. If we accept the official estimate, which in 1929 put the number of members in French Equatorial Africa at 13,000, the success of the association must have been considerable.

It was at this time that Matswa wrote to the President of the Council, protesting against the Native Code, as symbolizing the African peoples' inferiority, and in a second letter, criticizing a certain business firm in Brazzaville, he denounced the economic stagnation of French Equatorial Africa, contrasting it with 'the tremendous expansion' in the Belgian Congo.[45] Thus, the association began to outline a rudimentary political programme, which took the form locally of a campaign of passive disobedience against the official authorities. At the end of 1929, the latter reacted by securing the arrest of Matswa, who was still living in Paris. His trial, on a charge of embezzlement, took place in Brazzaville in the early part of April 1930.* As President of the *Amicale*, he was sentenced to imprisonment and later, with the three Ba-Lali who were considered to be his most active lieutenants, was exiled from French Equatorial Africa. During the two days of the trial there were outbreaks of violence in the European parts of the

* It is difficult to understand precisely the nature of his involvement. Certain letters from Matswa's friends appear to put the blame on the delegates, who disobeyed his instructions.

town, which were thronged with Africans from the native town-ship of Bacongo. From then on Matswa became the symbol of every form of protest and hostility expressed against the coloniz-ing society, and the fact that he was living in exile in Central Africa did nothing to destroy the movement he had launched, which was proving to be more successful than he could have hoped. It was at this stage that what was officially known as the 'Ba-Lali affair' really began to develop: a steady deterioration of relations with the Europeans, resulting in a series of intermittent crises, the most serious of which occurred at the time of France's defeat in 1940. Arrested for a second time in April 1940, Matswa was sent back to Brazzaville and again imprisoned, this time at Mayama.* There, while still serving his sentence, he died, on January 14, 1942 – according to the post-mortem, of dysentery. The people in the villages utterly refused to believe that he was dead, and at the 1946–7 elections, 'when, as a demonstration of unity, the Ba-Lali voted for a dead man, he won an absolute majority';[46] even ten years later, at the elections in January 1956, almost 5,000 people still cast their vote for Matswa. Meanwhile, under the influence of local messianic movements, Amicalism had assumed a religious character; the dead leader had become trans-formed into 'Jesus Matswa'.

André Matswa and the principal leaders

It is only possible to reconstruct a biography of Matswa on the basis of scattered facts patiently collected from official documents. He was born on January 17, 1899, at Mandzala-Kinkala on the outskirts of Brazzaville. Of his childhood we know little except that he was baptized and had the opportunity, unusual in those days, of attending school. Brought up by Catholic missionaries, he first became a mission teacher in the Mayama district,† but

* See the well documented unpublished study by M. Sinda: Le messianisme congolais et ses incidences politiques, to which reference has already been made. Sinda says: 'Matswa Grenard was arrested for the second time on April 5, 1940. Accused of having intelligence with the enemy, he was transferred to the Congo.'

† M. Sinda presents a somewhat high-flown portrait of the young André Matswa: 'An eloquent and brilliant orator ... admired by all the outstanding personalities of the region, Matswa Grenard was esteemed by everyone, and his popularity continu-ally grew. ... He longed to raise himself, to become something more than a small country preacher ...', op. cit., pp. 162–3.

being ambitious and energetic he gave up this position and moved to Brazzaville, where he was to find employment as a clerk in the customs department. In all this there was nothing exceptional, he was simply behaving like a typical évolué.

In 1923, anxious to widen his experience, he set out for Europe, first to Antwerp, then to Bordeaux and Marseilles. This was his first harsh contact with a world that was always to remain alien to him; but what seems to have affected him most deeply was his army service in Morocco in 1924–5, and the fact that he was involved in a colonial war. At the end of the campaign, in the course of which he was promoted to non-commissioned rank, Matswa settled in Paris. The effect of this experience can be gauged by the fact that shortly after his return he began to organize the *Amicale*: by this time he had come to realize the possibility of organized opposition to colonialism, and he may even have felt that by founding such an institution he was in some way atoning for having participated in a war against other victims of colonialism.

In Paris he found work as a book-keeper, managed to obtain French citizenship and began to take an interest in politics – at least to the extent of making contact with other African emigrants. His lawyer, who came from the Antilles, was more or less directly associated with the Pan-Negro movement; and it was about this time that the editor of the *Cri des nègres* invited him, as founder of the *Amicale*, to help in amalgamating a number of different organizations in the *Union des Travailleurs nègres* – a Communist organization of some standing. The Congolese association, jealous of its independence, seems to have held back, but as a result of this experience Matswa received a political education that had so far been denied to his compatriots in the Congo.

His stay in France also affected him in other ways. From the discussions he had with Africans living in other towns he was able to form a pretty clear idea of the problems confronting *all* colonial peoples; and, as may be seen from his correspondence, this served to strengthen his consciousness of the enormous gulf between the position of Africans living in the metropolitan country and their status in the colonies. Influenced particularly by the Senegalese emigrants that he met, Matswa imagined that by obtaining French citizenship he would be able to bridge this gulf and throw off his inferiority. There is a widely held illusion about citizenship and the instantaneous effect it will produce, as the attitude of the Ba-Kongo demonstrators clearly revealed at the time of the Brazzaville riots in 1930. And it was around the question of citizenship that the Amicalist campaign was launched in the villages.

Undoubtedly, the most remarkable feature of this biography is the quite exceptional nature of the relationship that Matswa succeeded in establishing with the Kongo people. Apart from occasions likely to appeal to the imagination, like his attempted escape from the ship taking him to Pointe-Noire, or his two successful escapes from internment in the Chad, the only times they actually saw him were when he appeared as the victim of injustice. It was not he who went to Africa to inaugurate the *Amicale*, he sent two delegates; his only public appearances were at the time of his trials. In these circumstances, it is easy to understand how people came to idealize him, to see him as a symbolic figure of unusual power. When the authorities tried to induce the Ba-Kongo chiefs to denounce him, they replied by praising his achievements: 'All Matswa is trying to do is to bring us French civilization, to improve the look of our villages and find out the best way of making our land fertile . . .'*

The only period when relations between the Ba-Kongo and the Europeans were not strained was during the first phase of the Second World War, when many of the former, especially the Ba-Lali, volunteered for the armed forces. But this did not last long. Matswa was arrested again – apparently on the grounds of conniving at secret German propaganda – and imprisoned at Mayama, where he died in 1942. But it was precisely at that moment that, for the Ba-Kongo, he began to live with an extraordinary intensity; regardless of the facts, they endowed him with every noble quality. Confronted by a phenomenon that they were powerless to control, the authorities were completely at a loss. After his death, the man they had looked upon simply as a political agitator was transformed into an illusive personality whose

* Quoted from a document in the archives. At the end of March 1930, before the leader's trial, the chiefs wrote to the Attorney-General, protesting against Matswa's detention and demanding that the Mayor of Brazzaville should be brought to trial for abusing his powers.

popular appeal was tremendously enhanced by all the accumulated energy of traditional myth. He became associated with
everything that stood for strength and independence – especially
during the war years with General de Gaulle; every success was
attributed to him, the ultimate victory, as well as the political
reforms that were promulgated in 1945.* Thus in the space of a
dozen years or so – by a process of such general scientific significance, particularly in the field of religious sociology, that we
must attempt to explain it – he had become a symbolic figure, in
certain respects a god.

How firmly established the movement became in the rural areas
as well as in the towns may be gauged by the diversity of its
leaders' social background. We were not able to carry out a
complete check, but a brief examination of the lists drawn up by
the authorities was enough to enable us to pick out the most
active members. The social categories to which these 70 men
belonged is shown in the following table.

TABLE I

Social classification of the principal leaders

Chiefs (village, territorial, tribal) or ex-chiefs	... ...	24
Civil servants and employees of the C.F.C.O.	... ...	19
Business men and artisans	... ...	17
Peasants (or occupation not specified) ...	... ...	10

From these figures it is clear that the two predominant social
categories are those whose members would inevitably be most
closely in touch with the colonial authorities (chiefs and clerical
workers); and this is borne out by a 1933 report which stresses
'the important part played by the native personnel of the administration'. In addition to this, 'modernists' and 'traditionalists' are
almost equally represented; which goes to show that the distinction which some of the official reports sought to establish between
the 'Europeanized' and 'primitive' leaders was superficial. What,

* Cf. Political Report for the Kinkala District, 1946. 'Some of the more educated
natives fully agree that Matswa died at Mayama, but he has become the symbol of
emancipation. It is thanks to him that they succeeded in winning political concessions
(thanks, that is to say, to his intervention in the other world). At various elections in
1946 he won by large majorities.'

in fact, the figures reveal is the reciprocity of influence between the two, to which we have drawn attention in other contexts, rather than any predominance. The main point that emerges is the preponderance of those elements most concerned with compensating for the inferiority – the limitations of authority and economic opportunity – that the colonial situation creates. These were the men who formed the general staff of the local organization set up by the *Amicale*.

After Matswa's death, when the movement was beginning to take on a religious rather than a political character, this overlapping of its modernist and rural aspects persisted; which partly explains the syncretistic form that it assumed locally. But it should also be realized that the way in which the outlook of some of the leaders was formed, the knowledge and experience they were able to acquire, also contributed to this syncretistic orientation. A typical example of this was Pierre K., who for a short time had been the Ba-Lali 'delegate' to the administrative authorities. An ex-soldier, who had lived in France and was later employed in the customs service, he was looked upon by his employers as 'a semi-literate native who, when he tries to write in French, does not even understand the correct meaning of the words he uses'. In addition to this makeshift education, Pierre K. had acquired what, to judge from the list of books in his possession, can only have been a jumble of ill-digested information; they included a French grammar, a dictionary, a Dalloz law manual, a couple of parish magazines, a collection of prayers, a compilation called *The Book of Atonement* in 23 volumes, four pamphlets on magic, an army manual for non-commissioned officers and a selection of speeches by the Governor-General.* If we are to understand the nature of syncretism, we must never lose sight of the extremely elementary sources of information that were available to the semi-literate men through whom it was expressed. Any satisfactory study of it would entail a thorough examination of the intellectual models they based themselves on.[47] The way in which they equipped themselves mentally was, in some respects, like the development of baroque art. The ablest of Matswa's local disciples were no exception to this rule.

* A few sheets of notepaper, with the heading 'Ecole Universelle', seem to indicate that he engaged in correspondence courses.

Organization and achievements of the Amicalist Movement

Amicalism, as it was generally called in the Congo, had a rudimentary form of organization. Until comparatively recently, this
consisted of a hierarchy of officials – commune leader, section
leader, sub-section leader, etc. – who succeeded in maintaining
some measure of coordination, and a number of itinerant dues
collectors. An official map of the Kinkala region drawn up in 1937
shows that there were then some fifteen leaders known to the
local authorities, who were doing their best to extend their
influence beyond the Ba-Kongo frontier to the neighbouring
Ba-Téké groups. The ambition to bring together the largest
possible number of villages in the southern Congo in a single
organization under the control of the Ba-Kongo was a distinctive
feature of the movement. In this way they hoped to overcome
any particularism and achieve a measure of unity among the
Congolese people.*

It was not possible to make a sufficiently accurate numerical
estimate to produce a map showing those parts of the country
that were most sympathetic to Amicalism. But from the scattered
facts that are to be found in official reports, it is fairly clear that
the most dynamic groups were those nearest to Brazzaville and
in the nearby Congo, since this was an area where, despite the fact
that it had the best system of communications, control was most
difficult. The replies to an official questionnaire that was circulated in the old Kinkala district in 1949 are significant: they reveal
not only the considerable number of people that were still active,
but also the persistence of a movement which, for almost twenty
years, had been bitterly persecuted. According to this document:
'While the number of active members is less than 4,000, approximately 10 per cent of the population, the number of sympathizers
on the other hand amounts to 90 per cent. . . . Thanks to skilful
propaganda . . . the masses still look forward to some change for
the better.'[48] In other words, the membership was still active, at
least in the sense of being opposed to colonization.

* The nature of this ambition may be seen from the administrative protests it gave
rise to: 'The authorities must never allow one tribe, more independent than the
others, to arrogate to itself the leadership of any part of the population.' Annual
Report for the Moyen-Congo, 1933.

Tension between the colonizing society and the colonized society had reached its highest point during the trial of André Matswa in April 1930. From then on, the 'Affair', as it came to be known, was completely misunderstood. The authorities insisted upon treating it as a movement inspired by 'agitators' whose honesty was suspect, but all their efforts to persuade the villagers to see them in this light proved futile; we were convinced of this, after a careful study of the archives, by the very small number of complaints that were addressed to the administration. The Ba-Kongo saw it as a developing process, consistent moreover with *traditional models*, that would eventually free them from oppression and put an end to their alienation. By 'paying their dues' (the word 'dues' became part of the Ki-Kongo language), they believed they were buying French citizenship, in the same way that a slave could buy the *ki-mfumu* that changed him into a free man enjoying the full rights of the clan community. In the old days, the loss of legal rights implicit in the law of conquest was not definitive; with the coming of peace they might be restored in return for a payment in kind. It is from this point of view that we have to see the financial measures taken by the *Amicale*. And a similar procedure traditionally applied to the ceding of territorial rights; if they were redeemed they reverted to the previous owner. Victory did not create a situation that was entirely in the victor's favour, leaving the defeated with no resources at all; negotiation and compromise, especially in traditional society, were always possible with a view to the revival of 'trading'.

It is not a question of maintaining that the organizers of the Amicalist movement believed that their policy was consistent with these customary practices, but simply of pointing out that they managed to convince people that it was in order to justify their actions. It was this conviction the colonial authorities were up against when they found that they were unable to refund the money that they had seized after Matswa's trial. For a considerable time, any attempt by a European to give an African a present was regarded as an indirect attempt to make restitution. For example, in 1933, the Ba-Kongo women attending the Catholic mission refused to accept the little medals they were offered, on the grounds that they must have been bought with 'dues money'. Again, in 1936-7 the free distribution of ground-nut seed was turned down or in some places the seed burnt, lest it involved accepting a gift paid for with the money that had been seized in 1930.* And it was for the same reason that, in 1938, the Kinkala chiefs refused to accept a subvention from the Governor-General. There were many similar cases; these are only some of the most striking. The fact that such an attitude could be maintained, for ten years and by people belonging to very different social categories,† proves how deeply motivated it must have been. It shows that they were afraid of reversing a situation in which, from the Ba-Kongo point of view, the administration was obliged either to grant the rights they had 'won', or, by violating them, to expose the breakdown of relations between the Europeans and their colonial subjects. To accept, in one form or another, a gift that might be interpreted as a repayment of their 'dues money' would mean not only resuming contact, but also accepting a return to the old state of affairs. Completely unaware of these implications, the administrative authorities were faced by an insoluble problem, and nothing, not even force, could alter the fact.

From then on, there was permanent opposition. Any attempt to intervene in Kongo society was apt to meet with a rebuff. In 1938, the reorganization of the chiefdoms led to a demonstration outside the law courts in Brazzaville. The attempt to establish native insurance societies resulted in the 'three francs war' (*n'zingu ya frâka tatu*), that is to say the refusal to contribute to or make use of this new institution. A project for taking a census of livestock, and even quite minor government schemes, automatically met with objections, the purpose of which was clear: to prevent the administration of the Ba-Kongo groups *from outside*, simply on the orders of local colonial authorities. One of the leaders in the Mayama district put the matter bluntly: 'We've obeyed long enough, we're tired of obeying.' Often, and very effectively, opposition assumed an economic form – interference with the movement of labour, preventing the introduction of new crops such as rice growing, restricting production for the market –

* Thus certain villages in the regions we investigated were nicknamed *mwâga nguba* (literally, 'to throw away ground-nuts').

† Even the students, during the July 14th holiday in 1931, refused to accept the prizes they had won. For other examples of this attitude, see M. Sinda, *op. cit.*; and Father Jaffre: 'L'Afrique aux Africains: le "N'gounzisme" au Congo', in *Les études*, March 1934.

though by drying up the few available sources of ready money such actions tended to recoil upon the Ba-Kongo themselves. A report by a colonial inspector-general referring to some of these acts of insubordination, pointed out that, quite apart from the failure to carry out such legal obligations as the payment of taxes and levies, they were creating 'a wall of silence' between the Ba-Kongo and the Europeans.

In certain circumstances, this confrontation was bound to become more open and more brutal. In addition to the rioting at Brazzaville provoked by Matswa's trial (April 1930), there were frequent periods of tension. During the celebration of the fiftieth anniversary of the Catholic Mission at Linzolo, the rifle that had been buried beneath a tree as a symbol of peace was dug up, the chiefs attending the reception given by the missionaries were molested, and the bishop was unable to bestow his blessing upon the crowd because they refused to kneel. These demonstrations, in September 1933, were particularly significant in that they proved that opposition was not directed merely against the administrative authorities, but involved the colonizing society as a whole.* Finally, in December 1937, a threatened march upon Brazzaville by all the Ba-Lali villages in the neighbourhood led to a series of military measures being taken – though the danger was probably exaggerated. In the months immediately before and after the outbreak of the Second World War Ba-Kongo resistance reached new heights: for a short time in 1938 there was an attempt to prevent army recruitment, and in 1941 the number of incidents increased, owing to a rumour that German troops might arrive at any moment. It was said that they would support the Amicalists and recognize André Matswa as 'king' of the right bank of the Congo; the struggle became more bitter and was met by harsh repression, with sentences of deportation and death. There is one fact however which, since it distinguishes Amicalism from similar movements that were occurring elsewhere, deserves to be stressed: the struggle between Europeans and Africans was to have practically no racial after-effects; it never resulted in a policy of organized

* This is precisely the point made in the Political Report for the Moyen-Congo for the third quarter of 1933: 'For the first time there have been demonstrations against the ecclesiastical element, which has hitherto been spared owing to the flexibility of its attitude towards the natives.'

racial discrimination. At moments of tensions the colonizing society, being in a minority, tended to exaggerate the dangers it was facing, ringing the changes on the threat of revolution, arms smuggling and foreign intervention in the hope that drastic measures would be taken that would restore a feeling of security; yet once the crisis was over, relations returned to normal.

Moreover, it is important to note that it was precisely when economic activity was at its lowest ebb that the political crisis became most acute. A people like the Ba-Kongo were quickly affected by any sudden change that restricted the opportunities for trading and making money; and official reports provide abundant evidence of the connection between the political situation and the state of the local market: the least hint of a set-back to the economy soon became a tidal wave, threatening to overwhelm the equilibrium that had been temporarily restored. All three periods of acute conflict – one of which occurred before the setting up of the *Amicale* – coincided with economic crises: that of 1921–2, when there was a drastic fall in the demand for colonial produce, at that time the only source of financial income; that of 1930–31, caused by the world-wide depression; and the years of hardship and rising prices after 1940. In 1931, the administration complained of what it called the 'obtuseness' of the villagers: 'The natives seem to be quite incapable of taking in the explanations of economic phenomena that our officials provide in the course of palavers.'[49] Ba-Kongo tradition did not prepare the peasants to accept the vicissitudes of a market economy passively; on the contrary, their whole attitude to the relations between man and the fruits of his labour* led them to regard any decline in the value of the latter as a reflection upon themselves. Economic disaster affected them all the more acutely in that they did not regard it as being purely material. A movement such as Amicalism represented an organized protest against a particular kind of economy which disturbed traditional equilibria by intro-ducing a sense of insecurity. In traditional societies, where the conditions of life are precarious because they depend upon a

---

* Cf. *Et. Bk.*, p. 129. 'Justice is equally strict towards everyone, for to appropriate something in a sense identifies the object appropriated with the individual. To lay hands on anyone's property is to lay hands on the owner. The Ba-Kongo have a very lively and quite special sense of this extension of their personality, which in other spheres is so restricted.'

money economy which nevertheless remains at a primitive level, any shock to it has immediate repercussions, the intensity of which we entirely fail to appreciate.

The means of expression

In the society in which Amicalism took root, primary education of a sort was relatively widespread, and Ki-Kongo had become established as a written language – thanks mainly to a translation of the Bible which gave it an almost sacred authority. One of the aims of the movement was the rapid extension of education with a view to producing as many technicians of Ba-Lali origin as possible. A letter from one of the leaders that was circulated in 1934 insisted that 'from now on, young Ba-Lali students, despite their backwardness, must do everything they can to study, so that they may become lawyers, engineers, doctors . . .'. Because of the prestige attaching to literacy and the acquisition of knowledge the part played by written propaganda was considerable, though the language in which it was expressed, mainly derived from official documents and political pamphlets though also from works of piety, was often very crude. Thus the first *written* literature to appear, and to have a wide popular audience, was directly connected with political and religious emancipation; it was born of opposition. In addition to the songs that were used to popularize slogans and protest, which were inspired by traditional models,* there were more elaborate works, usually utopian in outlook, whose rationalism was still deeply influenced by mythical thinking.

The fact that this verbal activity played a larger part than direct confrontation, was undoubtedly due to the unequal relation of forces – a weakness of which the majority of Amicalist leaders were fully aware. It led to an attitude of systematic rejection, reminiscent of the tactic of passive resistance; an attitude of utopian expectation transcending present difficulties, a kind of harmless violence, that could not be transformed into action

* There are many of these spontaneous and beautiful songs. They express nostalgia for the past ('Once we were really men . . .'), struggle ('For three francs, the Whites declared war on us . . .'), despair ('Weep, weep, for our ruined Congo . . .'), readiness to fight ('Even if all is lost, we'll start again at the beginning . . .') and expectation of Matswa's return ('Those who do not wish to believe that Matswa is still alive . . .'). An interesting selection of them may be found in M. Sinda, *op. cit.*

without serious risk. Moreover, the 'war of words' is not unknown in certain customary observances, where language serves as a substitute for physical aggression; and these are to be found in any area of civilization where speech possesses its own particular efficacy.

Such acts of aggression as were carried out in practice were in general of an *indirect* kind. They were directed not against individual members of the colonizing society, but against native elements who had become involved with that society. Moral pressure and physical violence were employed against chiefs who collaborated with the administration, while villagers who refused to operate the policy of passive resistance were ostracized. During the period of acute tension in 1940 the native police in the Boko and Pangala regions were attacked, and in 1945 one of the most active leaders organized an armed coup against the *native* administration of Bacongo. On the other hand, the few direct demonstrations that did take place were not aimed at individuals, but at weakening the colonizing society economically: opposition to public works undertaken by local bodies, refusal to grow certain commercial crops, working to rule on government contracts and, after 1945, incitements to strike. Later on, when Amicalism entered its politico-religious phase, the attitude of its members was influenced by the example of the early Christian martyrs; they began to base their behaviour on such notions as the efficacy of suffering and the redemption of sins. We are not here concerned with trying to assess the sincerity or spontaneity of this spirit of personal sacrifice, but of noting objectively the extent to which it inspired all activity directed against the European minority. Nor is it a question of judging whether or not the motives of the founders of Amicalism were suspect (as was maintained at every political trial), but of observing how firmly the movement had taken root and the way in which it encouraged innovation. It is impossible to underestimate its creative value.

In the next chapter we shall be studying the developments of the movement after Matswa's death, as well as local examples of Messianism. We have already stressed the fact that, for a minority, the dead leader became the very symbol of emancipation, while for the masses of the Ba-Kongo people he was transformed into the 'Saviour'. As his personality acquired mythological status and his influence continued to grow, opposition to colonization in his name came to be seen as a religious duty. In Brazzaville, meetings glorifying 'Jesus Matswa' were repeatedly held on the banks of the river Congo, on private premises and in chapels specially consecrated to the new cult (1948). At Mayama, clandestine ceremonies were organized in the vicinity of his grave in the form of pilgrimages, processions of ritual observances evoking the stations of the cross. The death of the leader had left his successors with an instrument of incomparable power – as well as an ideological system, and cadres capable of ensuring the rapid mobilization of the majority of the Kongo communities.*

Multiple implications of the phenomenon

The first point to be noted is that here we are dealing with a unifying movement that affected almost the entire Ba-Lali and Ba-Sundi peoples. Almost every social category was intimately involved in it: school children demonstrated in support, and the part played by women was so effective that an official report saw fit to attribute it to 'the system of matriarchy'.† The latent antagonisms between villager and townsman, traditionalist and modernist, yielded to its unifying influence. A revealing example of this was the attempt by a government official in 1938 to affect a split by organizing 'a local association in competition with the one from Paris';[50] it had been immediately nicknamed 'the toadies' association', and turned out to be a complete failure.‡ Official investigators invariably found themselves faced with a conspiracy of silence, and such information as they were able to obtain showed that this attitude was not simply due to fear. Only the specifically Ba-Kongo villages, which had been the first to react by creating a separatist church, for a time hesitated about joining.

* This opinion, which we first expressed in 1954, was borne out several years later by the political success of Abbé Youlon (who was identified with André Matswa) and the decisive political role of the Ba-Kongo.

† Obviously a very inadequate term, as we have already pointed out.

‡ A very explicit passage from a 1939 report states: 'The "toadies" have been reduced to their simplest expression. They are left with only one chief in the Brazzaville sub-division, two in the Mayama sub-division and one in the Boko sub-division, which makes a total of four tribal or cantonal chiefs out of eleven in the Department. And it must be added that these four chiefs are not supported by the great majority of those they are responsible for, who pay no attention to them.'

For nearly twenty years, the tendency to unity progressively over-
came differences that were partly accidental, partly connected with
tribal particularisms.

The size of the Amicalist movement and its persistence – from
1928 to 1956 its influence on local politics was continuous – are
sufficient proof that it cannot be regarded as an aberrant phenomenon. It succeeded and persisted because, to a very large extent,
it expressed all that was new in Kongo society, and also offered
the beginning of a solution, or at least the illusion of a solution, to
urgent problems. It was more than a political reaction against
subjection: it was also a cultural reaction against ready-made
political and religious systems imported from abroad; and it is
important to appreciate the relation between these two aspects.
The first reforms introduced after 1945, permitting the formation
of trade unions and political parties, turned out to be inadequate;
they were felt to be merely a further example of encouraging
foreign models – for a long time 'trade union' was a term used to
describe any official innovation or anyone who collaborated with
the administration. An official questionnaire that was issued in
1949 suggests the twofold significance of this attitude: 'The chiefs
do not belong to any political party or trade union, even native
ones, as anything of the kind is looked upon as "collaboration".
They believe in *Nzambi Pungu*, the God of their ancestors, whose
Christ is Matswa.'[51] What attracted people about Amicalism, why
they considered it to be effective, was that it seemed to be an
exclusively Kongo creation; it was the Ba-Kongo answer (whether
valid or not scarcely mattered) to the problems created by social
change; and it had managed to adapt itself sufficiently to become
firmly rooted in a familiar sociological environment. For better
or worse, the Ba-Kongo were anxious to find their own solutions,
and their example proved to be contagious; in the 1950s a dynamic people in the Haut-Congo, the Mbochi, launched a similar
movement throughout the whole area to which their influence
extended.[52] What they particularly demanded was a new kind of
constitution that would create a Mbochi dependency under the
authority of 'a commander' belonging to the tribe. This twofold
manifestation of initiative, at the two poles of the Congo, and
the emulation it gave rise to, at first had a positive effect by increasing the demands made on the government. Later on, however,

their aspirations became dangerously competitive: the leaders, Abbé Youlou and J. Opangault, fell out, and their followers became violently hostile, particularly during the bloody rioting that took place at Brazzaville in January 1959.

Protest, which we regard as the essential element of all Amicalist demonstrations, also seems to have been concerned with more everyday matters. Among the Kongo peoples there was no single agrarian question capable of playing a decisive role, as there was in the case of the Kikuyu in Kenya (where according to Leakey the main cause of the Mau-Mau revolt was over-population of the native reserves),[53] but a whole number of less serious socio-economic problems. Since 1930, the effect of these problems had been to strengthen the *will to change* manifested by many of the Ba-Kongo; and the failure to deal with them had only intensified them. A note from the Governor-General of French Equatorial Africa in 1946 drawing attention to this concluded: 'In tackling the Ba-Lali problem, we have not always provided the most necessary and opportune socio-economic and political solutions.'

The violent incidents that occurred in 1930, as a result of Mat-swa's trial, had been a brutal reminder to the administration of the need to carry out a programme of modernization and development. In 1931, they indicated the measures decided upon to encourage 'a return to order': 'Twenty hectares of land ploughed by tractor, irrigation, public relief, building subsidies for the best equipped huts, provision of local medical services, etc., have proved most effective in this respect.'[54] But this was only a very restricted and provisional programme. The *economic* causes of discontent remained, varying according to the acuteness of the crisis in the relations between the colonizing and colonized societies. A document dated 1943, which was a period of recovery, explicitly drew attention to this relationship: 'The Ba-Lali affair appears to have died down. . . . At the present time the Ba-Lali seem much more inclined to make money than to revive old quarrels. . . . The consequent prosperity is certainly not unconnected with the improvement in the political situation.'[55] On the plane of economic motivation, the following points should be particularly noted: money incomes remained low, those derived from farming were still inadequate and unreliable, while wages

scarcely sufficed to support the workers who could find employment, and inevitably fluctuated owing to the instability of the
labour market;[56] at the same time there was an increasing demand
for money, since the 'modernist' outlook of many Ba-Kongo made
them impatient to have access to the manufactured goods
imported by Europeans.* The difficulty of satisfying these needs
was intensified by the system of transport and distribution, which
kept prices high and encouraged speculation, by the amount of
money spent on display and personal rivalry (for example, at the
malaki) and by the unproductive methods of accumulating wealth.
Economic progress was still far from reaching the stage at which
it would be sufficiently dynamic to effect a genuine social mutation.
The recent developments of the Congolese economy have given
rise to aspirations rather than to lasting satisfaction; the dangers
threatening the 'security' obtained by traditional techniques still
outweigh the prospects of immediate advantage.†

A second series of reasons for discontent arose from the very
nature of the processes of change. This was stressed in the
Annual Report for 1930, which admitted in reference to the incidents at Brazzaville that there had been a failure to consider the
problems of development. It is significant how frequently such
expressions as 'semi-literate', 'semi-urbanized', 'semi-wage
earners' recur in official documents; they indicate processes as
yet not fully developed, and the haphazard nature of the attempts
to adapt to modern conditions. The failure to implement plans
for economic and social betterment helps to explain this situation;
though it was partly due to inadequate finance, there was no real
drive to carry them through. From this point of view, the native
townships, especially Poto-Poto, were particularly revealing: at
first sight they looked like temporary camps for workers attracted
by the hope of casual work; the harsh conditions of existence and
the precarious opportunities of obtaining cash incomes restricted
the possibilities of effective urbanization and encouraged mobility,

* Certain religious works that have appeared recently are concerned that more
manufactured goods, as well as the techniques for producing them, should be made
available.

† Cf. G. Balandier: *Ambiguous Africa*, Eng. trans., London, 1966, p. 258: In a
study trip to the Congo in May 1961, the agronomist, R. Dumont, recorded the
complaints of the peasants, and observed their disillusionment with the leaders living
in Brazzaville. "Independence is for them, not for us", he was told'.

with the result that these semi-townsfolk lived in a continual state of insecurity and carried this back with them to their villages.* In his study of the Kikuyu problem, Leakey rightly insists upon the failure to create 'a genuinely urbanized native population' and the tremendous importance of providing conditions that would encourage those who wished to do so to settle in the towns.[57] And what he says there applies equally to Central Africa.

Another example of this kind of incomplete evolution is provided by the social category described as 'literates'. Until very recently, they were unable to obtain the necessary qualifications to become technicians – and some of them were well aware of this. The only openings for them were minor positions in public administration or private firms, and in any case these were far too few to satisfy all the demands for employment: again and again official reports spoke of literates returning to their villages 'because of their inability to obtain work in the administration' (1935), or of their being expelled from the centres as 'suspects' (1940–41). It was only with the winning of political power that the 'Africanization' of cadres and their promotion to senior positions in the administration became essential. A similar position obtained as regards the évolués in the business community: the fact that the economy was still considerably influenced by a 'trading out-look' led to their numbers increasing, but their activities were restricted to the lower levels of the economy. Two facts help to explain a situation of this kind: on the one hand the immense difficulties of achieving technical and economic progress in an under-populated country requiring a high level of investment; and, on the other, the state of dependence, which restricted the advance of the most dynamic elements and gave rise to a kind of transference phenomenon by which the responsibility for every difficulty encountered was attributed to the Europeans. While these problems encouraged the emergence of a spirit of national-ism, the achievement of Independence did not suffice to abolish them.

The political significance of the Amicalist movement is not

* According to an investigation carried out in 1957, 'the lack of work is certainly the main preoccupation of Africans in Brazzaville, either because they have to feed those who are out of work, or because they themselves cannot find a job. Few of those who are unemployed expect the crisis to end'. Cf. R. Devauges: *op. cit.*, p. 244.

simply that it represented the rejection of direct control and an assertion of hostility towards the colonial situation. It was also a manifestation of a sense of solidarity, transcending existing frontiers, which was directly associated with the personality of the leader as 'King' and 'Saviour', as well as with the river that had symbolized Congolese unity in the past – an attitude that eagerly fed on all that was known about the ancient kingdom of Kongo. As a result, the very notion of chief has been transformed. He is no longer merely the most powerful individual at the head of the most powerful lineage (a clan outlook that could only encourage particularisms) but a man capable of arousing a spirit of unanimity, of dominating social and cultural change and orienting progress in conformity with the Ba-Kongo spirit. He inspires every initiative designed to promote solidarity. He helps to establish an authority better adapted to the needs of today than the type of power inherent in traditional society, less compromised than that created by the colonial government. He becomes the driving force in a total reconstruction of the social order: Amicalism had stimulated activity in the sphere of political relations as well as at the level of religious attitudes. Abbé Fulbert Youlou was obliged to adapt his activities to this new conception of the chief, of which in many ways Matswa remains the prototype;[58] and although later on he had to oppose the 'Matswanist religion', his outright victory in 1958 was seen as the outcome of the struggles that Matswa had led[59] and as a confirmation of Ba-Kongo pre-eminence. And lastly, the eventual disappearance of the traditional authorities (in the event, of the 'crowned chiefs') encouraged the competition for power: the new social categories (especially the literates and business men) sought to achieve leadership through the Amicalist movement; and it was mainly this aspect of the movement that government critics were referring to when they spoke of the 'moral constraint' exercised by the évolués.

The study of anthropology has revealed that the various elements of a culture are so closely interwoven that intervention at any one point produces a chain reaction whose effects are almost impossible to foresee. In this sense, Amicalism must be seen as an essentially *global* manifestation, effective at every level and involving all the constituent elements of socio-cultural reality. It was a reaction that affected the whole pattern of behaviour, the beliefs and material symbols associated with them as well as the organizational forms. In this sense, therefore, it was a phenomenon of outstanding importance, revealing the major social changes that were taking place as well as expressing a revival of initiative. These aspects will be seen more clearly in the following chapter, where we shall be considering the question of Ba-Kongo Messianism.

III
BA-KONGO MESSIANISM

In many parts of Black Africa where Christianity had obtained a footing, one of the most characteristic phenomena of the changes that occurred during the colonial period was the spread of Messianic movements leading to the emergence of more or less ephemeral *Negro churches*. Though apparently an essentially religious phenomenon, it rapidly assumed a political aspect, becoming the basis of a rudimentary form of nationalism, the significance of which was unmistakable. At the beginning of this century Leenhardt was already drawing attention to the development of the 'Ethiopian churches', which first appeared, around 1890, in South Africa; and his book, which provides a detailed chronology of events and biographies of the most outstanding leaders, shows a lively awareness of the importance of this development. Summing up the 'theses' that had oriented his approach to the subject, he writes unambiguously: 'Ethiopianism is a social movement of a people demanding its rights at the very moment that it is becoming conscious of itself and of the oppression to which it is subjected by a foreign government. It is caused by the restrictive laws of the English Native Code, by the animosity of the Whites and by the lack of flexibility and teaching skill on the part of many of the missionaries.'[1] This brings out clearly that it was a *total* reaction to the political situation, to the inequality existing between the two races and to the ill-conceived approach of the missionaries.

The area affected by this early form of Messianism was, broadly speaking, South Africa and Central and East Africa (Kenya) though it also sprang up among the peoples settled on the Gulf of Guinea, under the leadership of a Liberian prophet, Wade Harris, who claimed to have *been sent by God*, his mission having been revealed to him by the angel Gabriel. In the Ivory Coast alone, his teaching was widely supported by the ethnic groups of the lake region, and by about 1910 his following amounted to some 100,000–120,000 people.[2] Everywhere it displayed the same features: a moral and religious revival (in a sense that was not opposed to the local cultures), and a political reaction against the dominant colonial minority. Because it satisfied a deeply felt need, this teaching has not disappeared: there is a study by the ethnologist, Holas, of a sect that still accepts the doctrines of the Liberian prophet and has maintained much of its ritual – particularly baptism and public confession. As to its unifying tendencies, with their implication of a sudden revival of religious life, there is some evidence of their early appearance in Central Africa: for example, the *Kiyoka* movement, first observed in northern Angola around 1872, as a result of which all the 'fetishes' and implements of magical techniques were enthusiastically burnt (*yoka*).[3] Owing to its earlier economic and social development and the fundamental breach between the colonists and the native people, it was in South Africa, however, that the phenomenon expanded most rapidly and appears to have been most deeply rooted. In his study of the Union of South Africa, Marquard,[4] while emphasizing the unstable character of the illegal churches and the unreliability of the statistics, estimates their number at not less than 800, with a membership of around 760,000 – more than a quarter, that is to say, of the Bantu membership of the Christian churches.* It was not until later, after the First World War, that prophetic movements of this type developed in the Congo, where they have persisted, though not always on the same scale, ever since. Thus messianic churches are to be found throughout a large part of the Negro African world and, despite all their vicissitudes, continue to attract a very considerable membership. It is impossible therefore to regard them as an aberrant phenomenon, or as the work of leaders who are primarily concerned with furthering their personal ambitions. In this respect, the reports of the political information services are by no means convincing.

Thus it may be seen that the distribution of Negro churches largely coincides with that part of Africa inhabited by the Bantu peoples. But while it would be possible, according to a widely

* The number of churches officially recorded in 1954 was 1,286.

held preconception, to relate this to the smaller powers of resistance of Bantu societies and cultures, it is even more important to point out that it also corresponds with those areas where evangelization has been most intense and racial discrimination most marked – i.e. between the Cape and the river Congo – and where, owing to the exploitation of mineral wealth, modern economic development is still most actively pursued.* It is therefore an area where the causes of social change have been most numerous and decisive, and where the condition of domination has been most harshly experienced. In addition to this, the very manner in which Christianity was imposed upon the Africans has to be taken into account; the way, that is to say, that it was introduced by a variety of competing churches, whose own disputes were a cause of further division – a fact that was not lost upon our Congolese informants. Not only did it make demands that were radically hostile to African organizations (in the struggle against polygamy) and to African cultures (in its active hostility to everything that might encourage the traditional cults), but it also imported new elements of differentiation and antagonism. In South Africa, for instance, there were eight main missionary groups, divided between three major branches of Christianity, with a sharp distinction between the churches of Dutch and British origin. Or to take an example from the area with which we are concerned, the Congo, one has only to remember the hostility that existed between the Catholics, who considered themselves to be the 'national' church because of their connections with the government, and the 'foreign' Protestants represented by the Swedish evangelical missions, and between both of these and the Salvation Army. Thus the Kongo people were split up into Christians and traditionalists on the one hand, and, on the other, into offshoots of the Christian churches who were frequently in competition with one another.

There was yet another foreign movement, which we propose to deal with separately: the Watch Tower Congregation. Having first taken root in South and West Africa, it appears to have spread considerably; it attracted attention by the incidents it gave rise to in Nyasaland (1925) and the Belgian Congo (1931–5); and again, after the Second World War, by more serious risings in East

---

* The serious incidents, led by the Negro churches, which occurred in the Belgian Congo in 1931, 1941 and 1944, were precisely in the main mining areas.

Africa and the Belgian Congo. Its influence also made itself felt on the right bank of the Congo, especially in the urban centres (Brazzaville, Dolisie and Pointe-Noire), where the movement adopted the name of *Ki-Nsinga*, as well as throughout the Bantu country, where it was known by different names – *Ki-Tower*, *Ki-Tawer*, *Ki-Tawala*, etc. – though everywhere preserving its character as a *radical* movement that completely rejected the established order. The apocalyptic type of teaching elaborated by its founder was well adapted to provide mythical support for attempts at subversion. In this respect, the views expressed in Uganda during the 1942 incidents are revealing. Its members declared in effect: 'We are the children of God and we therefore refuse to accept man-made laws. . . . Times have changed; let us no longer obey earthly laws, for obedience to men is obedience to the devil.'[5] Even a superficial study of the question is enough to show the similarity between the *Ki-Tower* and the Bantu Messian-isms: the same opposition to sorcery and specialist cults, the same 'metaphysical' threats against reluctant villagers, the same assurance of invincibility and of a golden age that would put an end to every form of alienation. There can be no doubt that these movements, whose membership moreover was based on the same type of motivation, had a reciprocal effect upon one another; the *Ki-Tower* influence accentuated the aspects of radical subversion and encouraged the creation of apocalyptic myths.[6]

Despite their internal and external rivalries and their efforts to differentiate themselves, the Negro churches had sufficient features in common to enable them to achieve at least temporary unity. These may be defined provisionally and schematically as follows: they were religious groups formed either by secession from the Christian missions (which is why they were known as 'separatist' churches) or else created in imitation of them, and their central feature was a prophetic personality whose 'message' referred to some kind of 'golden age'.* Groups of this kind, though exercising considerable powers of attraction, appear to have had little organizational stability, but from the point of view

---

* For example, during the incidents in the Belgian Congo, the leaders spoke of a complete reversal of the position, as a result of which the white men would become the servants of the Congolese.

of the needs they satisfied and the aims they proclaimed their influence was lasting. Thus, though churches came and went, the messianic movement itself persisted for several decades. It represents both a *cultural* phenomenon, a reaction to the intro-duction, largely under compulsion (of foreign cultural elements, and a *sociological* phenomenon, in the sense that it expresses a revival of initiative and an attempt at social reconstruction on the part of the subject society.

I. THE BIRTH OF BA-KONGO MESSIANISM: SIMON KIMBANGOU, THE 'SAVIOUR'

Since 1920 there has been a succession of messianic movements in the Congo, sometimes on a religious, sometimes on a political plane (through the organization of resistance to the colonial administration); and the effect of repression was only to strengthen them by creating martyrs. In addition to its persistence, the second remarkable feature of the movement is the fact that its development was concerned with ethnic rather than with national frontiers; it expressed the profound reactions of a people that was beginning to recover its sense of unity – the 'messages' issued by the Congolese churches all referred to 'spreading knowledge' among the faithful in the two Congos and Angola. There can be no question but that this new religious movement was the starting point of a 'national' awareness, of a conscious striving to transcend the restricted limits of the clan or tribe.

The first messianic manifestations occurred in 1921, centring round the figure of Simon Kimbangou. This was a period when the aftermath of the First World War had begun to make itself felt; when a country as largely dependent upon the export trade as the Congo was inevitably affected by the falling demand for colonial produce. According to the literature glorifying the 'Saviour' which was distributed to members, Simon Kimbangou was born in September 1889 at Nkamba, to the north of Thysville, in the Belgian Congo, and was educated in a local Baptist Mission where, as well as the usual subjects, he acquired a good knowledge of the Old Testament. According to Leenhardt, it was here, too, that Simon Kimbangou had the first decisive experience with regard to his vocation: he failed to pass the examinations that would ultimately have enabled him to become a pastor, and had to be content with the inferior position of 'catechist'. It was this setback that eventually led him to break with the official church, and, to some extent, to oppose it. Simon believed that he had been touched by the grace of God' on March 28, 1921, which not only revealed his vocation to him,* but also gave him unusual powers that were the outward and visible signs of his election: he was recognized as being able to cure the sick and to restore life. His miracle-working was modelled on Christ's, and the village of Nkamba, where most of his miracles occurred, became known as the 'New Jerusalem'. Simon spoke of himself as Prophet, Messenger of God and Son of God, attempting in this way to associate himself with the symbol of the Trinity, and he took the name *Gounza* (which in the Ki-Kongo language means 'all these at once'). The word is also the Ki-Kongo equivalent of *Messiah*, as distinct from *mwatuma*, the term applied to any prophet, including the least gifted visionaries. For this reason the movement is sometimes known as *Gounzism*. Kimbangou taught the villagers in the Thysville region with great success, and apparently with real talent; the movement spread very rapidly, particularly in the frontier region of the Moyen-Congo where the government had some difficulty in maintaining its authority. The catechists of the Protestant missions, as well as some of the black pastors,† proud of having a Messiah who belonged both to their ethnic group and their religion, became his devoted disciples and propagandists and, together with Simon, created a body of devotional literature which we shall return to later.

One of the most significant aspects of Kimbangou's success was the widespread destruction of magic figurines (*mi-kisi*) that it led to, even beyond the area where he preached. In a society in which social upheaval had resulted in a proliferation of aggressive

---

* After leaving the mission where he was brought up, Kimbangou went to Leopoldville where he experienced his first 'visions'. For a time he resisted them, then resigned himself to returning to his own village, Nkamba. It was while he was there that he had a decisive dream: he received orders to go out and teach the Bible and to visit a nearby village to cure a sick child by the laying-on of hands. For a critical interpretation of Simon Kimbangou's biography, the reader should consult E. Andersson: *Messianic Popular Movements in the Lower Congo*, Uppsala, 1958, p. 48ff.

† A document published in the French Congo claims that sixty black pastors and catechists were imprisoned during the repression of Kimbangism.

magic and sorcery, this achievement was welcomed by everyone. It inspired confidence, restored the sacred bonds that had been broken, and canalized propitious 'forces'. In certain regions, such as Kipako, his disciples publicly identified the sorcerers (ba-ndòki) and refused to accept them into the 'church of the elect' – anyone whose hair did not absorb the water when he was baptized was rejected on these grounds.[7] In this way the new cult provided a method of coping with a danger that had only arisen because the Europeans had prohibited the traditional methods of dealing with the ki-ndòki. This in itself was bound to attract a considerable membership – and, on occasion, the Salvation Army missions did not hesitate to adopt similar methods for the same purpose. The problem of the extension of sorcery, that is to say of the multiplication of antagonisms that can neither be controlled nor compensated for, first forces itself upon the attention of sociologists when they find themselves confronted by a society in transition. Simon Kimbangou's teaching was effective at another level: it restored order, and introduced a measure of rationalization to debased religious systems that had encouraged the appearance of a variety of contradictory cults and beliefs; it retained only one fundamental element, the *ancestor cult*, on which it relied heavily. This is confirmed by Van Wing, who refers to the considerable importance accorded to the ancestors both in the ritual and the dogma formulated by the leaders of the movement: 'Neither Kimbangou nor any other leader ever appealed to the people to abandon the ancestor cult: their burial grounds were always kept tidy and the paths leading to them were cleared, for their return to life would initiate the golden age.'[8] This fact illustrates the central importance of the ancestor cult in Kongo society, and its *persistence* at a time when many other elements of the ancient religious system were disappearing; together with the organization of the clan and the kinship structures with which it was indissolubly connected, it proved to be the least vulnerable part of the system, despite the effect of multiple processes of change.

The Kimbangou ritual included baptism, confession and services at which hymns were sung. The latter were inspired by the Bible, which had been translated into Ki-Kongo, and the leaders of the movement made skilful use of the themes of protest and revolt in it that could easily be turned against the Europeans.

The new church could only grow through opposition;* so rapid was its success that there was very little possibility of controlling its members and the reactions that it had suddenly unleashed, which took the form of a primitive kind of xenophobia and led to incidents that soon provided an excuse for the Belgian administration to take action. The *Gounza* was arrested at Nkamba (then known as N'kamba-Yélusalèmi) on September 14, 1921 and condemned to death, but later he was pardoned and deported to Katanga in November 1921. Having thus become a martyr, he was now regarded as typifying resistance, and all relations with the official missions – who were accused of having helped in his arrest† – were broken off.

Kimbangou's imprisonment and deportation did more to increase his authority than to destroy the movement he had created. As happened with Matswa after his arrest,‡ the imprisoned leader became the symbol of opposition; removed from direct contact with his followers, there was nothing to hinder the process of idealization, and his example served to encourage intense devotion.

As we have already pointed out, Kimbangou was essentially both *Gounza* (a term connected with the symbolism of the Trinity and expressing his personal divinity) and 'Saviour' (an assertion of his role as liberator of the Kongo ethnic group). These two major qualifications show how closely the religious and political aims of the movement were associated. A Belgian document that appeared later was quite right not to make any distinction between his aspiration to found a 'Congolese religion' and his aspiration to create an independent 'Congolese state'. Similarly one finds the expressions 'Jehovah's Witness' and 'King' used alternatively – the latter connoting the idea of 'kingdom' in its Biblical sense of a just and prosperous 'country' because of its dependence upon God. On other occasions, Kimbangou was referred to as 'Simon

* This opposition was unavoidable, although Kimbangou maintained that, in certain circumstances, he would have preferred not to break with the missionaries. He lost control of the movement he had created and was swept along by the more radical members.

† A document that appeared after the 1921 events could still say: 'The Protestant Mission at Gombé Lutété began our education and made us pray to God to send us a Saviour; yet when our Saviour arrived this Mission became our enemy. It denounced him like the Catholic Missions, which demanded that he be arrested and put to death.'

‡ See previous chapter.

14

the Great', and his power was exalted because of the apocalyptic catastrophes that he would unleash, and then master, in order to establish 'the kingdom of God'; as a rule, the references to the Prophetic Books and the Apocalypse were very explicit.

It was not until later, however, with the creation of the *Mission des Noirs* in 1939–40, that the doctrine elaborated by the *new* organizers was implicitly based upon the conception of the 'King and Saviour of the Black people'; an elaboration that indicates how far the Kimbangist church had developed in the course of twenty years of violence and repression. Here Simon no longer appears as sharing in the person of Christ, as implied in the earlier writings, but as the founder-martyr of a religion directly revealed to the Black people without the assistance of 'foreigners', who only betrayed the divine message by acting in the interests of the government. In several instances, emphasis was placed upon the similarities between Kimbangou and the founders of the universal religions, as well as upon the racial nature of the revelations that had led to their emergence: 'God promised us to pour out his Holy Spirit upon our country. We besought him, and he sent us a Saviour of the Black peoples, Simon Kimbangou. He is the Leader and Saviour of the Black people in the same way as the Saviours of other races, Moses, Jesus Christ, Mahomet and Buddha.'[9] And again: 'God did not wish us to hear his word without giving us proof of it. . . . He has sent us Simon Kimbangou, who is to us what Moses was to the Jews, Christ to the foreigners and Mahomet to the Arabs.'[10]

The movement represented a form of racial reaction, as well as an endeavour to provide the Congolese with a major religion that they could look upon as their own. It opposed the Christianity imported by the colonists in the same way that it rejected the colonial situation, and it was in this sense that the messianic movements implied both religious emancipation and nationalist awakening.* The dynamic that the Kimbangist church derived from its *absolute* opposition (based upon its exposure of the gulf between official Christianity and its Ba-Kongo converts) it sought to use in a way that would promote the unity of the Kongo tribes

---

* During the 1930s various disciples proclaimed the departure of the Whites and the need to hurry it up. Then, it was said, Simon Kimbangou would be able to return and take possession of the Kongo throne.

and their supremacy throughout the Congo. This external stimulus, the presence of the colonist, was necessary if the new church was to develop: without this favourable condition for broadening the basis of the religious groups (hitherto bound up with kinship or specialized activities) it could never have taken root and lasted without deteriorating. It triumphed because, at least at the start, it could only exist in opposition, and because it was distinguished by the universal outlook of the revealed religions. It attracted a large membership because it constituted a third term, so to speak, distinct from the traditional cults (debased and partly abandoned because the progressive Mu-Kongo was afraid of appearing uncivilized if he sought to maintain them as they were) and also from Christianity (which it opposed as being associated with colonialism and incapable of assimilation unless adapted.)*

The analogy between Simon Kimbangou's martyrdom and the passion of Christ was unmistakable. The instruction that was later provided by the *Mission des Noirs* described his condemnation by the authorities, his resurrection and the teaching of his Apostles, all of which are briefly referred to in the following text:

'He whom God sent as Saviour of the Blacks was handed over to the Authorities, who sent him to Elizabethville, where he was imprisoned and enslaved for many years.†
Later the Authorities decided to have him shot. But no sooner did they make him stand up and begin to fire at him than he appeared in our country. He came to Kinzwana and to Kituengé where he made himself known to P.M., to Dembo, Kwanga and Kinhoni. It was then that he himself chose the Apostles, and ordered them to build houses of prayer.'[11]

The prophet's personality was also based upon that of Moses bringing the Jewish people the tablets of the law. No decision could be taken without reference to the founder of the church – because of the teachings he had received direct from God:

* In a quite different part of the country, Ghana, Nkwame Nkrumah, then leader of the opposition, maintained that, in the colonial countries, missionary activity 'is identified with the political and economic exploitation of our people.' See *Towards Colonial Freedom*, London, 1947.

† It may be noted in passing that those societies that have experienced slavery are much more sensitive about the *subordinate* position created by colonization.

'The chief of the Apostles . . . must bear in mind the rules issued by the founder of the church. He can give no order that did not emanate from him. The founder of the *Mission des Noirs* received the laws from God.'[12]

The inspiration of the Bible, derived from the book of Exodus rather than Leviticus, was regarded as binding, even as to the way in which the laws were conveyed to members; they could only be taught 'in the chamber of obedience where the original rules (*nanku dya nlamfo*) are expounded'.[13] The history of the people of Israel – who, according to Freud, 'resisted misfortunes and ill-treatment with unexampled tenacity'[14] – made a profound impression upon the minds of the leaders of the Congolese church. The sense of superiority, of being the chosen people expressed by the Jews could easily be translated into the Ba-Kongo context: the richness of their past, due to their connection with São Salvador and their privileged position as a people who, from very early times, had been leaders of local trade, had often led the Ba-Kongo to assert their supremacy. And this applied on at least two levels. Because of their direct relationship with God (a traditional God moreover, *Nzambi Pungu*) it attributed their authority to a sacred source, thus serving to fill the gap left by the decline of their one-time authority. In Freud's words, it proved that it was possible 'to achieve the extraordinary feat of creating a united people out of a diversity of families and individuals'.[15] This need for solidarity, moreover, was encouraged by ancient memories: behind the Kongo kings and the centralized government they had established, stood the figure of a culture hero, 'a highly skilled craftsman who had invented the art of working in iron'.[16] In a rough and ready way, the themes of the hero, the prophet and the 'great man' were amalgamated.

The *Mission des Noirs* composed and taught litanies exalting the twelve persons* of Simon Kimbangou, attributes that served to mark the rhythm of the seasons, since they were connected with the twelve months of the year, and which were one of the methods used to manifest the omnipresence of the Saviour. Simon was at once the Prophet, the Holy One, the Saviour, the

* An obvious example of the importance of the idea of personality in the minds of Negro religious thinkers.

Chief, the Flag, Jacob's Ladder, the Heavenly Gates, the Boat that takes the Soul on its last voyage, the Way of the Spirit, the River and the Priest. These designations, full of echoes of the Bible, clearly reveal the functions that were attributed to him, religious and political, celestial and terrestrial. Some of them indicate the part played by the concept of salvation introduced by Christianity, just as one finds in other texts the idea of the redemption of sins, both of which were teachings that Kongo culture was more or less prepared to accept because of the sense of guilt inherited from the past. In addition to this, the personality of Kimbangou was often associated with notions of material power. In some texts he is shown returning to the country with the other deportees, 'in the new King's locomotive'; in others, God was said to have given him a lorry so that he could go wherever he was needed; while in yet other 'messages' his image is associated with that of the river steamer and the aeroplane. As Tempels has shown, Bantu thought is dominated by the notion of full participation in the system of universal forces[17] – a way of compensating for their manifest inferiority with regard to European technology. A number of their teachings show clearly that the founders of the Congolese church aspired both to religious and political emancipation, and to the acquisition of technical ability. The church was concerned with material victory, as well as spiritual.

Obviously Kimbangou, separated from his disciples, was in no position to create this personality for himself. It was built up as circumstances required by the more or less disinterested men who carried on his work. But the fact of the matter is that it was the organized repression of the Belgian authorities that really put the new church on its feet: having provided it with a martyr, it gave free rein to the idealization of a leader who was free from any obligation to appear in the flesh. It is also important to appreciate the functional use that was made of borrowings from Christianity: the knowledge obtained from the missionaries, and even the way their churches were organized, were used as 'models' for the satisfaction, real or illusory, of specifically Ba-Kongo needs. And what made this all the easier was that many of the situations described in the Old Testament could readily be assimilated to those of the African peoples: as Leakey rightly points out, the use they made of the Bible was often entirely different from that envisaged by the missionaries. Moreover, in South Africa, this procedure is typical of the colonizing society as well as of the colonized: the Dutch Reformed Church claims to find there theological justification for the policies of the Nationalist Party, deriving the notion of apartheid from the Bible and using religion for political purposes.* Whether this is due to reciprocal influence, and if so in which direction, is by no means clear, but the fact itself is worth noting.

Even the briefest study of Kimbangist literature confirms these preliminary observations. Working through the collected texts soon becomes monotonous, for original works are rare and many of them appear to be merely variants of stereotyped versions. The reason for this is the small number of creative writers (though the *Mission des Noirs* eventually tried to create a body of writers, under the direction of a 'Great Writer') and the exclusive nature of the models on which they based themselves – the Bible and religious hymns. In addition to this one has to take into account the difficulties involved in publication, whether in the form of duplicated copies, or by the method known as 'the chain of happiness', or by purely oral means. Any classification of them is bound to be simplified and reflects this comparative poverty.

Since they formed part of the ritual, we will first consider the hymns, some of which have been collected under the general title *Songs of Heaven*, and which, despite their 'Christian' approach, constitute a literature of 'resistance'. The political authorities were quite right when they pointed out that the Christmas hymns to *Gounza* in 1923 were mainly allusions to the struggle against white domination, 'and are concerned with little else than the trials and suffering endured, and the struggles against the enemy'.[18] Here we must restrict ourselves to a few brief quotations, though these will suffice since the number of themes is restricted. Some of these hymns are simply a glorification of the 'Prophet', of his participation in God's omnipotence and invincibility:

* It also has some of the characteristics of a secret society. The *Afrikaner Broederbond* which is linked both with the Party and the Church represents an extremely powerful group, distinguished by its strict insistence upon secrecy, which, after taking action against non-Afrikaans Europeans, has now joined the racialist movement led by the Nationalist Party.

1 God created the world.
2 No one can set himself above Him.
3 He who listens to his message will be rewarded with eternal life.
4 He bequeathed his 'staff' to his prophets . . .
11 You, our Saviour, must not forsake us
12 Jesus Christ, you who were the first to suffer
13 Must not forsake us . . .
17 The White Men are tired of snatching the 'staff' of Jesus.
18 From the hands of our Saviour Kimbangou.
19 They tried to kill him, but they could not do so.

The 'staff' is an allusion to the one that was turned into a serpent, which God gave to Moses to prove that he was a prophet,[19] but it is primarily related to the traditional Congo context: the staff, or walking-stick, usually carved, was one of the insignia of royalty, and was for a long time the symbol of authority of the 'old-style chiefs'.[20] The 'kingdom of Christ', later to become that of the Black Messiah, is conceived of as being real, but adapted to a society in which an independent Congolese Church and State would coexist. In a more or less complementary sense, the 'staff' indicates that Simon Kimbangou was both King and Prophet. In addition to this, there is a repeated theme running through this particular text: that of *abandonment* and *isolation*. In this way, the victim of colonization expresses his feeling of weakness when faced by a situation that condemns him to a position of inferiority from which the only chance of escape is illusory and utopian. In his analytical study of South Africa Sachs shows the part that this sense of weakness and hopeless isolation has in creating what he calls 'black anger.'*

In other hymns, the exhortation to outright resistance and struggle is scarcely concealed by the religious symbolism. In the following text no one was likely to mistake the significance of such expressions as 'soldiers of Jesus' or 'lost unto all eternity'.

1 O Jesus, Saviour of the World, we come to seek refuge in Thee.

* Cf. Wulf Sachs: *Black Anger*, 1938, in which the hero uses these words in a discussion with a friend who is about to set out for the U.S.A.: 'He merely asked me to tell the people in the United States, specially the Negroes, how it is with this people in Africa, *how alone, how isolated* they are in their misery, *with no one in the world to appeal to*' (our italics).

2 We put our trust in Thee, and we shall not be lost to all
   eternity . . .
4 Do not lose heart, O soldiers of Jesus. Pluck up courage . . .
6 The Kingdom belongs to us. It is ours!
7 The White Man no longer possesses it . . .
12 Let none of us lose heart.
13 Let us praise God, our Father, who will come upon the clouds.

Lastly, some of these hymns associate with endlessly repeated
expressions of rejection religious and moral precepts that show
the priests' concern with teaching, their determination to create an
ethic that will prevent the most serious disorders arising from
social change. There is no such thing, they maintain, as 'secret
activities', everyone is responsible for everything that he does.

1 Heaven and Earth are witnesses of everything we do.
2 God knows everything . . .
3 On the day when Jesus Christ shall come to give judgement,
   everyone will be afraid . . .
8 The young women will be punished because they lust after
   other women's husbands.
9 O God our Father.
10 And the young men, too, shall be punished because they
   dream of sleeping with other men's wives.
11 O God our Father . . .
20 The chiefs will be punished because they set too high a value
   upon money.
21 O God our Father.
22 The police shall be punished because they make other people
   suffer.
23 O God our Father, forgive us all, that we may be delivered!

This last text is doubly significant: not only does it show the
concern felt by the religious leaders for establishing rules of conduct, it also emphasizes the important part that the theme of
guilt continued to play in Kongo culture. Confession still had
an important place in the life of the Kimbangist church, and its
expansion coincided with a more genuine and widespread
assimilation of the concepts of sin (which, to a considerable extent,
impinged upon the Ba-Kongo notion of infringing the prohibitions laid down by *Nzambi Pungu*) and of grace. This responsibility, established at the level of the ordinary man and no longer

restricted to those in positions of authority and leadership, was part of the whole process leading to 'recognition' of the individual. By transferring responsibility to the ordinary man, it had a subversive effect, for it made him active and capable of choice instead of passive and submissive. It freed the individual from his old allegiances and thus made it possible for him to join new organizations. For instance, at the time of the Gounzist demonstrations in 1923–4, it was in the name of the grace that only God can grant that certain villagers rejected unconditional submission to the orders of the official chiefs. They declared: 'You may as well hold your tongues, officials cannot give grace. We don't owe obedience to them, but only to God.'[21] By modifying the entire system of moral reference, Kimbangism challenged the whole basis of authority, not simply that of the official chiefs as in this case, but that of the old-style chiefs as well.*

Associated with these hymns, which, in imitation of the Salvation Army, played such an important part in their services, were the prayers that glorified not only outstanding personalities of the past but also the contemporary leaders of the church. Consider, for example, the following 'Prayer to God and the Saints':†

'Oh Almighty God, the one true light, God of the true gods, come to our aid and free us from all the evils that afflict us. Rid our country of all those who do us harm.

'Oh Supreme Chief, Bwéta M'Bôgo, defend our faith and our fatherland. Oh Ngoma, you who are the true intercessor . . . pray for us night and day . . .

'Nkampa, defender in all our difficulties . . . Our liberator, Mi-pâgala,‡ deliver us swiftly . . .

'N'Gabâdumu be unto us a faithful guardian . . .

'Myahunga, valiant defender of the world, save our country which is today in the hands of our enemy . . .'

The series of invocations continues, exalting some twenty individuals by name. In this way, they fulfil the traditional function of the 'verse-mottoes' applied to clans and legendary or

---

* Some of these songs condemn the chiefs for being more concerned with their own interests than those of the people: 'O God, our Father, the Chiefs are going to be punished because they worry too much about their money.'

† The words of this prayer were used in a Kimbangist church in the Boko region.

‡ Mi-pâgala was the supreme authority of the Ki-Mpâga clan and other parallel clans.

powerful individuals, though in this case it is the church and not the clan whose mighty deeds are proclaimed.

A second category of texts consists of *messages to the faithful*, directives and commentaries on day-to-day events, to sustain hope in 'the good news' in a form borrowed from the biblical works in most common use. Many of these use similar themes, which makes them tedious to read; but though, as noted in official reports, they contain no definite indication 'of opposition to established authority', they nevertheless contribute in one way or another to the spirit of revolt. Their verbal violence and the 'victories' they proclaim often appear to be a form of 'compensation'. The following one is typical:

> 'My brothers of Jerusalem, help one another. The business*
> will be finished with in June. It will be finished with by the
> beginning of the rainy season. We, the Apostles, shall by then
> have gone out to announce the Kingdom of God to the nations
> of the world. Matchets and axes are coming with the soldiers.
> We shall cut down the plantations of our Lord Jesus Christ.
>
> 'Simon Kimbangou has just arrived. He will return to
> Jerusalem. I, too, shall be going to the Jordan to baptize the
> people.
>
> 'Be ready in the villages, war is near.'†

Here it is worth noting that the *theme of expectation* is frequently associated with that of *abandonment*, already mentioned with reference to one of the preceding texts. It is expressed in the announcement of the 'end of the business', of the return of the deported Saviour and Apostles, of the catastrophes that will 'wipe out' the European,‡ of the providential alliances – like that

---

* This was the word that was used to describe the disturbances that broke out when Simon Kimbangou was sentenced in 1921; but, in a wider sense, it also refers to the whole range of antagonisms that existed between the Blacks and Whites in the Congo.

† This document was published in 1930, at the time when the trial of the leader, André Matswa, was causing violent reactions. We should add, perhaps, that the revolt it speaks of remained strictly verbal.

‡ For example, in December 1939 it was announced that Brazzaville and Leopold-ville would be destroyed by floods on January 1st; thereupon the Ba-Kongo fled from both towns to escape the catastrophe and to listen to the words of the Apostles. See *Rapport sur le mouvement gounziste*, published by the Boko sub-division, 1931.

of the Germans after the defeat of 1940, etc. All the Christian
literature proclaiming the 'good news', and the last judgement
when everyone will receive their due reward, helped to feed
this twofold hope. The transition from one theme to another
was not accidental; it restored in an almost mythical way –
Christian teaching providing what was lacking in Bantu mythology – a position which the first of the two themes represented as
being hopeless, and it implied that complete submission would be
followed by a positive phase. The colonial administration was
keenly aware of this revival of initiative, and reacted swiftly and
energetically. Though it is impossible to summarize the contents
of these many messages to the faithful it is nevertheless worth
listing some of them to indicate the principal themes. First of all
there are those proclaiming the omnipotence of God, that
represent the Trinity in the form of God (*Nzambi Pungu*) – Jesus –
Kimbangou. They speak of God 'having now arrived in the
Congo', as the 'liberator' of the Congolese. God's presence 'does
away with fear', it justifies putting up with every kind of suffering
and makes it possible to reject all other authority. God will reward
the 'elect', that is to say, the most zealous members, by giving them
'the first places'. Thus, by returning to its origins, Christianity will
recover the subversive energy it used to have in ancient Graeco-
Roman society; it proclaims the victory of the 'new kings' over the
'old kings'. Next comes a group of prayers expressing the need
for *power* and *physical force*. This kind of demand – for which the
system of traditional beliefs, based upon the idea of force and
power, were a preparation – is to be found in various texts that
were circulating in 1930, of which the following is typical: 'Rejoice
that you are practising the religion of God, that he may give you
power and strength to conclude this business and surpass all
white men.' Some of the 'letters to the Faithful', written at the
beginning of 1941 and bearing the stamp of the disturbances that
followed upon the French defeat, are even more explicit. After
announcing that a 'new reign' is imminent, one of them goes on:
'The Blacks will go into the workshops and factories of this new
king to learn how to make all the things that we see in the shops
but only possess with our eyes.' Other texts of this period predict
that Germany will be victorious and 'occupy the country for
twenty years at most, during which time they will teach the Blacks

how to derive greater benefit from the resources of their land and help them to put up factories where they can manufacture what the country needs, particularly motor cars, etc.'[22] The Congolese wanted modern technology and the goods it can produce, which had hitherto been unavailable to them; and not only did they aspire to a higher standard of living but, even more important, they recognized that any possibility of social and political progress depended upon the possession of material power. Lastly, a third group of themes emphasizes the gulf between the Whites and the Blacks – 'Whites and Blacks are kept apart; they on their side, we on ours' – and reveal the emergence of a kind of 'counter-racism' among the Congolese. These publicize the 'trials and persecutions' to which the Blacks had been subjected, and glorify their racial solidarity with 'the Negroes who are now living in America, but who will return to their own country, the Congo'. They warn of the dangers, both physical and metaphysical (being carried off 'into the country of the dead') that threaten all those 'who attend the white man's cults' and compromise with the 'government'. The racial attitude here expressed seems also to include sexual elements: one or two of the later texts refer to white women as a source of degradation (comparable in some respects with prostitutes), or as destroyers of the black race.*

It is clear, therefore, that these three groups of themes did not occur separately, but were logically related to one another. It is difficult to determine how far they represented the views of a minority of leaders, or how far they expressed a collective feeling; but we do know that they played a vital part in the Ba-Kongo revolt against the colonial situation. Popularized and widely discussed, they inspired the reactions in the countryside at every

* As an instance of this, consider the following unusual document, distributed by Simon-Pierre Mpadi in 1940: 'The second test is this. . . . The Blacks will have to marry all the Missus-ladies without husbands . . . Some of them will open houses for prostitutes so that the Black men will go there and debase themselves. These girls will all come from European countries. They will worry the Black wives who live in their husband's houses, and try to take their place. This marriage with the Missus-ladies will be a harsh test for the Blacks. Many of the Black men will cast off their Black wives to marry Missus-ladies. But I appeal to the Apostles, and to all those who believe in the Saviour, not to do such things.' It is in this context that one has to consider some of the acts of violence, especially the raping of white women, that occurred in 1960, after Congolese Independence. Throughout the area affected by Kimbangism (the Thysville region), the sudden relaxation of tension set free forces and illusions that had been held in check for forty years.

moment of crisis. Their very persistence indicates that they were typical of the new myths that were springing up, which included Christian elements; and, in this respect, it is revealing that they incorporate both revelations of an esoteric nature* and such legendary exploits as the imaginary journeys of the Saviour. This Kimbangist literature, standing as it does midway between traditional oral literature and the earliest formulation of political ideologies, still has something of the effectiveness hitherto attributed to myth.

II. THE VICISSITUDES OF KIMBANGISM; AND THE 'MISSION DES NOIRS'

On its first appearance, the effect of the Kimbangist movement on the villagers in the French colonies was comparatively slight; it reached them in the course of trade and as a result of their connections with their kinsmen settled on the other side of the river Congo; and at first it only affected the *Ba-Kongo* (i.e. the Ba-Kongo of the Boko region), whose groups were in direct contact with those of the Belgian Congo† and who had so far escaped the influence that the Catholic missions of Linzolo and Mbamou then exercised over the Ba-Sundi and Ba-Lali.‡ In its early days, Kimbangism did not extend beyond the frontiers of particularism (it was regarded as an innovation from outside peculiar to the *Ba-Kongo* tribe) and was looked upon as the sort of reaction typical of people who had accepted the teaching of the Protestant missions. Taking advantage of this limited development, the colonial administration quickly intervened and deported three of the most active leaders to the Chad.

But in 1923, during the Christmas festivities, hymns in praise of the *Gounza* were heard in every village church in the Belgian-controlled Congo, as well as in the vicinity of Boko. Opposition

* Here is an example taken from a message to the members: 'I saw the kingdom in the shape of an O. . . . This sign was as clear as the sun, almost as big as the sun, and shining like the sun itself.'

† The old Boko district was across the river from the most vital centres of Kimbangism: Nkamba, Kimbangou's village, and Ngombé-Lutété.

‡ Their reactions to Kimbangism set the Protestant and Catholic Missions at loggerheads, the latter being accused by the former of strengthening the 'calumniators' and agents of oppression. Cf. E. Andersson: *op. cit.*, p. 84 ff.

to the policy of repression carried out in 1921–2 led to demonstrations, and more and more frequently the songs that were sung referred to the 'first victims', and especially to the Saviour, who 'in spite of everything will come back and put an end to the white man's domination'. The sufferings that were endured strengthened the nature of the movement as a national awakening. From that time on there could no longer be any doubt that the freedom it sought on the religious plane would inevitably assume a wider significance. In the Boko region no one could fail to realize that Kimbangism was rapidly gaining ground. An official report pointed out that when 'recalcitrant catechists are arrested ... they are escorted by many hundreds of members'; and it also noted that the movement was affecting the women as well as the men.* At this stage, however, there was as yet no fundamental breach between the followers of the *Gounza* and the Protestant missions: of the latter it was said officially that 'their attitude proves that they regard Gounzism as a younger offshoot of the ancient tree of Protestantism', while the leaders of the movement maintained that it was 'the missionaries who taught us all we know'. It was only the completely hostile attitude of the administration that led to a final breaking-off of relations, thus helping to strengthen its racist and xenophobic tendencies.† The official reaction was extremely ill-advised, and the injudicious repression of the movement only served to reveal the government's bewilderment at finding itself confronted by a new religion which refused to obey its orders on the grounds that it owed primary obedience to God. Moreover, this refusal of unconditional submission, based upon a transcendental obligation, contributed greatly to the success of Kimbangism – as did its determination to establish an authority whose legitimacy derived directly from God at a time when the official chiefs were simply agents of the local administration.

The demonstrations continued from December 1923 to May 1924, when they stopped completely, partly as a result of the repression that was breaking up the movement, and partly from

* See *Mouvement gounziste en 1924*. Between January 9 and 14, 1924 the government post at Boko was threatened by more than 1,000 women members, organized in a succession of 'bands'.

† A rupture to which the Protestant missions (foreigners, and therefore immediately suspect) had to agree, though unwillingly. Cf. E. Andersson: *op. cit.*, pp. 84–95.

exhaustion. The incidents that had occurred had been a kind of explosion, that contained within itself both the chance of immediate success and the weakness that prevented it from producing lasting results. Between October 1926, when the principal leader of the local church returned from exile, and December 1929, the movement was gradually reorganized, but it restricted itself to clandestine activity. At this point, messages began to arrive from the Belgian Congo, professing to come from 'John the Baptist', which once again announced the coming of the 'Saviour'* and called upon the people to prepare for battle: 'Get ready, brothers, war is close upon us. . . . The time of red blood has come.' At Christmas, meetings and public ceremonies started up once more, and it was rumoured that on January 1st a flood would destroy both Brazzaville and Leopoldville, and sweep away all the Ba-Kongo who had opposed the movement. In 1929 and again in 1930, as in 1923, the feast of the Nativity gave rise to serious incidents. The identification of the *Gounza* with Christ encouraged a mood of exaltation, accentuating the tension between the European churches with their Christmas good cheer and the Negro church which could only hope for the freeing of its Saviour.† Every Christmas-time brought with it a conviction that the 'good news' was coming, only to be followed by a mood of deep disappointment. It was always in January that tension reached its highest point, as may be seen from the emergency measures taken at Boko in January 1931, revealing the authorities' profound sense of insecurity: churches were closed and all meetings forbidden, fire-arms had to be licensed, there were patrols day and night and the post was intercepted.[23]

Throughout the period 1930–31 there was intense activity and religious fervour. Orders were issued from the four villages where the leaders of the Gounzist church in the *Ba-Kongo* country lived. Their hold over the people may be seen not only from the number of 'confessions' they received but also from the type of religious observances that they succeeded in imposing. The services were

* The plagiarism from the Gospels is unmistakable.

† The reason for the dispute is clear from the official report: 'The great majority of members are convinced that sanctions against them were enforced at the instigation of the Missions . . . who look upon the new religion as a serious threat to their own teaching.' Political Report for the Brazzaville Sub-division, 1931.

held at night, from eight o'clock to eleven, although on Wednesdays (Saviour's day) and Sundays (Christ's day) the singing of hymns sometimes continued until the following morning. Obligations of this kind indicate how intense was the teaching to which the faithful were subjected; and, in addition, they were given a kind of 'psychological treatment' that was certainly very effective. Once the incidents were over, and the movement had again been deprived of its leaders, the religious fervour declined, though the church itself did not completely disappear. Each phase of serious conflict resulted in a more rigorous form of reorganization being adopted, revived the feelings that had originally led to the emergence of the church and widened the gulf between colonized and colonizers. An administrative report for the second quarter of 1931 declared: 'There are still many followers of the new religion who remain faithful to its doctrine and make no attempt to hide the fact. At the same time, as they are unaware of the political aims pursued by the leaders, the great majority of members practise its rites peacefully.'[24] By this time there could be no doubt that the roots of the Congolese church had struck deep enough to ensure its permanence, if not its effectiveness.

From the point of view of the groups living in the French colonies, the years 1929–31 were of exceptional importance. The serious economic situation brought about by the world crisis had created a feeling of uneasiness that crystallized discontent. It accentuated the sense of insecurity, raised the whole question of the temporary order that had been established and revived the anxieties of the authorities, though it was no longer possible for them to resort to the old methods of protection. It was a critical moment in the growing awareness of the colonial situation and of the problems posed throughout the Congo by the rapid pace at which change was taking place. Indeed, it was precisely during this period that Amicalism began to take root among the Ba-Lali and Ba-Sundi; the trial of André Matswa took place on April 2 and 3, 1930, and started a riot in the native townships of Brazzaville. Thus the majority of the Ba-Kongo on the right bank had their own movement, but though this satisfied the particularism of the Ba-Lali and Ba-Sundi it made no attempt to isolate itself from Kimbangism – in fact it strengthened it by introducing the techniques of political organization; furthermore, some of the

:aders of the Congolese church reacted to the April events by
xtolling the victims and distributing copies of 'Lamentations'. *
Jntil about 1939 Amicalism continued to dominate all activities
irectly opposed to colonialism, and served as a kind of 'relay
tation' for some of the Congo groups in the neighbouring
:rritory, whereas the members of the Congolese church sought
:fuge in the Salvation Army. Here, too, the two movements,
ir from conflicting, tended to act jointly and so maintained an
pposition that could not be put down.

  Before leaving this aspect of the subject, it is worth considering
few facts about the most active Kimbangist leaders in the Boko
egion. At that time the director of the local church was Samuel
I., a former 'Catechist Inspector' for the Swedish Evangelical
Iission, who, after his return from deportation in 1926, oddly
nough received the title of 'Bishop'. From the beginning of the
;ounzist movement he had been an active organizer and was one
f the first three victims of repression in 1921 – an official enquiry
poke of him as being 'the most disaffected of the illuminati, and
he most to be feared'. His centralizing role, and his responsibility
or local cadres, were described in some detail in the official
eports: 'Seated behind his official desk in his huge living quarters
.e presides over meetings; it is here that his subordinates gather
o learn hymns; and it is to him that the written confessions of
ther leaders and literate members are addressed.'[25] He directed
he movement from the village of Gombé with the help of Jacob
I., formerly a pupil of the school in Brazzaville and a government
iterpreter, who composed the 'Lamentations' of April 3, 1930
uoted above. In addition to these two there were: Jean B., a
atechist dismissed from the Swedish Evangelical Mission, under
olice supervision from 1924 onwards; Moses M., who had had
arious jobs in the Belgian Congo and was in touch with many
f the churches there; Paul M., who was later to play an important

  * See, for example, 'Lamentations of April 3, 1930, for those who were struck
own, flung into the river and imprisoned in the town of Brazzaville'. 'April 3, 1930
as a day of great persecution, punishment, outrage and insult. Those who have only
ıst been born are as yet without strength. But they came with their guns, their
ırtridges and all their soldiers, while we had nothing to fight with. Alas Lord!
he sound of tears and lamentation was heard. How they were beaten! How they
ere flung into the river! How they were outraged! They are the people of the living
;od. . . .' The rest of the document is inspired by, and draws heavily upon, the *Book
f Jeremiah*, XXXI, XXXIII and XXXIV.

part in the revival of the Kimbangist movement (1940–41), and
who for the time being acted as liaison with the Kimbangis
leaders in the frontier region. Together with two other les
influential leaders, they formed a leadership of seven (a deliberat
figure, perhaps), carrying on their activity in spite of numerou
difficulties; from 1921 until comparatively recently, one or othe
of them always managed to keep Kimbangism alive. From thi
account of the local cadres certain distinctive features of th
movement emerge. Until the 1930s, the movement remained
strongly influenced by its Protestant origins, from which it derived
themes taken from the Bible that stimulated the spirit of Messian
ism and provided it with cadres capable of original thinking. Th
movement was led by men who had assimilated many aspects o
European culture, and whose modernist outlook and concern
for progress were never in doubt. Then, too, the church the
created was closer to the 'Ethiopian' type, as defined by D
Sundkler, than to the 'Zionist'; it was more concerned with pro
gress than with a return to traditional values and attitudes.

From 1932 to 1939 the initiative seems to have been mainl
in the hands of the Amicalists – not only among the French Ba
Kongo, but also among the Belgian, some of whom temporaril
adopted this form of protest. This was partly due to circumstances
in the Belgian Congo the economic crisis had led to seriou
revolts,[26] and the savage repression that ensued had destroye
the leadership of any form of opposition, particularly that of th
Kimbangist church. After a feeble resurgence in the Boko regior
in 1935, Gounzism had declined, and was not to reappear unt
1939, by which time it was stronger and better organized, thank
to a new leader, Simon-Pierre Mpadi.

This man was a Mu-Kongo from the Belgian Congo. Few fact
about his life are available, but we know that he first worked fo
a Baptist mission, then for the Salvation Army, where he was ser
on an officers' course and was given a responsible position; an
that he experienced 'the call of God' at a time when Kimbangis
was at a low ebb (1936). He thereupon made contact with som
of the old followers of the *Gounza*, whose work he had come t
fulfil. His Christian name, Simon Peter, which had been given hir
quite by chance, was looked upon as confirming both his associa
tion with the Congolese Messiah and his status as a foundin

postle of the church. His aim was to carry through his work of organization by capitalizing the appeal attaching to the name of Simon Kimbangou. The essence of his doctrine was the exaltation of the Saviour's twelve persons, though it also involved rejection of the missionary churches and of the degraded practices of the traditional magical cults. It was not until December 1939, however, that the new organization – first called the *Mission des Noirs*, then *Nzambi ya Kaki* (the Khaki God) because of the colour of the prescribed uniform – was actually founded; that is to say, at a moment when colonialism was faced with considerable difficulties and the opposition could see the possibility of taking the initiative. On September 5th, Simon-Pierre Mpadi summoned the elders of the Gounzist church, and together they formulated the basis of the new organization; on the 7th he informed the local authorities of what he had done and, two days later, broke with the Salvation Army. On September 10th and 12th the first meetings of the faithful were held at Leopoldville and Kinkoni, and on the 13th the Council of the Apostles was elected. These dates were easily remembered since they more or less corresponded with the anniversary of the *Gounza*'s arrest. From then on Mpadi was to experience all the vicissitudes of the earlier leaders of the Congolese church; he was deported to Befalé, made several escapes, and finally crossed the frontier into the French Congo, where he was arrested in 1944, and again in 1945, being extradited on both occasions. Once more he suffered the kind of persecution that Simon Kimbangou and his disciples had had to bear, which helped to strengthen the similarity between the two men. Each time he was deported, however, Mpadi managed to find enough members of the old Kimbangist church to form a staunch network of believers to collect information and pass on the founder's commandments'.

Among the slogans that he sent to his followers there was one that the local Belgian authorities found particularly discouraging: 'The Chief of the Apostles has been exiled, but this will not prevent him from leading our Church.' In fact, Mpadi succeeded, often by remote control, in creating a church which the colonial administration recognized as being 'marvellously staffed', consisting of a group of individuals prepared to sacrifice everything'.[27] At the head of it was the Chief of the Apostles (*nkuluntu wa zintumwa*), assisted by three deputies, then a council of twelve 'Apostles' (*ba zintumwa*) having an equal number of assistants. The function o the Council was to act as a general staff, to teach, coordinate an control. Under them were 120 disciples who had regional responsi bilities, and 300 catechists who operated at village level. Thi organization, based on the symbolism of the three persons of th Trinity and the twelve persons of Simon Kimbangou, formed hierarchy, its members being distinguished both by their behavi our and in material ways.* Their khaki uniform – which Mpad spoke of as 'the uniform of hope and victory' – had a number o stripes on the sleeves indicating the wearer's position (the Chie of the Apostles had seven). On the other hand, the 'three hundred had no distinguishing mark except for a red scarf, chosen becaus of its symbolic colour which was associated with the idea of vita force (in the sense that the blood is 'the seat of the soul'), with th notion of power and with the memory of the first *voluntary* agree ments arrived at with the Europeans, which had been 'sealed' b a gift of red blankets.† This symbolism was to be found in all th Congolese churches.

At this point, it is possible to draw certain conclusions. In th first place, it should be noted that the church provided a *framewor of social organization*. It made it possible to establish a regrouping outside the particularisms and intermixtures of the fragmented clans, on the basis of voluntary membership and an agreement t settle in the vicinity of a particular village. Thus resettlement, th necessary condition for any progress or modernization of villag administration, which the colonial authorities had failed to impose was here undertaken thanks to the politico-religious functions o the *Mission des Noirs*. In the second place, the Salvation Army whose organization Mpadi had studied with the greatest care provided the model for a militant type of church; it was a mode that was immediately attractive because it established a strict an quite obvious hierarchy, and because it reinforced the tendency o the Congolese church to monopolize the basic social functions –

* There were regional variations of this hierarchy; and the qualifications for ran were not only connected with the levels of responsibility but also with specialize ritual duties (protection against sorcery, confession, religious instruction, etc.). C E. Andersson: *op. cit.*, p. 154 ff.

† The treasure chests of some of the chiefs still contained the red blankets tha had been given them as 'presents' by de Brazza and Mgr. Augouard.

eligious, political, and in this case, though in a still very embryonic form, military. And, finally, it should be emphasized that, in
its main aspects, the new church represented not some empty
formalism, but an interrelated whole of meanings and symbols
that owed little to borrowings or gratuitous creations. For instance
the symbol 12, which recurred in Kimbangou's twelve persons,
in the Council of twelve Apostles, and in the observance of the
first twelve days in June as 'days of grace', etc., was connected
not merely with Biblical tradition (the twelve tribes of Israel), but
with a whole network of obligations to which the faithful were
committed: participation in the qualities of the Saviour, in the
rhythm of the year, in the twelve fundamental commandments,
in the tradition of the people of Israel (because of their resistance
to slavery and relations with God), and finally, in the religion
founded by the sacrifice of the *Gounza*, which was held to be the
twelfth of the great religions.

From the outset, Simon Mpadi and his disciples were determined to prevent any misunderstanding and to assert the *totali-
tarian* character of the new church. For a Congolese it entailed a
complete break both with the European missions* and with
traditional practices, although it found a place for the ancestor
cult. We have already referred to the way in which anyone who
refused to break with the missionaries or government representatives was threatened; and these threats were bound up with a
whole process of de-Christianization worked out by Mpadi himself. One precept declared: 'We have abandoned the cross because
God has separated us from Jesus Christ.' Certain passages in the
Cahiers written by the 'Chief of the Apostles' clearly bring out
the meaning of this policy. We will quote a passage from notes
for a sermon to be used by preachers in the 'parishes': 'The pictures you are shown, and which you take to be photographs, are
inventions of the White Man. Neither in the time of Jesus Christ
nor of Adam was there any such thing as photography. The crosses
that you see all over the Congo are contrivances of Satan, for the
true cross was in Judaea and Jesus was taken down from it: never

---

* The *Nzambi ya kaki* claimed to be the only true church on the grounds that its
founder was 'chosen by God'. It was said that it would triumph over all its rivals.
Moreover, any contact with the Christian missions was strictly forbidden, and those
Congolese who were associated with them were denounced as sorcerers (*ba-ndoki*).

kneel before a cross. The Jews who belong to the church of Moses have no pictures or crosses in their churches, and we don't want any either. Moreover, God has separated us from Jesus Christ and given us a Black Saviour, whom the Whites shot dead, or tried to.'[28] Some of the texts tend to represent the Christianity of the missionaries as a deception, a means of mystifying the Congolese. On the other hand, the 'commandments' insist upon the rejection of the traditional cults (apart from that of the ancestor cult) and magical techniques, and at the same time recommend the spiritualizing of religious practices by ridding them of any kind of material symbolism. Two of the precepts teach that people should 'give up the fetishes of our fathers', and that they should 'pray to God, instead of to idols, statues, pictures and crosses'. This rejection was part of the religious and magical rivalry made possible by the deterioration of the old religious system, as well as by the process of differentiation that had given rise to new needs and new antagonisms. Throughout the whole of Central Africa, it is difficult to distinguish between proselytizing on behalf of new or imported cults and competing for power. The *Mission des Noirs* acted energetically, and revived the campaign for the destruction of fetishes that the missionaries had for so long pursued. In some of the least Europeanized areas (around Mayama, for example) it even attempted to separate the ancestor cult from its old material forms of expression in order to associate it with a purer form of symbolism implying a more direct communication.

In this way, which did not exclude the use of force, *Kakism* endeavoured, by regrouping and uniting people, to create a religious order that would at the same time provide a form of social organization. In a confused way it tended to become a commitment both to religious federation and, because of its opposition to the white man who was at once politically dominant and the defender of colonial Christianity, to a kind of religious racism. The aspect we wish to emphasize once again is that, on the part of the founders, it represented a serious attempt at rationalization. Its doctrine insisted that religious practice should be seen as an inner experience, rather than as an effective form of 'manipulation' – for example, it looked upon faith as the only sure guarantee of healing. This work of purification was facilitated by adopting as a model the Hebrew religion, as revealed in the Pentateuch. It corresponded, at least in our opinion, to a period of change for Kongo culture – to a transition from a culture based upon material symbols and oral tradition to one based upon writings and books. And though this change was due to the education provided by Europeans and the importance that this attributed to the written word, it was rendered easier by the determination of the leaders, and many of their followers, to participate in an accepted and indisputable 'civilization'. There can be no mistaking their intention to have done once and for all with the accusation of 'savagery' – which was regarded as the justification for all the forms of inferiority they were subjected to.

This endeavour to create a new religious system, in an attempt to offset the decline of the old cults and the insecurity resulting from the increasing and unrestricted recourse to magic practices, had its counterpart in a reorganization of the system of duties and prohibitions. Here, too, the example of the Pentateuch seems to have been decisive. The rules relating to ceremonial and the dress to be worn by members were mixed up with those concerned with impurity and the limitation of profit. In some cases the plagiarism is immediately discernable – as, for example, with the precepts relating to impurity: 'When a woman has a flux of blood she will remain impure for seven days: during this time she shall not wear her uniform. If a man has relations with a woman when she is in this state, he too will be impure for seven days. Such impurity can only be got rid of by bathing in running water.'*

As regards those obligations concerned with strengthening the church's cohesion, the most important was a form of endogamy, which restricted marriage to other members of the church instead of to those of the clan, tribe or even ethnic group. Those with whom marriage was prohibited were, in the first place, anyone connected with the European missions or the Salvation Army, but also 'strangers' to the sect: 'Wives who are not members would lead their husbands into sin; God turned away from Isaac and from Solomon because of their wives.' Next in importance was

* Cf. *Leviticus*, XV, 19 ff: 'And if a woman have an issue, and her issue in her flesh be blood, she shall be put apart seven days; and whosoever toucheth her shall be unclean until the even. . . . And if any man lie with her at all . . . he shall be unclean seven days.'

the injunction to secrecy, which applied even to one's immediate
kinsfolk unless they belonged to the church.* Some priests
maintained that this was only a temporary measure. One of them
said: 'As soon as we are no longer afraid of being sent to prison
for practising our religion we shall hold our meetings in public,
so that everyone can attend them.'[29] Though this secrecy was in
contradiction to the proselytizing aims of the movement, it
nevertheless helped to maintain its cohesion and vitality.

The remaining 'commandments' were for the most part concerned with ritual observances, some of which have been mentioned already: the *complete* prohibition of material symbols; the
obligatory confession of sins as a condition of membership; rules
relating to prayer and the way animals should be slaughtered,†
while the eating of certain animals was prohibited altogether,
partly because of their connection with traditional tribal emblems,
partly because of the passage in Leviticus (V.2) about 'pure and
impure animals'. There were also regulations concerning the
marriage ceremony, which could only be celebrated by an 'Apostle'
and consisted mainly of hymns and prayers; and finally a whole
number of rules relating to 'holy days' and 'days of grace'. On
the former, either Sundays or Wednesdays (the day decreed by
Simon Kimbangou), no secular activities were allowed: 'No
markets, festivities or *matâga*, no law suits, and women are forbidden to prepare *chickwangues*.' The *matâga* commemorated significant events in the history of the movement: the first twelve days
in June, recalling the time when Kimbangou began to teach and
also the 'June days' when Matswa was tried at Brazzaville; the
period from September 23rd–26th (the days of Simon Kimbangou's
'martyrdom') was more and more closely connected with December 23rd–26th as the *Gounza* was associated with, then gradually
took the place of, Christ. During these periods uniforms had to
be worn and religious observances were intensified, thus providing
a series of solemn occasions corresponding to the major festivals
of the Christian year.

The strictly moral prescriptions throw considerable light upon

---

* Cards (sometimes decorated with symbolic motifs) were issued to 'children of
the Church' (*mwana a Nzambi ya kaki*), and regarded also as 'passports to heaven'.
† The traditional method of killing an animal for sacrifice was to cut its throat –
yet another instance of Ba-Kongo tradition coinciding with that of the Bible.

some of the areas of social disequilibrium referred to in the preceding chapter. They were primarily concerned with relations between the sexes within the family group. Polygamy was not openly attacked – this major obstacle to conversion to Christianity had acquired a symbolic value, implying all the forms of incompatibility with European civilization[30] – though it was *limited*. Only the leaders and 'Apostles' were allowed to have three wives, thus indicating that polygamy was still regarded as the chief mark of social pre-eminence. Adultery was condemned: 'A wife who commits adultery can be put aside, but not on the first occasion, since women have a tendency to succumb'; on the other hand, a wife could have her marriage annulled if her husband misbehaved, though the money paid as compensation for adultery could not be spent by the husband. In addition to these major precepts, there were a number of others relating to theft, fraud and illicit profit, which were certainly justified, as was the church's fight against alcoholism and the sale of palm wine: 'To make palm wine is a sin, but to sell it or offer it to anyone else is to spread that sin.' Finally, the eleventh and twelfth commandments reaffirmed the Christian precept of loving one's neighbour: 'He who has love in his heart is sure to respect God's commandments.' The teaching in this respect encouraged the struggle against antagonisms and particularisms, and thus helped to promote unity; it insisted that people 'should love their neighbour, even their enemies, even the Ba-Yaka and the Ba-Ngala' – peoples with whom the Ba-Kongo had frequently been at war before the modern colonial period. The model of the Christian church, with its claim to universality, led to a form of reorganization that extended the limits of ancient clan society. This was of the greatest importance, for it revealed the possibility of creating still larger political units, extending beyond tribal divisions and colonial frontiers. Once they grasped these underlying tendencies of the movement, the colonial authorities reacted immediately, for they recognized in them the seeds of a rapidly approaching nationalist upsurge.

Such then were the outstanding features of the religious and ethical system elaborated by Simon-Pierre Mpadi and his assistants on the basis of the experiences of the first Kimbangist movement. Obviously, there was a considerable gulf between the theoretical conception of the founders and the adaptation of it in practice by the members, but the fervour of the latter shows that it was not too wide to prevent the essential part of the teaching from getting across. Thus monotheism was effectively established as a result of a transference, occurring at the very heart of traditional beliefs, which reoriented religious experience towards 'a higher spirit', instead of towards mediating or specialized 'spirits'. The superior being, *Nzambi Pungu*, became accessible, and this tended to deflect attention from the shades of the ancestors, as may be seen from the desperate complaints of the old crowned chiefs. In the traditional religious system, on the contrary, *Nzambi Pungu* had been regarded as 'an invisible and all-powerful being, who had created everything, both men and things', an 'unapproachable sovereign Lord', against whom mankind had 'no recourse', as Van Wing puts it.[31] According to the authors of *Notes sur les coutumes lari*, the *Nzambi Pungu* 'is in no way involved in religious and magic manifestations'; though when they go on to represent him as comparable, 'because of his attributes of power and goodness',[32] with the God of Christianity, they are in fact implying that the position was changing. This gradual transition from a pluralist to a unitary religion is understandable on the part of the leaders, for they were concerned to win acceptance for a higher unity (in which the concept of a Congolese church would merge with that of 'a Congolese kingdom') in place of a diversity that could only lead to isolation and antagonism. But how was this to be achieved for any considerable part of the peoples living in the Congo?

To understand this, we have to envisage the interplay of various kinds of mechanism. The first attempt to convert the country to Christianity, in the time of São Salvador, had undoubtedly left its mark upon Kongo culture, but in the main it was the more recent missionary activities that had integrated the idea of the Christian god with the body of traditional beliefs – and this in two ways. On the one hand, by their ruthless struggle against 'fetishism' the missionaries eventually made the practice of the basic cults almost impossible; and in so doing they created favourable material conditions for a reorientation of religious manifestations. On the other, in their attempt to provide a religious literature in the native tongue they had either to rely upon linguistic equivalents (for example, 'God' = *Nzambi*), which involved distorting the meaning, or to borrow concepts that had a special connotation for the Ba-Kongo; for instance, the Ba-Kongo word for guardian angel, *nkadi*, associated with the three elements, body (*nitu*), breath (*mwéla*) and soul (*lunzi*), constituting the individual. Even the notion of a superior being was affected by this kind of distortion. Above all, by introducing the concept of mediation, Christianity made it possible for human beings to communicate with *Nzambi Pungu* – a communication all the more to be desired in that *Nzambi* was the sole instance of a power which was exempt from the influence of the magical techniques that were now getting out of control. By the time the mediator had been identified with a Black Messiah the process of adaptation was complete. This new conception of divinity (in which traditional features were associated with others borrowed from the Christian idea of the Trinity and, later on, with that of a 'national' God as envisaged by the Jewish people) was accepted by the majority of the Ba-Kongo because it corresponded to their most urgent needs: it enabled them to emerge from a state of religious decline that had been brought about by the proliferation of magic and sorcery; and it provided a solution, albeit illusory, to the state of subjection resulting from colonialism. The assurance of a special relationship with God – which was by no means alien to the ideas of village folk, taught by custom to accept the bonds between clan group, ancestors and clan emblem – and the conception of a terrible God whose wrath strikes down the 'oppressor', provided psychological compensations that should certainly not be underestimated.

With regard to the leaders, who had worked out the most elaborate dogmas, we believe that this development was foreseen and planned. The superior being known to the traditional religions became 'accessible' thanks to the influence of Christianity, which explained how the relationship with God was brought about; and later on, the model of the Hebrew God was imposed because it corresponded even more closely to the needs of a people in a colonial situation and to the confused attempts of the leaders to transcend the idea of the clan by that of the nation. In the course of our enquiries, we were often struck by the frequent references to the Pentateuch. The founders of the Congolese church fully appreciated the parallels between the position and social characteristics of the Jewish and Kongo peoples and the related societies with which the latter were in touch. The teaching of the Pentateuch and the historical books of the Bible seemed to them far more significant than that of the European missionaries, for in them they found a solution to problems similar to those with which they were confronted: the evolution from tribe to nation and, at the same time, from personal divinities to an exclusive God;* the development from tradition to written law; the remedies applicable to Israel's moral and social crisis; the reaction to the experience of 'captivity'; the examples of religious initiative (Abraham, Moses, the Prophets and Jesus) as a response to the mutations of civilization. The teachings of the Bible were contrasted with those of the missionaries, which they regarded as being one-sided and incomplete; and one of their most frequent complaints was precisely that the missionaries had withheld significant knowledge. The Old Testament provided a body of ideas that were susceptible of immediate application. It underlined the Ba-Kongo's vocation as leaders of other peoples, and it encouraged their determination to fight against oppression.

Owing to their semi-clandestinity, the continual suppression of their cadres and the difficulties of communication, the various local churches that emerged from Kimbangism and Khakism could not be strictly controlled by the original leaders. They enjoyed a considerable measure of autonomy, often relying upon the initial inspiration and then dealing with the situation in the way that seemed best to them. This individual activity explains why both their doctrine and ritual differed from Mpadi's original system. In some of the churches, particularly those in the most remote areas, there was a revival of spontaneity and of certain specifically Kongo cultural features. In the Kinkala-Mayama region, for example, the movement was unable to maintain its strict attitude towards idolatry; it resorted to religious practices that were in some ways ambivalent – the innovations incorporating old meanings. Thus the sacred staff carried by the faithful, the liturgical bough with which people were blessed, the red and white 'banner', the device for trapping 'evil spirits', (a kind of

* Cf. A. Moret: *Histoire de l'Orient*, II, p. 644: 'According to the authors of the Bible, national unity, achieved by the confederated tribes under a single king, led to religious unity in the name of Jehovah.'

box with five holes pierced in the sides) were all traditional, though they were used in the new context. The material symbol that was placed on the altars was a large wooden V, between the arms of which was a wooden cross with a fragment of glass embedded in it – and here too, apart from the V, it was a question of cultural features belonging to a period prior to the recent attempts at evangelization.* The difficult concept of the Trinity was not only expressed in material form, but in a form that had local and temporary variants. In the parishes near Brazzaville the cross was at first surrounded by portraits of General de Gaulle and Matswa, then by a painting of the cock (symbol of Simon Peter, that is to say, Mpadi) and a photograph of Matswa.[33]

In the same way, religious services were no longer restricted to sermons on the teachings of the 'Apostles' and hymn singing. Most of the time, at least during our investigation, they were an occasion for *psychological liberation*. The hymns were sung in a very lively fashion, sometimes accompanied by the beating of drums and clapping of hands. The sacred dance, leading up to the moment at which the adept could surrender himself to the power that possessed him, was regularly repeated. One woman told us: 'Men and women are drawn up in two separate rows. Prayers and songs excite all the faithful. Then people start dancing and go into a trance, and everyone runs about waving his hands in the air without so much as touching the person next to him.' Unlike many traditional celebrations, their abandon did not lead to any relaxation of sexual control. Another woman member reported: 'In the course of three all-night sessions at which I was present, none of the men ever tried to sleep with me or any of the other women.' The crisis of possession, which ultimately meant communion with *Nzambi Pungu*, did not involve a direct relationship however; that was a step that the Ba-Kongo villagers were not yet prepared to take. There was an intermediate term, comparable to the Black Messiah on the doctrinal plane, which was that

* A surprising example of the persistence of cultural features. The cross, introduced by the first Christian missionaries, most of whom had disappeared by the middle of the eighteenth century, became a prophylactic sign or symbol of the ancestors. Today its symbolism is enriched by new and exclusively Ba-Kongo meanings; imitations of the European reliquaries of the fifteenth and sixteenth centuries, which used to be found in the magic figurines with small ventral receptacles covered with a fragment of glass, are to be seen here in the glass splinters embedded in the cross.

nameless force, inexhaustible yet susceptible of influence, that imbued the whole body of ancestors. With regard to this, a document exists that contains some interesting material; it shows what powerful affective reactions occurred as the moment for *Nzambi* to manifest himself gradually approached: 'The meetings take place at night, in the forest, by the light of candles and storm lanterns. Sometimes they are held near a grave, in which case the "pastor" forces a hollow stick into the earth until it touches the dead man. Then he sucks out a mixture of water and earth, dilutes it and invites the faithful to drink it as a sign of communion. The latter, drawn up in two rows, men and women, then come forward, dancing and trembling all over. Several of the faithful who were subjected to this test were unable to face it, and preferred to give up the Khakist religion.'*

Sometimes the quest for possession by the holy spirit was accompanied by an initiatory retreat and a veritable *spiritual hunt*. In 1946, the following facts were put together by a disciple who had 'received the faith' at one of the semi-clandestine centres in the Kinkala region, where, at the time, twenty-seven other people were staying, twenty-four men, one woman and two children. No one was accepted at the centre unless they had first undergone various purification rites, which in the new Christianized context involved the 'Calvary test' and baptism by immersion. Our informant's account was remarkably clear: 'Before I was allowed to join this order, I was led away and placed between two posts, indicating the place of purification. Two converts held my arms, while a third beat me on the back with a stick. The place where this punishment was administered was called the *Calvary*. When it was over I went back to the centre, and the leader of the group promised to baptize me at the end of my stay. . . . Baptism was performed in a pond that was some distance away.'

The initiation entailed giving up all normal activities, relying for food entirely upon gifts and foregoing any personal hygiene. 'None of the adepts had had a bath for several months, and they were covered from head to foot with a thick layer of filth that

* Political Report for the Boko District, 1948, under the heading 'Khakist Movement'. This 'sacred water' (*maza ma Nzambi*), like the Holy Water of the Catholic church, was supposed to have healing properties and to drive away evil spirits.

gave off a suffocating smell.' The rules required almost continuous worship. Every morning and evening there was a service, and every day the head of the centre preached a sermon on a text from the Gospels, then raised his hands to heaven and invoked the names of Matswa and Kimbangou; while the rest of the time was devoted to the singing of hymns and various solemn observances, particularly the lighting of candles. Sometimes these sessions would be interrupted by one of the adepts suddenly becoming possessed 'by the invisible spirit of God and his two Saviours' and rushing off into the bush. According to our informant: 'Such disappearances lasted for thirty or forty minutes, and when they got back everyone had to account to the leader for whatever he had managed to find during the hunt.'[34] Clearly, this 'spiritual hunt' (to use our informant's own expression) was nothing more nor less than an example of cultural reversion. It is similar to one of the major themes of initiation to the *Matômpa* (a ritual for warding off sleeping sickness, which is spread by evil spirits or *bakuyu*) that had been observed by Bonnefond several decades previously. He says: 'During the dance, some of those taking part, called *bituntuki*, break away from the group to chase the *bakuyu*. They run all over the village, and come back with little bundles (bits of mother-of-pearl, leaves, yellow or white earth or knuckle bones) which they are supposed to have received from the *bakuyu*.'[35] The parallel is unmistakable: it shows the continuity of a form of initiation which persisted despite the borrowings from Christianity.

These facts indicate that although the Khakist movement wanted to break away from the ancient magical and religious techniques as well as from the Christian missions, it was unable to prevent this harking back to themes that had been a part of Congolese culture in the remote past. The leaders could not suddenly impose a total rupture with the past; old forms persisted, adapted to new ends. The necessity for creating a religious system that would have immediate significance for everybody, and the limits of the faculty of innovation, tend to have the same effect. Moreover, such persistence shows that a typical culture has just as many resistant elements as it has fundamental attitudes. The study of religious behaviour reveals that novel features coexist alongside traditional requirements. Religious activity remains partly utilitarian, and tangible results are expected from it: for instance, curing illness by the laying on of hands, protection against the *nkundu* and the machinations of sorcerers, or the ending of European domination. In addition to this, however, there were indications of the emergence of a religion of salvation, effective in the after-life, a personal religion experienced by the individual independently of such moments of collective exaltation. The purely personal communication that had hitherto been the privilege of rank (the *mfumu mpu* alone was entitled to commune with the ancestors and derive strength from their contact) had now become common property; relations with God no longer had to be 'delegated'. Here we have an example of the individualization of the relationship with the divinity due to the influence of Christianity; but the process was also stimulated by circumstances, the semi-clandestine nature of the movement and the difficulty of organizing large public gatherings. In many villages in the vicinity of Brazzaville, every member of the movement stuck a pole in the ground outside his hut, and fixed a candle to it* to indicate that this was where he and the other members of his family group prayed. During the time that we were there, this easily distinguishable sign made it quite impossible to mistake the success of the Congolese church or the extent to which religious practice had become a personal matter.

Khakism derived its main importance from the new tendencies it expressed and its comparatively efficient organization. There was practically no sphere of social existence that was not in some measure influenced by it: morals, customary law, beliefs and symbols, attitudes towards power. At the time, no organization based on Congolese initiative had proved so successful. For instance, it was much more effective than André Matswa's during the early period of Amicalism; so much so that, after his death, the movement he had founded adopted the Congolese church as a model, and the activities of the two organizations tended to merge. More than this, it was this success, this ability to control spontaneous reactions, as well as the hierarchy that it had copied from that of the Salvation Army, that alarmed the

---

* The Ba-Kongo word for candle is *mpévé*, whence the expression *Nzambi mpévé* (the God with the candle), which was used ironically by practising Christians. The candle symbolizes the actual church building, as well as the Church of the faithful.

colonial administration. By 1941, Khakism controlled sixteen organized parishes, one of them (Kilanga) in the Boko region, and was trying to gain control of a further eight; and it was also rapidly extending its influence to other ethnic groups. Various documents of the time stress the role of the church as a means of federation, and the role of the Saviour (*mvukisi*) as the symbol of unity: 'Simon Kimbangou will be king of the whole country, and he has ordered all his Apostles to recruit members throughout the colony.'[36] In the then French Congo, churches either belonging to the Khakist movement or inspired by it and leading a semi-autonomous existence were soon reported to have appeared as far away as the borders of the Kongo country, in the old districts of Mindouli and Madingou.

For most members, the principal attraction was the fact that here was a religion comparable with the established religions but created entirely by the work of black founders. As one of them put it: 'It's better to join the *Nzambi Kaki*, it's a religion where we can be on our own.' But the movement had a further attraction in that it expressed a racial reaction, and encouraged a recovery of the initiative in respect of all the inferiorities revealed or created by colonialism. As a result of the French defeat, the years 1940–41 were a period of growing tension which exacerbated racial feeling. The ultimate victory of Germany was looked forward to as a decisive event that would overthrow the existing state of affairs and lead to emancipation: the kingdoms of Simon Kimbangou and André Matswa were proclaimed on either bank of the Congo. A Belgian document of this period, which makes little attempt to conceal its anxiety, observes: 'This movement is directed against the white man, and more especially against the Belgians. They expect us to quit the Congo so that they can establish their own Black church and state. They long for a German victory, believing that it would mean their liberation. With us will disappear the missionaries, who will have been driven out, and the official chiefs, who will have joined the tribe of Judas.'[37] The idea of salvation, insofar as it caught on, was seen in temporal terms: it kept alive the hope of a coming end to all the alienation the Africans suffered from, and offered a glimpse of the new society (based on the Negro church) that would abolish their insecurity and poverty. Its influence was directed against European domination, and against the distorted form of society that resulted from the colonial situation.

III. BA-KONGO MESSIANISM AND ITS SOCIAL IMPLICATIONS: THE NEW CONGOLESE 'CHURCHES'

To complete this study, while limiting it geographically and restricting it to the cases we have studied most intensively, we shall confine ourselves here to interpreting the results of investigations carried out in the neighbourhood of Boko and Mayama. This does not imply that these places represented the frontiers of the new faith: the native townships in Brazzaville and the Kinkala region had very active churches which succeeded in branching out beyond the limits of the Kongo ethnic group.

During the 1950s, Messianism was characterized by its power of expansion: it attracted not only one-time Kimbangists and deserters from the Protestant missions and the Salvation Army, but also those who had hitherto remained faithful to Catholicism, as well as younger folk who, having grown up during a period of confusion, had only known a kind of freedom that weighed upon them. So strong was the movement that the political groups in the Congo tried to obtain its support by demanding its official recognition on the grounds that the Constitution guaranteed freedom of religious expression.* An administrative note in 1949 insists: 'The movement is not connected with the political parties, although some of them (particularly the *Parti progressiste congolais*) are trying to win it over by insisting on their right to religious freedom.' In several places churches sprang up more or less spontaneously, and approached the authorities with a view to obtaining recognition. The following is from a report of January 1946: 'On Sunday, January 27th, a group of natives presented themselves at the Governor's residence in Kinkala, led by an individual shouting and singing prayers, while the rest of them joined in the chorus and some of them rolled on the ground invoking the Messiah. Their leader wanted to see the Governor

---

* In 1950, some of the leaders of the Congolese church approached the Governor-General with a view to leasing a plot of land in Brazzaville where they could build their 'cathedral'.

in order to demand official recognition of the religion that he had just founded.'[38]

Despite the number of new churches, however, Congolese Messianism began to exert a unifying tendency. Relations between the inhabitants of both Congos became closer: from 1941 to 1944 government reports were full of allusions to groups of proselytes and priests migrating, to members regarded as suspects (young men and women, for the most part) running away,* and to two visits to French territory by Simon Mpadi. At the same time, the death of Matswa, by bringing out the religious aspects of Amicalism, also contributed to unity, the Congolese leader taking his place alongside Simon Kimbangou, and thus giving the Trinity its definitive form. This gradual fusion of the two movements minimized the effects of the particularisms of the *Ba-Kongo* (hitherto more strongly oriented towards their kinsfolk in the neighbouring Congo and Kimbangism) and of the Ba-Lali/Ba-Sundi (at first influenced exclusively by the Amicalist movement); and it also helped to overcome the longstanding antagonism between the areas under Protestant influence and those under Catholic influence. This last point is particularly important. It shows that although Congolese Messianism was, to begin with, created by Christians influenced by Protestant teaching, later on it succeeded in attracting members who had been educated by Catholic missionaries. The repression of Amicalism, which started as an essentially secular movement, gave rise to a growing opposition which affected the entire colonial society, whereas reaction against the Christian missions became dominant as soon as they were suspected of being connected with the administration, as soon as the movement itself became a religious one and saw every mission as a hostile rival to its expansion. This crisis of confidence, which later led to a definite rupture, was what caused hostility towards the missionaries: during our investigation, a church that had been inaugurated by the former Catholic catechist Nganga E., attempted to set fire to the neighbouring Catholic mission, although its founder had worked there for almost ten years.

* In 1944 the Belgian authorities sent back to Boko several groups of people aged from seventeen to thirty-five, typical representatives of the younger and most active elements.

This church that Nganga E. established in the Mayama region is a good example to consider. Well away from the road, the sacred 'precincts' (known as *Galamboma*) consisted of a huge building, constructed by the faithful in imitation of the bush chapels, and a series of huts that served as dwellings. At one end of the chapel was a raised altar, separated from the worshippers by a wooden balustrade, behind which the priest stood when preaching. On the altar, which was covered with a red blanket, was a photograph of Matswa, a dagger dating from the days of the 'ancestors', and a lamp that was always kept burning. Behind this was the special emblem of the new religion: a V, with the cross of Lorraine fixed between the two arms. The same emblem, though in this case painted, was repeated on the wall, together with representations of a star and a cock.

Most of the symbols referred to have been mentioned before. The V stood for victory over suffering and poverty (as well as over the colonialists); it was associated with the cross of Lorraine, replacing the portrait of General de Gaulle that had been used previously, and connoted the idea of material power and success by physical force. The symbolism of the red blanket, apart from its traditional implications, recalled the martyrdom of the 'Saviour' and the first disciples. The old-fashioned dagger was an assertion of loyalty to the ancestors and a promise to restore the past splendours of the tribe; and at the same time, since it resembled the ceremonial knife worn by the traditional chiefs, it suggested the royal status of André Matswa. As regards the star, Nganga E. said it was 'God who lights up the world', confirming God's omnipresence and the protection he would give to true believers during the night, that is to say at the time of maximum danger. Finally, the cock symbolized the two Simon Peters (Kimbangou and Mpadi), and was a warning to the members not to betray their 'Saviour'.

One sees, therefore, that although the symbolism of the new church was limited, the essential meanings were preserved. Nganga E. insisted upon the destruction of fetishes, and himself led the campaign against magic and residual cults. When talking to us, he pointed out that 'these practices are too full of past history and past quarrels', and clearly showed that he was anxious to become a reorganizer and peacemaker. But he made no attempt to create a community by example and persuasion; he relied upon compulsion ('Didn't the Christian missions do the same?' he asked) and apocalyptic threats of floods and tornadoes that would destroy the unbelievers. He also maintained that those who did not belong to one of the great religions were 'evil' and 'dangerous' – which amounted to denouncing them as sorcerers.[39]

There can be no religious group without its specific taboos. In this case, the *nlôgo* as they were called were expressed in a traditional manner in a Christianized context. They were connected with the vampire, because he has wings like the devil, with the monkey, who is made in the likeness of man, and with the serpent, who successfully tempted the first woman. The basic obligations belonged, at least formally, to a familiar system. They comprised a body of moral precepts similar to those drawn up by Simon Mpadi: 'Men must love one another; they must help each other and never use magic or any other weapon to attack one another; stealing, committing adultery, etc. are forbidden' – nothing very original here, after all we have been saying. The notion of personal salvation was introduced to encourage submission. According to Nganga E., the faithful knew that so long as they strictly carried out God's will they would ultimately be accepted by him and the two Congolese 'Saviours' – in other words, the Road to Heaven (*Nzila ia Zulu*) was open to them. Although the founder of the church of *Galamboma* was scarcely aware of the fact, those who joined it were in large part motivated by the promise it held out of victory over the colonialists, and of a golden age that would eventually compensate for all the injuries they had suffered – the latter being emphasized by the name adopted by members: *bana-bansana* (orphan children).

Unlike the founder of the *Mission des Noirs*, Nganga E. did not establish an elaborate dogma and system of laws, although in a formal sense he borrowed from the former. He claimed originality for his decision to allow Catholic renegades to join a 'tribal' religion that was not exclusively influenced by Protestant teaching. He was quite determined to amalgamate with the Khakist 'churches', despite his differences with them, in order to strengthen the unity of all the Congolese movements. As opposed to the latter, he was against his church going underground and was ready to run considerable risks (his 'encampment' and one of the chapels were destroyed) in order to maintain it on a public footing and

gain recognition in fact if not in law. These were his most important contributions.

The elements of plagiarism in Nganga E.'s system are clear
enough, and it is easy to distinguish the borrowings from
Christianity. Making the sign of the cross (*dimbu dyala krwa*) was
retained, but the words were changed to: 'In the name of the
Father and of André Matswa and of Simon Kimbangou.' The
faithful were expected to kneel during prayers: the 'choir boys'
(*bitâgi*), who served the priest, recited the antiphons and the whole
congregation joined in the responses. During the services, the
priest wore a long robe, with a kind of chasuble over it, em-
broidered with the V sign and the cross of Lorraine; and in
church the women had to wear veils like those worn by nuns. The
use of candles – said to signify praying to God – was obviously
derived from Catholic ritual, though in our view it was not
merely imitative: in the first place it was a more or less conscious
reminder of the traditional significance of fire;* and, secondly,
one of the last manifestations of the traditional religious attitude,
according to which no sacred bond was effective that did not
involve *manipulation*. To make the flame spring up from the
candle was to give the sign that established communication, and
thus to evoke the power of the church. This simple material
feature was more, therefore, than a gratuitous borrowing. And this
view is borne out by the comment of a young Congolese writer:
'To the Ba-Lali mind, the correlation between the traditional fire
ritual and the lighting of candles would be immediate.'

The religious service (*mès*) prescribed by Nganga E. consisted
essentially of hymns, prayers and a sermon by the priest. It was
held on Thursdays – a day associated with Matswa's death† and,
in the Catholic church, with Maundy Thursday – and Sundays, a
day of rest dedicated to the worship of *Nzambi Pungu*. On both
these days the dress worn by the faithful was distinguished by a
different symbolic colour: black on Thursdays, as a mark of

---

* With regard to the Fang *Bwiti*, we noted the part that fire played in the ritual –
and also the fact that it contained cultural features belonging to various tribes,
especially to those related to the Ba-Kongo (living to the south and west) who had
preserved them.

† According to the official account, Matswa died on January 14, 1942, that is to
say, a Wednesday; but the news of his death was not made public until the next day,
Thursday.

mourning, and white on Sundays. In addition to this, a number of other feast days were observed, the services attracting hundreds of worshippers, so that the chapel was not large enough to hold them. Of these, the only specifically Kongo occasion was the anniversary of Matswa's death, on January 15th; the others were taken from the Christian calendar, though in some cases they might also have an additional justification. Easter celebrated 'the resurrection of the Saviour', and announced the coming of 'victory'; the Ascension marked the beatification of Kimbangou and Matswa, who had been summoned to sit beside *Nzambi Pungu*; All Saints' Day was set aside for prayers for the dead, and though observed on a different date it was a reminder of the traditional yearly ceremony in honour of the ancestors, when their help was sought on behalf of the lineage.[40] More than this, now that it was possible to pray direct to an accessible God, it involved the notion of recriprocity affecting *all* the ancestors and not only those of the clan, thus expressing the unitary tendency of the Congolese movement.* The other feasts that were kept, Christmas Day, Pentecost and Corpus Christi, did not lend themselves to this kind of reinterpretation. They were mainly a pretext for the periodical public festivities that are necessary for a religion that seeks to encourage the individualization of spiritual exercises. Indeed, if there was no dignitary of the church in a village to lead communal prayers, it was the duty of the faithful to pray on their own three times a day: first thing in the morning, at midday and again at night. This shows that, for the individual believer, the notion of salvation learnt from the missionaries did not imply simply acting under the guidance of a priest, but also personal initiative; on the level of religious innovation it reflects the increasing importance attached to the individual owing to the pressure of social change.

According to the particular festival being celebrated, the church required its members to wear a special garment, as well as membership badges (*siñö*) and insignia of rank – triangular tabs with the cross of Lorraine or the V sign, and an arrangement of stars – and to display the post and candle, referred to above, outside their huts.

* We have already drawn attention to a similar fact with regard to the Fang: the *Biéri* cult, which was devoted solely to the ancestors of the lineage, was replaced by the *Bwiti* cult with its appeal to all those who had died; and this, with the same end in view – unity.

At every moment of his life the believer was convinced that his faith not only afforded him personal protection, but was also an effective recourse against any social disturbances that might affect him; he was continually assured that the new religion provided greater safety than the traditional religious and magical therapeutic practices. This, as we have already suggested, was the most vulnerable point of the system, which is why Nganga E. and the leaders of other churches took care to complete the 'equipment' of their followers. Each of them was given a long, plain stick (*nkawa*, *mikawa*), similar to the staff traditionally carried by military leaders and notables, which had been consecrated on the ancestral graves. This conferred the traditional type of protection, and was even considered to be more effective – in some 'parishes' the *nkawa* was supposed to be the equivalent of the atomic bomb.* Clearly, this was looked upon as a minimal, though necessary, concession to the spirit of tradition.

There is one incidental but important point that remains to be made. Despite the fact that it was built up in an original manner on the basis of multiple borrowings from Catholicism, this church did not accept the cult of the saints, which plays such a large part in the syncretistic religious manifestations of the Brazilian Negroes. This is due partly to the fact that the first Congolese church to be established took as its model the teaching of the Protestant missions and, in its second phase of development, turned directly to the Old Testament. This phenomenon is especially remarkable because the historians of the Congo have come across objects and documents which prove that, during the first period of evangelization in the fifteenth century, saints (mainly of Portuguese origin) played a considerable part; and, at least on the left bank of the Congo, small statuettes of saints have recently been discovered among the ritual objects used in certain specialized cults.† These old examples show that the assimilation

* They used to say: 'If you are attacked by an aeroplane, all you have to do is to wave your holy staff and the plane will crash.'

† Particularly at the beginning of the eighteenth century, when a Congolese woman 'of the highest rank' (Dona Béatrice) identified herself with Saint Anthony, in order to found a new syncretistic cult as a rival to colonial Christianity, which was by that time seriously compromised. This religion, a forerunner of modern Zionism, was also of political significance, since it sought to re-establish national unity throughout the kingdom. See Father Laurent de Lucques: *Relations*; and L. Jadin: *Le Congo et la secte des Antoniens*.

of popular Catholic saints was not completely out of the question. At the same time, however, they show how they were used: because they were considered to have greater efficacy, the statues of the saints supplanted the statues (*nkisi*) that had hitherto been an essential part of the specialist cults; and since the basic feature of the religious system was still the ancestor cult, the way in which they were connected with these cults and techniques, in which religion and magic were scarcely distinguishable, was to some extent competitive. Now, as one of its primary tasks, the Congolese church took upon itself the destruction of fetishes and the rival cults that these often gave rise to; it sought to establish itself exclusively. By retaining as the only mediator the 'Black Saviour' who had given his life for the salvation of the ethnic group, it was excluding any possibility of rival innovations – which would not have been the case had it resorted to homologues of the Catholic saints as intermediaries between man and God. This would have meant running the risk of a pluralism completely opposed to its aims. As Bastide clearly shows in his work on Negro society in Brazil, the equation of African gods with Catholic saints is liable to give rise to multiple variations.[41] This is directly relevant to the aims of the Congolese church. It shows that Ba-Kongo monotheism, by basing itself upon a reinterpretation of Catholic beliefs, required more than an intermediary term (not present in the traditional religion) between *Nzambi Pungu* and mankind. While it claimed to be one of the great religions, it was also an expression of political aspirations. The exclusive recognition of *Nzambi Pungu* was connected with its affirmation of a ritual and cultural unity over and above the diversity of the Kongo groups. A Messiah filled this requirement and the desire for liberation associated with it better than a saint, for a Messiah is not only an intermediary but also the symbol of unity, the 'Saviour'* who sacrifices himself for the benefit of an entire people. It must be remembered that the modern position of the Ba-Kongo people almost inevitably determined the nature of any new religious movement, whether its original inspiration happened to be Protestant or Catholic.

Finally, it is important to show how Nganga E.'s church became the basis for a new type of social cadre. At the head of the

* 'Jesus-Saviour' was often used as a translation of Jesus.

hierarchy was the 'Head of the Church' (*mfumu bundu*), who, in each of the villages subject to his influence, appointed a representative (*sökur*) responsible for teaching, taking services and in general looking after the local *bana-bansana* (ordinary members). In villages where the headmen belonged to the movement they were given a special position and insignia, and in such cases their authority was superior to that of the *sökur*, but otherwise not. The older children were known as *bana-bankédi* or 'young guards' and were supposed to be like Boy Scouts, though in fact they were more like seminarists. They were chosen from the families most devoted to Amicalism and were organized in groups of twelve (as usual, the figure had a symbolic significance), while their food and clothing was provided by the *sökur* and came from collections or gifts, or even from forced levies. Periodically they had to attend a course of training at *Galamboma*, the sacred precinct – a form of retreat reminiscent of the traditional initiation rites. As regards this aspect of the organization, however, there seems to have been some uncertainty as to whether its purpose was to provide selective training, aimed at creating a 'clergy' freed from all the obligations of daily life, or a broader education open to all the children in the 'parish'. Owing to the lack of cadres and the hostility of the administration, the first alternative was adopted; but this did not mean that the second, which would eventually have provided a religious and political education by age groups, was therefore rejected.

In addition to this, another hierarchy was established for the women: at the head of it was the *mam ngudi*, the wife of Nganga E., who in turn was responsible for the other women members and for providing food for the *bana-bankédi*. This terminology was adopted from the traditional social system. According to Van Wing, *ma(m)*, which occurs in the expression *mamfumu* often applied to the crowned chiefs, was 'a title of respectful affection'.* As to the term *ngudi*, it is closely connected with the structure of the clan: in the traditional system it designated both the origin of the lineage and the lineage itself, both the founder of a descent group and the group. What is interesting here is, on the one hand, the importance accorded to women – more

* *Et. Bk.*, p. 139. The terms *mani*, *né*, *ni* and *na* were applied to the Kongo kings; *mani*, in particular, was used to indicate any political superior.

marked than in the Khakist churches – and, on the other, the conservative attitude displayed in the organization of this category of believers. It is as though these women members represented the persistence of a whole area of the traditional context, for it was their hierarchy that tended to assimilate most closely the 'birth' of the church to the 'birth' of the founder clans. Here, once again, one sees the impossibility of getting any completely new socio-cultural entity accepted. In this case, the concessions to tradition were more marked than in the case of the *Mission des Noirs*; but it is a fact, clearly established by Dr Sundkler, that the 'variants' that differentiate the Negro churches are indicative of the degree of evolution of the communities to which they owed their existence.

Before drawing the conclusions suggested by this analysis of one particular case, we must first try to find out which elements of the new organization and beliefs 'find support in', or 'correspond to', the traditional system. For example, we cannot exclude the possibility that, in its local form, the notion of 'Saviour', of a man chosen to suffer and, through his suffering, to ensure the advancement of the Kongo tribes, was due to the influence of Judaeo-Christian teaching and the old beliefs. The function of the *ba-nkita*, upon whom until recently the efficacy of certain magical and religious techniques depended, cannot have been obliterated without leaving some traces behind. In his work on the religious life of the Ba-Kongo, Van Wing states specifically: 'The *ba-nkita* were men who had suffered violent death. The most important of them were the *founding ancestors*, who had either been killed in war, committed suicide, or been assassinated. . . . The *ba-nkita* were white and extremely strong, they played an important part in fetishism, and they lived on in a large number of very powerful *nkisi* . . .'[42] Such a notion implied elements – an ancestor connected with the origin of the clans,* a dead man whose influence was

* The modern *Munkunguna* rite also appealed for the help of the ancestors at the beginning of, and before, colonization; they operated *together* in the same way that the Messiah of the Congolese churches operates *alone*. So much so, indeed, that this rite, which has now disappeared, may be seen as an intermediate stage between the traditional situation described by Van Wing and the situation resulting from the foundation of the Negro churches.

still effective because he had died violently, power and 'whiteness'
– calculated to give meaning to the concept of a Saviour whose
sacrifices result in the salvation of the people he leads; elements
which, at least to begin with, also encouraged acceptance of the
Messiah of Christian tradition and the Congolese Saviours. We
are not claiming that the two concepts are identical, but simply
that there are sufficient traditional cross-references to make the
borrowed concept generally meaningful. The following table is
an attempt to represent these references schematically.

TABLE I

Traditional references	References to missionary teaching and organization	Form adopted by the Congolese church
Ba-nkita	Messiah and Saviour	Black Saviour, founder of the church, who gave his life for the salvation of the church and the ethnic group
Nzambi Pungu	Affirmation of monotheism	*Nzambi Pungu* becomes 'accessible' through the mediation of the Congolese Saviours
Widespread symbolism of the figure 3 *	Affirmation of the Holy Trinity	Indigenous form of the Trinity: *Nzambi Pungu* and the two Congolese Saviours
Creative force and hierarchy of forces	Divine omnipotence	Healing by faith: help asked for in the form of intervention by *Nzambi Pungu*
Symbolism of red — the role of blood	The blood of Christ	Martyrdom of the Saviours and first disciples: incitement to opposition and sacrifice
. . . .	Concept of salvation	Access to the 'Heavenly Road'
Essential role of taboos	Biblical taboos	Definition of taboos in Christianized form

* In particular, two facts should be noted: in the first place, at an early age, the
child becomes part of a system in which parental control is exercised by three people
– its mother, its maternal uncle, and its father; in the second place, when a man grows
up and marries, he belongs to a system in which three clan segments are involved.

Traditional references	References to missionary teaching and organization	Form adopted by the Congolese church
Annual festival of the ancestors	All Saints' Day	All Saints' Day becomes the annual festival of the tribal ancestors
Possibility of giving a favourable direction to intervention by the ancestor	. . . .	Consecration of staffs on the ancestral graves: a complementary technique for protecting the individual
. . . .	Cult of the Saints	No cult of the Saints nor any equivalent
Fear of sorcery	The role of Satan	Not to belong to one of the great religions is 'evil' and 'dangerous'
The significance of fire	Catholic ritual	The role of candle flames (the 'Candle-God')
Absence of clergy	Hierarchized clergy	Hierarchy among the faithful; tendency to create a clergy
Fundamental clan hierarchies: *ma ngudi, ma mfumu*, etc.	. . . .	Organization of women members preserving the traditional context; assimilation of the origin of the church to the origin of the clans
. . . .	Material aspects of the church	Borrowing of material features from Christianity

Here we have only indicated the most important of these references, but imperfect as the table may be it does show that, in introducing innovations, the founders acted prudently. In many cases, the significance of the borrowed 'model' and concept is based on traditional beliefs; and there are practically no alien features that have not been recast in terms of the most closely related of these beliefs. On the other hand, there is a measure of selection, as we showed with regard to the cult of the Saints, which was not incorporated despite the fact that the 'parish' concerned was strongly influenced by Catholicism; the reason for this is the position of the 'receiving' society, and the precise needs to which the innovation corresponds. Apart from the main attractions that explain the success of the Congolese churches, this *adjustment*, which did not exclude modernization of the social context from within, was undoubtedly another factor contributing to their success. They remained an essentially Ba-Kongo achievement, whereas political parties and trade unions were at first looked upon as alien institutions and, in the eyes of the villagers, were therefore suspect. Moreover, those country folk who had become occasional city dwellers also contributed to the development of the churches in the native townships, where for a long time they were more powerful than any other 'modernist' group.

Locally, no one questioned the credit due to Nganga E.; the Catholic missionaries in the vicinity of *Galamboma* recognized 'the power of the native religious movement', and assured us that the prohibition of public services* had done little to prevent the extension of the cult through private gatherings. In villages where its members constituted a minority, secession sometimes occurred; in which case the members of the Congolese church would then break away and set up camp elsewhere so that they could continue to practise their religion in freedom, which shows that the religious phenomenon was sufficiently dynamic to affect the masses. This was true also with regard to the 'pilgrimages' to places where there was a branch of the mother church, which had all the characteristics of temporary religious migrations: some groups, including both men and women, were in the habit of spending a week or more at the *Galamboma* encampment.

From questions we put to various categories of members, it appears that the basic reason for membership was the desire to belong to a real religion 'like the Catholics and Protestants'. This is why official recognition remained the first objective of the Congolese church – so that the latter might be placed on the same plane as the missionary churches.

Thus, in the study of social change, the religious problem is seen to be of primary importance. It is at the heart of the irreducible conflicts and antagonisms resulting from the coming together of radically different civilizations. Above all, it is a pledge

* This was necessary during a period of direct colonial administration, owing to a number of serious incidents.

of the transition from 'barbarism' to 'civilization': whatever adaptations might be permissible elsewhere, the Congolese church was as opposed to magical and religious techniques as were the Christian missions; it was Nganga E. himself who inspired the campaigns for destroying fetishes. A 'great religion' was bound to be influenced by monotheism, to manifest tendencies to unification and to proclaim the superior efficacy of faith and prayer compared with ritual techniques. In the opinion of the most creative of its leaders, it was by building up this religion that the Ba-Kongo would eventually succeed in creating the kind of civilization that had enabled the Europeans to achieve superiority.

At the same time, it is not enough to consider the phenomenon solely from this point of view; it had definite sociological and political implications. It was predominantly a reaction to the colonial situation, an innovation profoundly influenced by the nature of the social and racial relations between the colonizers and the colonized. It was because it polarized every form of resentment that the Congolese movement was able to attract the most vital forces. The assimilation of Amicalism during the latter years helped to strengthen this tendency. How sensitive these reactions were may be seen from the fact that the history of the movement was closely bound up with the fluctuations (often economic in origin) in the relations between the Ba-Kongo and the Europeans. The group reacted on the plane where it felt itself to be most directly threatened – that of its fundamental beliefs and attitudes; on the only plane, that is to say, where it was able to take the initiative, since elsewhere it could only submit, more or less passively,* to the economic and political imperatives of the colonial powers. This transference of political activity to the plane of religious activity, moreover, occurs frequently in a situation of dependence, for to some extent the latter serves to conceal the former.

This essentially religious emphasis is also to be attributed to causes of a mainly internal order. Colonialism affects those areas of equilibrium that are vulnerable, creating a state of insecurity that gives rise to attempts to discover appropriate techniques for

* The idea of 'passive resistance' was already familiar in the Congo. The example of Indians working in South Africa had impressed the Bantu, whence it had been spread by migratory workers.

counteracting it; innovation therefore occurs on the plane at which it traditionally operates whenever general problems of security are involved – that of religious techniques. On the other hand, we have to realize that here we are dealing with a type of civilization in which opposition is expressed in a very attenuated form by means of oral literatures (as yet not 'desacralized') or, in a crude form, by religious and magical innovations. These, then, are the models upon which the opposition to colonial domination is at first organized. The administrative reports of the period show that, over a long period, the conflict set government officials against 'fetishists' and 'miracle workers'.* Lastly, the religious revival may be seen as a correlative of changes that were taking place in the relations between differentiated social categories within Kongo society; it was encouraged by the rise of new categories, for whom religion in one form or another was the only way of achieving power (or of justifying such power as they managed to achieve).

The Congolese movements brought about a revival of initiative and, at the same time, an attempt to reorganize society. They helped to counteract the processes responsible for the breakdown of communities and the weakening of cohesion which we have already discussed: antagonism between pagans and Christians, and between Christians themselves; growing individualism among the ever increasing modernist elements; new sources of conflict between the sexes; intensified competition as a result of the establishment of a money economy; disintegration of clans, lineages and villages. More or less consciously, the new movements sought to restore the broken ties and rebuild the community. They brought people together, unified them, tried to establish a more broadly based 'fraternity' than that of the old clans, which had almost broken down. In this way, an entire ethnic group began to discover a sense of unity and become conscious of its position. The only way in which it could recreate itself socially was by opposing all forms of foreign authority, especially religious and political; and this led to outbursts of xenophobia and a kind of racism. But the essential fact remains that here was a movement in which nationalism went hand in hand with monotheism, in

---

* In 1940 the head of the Stanley Pool Department said in an official report: 'I will not put up with any miracle worker in this Department.'

which political organization was bound up with the organization of the church. It was by extending the limits of the church that those leaders most conscious of their aims found a way of bringing together the various fragments of the Ba-Kongo people, and therefore of widening the sphere of influence of a dynamic ethnic group that had become convinced of its liberating mission.

On the other hand, this attempt by the Congolese movements to bring things up-to-date brought out the uneven capacity for resistance of the constituent elements of the old socio-cultural system. It showed, for instance, that the religious attitude persisted, despite the fact that the cults through which it had found expression had deteriorated or disappeared; and this also was the case with current conceptions of power, at a time when the traditional political institutions had almost ceased to have any meaning. Again, traditional reactions to polygamy and the machinations of the sorcerers still continued, though the social and religious contexts were actually undergoing profound changes. At a higher level – the attitude towards causality for instance – one finds a similar continuity, despite the increasing rationalization of the cultural context and the realization that technical efficiency is the basis of material power. This continuity was apparent during our investigations in 1950, when we discovered that even such progressive elements as the local school teachers reacted to the apocalyptic threats of Nganga E.* in much the same way as the inhabitants of Leopoldville and Brazzaville in 1929 had reacted to the prophecy that both cities would be swept away by floods on New Year's Day, merely displaying a measure of 'doubt' as to their reality. And the case is the same with regard to the powers attributed to the sacred staff, in a context involving such modern techniques as the aeroplane and atomic bomb.

Though we have only mentioned a few of these 'centres of resistance', it would be a mistake to see them simply as chance survivals; in fact, they represent the most persistent part of the old socio-cultural system. At a time when new forms of organization are the order of the day, when new economic and social relations are being established, certain fundamental ways of life

* One of them told us: 'Nganga E. had threatened to cause a great wind and flood that would sweep away those who refused to join his movement. When nothing happened, people began to doubt.'

and collective attitudes ensure a basis of stability, and serve as a kind of retreat position. Those we have identified as most persistent were also the best 'concealed' – inasmuch as organizations are more adaptable than collective attitudes or values. It is important to emphasize the uneven rate of social and cultural change, according to the level at which it occurs. To attribute some kind of stupidity or 'emotional inertia'[43] to those who are slow to change would be the greatest mistake, for there is in fact a kind of hesitancy that is *functional*. In the process of reorganization that the Congolese movements were attempting to effect, the fundamental problem was to arouse a sense of innovation and persuade people to accept it. This could only be achieved by making use of certain traditional ideas and relying upon the dynamic of certain typical attitudes. This is what we were alluding to when we contrasted the new structures emerging within the old cultural framework with those that were imported ready-made. On the other hand, as we have frequently pointed out, the Congolese movements succeeded in bringing about a revival of initiative, and a pride in Ba-Kongo achievement in face of all the pressures and influences arising from the colonial situation. This affirmation of values was only possible in terms of specifically Kongo beliefs: the 'survivals', that is to say, were used in the interests of emancipation. As long as a dependent people, subjected to colonialism, has no opportunity of competing with the foreigner in the sphere in which he excels, their only solution is to make use of their specificity – in the early stages of colonization either to remain hidden, or, as we have just seen, to encourage and justify their recovery of the initiative.

Faced by a new test, that of Independence, the Congolese churches made their final adaptation. Shortly before 1960, in both the Congos, they were officially recognized; and while this was an admission of their political influence and moral prestige, at the same time it forced them to define more clearly their attitude towards the political parties and the first African governments.

In Leopoldville, Kimbangism was given civic recognition on September 24, 1959, and the church – now known as 'The Church of Christ on Earth and of his son Kimbangou the Prophet' – was quickly organized under the direction of Joseph Diangienda, the founder's son. It now had its holy city, Nkamba, where the prophet was buried in a vast mausoleum guarded by six members of the church dressed in white. It could appeal to published works exalting the 'passion' of Simon Kimbangou[44] as well as to a published catechism, and its leaders were invited to express their views on the radio. It had a constitution, and a clearly defined administrative structure with 60,000 members.

By the time the Belgian Congo became independent, it was a force to be reckoned with, especially as the newly formed parties were still weak and had not yet acquired a national audience. According to popular opinion, the Congolese political leaders derived their authority from the Prophet. ABAKO (Alliance des Ba-Kongo), a political party that had been founded in 1950, was firmly established on ground prepared by the Congolese church; and by 1955 its leader, N. Kasavubu, who later became the first President of the Republic of the Congo, was regarded as 'a second Messiah', even a demi-god, taking his place beside Kimbangou.[45] Against the background of confrontations and rivalries that marked the early days of Congolese Independence the strength of Kimbangism was so highly respected that Patrice Lumumba, the head of the first government, appealed to the new church for its spiritual help in the difficult task of running the country's affairs. One of Kimbangou's sons and some members of the church were for a time members of the government.

As a result of coming out into the open and, with the end of colonialism, losing its main political characteristics, Kimbangism was bound to undergo modification. It began to operate purely on the religious plane, and devoted its enterprise and dynamism to the integration of the various sects. Its organization was improved, its teaching was rationalized and its doctrine and ritual purified, with the result that though it gained in 'respectability' it lost much of its spontaneity – so much so, in fact, that one Congolese writer actually maintains that 'Today the new sect is unrecognizable', and can only be regarded 'as an African religion on the completely false grounds that it is controlled by a "Black Prince" '.[46]

As for the right bank of the Congo, once Kimbangism ceased to be an underground movement, it was reorganized and started building a 'cathedral' on the outskirts of Boko. But the transformation of the Messianic movements was not fully completed, mainly owing to the intervention of Matswanism. Subsequent political development required a veritable *transference*: loyalty to André Matswa had to be transformed into loyalty to President Fulbert Youlou, and the principal political party – *L'Union de Défense des Intérêts africains* – had to take the place of the organizations inherited from Matswa. Certain influential priests refused to make this change and maintained the radical demands of the original 'prophets'. For them, the Congolese Government was usurping the achievements of Matswa and his comrades. They therefore advocated civil disobedience, refusing to pay taxes or vote, rejecting government assistance and claiming that the reward for such intransigence would be the coming of a golden age. In 1959, violent incidents occurred between them and the President's supporters, and eventually they were sentenced to prison. The fact of the matter was, the Congolese movements were now faced by a difficult choice: either they had to transform themselves into a national church and renounce any overt political action, or they would simply remain a sect, divorced from reality and passionately committed to a utopia that would involve the overthrow of the new order.

IV. MESSIANISM, A PRIVILEGED FIELD OF OBSERVATION

The movements whose historical impact throughout the Congolese zone we have been considering had their counterparts in certain countries of Black Africa exposed to Islam.[47] In their case, it is true, the 'great religion' had one specially favourable feature: the tradition that, as the end of the world approached, a man would appear, the Mahdi, who would be responsible for leading the faithful back into the fold and imposing justice. In this sense, Islam contains within itself a message that social reformers can utilize, a doctrine conducive to thoroughgoing radicalism, and which one of the Mahdis who appeared in East Africa expressed in the words: 'I shall destroy this world, and out of it I will create another.' What is interesting here is that this religious tendency, though it remained marginal to Islam itself, always became exceptionally powerful in *situations* similar to those we have been describing. The first of these Mahdis to appear in Black Africa created a theocratic state, restricted to the upper valley of the Nile, in the second half of the nineteenth century. In a study which shows him to have been both a liberator and a promoter of unity, the conditions under which he appeared are defined as follows: 'The Mahdist movement in the Sudan was, primarily, the result of the excesses of the Khedive of Egypt's agents. . . . It was the people's grievances . . . that led to the appearance of the Mahdi. He was the religious bond that united the rebels, despite their tribal disputes, racial differences and divergent interests.'[48] In Somaliland, the Mad Mullah, who was active at the beginning of this century, preached against any relaxation of the faith; he sought to overcome tribal particularism by imposing religious unity, and led the struggle against the British for almost twenty years without once laying down his arms. Nevertheless, all his efforts as a reformer and creator of unity suffered a considerable setback, for a reason that it is essential to grasp: 'Somaliland did not offer such a favourable sphere of activity as Eastern Sudan, because unlike the Sudanese the Somalis could hardly feel that they were oppressed by foreigners, since to all intents and purposes their country had not actually been invaded.'[49] We have to remember, on the one hand, the direct connection between the strength of the movement and the harshness of foreign domination; and, on the other, the utilization of an imported religion or a unifying influence (it helps to prevent the process of fission typical of tribal societies) at a time when foreign domination is giving rise to disturbances and resentment. 'God's messenger' arouses hopes of challenging the social order, and encourages an opposition to foreign domination that will help to create a broader based social system, comprising both political and religious unity. The comparison we have here outlined can be taken further. Within the confines of Muslim Africa we find two types of Mahdism corresponding more or less to the two types of Negro church distinguished by Dr Sundkler. In Eastern Africa (the Nile area) the movement is organized, makes some show of being an established power and provides a basis for nationalist aspirations – the Umma Party, which demanded that the sovereignty of their country should be restored to the Sudanese, was seen as the modern fulfilment of the Mahdi's efforts. In the west, on the other hand, Mahdism tends to be intermittent, inspired by less outstand-ing leaders; it is often a form of protest against a social situation that people are no longer prepared to accept passively; and in this case attempts at subversion, talk of Utopia and the reign of justice predominate. It has correctly been pointed out that all forms of Mahdism have three common features: the appearance of the phenomenon 'wherever there is a general feeling of dis-satisfaction' (in other words it is a response to a *crisis situation*); its success as a form of political and cultural *opposition*; its prestige as a movement announcing a reconstruction of society *in line with popular demand* – in contrast to the reformism of some modern leaders, which sometimes has little meaning for the relatively unsophisticated majority.

However, during the last few decades, the movements in the Moslem areas have not had the strength and staying power that similar movements have shown in the Christian areas. The reasons for this are, firstly, that the rise of Black Islam was not associated with colonial expansion, quite the contrary; and, secondly, that far from being a religion open both to colonized and colonizers, Islam is essentially an indication of fundamental differentiation and an instrument of opposition. It is understand-able, therefore, that in this case there is not the same concern with liberation that one finds in the colonial churches. Moreover, Islam lends itself more readily than Christianity to the adaptation and incorporation of individual contributions: the study of Black Islam shows the considerable use to which this tolerance has been put. The Christian Church, on the contrary, appears to create discord, and is associated with a definite political system which tends to hinder its growth. Moreover, there is an obvious contra-diction between the teachings of the colonists and the situation they create, which has done a good deal to help the African to grasp the reality of his own position. It was the Catholic mission-aries who, almost involuntarily, *began* to educate him politically; and it was through reading the Bible that his protests and resis-tance acquired a semi-mythical semi-literary form. In addition to this, the demands of Christianity were essentially hostile to the traditional socio-cultural context: it did its best to destroy the existing cults and suppress polygamy, and sought to influence the most deprived social categories, the women and younger men.

Above all, as far as the Catholics were concerned, it was opposed to any traditional religious formulation that challenged the orthodoxy of their teaching. In this sense, Christianity deepened the conflict between colonized and colonizer, and thus helped to stimulate reaction on the part of the former. Islam, on the other hand, made no such radical demands. It was capable of absorbing certain major divinities and magical techniques; it allowed fundamental attitudes to be maintained; and, apart from the minimum demands upon its members compatible with its continued existence, it provided very considerable opportunities for assimilation. Moreover, Islam made no attempt to interfere with the fundamental principles of social organization; it proclaimed itself to be a religion for men and so, as we ourselves observed in Senegal,[50] made no attempt to interfere with the traditional cults affecting women; thus it respected the spirit of the old hierarchy and, by a kind of division of religious labour between the sexes, made adaptation possible. This, and the opportunities for opposition inherent in Islam, explains the very different position of these two great religions in Africa south of the Sahara.

Finally, it has to be realized that the number of people belonging to the Negro churches is considerable: they cannot therefore be regarded as an abnormal phenomenon. Broadly speaking, their distribution coincided with those areas where the causes of social change were most active, where the colonial situation was experienced most harshly. Thus, for sociologists, the neo-Christian movements have to be seen as a *global* reaction to this situation. They represent a total response to a situation that has proved to be productive of internal 'crises' and conducive to continued alienation. They constitute a *real* field of observation, within which mechanisms occur which those anthropologists concerned primarily with the study of *acculturation* have persisted in treating in isolation. Above all, they lead to the study of the beginnings of nationalism.[51] In the Congo (Brazzaville) alone, we saw, in the 1950s, a new example of this phenomenon in one of the southern, and essentially Catholic, districts dominated by the Mbochi tribe. The emergence of the so-called 'Great Leader of the Mbochi'*

* A leader who proclaimed significantly: 'I shall die for this country like Jesus Christ.'

was connected with reactions against the missionaries and Catho-licism, with an attempted religious revival inspired by Catholicism, with united demonstrations against colonialism and with the dynamic and ambitious ethnic groups of the south.

Having suggested the widespread nature of such phenomena, it is worth recalling that, in comparable situations, *heresies* once served the cause of emancipation. In a very different geographical area, North Africa, Arab domination and conversion to Islam, imposed upon the particularisms and culture of the Berber tribes in the eighth and ninth centuries, produced reactions of the same nature. The heretical doctrines of the Kharijites inspired a revolt against the Arab bureaucracy, and the appearance of a prophet in the Baraghwata tribe led to the creation 'of an original religion adapted to the outlook of the tribesmen'. These movements, which incidentally were related, both resulted in the setting up of 'theocratic states' that succeeded in resisting the Arab armies for a considerable time.[52] We mention these facts because they help to 'place' Ba-Kongo Messianism, to show that neither geographi-cally nor historically is it in any sense an isolated phenomenon; and also because they demonstrate that *situations* of the same kind, even in societies with very different cultures, produce comparable *reactions* and lead to a very similar use being made of cultural material imposed from without.

CONCLUSION:
DYNAMIC SOCIOLOGY
AND SOCIAL CHANGE

In the two sections of this book devoted to the Fang and the Ba-Kongo, we have drawn attention to the changes and consequent disequilibria peculiar to each of these societies. At the same time we have indicated those tendencies and processes that seem to be of major importance inasmuch as they permit of some measure of generalization. It now remains to draw the conclusions that a comparison between the two cases makes possible.

I. COMPARATIVE DYNAMIC

It is clear that these two societies could not react to the colonial situation in the same way or with equal intensity. The Ba-Kongo were not faced with the same disequilibria and problems as the Gabonese Fang. Their greater adaptability may be seen from the fact that their reactions were directed to the outside world (with the demand for autonomy) rather than to internal problems, and this is particularly apparent if we examine *all* levels of social reality: their fairly satisfactory demographic position, a more or less progressive economy and a still effective institutional system. All these aspects are unmistakably interrelated; and this is borne out by a comparative study of the very different regions comprising the Fang country. For instance, owing to its demographic characteristics, its relatively high population, its economy and its greater 'clan vitality', the Woleu-Ntem is quite unlike the Moyen-Ogooué region, where the disintegrating groups seem to be almost completely resigned to progressive decline.

This first point needs clarifying; despite the specific differences, it introduces factors that are common both to the Ba-Kongo groups and to the most favourably situated of the Fang groups.

473

If we compare them in this way, we find that the Woleu-Ntem area and the most dynamic Ba-Kongo districts are the *only* ones that are able to support a relatively high population; and this means taking into account a number of *quantitative* features. The social units, in this case villages, have declined numerically less than elsewhere; they are less dispersed and less remote from one another; and the mutual ties they have preserved have prevented them from becoming turned in upon themselves. In both cases, the size of population they have maintained is not only conducive to greater social vitality, it also makes possible certain solutions that are only possible for village groups of a minimum size and in touch with the outside world. The capacity for reorganization and initiative is bound up with these quantitative aspects, with the scale of social intercourse that is available to the villages.

We find a kind of counter-proof of this in the most demoralized areas of the Fang country, with their multiplicity of isolated *micro-villages* – conditions that exist also among other ethnic groups. In the Mouila districts of Gabon, for instance, the Ba-Pounou suffer from a similar multiplicity of small groups and lowered vitality – due, incidentally, as with the Fang of the Moyen-Ogooué, to a policy of intensive forced labour.[1] In contrast to this, the effect of establishing a successful cash crop in the Woleu-Ntem was to strengthen the groups, while the connection of the Kongo country with Brazzaville and other railway centres led to economic developments that enabled it to sustain a high level of population. Under such conditions, effective planning at a higher level became possible.

It is necessary, therefore, to consider the *nature of the economy* that was established in each of the two regions. In both cases it is a question of areas where, even before the colonial period, there had been considerable commercial activity and a settled market agriculture, and where economic interests (however undeveloped) existed at village level. Apart from the fact that the earnings from these enterprises make it possible to meet some of the most pressing financial needs, it is important to bear in mind their customary or para-customary character. They are organized either within the traditional social framework or on traditional models adapted to the new requirements, so that, even if they lead to the appearance of new social categories and modify the existing social structures, these changes arise from the village and operate at village level. They are therefore amenable to some measure of control, which is not the case when the centres of economic interest are outside the village unit. The capacity for adaptation is to be seen most clearly in those Ba-Kongo groups where the family economy is at once semi-rural and semi-urban. In the Woleu-Ntem, as in the Kongo communities, opportunities for economic progress exist at the *level of the village group* – a state of affairs to which a whole number of British studies of 'community development' attribute outstanding importance.

The demographic and economic characteristics of the groups are closely connected; together they help to create a favourable situation for social and cultural reorganization. This seems to have been appreciated by certain local individuals, who envisaged the possibility of providing help to the demographically and economically developed areas within the vast underpopulated territory of the Gabon-Congo, with a view to extending their power of attraction and facilitating their modernization. They implicitly recognized their inability to function usefully in other areas. Apart from any reservations this point of view may call for, one has to remember the contradictions that existed between the economic aims of the colonized society (specifically, a modernized agriculture controlled as far as possible by the villagers) and those of the colonizing society (primarily concerned with mining and forestry, and to a lesser degree with the development of planta- tions and trade). Only very occasionally was it possible to recon- cile these conflicting interests, and this explains why the Central African communities, even those most favourably situated, were so sensitive to the vicissitudes of the colonial economy. The period of the war effort was enough to endanger the equilibrium that had been re-established in the Woleu-Ntem from 1935 onwards; while the massive reactions that economic crises produced among the Ba-Kongo show that they felt themselves to be threatened on every side. As a result, the stability, and even the composition, of the groups (because of individual migration and collective displacement) again became an issue, as did the financial status of the villagers and the efficacy of the adjustments achieved; and hostility to the colonizing society broke out once more. Reper- cussions on this scale prove that, in transitional societies, economic decisions have an *immediate* effect which affects social existence at every level. And this is so, not merely because African economies are vulnerable, but also because the economic processes are bound up, much more closely than in our own society, with all the other elements that constitute both culture and social organization. If it is true to say that in African society everything is connected with religion, it is equally true that everything is related to the economy.

This view is fully justified, provided one makes it clear that here, even more than elsewhere, the state of the economy is inseparable from the demographic facts. In addition to the variations resulting from the types of organization and cultural system that are adopted, it is essential to appreciate the relation between the quantitative features of the villages, the potentialities of the *local* economy, and the ability of the groups to adapt themselves to the latter; and while the third of these terms is the most difficult to define, it is just as important as the other two. In the Woleu-Ntem, so long as the groups were unable to adapt themselves (in such matters as the redivision of farm work between the sexes* and the extension of cocoa growing) there was only a slow improvement in the demographic position, in the growth of the villages and the widening of social relations. The parallel application of these three terms to a series of specific societies belonging to the major ethnic groups would enable us to classify in a meaningful way the capacity of the latter for planning and development. At the same time it should be noted that intervention by the colonist often contributed to disequilibrium by modifying one or all of these terms in a quite external way, primarily concerned with the requirements of the colonist. This happened when the result of his activities was to modify the demographic position without providing the necessary compensations, or when he sacrificed the local economy to the exigencies of the colonial economy.

This first group of inferences shows that, apart from the problems arising from the bringing together of different cultures and races, there are basic problems that cannot be adequately studied simply in terms of cultural anthropology. In this sense, the help of the sociologist and the economist is indispensable. From another angle, this approach leads to the conclusion that

* In other words, unless the Fang villager was prepared to play a more active part in agriculture.

the same type of *situation* produces the same effect on social change, despite the differences typical of the societies and cultures exposed to the processes of change. Each situation contains possibilities and impossibilities that the observer must take into account. For example, there is a certain set of circumstances that is conducive to movements of unification, as may be seen from their appearance and persistence in the Kongo country, in the north of the Woleu-Ntem and in the adjoining parts of Cameroun, whereas they do not occur, or at least do not succeed, in areas where the situation is quite different. Lastly, and it is a conclusion that bears out the previous ones, one finds that the modifications affecting incomplete structures have a certain independence as regards social organization. This independence is well brought out by Gurvitch in his essay on the differential typology of groups.[2] It is especially applicable to transitional African societies. At the level of incomplete social structures, the influence of the colonist, whoever he might be, had many common results, which explains why the problems posed by modern Africa are relatively uniform, despite its long-standing and marked cultural diversity. This may be seen from a single example: wherever labour policy and the tendency to urbanization have entailed a marked numerical imbalance between the sexes, as they did in Gabon, the status of women tends to improve, despite the diversity of institutional relationships that exists in traditional society. The maladjustment between changes affecting structures and the 'delayed' modifications affecting social organizations is one of the characteristics of societies exposed to multiple and rapid processes of change.

These observations remain valid outside Africa, they apply to so-called 'underdeveloped' societies which are at present being developed and modernized. Urbanization, migration of workers, improvement of communications and increasing mobility, reduction in the size of village groups owing to permanent security, etc., are all processes that involve the same type of problems, despite considerable cultural differences. Our inadequate understanding of these questions is due not merely to the material difficulties of research, but also to the fact that the majority of studies have for too long been conducted from the point of view of classical anthropology. For the sociologist they represent an extremely rich field of observation, and one that requires his most serious consideration.

II. DEPENDENCE AND SOCIAL CHANGE

We must now consider how 'the colonial situation' or 'the situation of dependence' affects social change – whatever cultural diversity may exist. This is a field we have already touched on, in an article that attempted to define a 'sociology of dependence'.[3] There we showed that this situation gives rise to specific antagonisms and reactions, leads to the intellectual awakening from which 'national' movements are born, and provokes a kind of *evasion* by means of cultural techniques that are essentially alien to the colonizer.

The material strength of the colonizing society, which Wirth insists upon in his analysis of the problems of minorities, as well as its superior administrative ability, explains the importance of what one might call *clandestine* or *indirect* reactions. Opposition has little or no opportunity of expressing itself openly and, at least until the national movements attain sufficient size, violent demonstrations remain the exception. Clandestinity may be of a simple kind, giving rise to more or less effective organizations that are unknown to the colonial authorities and only come into the open when there seems to be a chance of acting with impunity. At the beginning of this work we mentioned a religious association, the *Labi*, whose members were obliged to live in isolation and to refuse contact, even visual, with the white man, which nevertheless was to play a decisive role in the revolts in the Haute-Sangha in 1928–9. More often, however, clandestinity is due to the tremendous cultural gulf that exists between the colonized and the colonizer. This makes it possible for the opposition to organize itself, with the minimum of danger, within apparently traditional social bodies, engaged in various customary activities much of whose significance completely escapes the Europeans. It was in this way that the religious associations were used (or sometimes formally reorganized) in order to conceal the reactions to the colonial situation that they were in fact stimulating. Wherever an opposition party was banned, its place was effectively taken by some customary religious association.

As regards the Fang, we recall the role played by the members of the *Bwiti*, and how the most dynamic leaders were able to use this cult as a means of political expression. But the most revealing ind at the same time the most tragic, example was that of the Mau-Mau movement, which inspired the Kikuyu rising in Kenya.[4] It is important to note that, in all such movements, the most active elements belong to the social category known as 'évolués'. Owing to the lack of modern means of political expression, they are driven to make use of traditional organizations, since this enables them to carry on their work in a semi-underground manner. Moreover, the leaders are obliged to take this step if they want to obtain a large membership; they have to resort to a type of organization that will have an immediate significance for the peasants, and make it easy for them to join. Thus institutions of a traditional form are put to completely new uses. This is a phenomenon that can only be correctly understood in reference to the situation of dependence, for it is clear that to regard them as essentially a manifestation of counter-acculturation, an 'offensive' return to traditional values, leads to a completely inadequate evaluation.

The reactions we describe as *indirect* involve mechanisms that operate in very different ways. It might be, for example, by a calculated manifestation of passivity, as among the Kongo, where the Amicalist movement insisted upon its members taking an oath of resistance to the administration's demands. Or again, as Dr Sachs has shown in an independent study of the South African Bantu, it might take the form of an agreed decision to make the minimum amount of effort when working for Europeans. And furthermore, as we have noted on a number of occasions, there is the part played by *duplication* – especially with regard to the chieftainship. Underlying the apparent fulfilment of administrative orders or exaggerated professions of cooperation, independent activities are organized and basic opposition is manifested. But here the fact that so large a part of social activity is concealed, prevents or retards adaptation and creates tensions and conflict within the colonized society itself. And, finally, we have several times referred to the phenomenon of *transference* that operates as a result of the colonial situation.

Transference may take place between one group and another, in which case the colonizing society is attacked through a substitute: the body of appointed chiefs, those in favour of full cooperation with Europeans (whom at one time the Ba-Kongo nicknamed *sindikats*), half-castes or 'stranger' minorities. More often, and because conditions afford no other outlet, transference occurs between two different levels of existing society. Pent-up violence finds expression in terms of modern myth and Utopia building:[5] in this respect, the various forms of Messianism and the movements inspired by apocalyptic visions that are to be found in Central and Southern Africa, are revealing, and this is true of other parts of Africa. Linton, for example, speaks of the development of Messianism as 'a fairly common consequence of the relationship of domination and dependence';[6] and it is well-known that Max Weber used to interpret prophetic Messianism as a reaction against frustration. There can be no doubt that here, too, the 'situation' has a decisive influence; it leads to the same use being made of cultural material available to the dominated society – whether this consists of its own culture (myths involving the intervention of a mediator) or of cultural borrowings from the dominant society, (in which case the influence of the Bible is decisive).

This is a reminder that such 'borrowings' from the colonizing society are not simply reinterpreted, as the cultural anthropologists maintain, but *are treated in terms of the situation*, in terms of the reactions towards independence caused by this situation. In this respect, the so-called 'separatist' Negro churches are revealing. We have tried to demonstrate this by studying Ba-Kongo Messianism. This, like all similar movements, has to be analysed on the basis of the cultural facts (its syncretistic character emphasizes the 'unchanging' part of the traditional religions and the attitudes least susceptible of modification) and from the point of view of its being a reaction to dependence. It occurs as an attempt to revive, first of all religious autonomy, and later on political autonomy. This reassertion of initiative is only possible by using the Christian church as a model, while at the same time differentiating it (by indigenous contributions) and making it serve as a means of glorifying 'race'. In many places, colonial Christianity has resulted in the emergence of a sacral nationalism. And we have seen how widespread similar phenomena have been, not only in space but also in time. There are many examples of heresies from a dominant religion playing a part in the emancipation of colonized societies[7] and inspiring their first attempts to reorganize.

History also provides numerous examples of heresies being used by peasant uprisings as a way of asserting their rejection of an essentially inferior position; and, as we may see from contemporary history, the same process applies to a constricting and dominating ideology once the will to freedom asserts itself. Thus we are concerned with a sphere of activity in which, to use an expression of Gurvitch's, 'new and restless collective attitudes' are likely to occur.

Most social movements in dependent countries show that attempts to reorganize society are bound up with attempts to achieve independence; there is a direct relationship between the two. By its economic, political and cultural activities, the colonizing society stimulates processes of change at every level; yet in order to maintain its dominant position, it endeavours to exercise maximum control over them. We have given numerous examples of how it seeks to control movements of social reconstruction which, if successful, would inevitably threaten its position. Any modernist form of reorganization, as we noted particularly with regard to the 'regrouping' attempted by the Fang, soon constitutes a threat to the dominant society, which proceeds to suppress it. And, in addition to this fundamental difficulty, there are others. The *instability* of groups (all the more marked because their material basis remains precarious), as well as of institutions (owing to the changes that are necessary and the multiplicity of novel experiments), is, in certain circumstances, used as a means of restricting colonial control. But its persistence appears to prevent any effective adaptation. The same effect is produced by the *ambiguity* and *tactical formalism* that we emphasized when speaking of the Fang, who seek to preserve certain socio-cultural features as a screen between the colonists and themselves. All these are processes that retard the adoption of genuine solutions and maintain a state of 'crisis'. Failure to pay sufficient attention to these facts leads to attributing solely to cultural incompatibility a delay in adaptation that can *also* be explained by the nature of the relations between colonizers and colonized.

III. TRANSITION AND SOCIAL DISEQUILIBRIA

Comparative study has enabled us to distinguish certain forms of

16

maladjustment peculiar to so-called 'transitional' societies.[8] In the first place, it has to be realized that, in their traditional form, these African societies are far from constituting a *perfect system*. As a result of the many vicissitudes arising from migration (which continued until recently), from inter-tribal wars, from the slave trade and the long-standing influence of the West (even where only exerted from a distance), they all suffer from discord. In the words of Lévi-Strauss, they all 'bear the unmistakable imprint of the *event*'.[9] Like any other society, they represent an approximation; in varying degrees they miss opportunities for compromise and put up with failure. We have shown this, in both our examples, with regard to the rules ensuring the devolution of power, rank and 'specialization' – which nevertheless provide scope for social mobility and competition. Similarly, the Fang make allowances with respect to such fundamental principles as those governing the circulation of wives and the prohibition of incest. All these discrepancies, all these compromises are so many 'weak spots', and are the first to be affected by contact and exposure to the processes of change.* Failures with regard to the transmission of political responsibility, *as well as* government intervention, have encouraged competition and the emergence of rival authorities – thus contributing to the almost complete lack of authority observed among those most deeply affected. The commercialization of wives among the Fang could not have developed so rapidly (it only began in the first decade of this century), and assumed such grave proportions, had it not been for the possibilities already inherent in tradition. Moreover, the colonizers often endeavoured to strengthen their authority by acting upon these 'weak spots', the most sensitive areas of equilibrium in the colonized society; while the effect of micro-particularisms and the reaction of those elements most subject to traditional constraint (the women and younger men) both contributed to this end, at least during the early phase of colonization.

* Indeed, if we are to have any real understanding of the dynanisms resulting from 'contact' it would be necessary *first of all* to interpret the traditional social structures dynamically. These have potentialities that can only be realized under certain social conditions. To interpret structures in terms of position rather than of opposition only impoverishes and 'freezes' them, and ultimately falsifies them. It is in the hope of avoiding this that we are attempting to create an anthropology which will be at once *dynamic* and *critical*.

The introduction of a money economy, of a class of wage workers and of economic competition, in a context to which all these phenomena were completely alien, has given rise to numerous studies. But none of their authors appear to have devoted sufficient attention to a social change of capital importance: the decline of *primitive planning* peculiar to traditional society; a decline resulting from the extension of social relations and the development of a modern economy (the control of which remains entirely in the hands of the colonizing or dominant society), with its appeal to individuals rather than to groups. It was when studying the critical phases of Fang society that we first came to appreciate the full significance of this phenomenon. The connection which still exists, between social status (depending upon the size of group a man controls) and the mechanisms ensuring the circulation of wives and property involved careful planning. And this could only be effective within a framework in which the field of social relationships was restricted, where the volume of goods remained limited and where it was possible to control external influences. The development of a money economy and a class of wage earners, and the increase in competition, radically modified this combination of circumstances. Tactical recourse to traditional rules and principles of organization, which were continually losing their efficacy, encouraged abuses and retarded adaptation to the new economy. Similarly, as regards the Ba-Kongo, we have also stressed the weakening of this primitive planning; faced by competition from restricted groups and individuals, it is gradually disappearing. As a result, there is now a gap between traditional authority and economic power; and consequently an even more rapid decline of the chieftainship. The breakdown of this planning, at a time when new adjustments have not yet begun to function properly, is a phenomenon that may well have most serious consequences for people whose traditional organization used to be adjusted to a genuine social plan.*

At this point, it is necessary to recall briefly, and still in terms of economic processes, the extent to which the societies of Central

---

* In a very different field, with regard to the research he is carrying out on the religion and metaphysics of the Sudan, M. Griaule emphasizes the fact that these civilizations allow no room for improvisation; every phenomenon is noted and classified – submitted to a higher order.

Africa continue to be influenced by *a civilization in which a man's prestige is determined by the number of people, rather than the amount of property, that he controls.* But these two forms of saving can scarcely be separated, so that the new economic relationships tend to upset those of power and rank. Thus a contradiction develops between the traditional authorities who can only maintain their position by taking part in the economic struggle, and those individuals who, having attained considerable economic status, are at first unable to assert their prestige except by recourse to traditional 'procedures'.*

In addition to this form of rivalry, arising from the fact that rank and power no longer coincide, other maladjustments are apparent within these old political systems which are determined by more general processes. In their Preface to *African Political Systems*, Fortes and Evans-Pritchard maintain that the social structure should not be considered statically, but as a state of equilibrium that can only persist if it is continually renewed.[10] It is precisely the opportunity of returning to a state of equilibrium that is *disappearing* (or becoming less and less effective): the old compensatory relationship that existed between the authority of the 'chiefs', or those whose position was accepted by the lineage, and the authority of the 'associations' can no longer establish itself normally; the chiefs, having been so long controlled by the administration, are all losing their authority, while the 'associations', attacked by the missionaries or the administration, have in many cases disappeared. In this respect, both the Fang and the Ba-Kongo afford significant examples.

The difficulties experienced by the new social types (literates, "economic évolués and young workers) when they want to become members of organizations that appreciate their role, are also a cause of maladjustment. Despite their dynamic qualities, they were at first obliged to remain on the fringe of the organized groups – the 'traditional' groups were hardly likely to recognize their importance, while the position of the 'modernist' groups was for a long time precarious – and the vicissitudes of the clan regroupment carried out by the Fang showed how difficult it was for them to become accepted. What we have here is a form of the

---

* In recent years, the introduction of modern political structures and the decisive role of party leaders and cadres have modified this situation without eliminating it.

disequilibrium typical of the gap between the existing state of social organization and social structures to which we have already referred. It will only be when this gap has been reduced that African society can be regarded as being better adapted to its modern obligations, and as having passed beyond the negative phase of transition. Since achieving Independence, the political parties that provide the governments of the new states have been attempting to create homogeneous social cadres within which both 'modernist' and 'traditionalist' elements are associated, the party, to some extent, serving as the largest common cadre.

To this we should add, however, that the margin of tolerance of maladjustment appears to be a wide one: firstly, because there are definite 'fixed points', by which we mean the most resistant elements of the social system and the most persistent attitudes; and secondly, because there are incidental compensatory factors. Sometimes, for instance, relative economic prosperity obscures the gravity of the problems (one of the officials in the Cameroun used to say 'As long as cocoa is doing well, everything's all right'); or again, illusory compensations operate (ephemeral innovations, Utopia building, or increasing recourse to magic as a means of reducing insecurity). The old cultural orientation undoubtedly made such 'comforting' illusions effective.

This state of societies 'in transition' corresponds to a 'moment' that calls for their inclusion in a much wider field of relations than previously. The modification affects the space-scale they are connected with, the intensification of relationships and the volume of wealth' that they have to produce and handle. There is, in fact, a change of scale that involves new techniques for exploiting nature and organizing space. Instead of thinking in the usual terms of social evolution it would be more accurate to speak of social mutation. This crucial period has its negative and positive phases, movements of *destructuration* and *structuration, disorganization* and *reorganization*; but, apart from the possibility of complete physical destruction, whatever the obstacles and difficulties may be the second phase always occurs sooner or later. It would be useful if we could establish certain criteria that would make it possible to measure the levels of reconstruction in different societies.

In this respect, the cases of the Fang and Kongo are informative examples. True, all that they can contribute are pointers to research, and any detailed examination would require much more exhaustive comparative material. Nevertheless, the parallel treatment we have attempted indicates that the following aspects should be borne in mind: (1) the reduction of the instability of residential groups and the increase in their size; (2) an economy which, on a *local* scale, releases a certain volume of money and ensures the *local* circulation of a certain volume of agricultural produce and manufactured goods; (3) a tendency to technical and social adaptation, in an expanding field of relationships; (4) the reduction of the gap between the existing social structures and social organizations; (5) overcoming existing 'micro-particularisms, and substituting a 'spirit of public service' for the 'clan spirit'; (6) the degree of literacy and use of printed material; (7) the intensity and effectiveness of reactions to the 'alien' forces of political and economic subjection. These criteria apply at different 'levels' of social reality, and to the most important relationships. They confirm the point we have just made about 'social mutation'. They would enable us to present the situation quantitatively without undue difficulty or artificiality, and therefore to construct a scale that would make the comparison of different societies more fruitful – thus helping to clarify the notion of 'transition'. That such an undertaking is not impossible may be seen from the essays of S. C. Dodd of the University of Washington, particularly his project for a scale 'for assessing the aptitude for autonomous government'. With an instrument of this kind, it would be easier to appreciate the variations resulting from different social conditions, as well as the differences due to the political type of society under discussion.

IV. TOTAL SOCIAL PHENOMENA AND SOCIAL DYNAMICS

We shall now attempt to elucidate the relationship between total social phenomena and total social dynamics, in terms of two institutions that have already been briefly mentioned: the *bilaba* of the Fang and the *malaki* of the Ba-Kongo. Though they occur in dissimilar contexts and have experienced different vicissitudes, they are both of the same kind; they entail an exchange of gifts (a 'voluntary-obligatory' exchange, according to Mauss's classification), and the gift implies a challenge; they require a massive consumption of wealth; they call for public display on a large scale; and they create or reinforce certain social relations, while at the same time expressing latent antagonisms and competition for prestige. Moreover, both are based upon the same dialectic, which consists in transforming a real or potential conflict into a relationship of cooperation and alliance, an ambiguous relationship into one of friendship, a questionable prestige into one that is generally accepted. This transformation is achieved by enacting the conflict and confrontation in the form of a social drama, which is what every *bilaba* or *malaki* in effect amounts to. But the enactment is never simple, nor the outcome predetermined: because the themes involved in these institutions are multiple and complex, the emphasis varies according to time and circumstance and the results differ according to the motives of the individuals and groups concerned. To attempt to study such institutions in static terms would be to impoverish and falsify them; only by a dynamic approach* is it possible to see them as 'indicators' of a partly hidden social existence.

All our informants described the *bilaba* as 'a battle of insults', 'an exchange of gifts' and 'a period of rejoicing', distinguished by the wearing of special costumes, dancing and an abundance of food and palm wine. The diffusion of the *bilaba* among the Fang† appears to date from the second half of the eighteenth century, when they were still acquiring the territory where they now live and when the slave trade was aggravating competition and multiplying friction. Thus the institution came as an answer to the problems arising from these events. It helped to ensure peace and establish regular contact between peoples who were both 'strangers' to one another and hostile – the exchange of gifts leading first to pacification, then to close friendship (as may be seen from the fact that they used the so-called 'joking language') and eventually to alliance based on the exchange of wives. At

---

* Mauss himself was fully aware of the necessity. As he unequivocally said: 'We considered societies in their dynamic or physiological state. We did not study them as though they were inert, in a static or corpse-like state. . . . It is only by studying them as a whole that it is possible to grasp their essence, the living movement of the whole . . .' *Sociologie et anthropologie*, Paris, 1950, p. 275.

† Who seem to have adopted it from peoples now living in the coastal region of the Cameroun (Kribi).

the same time it reduced competition for rare and highly prized imported goods by organizing their distribution, and provided a means of organizing the economy in an area where regular markets were unknown.

In the course of evolution the *bilaba* preserved some of its original features; most importantly, it still involved 'strangers'. But in its modern, everyday form, it mainly takes the form of a challenge between two notables of the same tribe, who become friends through competing. The proceedings start with the sacrifice of a sheep, which is then eaten in common; the two protagonists thus publicly demonstrating their agreement to take part in the cycle of gifts and counter-gifts. The two camps then compete in public festivities, involving the consumption of large quantities of goods, in the course of which gifts are exchanged to the accompaniment of insults and mockery – the value of each gift having to exceed that of the one just received. The time the confrontation lasts varies: if it is prolonged, relations between the two notables are maintained on terms of friendship and equal prestige; if it ends by agreement, the one who finds himself in economic difficulties is regarded as the loser, both from the point of view of prestige and of authority; if it is broken off unilaterally, the issue is settled by recourse to violence, though this is now very unusual.

These, then, are the rules governing an institution that was already dying out as long ago as 1930, though it still survives in a 'mocking dance' of the same name, which is accompanied by an exchange of gifts between families related by marriage. From the point of view of its symbolism and rules, the *bilaba* is the expression of a fundamental dynamic relationship, which undoubtedly underlies all social manifestations of the same nature. It takes place between two men, well-known in their groups, who are either rivals or not yet on good terms – the zero relationship, like that of 'otherness', implying a potential antagonism and danger. It operates at a level of hostile dualism. It transforms a 'stranger' into an ally, an enemy into a friend, a relationship of uncertainty as to relative prestige into a hierarchy of prestige and authority. It binds by opposing; it creates a new social relationship, free of contradictions though arising from them; and, like any other system, it draws together antagonistic forces within a single system.

The two protagonists, the two opposed 'camps',* adopt
ontrasting symbols and notions. Each of them is associated with a
.eries that is the opposite of his rival's:

North (or West)	Right	Male	External	Imported goods
outh (or East)†	Left	Female	Internal	Traditional goods

This polarity is also found in the differentiation between clans
with names in *ésa* (male) and those with names in *ye* (female), who
ntermarry by preference; in the framework of the 'joking relationship' (*awusô*); and, possibly, in the old national initiation rite known
is *sô*.[11] Always, underlying it, is the same principle, which emerges
is an organizing antagonism, the prototype of which may well be,
it this level of economic and social development, the man-woman
relationship of otherness that marriage transforms into unity. The
ilaba, which in a sense achieves a 'marriage of contradictions',
ilso creates complex forms of social unity; areas of peaceful
existence (before the colonial 'pacification' policy was imposed
rom outside), of cooperation and intermarriage, as well as networks of economic activity; and, in addition, it may confer
political rank and authority.

On the face of it, the Ba-Kongo *malaki* affords no such wealth
of scientific implications. We shall try to define it in terms of its
differences. The society in which it is found is more highly
developed, with chiefdoms, regular markets and savings associa-
ions – a society that has made better use of the land and still looks
back to the legendary days of the old Kongo kingdom. It is part
of a more complex and stable social system than the Fang's,
hough it, too, suffered from the effects of the slave trade. In its
old form, the *malaki* was looked upon as a 'festival of the lineages
nd affines', which was held annually during the dry season. It
nvolves social groups – clans and lineages – as well as their leaders,
each of whom becomes *mfumu malaki* (chief of the *malaki*) when
his own village acts as host. The institution helps to provide a
periodic renewal of two systems of relations, which are fundamen-
al though vulnerable; it brings together the dispersed members of

* Though under modern conditions it may *start* as a personal contest, the extended
amily groups, the lineages, and even the clans of the two rivals soon find themselves
nvolved.
† According to which direction is agreed upon.

the clan and lineage; and it revives alliances and gives rise to new ones. The kinsfolk (to avoid being accused of sorcery) and the affines (to avoid breaking up marriages and thus destroying the alliance that depends upon them) *have* to accept the invitation of the 'giver of the *malaki*'. But, in addition to these obligatory guests, the host also invites his friends and anyone who either aspires to be on terms with a man of his standing or else openly challenges his economic position by accepting the contest of gifts and counter-gifts.

The *malaki* constitutes a 'system of total prestations', in the sense understood by Mauss. The key-note of the proceedings is ostentation and prodigality since the rules require that the host shall provide more food, goods and entertainment than he himself received on a similar occasion.[12] As against this, however, nowadays he benefits from the *cash* gifts that are given by 'strangers', and are not accompanied by mockery and insults. The festival is associated with the rites that are observed either in honour of the ancestors, or to mark the end of a period of mourning for some important person; it therefore has a religious significance. It is also an occasion on which property is transmitted and appointments confirmed; the lineage or clan thereby demonstrating its permanence and continued wealth, and publicly choosing its new 'leader' in the presence of all its members, relations by marriage and friendly 'strangers'.

In the case of the *malaki*, the polarity is not as marked as it was shown to be in our assessment of the *bilaba*. This is because it does not involve two protagonists only, but a whole number, depending upon the number of lineages related by marriage or in a position to compete; and also because it is held regularly, and not simply as occasion demands. Its function, however, remains the same: while strengthening existing bonds, it also includes 'strangers'; it organizes competition; and it adjusts a subsistence economy first of all to a trading economy, then to a money economy. It also has the same outcome: the cycle of gifts and counter-gifts guarantees solidarity; an agreement to abandon it entails loss of prestige; a unilateral breaking off gives rise to conflict.

Despite the differences between them, their common basis makes it permissible to treat both institutions as 'indicators' of number of economic, social and political forces; some traditional, others modern. As we have seen, they are based upon antagonisms which, thanks to them, can be contained, precisely because the way they function changes them into organizing antagonisms. They are sensitive to any situation that endangers established equilibria, and they enable certain new economic adjustments to be made.

This last point needs elaborating. The obvious symbolism of the *bilaba* makes the analysis easier. Of the two participants, one, the so-called 'outsider', provides durable manufactured goods (loin cloths, rifles, ironmongery, etc.) and the 'iron money' used in the past for marriage payments, while the host, or 'insider', provides goods produced traditionally and primarily for consumption (sheep, chickens, palm-kernels, ground-nuts, etc.), as well as such trade goods as ivory and, in modern times, cocoa. In this way, two different types of economy are brought together and seek to adjust themselves, to become complementary instead of being a source of conflict. From this point of view, the *bilaba* represents a positive response to a dangerous situation – a situation in which commercial activities exacerbate competition between rival groups, and which also, by introducing more and more highly valued goods that can be hoarded, upsets the market, especially the marriage market. The purpose of the *bilaba* is to ensure the circulation of wealth and to control its movement over wider economic areas, thereby creating areas of peaceful cooperation where new alliances may be arranged. From this point of view, it is easy to understand why the value of the counter-gift must always be *greater* than that of the preceding gifts; it is essential for the last recipient to be left in debt, since this guarantees that the cycle of gifts and counter-gifts will continue. It is the same with the *malaki*: the 'host' provides goods to be consumed communally, the 'guests' respond with gifts of money;* and the duration of the proceedings is also determined by the obligation to give more than one receives, doubling the amount in the case of cash gifts. In both cases, 'secondary' challenges develop out of the 'primary' challenges between the wealthiest and most eminent men, thus strengthening the network of economic relations and accelerating the circulation of those goods that are most in demand.

* At the beginning of the century these were mainly trade goods, especially red blankets.

Institutions of this kind also represent a definite way of using accumulated wealth, and a definite attitude towards such wealth, in societies where individual material advantage is not yet accepted and where relations within the kinship groups and lineages tend to promote equality. They entail a massive consumption of goods, from which the kinsmen and 'lineage brothers' of the 'host' benefit, without themselves having to contribute anything in return. Insofar as they have become a kind of *speculative gamble*, they create a common interest between them. Each of the rivals hopes, indeed, to force the other into difficulties and to gain advantage from the friendly settlement that will ensue. He tries to hold out as long as possible by obtaining help from his immediate kin and 'lineage brothers', with regard to whom he plays the part of banker, striving to interest his clients in a promising undertaking and hoping to induce them to risk a profitable investment, for if his side wins they will receive a share of the profit.

This aspect is accentuated, to the detriment of other aspects of these complex manifestations, when a money economy is sufficiently developed to endanger the old social relations. Nevertheless this does not yet affect the underlying significance of the phenomenon. On the one hand, large amounts of wealth are either consumed, or else 'frozen' with a view to forthcoming exchanges; they cannot, therefore, be used to create a position of supremacy (*de facto* to begin with, then *de jure*) within the lineage – or at least not for some time. On the other hand, the system is such that it makes the kinsmen and members of the lineage jointly responsible for the 'gamble', and so tends to establish supremacy with regard to an *outside* group (the one represented by the other competitor), though not within the lineage, where equality appears to be maintained.

Lastly, it is important to note that these manifestations not only ensure partial control of the traditional economy; they also help to activate it. This latter feature is especially noticeable in the case of the *malaki*: because it occurs annually, it requires a steady accumulation of goods; it stimulates dealings during the dry period, when the festivities take place; and, in addition, it leads to temporary markets being set up in the neighbourhood of the places where the *malaki* is held.

Another aspect to be considered is the way in which both these institutions *dramatize economic and social relations*. The collective manifestations associated with the *bilaba* and the *malaki* present a veritable pageant of the basic social relationships, providing as it were a visual summary of society as a whole. By using those forms of expression available to a society without writing – symbolic behaviour, special dances, conventional forms of speech, etc. – they enable people to grasp the nature of the social system. And furthermore they have a therapeutic effect, since their purpose is to control or modify serious antagonisms, potential or actual conflicts.

At first sight, it is the business of economic relations that occupy the centre of the stage. Once the *bilaba* starts, the guests' demand for presents is satisfied according to strict protocol; the 'donor-host' pretends to refuse, the beneficiary insults and mocks him.* During the final stage of the proceedings the gifts that have been received are scrupulously checked, and the evaluation of them leads to a protracted process of bargaining; then they are taken away by a caravan of bearers, led by the notable to whom they have been given, accompanied by men playing drums; and finally, when they get home, part of them is distributed to certain members of the kinship group and lineage at a specially summoned meeting. During the festivities that are a feature of the *bilaba*, the consumption of goods and entertainment clearly complies with established precedent; and in the course of the proceedings there is also a secondary exchange of goods, so that for a time the place where the *bilaba* is held becomes a centre of economic activity. The *malaki*, despite certain differences, is much the same, though 'market' activities are even more clearly associated with it.

Facts like these betoken a state of society in which economic relationships are not yet those of partners who efface themselves, as economic 'agents', behind the goods exchanged; on the contrary, the relationships are highly personalized, and above all the goods themselves represent non-economic values. At this stage of social development, economic activity, as yet scarcely

* The following is an example of this: 'Today, I, Mbutu, Mighty Chief of Sangmélima am dancing at little Owona's place, who is as poor as a dog and has nothing to give me. I shall take him home in chains and make him one of my servants. He'll be much better off with me than he is here. . . .'

separable from the general context, is still ritualized, still enacted in a veritable collective drama. The reality of the drama is accepted, and not only for the reasons just mentioned: those who take part in it are playing a dangerous game in which their property, their prestige and their relations of 'friendship' are all at stake; the lineage is struggling against a form of *economic* inequality that would change its entire nature; while society is trying to find a way in which the old subsistence economy can coexist alongside a market economy, which is seen as an intruder responsible for creating disorder and competition.[13]

We have already spoken of the therapeutic function of these total institutions which help us to perceive what Mauss describes as 'the movement of the whole'. The comments of the native exponents of the Congolese *malaki* are unequivocal. Periodically it leads to the 'regrouping' of related lineages that have become dispersed; it helps to counteract fission, strengthens the ties of 'blood' and restores the sacral communion with the common ancestors. It prevents the scattered members of the clan from becoming 'strangers' to one another, dangerous rivals who would not hesitate to resort to sorcery. It is a means of protection against hidden conflicts, for it links together real friends, puts the affines to the test and eventually creates new relations of co-operation. It enables accumulated wealth to be dealt with publicly, in association with the kinship group and certain members of the lineage. And lastly, like all institutions of this type, it provides an opportunity for the notables of rival lineages to compete for prestige without endangering peace. The very fact that their antagonism is displayed publicly means that it can be controlled, since it is transformed into a force involving both agreement and opposition. From this point of view, such institutions may be compared with the rituals of rebellion in the societies of southern Africa described by Gluckman. The tensions inherent in inequality of status and the existence of privilege are thereby liberated, as if the social relations had been suddenly inverted; but this inversion, by which the ruler becomes symbolically the first victim, is controlled because it is part of a minutely regulated annual rite; it tends to transform the controlled and sacralized 'protest' into a factor for strengthening the social and political structures.[14]

On a number of occasions we have referred to the obligation to provide a counter-gift of superior value to the original gift. This is both a guarantee of the duration of the cycle of exchange and a requirement that gives the latter the 'agonistic quality' so well brought out by Mauss; in fact, with its multiplicity of functions and meanings, the institution is primarily based upon this struggle for wealth. Before long, the counterpart of the gift received is in danger of reaching a high level. In addition to the problems of evaluation this gives rise to (since the value of subsistence goods has to be expressed in terms of imported manufactured goods), the rules of the *bilaba* require that every counter-gift shall include as impressive a surplus (*ngom*) as possible; while those of the *malaki* insist upon the doubling of the cash gifts (*fundu*). As a rule, therefore, the kinsmen and lineage are called upon to help. In this struggle, though it may be agreed that the friendship established by the exchange of gifts should be maintained, the side that gives in first is nonetheless the loser, from the point of view both of prestige and of wealth. The cycle is stopped, but the loser has to return the equivalent of the last gifts received by him. His opponent benefits substantially from having weakened him economically: if the procedure stops at the *nth* exchange, his profit amounts to $(n - 1)$ times the surpluses received in the case of the *bilaba*; and in the case of the *malaki* of $(n - 1)$ times the gifts made to the other side.

However, the strategy is neither simple nor invariably the same. The participants can regulate the rhythm of exchange. If they are primarily concerned to remain on good terms, they will choose a slow rhythm, thus ensuring that the cycle will continue for a long time. This is clearly seen in the Congolese institution: as soon as the amounts demanded threaten to become too large, the organizers of the *malaki* sometimes agree to equalize their contributions, in which case they are said to have 'withdrawn the *malaki*'. Thereupon they immediately start up a new cycle, and their alliance is maintained on an equal footing. If, on the other hand, the main purpose of the confrontation is to assert precedence and have it publicly recognized, the cycle tends to be shorter; a quick victory increases the prestige of the winner. On the other hand, during the last few decades, the wealthier notables have been able to help those engaged in minor challenges, thus making the latter dependent upon them, especially if the former refuse to accept any return for their assistance.

In this way, a hierarchy of challenges is created, which roughly corresponds to the hierarchy of prestige and the degrees of moral and political influence. These competitive institutions are undoubtedly, though not exclusively, useful politically. The manifestations of the *malaki* are moreover associated with the traditional Ba-Kongo system of authority: they ensure the laws of succession and the solemn transmission of office; and they strengthen the authority of the '*malaki* chief' within his lineage. In the last resort, they raise the whole question of the hierarchies of clans and lineages prescribed in the past. On the other hand, in Fang society, there were only very few positions of varying importance: some permanent, but effective only at the level of the lineages; others of greater scope, but only temporary, since they were based upon military skill, knowledge of custom or a talent for oratory. The *bilaba* was an attempt to establish a lasting and relatively widespread authority; and, though this was not its sole aim, it was certainly one of the most important.

In the conditions of modern life, there is even more to these institutions. They sometimes actually make it possible to transform economic superiority into moral and political superiority: a wealthy man, for example, finding himself in an ambiguous and dangerous position, is turned into a respected and influential notable. Among the Ba-Kongo, the *malaki* has resulted in quite spectacular examples of social promotion: 'It is by this means that one-time domestic slaves have succeeded in achieving "freedom" (i.e. obtaining the status of free men by purchase), as well as wealth and power.'[15] The accumulated property provides a basis for genuine 'sociological' investments; the profit from the transaction being expressed primarily in terms of prestige and a greater opportunity to play an active part in public and private affairs. In this way, the traditional social logic remains more important than mere economic advantage.

Total social phenomena, of which we have just given two African examples, bring out the dynamic forces underlying 'official' structures, the evolutionary tendencies that are beginning to take shape.[16] Their very complexity allows for different emphases according to different significant circumstances. What appears to be *primarily* at stake is sometimes the establishment of economic relations, the speeding up and regulation of exchange; sometimes the widening of the network of alliances; sometimes the desire to achieve fame, prestige, etc. Thus the same institutional framework adapts itself to circumstances, taking on functions and meanings that differ according to the situation to which it is applied; it both obeys and reveals the changing strategy of outstanding individuals and of the groups attached to them; and as well as obeying the processes of social change determined by history, it manifests the consequences of them.

Because of the considerable number of social factors they set in motion, these 'competitive institutions' make it possible *to comply with the profound underlying forces on which society is based*. The Fang *bilaba* provides what is almost a caricature of this: consisting, as it does, of two hostile protagonists, it transforms the multiple disputes between them into the elements of a unifying dualism, ensures the 'marriage' of the contradictions and, thanks to this, creates social entities of a new kind. These total manifestations serve not only to 'expose' the social system – by acting it out, so to speak, in public – they also have a therapeutic effect. They are an attempt to control antagonisms directly they appear – for instance, those that a market economy, and later a money economy, give rise to when they are first introduced. But the most remarkable fact is that this transformation of a dangerous, or negative, social relationship into a positive one, is effected by bringing about a change in the relationship which eventually *identifies* it with the relations of affinity and kinship; and, in those societies in which kinship and affinity still constitute the firmest basis, it is only at this point that the antagonism seems to be totally under control. Thus, for a considerable period, the clan system reveals a surprising capacity for assimilation.*

* In *The Savage Thought*, Eng. trans., London, 1966, p. 235, C. Lévi-Strauss makes some surprising comments on these arguments. His fragmentary and incomplete quotations almost inevitably misrepresent my interpretation. The phenomena described above are seen as: (1) instruments of social preservation; (2) signs of hidden dynamisms; (3) attempts to master and control modern developments. But it is essential that *all three* aspects should be considered *together*, as a careful reading of this study makes abundantly clear.

Finally, these institutions show that, owing to modern economic conditions, it is not easy to create new political powers; here, too, it is a question of bringing about the unmistakable transformation of turning a wealthy man into an influential and respected one by *traditional means*. Furthermore, this transformation will not be accepted until a considerable part of the wealth has been consumed, because, in these societies, it is still true that any attempt to acquire wealth on a purely individual basis is regarded as the height of immorality.

V. MESSIANISM AND SOCIAL DYNAMICS

At this point, rather than return to questions that have already been discussed, we propose to make one or two further observations about Congolese Messianism and to consider certain of its aspects in a new light.

At the outset, certain questions demand an answer. Why is it that in the Congo and adjacent areas peoples who are either closely related or have long been in touch with one another, and who have been subjected to the same kind of colonization and missionary activity, have not *all* reacted to the identical problems that confront them with movements of a Messianic nature? Why is it that the spread of Messianism has been restricted, whereas quite minor ritual innovations* have succeeded in transcending ethnic boundaries? Why do certain peoples adopt this type of reaction, while others resort to simple syncretism?

In an attempt to answer this question we shall compare the Fang, as inventors of syncretism (for example, the *Bwiti* and other religious innovations derived from it), with the Ba-Kongo, who have been creating Messianic movements for more than forty years. In certain respects, these two approaches are comparable. Both definitely break the sacral bond between the lineage and the ancestors, which is the guarantee of the permanence, fecundity and cohesion of the group. Both involve, though in varying degree, the integration of Christianized elements within a religious framework that is either new (the Congolese churches), or has been revived (the *Bwiti*). In both these ways they display an

* Such as the *Ngol*, which appeared in the Haut-Ogooué after 1945 and spread to a large part of Gabon and the Congo.

evolutionary tendency to rid themselves of narrow particularism: they express an extension of religion by extending the organization of religious life to larger social units – the ethnic group in the case of the Fang; a historically stabilized area, the Congo, in the case of the Ba-Kongo. Here then we have a first, though *not specific*, feature of Messianic movements. As religious phenomena, they are the result of an evolution that involves the breakdown of the clan system – a system that was distinguished by its more or less self-contained nature and by the smallness of the groups whose organization and structure it determined. But this dynamism, which in a sense represents an orientation towards the universal, also show how the transition is effected from a state of society preoccupied with conformity (by its acceptance of tradition) to one in which the forces of change and the impact of history are becoming more and more effective.

These observations should help us to appreciate more clearly the differences between them. Until comparatively recently, the Fang, a warlike and exceptionally mobile people, had only established very tentative relations with the territory they occupied; the impression they made upon the land itself was slight; and they had not created a genuine 'Fang country'. With the Ba-Kongo the position is quite different. They still cherish stirring memories of the kingdom created by their forbears, a vast territory symbolized by the river Congo. At the centre of their social and cultural system is an intricate complex of relations between lineage, ancestors and land. From various points of view, the latter is the equivalent of the ancestors, just as ownership of it ensures the status of a man 'born in the clan' and his dignity as a free man. Colonization, though it did not lead to any large-scale eviction of the peasantry, nevertheless produced a sense of dispossession, and therefore of infringement of their dignity. So much so, indeed, that the Amicalist movement, with its professed aim of buying back the land belonging to the Kongo and so winning the rights of citizenship for them, was undeniably successful in the area around Brazzaville. In his *Messianisme en Afrique du Sud*, Eberhardt rightly insists upon this essential point: the Messiah is first and foremost the man who can restore the territories no longer affected by slavery.[17] Physically, the promised land is that handed down by the ancestors, and among the Ba-Kongo the function of the 'crowned chief' was to defend its integrity and to mediate between the members of the lineage and the community of ancestors. This was the model on which the Congolese churches could be built: the 'parish' took the place of the fragmented clan territories, and the modern religious leader that of the old 'crowned chief'. In this way, stabilized relationships, those that give meaning and specificity to the Ba-Kongo organization of society, are revived in a different form on the basis of the division of the country into areas that have religious sanction. *This deep attachment to the land seems to be one of the conditions conducive to the emergence of Messianism.* As opposed to the Congolese, the religious innovations of the Fang were oriented upon the outlook of the *uprooted* and *homeless* Blacks: the *Bwiti* is comparable to the syncretistic manifestations that have been studied both in the West Indies and Brazil.[18]

To take another aspect, if one accepts the concept of *guilt culture* employed by American anthropologists, it can be applied to the Kongo. Serious social disorders are attributed to one or more 'guilty men', who admit their responsibility and are prepared to sacrifice themselves in order to restore order; and in certain clearly defined circumstances public confession is also practised with the same end in view. The Mu-Kongo is therefore made acutely conscious of the fact that his 'sins' affect society, and is ready to accept techniques designed to restore normality. Christianity, long established in this part of the Congo, accentuated this tendency. A culture of this kind seems to be unusually alive to any threat of disturbance; it makes the individual keenly aware of insecurity, whether real or assumed. Thus the upheavals due to colonization and the weakening of respect for customary obligations have generalized anxiety. Everyone feels guilty, responsible for the disorders resulting from the breakdown of the old order, and threatened by everyone else;* as may be seen from the increase in sorcery. Therapies claiming to cure anxiety therefore enjoyed considerable success during this period, and the Congolese prophets were looked upon primarily as *'restorers of confidence'*. The followings they attracted – and, from the start, public confession was a condition of membership – made it possible to restore order, to establish a rough and ready distinction

* Cf. Part III, ch. II, above.

between 'good' people and 'bad', between those who had 'heard the call' and those who had not. This summary dichotomy seemed to be a way of dealing with a confused and dangerous state of affairs. It localized the ills from which society appeared to be suffering.

It is matched by the dichotomy between the Ba-Kongo and the Europeans and those groups associated with them, as may be seen from the pairs of antagonistic terms in which it finds expression: Saviour of the Black Race and Christ, oppressors and oppressed, 'orphaned children' and those who wield material power, the chosen and the damned, etc. This realization of the inferiority to which they were condemned, of being relegated to the outskirts of the new kingdom founded by the white man and exiled from that of their ancestors, takes place in the *towns*. It is there – in Thysville and Leopoldville on the left bank; in Brazza- ville on the right – that the dividing line between the two is most clearly felt. That this is a necessary condition for the emergence of Messianism is borne out by the fact that certain groups, closely related to the Ba-Kongo but protected from the main currents of modern influence by the high mountains of the Mayombe, remained immune from Messianic tendencies, whereas these move- ments grew from strength to strength in the rapidly developing town of Pointe-Noire, although it, too, was inhabited by elements ethnically and culturally related.

In his study of ancient Judaism, Max Weber showed that the combination of town life, resulting from conquest, and the fact of being a 'people of outcasts' played an important part in the development of Messianism,[19] and the same is true of the Congolese. It was in the cities and their vicinity that the Ba-Kongo were most acutely aware of their twofold exile: for it was there they found themselves pulled in two opposite directions, return to an idealized past on the one hand and, on the other, total access to a modern civilization that could provide them with the material prosperity they longed for; they were therefore confronted by a twofold impossibility. One has only to study the various forms of Negro Messianism, particularly in South Africa, to realize that this connection exists between all such movements and a situation typified by a more elaborate modern development, intensive Christianization and a profound split between dominant 'foreig- ners' and native peoples.

This dichotomous outlook is very like the attitude one finds in many folklores and in the militant ideology of popular revolt. It corresponds to the same need for protest, rejection and hope. But its *Christian form remains to be explained.* The themes provided by traditional folklore and the myths associated with ancient rituals were scarcely suitable: they called for submission and agreement, rather than for revolutionary deeds that would change the course of history. In fact, only Christianity enabled the Ba-Kongo to create an ideology; it inspired them and provided them with the intellectual tools they lacked. This is easily understood when one remembers how large a part the teaching of the missionaries played until quite recent times, and that the Scriptures were almost the only literature to which the first generation of 'literates' had access. The Ki-Kongo translation of the Bible became *the* book, the basis of their modern thinking. It provided the arguments that made social criticism effective; it enabled the Congolese to justify, in their own eyes, modes of behaviour apparently similar to those described in the Old Testament; and it revealed the revolutionary significance of the exploits of the Prophets. Thus the influence of Jewish Messianism became paramount, and Christianity was restored to its original vitality. This is also true of the sacral revolts that occurred in other parts of Black Africa: for example, speaking of the Kikuyu of Kenya, Leakey points out that their independent churches were also based upon, and justified by, texts from the Old Testament. It is not enough, however, merely to show that the phenomenon of Messianism is due to the combination of conditions just referred to; it has to be seen as a global and ambiguous response to an ambiguous situation globally perceived.

The pace of evolution resulting from colonization has not been the same in all parts of the Kongo country; a modern diversity was superimposed upon the old diversity that was due to previous migrations, to cases of isolation and local rivalry. It is understandable, therefore, that the Messianic movement should have acquired different characteristics in different places. At the periphery of the most progressive areas it seems to be more strongly influenced by traditional themes and attitudes; it remains closer to the past and clings to models inherited from the past: the 'prophet-founder' is seen as a guide, planning an escape from the present which is nevertheless accepted as a step towards the golden age. The sacral bonds are restored and the feeling of weakness overcome, with the result that the faithful feel themselves to be safe from every threat, whether material or spiritual. Relying upon ancient methods, the head of the church has restored order, but on a new basis since it extends far beyond the narrow frontiers of the clan; an order that is all the more stable and promising in that it has produced its own martyrs. In those areas where the evolution is more advanced, the Messianic movement breaks more definitively with tradition: it takes the missionary churches as its model of social organization, it seeks to identify its field of action with the legendary kingdom of Kongo, and its teachings are inspired by the Bible. It is an attempt to create a new society: a theocracy based upon a politico-religious hierarchy and a sacral organization of the land reviving the debased clan organization. The founder seeks to restore the strength of native authority by recentralizing and resacralizing it, and to this end he gathers around him a small group of militant believers. He is seen as the creator of a long-awaited kingdom, setting in motion the forces of a sacred nationalism.

These different ways of interpreting Congolese Messianism make any single and one-sided explanation of it useless, especially as the movement is affected by all the incompatibilities and contradictions inherent in a society whose structures are in process of radical transformation. It was born in the period after the First World War, when the first 'modernist' generation was coming to the fore, and its originators immediately found themselves up against some of the traditional authorities. It seeks to achieve unity, but is thwarted by the existence of still active particularisms and increasing competition for power. It is an attempt to bring Kongo society up to date, but on an exclusively religious plane, at a time when economic and political developments and modern education are 'desacralizing' large areas of society. It offers the 'elect' a means of attaining the far-off Kingdom of God – and of the ancestors who dwell there – but it also wants the kingdom to be of this world, and rich in material possessions.

Precisely for this reason, the Messianic movements of Africa have tremendous possibilities. The plane on which they exist may be essentially religious. They may serve as a refuge for those in total opposition – as was the case in the Ivory Coast after the change in the political orientation of the R.D.A.;[20] or, on the contrary, if they come under the control of a successful political movement, they may lose their militancy – as happened in the Congo with the electoral success of the Abbé Fulbert Youlou, chosen as the new symbol of unity and rebirth. At the start, however, their significance is unmistakable. They betoken the awakening of a people that sees itself as having neither past nor future, that reacts against the slurs upon its dignity. They express a passionate desire for change; and because they assert the universal nature of human dignity, they represent a step towards universality.

References

REFERENCES

PART I CHAPTER I

(1) O. Mannoni: *Psychologie de la colonisation*, Paris, 1950.
(2) L. Joubert: 'le fait colonial et ses prolongements', in *Le monde non chrétien*, 15, 1950.
(3) Cf. R. Kennedy: 'The colonial crisis and the future', in *The Science of Man in the World Crisis*, pp. 308–9.
(4) For instance, the displacements of population in the interests of the Niger Office, which were the occasion of violent polemics. See P. Herbart's pamphlet *Le chancre du Niger* (with a Preface by André Gide), Paris, 1939.
(5) E. Chancelé: 'La question coloniale', in *Critique*, No. 35, 1949.
(6) Cf. L. P. Mair: 'The Study of Culture Contact as a Practical Problem', in *Africa*, VII, 4, 1934.
(7) Cf. J. Harmand: *Domination et colonisation*, Paris, 1910, as a classical example of justification by the laws of nature.
(8) Quoted in H. Brunschwig: *La colonisation française*, Paris, 1949.
(9) *Op. cit.*, p. 265.
(10) In *The Science of Man in the World Crisis*, ed. Ralph Linton, 1945.
(11) G. Balandier: 'Aspects de l'évolution sociale chez les Fang du Gabon', in *Cah. Int. de Sociologie*, IX, 1950, p. 82.
(12) R. Montagne: 'Le bilan de l'œuvre européenne au-delá des mers', in *Peuples d'outre-mer et civilisation occidentale*, Semaines sociales de France, 1948.
(13) G. Balandier: *op. cit.*, p. 78.
(14) G. Balandier: *op. cit.*, p. 78.
(15) Cf. the polemical pamphlet by Nkwame Nkrumah: *Towards Colonial Freedom*, London, 1947.
(16) Ch.-A. Julien: 'Impérialisme économique et impérialisme colonial', in *Fin de l'ère coloniale*, p. 25.
(17) P. Leroy-Beaulieu: *De la colonisation chez les peuples modernes*, 1874; J. Ferry: Preface to *Le Tonkin et la Mère-Patrie*, 1890.
(18) Cf. A. Conant: *The Economic Basis of Imperialism*, 1898, and J. A. Hobson: *Imperialism, a Study*, 1902.
(19) See the papers by J. Guitton and P. Reuter in *Peuples d'outre-mer et civilisation occidentale*, pp. 61 and 142 notably; and more recently, the book by P. Moussa: *Les nations prolétaires*.
(20) Cf. Joseph Stalin: *Marxism and the National and Colonial Question*.
(21) R. Kennedy: *op. cit.*, pp. 309–11.
(22) As regards French Africa, see the admirable studies by the geographer Jean Dresch.

(23) Cf. particularly C. Robequain: *L'évolution économique de l'Indochine française*, Paris, 1940, and P. Gourou: *L'utilisation du sol en Indochine française* and *Les pays tropicaux*, Paris, 1948.

(24) For an all-round study of this phenomenon, see V. Liversage: *Land Tenure in the Colonies*, London, 1945.

(25) Cf. C. Robequain: *op. cit.*

(26) J. Borde: 'Le problème ethnique dans l'Union sud-africaine', in *Cahiers d'outre-mer*, No. 12, 1950.

(27) Cf. W. G. Ballinger: *Race and Economics in South Africa*, 1934.

(28) K. L. Little: 'Social Change and Social Class in the Sierra-Leone Protectorate', in *American Journal of Sociology*, 54, July 1948. It was not until recently (after 1955), and particularly since many African states became independent, that these phenomena have been studied scientifically; political sociology especially is progressing fast, thanks to the work of D. Apter, L. Fallers, T. Hodgkin, J. Coleman, J. Maquet, ourselves and various other specialists.

(29) Cf. H. G. Barnett: *Anthropology in Administration*, Evanston, 1956; and particularly, for Africa, L. P. Mair: *Studies in Applied Anthropology*, London, 1957.

(30) R. Delavignette: *Les vrais chefs de l'Empire*, Paris, 1939, a revised edition of which has been translated into English under the title: *Freedom and Authority in French West Africa*, London, 1951.

(31) G. d'Arbousier: 'Les problèmes de la culture', in *Europe*, special African number: *Afrique noire*, May-June 1949.

(32) Cf. R. Delavignette: *op. cit.*, p. 130.

(33) Cf. P. Mercier: 'Remarques sur la signification du "tribalisme" actuel en Afrique noire', in *Cah. Int. de Sociologie*, XXI, 1961.

(34) *Les colonies, passé et avenir*, see the chapter 'Colonies tropicales et sociétés plurales'.

(35) H. Laurentie: 'Notes sur une philosophie de la politique coloniale française', in *Renaissances*, special number, October 1944.

(36) J. Borde: 'Le problème ethnique dans l'Union sud-africaine', *op. cit.*, p. 320.

(37) L. Wirth: 'The Problem of Minority Groups', in *The Science of Man in the World Crisis*, pp. 347-72; and also by the same author: *The Present Position of Minorities in the United States*.

(38) *Op. cit.*, revised edition, ch. II, 'La Société coloniale'.

(39) *Op. cit.*, p. 353.

(40) Cf. A. Siegfried: *Afrique du Sud*, Paris, 1949, p. 75. Also *Handbook on Race Relations in South Africa*, ed. E. Hellmann, 1949; and J. Borde: *op. cit.*, pp. 339-40.

(41) Cf. R. Maunier: *Sociologie coloniale*, pp. 19, 30, 33.

(42) J. R. Ayouné: 'Occidentalisme et africanisme', in *Renaissances*, special number, October 1944, p. 204.

(43) Cf. L. Aujoulat: 'Elites et masses et pays d'outre-mer', in *Peuples d'outre-mer et civilisation occidentale*, *op. cit.*, pp. 233-72.

(44) Memorandum XV, International Institute of African Languages and Cultures, 1938.

(45) M. Gluckman: 'Malinowski's Functional Analysis of Social Change', in *Africa*, XVII, 2, April 1947, pp. 103-21.

(46) *The Dynamics of Culture Change*, New Haven, 1945, VIII, pp. 84-5.

(47) Cf. G. Balandier: *Sociologie des Brazzavilles noires*, Paris, 1955, ch. IV.

(48) *Op. cit.*, p. 23.

(49) Cf. the concluding pages of *The Dynamics of Culture Change*, pp. 160-62.

(50) Cf. M. Gluckman: 'Tribalism in Modern British Central Africa', in *Cah. Et. africaines.*, I, 1960.
(51) Cf. *The Dynamics of Culture Change*, ch. VII, p. 73 ff.
(52) B. Malinowski: *A Scientific Theory of Culture*, Chapel Hill, 1944.
(53) *The Dynamics of Culture Change*, p. 65.
(54) *Op. cit.*, ch. VI, p. 64 ff.
(55) Cf. *La vocation actuelle de la sociologie*, Paris, 1950, pp. 98–108.
(56) Cf. L. Achille: *op. cit.*, pp. 211–15.
(57) At a conference on Ethnography and Colonialism, M. Leiris contributed a closely argued paper on this question, which was subsequently published in *Les temps modernes*.
(58) Cf. R. Bastide: *Sociologie et psychanalyse*, ch. XI: 'Le heurt des races, des civilisations et la psychanalyse', Paris, 1950.
(59) O. Mannoni: *op. cit.*, ch. II: 'La situation coloniale et le racisme'.
(60) Cf. R. Bastide: *op. cit.*, and 'Interpénétration des civilisations et psychologie des peuples', in *Revue de psychologie des peuples*, No. 3, 1950.
(61) H. de Saussure: *Psychologie de la colonisation française dans ses rapports avec les sociétés indigènes*, Paris, 1899.
(62) G. Hardy: 'La psychologie des populations coloniales', in *Revue de psychologie des peuples*, No. 3, July 1947.
(63) A. Irving Hallowell: 'Sociological Aspects of Acculturation', in *The Science of Man in the World Crisis*, ed. R. Linton.
(64) E. Stonequist: *The Marginal Man*, New York, 1937.
(65) F. Fanon: *L'an V de la Révolution algérienne*, Paris, 1959.
(66) F. Fanon: *Les damnés de la terre*, Paris, 1961; translated into English under the title *The Wretched of the Earth*, Penguin, 1967.
(67) Cf. P. Worsley: *The Trumpet Shall Sound*, London, 1957.
(68) Manchester, 1954.
(69) For a short review of works by English authors see P. Worsley: 'The Analysis of Rebellion and Revolution in Modern British Social Anthropology', *Science and Society*, XXV, I, 1961.
(70) Cf. M. Gluckman: 'Analysis of a Social Situation in Modern Zululand', in *Bantu Studies*, XIV, 1940. Also his controversy with Malinowski on the subject in *The Dynamics of Culture Change*, p. 14 ff.
(71) Cf. F. M. Keesing: 'Applied Anthropology in Colonial Administration', in *op. cit.*, ed. R. Linton.
(72) V. W. Turner: *Schism and Continuity in an African Society*, Manchester, 1957.
(73) H. Lefebvre: 'Perspectives de la sociologie rurale', in *Cah. Int. de Sociologie*, XIV, Paris, 1953.
(74) J.-P. Sartre: 'Questions de méthode', in *Les temps modernes*, 139, Paris, 1957.
(75) F. Boas: 'The Method of Ethnology', in *American Anthropologist*, 22, 1920.

PART I CHAPTER II

(1) J. Weulersee: 'L'Afrique noire', in *L'Afrique centrale française*, Paris, 1934, p. 241.
(2) Cf. H. Labouret: *Histoire des Noirs d'Afrique*, Paris, 1946.
(3) Gaston Martin: *Histoire de l'esclavage dans les colonies françaises*, 'Colonies et Empires', Paris, 1948, pp. 52–61.
(4) For an account of the Kongo based upon the most up-to-date sources see

G. Balandier, *Daily Life in the Kingdom of the Kongo*, translated by Helen Weaver, London, 1968.

(5) Cf. J. Van Wing: *Études bakongo, Histoire et sociologie*, Brussels, 1921.

(6) Van Wing: *op. cit.*, pp. 20-4. He relies mainly on O. Dapper: *Nauwkeurige beschrijving der Afrikaansche Gewesten*, Amsterdam, 1676; and Paiva Manson: *Historia da Congo*, Documentos, Lisbon, 1877.

(7) The best recent works on the history of the Kongo are those by J. Cuvelier: *L'ancien royaume de Congo*, Brussels, 1946; and J. Cuvelier and L. Jadin: *L'ancien Congo d'après les archives romaines*, Brussels, 1954.

(8) For this and other quotations from Van Wing in this paragraph, see *op. cit.*, ch. I.

(9) *Op. cit.*, p. 36. The whole of chapter II is a detailed study of the activities of the Congolese missions up to the beginning of the colonial drive in the nineteenth century.

(10) For the Loango missions, see Proyart: *Histoire de Loango, Cacongo et autres royaumes d'Afrique*, 2 vols., Paris, 1776; and particularly *Documents sur une mission française au Kakongo*, Brussels, 1953.

(11) Antonio Cavazzi: *Istorica descrizzione degli tre regni Congo, Angola e Matamba*, Bologna, 1687.

(12) *Op. cit.*, p. 37.

(13) *Ibid.*, pp. 20-73 *passim*.

(14) Tata Nsiesie: '*Notes sur les Christs et statues de l'Ancien Congo*', in *Brousse*, No. 3, 1939, p. 34.

(15) H. Cuvillier-Fleury: *La mise en valeur du Congo français*, Paris, 1904, p. 99.

(16) Annual Report for the Moyen-Congo, 1931.

(17) *Ibid.*

(18) Cf. G. Balandier, *Sociologie des Brazzavilles noires*, ch. I.

(19) Cf. G. Balandier, *Les villages gabonais*, p. 44.

(20) See G. Balandier, *Sociologie des Brazzavilles noires*.

(21) See the Annual Reports for the Moyen-Congo for 1932, 1933 and 1934.

(22) See the remarkable study by the P. R. Bureau on the 'Sociology of Conversion in Southern Cameroun', 1962.

(23) See the Annual Reports of the Inspector-General of Labour for 1947 and 1949, which do not include domestic servants.

PART II CHAPTER I

(1) A. Fourneau: *Au Vieux Congo*, published by the Comité de l'Afrique française, 1932, pp. 41-2.

(2) Cf. I. Dugast: *Inventaire ethnique du Sud-Cameroun*, I.F.A.N., Douala, 1949; see also *Bull. Soc. Et. camerounaises*, 21-2, 1948, 'Esquisse ethnologique pour servir à l'étude des principales tribus du Cameroun français. . . .'

(3) E. Trezenem: 'Notes ethnographiques sur les tribus Fan du Moyen-Ogooué', in *Journ. Soc. des Africanistes*, vol. VI, I, 1936

(4) *Rapport de la Commission d'Enquête historique*, Libreveille, 1949.

(5) Gabon archives: 'Rapports du Poste de Setté-Cama.'

(6) Dugast: *op. cit.*; and for an overall view: 'Essai sur le peuplement du Cameroun', in *Bull. Soc. Et. camerounaises*, 21-2, 1948

(7) J. Despois: 'Les genres de vie des populations de la forêt dans le Cameroun oriental', in *Annales de géographie*, 297, 1946.

(8) Cf. Trezenem: *op. cit.*

(9) A relationship confirmed by L. Homburger in *Les langues négro-africaines*, Paris, 1941, p. 35.

(10) Captain Maignan: 'Etudes sur le pays pahouin' (1912) in *Bull. Soc. Rech. congolaises*, 14, 1931; and L. Mba: 'Essai de droit coutumier pahouin', in *Bull. Soc. Rech. congolaises*, 25, June 1938.

(11) G. Tessmann: *Die Pangwe*, 2 vols., Berlin, 1913; I. Dugast: *Inventaire ethnique* ..., section devoted to the Pahouin.

(12) H. Trilles: *Le totémisme chez les Fán*, Bibliothèque Anthropos, vol. I, 4, 1912, p. 12.

(13) Captain Maignan: *op. cit.*

(14) *Ibid.*

(15) Captain Périquet: *Mission d'étude du chemin de fer du Nord*, 1910–11, Brazzaville archives.

(16) *Tradition des Ožip*, official archives of Oyem.

(17) Tessmann: *op. cit.*

(18) Captain Curault, 'Monographie du secteur de N'Djolé au Gabon', in *Rev. des troupes colon.*, 1908.

(19) *Tradition des Yénžòk*, official archives of Ebolowa, French Cameroun.

(20) Table of 'Tribes and sub-tribes' drawn up by the Fang of southern Gabon for the Commission for Historical Research of Libreville.

(21) L. Martrou: 'La langue fan et ses dialectes', in *Journ. Soc. des Africanistes*, VI, 2, 1936.

(22) L. Martrou: *op. cit.*; Captain Maignan: *op. cit.*; and L. Mba: *op. cit.*

(23) General Le Dentu: *Démographie de l'A. E. F.*, 1937; archives of the Brazzaville Health Service. For a more recent demographical and medical survey, but relating only to the Woleu-Ntem, see H. Estève: *Enquête démographique en pays fang, district d'Oyem*, Gabon, 1952–5.

(24) G. Bruel: *Notes géographiques sur le bassin de l'Ogooué*, Paris, 1911.

(25) Captain Périquet: *Mission d'étude du chemin de fer du Nord*, Brazzaville archives.

(26) G. Sautter: 'Essai sur le peuplement et l'habitat au Woleu-Ntem', *Cah. d'outre-mer*, 14, April-June, 1951.

(27) Cf. G. Sautter: *op. cit.*

(28) Population Commission. Minutes of the session of August 8, 1946.

(29) From a report by a leading member of the Yémödâg tribe, Mitzik, 1949.

(30) A study carried out with the help of material compiled particularly from among the Fang in the Woleu-Ntem, and especially in the Oyem region where the vitality of the Fang is most noticeable.

(31) H. Trilles: *Le totémisme chez les Fán*, notes to pp. 109, 111 and 180.

(32) The latter are carefully noted by Trilles, Largeau and especially Tessmann (*op. cit.*).

(33) *Légende des Yévò*, Ebolowa archives.

(34) H. Trilles: *op. cit.*, p. 130.

(35) *Ibid.*, p. 113.

(36) A. Van Gennep: *L'état actuel du problème totémique*, Paris, 1920, p. 35.

(37) Cf. L. Martrou: *Lexique fân-français*, Paris. No date.

(38) See particularly E. Trezenem: 'Notes ethnographiques sur les tribus Fan du Moyen-Ogooué,' in *op. cit.*

(39) H. Trilles: *op. cit.*, p. 88.

(40) Cf. M. Bertaut: *Le droit coutumier des Boulous*, the chapter on 'Successions'; and L. Mba: *op. cit.*, p. 39.

(41) L. Martrou: *Lexique fân-français*.

(42) Captain Curault: 'Monographie du secteur de N'Djolé au Gabon', in *Rev. des troupes colon.*, 68, February 1908.
(43) Minutes of the meeting of twenty-five Yémisèm villages at Afenané, July 12–19, 1948, Oyem archives.
(44) Cf. L. Mba: *op. cit.*, pp. 32 and 41.
(45) H. Trilles: 'Proverbes, légendes et contes Fang', in *Bull. Soc. neuchâteloise de Géographie*, 1905, pp. 49–295.
(46) A. Cureau: *op. cit.*, p. 118.
(47) L. Mba: *op. cit.*, p. 29.
(48) R. Bastide: *Sociologie et psychanalyse*, Bibl. de Sociologie contemporaine, Paris, 1950.
(49) E. Trezenem: 'Notes ethnographiques', in *op. cit.*, p. 87.
(50) L. Mba: *op. cit.*, p. 29; and V. Largeau: *Encyclopédia pahouine*, the article on 'Adultery': 'A husband is always free to lend his wife in return for some payment.'
(51) Cf. R. Bastide: *op. cit.*, pp. 160–61.
(52) Cf. E. Trezenem: *op. cit.*, p. 89.
(53) Cf. L. Mba: *op. cit.*: 'In the old days, the opinions of the interested parties were of little importance. The proposal was made by the head of one family to the head of the other.'
(54) V. Largeau: *op. cit.*: the article on 'Marriage'.
(55) M. Leenhardt: 'Cérémonie et sceau du mariage', in *Le monde non chrétien*, 15, 1950.
(56) Cf. François Méyé: 'Pour la jeunesse fang', in *Journal A. E. F.*, 25, July 1948.
(57) On the importance of these acts of reciprocity and the part they play in so-called primitive societies, see the remarkable work by C. Lévi-Strauss: *The Elementary Structure of Kinship*, Eng. trans., London, 1968.
(58) A. Fourneau: *op. cit.*, p. 77.
(59) A. Cureau: *op. cit.*, p. 119.
(60) Cf. V. Largeau: *op. cit.*, the article 'Femme'.
(61) L. Mba: *op. cit.*, p. 21.
(62) Cf. L. Mba: *op. cit.*, p. 17.
(63) *Op. cit.*, the article on 'Incest'.
(64) Libreville archives for 1905.
(65) V. Largeau: *op. cit.*, the article on the 'Village'.
(66) L. Martrou: 'Le nomadisme des "Fangs" ', in *Revue de géographie*, III, 1909.
(67) *Ibid.*
(68) J. Brunhes: *Human Geography*, abridged edition, London, 1952, p. 156.
(69) G. Sautter: 'Les paysans noirs du Gabon septentrional', *op. cit.*, pp. 126–8, 158.
(70) Cf. M. Bertaut: *op. cit.*, the chapter on 'Les biens'.
(71) Cf. the legends quoted by L. Mba. *op. cit.*, and V. Largeau *op. cit.*
(72) A. Cureau: *op. cit.*, p. 294.
(73) F. Grébert: *Au Gabon*, Paris, 1922.
(74) Quoted by G. Sautter: *op. cit.*, p. 124.
(75) *Travels in West Africa*, p. 154.
(76) *Op. cit.*, p. 332.
(77) *Ibid.*, p. 326.
(78) Minutes of the fifth session.
(79) Customs defining the powers of the chiefs and their appointment (Political Report from the Djouah, 1938).
(80) L. Mba: *op. cit.*, p. 12.
(81) Le Testu: 'Le N'gwéna, in *Bull. Soc. Rech. congolaises*, XII, 1930.

(82) M. Briault: *Sur les pistes de l'A. E. F.*, 1948, pp. 37–8, 42–3.

(83) The last part of 'Essai de droit coutumier pahouin', in *Rapport de la Commission d'Enquête historique*, Libreville, 1949.

(84) *Tradition des Yénżòk*, Ebolowa archives, Cameroun.

(85) E. Trezenem: *op. cit.*, III: *Le biéri*, pp. 74–6.

(86) H. Trilles: *op. cit.*, p. 62.; Captain Maignan: *op. cit.*; Lieutenant Poupard: 'Le fetichisme et la barbarie au Congo', in *Renseignements coloniaux*, March 1908. Especially L.-C. Leroux: 'Etude sur le Ngil', in *Bull. Soc. Rech. congolaises*, 6, 1925.

(87) L.-C. Leroux: *op. cit.*

(88) Cf. the descriptions, given in articles by Leroux, *op. cit.*, and Poupard, *op. cit.*

(89) Cf. A. Maclatchy: 'Organisation sociale des populations de la région de Mimongo', in *Bull. Inst. Et. centrafricaines*, I, 1, 1945.

(90) Cf. E. Trezenem: *op. cit.*, p. 79.

(91) L. Martrou: 'Les "Eki" des Mfang', in *Anthropos*, I, 1906.

(92) Cf. H. Lavignotte: *L'évur*, Société des Missions évangéliques, 1947; E. Trezenem: *op. cit*, II: *L'évur*, pp. 68–74; M. Briault: *op. cit.*; Captain Maignan, *op. cit.*

(93) E. Trezenem: *op. cit.*, p. 72.

(94) See the analysis of Dinka sorcery by the English anthropologist, G. Lienhardt: 'Some Notions of Witchcraft among the Dinka', in *Africa*, XXI, 4, October, 1951.

(95) The differentiating function of magic is discussed by G. Davy in *La foi jurée*, 1922, and by G. Gurvitch in *La vocation actuelle de la sociologie*, ch. VII, where he also refers to the changes in social organization, 'the margin of freedom' that arises from disputes between the clan and the magic brotherhoods: see particularly, pp. 412, 436, 503, 523–4.

(96) See H. Trilles: 'The Legend of the Nsas', in 'Proverbes, légendes et contes fang', *op. cit.*

(97) H. Trilles: *op. cit.*, p. 109n.

(98) *Op. cit.*, p. 89.

(99) *Cahiers de Daniel Ngéma Ondo.*

(100) Cf. C. Lévi-Strauss: *The Elementary Structure of Kinship.*

(101) Cf. L. Mba: *op. cit.*, p. 35, for the actual words of the curse.

(102) Unpublished papers by Abbé A. Walker, a native of Bas-Gabon whose knowledge of local ethnology is profound.

(103) P. du Chaillu: *op. cit.*, p. 296.

(104) Abbé A. Walker, unpublished notes.

(105) Libreville archives, 1909.

(106) L. Mba: *op. cit.*

(107) L. Martrou: 'Les "Ekis" des Mfang', *op. cit.*

(108) V. Largeau: *op. cit.*, the article on 'Prohibitions'.

(109) Cf. M. Briault: *op. cit.*, pp. 183–4.

(110) M. Briault: *op. cit.*, p. 183 ff.

(111) 'Les *E-Tchi*', an unpublished paper attached to the *Rapport de la Commission d'Enquête historique.*

(112) L. Martrou: 'Les "Ekis" des Mfang', *op. cit.*

(113) *Op. cit.* pp. 70–71.

(114) *Op. cit.*, the article on 'Education'.

(115) *Op. cit.*; particularly 'Blacks and Whites' and 'The Legend of the Nsas'.

(116) *Cahier des réunions*, the Yémisèm of Oyem.

(117) *Explorations and Adventures in Equatorial Africa*, London, 1861, pp. 36 and 48.

17

(118) *Op. cit.*, pp. 294–5.
(119) Annual Report for 1907, Gabon archives.
(120) *Op. cit.*, the article on 'Education'.
(121) *Op. cit.*, 'Légende du Nsas'.

PART II CHAPTER II

(1) For the Catholic missionary movement, see Sister Marie-Germaine: *Le Christ au Gabon*, Louvain, 1931.
(2) Report for the Ngounié, 1903, in which there is a description of the trial of an agent who had killed 'several natives' and burnt down 'one or two huts'.
(3) Annual Report, 1907: charges against the C.F.C.O. Company.
(4) *Le Gabon*, Agence des Colonies, 1948.
(5) Sister Marie-Germaine: *op. cit.*
(6) Quoted from the report of M. Guibet in the minutes of the session of March 7, 1918.
(7) G. Le Testu: *Rapport sur le Woleu-Ntem*, no date, quoted by G. Sautter in 'Les paysans noirs du Gabon septentrional', *op. cit.*, p. 132.
(8) *Ibid.*, p. 132.
(9) The Commission on Population, August 1946: Maclatchy report.
(10) Cf. the preceding chapter: 'The demographic situation of the Fang'.
(11) Facts obtained from G. Sautter, *op. cit.*, and local political reports.
(12) A document produced by the Commission for the Study of Marriage and the Family.
(13) Report by General Le Dentu.
(14) G. Le Testu: *Rapport de tournée en Guinée espagnole*, 1933.
(15) Report for the Woleu-Ntem, 1933, third quarter.
(16) Report for the Woleu-Ntem, 1934, third quarter.
(17) Report for the Woleu-Ntem, 1942, second quarter.
(18) Political Report for the Woleu-Ntem, 1937, first quarter. 'Many villages consist of natives belonging to tribes that have no connection with one another, mainly in the Mitzik and Minvoul sub-divisions.'
(19) P. du Chaillu: *Explorations and Adventures in Equatorial Africa*, p. 86.
(20) Curault: 'Monographie du secteur de N'Djole au Gabon', *op. cit.*
(21) *Travels in West Africa*, pp. 262ff., 229ff.
(22) 'Marriage among the M'Pongoué and the M'Fan', from a letter dated January 3, 1918.
(23) Report of a tour of inspection made by M. Soalhat, Inspector of Administrative Affairs.
(24) Figures taken from the *Bulletin d'informations économiques et sociales*, A.E.F., No. 20, February 1950.
(25) 'Les paysans noirs du Gabon septentrional', in *op. cit.*, pp. 146–56.
(26) Cf. L. Martrou: 'Le nomadisme des "Fangs" ', in *op. cit.*
(27) Report from Botika in the Libreville region, 1905.
(28) See 'Visage africain d'une coutume indienne et mélanésienne', by C. Zoll' Owanbe, in *Bull. Soc. Et. camerounaises*, 19–20, 1947; and J. Guilbot: 'Le bilaba', in *Journ. Soc des Africanistes*, XXI, No. II, 1951.
(29) See the passages devoted to the *Bilaba* in section 4 of the Conclusion of the present work: 'Total social phenomena and social dynamics'.
(30) F. Meyé: 'Pour la jeunesse fang: La femme africaine', *op. cit.*
(31) Political Report for the Djouah, 1938, first quarter.

(32) Annual Report for Gabon, 1922.

(33) Report for the Woleu-Ntem, 1934.

(34) Report for the Woleu-Ntem, 1929, third quarter; Report for the Ogooué-Maritime, 1935, third quarter.

(35) Letter from the Governor of Gabon to the President of the Commission, January 3, 1918; and minutes of the session held on March 7, 1918.

(36) *Projet d'arrêté réglementant le mariage indigène en pays fang*, December 1936.

(37) *Le canton Ndou-Libi (subdivision de Sangmélima)*, an unpublished paper by J.-M. Soupault, 1948, in the Ebolowa archives.

(38) See the investigation by Le Dentu, 1938.

(39) F. Meyé: 'La femme africaine', in *op. cit.*

(40) F. Grébert: 'La famille pahouine en 1931', in *Africa*, V, 2, 1932.

(41) *Ibid.*

(42) Cf. L. Mba: *op. cit.*; and E. Trezenem: *op. cit.*

(43) For this expression, cf. C. Lévi-Strauss: *The Elementary Structure of Kinship*, ch. XV.

(44) Cf. G. Balandier: 'Actualité du problème de la dot en Afrique noire', in *Le monde non chrétien*, January–March 1952.

(45) Minutes of the session of August 8, 1946.

(46) Letter from the Governor-General to the Governor of Gabon, April 1947.

(47) Cf. a pamphlet published by the Gabon Bureau des Affaires politiques et sociales.

(48) Cf. *Vœux*, II, 4: 'That a struggle should be instituted against the *Bwiti* cult'.

(49) Report by the Secretary of the Pahouin Congress.

(50) Circular letter to the chiefs of the region, commenting on the proposals of the Pahouin Congress.

(51) Political Report for the Djouah, 1938, first quarter; and Political Report for the Woleu-Ntem, 1937, first quarter.

(52) Introductory Report to the Representative Council of the Project for the Reform of the Chieftainships, 1948.

(53) Annual Report for Gabon, 1933.

(54) Report of a tour of inspection of the Oyem district, January 1948.

(55) Annual Report for the Woleu-Ntem, 1934.

(56) Political Report for the Oyem District, 1947.

(57) Cf. G. Balandier: 'L'utopie de Benoît Ogooué Iquaqua', in *Les temps modernes*, 84–5, 1952.

(58) See, for example, the Report for the Ogooué-Ivindo, 1944, first quarter.

(59) Cf. G. Balandier and J.-C. Pauvert: *Les villages gabonais*, memorandum of the Institut d'Etudes Centrafricaines, 5, 1952.

(60) Report for the Estuary District, 1937, second quarter. In fact, the writer was concerned about 'the state of mind of the small native planters who felt that they had risen in the social scale'.

(61) Quoted from the meeting book of a dignitary of the Yémisèm of Oyem.

(62) See F. Grébert: 'Arts en voie de disparition au Gabon', in *Africa*, VII, 1, 1934; also G. Balandier: 'Les conditions sociologiques de l'art noir', in *Présence africaine*, 10–11, 1951, a special number on *L'art nègre*, edited by G. Balandier and J. Howlett. Whereas Mary Kingsley, *op. cit.*, refers to a flourishing class of craftsmen in the last century.

(63) Report of an official visit to the canton of Ndou-Libi.

(64) We are extremely grateful to Abbé Walker, not only for the information he gave us personally, but also for allowing us access to his unpublished papers,

Le Bouiti and *Explication de quelques termes de sorcellerie gabonaise.* See also: '*Le Bouiti*', in *Bull. Soc. Rech. congolaises*, 4, 1924.

(65) E.g. Abbé Walker's papers, facts contained in Father Trilles's book, and some notes by Mgr Tardy quoted in part by M. Briault: *Sur les pistes de l'A.E.F.*

(66) du Chaillu: *op. cit.*, pp. 134 and 331ff.

(67) Unpublished documents, collected by the Commission for Historical Research, Libreville, 1949.

(68) A. Maclatchy: 'L'organisation sociale des populations de la région de Mimongo', in *Bull. Inst. Et. centrafricaines*, I, 1, 1945.

(69) See the works of Curault and Maignan cited in the Bibliography. In their *Rites et croyances*, Paris, 1962, Walker and Sillans emphasize the part played in spreading the cult by the Fang traders belonging to the Haut-Ogooué Company.

(70) Unpublished notes.

(71) Cf. E. Trezenem: 'Notes ethnographiques sur les tribus fang du Moyen-Ogooué', in *op. cit.*, p. 78.

(72) These facts are taken from Abbé Walker's study quoted above.

(73) Cf. A. R. Walker: *Dictionnaire mpongwé-français.*

(74) One of our students, a Galwa by birth, informed us of the recent effects of Islam upon certain *Bwiti*.

(75) The work by Walker and Sillans, *op. cit.*, scarcely mentions the Fang *Bwiti*, which they consider to be unauthentic. J. W. Fernandez's work has not yet been published.

(76) E. Trezenem: *op. cit.*

(77) H. Trilles: *Le totémisme chez les Fân, op. cit.*

(78) See also G. Balandier: *Ambiguous Africa*, Eng. trans., London, 1966, pp. 218–23, for certain further considerations.

(79) Letter from the Governor of Gabon to the Governor-General, Brazzaville, April 3, 1938.

(80) Report for Gabon, 1922, ch. II: 'Situation politique'.

(81) Report from the Governor of Gabon, January 1938.

(82) Statutes of the Ntem-Kribi Tribal Union, Ebolowa archives (Ebolowa being the capital of the Ntem region).

(83) Cf. the *Book of Samuel*, II, 11.

(84) Influences that are not only characteristic of clan literature. See, for example, P. Bekale: 'Du mal ou de la sorcellerie noire', in *Cah. Et. africaines*, 6, 1961.

(85) Statutes of the Yémvâg of Booué.

(86) Report of a tour of inspection, Ndou-Libi canton (Sangmélima).

(87) A. Métraux: *L'homme et la terre dans la vallée de Marbial* (*Haiti*), UNESCO, 1951.

(88) Cf. Annual Report for the Dagana Sub-division, 1944. Also a short paper in the journal *Farm and Forest*, 1945, Ibadan, Nigeria.

(89) Cf. M. Bertaut: *op. cit.*

(90) Translated from a report drawn up by the Spanish authorities at Ebebeyin (Spanish Guinea), December 1948.

(91) See J.-H. Aubane: *Renaissance gabonaise*, Brazzaville, 1947; and also G. Balandier and J.-C. Pauvert: *Villages gabonais*, published by the Institut d'Etudes Centrafricaines, Montpellier, 1952.

(92) Cf. G. Balandier and J.-C. Pauvert: *op. cit.*

PART II CHAPTER III

(1) Report by the Inspector of Administrative Affairs, January 4, 1937.
(2) Quoted from the meeting book of a Yémisèm president in the Oyem district.
(3) Documents relating to a judicial inquiry at Libreville tend to prove this.
(4) Minute book of the Yémisèm tribe, 1948.
(5) Cf. G. Perrault: 'Les Fang du pays Yaoundé', in *op. cit.*, p. 332.
(6) For further details, see the Annual Reports for the Ntem Region from 1947 onwards.
(7) Minutes of the meeting of twenty-five Yémisèm villages at Afenané, July 12–19, 1948, Oyem archives.
(8) See the admirable work by R. Bastide: *Les religions africaines au Brésil*, Paris, 1960, particularly p. 334ff.
(9) S. Reinach: 'L'origine des prières pour les morts', in *Cultes, mythes, religions*, Paris, 1905, vol. I. 'Pagans prayed to the dead, whereas Christians prayed for the dead.'
(10) A phenomenon that is even more marked in an urban environment; see G. Balandier: *Sociologie des Brazzavilles noires*.
(11) Cf. G. Balandier: *Les villages gabonais*, ch. V.
(12) See above, Part II, ch. I, section 5; as well as Father Trilles's collection of 'Proverbes, légendes et contes fang'.
(13) Cf. Part II, ch. II, section 2, above.

PART III CHAPTER I

(1) Documents relating to the Boko district, from the historical inquiry we made for the Ministry of Local Government of French Equatorial Africa.
(2) J. Van Wing (S. J.): *Etudes bakongo: Histoire et sociologie*, Brussels, 1921. As we shall be quoting frequently from this work, it will be referred to henceforth as *Et. Bk.*
(3) F. Rouget: *L'expansion coloniale au Congo français*, Paris, 1906.
(4) 'Projet de chefferies', an unpublished study, Boko sub-division November 1937.
(5) As well as more recent monographs: K. Laman: *The Kongo*, vol. I, 1953, vol. II, 1957; and M. Soret: *Les Kongo nord-occidentaux*, 1959.
(6) All our field work was carried out among the Ba-Lali and Ba-Sundi of Boko, Mayama-Pangala and Kinkala. The *Ba-Kongo* group was studied in less detail in view of the considerable number of works devoted to its homologues in what was once Belgian territory.
(7) *Et. Bk.*, p. 118ff.
(8) *Ibid.*, pp. 124–5.
(9) 'Projet de chefferies', *op. cit.*
(10) *Et. Bk.*, p. 127 ff.
(11) Cf. 'Some Types of Family Structure amongst the Central Bantu', in *African Systems of Kinship and Marriage*, ed. A. R. Radcliffe-Brown and Daryll Forde, London, 1950.
(12) *Et. Bk.*, p. 131.
(13) *Ibid.*, p. 135.
(14) *Ibid.*, p. 137.

(15) For example, among the Ba-Pounou of Gabon, cf. G. Balandier: *Les villages gabonais*, Brazzaville, 1952.

(16) *Et. Bk.*, p. 133.

(17) V. Mertens: 'Détermination des relations de famille chez les Bakongo', in *Zaïre*, III, 1, 1949.

(18) P. Bonnefond and J. Lombard: 'Notes sur les coutumes lari', in *Bull. Inst. Et. centrafricaines*, II, 2, 1946.

(19) C. Lévi-Strauss: *The Elementary Structure of Kinship*.

(20) *Op. cit.*, p. 246.

(21) E. Torday: *Causeries congolaises*, 1925, p. 103.

(22) *Et. Bk.*, p. 31.

(23) Map accompanying the report by the chief of the Bas-Congo Region, 1934, Brazzaville archives.

(24) Cf. V. Mertens: 'Le mariage chez les Bambata (Bakongo) et ses leçons sociales', in *Zaïre*, II, 10, 1948.

(25) P. Bonnefond and J. Lombard: *op. cit.*

(26) N. de Cleene writes, with reference to the Ba-Yumbé: 'Marriage comes to an end, kinship does not.' See his article 'La famille dans l'organisation sociale du Mayombe', in *Africa*, X, 1, 1937.

(27) It is not possible for us here to pursue a question which has already been dealt with by the authors referred to, particularly Van Wing and Mertens. Readers should consult their monographs.

(28) Cf. *Et. Bk.*, ch. V; and particularly the detailed study by J. Mertens: *Les chefs couronnés chez les Bakongo orientaux: Etude de régime successoral*, Mém. Inst. Roy. Col. Belge, XI, 1, 1942.

(29) Many of these were recorded by H. Pepper, musicologist at the Institut d'Etudes Centrafricaines, and translations of them will be found in a short, unpublished study: *Chants des 'Mfoumou Mpou'*, I.E.C., 1951.

(30) Cf. de Cleene: 'Les chefs indigènes au Mayombe', in *Africa*, VIII, 1, 1935.

(31) See examples in H. Pepper: *op. cit.*

(32) *Et. Bk.*, p. 146.

(33) For a description of the procedure adopted, see the remarkable work of J. Malonga: *La légende de M'Pfoumou Ma Mazono*, 1954, p. 55 ff.

(34) Cf. J. Mertens: 'La juridiction indigène chez les Bakongo orientaux', in *Kongo-Overzee*, XII–XIII to XVII inclusive, 1946–7 to 1951 – a careful and well-documented study, though sometimes open to criticism on account of its implied philosophy.

(35) *Ibid.*

(36) E. de Jonghe: *Les sociétés secrètes au Congo belge*, Brussels, 1907.

(37) J. Van Wing: *Etudes bakongo*, II: *Religion et magie*, Brussels, 1938.

(38) *Ibid.*, ch. VI, devoted to the *Kimpasi* society.

(39) *Et. Bk.*, pp. viii–ix.

(40) *Op. cit.*, pp. 147–51.

(41) Cf. G. Balandier: *Sociologie des Brazzavilles noires*, ch. IV.

(42) Cf. E. Torday: 'Dualism in Western Bantu Religion', in *Journ. Roy. Anthr. Inst.*, LVIII, 1933, pp. 225–45.

(43) *Et. Bk.*, p. 228.

(44) For instance, M. le Bourhuis: 'Du matriarcat dans le Niari-Ogooué', in *Bull. Soc. Rech. conqolaises*, 21, 1935.

(45) *Et. Bk.*, p. 231.

(46) *Ibid.*, pp. 263–311.

(47) Placide Tempels: *La philosophie bantoue*, Elizabethville, 1945, p. 42.

(48) Van Wing: '*Nzo longo* ou les rites de la puberté chez les Bakongo', in *Congo*, I and II, December 1920.

(49) J. Mertens: *op. cit.*, p. 205.

(50) *Et. Bk.*, pp. 286–7.

(51) G. Sautter: 'Economie du pays bacongo', in *op. cit.*; and by the same author: 'Une économie indigène progressive: les Bacongo du district de Boko (Moyen-Congo)', in *Bull. Assoc. Géogr. français*, March–April 1951.

(52) Annual Report for the Moyen-Congo, 1916, under the heading: 'Marchés at courants commerciaux'.

(53) *Et. Bk.*, p. 183, n. 1.

(54) P. Huvelin: *Essai historique sur le droit des marchés et des foires*, Paris, 1897, p. 346.

(55) This technique is described by H. Nicolai in *Luozi*, Brussels, 1961, I, ch. IV. He points out that the domesticated Kongo countryside 'is real "country" in the European sense of the word'.

PART III   CHAPTER II

(1) G. Sautter: 'Aperçu sur les villes africaines du Moyen-Congo', in *op. cit.*

(2) See the detailed study by R. Devauges: *Le chômage à Brazzaville, étude sociologique*, Paris, 1959.

(3) Annual Report for the Ba-Kongo Region, 1917, under the heading 'Mouvement commercial et industriel'.

(4) According to G. Sautter's figures in *Economie du pays bacongo*.

(5) *Ibid.*

(6) Cf. G. Balandier: 'Evolution de la Société et de l'Homme', in *Afrique équatoriale française*, vol. IX of the *Encylopédie française de l'Afrique*.

(7) *Et. Bk.*, pp. 74–6 and 110–13. See also Part I, ch. III above.

(8) For some years past it has been reinforced by the publication of a paper, *La semaine africaine*, which is the best source of information available to the people of the Congo (Brazzaville).

(9) Note entitled 'Les Balalis et l'enseignement primaire', February 1934.

(10) Quoted from a report dated March 1945.

(11) Report for the District of Mayama, September 1949.

(12) Annual Report for the Djoué Region, 1917.

(13) See, for example, the Annual Report for the Stanley Pool Region, 1935: 'Throughout the year the policy of destroying all encampments has been consistently pursued.'

(14) Annual Report for the Moyen-Congo, 1932.

(15) Annual Report for the Stanley Pool Region, 1935.

(16) G. Hubschwerlin: 'Le régime foncier indigène dans la région de Boko', in *Bull. Soc. Rech. congolaises*, 24, 1937.

(17) For example, see G. Hubschwerlin: *op. cit.*

(18) Cf. the 'church' of Emmanuel Ng., in the following chapter.

(19) Annual Report for the Ba-Kongo Region, 1917. For further detailed information, see the Annual Report for the Moyen-Congo, 1916.

(20) J. Chaumeton: *La parenté et la propriété foncière chez les Balali-Bassoundi*, unpublished, Institut d'Etudes Centrafricaines, 1947.

(21) A number of incidental observations to the same effect, but relating to the Ndembu of Rhodesia, will be found in V. W. Turner: *Schism and Continuity in an African Society*, Manchester, 1957.

(22) Under the heading 'Quelques circonstances particulières de la mort', p. 176.

(23) R. Bastide: 'Le suicide du nègre brésilien', in *Cah. Int. de Sociologie*, XII, 1952.
(24) For an example of this drawn from life, see G. Balandier: *Sociologie des Brazzavilles noires*, ch. VI,' "M" B and fear of the customary environment'.
(25) Figures taken from the Boko district archives, 1935.
(26) For details, see *Et. Bk.* II: *Religion et magie*, p. 290.
(27) See the Mitoundidi case, 1932, Boko archives.
(28) A useful critical review of the question will be found in G. Piers and M. B. Singer: *Shame and Guilt, a Psychoanalytic and Cultural Study*, Springfields, 1953.
(29) *Et. Bk.*, pp. 203–5.
(30) Cf. *Et. Bk.*, pp. 173–4; and J. Mertens: *op. cit.*, D, ch. I, 'Sanctions'.
(31) *Et. Bk.*, p. viii.
(32) This is referred to in the 'Projet de chefferies', Boko, 1937.
(33) *Et. Bk.*, pp. 78–9; and various 'Chronicles'.
(34) G. Balandier: *Les villages gabonais*, pp. 30–41.
(35) 'Projet de chefferies', Boko, 1937.
(36) P. Mus: *Viêt-Nam: Sociologie d'une guerre*, 1952, particularly ch. II.
(37) Cf. Report for the Stanley Pool Region, 1935, quoted above.
(38) *Et. Bk.*, p. 280.
(39) Annual Political Report for the Moyen-Congo, 1932.
(40) Annual Report for the Moyen-Congo, 1928.
(41) *Ibid.*, 1929.
(42) *L'Affaire Balali*, 1945, archive document.
(43) Note on the political and economic situation in the Kinkala district, July 1948.
(44) Ch. IV: 'Les types de groupements sociaux'.
(45) Letters dated June 4 and October 12, 1928.
(46) Note on the political and economic situation in the Kinkala district, July 1948.
(47) See G. Balandier: 'L'utopie de Benoît Ogoula Iquaqua', in *Les temps modernes*, 84–5, 1952.
(48) 'Questionnaire sur les sectes secrètes', Kinkala, December 1949.
(49) Annual Report for the Moyen-Congo, 1931.
(50) See the Annual Political Report for the Stanley Pool Sub-division, 1942.
(51) 'Questionnaire sur les sectes secrètes', Kinkala, December 1949.
(52) See the unpublished study by a colonial official, Le Guen, now in the archives of the Centre des Hautes Etudes d'Administration Musulmane.
(53) See L. S. B. Leakey: *Mau-Mau and the Kikuyu*, London, 1953; also an *Historical Survey of the Origins and Growth of Mau-Mau*, published by the Colonial Office, 1960.
(54) Annual Report for the Moyen-Congo, 1931.
(55) Annual Report for the Stanley Pool Region, 1943.
(56) See G. Balandier: *Sociologie des Brazzavilles noires*, ch. III, dealing with labour problems.
(57) *Op. cit.*, pp. 109–11.
(58) Abbé Fulbert Youlou, whose knowledge of the movement is profound, has written a study of the subject: *Le Matsouanisme*, Brazzaville, 1955.
(59) Cf. M. Sinda: *op. cit.*, p. 332.

PART III CHAPTER III

(1) M. Leenhardt: *Le mouvement éthiopien au sud de l'Afrique, de 1896 à 1899*, Cahors, 1902.

(2) The figure is given by G. Joseph, in his book *Côte-d'Ivoire*, Paris, 1944.

(3) See J. Van Wing: *Et. Bk.*, II: *Religion et magie*, pp. 168 and 290.

(4) L. Marquard: *The Peoples of South Africa*, London, 1952, pp. 203–5.

(5) These words are quoted from an unpublished study of the Watch Tower by Captain G. de Beauregard.

(6) See E. Andersson: *Messianic Popular Movements in the Lower Congo*, Uppsala, 1958, pp. 247–50, where the probable relations between the Watch Tower and the Congolese messianisms are discussed.

(7) *Et. Bk.*, II, p. 290.

(8) *Et. Bk.*, p. 168.

(9) Quoted from a collection of documents put together in 1940–41, and translated by the administrative authorities of the Belgian Congo; we shall refer to it henceforth as *Doc. Blg.*

(10) *Doc. Blg.*

(11) *Ibid.*

(12) *Ibid.*, Regulations of the *Mission des Noirs*.

(13) *Ibid.*

(14) S. Freud: *Moses and Monotheism*, St. Ed. vol. 23, London, 1964, p. 105.

(15) *Ibid.*, p. 161.

(16) *Et. Bk.*, p. 18.

(17) In *La philosophie bantoue*, ch. II, sections 3 and 4.

(18) *Mouvement gounziste en 1924*, Brazzaville archives.

(19) The *Book of Exodus*, IV, 1–5.

(20) *Et. Bk.*, p. 28.

(21) Quoted in *Mouvement gounziste en 1924*.

(22) *Doc. Blg.*

(23) Report from the Brazzaville Sub-division, 1931.

(24) *Ibid.*

(25) Appendix to the *Rapport sur le mouvement gounziste*, 1931, Boko sub-division.

(26) Annual Political Report for the Moyen-Congo, 1932.

(27) *Doc. Blg.*

(28) *Ibid.*

(29) Boko administrative archives.

(30) In 'L'utopie de Benoît Ogoula Iquaqua', *Les temps modernes*, October-November 1952, we showed how, in a particular case, the conflict could be schematized by the impossibility of being at one and the same time a Catholic and a polygamist.

(31) See *Et. Bk.*, I and II: and his article 'L'Etre suprême des Bakongo', in *Rech. de sciences religieuses*, May-August 1920, pp. 70–81.

(32) *Op. cit.*, p. 142.

(33) See also the descriptions given in G. Balandier: *Ambiguous Africa*, London, 1966, ch. VII.

(34) All these facts were obtained from an ex-initiate, who subsequently prepared a detailed report of the 'tests' to which he had been submitted. Coma-Tsé-Tsé, March 1946.

(35) *Notes sur les coutumes lari*, p. 149.

(36) *Doc. Blg.*

(37) Report on the *Mission des Noirs* in the Bas-Congo region, August 1941.

(38) Political Report, Brazzaville, May 1946.

(39) See also *Ambiguous Africa*, ch. VII.

(40) *Et. Bk.*, pp. 149–51.

(41) Cf. R. Bastide: *Les religions africaines au Brésil*, Paris, 1960.

(42) *Et. Bk.*, II, pp. 18–19 (our italics).

(43) This is the expression used by F. Alexander in *Our Age of Unreason*, New York, 1940.

(44) J. Chome: *La passion de Simon Kimbangou*, Brussels, 1959.

(45) M. Sinda: *op. cit.*, p. 136ff.

(46) *Ibid.*, pp. 131 and 134.

(47) In her interesting and very detailed book, *Propheten in Africa*, Braunschweig, 1949, K. Schlosser attributes considerable importance to 'prophetic manifestations' in African Islam.

(48) A. Le Grip: 'Le mahdisme en Afrique noire', in *L'Afrique et l'Asie*, 18, 2nd quarter, 1952, pp. 3–16. See also J.-C. Froelich: *Les Musulmans d'Afrique noire*, Paris, 1962, pp. 200–10.

(49) Froelich: *op. cit.*

(50) See G. Balandier: *Particularisme et évolution: Les pêcheurs lébou*, published by the Institut Français d'Afrique Noire, 1952, in which attention was drawn to these particular features of syncretism.

(51) In this respect, see R. Bastide: 'Messianisme et développement économique et social', in *Cah. Int. de Sociologie*, XXI, 1961, in which he attempts to evaluate the recent vicissitudes of Messianism.

(52) See the important studies by Charles A. Julien and especially his *Histoire de l'Afrique du Nord*. Information with regard to the Berber heresies is also to be found in G. Drague: *Esquisse d'histoire religieuse du Maroc*, Paris, 1952.

CONCLUSION

(1) Cf. G. Balandier: *Les villages gabonais*, 1952.

(2) See *La vocation actuelle de la sociologie*, p. 285ff.

(3) G. Balandier: 'Contributions à une sociologie de la dépendance', in *Cah. Int. de Sociologie*, XII, 1952.

(4) Cf. L. S. B. Leakey: *op. cit*; and my Preface to the French translation of Jomo Kenyatta: *Au pied du mont Kenya*, Paris, 1960.

(5) Cf. G. Balandier: 'Les mythes politiques de colonisation et de décolonisation en Afrique', in *Cah. Int. de Sociologie*, XXXIII, 1962.

(6) R. Linton: Introduction to *Acculturation in Seven American Indian Tribes*, New York, 1940.

(7) In this respect, see V. Lanternari's admirable work, *Movimenti religiosi di liberta e di salvezza*, Milan, 1960.

(8) See G. Balandier: 'Déséquilibres socio-culturels et modernisation des pays sous-développés', in *Cah. Int. de Sociologie*, XX, 1956.

(9) C. Lévi-Strauss: 'La notion d'archaïsme en ethnologie', in *Cah. Int. de Sociologie*, XII, 1952. A revised version appeared in *Structural Anthropology*, Eng. trans., Harmondsworth, 1968.

(10) M. Fortes and E. Evans-Pritchard: *African Political Systems*, London, 1948.

(11) P. Alexandre and J. Binet: *Le groupe dit Pahouin*, Paris, 1958, p. 47.

(12) For an account of a *malaki*, see G. Balandier: *Ambiguous Africa*, London, 1966, p. 137ff.

(13) Cf. the article by H. G. Barnett, in which he explains the elaborate developments of the old form of potlatch introduced by the Kwakiutl Indians under the influence of an exchange economy: 'The Nature of the Potlatch', in *Am. Anthropologist*, 40, 3, 1938.

(14) M. Gluckman: *Rituals of Rebellion in South-East Africa*, Manchester, 1954.

(15) G. Balandier: 'Structures sociales traditionnelles et changements économiques' in *Cah. Et. africaines*, I, 1960.

(16) There are a number of further examples in Africa. F. Rehfish has studied competitive gifts among the Mambila, in what used to be the British Cameroons: see *Cah. Et. africaines*, III, 1, 1962; and Miss J. Thomas has described the *yé lé* of the Ngbaka of the Lobaye (Republic of Central Africa), which are similar in principle and subject to the same process of evolution.

(17) In *Archives de Soc. des Relig.*, 4, 1957.

(18) Cf. R. Bastide: *Les religions africaines au Brésil*, Paris, 1960, especially p. 79ff.

(19) See the English translation: Weber, *Ancient Judaism*, Glencoe, 1952.

(20) The churches based on 'Harrisism' experienced a fresh influx of members when the R.D.A. (*Rassemblement Démocratique Africain*) normalized its relations with the colonial administration. For an admirable study of the question, see the Ms. thesis presented to the Ecole des Hautes Etudes by Amos Djoro.

Bibliography

BIBLIOGRAPHY

I. FANG

ALEXANDRE, P. and BINET, J.: *Le group dit Pahouin*, Paris, 1958.

AVELOT, R.: 'Recherches sur l'histoire des migrations dans le bassin de l'Ogooué et la région littorale adjacente', in *Bull. géogr. hist. et descr.*, XX, 1905.

BALANDIER, G.: 'Aspects de l'évolution sociale chez les Fang du Gabon, in *Cah. int. de Sociologie*, IX, 1950.

—— in collaboration with Pauvert, J.-C.: *Les villages gabonais*, memorandum of the Institut d'Etudes Centrafricaines, 5, Brazzaville, 1952.

—— *Ambiguous Africa*, Eng. trans., London, 1966.

BERTAUT, M.: *Le droit coutumier des Boulous*, Paris, 1935.

BÉTI, MONGO *Le pauvre Christ de Bomba*, Paris, 1956.

BOT BA NJOCK, H.: 'Prééminences sociales et système politico-religieux dans la société traditionnelle bulu et fang', in *Journ. Soc. des Africanistes*, 1960.

BRUNHES, J.: 'Exploitations de primitifs: type complexe de dévastation végétale et animale dans la forêt équatoriale: les Fang', in *La géographie humaine*, abridged edition, Paris, 1947, pp. 199–204.

CURAULT, CAPTAIN: 'Monographie du secteur de N'Djolé au Gabon', in *Rev. des troupes colon.*, 68, 1908.

CUREAU, DR A.: *Les populations primitives de l'Afrique équatoriale*, Paris, 1912.

DUGAST, I.: *Inventaire ethnique du Sud-Cameroun*, Douala, I.F.A.N., 1949.

FERNANDEZ, J.: 'Christian Acculturation and Fang Witchcraft', in *Cah. Et. africaines*, 6, 1961.

GRÉBERT, F.: *Au Gabon*, Paris, 1928.

—— 'La famille pahouine en 1931', *Africa*, V. 2, April 1932.

KINGSLEY, M. H.: *Travels in West Africa, Congo français, Corisco and Cameroons*, London, 1897.

—— *West African Studies*, London, 1901, 2nd ed.

LARGEAU, V.: *Encyclopédie pahouine*, Paris, 1901.

LAVIGNOTTE, H.: *L'évur, croyance des pahouins du Gabon*, Paris, 1936.

LEROUX, L.-C.: 'Etude sur le Ngil (confrérie Fan)', in *Bull. Soc. Rech. congolaises*, 8, 1925.

MAIGNAN, CAPTAIN: 'Etudes sur le pays pahouin', in *Bull. Soc. Rech. congolaises*, 14, 1931.

MARTROU, L.: 'Les "Eki" des Mfang', in *Anthropos*, I, 1906.

—— 'Le nomadisme des "Fangs" ', in *Revue de géographie*, new series, III, 1909.

—— 'La langue fan et ses dialectes', in *Journ. Soc. des Africanistes*, VI, 2, 1936.

MBA, L.: 'Essai de droit coutumier pahouin', in *Bull. Soc. Rech. congolaises*, 25, 1938.

PERRAULT, G.: 'Les Fang du pays Yaoundé', in *Cah. d'outre-mer*, 8, 1949.

SAUTTER, G.: 'Le cacao dans l'économie rurale du Woleu-Ntem', in *Bull. Inst. Et. centrafricaines*, 1, 1950.

—— 'Les paysans noirs du Gabon septentrional: Essai sur le peuplement et l'habitat au Woleu-Ntem', in *Cah. d'outre-mer*, 14, 1951.

SILLANS, R.: *Rites et croyances des peuples du Gabon*, Paris, 1962.

TESSMANN, G.: 'Ueber das Verhältniss der Fangneger zur umgebenden Tierwelt', in *Zeitschrift für Ethnologie*, XXXIX, 1907.

—— 'Religionsformen der Pangwe', in *Zeitschrift für Ethnologie*, XLI, 1909.

—— 'Kinderspiele der Pangwe', in *Baessler Archiv.*, IV, 1912.

—— *Die Pangwe, Volkerkundliche Monographie eines Westafrikanischen Negerstammes*, 2 vols., Berlin, 1913.

TRILLES, H.: 'Les Fang, croyances et religion', in *Bull. Soc. Géogr. de Lille*, XLVIII, 1907.

—— *Le totémisme chez les Fân*, Biblioth. Anthropos, Münster, 1912.

—— 'Proverbes, légendes et contes fang', in *Bull. Soc. neuchâteloise de Géographie*, 1905, pp. 49–295.

—— *Quinze ans au pays fan*, Paris, 1912.

TREZENEM, E.: 'Notes ethnographiques sur les tribus Fan du Moyen Ogooué', in *Journ. Soc. des Africanistes*, VI, 1, 1936.

WALKER, A.: Various articles in *Bull. Soc. Rech. congolaises*; and particularly those written in collaboration with R. Sillans (q.v.).

II. BA-KONGO

ANDERSSON, E.: *Messianic Popular Movements in the Lower Congo*, Uppsala, 1958.

BALANDIER, G.: 'Messianismes et nationalismes en Afrique noire', in *Cah. int. de Sociologie*, XIV, 53.

—— *Sociologie des Brazzavilles noires*, Paris, 1955.

—— *Ambiguous Africa*, Eng. trans., London, 1966.

BONNEFOND, R. P.: and LOMBARD, J.: 'Notes de folklore lari', in *Journ. Soc. des Africanistes*, IV, 1, 1934.

CABANAC, P.: 'Les tribus Ballali et Bassoundi de la subdivision de Mayama', in *Bull. Soc. Rech. congolaises*, 8, 1925.

CHAUMETON, J.: *La parenté et la propriété foncière chez les Balali-Bassundi*, I.E.C., Ms.

CLEENE, N. de: 'Les chefs indigènes au Mayombe', in *Africa*, VIII, 1, 1935.

—— 'La famille au Mayombe', in *Africa*, X, 1, 1937.

CUVILLIER-FLEURY, H.: *La mise en valeur du Congo français*, Paris, 1904.

DRESCH, J.: 'Villes congolaises: Etude de géographie urbaine et sociale', in *Rev. Géogr. hum. et ethno.*, 3, 1948.

EUCHER, R. P.: *Le Congo: Essai sur l'histoire religieuse de ce pays depuis sa découverte – 1884 – jusqu'à nos jours*, Huy, 1894.

HUBSCHWERLIN, G.: 'Le régime foncier indigène dans la région de Boko', in *Bull. Soc. Rech. congolaises*, 24, 1937.

JAFFRE, R. P.: 'L'Afrique aux Africains, le "N'gounzisme" au Congo', in *Les études*, March 1934.

JONGHE, E. de: *Les sociétés secrètes au Bas-Congo*, Brussels, 1907.

LAMAN, K. E.: *Dictionnaire kikongo-français*, Brussels, 1936.

—— *The Kongo*, 2 vols., Uppsala, 1953 and 1957.

MALONGA, J.: *La légende de M'Pfoumou Ma Mazono*, Paris, 1954.

MERTENS, J.: *Les chefs couronnés chez les Bakongo orientaux: Etude de régime successoral*, Mém. Inst. Roy. Col. Belge, XI, 1, 1942.

—— 'La juridiction indigène chez les Bakongo orientaux', in *Kongo-Overzee*, 1946–7 and 1951.

MERTENS, V.: 'Le mariage chez les Bambada (Bakongo) et ses leçons sociales', in *Zaïre*, II, 10, 1948.

—— 'Détermination des relations de famille chez les Bakongo', in *Zaïre*, III, 1, 1949.

PROYART, ABBÉ L.-B.: *Histoire du Loango, Kakongo et autres royaumes d'Afrique, rédigée d'après les mémoires des préfets apostoliques de la mission française*, Paris, 1776.

RICHARDS, A.: 'Some types of family structure amongst the Central Bantu', in Radcliffe-Brown, A. R. and Forde, D., *African Systems of Kinship and Marriage*, London, 1950.

ROUGET, F.: *L'expansion coloniale au Congo français*, Paris, 1906.

SAUTTER, G.: 'Une économie indigène progressive: les Bacongo du district de Boko (Moyen-Congo)', in *Bull. Assoc. Géogr. français*, March-April 1951.

SCHLOSSER, K.: *Propheten in Afrika*, Braunschweig, 1949.

SINDA, M.: *Le messianisme congolaise et ses incidences politiques*, Ms., 1961.

SORET, M.: *Les Kongo nord-occidentaux*, Paris, 1959.

TCHIKAYA, J.: 'Etude sur la race bassoundi', in *Bull. d'information et de documentation de l'A.E.F.*., 59, 1950.

TORDAY, E.: 'Dualism in Western Bantu Religion', in *Journ. Roy. Anthr. Inst.*, LVIII, 1933.

VAN WING, J.: 'Une évolution de la coutume bakongo', in *Congo*, II, 1926.

—— '*Nzo Longo* ou les rites de la puberté chez les Bakongo', in *Congo*, I and II, December 1920.

—— *Etudes Bakongo: Histoire et sociologie*, Brussels, 1921.

—— *Etudes Bakongo, II: Religion et magie*, Brussels, 1938.

YOULOU, ABBÉ F.: *Le Matsouanisme*, Brazzaville, 1955.

III. BIBLIOGRAPHIES

BRUEL, G.: *Bibliographie de l'Afrique équatoriale française*, Paris, 1914.

SANNER P. *Bibliographie ethnographique de l'Afrique équatoriale française*, Paris, 1949.

Bibliographie africaniste, published annually by the *Journ. Soc. des Africanistes*.

Bibliographie ethnographique du Congo belge et des régions avoisinantes, published by the Musée du Congo Belge, Tervueren Belgium).

INDEX

Grébert, F., 134, 196–7, 198, 205 *n*., 208, 218, 271 *n*.
Guibet report, 190
Gurvitch, G., 45, 53, 481

Haiti, 247
Hamon mission, in the Kinkala district, 353
Harris, Wade, 410–11
Haut-Congo, 70, 71, 329, 348, 349; people of, 60–1, 297
Haut-Gabon, 61, 229, 240
Haut-Katanga region (Congo), 247
Haut-Niari, 289
Haut-Ogooué, 164; people of, 60–1
Haut-Ogooué Company, 179
Haute-Ngounié, 222, 224
Haute-Sanga uprising, 74, 478
Hole in the *adzap* legend, 241

Incest, 130–1
Indians, of South Africa, 35, 36, 47
Indo-China, 27
Infant mortality, 100, 102
Islam, 468–72
Ivory Coast, 411, 504
Ivory trade, 62–3

Jacob M. (Kimbangist leader), 433
Jean B. (Kimbangist leader), 433
Jeune Gabonais, 166
John II, of Portugal, 63, 64
Jonghe, E. de, 59, 326, 327, 328, 342, 379
Judicial authority: Fang, 143–4; Ba-Kongo, 324–6

Kâda, or *nkâda* (clan; Ba-Kongo), 299
Kakism. See *Mission des Noirs*
Kango, 214, 223, 234
Karinou (Haute-Sanga religious leader), 74
Kasavubu, President, 386, 467
Kaunga clan (Ba-Kongo), 294, 296, 317
Kennedy, R., 23 *n*., 25, 27
Kenya, 49, 405, 407, 410, 479, 502
Khakist movement. See *Mission des Noirs*
Kharijites, 472
Kibouendé (in the old Kinkala district), Catholic mission at, 353
Kihinda, village of (near Boko), 362–3
Ki-Hinda clan (Ba-Kongo), 317
Ki-Kongo language, 348, 397, 401, 415
Ki-Kwimba clan, of the Congo, 294, 296, 317
Kimbangism, 66, 70 (*and see* Messianism)

Kimbangou, Simon, 386, 414, 422, 427, 435–7, 440, 447, 451–2, 455, 467; biography, 414–15; success of his teaching, 415–16; deported, 417; as *Gounza* and 'Saviour', 417–21
Ki-Mbèmbé clan, of the Boko country, 294, 317
Ki-Mpâga clan (Ba-Kongo), 315
Kimpala, 309–10
Kimpasi society (Ba-Kongo), 327
Kindaba (in the old Mayama district), Catholic mission at, 353
Ki-Ndâba clan (Ba-Kongo), 315
Ki-Ndâmba clan (Ba-Kongo), 296
Ki-Ngâdu clan (Ba-Kongo), 315
Kingship concept, 386
Kingsley, Mary, 121, 128 *n*., 135, 177
Ki-Nimbi clan (Ba-Kongo), 296, 317
Kinkala region, 351, 387; Ba-Kongo of the old district, 295; suicide, 369; and the Amicalist movement, 396, 398; Messianism, 446, 450
Kinkala-Mayama region, Messianism in, 444
Kinkoni, 435
Kinshasa, 297, 298
Kinship system: Fang, 116–21, 212; Ba-Kongo, 392–7
Ki-Nsundi clan (Ba-Kongo), 317
Kioka movement, in Angola, 66
Kipako region, 416
Ki-Sèngélé clan (Ba-Kongo), 315
Kitawale or Watch Tower movement. *See* Watch Tower Congregation
Kôgo dya Ntotila. See São Salvador
Kôjé people, 91, 112, 115, 195, 211, 212
Komo society, of western Sudan, 272
Kongo, kingdom of, 57–61, 63, 65, 292, 298, 489, 503
Kongo people, 348
Kribi, 183
Kyé-Nyé canton, 107, 195

Labi (religious association; Fang), 74, 478
Lali-Sundi people, 342
Lambaréné, 176, 223
'Lamentations' (Kimbangist document), 433
Land: rise in value, 359; disputes over ownership, 359–60; tied up with clan group, 360–1, 365
Largeau, V., 126, 131, 134, 150 *n*., 160, 162, 271
Lari people. *See* Ba-Lali people
Leakey, L. S. B., 405, 407, 421, 502
Lebanese, in West Africa, 35
Le Dentu, General, 94, 98, 100, 102, 194

402, 480, 501; its birth, Simon Kimbangou the 'Saviour', and its literature, 414-29; vicissitudes of Kimbangism, 429-34; the *Mission des Noirs* (q.v.); social implications, 450-9; and the traditional system, 459-63; sociological and political implications, 463-6; the new Congolese 'churches', 466-8; a privileged field of observation, 468-72; and social dynamics, 498-504; different characteristics in different places, 502-3; its possibilities, 503-4

Mévungö association (Fang), 154
Meyé, François, 126, 129-30, 134, 186
M'Fagne, village of, 137
Mikéngé people, of the Mayama region, 385
Mindouli District, 348; Ba-Kongo of the old district, 295
Mindzo, village of (on Mayama-Pangala road), 315
Minière, Compagnie (of Mindouli, Moyen-Congo), 68
Minorities, dominant and subordinate, 33-9
Minvoul, 200; Catholic Mission at, 179
Mission des Noirs (Khakist movement), 418-20, 422, 459; founded by Mpadi, 435; religious and ethical system, 435-441; the system in practice, 441-4; the local churches, 444-5; religious services, 445; possession by the holy spirit, 445-6; initiation, 446-7; persistence of old forms in, 447-8; importance and attraction, 448-50. *See also* Messianism
Missions and missionaries, 63-6, 165, 192, 213-14, 326, 327, 331, 352-3, 377, 383, 412, 413, 422, 470-2
See also Catholic missions; Christianity; Protestant missions
Mitshogo country, 225, 227
Mitshogo people, of Gabon, 60, 222, 224, 227, 228
Mitzik district, 96-100, 170, 174, 182, 209; enquiry on village regroupment, 257
Mixed Gabonese Committee, 201
Miyalu (shield; Ba-Kongo), 319
Mobility of social groups, 70-3
Monetary economy, introduction of, 184-7, 483
Mònòmvògò Esònò (the elder), 109
Moses M. (Kimbangist leader), 433
Mouila districts, of Gabon, 474
Moyen-Congo, 68, 75; social mobility in, 72; Haute-Sanga uprising, 74, 478;

slavery, 75; competition for labour, 79
Moyen-Ogooué, 473; Fang settlement in, 88, 90; *Bwiti* cult, 226; impact of colonialism, 282
Mpadi, Simon-Pierre (Kimbangist leader), 428 n., 434-7, 441, 445, 451-3
Mpongwé people, of Haut-Gabon, 61, 190, 222, 229, 230, 236
Mu-Kongo people, 366, 367, 375, 389, 500
Munkunguna movement (Ba-Kongo), 327
Musana (near Brazzaville), Swedish Evangelical Mission at, 353
Musitu (forest zone; Ba-Kongo), 345-6
Mutual Aid Society for the Fang People, 201
Muziri association (Ba-Kongo), 329
Mwiri association (Fang), 147, 222

Napoleon III, 24
Nd'è bòt (male kinship group; Fang), 135-9, 141-2, 156, 182, 209
Ndembu of Northern Rhodesia, 55
Ndjolé district, 165, 176
Ndôg tribe, 92, 241
Ndona-kèntò, woman-wife or female chief (Ba-Kongo), 322
Ndou-Libi, canton of (Sangmélima region), 194, 249
Negro churches, 31, 235, 410-14, 444-5, 449
See also Messianism; *Mission des Noirs*
Nganga E. (Messianic leader), 451-3, 456-8, 462-3
Ngil organization (Fang), 146-7, 150
N'Goko Sangha Company, 70
Ngòma (eight-stringed harp), 230
Ngonéki (in the Médouneu district), 234
Ngounié region, 147, 223
Nigeria, 32, 59
Njambai cult (Fang), 222
Nkamba, village of (the 'New Jerusalem'), 415, 417; becomes holy city of Kimbangism, 467
Nkasa ordeal (Ba-Kongo), 370-1
Nkazi (maternal uncle; Ba-Kongo), 375-9
Nkomé people, of Haut-Gabon, 61, 222, 236
Nkoum, Yéngwi village of, 109
Nkoumadzap, village of (Médouneu region), 214
Nkrumah, Nkwame, 30, 419 n.
N'*nup* association (Fang), 154
Notòtila (king, Ba-Kongo), 316
Nsim Esònò, 109
Ntem-Kribi Tribal Union, 239, 240, 254
Ntumu group, of the Fang, 92, 185